The Languages of Early Medieval Charters

Brill's Series on the Early Middle Ages

CONTINUATION OF THE TRANSFORMATION OF THE ROMAN WORLD

VOLUME 27

The titles published in this series are listed at *brill.com/bsem*

The Languages of Early Medieval Charters

Latin, Germanic Vernaculars, and the Written Word

Edited by

Robert Gallagher
Edward Roberts
Francesca Tinti

BRILL

LEIDEN | BOSTON

Cover illustration: An original charter of Æthelberht, 'king of the West Saxons and of the men of Kent', from 863, written in a combination of Latin and Old English (S 332, Canterbury, Dean & Chapter, ChAnt M. 14). Reproduced by kind permission of the Dean and Chapter of Canterbury.

Library of Congress Cataloging-in-Publication Data

Names: Gallagher, Robert, editor. | Roberts, Edward, editor. | Tinti, Francesca, editor.
Title: The languages of early medieval charters : Latin, Germanic vernaculars, and the written word / edited by Robert Gallagher, Edward Roberts, Francesca Tinti.
Description: Leiden ; Boston : Brill, 2021. | Series: Brill's series on the early Middle Ages, 1878-4879 ; volume 27 | Includes bibliographical references and index.
Identifiers: LCCN 2020035012 (print) | LCCN 2020035013 (ebook) | ISBN 9789004428119 (hardback) | ISBN 9789004432338 (ebook)
Subjects: LCSH: Law, Medieval—Language. | Europe, Western—Charters, grants, and privileges—History—To 1500. | Written communication—Europe, Western—History—To 1500. | Multilingualism—Europe, Western—History—To 1500. | Latin language, Medieval and modern—Europe, Western. | Germanic languages—History—Europe, Western. | English language—Old English, ca. 450-1100.
Classification: LCC KJ77 .L36 2020 (print) | LCC KJ77 (ebook) | DDC 349.409/02—dc23
LC record available at https://lccn.loc.gov/2020035012
LC ebook record available at https://lccn.loc.gov/2020035013

Typeface for the Latin, Greek, and Cyrillic scripts: "Brill". See and download: brill.com/brill-typeface.

ISSN 1878-4879
ISBN 978-90-04-42811-9 (hardback)
ISBN 978-90-04-43233-8 (e-book)

This book is printed on acid-free paper and produced in a sustainable manner.

Contents

Illustrations

Maps

Figures

Tables

Abbreviations

Abing	*Charters of Abingdon Abbey*, ed. S. E. Kelly, Anglo-Saxon Charters VII–VIII (Oxford, 2000)
ASChart	*Anglo-Saxon Charters*, ed. and trans. Agnes J. Robertson, 2nd ed. (Cambridge, 1956)
ASE	*Anglo-Saxon England*
ASWills	*Anglo-Saxon Wills*, ed. and trans. Dorothy Whitelock (Cambridge, 1930)
ASWrits	*Anglo-Saxon Writs*, ed. and trans. Florence E. Harmer (Manchester, 1952; 2nd ed. Stamford, 1989)
Bath	*Charters of Bath and Wells*, ed. S. E. Kelly, Anglo-Saxon Charters 13 (Oxford, 2007)
Burt	*Charters of Burton Abbey*, ed. P. H. Sawyer, Anglo-Saxon Charters II (Oxford, 1979)
BCS	*Cartularium Saxonicum: A Collection of Charters Relating to Anglo-Saxon History*, ed. Walter de Gray Birch, 3 vols (London, 1885–99)
CAAPi	*Carte dell'Archivio Arcivescovile di Pisa, Fondo arcivescovile. 1. 720–1100*, ed. Antonella Ghignoli, *2. 1101–1150*, ed. Silio P. P. Scalfati, *3. 1151–1200*, ed. Silio P. P. Scalfati, Biblioteca del « Bollettino Storico Pisano », Fonti, 11, 3 vols (Pisa, 2006)
CantCC	*Charters of Christ Church Canterbury*, eds N. P. Brooks and S. E. Kelly, Anglo-Saxon Charters 17–18 (Oxford, 2013)
CantStA	*Charters of St Augustine's Abbey, Canterbury*, ed. S. E. Kelly, Anglo-Saxon Charters IV (Oxford, 1995)
CDL	*Codice diplomatico Longobardo*, eds Luigi Schiaparelli et al., 5 vols (Rome, 1929–2003)
ChLA	*Chartae latinae antiquiores*, eds Albert Bruckner et al., 118 vols (Olten et al., 1954–2019)
CLA	*Codices latini antiquiores. A Palaeographical Guide to Latin Manuscripts prior to the Ninth Century*, ed. Elias Avery Lowe, 11 vols + supplement (Oxford, 1935–71)
EHR	*The English Historical Review*
EME	*Early Medieval Europe*
Glast	*Charters of Glastonbury Abbey*, ed. S. E. Kelly, Anglo-Saxon Charters 15 (Oxford, 2012)

KCD	*Codex Diplomaticus Ævi Saxonici*, ed. J. M. Kemble, 6 vols (London, 1839–48), paperback reprint, 6 vols (Cambridge, 2011)
LondStP	*Charters of St Paul's, London*, ed. S. E. Kelly, Anglo-Saxon Charters X (Oxford, 2004)
Malm	*Charters of Malmesbury Abbey*, ed. S. E. Kelly, Anglo-Saxon Charters XI (Oxford, 2005)
MGH	Monumenta Germaniae Historica
Auct. ant.	*Auctores antiquissimi*, 15 vols (Berlin, 1877–1919)
Capit.	*Capitularia regum Francorum*, eds Alfred Boretius and Victor Krause, 2 vols (Hanover, 1883–97)
Capit. episc.	*Capitula episcoporum*, 4 vols (Hanover, 1984–2005)
Conc.	*Concilia, Legum sectio III*, 6 vols (Hanover, 1893–2014)
D(D)	Diploma(s) of
Arnulf	*Die Urkunden Arnolfs*, ed. Paul Kehr, MGH Diplomata regum Germaniae ex stirpe Karolinorum 3 (Berlin, 1940)
Charlemagne	*Die Urkunden Pippins, Karlmanns und Karls des Grossen*, ed. Engelbert Mühlbacher, MGH Diplomata Karolinorum 1 (Hanover, 1906)
Lothar II	*Die Urkunden Lothars I. und Lothars II.*, ed. Theodor Schieffer, MGH Diplomata Karolinorum 3 (Berlin and Zürich, 1966)
Louis the German	*Die Urkunden Ludwigs des Deutschen, Karlmanns und Ludwigs der Jüngeren*, ed. Paul Kehr, MGH Diplomata regum Germaniae ex stirpe Karolinorum 1 (Berlin, 1934)
Louis the Pious	*Die Urkunden Ludwigs des Frommen*, eds Theo Kolzer, Jens Peter Clausen, Daniel Eichler, Britta Mischke, Sarah Patt, and Susanne Zwierlein, MGH Diplomata Karolinorum 2 (Wiesbaden, 2016)
Mer.	*Die Urkunden der Merowinger*, eds Theo Kölzer, Martina Hartmann, and Andrea Stieldorf, MGH Diplomata regum Francorum e stirpe Merovingica (Hanover, 2001)
Otto I	*Die Urkunden Konrad I., Heinrich I. und Otto I.*, ed. Theodor Sickel, MGH Diplomata regum et imperatorum Germaniae 1 (Hanover, 1879–84)
Zwentibold	*Die Urkunden Zwentibolds und Ludwigs des Kindes*, ed. Theodor Schieffer, MGH Diplomata regum Germaniae ex stirpe Karolinorum 4 (Berlin, 1960)
Epp.	*Epistolae (in Quart)*, 8 vols (Hanover and Berlin, 1887–2018)

Necr.	*Necrologia Germaniae*, 5 vols and supplement (Berlin, 1884–1920)
SS	*Scriptores in folio* (Hanover, 1826–)
SS rer. Germ.	*Scriptores rerum Germanicarum in usum scholarum separatim editi* (Hanover, 1871–)
SS rer. Merov.	*Scriptores rerum Merovingicarum*, 7 vols (Hanover, 1885–1920)
North	*Charters of Northern Houses*, ed. D. A. Woodman, Anglo-Saxon Charters 16 (Oxford, 2012)
OSFacs	*Facsimiles of Anglo-Saxon Manuscripts*, ed. W. B. Sanders, 3 vols (Southampton, 1878–84)
Pet	*Charters of Peterborough Abbey*, ed. S. E. Kelly, Anglo-Saxon Charters 14 (Oxford, 2009)
Roch	*Charters of Rochester*, ed. A. Campbell, Anglo-Saxon Charters I (Oxford, 1973)
S	P. H. Sawyer, *Anglo-Saxon Charters: An Annotated List and Bibliography* (London, 1968); revised as the Electronic Sawyer, www.esawyer.org.uk
Sel	*Charters of Selsey*, ed. S. E. Kelly, Anglo-Saxon Charters VI (Oxford, 1998)
Settimane	*Settimane di studio del Centro italiano di studi sull'alto medioevo* (Spoleto, 1953–)
Sherb	*Charters of Sherborne*, ed. M. A. O'Donovan, Anglo-Saxon Charters III (Oxford, 1998)
StAlb	*Charters of St Albans Abbey*, ed. J. Crick, Anglo-Saxon Charters XII (Oxford, 2007)
W	*Urkundenbuch der Abtei Sanct Gallen*, ed. Hermann Wartmann, 3 vols (Zürich, 1863–82)
Wells	*Charters of Bath and Wells*, ed. S. E. Kelly, Anglo-Saxon Charters 13 (Oxford, 2007)
WinchNM	*Charters of the New Minster, Winchester*, ed. S. Miller, Anglo-Saxon Charters IX (Oxford, 2001)

Notes on Contributors

Stefan Esders
is Professor of Late Antique and Early Medieval History at the Freie Universität Berlin, specializing in legal history. He has co-authored a book on an Old High German document (*Der althochdeutsche Klerikereid. Bischöfliche Diözesangewalt, kirchliches Benefizialwesen und volkssprachliche Rechtspraxis im frühmittelalterlichen Baiern*, 2000, with Heike Johanna Mierau), and has recently co-edited *East and West in the Early Middle Ages: The Merovingian Kingdoms in Mediterranean Perspective* (2019) with Yaniv Fox, Yitzhak Hen, and Laury Sarti, and *Using and Not Using the Past after the Carolingian Empire, c.900–c.1050* (2019), with Sarah Greer and Alice Hicklin.

Albert Fenton
obtained a BA in Anglo-Saxon, Norse and Celtic at Trinity College, Cambridge, followed by an MA in Medieval and Renaissance Studies at University College London, and is nearing the completion of his doctoral thesis entitled 'The Function of Writs in Anglo-Saxon England' at Trinity College, Cambridge under the supervision of Professor Simon Keynes. He has worked as a research assistant at the University of Oslo, the University of the Basque Country, and the Freie Universität Berlin. He has also taught extensively in early English history and diplomatic at the University of Cambridge.

Robert Gallagher
is Lecturer in Early Medieval History at the University of Kent. His primary research focus is the textual cultures of early medieval Britain, with special interests in documentary activity, Latin verse, and manuscript ownership and use. He gained his BA and MA from the University of York and his PhD from the University of Cambridge. He has held postdoctoral research positions at the University of the Basque Country and the University of Oxford.

Wolfgang Haubrichs
is Professor Emeritus in German Literature of the Middle Ages and History of the German Language at the University of Saarland, where he has worked since 1972. After gaining his PhD in 1967, he held a scholarship of the Deutsche Forschungsgemeinschaft (DFG) in 1967–69, became assistant professor at the University of Saarland in 1972, and gained his lecturing qualification (Habilitation) in 1975. He has directed several major research projects on medieval literature, historical semantics, and onomastics. He is a member of the

Akademie der Wissenschaften Mainz and of the Österreichische Akademie der Wissenschaften, head of the Mainz Academy-project Wörterbuch der Deutschen Winzersprache (WDW), and since 1970 founder and editor of the journal *Zeitschrift für Literaturwissenschaft und Linguistik* (LiLi). He is the author of many publications, including *Die Anfänge. Versuche volkssprachiger Schriftlichkeit im frühen Mittelalter* (2nd ed., 1995).

Charles Insley
is a historian of Anglo-Saxon England and the insular world, *c.*600–1100 who specializes in the study of charters. He is the author of a number of articles on Anglo-Saxon and Welsh diplomatics, as well as a forthcoming edition of the Anglo-Saxon Charters of Exeter Cathedral (Oxford University Press) and a biography of Æthelstan (Routledge). He undertook his undergraduate and doctoral degrees at Oxford, before holding academic posts at Bangor University, University College Northampton, and Canterbury Christ Church University. He moved to a Senior Lectureship in Medieval History at the University of Manchester in 2012, where he is currently head of department.

Kathryn A. Lowe
is Senior Lecturer in English Language & Linguistics at the University of Glasgow. She has published very widely on Old and Middle English, focusing on language, the history of literacy, and manuscript studies, including textual transmission. Her major project, an edition of the charters of Bury St Edmunds for the Anglo-Saxon Charters British Academy series, is close to completion. She is a Fellow of the Society of Antiquaries.

Rosamond McKitterick
is Professor Emerita of Medieval History in the University of Cambridge, a Fellow of Sidney Sussex College, and Chair of the Faculty of Archaeology, History and Letters of the British School at Rome. She has published many books and articles on Frankish history, early medieval manuscripts, literacy, and the writing of history in the early Middle Ages, such as *The Carolingians and the Written Word* (1989), *The Uses of Literacy in Early Mediaeval Europe* (1990), and *History and Memory in the Carolingian World* (2004). Her most recent book is *Rome and the Invention of the Papacy: The* Liber pontificalis (2020).

Rory Naismith
is a Lecturer in the History of England before the Norman Conquest in the Department of Anglo-Saxon, Norse and Celtic at the University of Cambridge, and a Fellow of Corpus Christi College. Previously he lectured at King's College

London, and before that received a BA, MPhil, and PhD at Cambridge. He was also a Junior Research Fellow at Clare College, Cambridge, a Leverhulme Early Career Research Fellow, and a Mellon Research Associate.

Janet L. Nelson
is Professor Emeritus of Medieval History at King's College, London. From 2000 to 2004 she was President of the Royal Historical Society. She is a Fellow of the British Academy, a corresponding Fellow of the Medieval Academy of America, and holds honorary doctorates from several universities in the UK. In 2019 she was awarded the Medlicott Medal for Service to History by the Historical Association. She has published widely on the early Middle Ages, her books including *Politics and Ritual in Early Medieval Europe* (1986), *Charles the Bald* (1992), *The Frankish World* (1995), *Courts, Elites and Gendered Power in the Early Middle Ages* (2007), and *King and Emperor: A New Life of Charlemagne* (2019).

Edward Roberts
is Lecturer in Early Medieval History at the University of Kent. He specializes in the history of Carolingian and Ottonian Europe, with particular interests in historiography, legal culture, bishops, and institutional change. He studied at Manchester and St Andrews and then held postdoctoral positions at King's College London, the University of the Basque Country, and the University of Liverpool. His first book, *Flodoard of Rheims and the Writing of History in the Tenth Century*, was published in 2019.

Annina Seiler
is an Academic Associate at the English Department of the University of Zürich, Switzerland, where she teaches and researches on various topics of English historical linguistics. She is the author of a monograph on *The Scripting of the Germanic Languages* (2014). Her research interests include Old and Middle English, the West Germanic languages, language contact and multilingualism, the functions of writing, Roman and runic script, historical lexicography and lexicology, and the history of linguistic thought.

Marco Stoffella
received his MA in Medieval History from Pisa University and his PhD from Ca' Foscari University. He was a postdoctoral researcher at IEMAN, Paderborn University, and Mitarbeiter at the Austrian Academy of Science. Since December 2008 he has taught medieval history at the University of Verona;

he has also been visiting scholar in several universities in Europe. His main research interests lie in early medieval social history, local societies, international relationships, minor local officers, and manuscripts, with an emphasis on the Verona Capitular Library and its networks in the early and high Middle Ages.

Francesca Tinti
is Ikerbasque Research Professor at the University of the Basque Country in Spain. She previously held research and teaching positions at the Universities of Cambridge and Bologna and has been principal investigator of several research projects financed by British, Italian, and Spanish funding agencies. She has published widely on early medieval religious, social, and cultural history, with a special focus on Anglo-Saxon England, its church, its documentary culture, and its relations with the European continent.

Kate Wiles
is Senior Editor of *History Today* and Associate Fellow of the Institute of Historical Research (IHR), School of Advanced Study, University of London. Her research interests are on scribal practice, Old English, and bilingualism. She gained her BA and MA from the University of Sheffield and her PhD from the University of Leeds, and held a postdoctoral research position at the University of the Basque Country. She is currently writing *Lost Voices: The Languages of Britain* (Allen Lane, forthcoming).

Bernhard Zeller
studied History, German Philology, Historical Auxiliary Sciences, and Archival Studies at the University of Vienna. He received his MA in 1999, MAS in 2001, and PhD in 2003. In the framework of a joint research project, he has been working on the facsimile edition of the St Gall charters for the *Chartae latinae antiquiores* series. In 2018 he received his Habilitation in Medieval History and Historical Auxiliary Sciences with his forthcoming thesis *Diplomatische Studien zu den St. Galler Privaturkunden des frühen Mittelalters* (ca. 720–980). He is Research Fellow at the Institute for Medieval Research of the Austrian Academy of Sciences and Lecturer at the University of Vienna, Austria.

CHAPTER 1

Latin and Germanic Vernaculars in Early Medieval Documentary Cultures: Towards a Multidisciplinary Comparative Approach

Francesca Tinti

This volume is one of the outcomes of a research project investigating the roles of, and interplay between, the languages employed in the documentary cultures of two regions of early medieval Europe: Anglo-Saxon England and eastern Francia.[1] It gathers contributions by the scholars who conducted the research for the project itself, along with others who were invited to present their work either at lecture cycles organized at the Universidad del País Vasco, where the project was based, or at the Leeds International Medieval Congress of 2016, in a strand of sessions on 'Languages and Literacy in the Early Medieval West'. The chapters in the book are therefore the result of the work of, and exchanges among, scholars of different nationalities, working in different European countries, at different stages of their careers (from PhD students to retired professors), and conducting their work in diverse research areas, covering primarily history and historical linguistics. The rationale for the volume and the research project behind it can be understood as a response to two major developments in (early) medieval studies: first, the production in the last thirty years or so of numerous publications dealing with early medieval literacy and the role played by charters in facilitating access to the written word at different social levels; and second, the current burgeoning of research into historical multilingualism in general, as well as medieval vernaculars and their interplay with Latin in particular.[2] These two research areas have largely

1 For more information on *The Languages of Early Medieval Charters* project, funded by the Spanish Ministerio de Economía y Competitividad and the Universidad del País Vasco UPV/EHU, see www.ehu.eus/lemc. The project was directed by Francesca Tinti and involved the work of three postdoctoral researchers: Robert Gallagher, Edward Roberts, and Kate Wiles.

2 Recent publications on ancient and medieval multilingualism include *Bilingualism in Ancient Society: Language Contact and the Written Text*, eds J. N. Adams, Mark Janse, and Simon Swain (Oxford, 2002); J. N. Adams, *Bilingualism and the Latin Language* (Cambridge, 2003); *Conceptualizing Multilingualism in Medieval England*, c.*800*–c.*1250*, ed. Elizabeth M. Tyler (Turnhout, 2011); *Mehrsprachigkeit im Mittelalter. Kulturelle, literarische, sprachliche und didaktische Konstellationen in europäischer Perspektive. Mit Fallstudien zu den 'Disticha Catonis'*, eds Michael Baldzuhn and Christine Putzo (Berlin, 2011); *Multilingualism in the*

 DOI:10.1163/9789004432338_002

moved along parallel paths, separated by the disciplinary boundaries that far too often prevent scholars from gaining useful insights from colleagues working in different, though hardly unconnected, fields.[3] In many respects this book represents the result of efforts made to overcome such obstacles, so as to bring the roles of languages and multilingualism into the study of early medieval documentary cultures, and, conversely, to encourage scholars of past multilingualism to engage further with the illuminating evidence provided by early medieval charters.

Charters, i.e. legal documents containing some kind of record,[4] have been at the centre of a remarkably fruitful area of historical research exploring the impact of the written word on different sectors of society. Social and cultural historians, taking their lead from anthropologists, have tested the validity of modern definitions of 'literacy' when applied to the early medieval world, often reacting to traditional assumptions about the limited role of the written word in these societies, not least the notion that charters were relevant only to the clerical minority who wrote them.[5] It has thus been shown, for instance, that

Graeco-Roman Worlds, eds Alex Mullen and Patrick James (Cambridge, 2012); J. N. Adams, *Social Variation and the Latin Language* (Cambridge, 2013); *Spoken and Written Language: Relations Between Latin and the Vernacular Languages in the Earlier Middle Ages*, eds Mary Garrison, Árpád P. Orban, and Marco Mostert (Turnhout, 2013). For studies that deal specifically with the main regions and periods covered by this volume, see, among others, Rosamond McKitterick, *The Carolingians and the Written Word* (Cambridge, 1989); Ernst Hellgardt, 'Zur Mehrsprachigkeit im Karolingerreich. Bermerkungen aus Anlaß von Rosamond McKittericks Buch "The Carolingians and the Written Word"', *Beiträge zur Geschichte der deutschen Sprache und Literatur* 118 (1996), 1–48; Scott Gwara, 'Second Language Acquisition and Anglo-Saxon Bilingualism: Negative Transfer and Avoidance in Ælfric Bata's Colloquia, ca. A.D. 1000', *Viator* 29 (1998), 1–24; Matthew Townend, *Language and History in Viking Age England: Linguistic Relations between Speakers of Old Norse and Old English* (Turnhout, 2002); Julia M. H. Smith, *Europe after Rome: A New Cultural History, 500–1000* (Oxford, 2005), pp. 13–50; Olga Timofeeva, 'Anglo-Latin Bilingualism before 1066: Prospects and Limitations', in *Interfaces between Language and Culture in Medieval England: A Festschrift for Matti Kilpiö*, eds Alaric Hall, Olga Timofeeva, Ágnes Kiricsi, and Bethany Fox (Leiden, 2010), pp. 1–36; Rebecca Stephenson, *The Politics of Language: Byrhtferth, Ælfric, and the Multilingual Identity of the Benedictine Reform* (Toronto, 2015); Emily Butler, *Language and Community in Early England: Imagining Distance in Medieval Literature* (London, 2017).

3 One of the most significant recent attempts at interdisciplinary cooperation between historians and philologists working in areas related to the theme of this volume can be found in *Sprache und Identität im frühen Mittelalter*, eds Walter Pohl and Bernhard Zeller (Vienna, 2012).

4 The term 'charter' is used in this volume in a maximalist, inclusive way, that is without specific implications concerning form or contents. For discussion of some terminological issues, see Kathryn Lowe's contribution.

5 Cf. Michael Richter, '"... quisquis scit scribere, nullum potat abere labore". Zur Laienschriftlichkeit im 8. Jahrhundert', in *Karl Martell in seiner Zeit*, eds Jörg Jarnut, Ulrich Nonn, and

laypeople did not necessarily need to be able to read the text of a Latin charter on their own in order to participate in documentary culture, since documents could be read aloud in their presence during proceedings often heavily imbued with ritual and within which communication was achieved through speech, text, and a variety of actions and gestures. Notions of pragmatic literacy and textual communities accommodating different levels of literacy have thus become customary in most investigations trying to establish how deep into society charters could reach.[6] These lines of research have been in part influenced by parallel studies in historical linguistics, such as those by Michel Banniard and Roger Wright. The latter's work in particular has drawn attention to the important act of reading charters aloud, for in Romance-speaking areas this very action often bridged the Latin of the charter and the early Romance pronunciation of the locality.[7] However, in non-Romance-speaking regions, such as England and eastern Francia, the gulf between the written and the spoken word was much bigger; while this has often been acknowledged, the impact of such a linguistic divide on the functioning of documentary culture deserves far more attention than it has hitherto received.

Anglo-Saxon England famously represents a peculiar linguistic case among the former territories of the western Roman Empire, as the Germanic populations who settled in lowland Britain in the fifth and sixth centuries continued to use their West Germanic language (or cluster of dialects) instead of adopting late Latin or some form of proto-Romance, as other originally

---

Michael Richter (Sigmaringen, 1994), pp. 393–404, and Matthew Innes, 'Memory, Orality and Literacy in an Early Medieval Society', *Past & Present* 158 (1998), 3–36; see also McKitterick in this volume, with further bibliography cited there. Recent analyses have shown that lay scribes played a more significant role in charter production than previously assumed and that the traditional lay/clerical divide can lead to misleading dichotomies in modern interpretations of early medieval documentary cultures: *Documentary Culture and the Laity in the Early Middle Ages*, eds Warren C. Brown, Marios Costambeys, Matthew Innes, and Adam J. Kosto (Cambridge, 2013); on lay scribes see also Stoffella in this volume.

6 Janet L. Nelson, 'Literacy in Carolingian Government', in *The Uses of Literacy in Early Mediaeval Europe*, ed. Rosamond McKitterick (Cambridge, 1990), pp. 258–96, at 269–70; Innes, 'Memory, Orality and Literacy'; Patrick J. Geary, 'Land, Language and Memory in Europe 700–1100', *Transactions of the Royal Historical Society*, 6th ser., 9 (1999), 169–84. For classic studies on pragmatic literacy and textual communities, see, respectively, Malcolm B. Parkes, 'The Literacy of the Laity', in *Literature and Western Civilization*, vol. 2: *The Medieval World*, eds David Daiches and Anthony Thorlby (London, 1973), pp. 555–77, and Brian Stock, *The Implications of Literacy: Written Language and Models of Interpretation in the Eleventh and Twelfth Centuries* (Princeton, NJ, 1983).

7 Michel Banniard, *Viva voce. Communication écrite et communication orale du IVe au IXe siècle en Occident latin* (Paris, 1992); Roger Wright, *A Sociophilological Study of Late Latin* (Turnhout, 2002).

Germanic-speaking peoples, such as the Franks or the Lombards/Langobards,[8] all eventually did following their migration and settlement.[9] The reasons for this different outcome have been and continue to be debated: the extent to which Britain had been Romanized and Christianized before the *adventus Saxonum*, the number of Germanic-speaking people who settled in Britain, the violence that characterized their takeover, and the limited amount of contact that they might have had with the Roman world prior to their migration (especially if compared with the Franks) have all repeatedly featured in the many discussions that historians, archaeologists, and linguists have dedicated to the topic.[10] Given the scarcity of both written and material sources to properly understand this transformative period, the debate is unlikely to settle any time soon.

Surviving runic inscriptions show that the Anglo-Saxons brought with them some knowledge of writing. Runic texts, however, were normally very short and an extensive written tradition only commenced with the introduction of the Roman alphabet within Old English-speaking communities following the late sixth- and early seventh-century activities of Italian and Irish missionaries. Runes were instrumental in the subsequent adaptation of the Roman alphabet to the representation of the Old English language, but within this early Christian context literary culture was, as far as we can tell, almost exclusively Latin, a language that the Anglo-Saxons had to learn as a foreign one.[11]

8 Both terms are used in this volume according to individual preference to refer to the same people.

9 Edward James, *Britain in the First Millennium* (London, 2001), pp. 60–64. See also Haubrichs and Stoffella in this volume. For a discussion placing the main areas explored in this book in a wider European framework, see Smith, *Europe after Rome*, pp. 13–50.

10 Cf., for instance, *The Anglo-Saxons from the Migration Period to the Eighth Century: An Ethnographic Perspective*, ed. John Hines (Woodbridge, 1997); James, *Britain in the First Millennium*; Richard Sharpe, 'Martyrs and Local Saints in Late Antique Britain', in *Local Saints and Local Churches in the Early Medieval West*, eds Alan Thacker and Richard Sharpe (Oxford, 2002), pp. 75–154; *After Rome*, ed. Thomas Charles-Edwards (Oxford, 2003); Catherine Hills, *The Origins of the English* (London, 2003); Richard Coates, 'Invisible Britons: The View from Linguistics', in *Britons in Anglo-Saxon England*, ed. Nick Higham (Woodbridge, 2007), pp. 172–91; Guy Halsall, *Worlds of Arthur: Facts and Fiction of the Dark Ages* (Oxford, 2013). See also further bibliography provided by Roberts and Tinti, below.

11 Though only preserved in later manuscripts, four seventh-century vernacular law-codes from Kent and Wessex represent important exceptions that must be borne in mind. Susan Kelly, 'Anglo-Saxon Lay Society and the Written Word', in *The Uses of Literacy*, ed. McKitterick, pp. 36–62; Andy Orchard, 'Latin and the Vernacular Languages: The Creation of a Bilingual Textual Culture', in *After Rome*, ed. Charles-Edwards, pp. 191–219; George Hardin Brown, 'The Dynamics of Literacy in Anglo-Saxon England', in *Textual and Material Culture in Anglo-Saxon England: Thomas Northcote Toller and the Toller Memorial Lectures*, ed. Donald Scragg (Woodbridge, 2003), pp. 183–212; Annina Seiler, 'Factual and

The earliest surviving examples of Anglo-Saxon charters are Latin royal diplomas dating from the late seventh century. They usually record a grant of land to an individual as a representative of a religious community or to a lay person who was willing to found one. Such royal diplomas testify to a growing importance in which the non-literate Anglo-Saxon kings of the time held written documents that were produced in their name by 'interested' ecclesiastical scriptoria, eager to secure full control of their landed properties. The language in which these documents were written and the uncial script used in the earliest, few surviving original single sheets attest to the role played by Christian culture in the Anglo-Saxons' adoption of documentary practices, even though there is no agreement as to who actually introduced charters in England: Augustine and Theodore, churchmen who were sent from Italy in the late sixth century and in the late 660s respectively to become bishops of Canterbury, have both been suggested as possible candidates because of the similarities that can be identified between late antique Italian charters and early Anglo-Saxon royal diplomas, though Merovingian and Celtic influences have also been hypothesized.[12] Irrespective of who was ultimately responsible for introducing charters into England, it is important to bear in mind the profound significance of these early phases, when a documentary culture was established through the acceptance of a foreign language that carried the authority of the Christian religion. As 'one essential function of the charter was to serve as a written record of an oral transaction',[13] the remarkable change of linguistic code that the passage from oral transactions to written records required in seventh-century England probably contributed to their becoming powerful symbolic instruments of royal authority.

Even at these early stages, however, as Annina Seiler's chapter in this volume clearly demonstrates, Anglo-Saxon charters were never written entirely in Latin, as from the very beginning place-names and personal names presented challenges for the scribes who had to accommodate vernacular elements in Latin contexts. Interesting forms of interplay between Latin and

---

Fictional Inscriptions: Literacy and the Visual Imagination in Anglo-Saxon England', in *Anglo-Saxon England and the Visual Imagination*, eds John D. Niles, Stacy S. Klein, and Jonathan Wilcox (Tempe, AZ, 2016), pp. 211–36, at 212–18.

12 Cf. Pierre Chaplais, 'Who Introduced Charters into England? The Case for Augustine', *Journal of the Society of Archivists* 3 (1969), 526–42; Kelly, 'Anglo-Saxon Lay Society', pp. 40–42; Ben Snook, 'Who Introduced Charters into England? The Case for Theodore and Hadrian', in *Textus Roffensis: Law, Language, and Libraries in Early Medieval England*, eds Bruce O'Brien and Barbara Bombi (Turnhout, 2015), pp. 257–89. See also Roberts and Tinti in this volume.

13 Rosamond McKitterick, 'Conclusion', in *The Uses of Literacy*, ed. McKitterick, pp. 319–333, at 320.

the vernacular, therefore, can already be observed in the earliest years of Anglo-Saxon charter production. As time went on and Old English started to be used for a variety of other literary purposes, Anglo-Saxon documentary culture became bilingual,[14] but its enormous potential for enhancing our understanding of the role of the written word in early medieval societies has only recently begun to be properly appreciated.[15] As is well known, Old English was particularly successful in making its way into the text of Latin charters when it was necessary to provide landscape descriptions, especially boundary clauses.[16] However, this was far from the only area in which the vernacular was employed in Anglo-Saxon charters. As Robert Gallagher has recently demonstrated, in the first half of the ninth century one can identify a period of special dynamism with Old English being used more frequently and in more varied contexts of Anglo-Saxon documentary production, from wills to endorsements to dispute memoranda, including even an exceptional Mercian royal diploma of the mid-840s written almost entirely in the vernacular.[17] In the later Anglo-Saxon period charters employing Old English became even more diverse and numerous.[18] Notwithstanding several normative trends which were more or less always at work (royal diplomas, for instance, were normally composed in Latin while wills were written in Old English), language choice and code-switching played a fundamental role in this bilingual documentary culture—a point that is emerging with increasing clarity in scholarship, not least in several of the chapters contained in this volume.[19]

---

14 Kelly, 'Anglo-Saxon Lay Society'; Kathryn Lowe, 'Lay Literacy in Anglo-Saxon England and the Development of the Chirograph', in *Anglo-Saxon Manuscripts and their Heritage*, eds Philip Pulsiano and Elaine M. Treharne (Aldershot, 1998), pp. 161–204; Robert Gallagher, 'The Vernacular in Anglo-Saxon Charters: Expansion and Innovation in Ninth-Century England', *Historical Research* 91 (2018), 205–35.

15 This is remarkable, because many of the studies presenting a maximalist view of literacy originated as responses to M. T. Clanchy, *From Memory to Written Record: England 1066–1307* (Oxford, 1979, with subsequent revised editions in 1993 and 2013), which in its first edition tended to downplay the role of written records in the early medieval period. However, although Clanchy's study centred on England, most of those who have emphasized the role of the written word in early medieval societies have done so by focusing on continental Europe, especially the Carolingian world.

16 Nicholas Howe, *Writing the Map of Anglo-Saxon England: Essays in Cultural Geography* (New Haven, CT, 2008), pp. 32–38.

17 Gallagher, 'The Vernacular in Anglo-Saxon Charters'; S 204 (*CantCC* 75).

18 Simon Keynes, 'Royal Government and the Written Word in Late Anglo-Saxon England', in *The Uses of Literacy*, ed. McKitterick, pp. 226–57, at 248–57.

19 Herbert Schendl, 'Beyond Boundaries: Code-Switching in the Leases of Oswald of Worcester', in *Code-Switching in Early English*, eds Herbert Schendl and Laura Wright (Berlin, 2011), pp. 47–94. Nicholas Brooks, 'Latin and Old English in Ninth-Century

Turning to the eastern Frankish territories, the situation one encounters would seem to be rather different. Although these regions were also predominantly inhabited by Germanic-speaking populations, their vernaculars do not seem to have been employed nearly as much as in England in the records from the period covered by this volume. However, this general observation needs to be qualified by looking more closely at the linguistic features of the documents produced in eastern Francia, while also bearing in mind that this area formed part of a much wider, multilingual polity. Although this is not the place for a detailed reconstruction of the origins of the Frankish Empire, it is necessary to cover at least some of the most salient developments that pertain to this volume.

Following their settlement of northern Gaul, Frankish expansion out of their Lower and Middle Rhine homeland was matched by a progressive adoption of many aspects of Roman administration and culture, including Catholic Christianity and, as was mentioned above, the Latin language. This linguistic shift, which appears to have started in the sixth century, was not unidirectional but also involved the absorption into late Latin of many terms of Germanic origin.[20] And as the Franks proceeded in their military, political, and cultural expansion to the south and the east, the linguistic constitution of their emerging empire became substantially more complex. The eighth century is often described as a turning point by both historians and linguists. As members of the Pippinid or Carolingian family asserted their control of the Frankish kingdoms, they embarked on a remarkable campaign of further expansion to secure their rule over such regions as Alemannia and Bavaria, which, though nominally under Frankish control, had hitherto enjoyed a certain degree of autonomy. Frisia was also brought under more direct rule, while Saxony, a territory well beyond the old Roman border, was only secured after a long period of conflict. By the end of the eighth century the Carolingian realms extended from northern Gaul to northern Spain and central Italy, and from the Atlantic

---

Canterbury', in *Spoken and Written Language*, eds Garrison et al., pp. 113–31; Gallagher, 'The Vernacular in Anglo-Saxon Charters'; Francesca Tinti, 'Writing Latin and Old English in Tenth-Century England: Patterns, Formulae and Language Choice in the Leases of Oswald of Worcester', in *Writing, Kingship and Power in Anglo-Saxon England*, eds Rory Naismith and David A. Woodman (Cambridge, 2018), pp. 303–27; Robert Gallagher and Francesca Tinti, 'Latin, Old English and Documentary Practice at Worcester from Wærferth to Oswald', *Anglo-Saxon England* 46 (2019 for 2017), 271–325.

20 Michel Banniard, 'Germanophonie, latinophonie et accès à la *Schriftlichkeit* (V^e^–VIIIe siècle)', in *Akkulturation. Probleme einer germanisch-romanischen Kultursynthese in Spätantike und frühen Mittelalter*, eds Dieter Hägermann, Wolfgang Haubrichs, and Jörg Jarnut (Berlin, 2004), pp. 340–58, at 349–51. See also the chapters by Haubrichs and by Roberts and Tinti in this volume.

to Pannonia.[21] The linguistic layout of this extensive territory was rather diverse, as a result not only of military success, but also of intensive cultural reforms and the emergence of a new empire-wide aristocracy. While the regions more to the south and the west of this vast polity can be safely assumed to have been part of the so-called Latin-Romance 'ensemble', and those far to the east and of more recent annexation (such as Saxony or Thuringia) were inhabited by Germanic-speaking populations, the nature of the situation in other, more central areas of the Empire is not so easy to determine. In fact, as Wolfgang Haubrichs also shows in his contribution to this volume, recent research has demonstrated that one should not think in terms of a linguistic frontier between the Romance- and the Germanic-speaking parts of the Frankish Empire, but rather of fluid contact zones characterized by a certain degree of bilingualism.[22]

Within the Latin-Romance 'ensemble' the eighth century has been identified as the period in which vertical communication between sophisticated writers and uneducated listeners was becoming more difficult because of the growing distance between *grammatica* and *rusticitas*. It would seem that the reforms promoted by Charlemagne and his advisor, the Northumbrian Alcuin, the leading intellectual of his day and someone who, like all Anglo-Saxons students, had learnt Latin as a foreign language, were fundamental in creating a clearer separation between correct Latin and spoken Romance, although the details and interpretation of what happened remain subjects of considerable debate.[23] Historians have traditionally placed special emphasis on the fact that the linguistic reforms of the Carolingians, which formed part of their ambitious plans for the reform of the liturgy, the clergy, and the education of the laity, sought to establish a universal Latin language, mastery of which was required of all members of the elite, irrespective of where they came from. Mayke de Jong has aptly described this as a 'Mandarin language' which differed notably

21 Paul Fouracre, 'Frankish Gaul to 814', in *The New Cambridge Medieval History, Volume II: c.700–c.900*, ed. Rosamond McKitterick (Cambridge, 1995), pp. 85–109; Walter Pohl, 'The Barbarian Successor States', in *The Transformation of the Roman World, AD 400–900*, eds Leslie Webster and Michelle Brown (London, 1997), pp. 33–47; Marios Costambeys, Matthew Innes, and Simon MacLean, *The Carolingian World* (Cambridge, 2011), pp. 1–30.

22 Jens Schneider, 'Langues germaniques', in *Les Barbares*, ed. Bruno Dumézil (Paris, 2016), pp. 843–49, at 846. See also Seiler and Zeller in this volume and further bibliography provided by Haubrichs, below.

23 Cf. Wright, *A Sociophilological Study*, pp. 127–57 and Banniard, *Viva voce*, pp. 305–68. See also Marc Van Uytfanghe, 'The Consciousness of a Linguistic Dichotomy (Latin-Romance) in Carolingian Gaul: The Contradictions of the Sources and their Interpretation', in *Latin and the Romance Languages in the Middle Ages*, ed. Roger Wright (London, 1991), pp. 114–29.

from the language used in informal communication.[24] Emphasis on these aspects and the fact that the Carolingian Empire considered itself the ideological successor of the Roman Empire has often led historians to overlook the importance of vernacular languages and communication among the Carolingian upper classes,[25] as well as the linguistic features of records produced in non-Romance-speaking areas such as the Middle Rhine valley, Alsace, Alemannia, or Bavaria.

These same features take centre stage in this volume, thanks in part to the results obtained within our research project with regard to the presence and significance of the vernacular in eastern Frankish documentary sources produced between the mid-eighth and the end of the ninth century.[26] Furthermore, one must bear in mind the remarkable connections which were established between eastern Francia and Anglo-Saxon England during the above-mentioned period of Carolingian expansion, which coincided with the arrival of numerous missionaries from Britain and Ireland in the eighth century. The most notable of these was Boniface, who, with Carolingian and papal support, spearheaded the Christianization of *Germania* and the regularization of its nascent church.[27] Insular missionaries brought with them expertise in using the vernacular to instil Christian teachings, and their arrival was soon followed by the initial textualization of Old High German and Old Saxon. The monastery of Fulda, founded by Boniface in 744, became the cradle of continental Germanic learning. The presence of insular script in manuscripts produced here and elsewhere in eastern Francia is a particularly clear manifestation of this influence.[28] Moreover, in the early 780s, another Anglo-Saxon,

---

24 Mayke de Jong, 'Some Reflections on Mandarin Language', in *East and West: Modes of Communication. Proceedings of the First Plenary Conference at Merida*, eds Evangelos Chrysos and Ian Wood (Leiden, 1999), pp. 61–69.

25 See, by contrast, Haubrichs' chapter in this volume on second-language acquisition among Carolingian elites. For the development of scholars' views as to whether there was ever 'official' interest in promoting Germanic vernaculars, see Hans J. Hummer, *Politics and Power in Early Medieval Europe: Alsace and the Frankish Realm, 600–1000* (Cambridge, 2005), pp. 130–33.

26 Edward Roberts, 'Boundary Clauses and the Use of the Vernacular in Eastern Frankish Charters, *c.*750–*c.*900', *Historical Research* 91 (2018), 580–604.

27 Ian Wood, *The Missionary Life: Saints and the Evangelisation of Europe, 400–1050* (Harlow, 2001), pp. 57–78; Joanna Story, *Carolingian Connections: Anglo-Saxon England and Carolingian Francia, c.750–870* (Aldershot, 2003); James T. Palmer, *Anglo-Saxons in a Frankish World, 690–900* (Turnhout, 2009); Janneke Raaijmakers, *The Making of the Monastic Community of Fulda, c.744–c.900* (Cambridge, 2012), pp. 19–40.

28 Herrad Spilling, 'Angelsächsische Schrift in Fulda', in *Von der Klosterbibliothek zur Landesbibliothek. Beiträge zum zweihundertjährigen Bestehen der Hessischen Landesbibliothek Fulda*, ed. Artur Brall (Stuttgart, 1978), pp. 47–98; Rosamond McKitterick, 'Anglo-Saxon

the aforementioned Alcuin, was invited by Charlemagne to head up his court school. Alcuin's renown as a teacher was such that promising pupils came to him from across the Frankish world, and he consequently trained many of the next generation's leading scholars and churchmen.[29] One of his students was Hrabanus Maurus, a monk of Fulda who studied with Alcuin at Tours, and who later became abbot of Fulda and eventually archbishop of Mainz.[30] Under Hrabanus' auspices, the reign of Louis the German (r. 840–76) witnessed the flourishing of vernacular literature.[31] Throughout this period, even though there were important differences between the relative presence of the vernacular in charters from England and the eastern Frankish Empire, it is possible to demonstrate significant parallels in the ways in which two predominantly Latin documentary cultures could and did accommodate Germanic vernaculars.[32]

Later developments, by contrast, show somewhat divergent trends. Whereas in the tenth and eleventh centuries England witnessed the consolidation of Old English as a literary and documentary code,[33] German did not become a language of written administration until much later. Scholars of German

Missionaries in Germany: Reflections on the Manuscript Evidence', *Transactions of the Cambridge Bibliographical Society* 9 (1989), 291–329, reprinted in Rosamond McKitterick, *Books, Scribes and Learning in the Frankish Kingdoms, 6th–9th Centuries* (Aldershot, 1994), IV; Gernot Wieland, 'Anglo-Saxon Culture in Bavaria, 739–850', *Mediaevalia* 17 (1994), 177–200; and Annina Seiler, *The Scripting of the Germanic Languages: A Comparative Study of "Spelling Difficulties" in Old English, Old High German and Old Saxon* (Zürich, 2014), pp. 36–47.

29 Michael Fox, 'Alcuin as Exile and Educator: "uir undecumque doctissimus"', in *Latin Learning and English Lore: Studies in Anglo-Saxon Literature for Michael Lapidge*, eds Katherine O'Brien O'Keefe and Andy Orchard, 2 vols (Toronto, 2005), 1:215–36; Mary Garrison, 'Alcuin of York', in *The Wiley Blackwell Encyclopedia of Anglo-Saxon England*, eds Michael Lapidge, John Blair, Simon Keynes, and Donald Scragg, 2nd ed. (Chichester, 2014), pp. 26–27.

30 *Hrabanus Maurus: Gelehrter, Abt von Fulda und Erzbischof von Mainz*, ed. Franz J. Felten (Mainz, 2006); *Raban Maur et son temps*, eds Philippe Depreux, Stéphane Lebecq, Michel J.-L. Perrin, and Olivier Szerwiniack (Turnhout, 2010); Michel Banniard, 'Rhabanus Maurus and the Vernacular Languages', in *Latin and the Romance Languages*, ed. Wright, pp. 164–74.

31 Wolfgang Haubrichs, 'Althochdeutsch in Fulda und Weißenburg—Hrabanus Maurus und Otfrid von Weißenburg', in *Hrabanus Maurus: Lehrer, Abt und Bischof*, eds Raymund Kottje and Harald Zimmermann (Wiesbaden, 1982), pp. 182–93; Wolfgang Haubrichs, 'Fulda, Hrabanus Maurus und die theodiske Schriftlichkeit', in *Hrabanus Maurus*, ed. Felten, pp. 93–120; Eric J. Goldberg, *Struggle for Empire: Kingship and Conflict under Louis the German, 817–876* (Ithaca, 2006), pp. 165–200.

32 See Roberts and Tinti in this volume.

33 Mechthild Gretsch, 'Literacy and the Uses of the Vernacular', in *The Cambridge Companion to Old English Literature*, eds Malcolm Godden and Michael Lapidge, 2nd ed. (Cambridge, 2013), pp. 173–294; Elaine Treharne, 'The Authority of English, 900–1150', in

literary history often refer to the so-called *große Lücke* ('wide gap') to describe the tenth and the first half of the eleventh century because of the near-total absence of texts written in the vernacular over that period.[34] Such divergent trends may appear to be reflected in the contents of this volume, as most of the chapters dealing with continental materials focus on the eighth and ninth centuries, unlike those on English records, which collectively span the entire Anglo-Saxon period through the Norman conquest of 1066 and beyond (as is the case with the vernacular records from Bury St Edmunds discussed in Kathryn Lowe's contribution). However, Stefan Esders's chapter on the use of Old Dutch and Old Saxon in tenth-century manorial records from Werden and Essen is a healthy reminder of the fact that Germanic vernaculars could be and were used on the continent for administrative purposes under specific circumstances even in the tenth century. Esders observes that the situations emerging from these records attest to a certain blurring of the line between Latin and vernaculars, which should not be seen as juxtaposed languages but rather as complementary media contributing to wider communicative contexts in which administrative records could reach far deeper into society.

Recent studies in historical linguistics and medieval literature are similarly moving away from notions of diglossia—still popular in the 1990s—preferring to refer instead to bilingualism and multilingualism.[35] The relationships between Latin and the vernaculars in the early medieval West have thus been shown to be far more complex and varied than previously thought. Whereas earlier interpretations tended to emphasize the contrast between the 'immense prestige of Latin' and the 'unlearned nature of vernacular culture' which would seem to emerge from contemporary sources,[36] more recently, important efforts have been made to qualify such apparent dichotomies and to point out the extent to which Latin and the vernaculars interacted in the (early) medieval period, while also highlighting the variety of literary genres for which Germanic vernaculars were employed: homilies, biblical poetry, prayers, baptismal vows, heroic poetry, charms, blessings, recipes, etc.[37] In the case of

---

The Cambridge History of Early Medieval English Literature, ed. Clare A. Lees (Cambridge, 2013), pp. 554–78.

34 Dennis H. Green, 'Die Schriftlichkeit und die Geschichte der deutschen Literatur im Mittelalter', *Literaturwissenschaftliches Jahrbuch* 30 (1989), 9–26.

35 *Spoken and Written Language*, eds Garrison et al., pp. vii–ix.

36 Cyril Edwards, 'German Vernacular Literature: A Survey', in *Carolingian Culture: Emulation and Innovation*, ed. Rosamond McKitterick (Cambridge, 1994), pp. 141–70, at 141–42.

37 Brian Murdoch, 'Textual Fluidity and the Interaction of Latin and Vernacular Languages', in *The Oxford Handbook of Medieval Latin Literature*, eds Ralph Hexter and David Townsend (Oxford, 2012), pp. 284–303; *Spoken and Written Language*, eds Garrison et al. See also *Latinity and Identity in Anglo-Saxon Literature*, eds Rebecca Stephenson and

Anglo-Saxon England, where a vernacular tradition has long been known to have thrived and encompassed an even wider variety of genres, recent studies have also played down earlier assumptions about Old English usage. Whereas the vernacular was once considered a poor substitute for Latin, employed to ensure comprehension, scholars now emphasize the confidence with which the educated elite used their native language.[38]

The evidence provided by charters and other administrative records for the study of the interactions between Latin and Germanic vernaculars and, more generally, early medieval multilingualism, has only just begun to be considered within this framework. Scholars of ancient bilingualism and multilingualism often refer to the limits of the written sources they have to rely upon when comparing their work to that of modern linguists who study the same phenomena through spoken forms.[39] Compared to other written sources, however, charters present a number of features that can lead to more fruitful outcomes. First of all, charters can normally be tied down to a specific time and place, so that collectively they furnish evidence for geographical variety and diachronic developments. Furthermore, virtually every charter can be linked to a specific event featuring some sort of agreement and whose participants would generally be recorded (often in witness-lists). Most importantly, because of their performative nature, charters provide an arguably unparalleled link between literacy and orality, so that even though they do not normally contain exact records of the oral exchanges that took place at the events from which they originated, they nonetheless provide important clues about those very exchanges.[40] In other words, even though students of early medieval multi-

Emily V. Thornbury (Toronto, 2016). For a succinct survey of literary texts in Old High German and Old Saxon, see Edwards, 'German Vernacular Literature'. For a more comprehensive literary history, see Wolfgang Haubrichs, *Die Anfänge: Versuche volkssprachiger Schriftlichkeit im frühen Mittelalter (ca. 700–1050/60). Geschichte der deutschen Literatur von den Anfängen bis zum Beginn der Neuzeit, I: Von den Anfängen bis zum hohen Mittelalter*, 2nd ed. (Tübingen, 1995), and for detailed treatment of all surviving works written in either Old High German or Old Saxon between the eighth and the eleventh century, see *Althochdeutsche und altsächsische Literatur*, ed. Rolf Bergmann (Berlin, 2013). For an overview on the emergence of a bilingual textual culture in Anglo-Saxon England, see Orchard, 'Latin and the Vernacular Languages'. For more detailed studies, see *The Cambridge History of Early Medieval English Literature*, ed. Lees.

38 Stephenson, *The Politics of Language*; Helen Gittos, 'The Audience for Old English Texts: Ælfric, Rhetoric and the "Edification of the Simple"', *ASE* 43 (2014), 231–66.

39 Adams, *Bilingualism and the Latin Language*, p. 3.

40 For charters as records of performances, see Geary, 'Land, Language and Memory'. Geary maintains that the use of the vernacular was most directly related to the performative nature of charters and the need to memorize boundary descriptions, especially in case of a future dispute. Cf., however, Roberts, 'Boundary Clauses', where it is proposed that

lingualism do not have access to spoken languages, in documentary sources they can catch glimpses of spoken forms. In Germanic-speaking regions such forms are made most visible through the employment of vernaculars which, as Patrick Geary has put it, can be seen to 'bleed through the Latin text'.[41] This is not to say that every single occurrence of Germanic words or passages in early medieval charters attests to spoken or colloquial forms as opposed to the written, learned role of Latin. In fact, it has been shown that different registers of both Latin and the vernaculars found their way into charters, depending on the function(s) of the records and of the relevant individual sections or passages in them. Opening introductory passages such as proems or *arengae* are normally written in a more formal Latin than the dispositive sections detailing the basic information regarding the recorded transaction.[42] In late Anglo-Saxon charters Old English could be used for different purposes and not just for 'practical information', such as that provided by boundary clauses. For instance, at Worcester, where the production of bilingual or entirely vernacular private documents is particularly well attested from the late ninth century, it is possible to encounter several examples of Old English verbal invocations at the start of the text.[43] Furthermore, in the important corpus of episcopal leases issued by Bishop Oswald in the second half of the tenth century, the vernacular was also regularly used for spiritual sanctions, i.e. the section normally found towards the end of the document comprising both a blessing for those who uphold what was established in the leases and an anathema condemning anyone who attempts to change it.[44] Similarly illuminating is the employment of alliterative and symbolic language in vernacular writs issued by late Anglo-Saxon kings, as discussed by Albert Fenton in this volume. Early medieval charters display a variety of uses and registers for both Latin and the vernaculars, thus showing the importance of language choice in their production.

---

vernacular boundary descriptions were not necessarily preserved for their juridical value but as rhetorical instruments reflecting the involvement of local landowners and the construction of local identities. On charters' performativity see Geoffrey Koziol, *The Politics of Memory and Identity in Carolingian Royal Diplomas: The West Frankish Kingdom (840–987)* (Turnhout, 2012), pp. 42–52, and Fenton, below. For possible evidence of charters recording oral depositions at court-cases held in late eighth- and ninth-century Tuscany, see Stoffella in this volume.

41 Geary, 'Land, Language and Memory', p. 176.

42 Alice Rio, *Legal Practice and the Written Word in the Early Middle Ages: Frankish Formulae, c.500–1000* (Cambridge, 2009), pp. 17–18; Scott T. Smith, *Land and Book: Literature and Land Tenure in Anglo-Saxon England* (Toronto, 2012), pp. 22–69.

43 Gallagher and Tinti, 'Latin, Old English and Documentary Practice', pp. 285, 297, 311, 316.

44 Tinti, 'Writing Latin and Old English, pp. 321–26.

In drawing scholars' attention to meaningful but little-discussed linguistic features of charters from Germanic-speaking territories of the early medieval West, the chapters contained in this volume acknowledge important quantitative differences between the documentary collections of Anglo-Saxon England and Francia; these are particularly evident when one considers, for example, that from the abbey of St Gall alone there survive *c.*800 charters up to the year 1000, while for the whole of England before the Norman Conquest there are only about 1500 surviving specimens. At the same time, Anglo-Saxon charters proportionally contain far more vernacular text than eastern Frankish documents. Quantitative approaches to the study of early medieval documentary cultures, however, have long been shown not to be particularly helpful,[45] especially if one bears in mind that our view of the linguistic differences between the two regions is very much determined by the situation at the end of the period here considered, characterized by, on the one hand, the above-mentioned continental *große Lücke*, and, on the other, the flourishing of Old English written production in the tenth and eleventh centuries. By contrast, in the eighth and ninth centuries, as demonstrated in the chapters by Annina Seiler and by Edward Roberts and Francesca Tinti, the linguistic features of Anglo-Saxon and eastern Frankish charters point towards several comparable strategies of conscious language use. These chapters stress that such strategies must be considered in their own right—that is, by avoiding hindsight bias as much as possible. Within such a framework Anglo-Saxon England can cease to be considered the exception to the rule of an overwhelmingly Latin documentary culture,[46] and be included in analyses that fruitfully compare and contrast the relationships between Latin and vernaculars in early medieval societies which shared an amalgamated Roman and Germanic linguistic and cultural heritage.

The complex interplay between spoken and written forms to which documentary sources attest often includes influences from Romance languages, as was the case at St Gall, thanks to the abbey's domain incorporating Romance-speaking Raetia, as Bernhard Zeller discusses in this volume. Elsewhere, Celtic vernaculars were important, as demonstrated by Charles Insley's chapter on surviving charters from Cornwall. In order to stress the importance of the variety of language contact revealed by early medieval charters, the volume includes a contribution by Marco Stoffella dealing with a region beyond eastern Francia or Anglo-Saxon England, namely northern Italy (and especially Tuscany) in the late Lombard and early Carolingian period. When the Lombards arrived in Italy in the mid-sixth century, they spoke a Germanic

45 See McKitterick in this volume.

46 Cf. Patrick Geary, *Language and Power in the Early Middle Ages* (Waltham, MA, 2013), pp. 56, 57, 59, 63.

language, but over the following centuries they abandoned their native tongue in favour of Latin and Italo-Romance. The inclusion of a study of this region becomes all the more relevant when one bears in mind the political and cultural ties that linked the Lombard kingdom to other Germanic-speaking territories, especially Alemannia and Bavaria. Various types of evidence, including inscriptions, place-names, and charter formulae, hint at the possibility of Lombard language survival among lay elites even after the Carolingian conquest of 774. Traces of possible Romance-Germanic bilingualism thus act as powerful reminders of the range of linguistic interactions that must be taken into account when addressing the social and political significance of the linguistic choices lying behind the production of early medieval records.

Further comparative insights are provided in Rory Naismith's chapter, which places the complex logistical operations and communicative interactions that characterized the Anglo-Saxon monetary system alongside those behind the production of royal diplomas. His comparative analysis usefully points out that charters are just one manifestation of early medieval literacy and multilingualism, as Rosamond McKitterick also notes in the volume's opening chapter. Moreover, coins place special significance on visual elements and on the positioning of both images and written text, suggesting further possible comparisons with the materiality of charters. For instance, while scribes tended to write out charter text on a single side of parchment, charters often provide crucial information on their production and subsequent uses on the other side, as Robert Gallagher and Kate Wiles demonstrate in their study of Anglo-Saxon charter endorsements.

Script, graphic choices, spelling, code-switching, endorsements, and many other features of charters explored in this volume indicate that the interactions between Latin and vernaculars could take place at different levels and that the choice to use one or the other language for any given portion of a charter could be determined by a variety of factors which were often due to specific circumstances of time and place. The different contexts of communication as well as the multiple forms of interplay between speaking, hearing, writing, and reading to which early medieval charters attest illustrate the range of crucial questions about early medieval societies that these materials can help us address. Doing that through the range of diverse expertise displayed by the contributors to this volume makes such an exercise especially rewarding.[47]

47 I am grateful to Robert Gallagher and Edward Roberts for reading and commenting on an earlier draft of this introduction. This chapter and the editing of this volume are part of the activities conducted by the University of the Basque Country Research Group GIU17/006 within the research project HAR2017-86502-P funded by the Spanish Ministerio de Ciencia e Innovación.

Bibliography

Secondary Sources

Adams, J. N., *Bilingualism and the Latin Language* (Cambridge, 2003).

Adams, J. N., *Social Variation and the Latin Language* (Cambridge, 2013).

Adams, J. N., Janse, Marke, and Swain, Simon (eds), *Bilingualism in Ancient Society: Language Contact and the Written Text* (Oxford, 2002).

Baldzuhn, Michael and Putzo, Christine (eds), *Mehrsprachigkeit im Mittelalter. Kulturelle, literarische, sprachliche und didaktische Konstellationen in europäischer Perspektive. Mit Fallstudien zu den 'Disticha Catonis'* (Berlin, 2011).

Banniard, Michel, 'Germanophonie, latinophonie et accès à la *Schriftlichkeit* (Ve–VIIIe siècle)', in *Akkulturation. Probleme einer germanisch-romanischen Kultursynthese in Spätantike und frühen Mittelalter*, eds Dieter Hägermann, Wolfgang Haubrichs, and Jörg Jarnut (Berlin, 2004), pp. 340–58.

Banniard, Michel, 'Rhabanus Maurus and the Vernacular Languages', in *Latin and the Romance Languages in the Middle Ages*, ed. Roger Wright (London, 1991), pp. 164–74.

Banniard, Michel, *Viva voce. Communication écrite et communication orale du IVe au IXe siècle en Occident latin* (Paris, 1992).

Bergmann, Rolf (ed.), *Althochdeutsche und altsächsische Literatur* (Berlin, 2013).

Brooks, Nicholas, 'Latin and Old English in Ninth-Century Canterbury', in *Spoken and Written Language: Relations Between Latin and the Vernacular Languages in the Earlier Middle Ages*, eds Mary Garrison, Árpád P. Orban, and Marco Mostert (Turnhout, 2013), pp. 113–31.

Brown, George Hardin, 'The Dynamics of Literacy in Anglo-Saxon England', in *Textual and Material Culture in Anglo-Saxon England: Thomas Northcote Toller and the Toller Memorial Lectures*, ed. Donald Scragg (Woodbridge, 2003), pp. 183–212.

Brown, Warren, Costambeys, Marios, Innes, Matthew, and Kosto, Adam (eds), *Documentary Culture and the Laity in the Early Middle Ages* (Cambridge, 2013).

Butler, Emily, *Language and Community in Early England: Imagining Distance in Medieval Literature* (London, 2017).

Chaplais, Pierre, 'Who Introduced Charters into England? The Case for Augustine', *Journal of the Society of Archivists* 3 (1969), 526–42.

Charles-Edwards, Thomas (ed.), *After Rome* (Oxford, 2003).

Clanchy, M. T., *From Memory to Written Record: England 1066–1307* (London, 1979, rev. editions 1993 and 2013).

Coates, Richard, 'Invisible Britons: The View from Linguistics', in *Britons in Anglo-Saxon England*, ed. Nick Higham (Woodbridge, 2007), pp. 172–91.

Costambeys, Marios, Innes, Matthew, and MacLean, Simon, *The Carolingian World* (Cambridge, 2011).

Depreux, Philippe, Lebecq, Stéphane, Perrin, Michel J.-L., and Szerwiniack, Olivier (eds), *Raban Maur et son temps* (Turnhout, 2010).

Edwards, Cyril, 'German Vernacular Literature: A Survey', in *Carolingian Culture: Emulation and Innovation*, ed. Rosamond McKitterick (Cambridge, 1994), pp. 141–70.

Felten, Franz J. (ed.), *Hrabanus Maurus: Gelehrter, Abt von Fulda und Erzbischof von Mainz* (Mainz, 2006).

Fouracre, Paul, 'Frankish Gaul to 814', in *The New Cambridge Medieval History, Volume II: c.700–c.900*, ed. Rosamond McKitterick (Cambridge, 1995), pp. 85–109.

Fox, Michael, 'Alcuin as Exile and Educator: "uir undecumque doctissimus"', in *Latin Learning and English Lore: Studies in Anglo-Saxon Literature for Michael Lapidge*, eds Katherine O'Brien O'Keefe and Andy Orchard, 2 vols (Toronto, 2005), 1:215–36.

Gallagher, Robert, 'The Vernacular in Anglo-Saxon Charters: Expansion and Innovation in Ninth-Century England', *Historical Research* 91 (2018), 205–35.

Gallagher, Robert and Tinti, Francesca, 'Latin, Old English and Documentary Practice at Worcester from Wærferth to Oswald', *Anglo-Saxon England* 46 (2019 for 2017), 271–325.

Garrison, Mary, 'Alcuin of York', in *The Wiley Blackwell Encyclopedia of Anglo-Saxon England*, eds Michael Lapidge, John Blair, Simon Keynes, and Donald Scragg, 2nd ed. (Chichester, 2014), pp. 26–27.

Garrison, Mary, Orban, Árpád P., and Mostert, Marco (eds), *Spoken and Written Language: Relations Between Latin and the Vernacular Languages in the Earlier Middle Ages* (Turnhout, 2013).

Geary, Patrick J., 'Land, Language and Memory in Europe 700–1100', *Transactions of the Royal Historical Society*, 6th ser., 9 (1999), 169–84.

Geary, Patrick, *Language and Power in the Early Middle Ages* (Waltham, MA, 2013).

Gittos, Helen, 'The Audience for Old English Texts: Ælfric, Rhetoric and the "Edification of the Simple"', *ASE* 43 (2014), 231–66.

Goldberg, Eric J., *Struggle for Empire: Kingship and Conflict under Louis the German, 817–876* (Ithaca, 2006).

Green, Dennis H., 'Die Schriftlichkeit und die Geschichte der deutschen Literatur im Mittelalter', *Literaturwissenschaftliches Jahrbuch* 30 (1989), 9–26.

Gretsch, Mechthild, 'Literacy and the Uses of the Vernacular', in *The Cambridge Companion to Old English Literature*, eds Malcolm Godden and Michael Lapidge, 2nd ed. (Cambridge, 2013), pp. 173–294.

Gwara, Scott, 'Second Language Acquisition and Anglo-Saxon Bilingualism: Negative Transfer and Avoidance in Ælfric Bata's Colloquia, ca. A.D. 1000', *Viator* 29 (1998), 1–24.

Halsall, Guy, *Worlds of Arthur: Facts and Fiction of the Dark Ages* (Oxford, 2013).

Haubrichs, Wolfgang, 'Althochdeutsch in Fulda und Weißenburg—Hrabanus Maurus und Otfrid von Weißenburg', in *Hrabanus Maurus: Lehrer, Abt und Bischof*, eds Raymund Kottje and Harald Zimmermann (Wiesbaden, 1982), pp. 182–93.

Haubrichs, Wolfgang, *Die Anfänge: Versuche volkssprachiger Schriftlichkeit im frühen Mittelalter (ca. 700–1050/60). Geschichte der deutschen Literatur von den Anfängen bis zum Beginn der Neuzeit, I: Von den Anfängen bis zum hohen Mittelalter*, 2nd ed. (Tübingen, 1995).

Haubrichs, Wolfgang, 'Fulda, Hrabanus Maurus und die theodiske Schriftlichkeit', in *Hrabanus Maurus: Gelehrter, Abt von Fulda und Erzbischof von Mainz*, ed. Franz J. Felten (Mainz, 2006), pp. 93–120.

Hellgardt, Ernst, 'Zur Mehrsprachigkeit im Karolingerreich. Bermerkungen aus Anlaß von Rosamond McKittericks Buch "The Carolingians and the Written Word"', *Beiträge zur Geschichte der deutschen Sprache und Literatur* 118 (1996), 1–48.

Hills, Catherine, *The Origins of the English* (London, 2003).

Hines, John (ed.), *The Anglo-Saxons from the Migration Period to the Eighth Century: An Ethnographic Perspective* (Woodbridge, 1997).

Howe, Nicholas, *Writing the Map of Anglo-Saxon England: Essays in Cultural Geography* (New Haven, CT, 2008).

Hummer, Hans J., *Politics and Power in Early Medieval Europe: Alsace and the Frankish Realm, 600–1000* (Cambridge, 2005).

Innes, Matthew, 'Memory, Orality and Literacy in an Early Medieval Society', *Past & Present* 158 (1998), 3–36.

James, Edward, *Britain in the First Millennium* (London, 2001).

de Jong, Mayke, 'Some Reflections on Mandarin Language', in *East and West: Modes of Communication. Proceedings of the First Plenary Conference at Merida*, eds Evangelos Chrysos and Ian Wood (Leiden, 1999), pp. 61–69.

Kelly, Susan, 'Anglo-Saxon Lay Society and the Written Word', in *The Uses of Literacy in Early Mediaeval Europe*, ed. Rosamond McKitterick (Cambridge, 1990), pp. 36–62.

Keynes, Simon, 'Royal Government and the Written Word in Late Anglo-Saxon England', in *The Uses of Literacy in Early Mediaeval Europe*, ed. Rosamond McKitterick (Cambridge, 1990), pp. 226–57.

Koziol, Geoffrey, *The Politics of Memory and Identity in Carolingian Royal Diplomas: The West Frankish Kingdom (840–987)* (Turnhout, 2012).

Lees, Clare A. (ed.), *The Cambridge History of Early Medieval English Literature* (Cambridge, 2013).

Lowe, Kathryn, 'Lay Literacy in Anglo-Saxon England and the Development of the Chirograph', in *Anglo-Saxon Manuscripts and their Heritage*, eds Philip Pulsiano and Elaine M. Treharne (Aldershot, 1998), pp. 161–204.

McKitterick, Rosamond, 'Anglo-Saxon Missionaries in Germany: Reflections on the Manuscript Evidence', *Transactions of the Cambridge Bibliographical Society* 9 (1989),

291–329; reprinted in Rosamond McKitterick, *Books, Scribes and Learning in the Frankish Kingdoms, 6th–9th Centuries* (Aldershot, 1994), IV.

McKitterick, Rosamond, *The Carolingians and the Written Word* (Cambridge, 1989).

McKitterick, Rosamond, 'Conclusion', in *The Uses of Literacy in Early Mediaeval Europe*, ed. Rosamond McKitterick (Cambridge, 1990), pp. 319–333.

Mullen, Alex and James, Patrick (eds), *Multilingualism in the Graeco-Roman Worlds* (Cambridge, 2012).

Murdoch, Brian, 'Textual Fluidity and the Interaction of Latin and Vernacular Languages', in *The Oxford Handbook of Medieval Latin Literature*, eds Ralph Hexter and David Townsend (Oxford, 2012), pp. 284–303.

Nelson, Janet L., 'Literacy in Carolingian Government', in *The Uses of Literacy in Early Medieval Europe*, ed. Rosamond McKitterick (Cambridge, 1990), pp. 258–96.

Orchard, Andy, 'Latin and the Vernacular Languages: The Creation of a Bilingual Textual Culture', in *After Rome*, ed. Thomas Charles-Edwards (Oxford, 2003), pp. 191–219.

Palmer, James T., *Anglo-Saxons in a Frankish World, 690–900* (Turnhout, 2009).

Parkes, Malcolm B., 'The Literacy of the Laity', in *Literature and Western Civilization*, vol. 2: *The Medieval World*, eds David Daiches and Anthony Thorlby (London, 1973), pp. 555–77.

Pohl, Walter, 'The Barbarian Successor States', in *The Transformation of the Roman World, AD 400–900*, eds Leslie Webster and Michelle Brown (London, 1997), pp. 33–47.

Pohl, Walter and Zeller, Bernhard (eds), *Sprache und Identität im frühen Mittelalter* (Vienna, 2012).

Raaijmakers, Janneke, *The Making of the Monastic Community of Fulda, c.744–c.900* (Cambridge, 2012).

Richter, Michael, '"... quisquis scit scribere, nullum potat abere labore". Zur Laienschriftlichkeit im 8. Jahrhundert', in *Karl Martell in seiner Zeit*, eds Jörg Jarnut, Ulrich Nonn, and Michael Richter (Sigmaringen, 1994), pp. 393–404.

Rio, Alice, *Legal Practice and the Written Word in the Early Middle Ages: Frankish Formulae, c.500–1000* (Cambridge, 2009).

Roberts, Edward, 'Boundary Clauses and the Use of the Vernacular in Eastern Frankish Charters, *c.*750–*c.*900', *Historical Research* 91 (2018), 580–604.

Schendl, Herbert, 'Beyond Boundaries: Code-Switching in the Leases of Oswald of Worcester', in *Code-Switching in Early English*, eds Herbert Schendl and Laura Wright (Berlin, 2011), pp. 47–94.

Schneider, Jens, 'Langues germaniques', in *Les Barbares*, ed. Bruno Dumézil (Paris, 2016), pp. 843–49.

Seiler, Annina, 'Factual and Fictional Inscriptions: Literacy and the Visual Imagination in Anglo-Saxon England', in *Anglo-Saxon England and the Visual Imagination*, eds John D. Niles, Stacy S. Klein, and Jonathan Wilcox (Tempe, AZ, 2016), pp. 211–36.

Seiler, Annina, *The Scripting of the Germanic Languages: A Comparative Study of "Spelling Difficulties" in Old English, Old High German and Old Saxon* (Zürich, 2014).

Sharpe, Richard, 'Martyrs and Local Saints in Late Antique Britain', in *Local Saints and Local Churches in the Early Medieval West*, eds Alan Thacker and Richard Sharpe (Oxford, 2002), pp. 75–154.

Smith, Julia M. H., *Europe after Rome: A New Cultural History, 500–1000* (Oxford, 2005).

Smith, Scott T., *Land and Book: Literature and Land Tenure in Anglo-Saxon England* (Toronto, 2012).

Snook, Ben, 'Who Introduced Charters into England? The Case for Theodore and Hadrian', in *Textus Roffensis: Law, Language, and Libraries in Early Medieval England*, eds Bruce O'Brien and Barbara Bombi (Turnhout, 2015), pp. 257–89.

Spilling, Herrad, 'Angelsächsische Schrift in Fulda', in *Von der Klosterbibliothek zur Landesbibliothek. Beiträge zum zweihundertjährigen Bestehen der Hessischen Landesbibliothek Fulda*, ed. Artur Brall (Stuttgart, 1978), pp. 47–98.

Stephenson, Rebecca, *The Politics of Language: Byrhtferth, Ælfric, and the Multilingual Identity of the Benedictine Reform* (Toronto, 2015).

Stephenson, Rebecca and Thornbury, Emily V. (eds), *Latinity and Identity in Anglo-Saxon Literature* (Toronto, 2016).

Stock, Brian, *The Implications of Literacy: Written Language and Models of Interpretation in the Eleventh and Twelfth Centuries* (Princeton, NJ, 1983).

Story, Joanna, *Carolingian Connections: Anglo-Saxon England and Carolingian Francia, c.750–870* (Aldershot, 2003).

Timofeeva, Olga, 'Anglo-Latin Bilingualism before 1066: Prospects and Limitations', in *Interfaces between Language and Culture in Medieval England: A Festschrift for Matti Kilpiö*, eds Alaric Hall, Olga Timofeeva, Ágnes Kiricsi, and Bethany Fox (Leiden, 2010), pp. 1–36.

Tinti, Francesca, 'Writing Latin and Old English in Tenth-Century England: Patterns, Formulae and Language Choice in the Leases of Oswald of Worcester', in *Writing, Kingship and Power in Anglo-Saxon England*, eds Rory Naismith and David A. Woodman (Cambridge, 2018), pp. 303–27.

Townend, Matthew, *Language and History in Viking Age England: Linguistic Relations between Speakers of Old Norse and Old English* (Turnhout, 2002).

Treharne, Elaine, 'The Authority of English, 900–1150', in *The Cambridge History of Early Medieval English Literature*, ed. Clare A. Lees (Cambridge, 2013), pp. 554–78.

Tyler, Elizabeth M. (ed.), *Conceptualizing Multilingualism in Medieval England, c.800–c.1250* (Turnhout, 2011).

Van Uytfanghe, Marc, 'The Consciousness of a Linguistic Dichotomy (Latin-Romance) in Carolingian Gaul: The Contradictions of the Sources and their Interpretation', in

Latin and the Romance Languages in the Middle Ages, ed. Roger Wright (London, 1991), pp. 114–29.

Wieland, Gernot, 'Anglo-Saxon Culture in Bavaria, 739–850', *Mediaevalia* 17 (1994), 177–200.

Wood, Ian, *The Missionary Life: Saints and the Evangelisation of Europe, 400–1050* (Harlow, 2001), pp. 57–78.

Wright, Roger, *A Sociophilological Study of Late Latin* (Turnhout, 2002).

Online sources

The Languages of Early Medieval Charters, www.ehu.eus/lemc.

CHAPTER 2

Charters, Languages, and Communication: Recent Work on Early Medieval Literacy

Rosamond McKitterick

Multilingualism, the display in many different literary and documentary genres of diverse language skills, and the promotion of Latin as the language of communication, government, religion, and law, are among the most striking aspects of early medieval European culture. For early medieval secular and clerical elites, the Latin language served as an instrument of cohesion in a highly diverse world. This book's focus on charters, the languages in which they were written, and the linguistic influences they betray, therefore yields fascinating case studies both of the variety of the linguistic situation in western Europe and its manifestations in the written record. Such manifestations, of course, presuppose 'participation in literacy' on a number of different levels. Study of this participation has become ever more concentrated in the past few decades, to the degree that particular emphases as well as new directions to pursue can be identified, as this chapter will demonstrate. First, however, it may be helpful to provide a summary of 'the story so far'.

It has become a commonplace in the past generation that charters and other administrative documents, alongside a kaleidoscopic range of literary, religious, and scholarly texts, furnish precious evidence for studying how individuals across the social spectrum used literacy. They thereby participated in a culture in which the written word clearly played a fundamental role and was fully integrated into the workings of society. These early medieval texts unequivocally attest to the communicative power of the written word in early medieval societies for transmitting information, ideas, and aspirations, in their sentences and in their very letterforms. That this understanding has become a commonplace is the consequence of a wealth of studies over the past thirty years in particular. The old assumption that this was an age of 'orality' in which the abilities to read and write were restricted to a small clerical elite has been demolished.[1] The documentary and literary sources from the Frankish

1 See, for example, Rosamond McKitterick, *The Carolingians and the Written Word* (Cambridge, 1989), and *The Uses of Literacy in Early Mediaeval Europe*, ed. Rosamond McKitterick

 | DOI:10.1163/9789004432338_003

regions, Spain, Italy, and the British Isles in the early Middle Ages, and most especially the manuscript evidence, simply contradict the negative assumptions about the role and manifestations of writing and about literacy in early medieval society that prevailed in the scholarly literature of the 1970s and early 1980s. Consequently, the regions of Europe where Latin was used alongside the Romance, Germanic, and Celtic languages, and whence written texts produced in whatever medium have survived, have engaged the attention of diplomatists, epigraphers, numismatists, palaeographers, historians, musicologists, and art historians. All explore the role of the written word and written notation in early medieval culture from their various perspectives, and with respect to their specific categories of evidence. Yet the way a culture fundamentally based on the written word coalesced in early medieval Europe is still not fully understood. This is precisely because it was such a multilingual world, with so many different local realities, in which oral communication also continued to play a significant role.

The question of continuity in legal practice from the late antique Roman Empire is one aspect that has been considered in a number of contexts,[2] as has the possibility of the continued archiving of legal records in local repositories

(Cambridge, 1990). For a comprehensive bibliography up to 2011 see Marco Mostert, *A Bibliography of Works on Medieval Communication* (Turnhout, 2012).

2 I single out here only a handful of studies in addition to those mentioned in McKitterick, *Carolingians*, pp. 23–24, such as the pioneering collection *Recht und Schrift im Mittelalter*, ed. Peter Classen, Vorträge und Forschungen 23 (Sigmaringen, 1977), augmented in a number of collaborative volumes as well as monographs, such as *The Settlement of Disputes in Early Medieval Europe*, eds Wendy Davies and Paul Fouracre (Cambridge, 1986); *Literacy, Politics, and Artistic Innovation in the Early Medieval West*, ed. Celia M. Chazelle (Lanham, MD, 1992); François Bougard, *La justice dans le royaume d'Italie: de la fin du VIIIe siècle au début du XIe siècle*, Bibliothèque des Écoles françaises d'Athènes et de Rome 291 (Rome, 1995); *Schriftkultur und Reichswervaltung unter den Karolingern*, ed. Rudolf Schieffer, Abhandlungen der Nordrhein-Westfälischen Akademie der Wissenschaften 97 (Opladen, 1996); Martina Stratmann, 'Schriftlichkeit in der Verwaltung von Bistümern und Klöstern zur Zeit Karls des Großen', in *Karl der Große und sein Nachwirken 1000 Jahre Kultur und Wissenschaft in Europa*, eds Paul Butzer, Max Kerner, and Walter Oberscherlp (Turnhout, 1997), pp. 251–75; *Law, Custom and Justice in Late Antiquity and the Early Middle Ages*, ed. Alice Rio (London, 2007); *Law before Gratian. Law in Western Europe c. 500–1100*, eds Per Andersen, Mia Münster-Swendsen, and Helle Vogt (Copenhagen, 2007); Alice Rio, *Legal Practice and the Written Word in the Early Middle Ages: Frankish Formulae,* c.500–1000 (Cambridge, 2009); Thomas Faulkner, *Law and Authority in the Early Middle Ages: The Frankish* leges *in the Carolingian Period* (Cambridge, 2016); Karl Ubl, *Sinnstiftungen eines Rechtsbuchs. Die Lex Salica im Frankenreich*, Quellen und Forschungen zum Recht im Mittelalter 9 (Ostfildern, 2017). The bibliographies of the most recent volumes cited here and of that in the next footnote provide guidance to the extensive literature.

and family archives.[3] This work has built on earlier studies of particular monasteries and bishoprics such as Farfa, Lorsch, Wissembourg, Fulda, Werden, and Canterbury,[4] regions such as Catalonia, Raetia, and Bavaria,[5] and the implications of particular and individual documents, such as the wills of Adalgisel-Grimo, Angelberga, Erkanfrida, and Ælfgifu, or the handbook of Dhuoda.[6]

---

3 *Documentary Culture and the Laity in the Early Middle Ages*, eds Warren Brown, Marios Costambeys, Matthew Innes, and Adam Kosto (Cambridge, 2013).

4 Among the many studies of these centres and the texts they produced it is primarily those from the Anglophone scholarly tradition that engage specifically with issues of literacy: Marios Costambeys, *Power and Patronage in Early Medieval Italy: Local Society, Italian Politics and the Abbey of Farfa, c.700–900* (Cambridge, 2007); Matthew Innes, *State and Society in the Early Middle Ages: The Middle Rhine Valley, 400–1000* (Cambridge, 2000); Hans J. Hummer, *Politics and Power in Early Medieval Europe: Alsace and the Frankish Realm, 600–1000* (Cambridge, 2005); Janneke Raaijmakers, *The Making of the Monastic Community of Fulda, c.744–c.900* (Cambridge, 2012); Rosamond McKitterick, 'The Uses of Literacy in Carolingian and Post-Carolingian Europe: Literate Conventions of Memory', in *Scrivere e leggere nell'alto medioevo*, Settimane 59 (Spoleto, 2012), pp. 179–211; Marco Stoffella, 'Aristocracy and Rural Churches in the Territory of Lucca between Lombards and Carolingians: A Case Study', in *774, ipotesi su una transizione. Atti del seminario di Poggibonsi, 16–18 febbraio 2006*, ed. Stefano Gasparri (Turnhout, 2008), pp. 289–311; and Marco Stoffella, 'Gli atti di permute nella Toscana occidentale tra VIII e XI secolo', in *Tauschgeschäft und Tauschurkunde vom 8. bis zum 12. Jahrhundert/L'acte d'échange, du VIIIe au XIIe siècle* (Limoges, 2013), pp. 129–57; Nicholas Brooks, *The Early History of the Church of Canterbury: Christ Church from 597 to 1066* (London, 1984); *CantCC*; *Archbishop Theodore: Commemorative Studies on his Life and Influence*, ed. Michael Lapidge (Cambridge, 1995).

5 Adam J. Kosto, *Making Agreements in Medieval Catalonia: Power, Order, and the Written Word, 1000–1200* (Cambridge, 2001); Jonathan Jarrett, *Rulers and Ruled in Frontier Catalonia, 880–1010: Pathways of Power* (Woodbridge, 2010); Warren Brown, *Unjust Seizure: Conflict, Interest and Authority in an Early Medieval Society* (Ithaca, 2001); Peter Erhart and Julia Kleindinst, *Urkundenlandschaft Rätien*, Forschungen zur Geschichte des Mittelalters 7 (Vienna, 2004); *Mensch und Schrift im frühen Mittelalter*, eds Peter Erhart and Lorenz Hollenstein (St Gall, 2006); *Die Privaturkunden der Karolingerzeit*, eds Peter Erhart, Karl Heidecker, and Bernhard Zeller (Dietikon-Zürich, 2009).

6 Wilhelm Levison, 'Das Testament des Diakons Adalgisel-Grimo vom Jahre 634', *Trierer Zeitschrift* 7 (1932), 69–85; reprinted in Wilhelm Levison, *Aus Rheinischer und Fränkische Frühzeit* (Düsseldorf, 1948), pp. 118–38; Régine Le Jan, 'The Multiple Identities of Dhuoda', and Cristina La Rocca, 'Angelberga, Louis II's Wife and her Will (877)', both in *Ego Trouble: Authors and their Identities in the Early Middle Ages*, eds Richard Corradini, Matthew Gillis, Rosamond McKitterick, and Irene van Renswoude, Forschungen zur Geschichte des Mittelalters 15 (Vienna, 2010), pp. 211–20 and 221–26 respectively; Janet L. Nelson, 'The Wary Widow', in *Property and Power in the Early Middle Ages*, eds Wendy Davies and Paul Fouracre (Cambridge, 1995), pp. 82–113; and *Dhuoda, Manual pour mon fils*, ed. Pierre Riché, Sources Chrétiennes 225bis (Paris, 1997). See also *ASWills*; and Linda Tollerton, *Wills and Will-Making in Anglo-Saxon England* (York, 2011).

All this research has highlighted the richness of the surviving evidence, the enormous diversity of deployments and manifestations of literacy, and the extent, above all, to which lay people and clerics shared a common documentary culture.[7] Early medievalists, moreover, have long since abandoned a futile effort at quantification. Instead, their qualitative assessments have sought to understand attitudes to writing and literacy as a social and cultural phenomenon. Scholars of the early medieval West have explored the interaction between literate media and other forms of human discourse, expression and communication, and the technical and cultural implications of the many manifestations of the written word. The work of Christian missionaries in introducing hitherto alien written practices as well as Latin to new peoples and regions in western and northern Europe adds a further dimension, as does the intervention of particular individuals in order to promote specific social practices. It is clear nevertheless how much still needs be done, especially at a local level, as the studies in the rest of this volume demonstrate.

The Evidential Base

The evidential base for current studies of charters and literacy was established, along with the principal characteristics of the discipline of palaeography, by Jean Mabillon and Ludwig Traube, with classic contributions to the study of diplomatic in their wake by Arthur Giry and Harry Bresslau.[8] These scholars emphasized the interconnection of script types, scribal skills, language, and cultural context. Thus the twentieth-century surveys in *Codices latinae antiquiores* of Latin manuscripts prior to 800 and Bernhard Bischoff's *Katalog* of ninth-century manuscripts[9] effectively appeared in tandem with similar projects tracing the production of charters, such as the *Chartae latinae antiquiores* for surviving 'original' charters from before 800. This remarkable enterprise continues, and now aims to produce in facsimile all extant original charters from the ninth century. To date, all the ninth-century charters in Italian

7 See especially Adam J. Kosto, 'Laymen, Clerics, and Documentary Practices in the Early Middle Ages: The Example of Catalonia', *Speculum* 80 (2005), 44–74, with an excellent review of earlier literature.

8 Jean Mabillon, *De re diplomatica* (Paris, 1681); Ludwig Traube, *Vorlesungen und Abhandlungen*, 3 vols (Munich, 1909–11); Arthur Giry, *Manuel de Diplomatique*, rev. ed. (Paris, 1925, originally 1894); and Harry Bresslau, *Handbuch der Urkundenlehre*, 2 vols, rev. ed. (Berlin, 1912, originally 1889, reprinted 1969).

9 CLA; and Bernhard Bischoff, *Katalog der festländischen Handschriften des neunten Jahrhunderts (mit Ausnahme der wisigotischen)*, 3 vols (Wiesbaden, 1998–2014).

archives and St Gall have been published, and a project to publish a survey and set of facsimiles of the ninth-century charters in French archives has recently been launched.[10] These volumes will augment existing volumes of royal diplomata already published in facsimile,[11] and the invaluable ARTEM (Atelier de recherche sur les textes médiévaux) inventory that appeared in 2001.[12] For Anglo-Saxon England, Peter Sawyer's handlist has been extensively updated in 'The Electronic Sawyer' website.[13] The ongoing British Academy series of Anglo-Saxon charter archives continues to publish scholarly editions and critical commentaries of all surviving pre-Conquest documents.[14] Meanwhile, the documentation of the astonishing wealth of material for Catalonia has been underway since Ramon d'Abadal i de Vinyals first launched his Catalunya Carolíngia charter project in 1926.[15] Over the past two hundred years, editions of many charters made from originals and later copies, especially those reproduced in cartularies, have thus provided the essential texts. National enterprises such as the Monumenta Germaniae Historica have played a crucial role. In recent years, for example, the massive editions of Merovingian charters and the diplomas of the Emperor Louis the Pious, both coordinated by Theo Kölzer, have appeared, buttressed by comprehensive studies of their diplomatic and the language of the formulae.[16]

---

10 *ChLA*, masterminded by Albert Bruckner and Robert Marichal, and that for the ninth century by their successors Guglielmo Cavallo and Giovanna Nicolaj, on the model of CLA, all with transcriptions, commentary and facsimiles: St Gall was the first to appear and then successive volumes on Great Britain, the United States, France, Italy, Egypt, Germany, Scandinavia, Greece, Russia, and Spain in the series up to 800. The second series, cataloguing charters of the ninth century, begins with vol. 50, covering Italy to vol. 99, Switzerland (including St Gall) in 14 volumes, and as of 2019 three volumes for Spain have appeared.

11 *Diplomata Karolinorum: Recueil de reproductions en facsimile des actes originaux des souverains carolingiens conservés dans les archives et bibliothèques de France*, eds Ferdinand Lot and Philippe Lauer, 10 vols (Paris, 1936–40) and *Diplomata Karolinorum: Faksimile-Ausgabe der in der Schweiz liegenden originalen Karolingerdiplome*, ed. Albert Bruckner, 4 vols (Basle, 1969–72).

12 Benoît-Michel Tock, *La diplomatique française du Haut Moyen Age. Inventaire des chartes originales antérieures à 1121 conservée en France*, 2 vols (Turnhout, 2001).

13 S.

14 For a full list, see www.thebritishacademy.ac.uk/anglo-saxon-charters.

15 *Catalunya Carolingia*, eds Ramon d'Abadal i de Vinyals et al. (Barcelona, 1926–2006), among many other editions of charters from particular Catalonian archives. See also Cullen J. Chandler, *Carolingian Catalonia: Politics, Culture, and Identity in an Imperial Province, 778–987* (Cambridge, 2019).

16 MGH DD Mer.; MGH DD Louis the Pious; Mark Mersiowsky, *Die Urkunde in der Karolingerzeit. Originale, Urkundenpraxis und politische Kommunikation*, MGH Schriften 60, 2 vols (Wiesbaden, 2015); Sarah Patt, *Studien zu den 'Formulae imperiales'. Urkundenkonzeption*

The international collaboration of scholars in order to tabulate and calendar the evidence available is one of the most striking aspects of the modern study of the Middle Ages.[17] It was in the 1950s that the Comité internationale de paléographie was founded, with its core members being among those responsible for both the journal *Scriptorium*, founded 1946, and the *Manuscrits datés* project launched in the late 1950s. Other enterprises at both a national and individual level have concentrated on inventories of particular categories of texts such as manuscripts with notable illumination or those containing music or vernacular glosses; texts such as classical authors, canon law,[18] or medical texts; surveys of special characteristics such as the chrismon (a symbolic invocation in charters);[19] or surveys of particular media such as collections of inscriptions[20] and charters extant on papyrus.[21] Earlier inventories of cartularies and monastic archives, such as that of Henri Stein, have been supplemented by more recent studies. Many editions of charters and cartularies have emanated from the École Nationale des Chartes in Paris and similar institutions elsewhere in Europe.[22]

---

und Formulargebrauch in der Kanzlei Kaiser Ludwigs des Frommen (814–840), MGH Studien und Texte 59 (Wiesbaden, 2016); Susanne Zwierlein, *Studien zu den Arengen in den Urkunden Kaiser Ludwigs des Frommen (814–840)*, MGH Studien und Texte 60 (Wiesbaden, 2016).

17 See the engaging surveys, for example, of the emergence of the *Patrologia Latina*, the Monumenta Germanica Historiae, and the Rolls Series by David Knowles, *Great Historical Enterprises: Problems in Monastic History* (London, 1963).

18 Lotte Kéry, *Canonical Collections of the Early Middle Ages (ca. 400–1140): A Bibliographical Guide to the Manuscripts and Literature* (Washington, DC, 1999).

19 *Graphische Symbole in mittelalterlichen Urkunden. Beiträge zur diplomatischen Semiotik*, ed. Peter Rück (Sigmaringen, 1996).

20 *Receuil des inscriptions chrétiennes de la Gaule antérieure à la renaissance carolingienne*, ed. Henri-Irénée Marrou and, from 1997, Luce Pietri and Nancy Gauthier (Paris, 1975-); Guglielmo Cavallo and Cyril Mango, *Epigrafia medievale greca e latina: ideologia e funzione* (Spoleto, 1995); Nicolette Gray, 'The Palaeography of Latin Inscriptions in the Eighth, Ninth and Tenth Centuries in Italy', *Papers of the British School at Rome* 16 (1948), 38–170; and Luca Cardin, *Epigrafia a Roma nel primo medioevo (secoli IV–X). Modelli grafici e tipologie d'uso* (Rome, 2008).

21 Jan-Olof Tjäder, *Die nichtliterarischen lateinischen Papyri Italiens aus der Zeit 445–700*, 3 vols (Lund and Stockholm, 1954–82).

22 Henri Stein, *Bibliographie générale des cartulaires français ou relatifs à l'histoire de France* (Paris, 1907); *Les cartulaires*, eds Olivier Guyotjeannin, Laurent Morelle, and Michel Parisse, Mémoires et documents de l'École des chartes 39 (Paris, 1993); *Charters, Cartularies, and Archives: The Preservation and Transmission of Documents in the Medieval West. Proceedings of a Colloquium of the Commission internationale de diplomatique, Princeton and New York, 16–18 September 1999*, eds Adam J. Kosto and Anders Winroth, Papers in Medieval Studies 17 (Toronto, 2002). Even a quick trawl of any substantial university library catalogue under 'cartulaire', 'cartulary', 'cartularium', 'Urkundenbuch', or

Formative Studies

Studies of this wealth of material in the earlier decades of the twentieth century tended to focus on the content of the documents, formulae, the development of diplomatic, and what the documents yielded concerning property and social networks, rather than their significance as written records and their implications for the uses of literacy. The *Namenforschung* group in Freiburg exploited charters alongside *Libri memoriales* to reconstruct social and family networks in the early Middle Ages.[23] Yet even in the 1950s, new emphases in research were emerging, and some of these were stimulated by the Centro italiano di studi sull'alto medioevo at its annual Settimane convened in Spoleto since 1954. This regular annual gathering began long before conferences such as the Kalamazoo International Congress on Medieval Studies and the Leeds International Medieval Congress became well established, when there were relatively few such opportunities for early medievalists to exchange ideas. The themes chosen for these meetings encouraged the integration of questions of manuscripts, art and scripts, charters and other legal and administrative documents, inscriptions, and coinage, into discussions by internationally renowned scholars of the historical and cultural issues of the early Middle Ages as a whole. They helped to create an unusual unanimity of purpose among early medievalists as well as worldwide networks of collaborative scholarship and friendship.

With hindsight, these separate studies in the Spoleto volumes clearly provided a rich potpourri of ideas and perspectives on which later studies of literate culture were able to draw. Scholars such as Bernhard Bischoff, Giorgio Cencetti, and Armando Petrucci considered letter forms and codices as primary pieces of historical evidence in their own right, not simply as vehicles of texts.[24] One of the pioneering contributions of the early years of the Spoleto Settimane, for example, was the demonstration by Giorgio Cencetti of the

'Traditiones' yields many separate editions of early medieval charters and cartularies too abundant to list here.

23 Gerd Tellenbach, 'Liturgische Gedenkbücher als historische Quelle', in *Mélanges E. Tisserant* 5, Studi e Testi 235 (Vatican City, 1964), pp. 389–99; Karl Schmid and Joachim Wollasch, 'Die Gemeinschaft von Lebenden und Verstorbenen in Zeugnissen des Mittelalters', *Frühmittelalterliche Studien* 1 (1967), 365–405; and Gerd Althoff, *Amicitiae und Pacta. Bündnis, Einung, Politik und Gebetsgedenken im beginnenden 10. Jahrhundert*, MGH Schriften 37 (Hanover, 1992).

24 See Rosamond McKitterick, 'Palaeography, Diplomatic and Codicology: The Last Fifty Years', in *Omaggio al Medioevo. I primi cinquanta anni del Centro italiano di studi sull'alto medioevo di Spoleto*, ed. Enrico Menestò (Spoleto, 2009), pp. 179–210, on which I draw in what follows.

influence exerted by Roman documentary cursive scripts on subsequent charter hands in the barbarian successor states of the early Middle Ages.[25] Armando Petrucci built on Cencetti's work by emphasizing letter forms and script as cultural expressions and symbols.[26] Their work was augmented by the classic study of the development of royal diplomas and charter practice by Peter Classen.[27] The Franks, for example, consolidated their Roman chancery heritage and contributed their own institutional, technical, and ideological innovations. They provided the foundation for the legal and documentary practice of governments throughout Europe for the rest of the Middle Ages.[28]

Despite these efforts, the topic of literacy as such was surprisingly absent in the early Spoleto volumes, even from considerations of conversion in the seventh and eighth centuries. The discussions of the significance of Wulfila's work and the provision of an alphabet for the written form of Gothic, for example, was the outcome of an exhibition in the Biblioteca Apostolica Vaticana.[29] Only in more recent volumes from the twenty-first century have the themes of communication and literacy been addressed. By then, the contributors were in any case members of a younger generation who had inaugurated the new work on literacy and manifestations of documentary culture.[30]

Gradually, the Settimane studies meshed with investigations of literacy and the written word in antiquity and the early Middle Ages more generally and became one stream among many contributions to wider scholarly discussion. A further extension of the context in which script is to be understood, for example, was promoted by Gugliemo Cavallo's insistence on the importance of the

25 Giorgio Cencetti, 'Dall'unità al particolarismo grafico. Le scritture cancelleresche romane e quelle dell'alto medioevo', in *Il passagio dall'antichità al medioevo in occidente*, Settimane 9 (Spoleto, 1962), pp. 237–64.

26 Armando Petrucci, 'Aspetti simbolici delle testimonianze scritte', in *Simboli e simbologia nell'alto medioevo*, Settimane 23 (Spoleto, 1976), pp. 813–44.

27 Peter Classen, *Kaiserreskript und Königsurkunde: diplomatischer Studien zum Problem der Kontinuität zwischen Altertum und Mittelalter* (Thessaloniki, 1977).

28 See, for example, on charter production, chrismons, and format, the Marburg Hilfswissenschaft contributions led by Peter Rück and Frank Bischoff: Frank Bischoff, *Urkundenformate im Mittelalter. Größe, Format und Proportionen von Papsturkunden in Zeiten expandierender Schriftlichkeit (11.–13. Jahrhundert)* (Marburg, 1996); *Graphische Symbole*, ed. Rück; *Methoden der Schriftbeschreibung*, ed. Peter Rück (Stuttgart, 1999).

29 *Tre alfabeti per gli Slavi. Catalogo della mostra allestita nella Biblioteca Vaticana per l'undicesimo centenario della morte di San Metodio*, eds Leonard Boyle and Vittorio Peri (Vatican City, 1985).

30 *Comunicare e significare nell'alto medioevo*, Settimane 52 (Spoleto, 2005); and *Scrivere e leggere nell'alto medioevo*, Settimane 59 (Spoleto, 2012).

audience and cultural milieu for all medieval written texts,[31] and the epigrapher Robert Favreau's demonstration of the social role of inscribed stones and the light they throw on those who commissioned them.[32] In explicit appraisals across different media, Cavallo and Giovanna Nicolaj assessed how books and charters mirror social and cultural change.[33] In considering the relationship between text and image, the impact of letter forms and literacy, Beat Brenk emphasized how the understanding of texts and writing needed to include not only their aesthetic qualities but also how one might read pictures. John Mitchell's work, furthermore, underscored the many different levels on which the uses of writing need to be understood, from brick stamps and tile-makers' marks to elaborate inscriptions on the lintels of buildings.[34] Both Favreau and Petrucci, moreover, highlighted the ideological importance of writing in whatever medium, the importance of appreciating the technical skill of the scribe or stonecutter, and the extra capacity of writing and letter forms to evoke the past.[35]

Literacy as a specific theme was also explored independently. Groundbreaking studies from different perspectives, but with crucial underlying principles about the role of writing in society, had been published by Léopold Delisle in countless studies of Merovingian and Carolingian manuscripts and by Ludwig Traube in the studies gathered together in his *Vorlesungen und Abhandlungen*.[36] Other early contributions have become classics: James Thompson's assessment

31 Guglielmo Cavallo, 'Libri scritti, libri letti, libri dimenticati', in *Il secolo di ferro: mito e realtà del secolo X*, Settimane 38 (Spoleto, 1991), pp. 759–94.

32 Robert Favreau, 'Les commanditaires dans les inscriptions du haut moyen âge occidental' in *Committenti e produzione artistico-letteraria nell'alto medioevo occidentale*, Settimane 39 (Spoleto, 1992), pp. 681–722.

33 Giovanna Nicolaj, 'Fratture e continuità nella documentazione fra tardo antico e alto medioevo. Preliminari di diplomatica e questioni di metodo', and Guglielmo Cavallo, 'Scrivere, leggere, memorizzare le sacre scritture', both in *Morfologie sociali e culturali in Europa fra tarda antichità e alto medioevo*, Settimane 45 (Spoleto, 1998), pp. 953–84 and 987–1008 respectively.

34 *Testo e immagine nell'alto medioevo*, Settimane 41 (Spoleto, 1994), especially Beat Brenk, 'Schriftlichkeit und Bildlichkeit in der Hofschule Karls d. Gr.', and John Mitchell, 'The Display of Script and the Uses of Painting in Longobard Italy', at pp. 631–82 and 887–954 respectively.

35 Robert Favreau, 'La mémoire du passé dans les inscriptions du haut moyen âge', and Armando Petrucci, 'Spazi di scrittura e scritte avventizie nel libro alto medievale', both in *Ideologie e pratiche del reimpiego nell'alto medioevo*, Settimane 46 (1999), pp. 937–76 and 981–1006 respectively.

36 Traube, *Vorlesungen und Abhandlungen*.

of the literacy of the laity in the Middle Ages,[37] Henry Chaytor's *From Script to Print*,[38] Herbert Grundmann's article '*Litteratus-illiteratus*',[39] Richard Hoggart's *The Uses of Literacy*, Stanley Morison's *Politics and Script*,[40] and the corpus of Bernhard Bischoff's work.[41] All these contributed fundamental discussions of a wealth of literary and palaeographical evidence. In terms of conceptualization and method, the work of the social anthropologists Ian Watt and Jack Goody, whose 'The Consequences of Literacy' of 1963 was reprinted in Jack Goody's edited volume *Literacy in Traditional Societies*, as well as Jack Goody's own *The Logic of Writing and the Organization of Society*, were hugely influential.[42] In the decade before my own *The Carolingians and the Written Word* was published, the justly famous and path-breaking study by Michael Clanchy, *From Memory to Written Record*, had appeared, first published in 1979. The second edition in 1993 (and a third in 2013) responded generously to the criticism that Clanchy had downplayed the evidence for literacy in either Latin or the vernacular Old English in the Anglo-Saxon period.[43] The first edition had been perhaps too much influenced by the rhetorically effective paper the young Patrick Wormald had published on 'The Uses of Literacy in Anglo-Saxon England and its Neighbours', but Clanchy and Wormald had, after all, been colleagues in the same department at the University of Glasgow at the time.[44] Of major importance, furthermore, was Brian Stock's immensely fertile idea of a 'textual community', that is, a group within society coalescing around the

37 James Westfall Thompson, *Literacy of the Laity in the Middle Ages* (New York, 1960); and Malcolm B. Parkes, 'The Literacy of the Laity', in *Literature and Western Civilization: The Medieval World*, eds David Daiches and A. K. Thorby (London, 1973), pp. 555–77.

38 Henry J. Chaytor, *From Script to Print* (London, 1945).

39 Herbert Grundmann, '*Literatus-illiteratus*. Der Wandel einer Bildungsnorm von Altertum zum Mittelalter', *Archiv für Kulturgeschichte* 40 (1958), 1–65; and Franz Bäuml, 'Varieties and Consequences of Medieval Literacy and Illiteracy', *Speculum* 55 (1980), 237–65.

40 Richard Hoggart, *The Uses of Literacy* (London, 1957); Stanley Morison, *Politics and Script: Aspects of Authority and Freedom in the Development of Graeco-Latin Script from the Sixth Century B.C. to the Twentieth Century A.D.* (Oxford, 1972).

41 Bernhard Bischoff, *Mittelalterliche Studien*, 3 vols (Stuttgart, 1966–81); and Bernhard Bischoff, *Die südostdeutsche Schreibschulen und Bibliotheken in der Karolingerzeit*, I: *Die bayrischen Diözesen*, 3rd ed. (Wiesbaden, 1974), and II: *Die vorwiegend Österreichischen Diözesen* (Wiesbaden, 1980).

42 *Literacy in Traditional Societies*, ed. Jack Goody (Cambridge, 1969); Jack Goody, *The Logic of Writing and the Organization of Society* (Cambridge, 1986). See also Harvey J. Graff, *Literacy in History: An Interdisciplinary Research Bibliography* (London, 1981); and Brian V. Street, *Literacy in Theory and Practice* (Cambridge, 1984).

43 M. T. Clanchy, *From Memory to Written Record: England 1066–1307* (London, 1979, rev. editions 1993 and 2013).

44 Patrick Wormald, 'The Uses of Literacy in Anglo-Saxon England and its Neighbours', *Transactions of the Royal Historical Society*, fifth series, 27 (1977), 95–114.

shared understanding of a text. This has achieved great resonance.[45] Stock also offered a provoking challenge to any early medievalist in his notion of a 'rebirth of literacy in the eleventh century'. I should here emphasize, however, that Stock's subsequent collection of essays, *Listening for the Text: On the Uses of the Past* was published in Baltimore in 1990, so that some of my own marking out of territory in relation to his earlier work in my *The Carolingians and the Written Word* was rendered very quickly both obsolete and inaccurate.[46] Nevertheless, any notion of a 'rebirth of literacy' as late as the eleventh century is now untenable and is one, moreover, locked into a quantitative understanding of how literacy in any society should be assessed. On the contrary, there has been a general acknowledgement that the qualitative assessment of the uses of literacy and role of the written word in any early medieval society was essential and has proven more enlightening than any attempt at quantification.[47]

New Interpretations

As a way to chart the developments in scholarship in the late 1980s and 1990s, it may be helpful to describe my own ventures and thinking which had culminated by the time I sent *The Carolingians and the Written Word* to press in 1988. I had been exploring many different aspects of the extant manuscript evidence from early medieval Europe in studies that were published both before and after the book itself. These studies included analyses of single codices as well as of secular law books from the Carolingian period; the production and dissemination of canon law manuscripts before 789 (that is, before the promotion of the *Dionysio-Hadriana* collection in the *Admonitio generalis*);[48] Merovingian scriptoria, the evidence for insular influence in manuscripts from Neustria between 650 and 850, the manuscripts from the Anglo-Saxon missionary centres east of the Rhine, women and literacy, and the existence of

45 Brian Stock, *The Implications of Literacy: Written Language and Models of Interpretation in the Eleventh and Twelfth Centuries* (Princeton, NJ, 1983).

46 Brian Stock, *Listening for the Text: On the Uses of the Past* (Baltimore, MD, 1990).

47 William Harris, *Ancient Literacy* (New Haven, 1989).

48 Rosamond McKitterick, 'A Ninth-Century Schoolbook from the Loire Valley: Phillipps 16308', *Scriptorium* 30 (1976), 225–31; Rosamond McKitterick, 'The Gospels of St Hubert', in *Art at Auction*, ed. Georgia Fogg (London, 1986), pp. 154–57; Rosamond McKitterick, 'Some Carolingian Law Books and their Function', in *Authority and Power: Studies on Mediaeval Law and Government presented to Walter Ullmann on his 70th birthday*, eds Peter Linehan and Brian Tierney (Cambridge, 1980), pp. 13–27; Rosamond McKitterick, 'Knowledge of Canon Law in the Frankish Kingdoms before 789: The Manuscript Evidence', *Journal of Theological Studies* n.s. 36 (1985), 97–117.

nuns' scriptoria;[49] Frankish uncial, Carolingian uncial, and Carolingian book production;[50] the library of Charles the Bald;[51] and orality and literacy.[52] Some of this work had begun in the course of my doctoral research which culminated in my book on *The Frankish Church and the Carolingian Reforms*, published in 1977.[53] But it was a year in Munich in 1974–75, studying palaeography under Bernhard Bischoff and looking at manuscripts daily in the Bayerische Staatsbibliothek, that consolidated my understanding of the importance of going beyond the printed texts to the original manuscripts, and of the necessity to think about both the cultural and social context in which these manuscripts

---

49 Rosamond McKitterick, 'The Scriptoria of Merovingian Gaul: A Survey of the Evidence', in *Columbanus and Merovingian Monasticism*, eds Howard Clarke and Mary Brennan, British Archaeological Reports, International Series 113 (Oxford, 1981), pp. 173–207; Rosamond McKitterick, 'The Diffusion of Insular Culture in Neustria between 650 and 850: The Implications of the Manuscript Evidence' in *La Neustrie. Les pays au nord de la Loire de 650 à 850*, ed. Hartmut Atsma, 2 vols, Beihefte der Francia 16 (Sigmaringen, 1989), 2:395–432; Rosamond McKitterick, 'Anglo-Saxon Missionaries in Germany: Reflections on the Manuscript Evidence', *Transactions of the Cambridge Bibliographical Society* 9 (1989), 291–329.

50 Rosamond McKitterick, 'Frankish Uncial in the Eighth Century: A New Context for the Work of the Echternach Scriptorium', in *Willibrord, zijn wereld en zijn werk*, eds Petty Bange and Antonius G. Weiler (Nijmegen, 1990), pp. 350–64; Rosamond McKitterick, 'Carolingian Book Production: Some Problems', *The Library*, sixth series, 12 (1990), 1–33; Rosamond McKitterick, 'Carolingian Uncial: A Context for the Lothar Psalter', *The British Library Journal* 16 (1990), 1–15.

51 Rosamond McKitterick, 'Charles the Bald (823–877) and his Library: The Patronage of Learning', *EHR* 95 (1980), 29–47; Rosamond McKitterick, 'Manuscripts and Scriptoria in the Reign of Charles the Bald, 840–877', in *Giovanni Scoto nel suo tempo. L'organizzazione del sapere in età carolingia. Atti del XXIV Convegno storico internazionale, Todi, 11–14 ottobre 1987* (Spoleto, 1989), pp. 200–33; Rosamond McKitterick, 'Frauen und Schriftlichkeit im Frühmittelalter', in *Weibliche Lebensgestaltung im frühen Mittelalter*, ed. Hans-Werner Goetz (Cologne, 1991), pp. 65–118; Rosamond McKitterick, 'Early Mediaeval Book Production and the Problem of Female Literacy', *Theoretische Geschiedenis* 19 (1992), 147–68; Rosamond McKitterick, 'Nuns' Scriptoria in England and Francia in the Early Middle Ages', *Francia* 19 (1992), 1–35.

52 Rosamond McKitterick, 'Text and Image in the Carolingian World', in *The Uses of Literacy*, ed. McKitterick, pp. 297–318; Rosamond McKitterick, 'Literacy in Alemannia and the Role of St Gall', in *St Gall as a Centre of Culture*, ed. Werner Vogler (Stuttgart and Zürich, 1991), pp. 217–26; Rosamond McKitterick, 'The Written Word and Oral Communication: Rome's Legacy to the Franks', in *Latin Culture and Medieval Germanic Europe: Proceedings of the First Germania Latina Conference Held at the University of Groningen, 26 May 1989*, eds Richard North and Tette Hofstra, Germania Latina 1, Mediaevalia Groningana 11 (Groningen, 1992), pp. 87–110. Most of the articles cited in nn. 48–51 above were reprinted in Rosamond McKitterick, *Books, Scribes and Learning in the Frankish Kingdoms, Sixth to Ninth Centuries* (Aldershot, 1994); and Rosamond McKitterick, *Frankish Kings and Culture in the Early Middle Ages* (Aldershot, 1995).

53 Rosamond McKitterick, *The Frankish Church and the Carolingian Reforms, 789–895* (London, 1977).

were produced and what the production and existence of these manuscripts implied. The communicative power of words and letter forms across time and space remains a topic of abiding fascination, and my own study of manuscripts introduced me to a world where scribes clearly engaged with the texts they were copying as much as readers did with the results of their labours. The letter forms and scripts the scribes set down on the page are in themselves historical and cultural artefacts and intrinsic elements of any text's message and meaning.

In order to take into account the remarkable diversity of scholarship on the artefacts of literate and documentary culture for the early Middle Ages, some of which I have summarized above, it became clear that any assessment of literacy had to take both pragmatic (legal, liturgical) and learned (literary, intellectual) contexts into account as well as the consequences and implications of language and communication. Hence my own discussions in *The Carolingians and the Written Word* of Latin and vernacular, of the implications of the capitulary and legal material, and of the St Gall charters. The significance of the channelling of wealth towards book production to such a spectacular degree in the Carolingian period also needed to be considered. In addition, the extant manuscripts and library evidence has important implications for the organization of written knowledge in the early Middle Ages. Finally, the issue of both lay and clerical literacy within society as a whole needed to be addressed.

Although William Harris' largely quantitative assessment in his *Ancient Literacy* had been published in the same year as *The Carolingians and the Written Word*, Rosalind Thomas' *Oral Tradition and Written Record in Classical Athens*, also published in 1989, took the discussion of ancient literacy in new directions. She too insisted that literacy depended on social attitudes and that we needed to investigate the uses and implications of literacy. Her *Literacy and Orality in Ancient Greece*, which came out three years later, engaged directly with the challenge of analysing oral material that survives only in written form.[54] Many more topics and categories of evidence were now opening up on all sides, such as the importance of forgeries and inscriptions,[55] the relationship between orality and literacy, and the discontinuities as well as continuities with the Roman past.[56]

Apparently in direct response to my own book there were broadenings of the enquiry, such as Ernst Hellgardt's study of multilingualism in the Carolingian

54 Rosalind Thomas, *Oral Tradition and Written Record in Classical Athens* (Cambridge, 1989); and Rosalind Thomas, *Literacy and Orality in Ancient Greece* (Cambridge, 1992).

55 *Fälschungen im Mittelalter*, ed. Detlev Jasper, MGH Schriften 33, 6 vols (Hanover, 1988–90).

56 Matthew Innes, 'Memory, Orality and Literacy in an Early Medieval Society', *Past & Present* 158 (1998), 3–38.

period,[57] and critical assessments such as that offered by Mark Vessey, who rightly emphasized the need to explore the uses of literacy in late antiquity as well.[58] Blunt refusals to take the arguments and evidence presented in *The Carolingians and the Written Word* on board were rare.[59] My own edited volume *The Uses of Literacy in Early Mediaeval Europe* augmented the evidence from the Carolingian realms with assessments of literacy in the British Isles, Spain, Merovingian Gaul, Byzantium, among the Jews across the Mediterranean region from the Cairo Genizah evidence, at San Vincenzo in central Italy, and within papal circles. Books, documents, and scripts were all considered as different aspects of the same historical problem.[60] These contributions were speedily followed by a number of studies, rightly recognizing how many different aspects still needed consideration. Among these were the collaborative volume on *Literacy and Power in the Ancient World* and Nicholas Everett's study of literacy in Lombard Italy.[61] The diverse uses of the written word in Italy in the early Middle Ages, especially Rome, have proved a rich source of material for study of epigraphy, syllogi, administrative and documentary culture, texts and coins, scripts, and graphic display.[62] Everett, for example, was able to take advantage of a number of studies published by Italian scholars, many of them in the more recent Settimane volumes mentioned above, who had identified many different manifestations of writing that needed to be incorporated into the discussion.

A major contribution to the understanding of literacy in its various manifestations has been the work stimulated by the Münster project on Pragmatische Schriftlichkeit and by Marco Mostert's 'Pionier Project' in Utrecht. The latter emphasized 'non-verbal, oral and written communication and their interrelationship'.[63] The range of themes Mostert and his colleagues addressed has nicely exposed and further explored the complexities of the topic. The very interesting possibilities for extending the kinds of problems identified in early medieval contexts into northern, central, and eastern Europe in the later

57 Ernst Hellgardt, 'Zur Mehrsprachigkeit im Karolingerreich. Bermerkungen aus Anlaß von Rosamond McKittericks Buch "The Carolingians and the Written Word"', *Beiträge zur Geschichte der deutschen Sprache und Literatur* 118 (1996), 1–48.

58 Mark Vessey, 'Literacy and *litteratura*, AD 200–800', *Studies in Medieval and Renaissance History* n.s. 13 (1992), 139–60.

59 Michael Richter, *The Formation of the Medieval West: Studies in the Oral Culture of the Barbarians* (Dublin, 1994).

60 *The Uses of Literacy*, ed. McKitterick.

61 *Literacy and Power in the Ancient World*, eds Alan Bowman and Greg Woolf (Cambridge, 1994); Nicholas Everett, *Literacy in Lombard Italy, c.568–774* (Cambridge, 2003).

62 *Roma nell'alto medioevo*, Settimane 48 (Spoleto, 2001).

63 *New Approaches to Medieval Communication*, ed. Marco Mostert (Turnhout, 1999).

Middle Ages have also been productively pursued.[64] Dorde Bubalo, for example, investigated not only the categories of written record but also the agents of literacy and the various uses of the written word in medieval Serbia.[65] There has been a useful engagement on a theoretical level with Ruth Finnegan's notion of an 'oral-written continuum',[66] and a collaborative exploration of the notions of 'visual literacy', building on the earlier work of Beat Brenk on 'Bildlichkeit', to understand the interaction between verbal and non-verbal means of communication and visual symbols other than writing.[67] Non-verbal gestures and especially legal rituals, or what are sometimes referred to as the 'performative' characteristics or 'verbal and visual semiotics' of charters, offer further extensions of the contexts in which writing is to be understood.[68]

Considerations of the materiality of the evidence, long familiar to archaeologists and epigraphers, were also applied to manuscripts and charters by authors in the Utrecht series. Issues of layout, choice of script in relation to linguistic features, lexical variation and code-switching, and the influence of layout and script on any manuscript's communicative potential have been topics of discussion among historians of the book for some decades.[69] In some

64 See, for example, *Charters and the Use of the Written Word in Medieval Society*, ed. Karl Heidecker (Turnhout, 2000); *Epigraphic Literacy and Christian Identity: Modes of Written Discourse in the Newly Christian European North*, eds Kristel Zilmer and Judith Jesch (Turnhout, 2003); *The Development of Literate Mentalities in East Central Europe*, eds Anna Adamska and Marco Mostert (Turnhout, 2004); Arnved Nedkvitne, *The Social Consequences of Literacy in Medieval Scandinavia* (Turnhout, 2005). See also *Language and Literacy in Early Scandinavia and Beyond*, eds Michael Schulte and Robert Nedoma, special issue of *NOWELE: North-Western European Language Evolution* 62–63 (Odense, 2011).

65 Dorde Bubalo, *Pragmatic Literacy in Medieval Serbia* (Turnhout, 2014); but compare the earlier contribution by Simon Franklin, 'Literacy and Documentation in Mediaeval Russia', *Speculum* 60 (1985), 1–38.

66 *Along the Oral-Written Continuum*, eds Slavica Ranković, Leidulf Melve, and Else Mundal (Turnhout, 2010); and compare *Orality and Literacy in the Middle Ages: Essays on a Conjunction and its Consequences in Honour of D. H. Green*, eds Mark Chinca and Christopher Young (Turnhout, 2005).

67 *Reading Images and Texts: Medieval Images and Texts as Forms of Communication*, eds Mariëlle Hagemann and Marco Mostert (Turnhout, 2005).

68 *Zwischen Pragmatik und Performanz. Dimensionen mittelalterlicher Schriftkultur*, eds Christoph Dartmann, Thomas Scharff, and Christoph F. Loeber (Turnhout, 2011); Geoffrey Koziol, *The Politics of Memory and Identity in Carolingian Royal Diplomas: The West Frankish Kingdom (840–987)* (Turnhout, 2012); and *Medieval Legal Process: Physical, Spoken and Written Performance in the Middle Ages*, eds Marco Mostert and Paul S. Barnwell (Turnhout, 2013).

69 See in particular *Mise en page et mise en texte du livre manuscrit*, eds Henri-Jean Martin and Jean Vézin (Paris, 1990); Armando Petrucci, *La scrittura. Ideologia e rappresentazione* (Turin, 1980); translated into English as *Public Lettering: Script, Power, and Culture*,

of this recent literature a misplaced confidence in 'new' developments from the eleventh century onwards is apparent. Examples are the monograph by Tjamke Snijders and the collaborative study of 'formal aspects of written communication' in the Middle Ages. Such misperceptions can only be counteracted by study of the work of the scribes and compilers of late antique and early medieval books, documents, and inscriptions. The contributions to layout, text structure and organization, and conventions of presentation, need to be assessed as further manifestations of literate culture.[70]

Current Preoccupations and Further Questions

From all this work on particular manifestations of writing and non-verbal symbols, as well as from the evocation of the social and cultural contexts in which they should be understood, it is clear that charters are only one manifestation of literacy. They can only be separated from books, inscriptions, graffiti, literary compositions, scholarly treatises, didactic works, legal and administrative texts, or coin legends for the convenience of discussion. Charters, in consequence, have been recognized not merely as records of oral transactions or decisions, but also as texts with symbolic weight; they act as complementary witnesses to human communication, social networks, and discourse. Literacy, in short, embraces the entire content of a written tradition as well as the levels of individual or collective skill and production in any one place and at any one time. Although space has only permitted this very impressionistic summary of

trans. Linda Lappin (Chicago, 1993); Armando Petrucci, *Writers and Readers in Medieval Italy: Studies in the History of Written Culture* (New Haven and London, 1995) (a collection of selected papers translated by Charles Radding); *Vom Nutzen des Schreibens. Soziales Gedächtnis, Herrschaft und Besitz*, eds Walter Pohl and Paul Herold, Forschungen zur Geschichte des Mittelalters 5 (Vienna, 2002); Roger Chartier, *Inscrire et effacere. Culture écrite et littérature (XIe–XVIIIe siècle)* (Paris, 2005).

70 Tjamke Snijders, *Manuscript Communication: Visual and Textual Mechanics of Communication in Hagiographical Texts from the Southern Low Countries, 900–1200* (Turnhout, 2014); *Ruling the Script in the Middle Ages: Formal Aspects of Written Communication*, eds Sébastien Barret, Dominique Stutzmann, and Georg Vogeler (Turnhout, 2017); *Verbal and Visual Communication in Early English Texts*, eds Matti Peikola, Aleksi Mäkilähde, Hanna Salmi, Mari-Liisa Varila, and Janne Skaffari (Turnhout, 2017). For earlier instances of such phenomena as are described in these volumes, see for example the suggestions made in Rosamond McKitterick, 'Glossaries and Other Innovations in Carolingian Book Production', in Erik Kwakkel, Rosamond McKitterick, and Rodney Thomson, *Turning Over a New Leaf: Change and Development in the Medieval Book* (Leiden, 2012), pp. 21–78 and plates 1–20 (pp. 169–93), but much more work needs to be done on these topics.

past work on literacy, many important questions have emerged from it, some of which can be addressed here.

The first is the issue of trust, that is, the degree to which writing conferred trust in what was written and whether that trust was dependent on an authority responsible for the written text.[71] Extant manuscripts and charters constitute an obvious body of material particularly relevant for such a concern. The specific authorization or origin of each text, the degree to which antiquity might confer authority on it and thus affect the status, perception, and reception of it, all need to be explored. A written work manifestly functioned as a particular expression of a mentality through which power could be constructed and influence exerted, and which affected and effected social practice in ways that can often be precisely delineated. The Frankish mayors of the palace and kings were certainly not alone in western Europe in promoting both documentary and literary culture, even though the remarkable amount of evidence that can be associated with their efforts has received a greater proportion of scholarly attention.[72] Nevertheless, the Frankish example serves as a reminder of the importance within western Europe of the wider cultural context in which kings and their officials worked, and of the expectations and assumptions implicit in the way the written word was deployed. The authority of texts and the effectiveness of government are thus inextricably linked to the expectations of literacy in wider society.[73] This is fertile ground for further cultivation.

Trust in writing is also related to memory, for literate modes of communication could invoke memory and the resources of the past in order to confer legitimation and authority.[74] This involves what I have termed elsewhere as 'literate conventions of memory'.[75] Isidore of Seville's explanation of the function of written letters emphasized the presentation of words through the eyes

71 See Rosamond McKitterick, *History and Memory in the Carolingian World* (Cambridge, 2004), pp. 218–44. The essays in *Strategies of Writing: Studies on Text and Trust in the Middle Ages*, eds Petra Schulte, Marco Mostert, and Irene van Renswoude (Turnhout, 2008) are an important set of articulations of the issues.

72 Pierre Riché, *Education and Culture in the Barbarian West*, trans. John J. Contreni (Columbia, SC, 1976) (original French edition 1962); Yitzhak Hen, *Roman Barbarians: The Royal Court and Culture in the Early Medieval West* (Basingstoke, 2007).

73 See, for example, *Images of Authority: Papers Presented to Joyce Reynolds on the Occasion of her Seventieth Birthday*, eds Mary M. Mackenzie and Charlotte Roueché (Cambridge, 1989); and Ildar H. Garipzanov, *The Symbolic Language of Authority in the Carolingian World* (*c*.751–877) (Leiden, 2008).

74 See *The Resources of the Past in Early Medieval Europe*, eds Clemens Gantner, Rosamond McKitterick, and Sven Meeder (Cambridge, 2015).

75 McKitterick, 'The Uses of Literacy', p. 180. I draw further on this paper in the paragraph that follows.

rather than the ears, and the invention of letters to remember things, 'bound by letters lest they slip away into oblivion'.[76] Written texts, therefore, are a form of communication across time as well as space, and the means by which memories as well as the actions, wisdom, and knowledge of the past were transmitted and preserved. History-writing and an enormous variety of forms of recording the past have long been a focus of lively discussion, with an emerging realization of charters' potential as historical narratives and repositories of memory as well. There remain many more texts and perceptions of particular aspects of the past to be explored, but the study of literacy has transformed the way in which such texts are approached. It is not just their content or context that are objects of study, important as these are, but also the precise motivation for their production: how they might have been written, disseminated, and preserved, and what the potential audience at any of these stages might have been.[77]

Similarly, the once comfortable understanding of the loss of the 'epigraphic habit' in early medieval Europe as a symptom of the 'decline in literacy' has been disrupted by new considerations of the inscription evidence from Gaul, Spain, and Italy.[78] The once publicly displayed inscriptions associated with Carolingian Melle and Bourges, as documented by Cécile Treffort and others, are important witnesses to the motives of those who first erected them in the early Middle Ages. The makers and commissioners of these monumental inscriptions believed in their immediate effectiveness as well as their potential

---

76 *Nam ne oblivione fugiant, litteris alligantur*: Isidore of Seville, *Etymologiae*, I.iii.1–2, ed. W. M. Lindsay (Oxford, 1911); English translation Stephen A. Barney, W. J. Lewis, J. A. Beach, and Oliver Berghof, *The Etymologies of Isidore of Seville*, 2nd ed. (Cambridge, 2010), p. 39.

77 *Bücher des Lebens—lebendige Bücher. Katalog zur gleichnamigen Ausstellung im Regierungsgebäude des Kantons Sankt Gallen*, eds Peter Erhart and Jakob Kuratli (St Gall, 2010); Helmut Reimitz, *History, Frankish Identity and the Framing of Western Ethnicity, 550–850* (Cambridge, 2015); and *Writing the Early Medieval West*, eds Elina Screen and Charles West (Cambridge, 2018).

78 On the epigraphic habit see Ramsey MacMullen, 'The Epigraphic Habit in the Roman Empire', *American Journal of Philology* 103 (1982), 233–46; but for the significance of the evidence from late antiquity and the early Middle Ages, see Mark Handley, *Death, Society and Culture: Inscriptions and Epitaphs in Gaul and Spain AD 300–750*, British Archaeological Reports. International Series, 1135 (Oxford, 2003); *The Inscriptions of Early Medieval Brittany*, eds Wendy Davies, James Graham-Campbell, Mark Handley, Paul Kershaw, J. T. Koch, G. le Duc, and K. Lockyear (Oakville, CT and Aberystwyth, 2000); Cécile Treffort, *Mémoires carolingiennes. L'épitaphe entre célébration mémorielle, genre littéraire et manifeste politique (milieu VIII*e*–début XI*e* siècle)* (Rennes, 2007); and Walter Koch, *Inschriftenpaläographie des abendländischen Mittelalters und der früheren Neuzeit* (Vienna, 2007). See also above, n. 20, and Wolfgang Haubrichs, this volume.

longevity. They were committed to the harnessing of this particular form of record to serve their social and political aims.

Inscriptions also appear to have coexisted with other and new practices of commemoration in written form, such as the *Libri vitae* or *Libri memoriales* and liturgical and musical composition, which were introduced in the course of the eighth and ninth centuries.[79] Occasionally we can catch a sense of the swiftness of the adoption of literate conventions of memory in recently conquered or Christianized regions, such as is yielded by the cartulary and extant manuscripts associated with Werden on the Ruhr, founded *c.*799.[80] Werden is but one example, but it needs to be seen against the backdrop of particular expectations and assumptions about the role of the written word in any one community, which as historians we need to determine.

The possible role of letters and writing as visual symbols is a fashionable theme currently under further investigation. Letters need to be assessed alongside other graphic symbols, carrying specific meaning in their own right, even though the inevitable subjectivity of such assessment may make many conclusions merely, if suggestively, speculative. The many layers of meaning in signs and symbols were explored, for example, in a recent volume on *Sign and Design* and 'the pictorial dimension of writing … the content of pictographs, ideograms and logographic writing systems as well as alphabetic scripts'. These are compared across the cultures and different religious systems of the Middle Ages. Ildar Garipzanov and others recently coordinated a series of papers which argue that graphic signs could communicate visual messages about identity, religious faith, and social power. Such signs could also explore the degree to which culturally specific norms and practices, as well as 'evolving perceptions and projections of authority' can be identified.[81] Garipzanov himself, moreover, has offered a cultural history of graphic signs, and how signs of the cross, christogrammes, and secular and religious monogrammes were used to communicate secular and divine authorship.[82] These essays connect sign, symbol, and language in creative ways that explicate symbolic designs too often overlooked in the past. To such new ventures can be added Evina

79 McKitterick, 'The Uses of Literacy', pp. 184–85. See also Julian Hendrix, 'Liturgy for the Dead and the Confraternity of Reichenau and St Gall, 800–950' (unpublished PhD thesis, University of Cambridge, 2007).

80 McKitterick 'The Uses of Literacy', pp. 189–207.

81 *Sign and Design: Script as Image in Cross-Cultural Perspective (300–1600 CE)*, eds Brigitte Bedos-Rezak and Jeffrey Hamburger (Cambridge, MA, 2016); *Graphic Signs of Identity, Faith, and Power in Late Antiquity and the Early Middle Ages*, eds Ildar H. Garipzanov, Caroline Goodson, and Henry Maguire (Turnhout, 2017).

82 Ildar H. Garipzanov, *Graphic Signs of Authority in Late Antiquity and the Early Middle Ages, 300–900* (Oxford, 2018). I am grateful to Professor Garipzanov for letting me read some of his chapters in advance of publication.

Steinova's examination of the wealth of graphic symbols and signs that scribes deployed in texts.[83]

It is hardly news that displayed letters can evoke power, authority, and the past.[84] All the same, the precise choice of letter forms in early medieval texts and inscriptions, and the timing and place of such choices, are of great significance. One obvious example is the use of monumental capitals and uncial script, and the visual evocation of the Roman past in manuscripts such as the Lorsch and Soissons Gospels, the Godescalc Gospel Lectionary, and the Dagulf Psalter produced by the court groups of scribes associated with Charlemagne.[85] The monumental capitals of the epitaph for Pope Hadrian I, produced *c.*795,[86] were part of the same fundamental transformation of letter forms, book script, and the emergence of Caroline minuscule in the last two decades of the eighth century. As David Ganz has put it, the theology of these gospel-books was completed 'by the majesty of the script in which their texts open'.[87] Ganz also emphasized that these 'ancient' letters forms, perhaps primarily based on sixth-century models, were actually discussed by contemporaries.[88]

At precisely the time when the new Caroline minuscule was being adopted within western Europe, and when there was such an extraordinary stress on writing and written records in the Carolingian world, musical notation was also devised with an even more complex relationship between sound and symbol than allowed by the alphabet system that records oral agreements in

83 Evina Steinova, '*Notam Superponere studii*. The Use of Technical Signs in the Early Middle Ages' (unpublished PhD thesis, University of Utrecht, 2016). On these topics, see also the contribution of Annina Seiler in the present volume.

84 Morison, *Politics and Script*; Petrucci, *Public Lettering*; and see above n. 34.

85 See Lawrence Nees, 'Prolegomenon to a Study of the Vienna Coronation Gospels: Common Knowledge, Scholarship, Tradition, Legend, Myth', in *Rome and Religion in the Medieval World. Studies in Honor of Thomas F. X. Noble*, eds Valerie L. Garver and Owen M. Phelan (Farnham, 2014), pp. 253–74, and the summary of the court groups' work with references to earlier scholarship in Rosamond McKitterick, *Charlemagne: The Formation of a European Identity* (Cambridge, 2008), pp. 345–63.

86 Joanna Story, Judith Bunbury, Anna Candida Felici, Gabriele Fronterotta, Mario Piacentini, Chiara Nicolais, Daria Scacciatelli, Sebastiano Sciuti, and Margherita Vendittelli, 'Charlemagne's Black Marble: The Origin of the Epitaph of Pope Hadrian I', *Papers of the British School at Rome* 73 (2005), 157–90.

87 Donald Bullough, 'Roman Books and Carolingian *renovatio*', in *Renaissance and Renewal in Christian History*, ed. Derek Baker (London, 1977), pp. 23–50; reprinted in Donald A. Bullough, *Carolingian Renewal: Sources and Heritage* (Manchester, 1991), pp. 1–33; David Ganz, '"Roman Books" Reconsidered: The Theology of Carolingian Display Script', in *Early Medieval Rome and the Christian West. Essays in Honour of Donald A. Bullough*, ed. Julia M. H. Smith (Leiden, 2000), pp. 297–316, at 316.

88 Ganz, '"Roman Books" Reconsidered', pp. 298–99; as well as his contribution, 'Early Medieval Display Scripts and the Problem of How We See Them', in *Graphic Signs of Identity*, eds Garipzanov et al., pp. 125–46.

written form in charters. The origin of neumes is a question that has preoccupied many musicologists, the most recent and most persuasive of whom is Susan Rankin.[89] Henry Parkes has also demonstrated, in the context of the liturgical books produced at Mainz in the tenth century, how the scribes responsible affected and effected changes in both ritual practice and written conventions for the music.[90]

The relationship of sound to sign may underlie the supposed changes in what was expected of a reader and reading practice, possibly indicated by the fascinating coincidental change from uncial to minuscule scripts in both the Frankish regions and the Byzantine Empire in the later eighth and early ninth centuries.[91] Any appreciation of written culture, therefore, has to embrace the implications of letter forms, scribal embellishments, technical omission signs and other devices for annotation, abbreviations, orthography, methods of preparing parchment and assembling a book, scribal formulae in documents, as well as the training, social position, and cultural context of scribes. Graphic signs are the primary evidence. They are the physical remnants of a past that cannot always be recaptured or reconstructed; events that shaped letters have often left us little else but the letters themselves. Letter forms, in short, are historical monuments in their own right; they map lines of cultural and intellectual contact. They prompt the questions, moreover, of how much importance one should attach to the abilities to read a script, to read a script in order to edit a text, or to read script as historical evidence.

The Franks and Their Scripts

In Frankish Gaul, the problems of eighth-century script development and the respective roles and status of uncial and cursive script on the eve of the emergence of Caroline minuscule need to be taken into account in confronting the

89 Kenneth Levy, *Gregorian Chant and the Carolingians* (Princeton, 1998), and review by Rosamond McKitterick, *Early Music History* 19 (2000), 279–90; Leo Treitler, 'The "Unwritten" and "Written Transmission" of Medieval Chant and the Start-up of Musical Notation', *Journal of Musicology* 10 (1992), 131–91; Susan Rankin, *Writing Sounds in Carolingian Europe: The Invention of Musical Notation* (Cambridge, 2018).

90 Henry Parkes, *The Making of Liturgy in the Ottonian Church: Books, Music and Ritual in Mainz, 950–1050* (Cambridge, 2015).

91 *Ancient Literacies: The Culture of Reading in Greece and Rome*, eds William A. Johnson and Holt N. Parker (Oxford, 2009); Guglielmo Cavallo, 'Leggere e scrivere. Tracce e divaricazioni di un percorso dal tardoantico al medioevo greco e latino', and Marco Mostert, 'Using and Keeping Written Texts: Reading and Writings as Forms of Communication in the Early Middle Ages', both in *Scrivere e leggere*, pp. 1–38 and 71–94 respectively.

evidence of the charters. It is in this context that the famously misleading claim by Einhard that Charlemagne was unable to write needs to be considered:

> [Charlemagne] also attempted to write and for this reason used to place both wax tablets and notebooks under the pillows on his bed, so that if he had any free time he might accustom his hand to forming letters. But his effort came too late in life and achieved little success.[92]

We know far too little about the process of learning technical writing skills and its relation to language acquisition in a multilingual world,[93] but Einhard's story appears to relate precisely to how one might learn to write in the early Middle Ages, and what resources or models were available for scribes to follow. Understanding Einhard's claim as proving Charlemagne's illiteracy, however, may only satisfy deep-rooted fantasies about barbarian rulers in western Europe. Medieval kings, of course, had notaries and secretaries to record their oral decisions, possibly actually from dictation, so would not often need to write themselves. Yet Charlemagne oversaw literate government. He may only have been able to read, without being able to write,[94] but it makes little sense in the light of all else we know about Charlemagne and his participation in the promotion of legal knowledge, Christian orthodoxy, correct texts, education, and learning, either to suppose he could not read, or to cast him as illiterate and unable to write at all on the strength of Einhard's comment. He was *litteratus* in Grundmann's sense of literate in Latin,[95] but it is Einhard again who highlighted the use of Latin in a diverse linguistic context, informing us elsewhere that Charlemagne himself invented names of the months and winds, in his own Germanic dialect, probably Rhenish Franconian.[96] Charlemagne was thus at least bilingual, and many at his court were possibly multilingual, given

---

92 'Temptabat et scribere tabulasque et codicellos ad hoc in lecto sub ceruicalibus circumferre solebat, ut cum uacuum tempus esset manum litteris effigiendis adsuesceret; sed parum successit labor praeposterus ac sero inchoatus': Einhard, *Vita Karoli*, 25, eds Michel Sot and Christiane Veyrard-Cosme, *Eginhard. Vie de Charlemagne* (Paris, 2014), p. 60.

93 See the fundamental comments by Armando Petrucci, 'Alfabetismo ed educazione grafica degli scribi altomedievali (secoli VII–X),' in *The Role of the Book in Medieval Culture*, ed. Peter Ganz, 2 vols, Bibliologia 3 (Turnhout, 1986), 1:109–32. Some useful comments are also to be found in *Teaching Writing, Learning to Write: Proceedings of the XVIth Colloquium of the Comité Internationale de Paléographie Latine*, ed. P. R. Robinson (London, 2010).

94 See Rosamond McKitterick, 'Introduction' and 'Conclusion', in *The Uses of Literacy*, ed. McKitterick, pp. 1–10 and 319–33 respectively.

95 Grundmann, 'Literatus-illiteratus'.

96 For some further comments see Rosamond McKitterick, 'A Landmark Figure in the History of German? Charlemagne, Language and Literacy', in *Landmarks in the History of the German Language*, eds Geraldine Horan, Nils Langer, and Sheila Watts, Britische und irische Studien zur deutschen Sprache und Literatur 52 (Bern, 2009), pp. 11–34.

their origins. Latin in this context, therefore, was literally the *lingua franca* and facilitated communication and record at every level, not least in the charters themselves.

Many have addressed the problem of Charlemagne's writing skills. Paul Dutton, for example, examined the issue scrupulously in 2004 in his '*Karolus Magnus Scriptor*',[97] but found nothing that demonstrated unequivocally to him that the king was literate, despite Charlemagne's patronage of scholars and reform. Such a position would have to discount several other key pieces of evidence: the anomaly of an illiterate king of a new dynasty in relation to the Merovingians' well-attested use of writing in government; the fact that Charlemagne's sister Gisela was clearly well educated; the reference to Benedict of Aniane's experience at the court of Pippin and Bertrada recorded by Ardo Smaragdus, where he was educated among its *scolares* (*tradidit inter scolares nutriendum*); and Charlemagne's recruitment of scholars to enhance his own knowledge. A supposedly illiterate father could of course still ensure that his sons and daughters should be taught the liberal arts, as Charlemagne did, according to his court poets, but Charlemagne's own father Pippin III had been educated at the monastery of Saint-Denis. Dutton's literary analysis of Einhard's account of Charlemagne's skills offered a further nuance in suggesting a textual progression in which writing with his own hand was part of the representation of a sequence of achievement from a *dicaculus* king of oral culture to the *labor inchoatus* of the written culture. Such a literary conceit, however, may not be especially helpful when considering the realities of that written culture.

Einhard's claim about Charlemagne's lack of skill could be read literally to refer to the forming not merely of letters but of a particular type of letters. If Charlemagne were indeed trying to form letters, they could have been those of the new Caroline minuscule, as well as the monumental capitals and elegant uncials which held such symbolic resonance, mentioned above. These were developed by court scribes such as Godescalc in the early 780s when Charlemagne was well into his 30s.[98]

The new minuscule, capitals, and uncials of the Carolingian court and the leading Carolingian centres of book production need to be seen against the

97 Paul Edward Dutton, *Charlemagne's Mustache and Other Cultural Clusters of a Dark Age* (London, 2004), pp. 69–92.

98 For example, Paris, Bibliothèque nationale n.a. lat. 1203 (*CLA* 5, no. 681), or Bibliothèque de l'Arsenal 599 (*CLA* 5, no. 517), Gospels 'written for royal presentation', late eighth century. See also Lawrence Nees, 'Godescalc's Career and the Problem of Influence', in *Under the Influence: The Concept of Influence and the Study of Illuminated Manuscripts*, eds John Lowden and Alixe Bovey (Turnhout, 2007), pp. 21–43.

background of the earlier, pre-Caroline scripts which would have been familiar to Charlemagne as a boy. A supposition of his possessing some basic writing skill is made on analogy with what else we know about teaching practice and implied by Latin grammatical instruction in antiquity and the early Middle Ages. It appears to have involved a certain amount of writing and alphabet learning, as well as learning from oral instruction by rote and memory.[99] How might Charlemagne have had to cope with the great variety of scripts and experimentation, let alone the varied pace of the evolution of Caroline minuscule in the second half of the eighth century? How might he have perceived the dramatic transition of script types and the emergence of Caroline minuscule in perfected form in the late 770s and early 780s? Does it make sense to suppose that he noticed the transformations in script and actually formed an aesthetic judgement about it? I suggest that it does. It was, after all, only well into Charlemagne's reign that the earliest dated examples of perfected Caroline minuscule appear, in the Maurdramnus Bible at Corbie *c.*780, the Godescalc Lectionary of 781–83, and the Salzburg *Liber vitae* of 784.[100] Before that there was a very great variety of scripts, both formal and informal, ranging from uncial and half uncial to a number of experimental minuscules and flowing, as well as clumsy, cursives.

It is conceivable, therefore, that scripts, both minuscule and majuscule and even cursive letter forms, were part of basic education in the early decades of the eighth century, not just for a young prince but for anyone. The range of Merovingian uncials, half uncials, and cursives to be found in books produced during Charlemagne's early years would have included scripts looking like the expert cursive from the turn of the seventh century in the copy

99 Eleanor Dickey, *Learning Latin the Ancient Way: Latin Textbooks from the Ancient World* (Cambridge, 2016). See also the classic accounts in Maurice Roger, *L'enseignement des lettres classiques d'Ausone à Alcuin. Introduction à l'histoire des écoles carolingiennes* (Paris, 1905); Pierre Riché, 'L'instruction des laïcs en Gaule mérovingienne au VIIe siècle', in *Caratteri del secolo VII in Occidente*, Settimane 5 (Spoleto, 1957), pp. 833–88; and Pierre Riché, 'L'enseignement de la culture des laïcs dans l'occident pré-carolingien', in *La Scuola nell'occidente latino dell'alto medioevo*, Settimane 19 (Spoleto, 1971), pp. 231–53, both reprinted in Pierre Riché, *Instruction et vie religieuse dans le Haut Moyen Âge* (London, 1981), chapters VI and VII.

100 For a succinct account see Bernhard Bischoff, *Latin Palaeography: Antiquity and the Middle Ages*, trans. Dáibhí Ó Cróinín and David Ganz (Cambridge, 1990), pp. 112–18. See also David Ganz, 'The Preconditions for Caroline Minuscule', *Viator* 118 (1987), 23–44; David Ganz, 'Book Production in the Carolingian Empire and the Spread of Caroline Minuscule', in *The New Cambridge Medieval History, Vol. II,* c.*700–900*, ed. Rosamond McKitterick (Cambridge, 1995), pp. 786–808; and Rosamond McKitterick, 'Script and Book Production', in *Carolingian Culture: Emulation and Innovation*, ed. Rosamond McKitterick (Cambridge, 1994), pp. 221–47.

of Jerome-Gennadius' *De viris illustribus* contained in Paris, Bibliothèque nationale lat. 12168;[101] the mixed uncial and half uncial of the *Chronica* known as the 'Barbarus Scaligeri' dating from the second half of the eighth century from northern Francia in Paris, Bibliothèque nationale lat. 4884;[102] the cursive minuscule reminiscent of the style of Luxeuil of the volume of Gregory of Tours' *Historiae*, Paris, Bibliothèque nationale lat. 17655, from the turn of the seventh century;[103] the *Martyrologium Luxoviense* written in a mixture of Frankish uncial, half uncial, and cursive minuscule from the first half of the eighth century (Paris, Bibliothèque nationale lat. 14086);[104] the copy of Cassiodorus on Psalms written in 'eN' type and early Caroline minuscule from the second half of the eighth century (Paris, Bibliothèque nationale lat. 12239);[105] or the script of annotations in Merovingian manuscripts such as Epinal, Bibliothèque municipale 149 (68), written at Tours in the third year of Childeric III's reign (744/45), and containing Jerome's Epistles.[106] Here one should heed geography as well as chronology. Neither for the household of Pippin as *maior* before 751 or as king thereafter, nor for Saint-Denis, can original manuscripts from the middle of the eighth century be identified in the crucial years in the middle of the eighth century (if we accept Charlemagne's birth year as 747 or 748).[107] The exception is a charter of Pippin recording a donation to Fulda. Fulrad's testament was produced later in the eighth century.[108] Yet the evidence of a habitual use of charters within the Arnulfing mayoral writing office and the indications of Pippin III's promotion of at least liturgical book

101 See also Paris, Bibliothèque nationale lat. 256, a gospel-book written in northern Frankish uncial beginning of the eighth century (*CLA* 5, no. 524), with 'liturgical entries in a Merovingian charter hand' adding a collect and preface of a mass for the dead on fol. 103v; Paris, Bibliothèque nationale lat. 1820 (*CLA* 5, no. 536), possibly written at Tours, containing Jerome's *In Ieremiam* written in early minuscule of the second half of the eighth century; Paris, Bibliothèque nationale lat. 2024, fol. 1309 from northeast France, written in Laon a-z type second half of the eighth century (*CLA* 5, no. 539) and containing Ambrosius, *De fide*.

102 *CLA* 5, no. 560.

103 *CLA* 5, no. 671.

104 *CLA* 5, no. 664.

105 *CLA* 5, no. 638 and compare Paris, Bibliothèque nationale lat. 12217 (*CLA* V 636), written in 'a–b script' and caroline minuscule; Paris, Bibliothèque nationale lat. 12226 (*CLA* 5, no. 637), written in Maurdramnus minuscule, end of the eighth century, at Corbie.

106 *CLA* 6, no. 762.

107 Karl-Ferdinand Werner, 'Das Geburtsdatum Karls des Großen', *Francia* 1 (1973), 115–57; and Matthias Becher, 'Neue Überlegungen zum Geburtsdatum Karls des Großen', *Francia* 19 (1992), 37–60.

108 Michael Tangl, 'Das Testament Fulrads von Saint-Denis', *Neues Archiv* 32 (1907), 167–217; and Alain Stoclet, *Autour de Fulrad de Saint Denis (v. 710–784)* (Geneva, 1993).

production need also to be taken into account.[109] Manuscripts and charters from the middle of the eighth century from the Austrasian and north-eastern writing provinces may give a better idea of the panoply of scripts Charlemagne or any Frank might have encountered in his youth, difficult as it is to be very precise about dates. The Gundohinus Gospels, dated to 754/55, is one of the few that can be pinned down by date, even though 'Vosevio', the place where the scribe was writing, has alas resisted identification.[110]

These pre-Caroline scripts, therefore, may have been what Charlemagne was taught to write in his youth, or were at least what he was accustomed to see. We might suppose therefore that it was something like the work of Godescalc and other court scribes whose work survives from the 780s onwards that the king tried to emulate, and demonstrated to him not only what a scribe could achieve, but also the significance of the majestic capitals, elegant uncials, and expert minuscule used in the gospel-books and psalters these court group scribes produced. Einhard's story then becomes more of a comment on the degree of skill the palace school scribes had attained in contrast to the king, even though working for him.

The diversity of script types in use at the time of Charlemagne's early education, moreover, constitutes a warning about the sheer diversity of practice and possibilities for the acquisition of literate skills in the early Middle Ages. Whatever his own skills as a scribe, or lack thereof, the young king Charlemagne inherited an assumption of the relevance of the written word to his role as king and to local and royal government, a functioning royal writing office, and a tradition of the active patronage of learning, liturgy, and law. That conviction of the role of the written word filtered out across the Frankish realms and was introduced to all the new peoples incorporated into the Carolingian Empire and its administrative networks. The comprehensive network of communications across Mediterranean Europe north of the Alps, and north and east of the Black Sea in late antiquity and the early Middle Ages, should also alert us to the possibility of cross-pollination or cross-fertilization in the techniques of charter production in the different regions, not least where there was contact with Muslim or Jewish communities.

The Carolingian rulers fostered the production of beautiful books on all manner of topics, but above all Christian texts, filled with majestic and superbly skilled writing. Charlemagne, for example, needed books in his chapel.

---

109 Ingrid Heidrich, *Die Urkunden der Arnulfinger* (Bad Münsterfeld, 2001); and Yitzhak Hen, *The Royal Patronage of Liturgy in Frankish Gaul to the Death of Charles the Bald (877)* (London, 2001), pp. 42–64.

110 Lawrence Nees, *The Gundohinus Gospels* (Cambridge, MA, 1987).

He commissioned books from some very skilful scribes and artists, such as Godescalc.[111] He had plans for lavish gifts for promoting correct and therefore orthodox texts. This included a new edition of the Gospels.[112] The palace chapel played a major role in promoting what was claimed as 'Roman' liturgy.[113] It is one of the best-known aspects of the Carolingian reforms that Charlemagne promoted correct Latin, but a great range of documents and literary texts was produced, both within and beyond the Frankish Empire, in regions once part of the Roman Empire as well as those which were not. Not the least of these texts are the charters which are the focus of this book with the wealth of evidence they offer for both documentary culture, legal practice, and linguistic variation. They reflect the many different styles of the written Latin in use in the early Middle Ages as well as, occasionally, indications of local vernaculars.

The complexity of the linguistic situation as well as the wonderful opportunities for linguistic study in the charter material are very apparent. The relationship between Latin and the vernaculars used to be framed according to the conventional understanding of diglossia and different linguistic registers, but it also needs to be considered in terms of bilingualism and the more recent emphasis on 'multilingualism'.[114] Even the notions of 'Latin' and 'vernacular' are themselves far from straightforward. There is a great diversity of Latin from the early Middle Ages, with contemporary usage varying from region to region as well as the many varieties of Latin from antiquity, Christian Latin,

111 Nees, 'Godescalc's Career'.

112 Bonifatius Fischer, 'Bibeltext und Bibelreform unter Karl dem Großen', in *Karl der Große. Lebenswerk und Nachleben*, eds Helmut Beumann, et al., 5 vols (Düsseldorf, 1965–68), 2:154–216; Wilhelm Koehler, *Die karolingische Miniatiuren, II: Die Hofschule Karls des Großen* (Berlin, 1958), and *III: Die Gruppe des Wiener Krönungsevangeliar / Metzer Handschriften* (Berlin, 1960).

113 See McKitterick, *Charlemagne*, pp. 295–380; and Rosamond McKitterick, 'Charlemagne, Rome, and the Management of Sacred Space', in *Charlemagne: les temps, les espaces, les hommes. Construction et déconstruction d'un règne*, eds Rolf Grosse and Michel Sot (Turnhout, 2017), pp. 165–79.

114 Again, the Utrecht series has contributed to this discussion for the early Middle Ages with *Spoken and Written Language: Relations Between Latin and the Vernacular Languages in the Earlier Middle Ages*, eds Mary Garrison, Árpád P. Orban, and Marco Mostert (Turnhout, 2013), though this volume was based on work completed in 1999. For more recent appraisals, see J. N. Adams, *The Regional Diversification of Latin, 200 BC–AD 600* (Cambridge, 2007); J. N. Adams, *Social Variation and the Latin Language* (Cambridge 2013); *Conceptualizing Multilingualism in Medieval England, c.800–c.1250*, ed. Elizabeth M. Tyler (Turnhout, 2011); *Multilingualism in the Graeco-Roman Worlds*, eds Alex Mullen and Patrick James (Cambridge, 2012); *Early and Late Latin: Continuity or Change?* eds J. N. Adams and Nigel Vincent (Cambridge, 2016); Pierre Flobert, 'Latin-Frankish Bilingualism in Sixth-Century Gaul', in *Bilingualism in Ancient Society: Language Contact and the Written Text*, eds J. N. Adams, Mark Janse, and Simon Swain (Oxford, 2002), pp. 419–30.

and 'informal Latin', all available in many different genres. For many of those producing these early medieval texts, this 'Latin' was either effectively the vernacular or an acquired second language learnt from books. Further, one of the most influential texts for written Latin was the Bible. Whether in the *Vetus Latina* or *Vulgate* version, it was still what has been described as 'a translation text, full of artificiality and translationese'.[115] James Adams' study of bilingualism and the Latin language, although devoted to the period up to the fourth century, offers many highly pertinent comparisons for the studies in this volume, with examples of code-switching, linguistic change as a consequence of different languages coming into contact with one another, the impact of Latin in conflict with a number of vernacular languages, the role played by language choice, and the importance of language for conveying and expressing a sense of identity, even if only in the form of personal and place names.[116] The work of Roger Wright, Michel Banniard, and others, moreover, has established the enormous diversity of Latin in early medieval Europe, with regional differentiation in vocabulary, formulaic phrasing, orthography, and textual reminiscences that need to be further investigated.[117]

Glossaries: A Potential Resource?

In relation to language use and acquisition, a recent but complementary resource is the myriad of eighth- and ninth-century manuscripts containing glossaries; they provide a relatively untapped source. An example of this category of evidence is a remarkable book produced in the late eighth century, apparently in the scriptorium responsible for 'a-b' script. This may have been Soissons, or one among the Seine valley constellation of monasteries with strong links to the royal court, such as Chelles. It is an encyclopaedia-like dictionary, organized into almost absolute alphabetical order, known as the *Liber glossarum*, and available in a digital edition coordinated by Anne

115 See J. N. Adams, *An Anthology of Informal Latin 200 BC–AD 900: Fifty Texts with Translations and Linguistic Commentary* (Cambridge, 2016), p. 643. For the discussion comparing *Vetus Latina* and Vulgate, see pp. 429–44.

116 J. N. Adams, *Bilingualism and the Latin Language* (Cambridge, 2003).

117 Roger Wright, *Late Latin and Early Romance in Spain and Carolingian France* (Liverpool, 1982); *Latin and the Romance Languages in the Early Middle Ages*, ed. Roger Wright (London, 1991); Roger Wright, *A Sociophilological Study of Late Latin* (Turnhout, 2002); Michel Banniard, 'Language and Communication in Carolingian Europe', in *The New Cambridge Medieval History II*, ed. McKitterick, pp. 695–708. Several of the chapters in this volume contribute substantially to this investigation.

Grondeux.[118] It is extant in what appear to be the original two huge volumes now in Paris and Cambrai, but with further copies also extant from Lorsch, Auxerre, Corbie, Tours, Fleury, and a 1070-page shorter (!) version copied at St Gall known as the *Glossae Salomonis*.[119] Entries vary between one-line synonyms and definitions to extended explanations covering several columns of text which in many places cite the authors from which they are drawn. This remarkable compilation forms the core of later dictionaries produced in the eleventh, twelfth, and thirteenth centuries such as those by Papias and Huguccio as well as the *Catholicon*.

The potential of the *Liber glossarum* and other glossary material to illuminate the understanding of Latin and German literacy in the Carolingian world is immense. The *Liber glossarum* is but one of many Latin glossaries and glossary collections, or 'glossary chrestomathies' as I have labelled them, produced in the late eighth and throughout the ninth century.[120] As I have remarked elsewhere, the corpus of early medieval Latin and bilingual dictionaries needs to be appreciated as a cultural and historical phenomenon in its own right. Early medieval glossaries are predominantly lists of Latin words with definitions also in Latin, either as single-word synonyms or explanatory short phrases of encyclopaedic character. Still other word definitions are allegorical, metaphorical, or symbolic. They are organized in anything from basic 'A' or 'A-B' order to virtually absolute alphabetical order. The words are culled from both classical and early medieval texts covering such topics as literature, philosophy, architecture, agriculture, military engineering, surveying, natural science, medicine, arithmetic, geometry, astronomy, music, law, theology, and history. Certainly, classical traditions of specialist word lists and *hermeneumata* were developed further, and many glossaries introduce transliterated Hebrew and Greek words into their word lists and definitions. The word lists thus reflect a succession of choices and selections of words that were thought to be necessary, appropriate, useful, or interesting for particular contexts within multilingual Europe at a crucial stage of its development in the aftermath of the Roman Empire.

118 http://liber-glossarum.huma-num.fr/index.html; see *CLA* 5, no. 611 (Paris, Bibliothèque nationale lat. 11529 + 11530).

119 St Gall, Stiftsbibliothek, Cod. Sang. 905; http://www.e-codices.unifr.ch/en/list/one/csg/0905.

120 McKitterick, 'Glossaries and Other Innovations', with references to earlier literature; Rosamond McKitterick, 'Glossaries and Their Functions in the Early Middle Ages: The Example of BAV lat. 6018' in *Faire Lien. Aristocratie, réseaux et échanges compétitifs. Mélanges en honneur de Régine Le Jan*, eds Laurent Jégou, Sylvie Joye, Thomas Lienhard, and Jens Schneider (Paris, 2015), pp. 307–14; Rosamond McKitterick, 'Le pouvoir des mots: les glossaires, la mémoire culturelle et la transmission du savoir au Haut Moyen Âge', *Les Cahiers columbaniens 2013*, ed. Pierre Riché (Luxeuil-les-Bains, 2014), pp. 16–58.

The bilingual glossaries are based on Latin but contain words in Old English, Old Irish, Old High German, Greek, Hebrew, and Arabic. Many early medieval glossaries have been associated with the missionary context of second-language learning by men and women working in England and east of the Rhine, whether of Latin or of Old High German and Old English. But a substantial majority of the earliest medieval glossaries and encyclopaedic collections extant from the later eighth and ninth centuries was produced in north-western France and the Loire valley.[121] These places were not just interested in the Latin language; we also find Greek-Latin, transliterated Greek-Latin, and Latin-Greek.

All these glossaries need to be seen not only against the background of the extraordinary assimilation and consolidation of Latin as the language of government, religion, law, and education within most of the barbarian successor states of post-Roman Europe, but actually as crucially constructive contributions to that process. The glossaries are dynamic sources, representing a reframing and structuring of particular 'resources of the past' for present concerns and becoming themselves a resource for the future. They survive in an astonishing abundance from the eighth and ninth centuries. I have so far identified over 200 manuscripts containing glossaries, mostly compiled and copied in the northern and western regions ruled by the Franks in the Carolingian period from such places as Rheims, Paris (Saint-Germain-des-Prés), Amiens, Fleury, and Tours. Some of the more famous glossaries were categorized by late nineteenth- and early twentieth-century scholars according to their first words: *Abavus*, *Ab absens*, *Abba*, *Abolita*, *Abstrusa*, *Affatim*. All these appear to have spawned similar kinds of collections. Some compilers mixed the words in different glossaries into new composite versions. Some kept the words but abbreviated, or otherwise altered, the definitions in small ways. Some used an older glossary but reorganized it, so that the same words occur but in a different order. Some even rationalized the word order.

It is necessary to move beyond simply cataloguing the existence and representatives of a lexicographical and encyclopaedic tradition in the early Middle Ages. Instead, the focus should be on the content of the compilations, what they reveal of attitudes to language, reading processes, the construction of knowledge, and their purpose, and how, if at all, they relate to the great range of texts in Latin being produced at the same time and often in the same place.

121 The four volumes in the Storehouses of Learning project directed by Rolf H. Bremmer Jr, Kees Dekker, and Patrizia Lendinara are a particularly important contribution, especially the fourth and final volume, *Fruits of Learning: The Transfer of Encyclopaedic Knowledge in the Early Middle Ages*, eds Rolf H. Bremmer Jr and Kees Dekker (Leuven, 2016).

The glossaries are an important category of evidence for any consideration of language in the early Middle Ages. They raise many questions about context, as well as the purposes for which new compilations were put together and Roman and late antique ones recopied. They may have acted as aids to reading, didactic tools for acquiring Latin vocabulary, or aids to learning Latin as a second language. Some might have been designed as sources of explanation for difficult and foreign words, such as Greek and Hebrew assimilated into Latin texts. They may have served as treasuries of information as well as of definition. A further function might have been as guides to new meanings of words in new contexts. Glossaries could also have functioned as aids to honing rhetorical skills. Early medieval glossaries and encyclopaedic miscellanies should be regarded as active participants in the creation of an intellectual and cultural tradition and thus a major contribution to the literate culture of the early Middle Ages.

Conclusion

Words represent essential and potent carriers of cultural memory in the early Middle Ages, a period too often overlooked by theoreticians of cultural memory. Words are the base elements of Aleida Assmann's category of functional memory, but they are not static.[122] Every word had its original context. Every word, and all the meanings associated with it, could be identified as potentially pertinent to new contexts. The acts of selection, de-selection, re-selection, organization, reassembly, and the thematic and subject-based classification of words from lists, or from whole texts, can all be recognized as attempts to order the world as well as represent the world. The words and the approach to language articulated in the glossaries are the keys to understanding the texts inherited from the past. They are also the tools with which new texts are forged and new ideas articulated. Without language, whether in writing or speech, how can the ideas and values of any culture be communicated? Without an understanding of the meaning of words, how can texts from one culture be understood and used in new contexts? This 'vast cultural archive of written memory' offers an arsenal for connecting the present with a distant past.[123] Words

122 Aleida Assmann, *Erinnerungsräume. Formen und Wandlungen des kulturellen Gedächtnisses* (Munich, 1999); and Aleida Assmann, *Cultural Memory and Western Civilisation: Functions, Media, Archives* (Cambridge, 2011).

123 Walter Pohl and Ian Wood, 'Introduction: Cultural Memory and the Resources of the Past', in *The Resources of the Past*, eds Gantner et al., pp. 1–14.

were the most basic form in which the ideas and values of the Greco-Roman, Judaeo-Christian, and Muslim traditions were transmitted to western Europe. Words from northern European traditions enriched this arsenal in the form of creative composition, translation, and names,[124] and have been transmitted to posterity in literary texts, glossaries, and documents such as those discussed in this volume.

The many studies cited in this chapter might be seen to be part of an interpretative and methodological cycle, in which topics and texts considered in one context then re-emerge with something more to reveal in response to new contexts and new questions. The history of literacy in Europe is not one of unbroken continuity from the Roman world to that of early medieval Europe. It is rather a variegated landscape of continuities and disruptions, transformations, creativity, adoption, and adaptation, and new forms of commemoration and record.

Examination of the many modes of literacy and manifestations of documentary culture in the early Middle Ages alluded to in this chapter has had a transformative impact on the study of the early Middle Ages more broadly. The realization of the interdependence of literacy, language, and communication with all other aspects of early medieval culture, furthermore, can be usefully considered within the concept of 'entanglement'. Entanglement, when technically deployed in the field of quantum mechanics, expresses the degree of interaction by any one particle that could not be fully described without considering those other particles with which it interacts; nothing within a system can be regarded as fully independent. Adapted by the social sciences, 'entanglement' has become a useful portmanteau notion to denote complex networks of interdependence.[125] Thus the charters and other documentary

---

124 For some important examples see D. H. Green, *The Carolingian Lord. Semantic Studies on Old High German, Balder, Frô, Truhtin and Herro* (Cambridge, 1965); *Latin Culture*, eds North and Hofstra; D. H. Green, *Language and History in the Early Germanic World* (Cambridge, 1998); and *Akkulturation. Probleme einer germanisch-romanischen Kultursynthese in Spätantike und frühen Mittelater*, eds Dieter Hägermann, Wolfgang Haubrichs, and Jörg Jarnut, Ergänzungsbände zum Reallexikon der Germanischen Altertumskunde 41 (Berlin, 2004).

125 Ian Hodder, 'Human-Thing Entanglement: Towards an Integrated Archaeological Perspective', *Journal of the Royal Anthropological Institute* n.s. 17 (2011), 154–77. I consider the notion of 'entanglement' more fully in Rosamond McKitterick, 'Migration and the Written Word in the Early Middle Ages', in *Europa im Geflecht der Welt. Mittelalterliche Migrationen in globalen Bezügen*, eds Michael Borgolte, Julia Dücker, Marcel Müllerburg, Paul Predatsch, and Bernd Schneidmüller, Europa im Mittelalter 20, Abhandlungen und Beiträge zur historischen Komparatistik (Berlin, 2012), pp. 71–86.

records considered in this volume, the words they contain, the scripts in which they were written, and the formulae they preserve, are among the building blocks of cultural memory, that is, of an inclusive understanding of the past articulated by learned men and women fully integrated into their own social and political worlds. Glossaries could be used to create new texts and, in this respect, they were also a bridge between the past and the future. Similarly, charters recorded the past but were destined for both present concerns and future record, quite apart from being precious remnants of language use and evolution, as we shall see in the chapters which follow.[126]

Bibliography

Primary Sources

Anglo-Saxon Wills, ed. and trans. Dorothy Whitelock (Cambridge, 1930).

Catalunya Carolingia, eds Ramon d'Abadal i de Vinyals et al. (Barcelona, 1926–2006).

Chartae latinae antiquiores, eds Albert Bruckner et al., 118 vols (Olten et al., 1954–2019).

Codices latini antiquiores. A Palaeographical Guide to Latin Manuscripts prior to the Ninth Century, ed. Elias Avery Lowe, 11 vols + supplement (Oxford, 1935–71)

Dhuoda, Manual pour mon fils, ed. Pierre Riché, Sources Chrétiennes 225bis (Paris, 1997).

Diplomata Karolinorum: Faksimile-Ausgabe der in der Schweiz liegenden originalen Karolingerdiplome, ed. Albert Bruckner, 4 vols (Basle, 1969–72).

Diplomata Karolinorum: Recueil de reproductions en facsimile des actes originaux des souverains conservés dans les archives et bibliothèques de France, eds Ferdinand Lot and Philippe Lauer, 10 vols (Paris, 1936–40).

Einhard, *Vita Karoli*, eds Michel Sot and Christiane Veyrard-Cosme, *Eginhard. Vie de Charlemagne* (Paris, 2014).

Isidore of Seville, *Etymologiae*, ed. W. M. Lindsay (Oxford, 1911); English translation Stephen A. Barney, W. J. Lewis, J. A. Beach, and Oliver Berghof, *The Etymologies of Isidore of Seville*, 2nd ed. (Cambridge, 2010).

Receuil des inscriptions chrétiennes de la Gaule antérieure à la renaissance carolingienne, eds Henri-Irénée Marrou, Luce Pietri, and Nancy Gauthier (Paris, 1975-).

Tjäder, Jan-Olof. *Die nichtliterarischen lateinischen Papyri Italiens aus der Zeit 445–700*, 3 vols (Lund and Stockholm, 1954–82).

126 I should like to thank the three editors of this volume, and especially Ed Roberts for the invitation to contribute this chapter, and for their very constructive and helpful comments.

Secondary Sources

Adams, J. N., *An Anthology of Informal Latin 200 BC–AD 900: Fifty Texts with Translations and Linguistic Commentary* (Cambridge, 2016).

Adams, J. N., *Bilingualism and the Latin Language* (Cambridge, 2003).

Adams, J. N., *The Regional Diversification of Latin, 200 BC–AD 600* (Cambridge, 2007).

Adams, J. N., *Social Variation and the Latin Language* (Cambridge 2013).

Adams, J. N. and Vincent, Nigel (eds), *Early and Late Latin: Continuity or Change?* (Cambridge, 2016).

Adamska, Anna and Mostert, Marco (eds), *The Development of Literate Mentalities in East Central Europe* (Turnhout, 2004).

Althoff, Gerd, *Amicitiae und Pacta. Bündnis, Einung, Politik und Gebetsgedenken im beginnenden 10. Jahrhundert*, MGH Schriften 37 (Hanover, 1992).

Andersen, Per, Münster-Swendsen, Mia, and Vogt, Helle (eds), *Law before Gratian. Law in Western Europe c. 500–1100* (Copenhagen, 2007).

Assmann, Aleida, *Cultural Memory and Western Civilisation: Functions, Media, Archives* (Cambridge, 2011).

Assmann, Aleida, *Erinnerungsräume. Formen und Wandlungen des kulturellen Gedächtnisses* (Munich, 1999).

Banniard, Michel, 'Language and Communication in Carolingian Europe', in *The New Cambridge Medieval History, Vol. II, c.700–900*, ed. Rosamond McKitterick (Cambridge, 1995), pp. 695–708.

Barret, Sébastien, Stutzmann, Dominique, and Vogeler, Georg (eds), *Ruling the Script in the Middle Ages: Formal Aspects of Written Communication* (Turnhout, 2017).

Bäuml, Franz, 'Varieties and Consequences of Medieval Literacy and Illiteracy', *Speculum* 55 (1980), 237–65.

Becher, Matthias, 'Neue Überlegungen zum Geburtsdatum Karls des Großen', *Francia* 19 (1992), 37–60.

Bedos-Rezak, Brigitte and Hamburger, Jeffrey (eds), *Sign and Design: Script as Image in Cross-Cultural Perspective (300–1600 CE)* (Cambridge, MA, 2016).

Bischoff, Bernhard, *Katalog der festländischen Handschriften des neunten Jahrhunderts (mit Ausnahme der wisigotischen)*, 3 vols (Wiesbaden, 1998–2014).

Bischoff, Bernhard, *Latin Palaeography: Antiquity and the Middle Ages*, trans. Dáibhí Ó Cróinín and David Ganz (Cambridge, 1990).

Bischoff, Bernhard, *Mittelalterliche Studien*, 3 vols (Stuttgart, 1966–81).

Bischoff, Bernhard, *Die südostdeutsche Schreibschulen und Bibliotheken in der Karolingerzeit*, I: *Die bayrischen Diözesen*, 3rd ed. (Wiesbaden, 1974), and II: *Die vorwiegend Österreichischen Diözesen* (Wiesbaden, 1980).

Bischoff, Frank, *Urkundenformate im Mittelalter. Größe, Format und Proportionen von Papsturkunden in Zeiten expandierender Schriftlichkeit (11.-13. Jahrhundert)* (Marburg, 1996).

Bougard, François, *La justice dans le royaume d'Italie: de la fin du VIIIe siècle au début du XIe siècle*, Bibliothèque des Écoles françaises d'Athènes et de Rome 291 (Rome, 1995).

Bowman, Alan and Woolf, Greg (eds), *Literacy and Power in the Ancient World* (Cambridge, 1994).

Boyle, Leonard and Peri, Vittorio (eds), *Tre alfabeti per gli Slavi. Catalogo della mostra allestita nella Biblioteca Vaticana per l'undicesimo centenario della morte di San Metodio* (Vatican City, 1985).

Bremmer Jr, Rolf H. and Dekker, Kees (eds), *Fruits of Learning: The Transfer of Encyclopaedic Knowledge in the Early Middle Ages* (Leuven, 2016).

Bresslau, Harry, *Handbuch der Urkundenlehre*, 2 vols, rev. ed. (Berlin, 1912, originally 1889, reprinted 1969).

Brenk, Beat, 'Schriftlichkeit und Bildlichkeit in der Hofschule Karls d. Gr.', in *Testo e immagine nell'alto medioevo*, Settimane 41 (Spoleto, 1994), pp. 631–82.

Brooks, Nicholas, *The Early History of the Church of Canterbury: Christ Church from 597 to 1066* (London, 1984).

Brown, Warren, *Unjust Seizure: Conflict, Interest and Authority in an Early Medieval Society* (Ithaca, 2001).

Brown, Warren, Costambeys, Marios, Innes, Matthew, and Kosto, Adam (eds), *Documentary Culture and the Laity in the Early Middle Ages* (Cambridge, 2013).

Bubalo, Dorde, *Pragmatic Literacy in Medieval Serbia* (Turnhout, 2014).

Bullough, Donald, 'Roman Books and Carolingian *renovatio*', in *Renaissance and Renewal in Christian History*, ed. Derek Baker (London, 1977), pp. 23–50; reprinted in Donald A. Bullough, *Carolingian Renewal: Sources and Heritage* (Manchester, 1991), pp. 1–33.

Cardin, Luca, *Epigrafia a Roma nel primo medioevo (secoli IV–X). Modelli grafici e tipologie d'uso* (Rome, 2008).

Cavallo, Guglielmo, 'Leggere e scrivere. Tracce e divaricazioni di un percorso dal tardoantico al medioevo greco e latino', in *Scrivere e leggere nell'alto medioevo*, Settimane 59 (Spoleto, 2012), pp. 1–38.

Cavallo, Guglielmo, 'Libri scritti, libri letti, libri dimenticati', in *Il secolo di ferro: mito e realtà del secolo X*, Settimane 38 (Spoleto, 1991), pp. 759–94.

Cavallo, Guglielmo, 'Scrivere, leggere, memorizzare le sacre scritture', in *Morfologie sociali e culturali in Europa fra tarda antichità e alto medioevo*, Settimane 45 (Spoleto, 1998), pp. 987–1008.

Cavallo, Guglielmo and Mango, Cyril, *Epigrafia medievale greca e latina: ideologia e funzione* (Spoleto, 1995).

Cencetti, Giorgio, 'Dall'unità al particolarismo grafico. Le scritture cancelleresche romane e quelle dell'alto medioevo', in *Il passagio dall'antichità al medioevo in occidente*, Settimane 9 (Spoleto, 1962), pp. 237–64.

Chandler, Cullen J., *Carolingian Catalonia: Politics, Culture, and Identity in an Imperial Province, 778–987* (Cambridge, 2019).

Chartier, Roger, *Inscrire et effacere. Culture écrite et littérature (XIe–XVIIIe siècle)* (Paris, 2005).

Chaytor, Henry J., *From Script to Print* (London, 1945).

Chazelle, Celia M. (ed.), *Literacy, Politics, and Artistic Innovation in the Early Medieval West* (Lanham, MD, 1992).

Chinca, Mark and Young, Christopher (eds), *Orality and Literacy in the Middle Ages: Essays on a Conjunction and its Consequences in Honour of D. H. Green* (Turnhout, 2005).

Clanchy, M. T., *From Memory to Written Record: England 1066–1307* (London, 1979, rev. editions 1993 and 2013).

Classen, Peter, *Kaiserreskript und Königsurkunde: diplomatischer Studien zum Problem der Kontinuität zwischen Altertum und Mittelalter* (Thessaloniki, 1977).

Classen, Peter (ed.), *Recht und Schrift im Mittelalter*, Vorträge und Forschungen 23 (Sigmaringen, 1977).

Comunicare e significare nell'alto medioevo, Settimane 52 (Spoleto, 2005).

Costambeys, Marios, *Power and Patronage in Early Medieval Italy: Local Society, Italian Politics and the Abbey of Farfa, c.700–900* (Cambridge, 2007).

Dartmann, Christoph, Scharff, Thomas, and Loeber, Christoph F. (eds), *Zwischen Pragmatik und Performanz. Dimensionen mittelalterlicher Schriftkultur* (Turnhout, 2011).

Davies, Wendy and Fouracre, Paul (eds), *The Settlement of Disputes in Early Medieval Europe* (Cambridge, 1986).

Davies, Wendy, Graham-Campbell, James, Handley, Mark, Kershaw, Paul, Koch, J. T., le Duc, G., and Lockyear, K. (eds), *The Inscriptions of Early Medieval Brittany* (Oakville, CT and Aberystwyth, 2000).

Dickey, Eleanor, *Learning Latin the Ancient Way: Latin Textbooks from the Ancient World* (Cambridge, 2016).

Dutton, Paul Edward, *Charlemagne's Mustache and Other Cultural Clusters of a Dark Age* (London, 2004).

Erhart, Peter, Heidecker, Karl, and Zeller, Bernhard (eds), *Die Privaturkunden der Karolingerzeit* (Dietikon-Zürich, 2009).

Erhart, Peter and Hollenstein, Lorenz (eds), *Mensch und Schrift im frühen Mittelalter* (St Gall, 2006).

Erhart, Peter and Kleindinst, Julia, *Urkundenlandschaft Rätien*, Forschungen zur Geschichte des Mittelalters 7 (Vienna, 2004).

Erhart, Peter and Kuratli, Jakob (eds), *Bücher des Lebens—lebendige Bücher. Katalog zur gleichnamigen Ausstellung im Regierungsgebäude des Kantons Sankt Gallen* (St Gall, 2010).

Everett, Nicholas, *Literacy in Lombard Italy, c.568–774* (Cambridge, 2003).

Faulkner, Thomas, *Law and Authority in the Early Middle Ages: The Frankish leges in the Carolingian Period* (Cambridge, 2016).

Favreau, Robert, 'Les commanditaires dans les inscriptions du haut moyen âge occidental' in *Committenti e produzione artistico-letteraria nell'alto medioevo occidentale*, Settimane 39 (Spoleto, 1992), pp. 681–722.

Favreau, Robert, 'La mémoire du passé dans les inscriptions du haut moyen âge', in *Ideologie e pratiche del reimpiego nell'alto medioevo*, Settimane 46 (1999), pp. 937–76.

Fischer, Bonifatius, 'Bibeltext und Bibelreform unter Karl dem Großen', in *Karl der Große. Lebenswerk und Nachleben*, eds Helmut Beumann, et al., 5 vols (Düsseldorf, 1965–68), 2:154–216.

Flobert, Pierre, 'Latin-Frankish Bilingualism in Sixth-Century Gaul', in *Bilingualism in Ancient Society: Language Contact and the Written Text*, eds J. N. Adams, Mark Janse, and Simon Swain (Oxford, 2002), pp. 419–30.

Franklin, Simon, 'Literacy and Documentation in Mediaeval Russia', *Speculum* 60 (1985), 1–38.

Gantner, Clemens, McKitterick, Rosamond, and Meeder, Sven (eds), *The Resources of the Past in Early Medieval Europe* (Cambridge, 2015)

Ganz, David, 'Book Production in the Carolingian Empire and the Spread of Caroline Minuscule', in *The New Cambridge Medieval History, Vol. II, c.700–900*, ed. Rosamond McKitterick (Cambridge, 1995), pp. 786–808.

Ganz, David, 'Early Medieval Display Scripts and the Problem of How We See Them', in *Graphic Signs of Identity, Faith, and Power in Late Antiquity and the Early Middle Ages*, eds Ildar H. Garipzanov, Caroline Goodson, and Henry Maguire (Turnhout, 2017), pp. 125–46.

Ganz, David, 'The Preconditions for Caroline Minuscule', *Viator* 118 (1987), 23–44.

Ganz, David, '"Roman Books" Reconsidered: The Theology of Carolingian Display Script', in *Early Medieval Rome and the Christian West. Essays in Honour of Donald A. Bullough*, ed. Julia M. H. Smith (Leiden, 2000), pp. 297–316.

Garipzanov, Ildar H., *Graphic Signs of Authority in Late Antiquity and the Early Middle Ages, 300–900* (Oxford, 2018).

Garipzanov, Ildar H., *The Symbolic Language of Authority in the Carolingian World (c.751–877)* (Leiden, 2008).

Garipzanov, Ildar H., Goodson, Caroline, and Maguire, Henry (eds), *Graphic Signs of Identity, Faith, and Power in Late Antiquity and the Early Middle Ages* (Turnhout, 2017).

Garrison, Mary, Orban, Árpád P., and Mostert, Marco (eds), *Spoken and Written Language: Relations Between Latin and the Vernacular Languages in the Earlier Middle Ages* (Turnhout, 2013).

Giry, Arthur, *Manuel de Diplomatique*, rev. ed. (Paris, 1925, originally 1894).
Goody, Jack, *The Logic of Writing and the Organization of Society* (Cambridge, 1986).
Goody, Jack (ed.), *Literacy in Traditional Societies* (Cambridge, 1969).
Graff, Harvey J., *Literacy in History: An Interdisciplinary Research Bibliography* (London, 1981).
Gray, Nicolette, 'The Palaeography of Latin Inscriptions in the Eighth, Ninth and Tenth Centuries in Italy', *Papers of the British School at Rome* 16 (1948), 38–170.
Green, D. H., *The Carolingian Lord. Semantic Studies on Old High German, Balder, Frô, Truhtin and Herro* (Cambridge, 1965).
Green, D. H., *Language and History in the Early Germanic World* (Cambridge, 1998).
Grundmann, Herbert, '*Literatus-illiteratus*. Der Wandel einer Bildungsnorm von Altertum zum Mittelalter', *Archiv für Kulturgeschichte* 40 (1958), 1–65.
Guyotjeannin, Olivier, Morelle, Laurent, and Parisse, Michel (eds), *Les cartulaires*, Mémoires et documents de l'École des chartes 39 (Paris, 1993).
Hägermann, Dieter, Haubrichs, Wolfgang, and Jarnut, Jörg (eds), *Akkulturation. Probleme einer germanisch-romanischen Kultursynthese in Spätantike und frühen Mittelater*, Ergänzungsbände zum Reallexikon der Germanischen Altertumskunde 41 (Berlin, 2004).
Hagemann, Mariëlle and Mostert, Marco (eds), *Reading Images and Texts: Medieval Images and Texts as Forms of Communication* (Turnhout, 2005).
Handley, Mark, *Death, Society and Culture: Inscriptions and Epitaphs in Gaul and Spain AD 300–750*, British Archaeological Reports. International Series, 1135 (Oxford, 2003).
Harris, William, *Ancient Literacy* (New Haven, 1989).
Heidecker, Karl (ed.), *Charters and the Use of the Written Word in Medieval Society* (Turnhout, 2000).
Heidrich, Ingrid, *Die Urkunden der Arnulfinger* (Bad Münsterfeld, 2001).
Hellgardt, Ernst, 'Zur Mehrsprachigkeit im Karolingerreich. Bermerkungen aus Anlaß von Rosamond McKittericks Buch "The Carolingians and the Written Word"', *Beiträge zur Geschichte der deutschen Sprache und Literatur* 118 (1996), 1–48.
Hen, Yitzhak, *Roman Barbarians: The Royal Court and Culture in the Early Medieval West* (Basingstoke, 2007).
Hen, Yitzhak, *The Royal Patronage of Liturgy in Frankish Gaul to the Death of Charles the Bald (877)* (London, 2001).
Hendrix, Julian, 'Liturgy for the Dead and the Confraternity of Reichenau and St Gall, 800–950' (unpublished PhD thesis, University of Cambridge, 2007).
Hodder, Ian, 'Human-Thing Entanglement: Towards an Integrated Archaeological Perspective', *Journal of the Royal Anthropological Institute* n.s. 17 (2011), 154–77.
Hoggart, Richard, *The Uses of Literacy* (London, 1957).

Hummer, Hans J., *Politics and Power in Early Medieval Europe: Alsace and the Frankish Realm, 600–1000* (Cambridge, 2005).

Innes, Matthew, 'Memory, Orality and Literacy in an Early Medieval Society', *Past & Present* 158 (1998), 3–38.

Innes, Matthew, *State and Society in the Early Middle Ages: The Middle Rhine Valley, 400–1000* (Cambridge, 2000).

Jarrett, Jonathan, *Rulers and Ruled in Frontier Catalonia, 880–1010: Pathways of Power* (Woodbridge, 2010).

Jasper, Detlev (ed.), *Fälschungen im Mittelalter*, MGH Schriften 33, 6 vols (Hanover, 1988–90).

Johnson, William A. and Parker, Holt N. (eds), *Ancient Literacies: The Culture of Reading in Greece and Rome* (Oxford, 2009).

Kéry, Lotte, *Canonical Collections of the Early Middle Ages (ca. 400–1140): A Bibliographical Guide to the Manuscripts and Literature* (Washington, DC, 1999).

Knowles, David, *Great Historical Enterprises: Problems in Monastic History* (London, 1963).

Koch, Walter, *Inschriftenpaläographie des abendländischen Mittelalters und der früheren Neuzeit* (Vienna, 2007).

Koehler, Wilhelm, *Die karolingische Miniatiuren, II: Die Hofschule Karls des Großen* (Berlin, 1958), and *III: Die Gruppe des Wiener Krönungsevangeliar / Metzer Handschriften* (Berlin, 1960).

Kosto, Adam J., 'Laymen, Clerics, and Documentary Practices in the Early Middle Ages: The Example of Catalonia', *Speculum* 80 (2005), 44–74.

Kosto, Adam J., *Making Agreements in Medieval Catalonia: Power, Order, and the Written Word, 1000–1200* (Cambridge, 2001).

Kosto, Adam J. and Winroth, Anders (eds), *Charters, Cartularies, and Archives: The Preservation and Transmission of Documents in the Medieval West. Proceedings of a Colloquium of the Commission internationale de diplomatique, Princeton and New York, 16–18 September 1999*, Papers in Medieval Studies 17 (Toronto, 2002).

Koziol, Geoffrey, *The Politics of Memory and Identity in Carolingian Royal Diplomas: The West Frankish Kingdom (840–987)* (Turnhout, 2012).

Lapidge, Michael (ed.), *Archbishop Theodore: Commemorative Studies on his Life and Influence* (Cambridge, 1995).

La Rocca, Cristina, 'Angelberga, Louis II's Wife and her Will (877)', in *Ego Trouble: Authors and their Identities in the Early Middle Ages*, eds Richard Corradini, Matthew Gillis, Rosamond McKitterick, and Irene van Renswoude, Forschungen zur Geschichte des Mittelalters 15 (Vienna, 2010), pp. 221–26.

Le Jan, Régine, 'The Multiple Identities of Dhuoda', in *Ego Trouble: Authors and their Identities in the Early Middle Ages*, eds Richard Corradini, Matthew Gillis,

Rosamond McKitterick, and Irene van Renswoude, Forschungen zur Geschichte des Mittelalters 15 (Vienna, 2010), pp. 211–20.

Levison, Wilhelm, 'Das Testament des Diakons Adalgisel-Grimo vom Jahre 634', *Trierer Zeitschrift* 7 (1932), 69–85; reprinted in Wilhelm Levison, *Aus Rheinischer und Fränkische Frühzeit* (Düsseldorf, 1948), pp. 118–38.

Levy, Kenneth, *Gregorian Chant and the Carolingians* (Princeton, 1998).

Mabillon, Jean, *De re diplomatica* (Paris, 1681).

Mackenzie, Mary M. and Roueché, Charlotte (eds), *Images of Authority: Papers Presented to Joyce Reynolds on the Occasion of her Seventieth Birthday* (Cambridge, 1989).

MacMullen, Ramsey, 'The Epigraphic Habit in the Roman Empire', *American Journal of Philology* 103 (1982), 233–46.

Martin, Henri-Jean and Vézin, Jean (eds), *Mise en page et mise en texte du livre manuscript* (Paris, 1990).

McKitterick, Rosamond, 'Anglo-Saxon Missionaries in Germany: Reflections on the Manuscript Evidence', *Transactions of the Cambridge Bibliographical Society* 9 (1989), 291–329.

McKitterick, Rosamond, *Books, Scribes and Learning in the Frankish Kingdoms, Sixth to Ninth Centuries* (Aldershot, 1994).

McKitterick, Rosamond, 'Carolingian Book Production: Some Problems', *The Library*, sixth series, 12 (1990), 1–33.

McKitterick, Rosamond, *The Carolingians and the Written Word* (Cambridge, 1989)

McKitterick, Rosamond, 'Carolingian Uncial: A Context for the Lothar Psalter', *The British Library Journal* 16 (1990), 1–15.

McKitterick, Rosamond, 'Charlemagne, Rome, and the Management of Sacred Space', in *Charlemagne: les temps, les espaces, les hommes. Construction et déconstruction d'un règne*, eds Rolf Grosse and Michel Sot (Turnhout, 2017), pp. 165–79.

McKitterick, Rosamond, *Charlemagne: The Formation of a European Identity* (Cambridge, 2008).

McKitterick, Rosamond, 'Charles the Bald (823–877) and his Library: The Patronage of Learning', EHR 95 (1980), 29–47.

McKitterick, Rosamond, 'The Diffusion of Insular Culture in Neustria between 650 and 850: The Implications of the Manuscript Evidence' in *La Neustrie. Les pays au nord de la Loire de 650 à 850*, ed. Hartmut Atsma, 2 vols, Beihefte der Francia 16 (Sigmaringen, 1989), 2:395–432.

McKitterick, Rosamond, 'Early Mediaeval Book Production and the Problem of Female Literacy', *Theoretische Geschiedenis* 19 (1992), 147–68.

McKitterick, Rosamond, *The Frankish Church and the Carolingian Reforms, 789–895* (London, 1977).

McKitterick, Rosamond, *Frankish Kings and Culture in the Early Middle Ages* (Aldershot, 1995).

McKitterick, Rosamond, 'Frankish Uncial in the Eighth Century: A New Context for the Work of the Echternach Scriptorium', in *Willibrord, zijn wereld en zijn werk*, eds Petty Bange and Antonius G. Weiler (Nijmegen, 1990), pp. 350–64.

McKitterick, Rosamond, 'Frauen und Schriftlichkeit im Frühmittelalter', in *Weibliche Lebensgestaltung im frühen Mittelalter*, ed. Hans-Werner Goetz (Cologne, 1991), pp. 65–118.

McKitterick, Rosamond, 'Glossaries and Other Innovations in Carolingian Book Production', in Erik Kwakkel, Rosamond McKitterick, and Rodney Thomson, *Turning Over a New Leaf: Change and Development in the Medieval Book* (Leiden, 2012), pp. 21–78 and plates 1–20 (pp. 169–93).

McKitterick, Rosamond, 'Glossaries and Their Functions in the Early Middle Ages: The Example of BAV lat. 6018' in *Faire Lien. Aristocratie, réseaux et échanges compétitifs. Mélanges en honneur de Régine Le Jan*, eds Laurent Jégou, Sylvie Joye, Thomas Lienhard, and Jens Schneider (Paris, 2015), pp. 307–14.

McKitterick, Rosamond, 'The Gospels of St Hubert', in *Art at Auction*, ed. Georgia Fogg (London, 1986), pp. 154–57.

McKitterick, Rosamond, *History and Memory in the Carolingian World* (Cambridge, 2004).

McKitterick, Rosamond, 'Knowledge of Canon Law in the Frankish Kingdoms before 789: The Manuscript Evidence', *Journal of Theological Studies* n.s. 36 (1985), 97–117.

McKitterick, Rosamond, 'A Landmark Figure in the History of German? Charlemagne, Language and Literacy', in *Landmarks in the History of the German Language*, eds Geraldine Horan, Nils Langer, and Sheila Watts, Britische und irische Studien zur deutschen Sprache und Literatur 52 (Bern, 2009), pp. 11–34.

McKitterick, Rosamond, 'Literacy in Alemannia and the Role of St Gall', in *St Gall as a Centre of Culture*, ed. Werner Vogler (Stuttgart and Zürich, 1991), pp. 217–26.

McKitterick, Rosamond, 'Manuscripts and Scriptoria in the Reign of Charles the Bald, 840–877', in *Giovanni Scoto nel suo tempo. L'organizzazione del sapere in età carolingia. Atti del XXIV Convegno storico internazionale, Todi, 11–14 ottobre 1987* (Spoleto, 1989), pp. 200–33.

McKitterick, Rosamond, 'Migration and the Written Word in the Early Middle Ages', in *Europa im Geflecht der Welt. Mittelalterliche Migrationen in globalen Bezügen*, eds Michael Borgolte, Julia Dücker, Marcel Müllerburg, Paul Predatsch, and Bernd Schneidmüller, Europa im Mittelalter 20, Abhandlungen und Beiträge zur historischen Komparatistik (Berlin, 2012), pp. 71–86.

McKitterick, Rosamond, 'A Ninth-Century Schoolbook from the Loire Valley: Phillipps 16308', *Scriptorium* 30 (1976), 225–31.

McKitterick, Rosamond, 'Nuns' Scriptoria in England and Francia in the Early Middle Ages', *Francia* 19 (1992), 1–35.

McKitterick, Rosamond, 'Palaeography, Diplomatic and Codicology: The Last Fifty Years', in *Omaggio al Medioevo. I primi cinquanta anni del Centro italiano di studi sull'alto medioevo di Spoleto*, ed. Enrico Menestò (Spoleto, 2009), pp. 179–210.

McKitterick, Rosamond, 'Le pouvoir des mots: les glossaires, la mémoire culturelle et la transmission du savoir au Haut Moyen Âge', *Les Cahiers columbaniens 2013*, ed. Pierre Riché (Luxeuil-les-Bains, 2014), pp. 16–58.

McKitterick, Rosamond, 'Review of Kenneth Levy, *Gregorian Chant and the Carolingians* (Princeton, 1998)', *Early Music History* 19 (2000), 279–90.

McKitterick, Rosamond, 'Script and Book Production', in *Carolingian Culture: Emulation and Innovation*, ed. Rosamond McKitterick (Cambridge, 1994), pp. 221–47.

McKitterick, Rosamond, 'The Scriptoria of Merovingian Gaul: A Survey of the Evidence', in *Columbanus and Merovingian Monasticism*, eds Howard Clarke and Mary Brennan, British Archaeological Reports, International Series 113 (Oxford, 1981), pp. 173–207.

McKitterick, Rosamond, 'Some Carolingian Law Books and their Function', in *Authority and Power: Studies on Mediaeval Law and Government presented to Walter Ullmann on his 70th birthday*, eds Peter Linehan and Brian Tierney (Cambridge, 1980), pp. 13–27.

McKitterick, Rosamond, 'Text and Image in the Carolingian World', in *The Uses of Literacy in Early Mediaeval Europe*, ed. Rosamond McKitterick (Cambridge, 1990), pp. 297–318.

McKitterick, Rosamond, 'The Uses of Literacy in Carolingian and Post-Carolingian Europe: Literate Conventions of Memory', in *Scrivere e leggere nell'alto medioevo*, Settimane 59 (Spoleto, 2012), pp. 179–211.

McKitterick, Rosamond, 'The Written Word and Oral Communication: Rome's Legacy to the Franks', in *Latin Culture and Medieval Germanic Europe: Proceedings of the First Germania Latina Conference Held at the University of Groningen, 26 May 1989*, eds Richard North and Tette Hofstra, Germania Latina 1, Mediaevalia Groningana 11 (Groningen, 1992), pp. 87–110.

McKitterick, Rosamond (ed.), *The Uses of Literacy in Early Mediaeval Europe* (Cambridge, 1990).

Mersiowsky, Mark, *Die Urkunde in der Karolingerzeit. Originale, Urkundenpraxis und politische Kommunikation*, MGH Schriften 60, 2 vols (Wiesbaden, 2015).

Mitchell, John, 'The Display of Script and the Uses of Painting in Longobard Italy', *Testo e immagine nell'alto medioevo*, Settimane 41 (Spoleto, 1994), pp. 887–954.

Morison, Stanley, *Politics and Script: Aspects of Authority and Freedom in the Development of Graeco-Latin Script from the Sixth Century B.C. to the Twentieth Century A.D.* (Oxford, 1972).

Mostert, Marco, *A Bibliography of Works on Medieval Communication* (Turnhout, 2012).

Mostert, Marco, 'Using and Keeping Written Texts: Reading and Writings as Forms of Communication in the Early Middle Ages', in *Scrivere e leggere nell'alto medioevo*, Settimane 59 (Spoleto, 2012), pp. 71–94.

Mostert, Marco (ed.), *New Approaches to Medieval Communication* (Turnhout, 1999).

Mostert, Marco and Barnwell, Paul S. (eds), *Medieval Legal Process: Physical, Spoken and Written Performance in the Middle Ages* (Turnhout, 2013).

Mullen, Alex and James, Patrick (eds), *Multilingualism in the Graeco-Roman Worlds* (Cambridge, 2012).

Nedkvitne, Arnved, *The Social Consequences of Literacy in Medieval Scandinavia* (Turnhout, 2005).

Nees, Lawrence, 'Godescalc's Career and the Problem of Influence', in *Under the Influence: The Concept of Influence and the Study of Illuminated Manuscripts*, eds John Lowden and Alixe Bovey (Turnhout, 2007), pp. 21–43.

Nees, Lawrence, *The Gundohinus Gospels* (Cambridge, MA, 1987).

Nees, Lawrence, 'Prolegomenon to a Study of the Vienna Coronation Gospels: Common Knowledge, Scholarship, Tradition, Legend, Myth', in *Rome and Religion in the Medieval World. Studies in Honor of Thomas F. X. Noble*, eds Valerie L. Garver and Owen M. Phelan (Farnham, 2014), pp. 253–74.

Nelson, Janet L., 'The Wary Widow', in *Property and Power in the Early Middle Ages*, eds Wendy Davies and Paul Fouracre (Cambridge, 1995), pp. 82–113.

Nicolaj, Giovanna, 'Fratture e continuità nella documentazione fra tardo antico e alto medioevo. Preliminari di diplomatica e questioni di metodo', in *Morfologie sociali e culturali in Europa fra tarda antichità e alto medioevo*, Settimane 45 (Spoleto, 1998), pp. 953–84.

North, Richard and Hofstra, Tette (eds), *Latin Culture and Medieval Germanic Europe: Proceedings of the First Germania Latina Conference Held at the University of Groningen, 26 May 1989*, Germania Latina 1, Mediaevalia Groningana 11 (Groningen, 1992).

Parkes, Henry, *The Making of Liturgy in the Ottonian Church: Books, Music and Ritual in Mainz, 950–1050* (Cambridge, 2015).

Parkes, Malcolm B., 'The Literacy of the Laity', in *Literature and Western Civilization: The Medieval World*, eds David Daiches and A. K. Thorby (London, 1973), pp. 555–77.

Patt, Sarah, *Studien zu den 'Formulae imperiales'. Urkundenkonzeption und Formulargebrauch in der Kanzlei Kaiser Ludwigs des Frommen (814–840)*, MGH Studien und Texte 59 (Wiesbaden, 2016).

Peikola, Matti, Mäkilähde, Aleksi, Salmi, Hanna, Varila, Mari-Liisa, and Skaffari, Janne (eds), *Verbal and Visual Communication in Early English Texts* (Turnhout, 2017).

Petrucci, Armando, 'Alfabetismo ed educazione grafica degli scribi altomedievali (secoli VII–X),' in *The Role of the Book in Medieval Culture*, ed. Peter Ganz, 2 vols, Bibliologia 3 (Turnhout, 1986), 1:109–32.

Petrucci, Armando, 'Aspetti simbolici delle testimonianze scritte', in *Simboli e simbologia nell'alto medioevo*, Settimane 23 (Spoleto, 1976), pp. 813–44.

Petrucci, Armando, *La scrittura. Ideologia e rappresentazione* (Turin, 1980); translated into English as *Public Lettering: Script, Power, and Culture*, trans. Linda Lappin (Chicago, 1993).

Petrucci, Armando, 'Spazi di scrittura e scritte avventizie nel libro alto medievale', in *Ideologie e pratiche del reimpiego nell'alto medioevo*, Settimane 46 (1999), pp. 981–1006.

Petrucci, Armando, *Writers and Readers in Medieval Italy: Studies in the History of Written Culture*, trans. Charles M. Radding (New Haven and London, 1995).

Pohl, Walter and Herold, Paul (eds), *Vom Nutzen des Schreibens. Soziales Gedächtnis, Herrschaft und Besitz*, Forschungen zur Geschichte des Mittelalters 5 (Vienna, 2002).

Pohl, Walter and Wood, Ian, 'Introduction: Cultural Memory and the Resources of the Past', in *The Resources of the Past in Early Medieval Europe*, eds Clemens Gantner, Rosamond McKitterick, and Sven Meeder (Cambridge, 2015), pp. 1–14.

Raaijmakers, Janneke, *The Making of the Monastic Community of Fulda, c.744–c.900* (Cambridge, 2012).

Rankin, Susan, *Writing Sounds in Carolingian Europe: The Invention of Musical Notation* (Cambridge, 2018).

Ranković, Slavica, Melve, Leidulf, and Mundal, Else (eds), *Along the Oral-Written Continuum* (Turnhout, 2010).

Reimitz, Helmut, *History, Frankish Identity and the Framing of Western Ethnicity, 550–850* (Cambridge, 2015).

Riché, Pierre, *Education and Culture in the Barbarian West*, trans. John J. Contreni (Columbia, SC, 1976).

Riché, Pierre, 'L'enseignement de la culture des laïcs dans l'occident pré-carolingien', in *La Scuola nell'occidente latino dell'alto medioevo*, Settimane 19 (Spoleto, 1971), pp. 231–53.

Riché, Pierre, 'L'instruction des laïcs en Gaule mérovingienne au VIIe siècle', in *Caratteri del secolo VII in Occidente*, Settimane 5 (Spoleto, 1957), pp. 833–88.

Riché, Pierre, *Instruction et vie religieuse dans le Haut Moyen Âge* (London, 1981).

Richter, Michael, *The Formation of the Medieval West: Studies in the Oral Culture of the Barbarians* (Dublin, 1994).

Rio, Alice, *Legal Practice and the Written Word in the Early Middle Ages: Frankish Formulae, c.500–1000* (Cambridge, 2009).

Rio, Alice (ed.), *Law, Custom and Justice in Late Antiquity and the Early Middle Ages* (London, 2007).

Robinson, P. R. (ed.), *Teaching Writing, Learning to Write: Proceedings of the XVIth Colloquium of the Comité Internationale de Paléographie Latine* (London, 2010).

Roger, Maurice, *L'enseignement des lettres classiques d'Ausone à Alcuin. Introduction à l'histoire des écoles carolingiennes* (Paris, 1905).

Roma nell'alto medioevo, Settimane 48 (Spoleto, 2001).

Rück, Peter (ed.), *Graphische Symbole in mittelalterlichen Urkunden. Beiträge zur diplomatischen Semiotik* (Sigmaringen, 1996).

Rück, Peter (ed.), *Methoden der Schriftbeschreibung* (Stuttgart, 1999).

Sawyer, P. H., *Anglo-Saxon Charters: An Annotated List and Bibliography* (London, 1968); revised as the Electronic Sawyer, www.esawyer.org.uk.

Schieffer, Rudolf (ed.), *Schriftkultur und Reichswervaltung unter den Karolingern*, Abhandlungen der Nordrhein-Westfälischen Akademie der Wissenschaften 97 (Opladen, 1996).

Schmid, Karl and Wollasch, Joachim, 'Die Gemeinschaft von Lebenden und Verstorbenen in Zeugnissen des Mittelalters', *Frühmittelalterliche Studien* 1 (1967), 365–405.

Schulte, Michael and Nedoma, Robert (eds), *Language and Literacy in Early Scandinavia and Beyond*, special issue of *NOWELE: North-Western European Language Evolution* 62–63 (Odense, 2011).

Schulte, Petra, Mostert, Marco, and van Renswoude, Irene (eds), *Strategies of Writing: Studies on Text and Trust in the Middle Ages* (Turnhout, 2008).

Screen, Elina and West, Charles (eds), *Writing the Early Medieval West* (Cambridge, 2018).

Scrivere e leggere nell'alto medioevo, Settimane 59 (Spoleto, 2012).

Snijders, Tjamke, *Manuscript Communication: Visual and Textual Mechanics of Communication in Hagiographical Texts from the Southern Low Countries, 900–1200* (Turnhout, 2014).

Stein, Henri, *Bibliographie générale des cartulaires français ou relatifs à l'histoire de France* (Paris, 1907).

Steinova, Evina, '*Notam Superponere studii*. The Use of Technical Signs in the Early Middle Ages' (unpublished PhD thesis, University of Utrecht, 2016).

Stock, Brian, *Listening for the Text: On the Uses of the Past* (Baltimore, MD, 1990).

Stock, Brian, *The Implications of Literacy: Written Language and Models of Interpretation in the Eleventh and Twelfth Centuries* (Princeton, NJ, 1983).

Stoclet, Alain, *Autour de Fulrad de Saint Denis (v. 710–784)* (Geneva, 1993).

Stoffella, Marco, 'Aristocracy and Rural Churches in the Territory of Lucca between Lombards and Carolingians: A Case Study', in *774, ipotesi su una transizione. Atti del seminario di Poggibonsi, 16–18 febbraio 2006*, ed. Stefano Gasparri (Turnhout, 2008), pp. 289–311.

Stoffella, Marco, 'Gli atti di permute nella Toscana occidentale tra VIII e XI secolo', in *Tauschgeschäft und Tauschurkunde vom 8. bis zum 12. Jahrhundert/L'acte d'échange, du VIIIe au XIIe siècle* (Limoges, 2013), pp. 129–57.

Story, Joanna, Bunbury, Judith, Felici, Anna Candida, Fronterotta, Gabriele, Piacentini, Mario, Nicolais, Chiara, Scacciatelli, Daria, Sciuti, Sebastiano, and Vendittelli, Margherita, 'Charlemagne's Black Marble: The Origin of the Epitaph of Pope Hadrian I', *Papers of the British School at Rome* 73 (2005), 157–90.

Stratmann, Martina, 'Schriftlichkeit in der Verwaltung von Bistümern und Klöstern zur Zeit Karls des Großen', in *Karl der Große und sein Nachwirken 1000 Jahre Kultur und Wissenschaft in Europa*, eds Paul Butzer, Max Kerner, and Walter Oberscherlp (Turnhout, 1997), pp. 251–75.

Street, Brian V., *Literacy in Theory and Practice* (Cambridge, 1984).

Tangl, Michael, 'Das Testament Fulrads von Saint-Denis', *Neues Archiv* 32 (1907), 167–217.

Tellenbach, Gerd, 'Liturgische Gedenkbücher als historische Quelle', in *Mélanges E. Tisserant* 5, Studi e Testi 235 (Vatican City, 1964), pp. 389–99.

Thomas, Rosalind, *Literacy and Orality in Ancient Greece* (Cambridge, 1992).

Thomas, Rosalind, *Oral Tradition and Written Record in Classical Athens* (Cambridge, 1989).

Thompson, James Westfall, *Literacy of the Laity in the Middle Ages* (New York, 1960).

Tock, Benoît-Michel, *La diplomatique française du Haut Moyen Age. Inventaire des chartes originales antérieures à 1121 conservée en France*, 2 vols (Turnhout, 2001).

Tollerton, Linda, *Wills and Will-Making in Anglo-Saxon England* (York, 2011).

Traube, Ludwig, *Vorlesungen und Abhandlungen*, 3 vols (Munich, 1909–11).

Treffort, Cécile, *Mémoires carolingiennes. L'épitaphe entre célébration mémorielle, genre littéraire et manifeste politique (milieu VIIIe–début XIe siècle)* (Rennes, 2007).

Treitler, Leo, 'The "Unwritten" and "Written Transmission" of Medieval Chant and the Start-up of Musical Notation', *Journal of Musicology* 10 (1992), 131–91.

Tyler, Elizabeth M. (ed.), *Conceptualizing Multilingualism in Medieval England, c.800–c.1250* (Turnhout, 2011).

Ubl, Karl, *Sinnstiftungen eines Rechtsbuchs. Die Lex Salica im Frankenreich*, Quellen und Forschungen zum Recht im Mittelalter 9 (Ostfildern, 2017).

Vessey, Mark, 'Literacy and *litteratura*, AD 200–800', *Studies in Medieval and Renaissance History* n.s. 13 (1992), 139–60.

Werner, Karl-Ferdinand, 'Das Geburtsdatum Karls des Großen', *Francia* 1 (1973), 115–57.

Wormald, Patrick, 'The Uses of Literacy in Anglo-Saxon England and its Neighbours', *Transactions of the Royal Historical Society*, fifth series, 27 (1977), 95–114.

Wright, Roger, *Late Latin and Early Romance in Spain and Carolingian France* (Liverpool, 1982).

Wright, Roger, *A Sociophilological Study of Late Latin* (Turnhout, 2002).

Wright, Roger (ed.), *Latin and the Romance Languages in the Early Middle Ages* (London, 1991).

Zilmer, Kristel and Jesch, Judith (eds), *Epigraphic Literacy and Christian Identity: Modes of Written Discourse in the Newly Christian European North* (Turnhout, 2003).

Zwierlein, Susanne, *Studien zu den Arengen in den Urkunden Kaiser Ludwigs des Frommen (814–840)*, MGH Studien und Texte 60 (Wiesbaden, 2016).

CHAPTER 3

The Multilingualism of the Early Middle Ages: Evidence from Peripheral Regions of the *Regnum orientalium Francorum*

Wolfgang Haubrichs

Two Types of Linguistic Acculturation

The migrations of Germanic peoples into the western, Latin-speaking parts of the Roman Empire during the fifth and sixth centuries produced strikingly varied linguistic results. We may distinguish between two basic processes.[1] The first concerns those regions where migrants ultimately formed a minority; here, linguistic acculturation to the Latin-speaking (or, later, Romance-speaking) majority was only a question of time, albeit with sociolectal and regional differences. This process applies primarily to the southern and western provinces, being far away from the *limites* of the western Empire.

The Italo-Dalmatian kingdom of the Goths, founded by Theoderic (493–526), offers an important model.[2] After Bishop Wulfila (d. 382/83) translated the Bible into Gothic (*c*.369), the Christianized Goths possessed a culture based on written texts supported by a special script invented by Wulfila.[3]

1 On linguistic acculturation in the former western Roman Empire, see Klaus Dietz, Maria Besse, Wolfgang Haubrichs, Stefan Sonderegger, Peter Wiesinger, and Martina Pitz, 'Romanisch-Germanische Sprachbeziehungen', in *Reallexikon der Germanischen Altertumskunde*, 35 vols, 2nd ed. (Berlin, 2003), 25:242–304; Wolfgang Haubrichs, 'Die verlorene Romanität im deutschen Sprachraum', in *Romanische Sprachgeschichte. Ein internationales Handbuch zur Geschichte der romanischen Sprachen*, eds Gerhard Ernst, Martin-Dietrich Gleßgen, Christian Schmitt, and Wolfgang Schweickard, 3 vols (Berlin, 2003), 1:695–709; Wolfgang Haubrichs and Max Pfister, 'La Romania submersa dans les pays de langue allemande', in *Manuel des langues romanes*, eds Andre Klump, Johannes Kramer, and Aline Willems (Berlin, 2014), pp. 224–44.

2 For the Gothic *regnum* of Theoderic, see Peter Heather, 'Theoderic, King of the Goths', *EME* 4 (1995), 145–73; Peter Heather, *The Goths* (Oxford 1996), pp. 216–76; Hans-Ulrich Wiemer, *Theoderich der Große. König der Goten—Herrscher der Römer* (Munich, 2018).

3 Elfriede Stutz, *Gotische Literaturdenkmäler* (Stuttgart, 1966); Jan-Olof Tjäder, 'Der Codex argenteus in Uppsala und der Buchmeister Viliaric in Ravenna', in *Studia Gotica. Die eisenzeitlichen Verbindungen zwischen Schweden und Südosteuropa*, ed. Ulf Erik Hagberg (Stockholm, 1972), pp. 144–64; Wilhelm Braune and Frank Heidermanns, *Gotische Grammatik. Mit*

 DOI:10.1163/9789004432338_004

The powerful influence of this new script among the Arian East Germanic peoples (the Ostrogoths, Visigoths, and Vandals) has recently been highlighted by the discovery of Gothic graffiti from the ninth or tenth century carved with Wulfila's characters in the capital of the Crimean bishopric of Gothia.[4] Of the Gothic texts that have been preserved—mainly manuscripts of the Bible translation—most were written in Ostrogothic Italy.[5] Theoderic's Goths were not simply a band of warriors; they also had in their ranks *bôkareis*, 'scholars', experts in script and book-production, as well as notaries responsible for writing out official documents, biblical codices, and liturgical texts. Theologians commented on the gospels (the *Skeireins*, a commentary of the Gospel of John), annotated homilies (the *Gotica Veronensia*), and wrote sermons in Gothic (the *Fragmenta Bononiensia*).[6] Although the Goths clearly remained a small minority, the language of both the state and people of Theoderic was deemed sufficiently important for some senatorial Roman families (such as that of the *referendarius*, *patricius*, and *vir illustris* Cyprianus) to let their sons study their conquerors' Germanic language.[7] There is a parallel for this in the kingdom of the Burgundians on the river Rhône, where a legal expert from a senatorial family named Syagrius learned the East Germanic language of the newcomers.[8] In Italy, therefore, we may suppose that there was a limited degree of bilingualism, mainly on the part of the Goths.[9] This interpretation is supported by the presence of a considerable number of Gothic loanwords in

---

Lesestücken und Wörterverzeichnis, 20th ed. (Tübingen, 2004), pp. 19–26; Carla Falluomini, *The Gothic Version of the Gospels and Pauline Epistles: Cultural Background, Transmission and Character* (Berlin, 2015).

4 Maksim Korobov and Andrey Vinogradov, 'Gotische Graffito-Inschriften aus der Bergkrim', *Zeitschrift für deutsches Altertum* 145 (2016), 141–57.

5 Stutz, *Gotische Literaturdenkmäler*, pp. 20–27; Braune and Heidermanns, *Gotische Grammatik*, pp. 6–15.

6 Carla Falluomini, 'Zum gotischen Fragment aus Bologna', *Zeitschrift für deutsches Altertum* 143 (2014), 281–305; Carla Falluomini, 'Zum gotischen Fragment aus Bologna II: Berichtigungen und neue Lesungen', *Zeitschrift für deutsches Altertum* 146 (2017), 284–94; *The Gothic Palimpsest from Bologna. Philological and Linguistic Studies*, eds Anita Auer and Michiel De Vaan, Cahiers de l'ILSL 50 (Lausanne, 2016).

7 *Cassiodori Senatoris Variae*, ed. Theodor Mommsen, MGH Auct. ant. 12 (Berlin, 1894), V.40, pp. 166–67; VIII.21, pp. 252–53: 'Pueri stirpis Romanae nostra lingua loquuntur, eximie indicantes exhibere se nobis futuram fidem, quorum iam videntur affectasse sermonem'. Cf. p. 491 (*Index personarum*).

8 Wolfgang Haubrichs, 'Akkulturation und Distanz. Germanische und romanische Personennamen im *regnum* der Burgunden', in *Völker, Reiche und Namen im frühen Mittelalter*, eds Matthias Becher and Stefanie Dick, Mittelalterstudien 22 (Munich, 2010), pp. 191–222, at 216, n. 124.

9 Cf. Nicoletta Francovich Onesti, *I nomi degli Ostrogoti* (Florence, 2007), pp. 9–10.

Italian dialects, and there are further parallels in the former Visigothic regions of Provence, Spain, and Portugal.[10] However, Gothic culture and literature quickly died out following the collapse of the Gothic kingdom and the eastern Roman Empire's 'reconquista' of Italy under Justinian in 553.

In the early-sixth-century African kingdom of the Vandals, we find comparable evidence and testimonies for a surviving East Germanic idiom, similar to Gothic, until the language died with the destruction of the realm and the expulsion of the Vandals in 533.[11] On the other hand, the Burgundian language seems to have survived the demise of their kingdom (443–534), lasting until the second half of the sixth century, as demonstrated by a runic inscription found at Charnay-lès-Mâcon (dep. Saône-et-Loire) and by several anthroponyms found in charters and inscriptions.[12] These witnesses imply a deep-seated bilingualism. Furthermore, the Visigothic language in Spain and the *Narbonensis* (the later *Gothia*), attested only by names and secondary documents, may have survived in a bilingual situation among the upper stratum of the *gens* until the later seventh century.[13]

10 The loanwords of Gothic origin in Italian language and dialects are collected in *Lessico Etimologico Italiano (LEI). Germanismi, Vol. I*, ed. Elda Morlicchio (Wiesbaden, 2015).

11 Hermann Reichert, 'Sprache und Namen der Wandalen in Afrika', in *Namen des Frühmittelalters als sprachliche Zeugnisse und als Geschichtsquellen*, eds Albrecht Greule and Matthias Springer (Berlin, 2009), pp. 43–120; Andy Merrills and Richard Miles, *The Vandals* (Chichester, 2010), pp. 94–95; Wolfgang Haubrichs, 'Nescio latine! Volkssprache und Latein im Konflikt zwischen Arianern und Katholiken im wandalischen Afrika nach der Historia persecutionis des Victor von Vita', in *Geschichtsvorstellungen. Bilder, Texte und Begriffe aus dem Mittelalter. Festschrift für Hans-Werner Goetz*, eds Steffen Patzold, Anja Rathmann-Lutz, and Volker Scior (Cologne, 2012), pp. 15–42; Konrad Vössing, *Das Königreich der Vandalen. Geiserichs Herrschaft und das Imperium Romanum* (Darmstadt, 2014), pp. 98–99, 175, nn. 138–45.

12 Wolfgang Haubrichs, 'Ein namhaftes Volk—Burgundische Namen und Sprache des 5. und 6. Jahrhunderts', in *Die Burgunder. Ethnogenese und Assimilation eines Volkes*, ed. Volker Gallé (Worms, 2008), pp. 135–84, at 172–75; Wolfgang Haubrichs, 'Sprachliche Integration, Sprachinseln und Sprachgrenzbildung im Bereich der östlichen Gallia. Das Beispiel der Burgunden und der Franken', in *Von der Spätantike zum frühen Mittelalter: Kontinuitäten und Brüche, Konzeptionen und Befunde*, eds Theo Kölzer and Rudolf Schieffer, Vorträge und Forschungen 70 (Ostfildern, 2009), pp. 61–100, at 80–81.

13 Cf. Joseph M. Piel and Dieter Kremer, *Hispano-gotisches Namenbuch: Der Niederschlag des Westgotischen in den alten und heutigen Personen- und Ortsnamen der iberischen Halbinsel* (Heidelberg, 1976), p. 277; Hermann Reichert, 'Die Bildungsweise der frühen germanischen Personennamen', in *Linguistica et Philologica. Gedenkschrift für Björn Collinder*, eds Otto Gschwantler, Karoly Redei, Hermann Reichert, and Helmut Birkhan (Vienna, 1984), pp. 355–67, at 364–67; Wolfgang Haubrichs, 'Ethnisch signifikante und andere sprechende Namen im wisigotischen Spanien und im gotischen Italien', in *Sprache—Rhetorik—Translation. Festschrift für Alberto Gil*, eds Vahram Atayan and Ursula Wienen, Rhethos 3 (Frankfurt, 2012), pp. 41–54, at 42–46.

The Franks in northern Gaul and the Langobards in Italy constitute special cases. For the Franks, we must envisage a long-lasting bilingualism from the last decades of the fifth century, especially in the districts near what later became the Romance-Germanic language border (Champagne, Picardie, Wallonia, Ardennes, and Lorraine). This is shown not only by the intensive Germanization of the personal names of Romance-speaking people in northern Gaul, but also by nests of Frankish toponyms and hydronyms, and by the high quantity of early Frankish loanwords in French and Gallo-Romance dialects of the contact areas, to which we shall return below.

One meets a similar situation with the Langobards, who invaded the Italian provinces in 568 and conquered northern and central Italy, from Friuli and Lombardy to Tuscany, and eventually Spoleto and Benevento.[14] The Germanization of the anthroponymy in the Langobard kingdom, in sharp contrast to the Byzantine parts of the peninsula,[15] as well as the high number of Langobardic loanwords in Italian and its dialects, testify to an enduring bilingualism of the *gens*.[16] Toponyms formed with genuinely Langobardic words also offer evidence of this long-lasting process: e.g. *fara*, 'travelling group', but

14 Jörg Jarnut, *Geschichte der Langobarden* (Stuttgart, 1982), Italian translation: *Storia dei Longobardi* (Turin, 1995); Paolo Delogu, 'Il regno longobardo', in *Longobardi e Bizantini*, eds Paolo Delogu, André Guillou, and Gherardo Ortalli, Storia d'Italia 2 (Turin, 1980), pp. 1–216; *Il regno dei Longobardi in Italia. Archeologia, società, istituzioni*, ed. Stefano Gasparri (Spoleto, 2004); *Die Langobarden. Herrschaft und Identität*, eds Walter Pohl and Peter Erhart (Vienna, 2005); *The Langobards before the Frankish Conquest: An Ethnographic Perspective*, eds Giorgio Ausenda, Paolo Delogu, and Chris Wickham (Woodbridge, 2009); Stefano Gasparri, *Italia longobarda. Il regno, i Franchi, il papato* (Bari, 2012); Claudio Azzara, *I Longobardi* (Bologna, 2015).

15 T. S. Brown, *Gentlemen and Officers: Imperial Administration and Aristocratic Power in Byzantine Italy A.D. 554–800* (Rome, 1984); Wolfgang Haubrichs, 'The Early Medieval Naming-World of Ravenna, Eastern Romagna and the Pentapolis', in *Ravenna: Its Role in Earlier Medieval Change and Exchange*, eds Judith Herrin and Jinty Nelson (London, 2016), pp. 253–95.

16 Federico Albano Leoni, 'Bilinguismo e coscienza del bilinguismo nell'Italia longobarda', in *Italia linguistica: idee, storia, strutture*, eds Federico Albano Leoni, Daniele Gambarara, Franco Lo Piparo, and Raffaele Simone (Bologna, 1983), pp. 133–48; Nicoletta Francovich Onesti, *Vestigia longobarde in Italia (568–774). Lessico e antroponimia* (Rome, 1999), pp. 39–50; Wolfgang Haubrichs, 'Langobardic Personal Names: Given Names and Name-giving Among the Langobards', in *The Langobards*, eds Ausenda et al., pp. 195–236, at 217–22; Wolfgang Haubrichs, 'Sprache und Schriftlichkeit im langobardischen Italien—Das Zeugnis von Namen, Wörtern und Entlehnungen', *Filologia Germanica—Germanic Philology* 2 (2010), 133–201, at pp. 182–88; *I Longobardi in Italia: lingua e cultura*, ed. Carla Falluomini (Alessandria, 2015).

later on 'parentela';[17] *stôde-garda*, 'stud farm' or 'place for horse-breeding';[18] or *theut-pacis* < **theuda-bakja-*, 'river under public control'.[19] Furthermore, we find place-names formed with the ethnonyms of groups coming into Italy with the Langobards (*Suebi, Gepidi, Sciri, Baiovarii, Bulgari,* etc.).[20] Many terms found in the Langobard laws attest to its continued use as a legal language. In the eighth century, however, the Romanization of the Langobards accelerated significantly, and we can consider their native language to have died out at the end of the century.[21]

These scenarios of progressive acculturation of the Germanic *gentes* and their gradual amalgamation with majority Romance-speaking societies have hitherto remained the focus of historical research. Too often, the simultaneous process of the integration of Romance-speaking people into Germanic-speaking societies is almost wholly overlooked. This constitutes the second basic type of linguistic acculturation. Mention here should of course be made of the linguistic and cultural transformation of large parts of Roman Britain, which was caused by the migrations of North Sea Germanic groups of Angles, Saxons, Jutes, Frisians, and others, and the subsequent assimilation of remaining Latin- or Britonnic-speaking populations.[22] One might also refer to the 'de-Latinization' of the northern parts of *Germania Secunda* and *Belgica Secunda*, that is to say, the later Low Franconian-, Dutch-, and Flemish-speaking parts of

17 Paul the Deacon, *Historia Langobardorum*, MGH SS rer. Germ. 48 (Hanover, 1878), II.9, p. 91: 'faras, hoc est generationes vel lineas …'. Cf. Francovich Onesti, *Vestigia longobarde*, p. 76; Haubrichs, 'Sprache und Schriftlichkeit', pp. 167–69.

18 Wolfgang Haubrichs, 'Langobardisch-fränkische Ortsnamen in Oberitalien: Zu den toponymischen Typen *Stuttgart, Gamundio* und *Herstall / Wardstall*', *Namenkundliche Informationen* 109–110 (2017), 269–90, at pp. 270–73.

19 Nicoletta Francovich Onesti, 'Toponimi di origine germanica della Val di Cornia', *A.I.O.N. Filologia Germanica* 30–31 (1987–88), 7–42; Francovich Onesti, *Vestigia longobarde*, p. 123.

20 Federico Belli, 'Etnici e nomi di luogo di origine germanica in Italia', in *A Torino. Atti del XII Convegno Internazionale di Onomastica e Letteratura*, eds Daniela Cacia and Chiara Colli Tibaldi (Alessandria, 2008), pp. 309–38.

21 Haubrichs, 'Langobardic Personal Names', pp. 217–22; Haubrichs, 'Sprache und Schriftlichkeit', pp. 185–88. See also the contribution of Marco Stoffella in this volume.

22 Cf. Alex Woolf, 'The Britons: From Romans to Barbarians', in *Regna and Gentes. The Relationship between Late Antique and Early Medieval Peoples and Kingdoms in the Transformation of the Roman World*, eds Hans-Werner Goetz, Jörg Jarnut, and Walter Pohl (Leiden, 2003), pp. 345–80; *Britons in Anglo-Saxon England*, ed. Nick Higham (Woodbridge, 2007); Klaus Dietz, 'Benennungen von Romanen und Kelten (und ihrer Sprache) im frühmittelalterlichen England', in *Walchen, Romani und Latini. Variationen einer nachrömischen Gruppenbezeichnung zwischen Britannien und dem Balkan*, eds Walter Pohl, Ingrid Hartl, and Wolfgang Haubrichs (Vienna, 2017), pp. 163–76.

the northern Rhineland, Netherlands, and northern France.[23] Space precludes discussion of these subjects here, however. The following investigation concentrates on the Germanic-Romance interference zones west of the Middle and Upper Rhine and south of the Upper Danube as a further significant example of such acculturation. This survey draws on names and words preserved in an array of sources, including charters, inscriptions, chronicles, saints' lives, bilingual phrasebooks, glosses, and more. Linguistic analysis of the word- and name-forms of such texts furnishes vital perspectives on questions of bilingualism and multilingualism in western Europe between the later Roman Empire and the beginning of the high Middle Ages.

Regions of Basic Language Contact and Interference West of the Middle and Upper Rhine

In late antiquity, after the loss of the *Agri Decumates* (*c.*260), the *limes* of the Roman Empire in the west opposite the so-called *Germania libera* was essentially formed by two large rivers, the Rhine and the Danube. After the river *limites* were also given up in the late fifth century and these regions were no longer protected by Roman administration and military forces, they came to be dominated by new Germanic settlers and developed complex structures of linguistic interference. In the Rhineland, these settlers were mainly Frankish and Alemannic groups, but there were also mixed zones featuring a 'pêle-mêle' of *Romani* and *Germani*. In addition, we find compact Roman relic areas of different consistency and temporal duration, especially in the surroundings of *civitates* and *castella*. Linguistic evidence for these developments is primarily offered by three things: first, residual Latin-Romance toponyms and early types of Germanic place-names; second, Latin loanwords in Germanic target languages and dialects; and third, Frankish loanwords in the dialects of eastern,

23 Luc van Durme, *Galloromaniae Neerlandicae submersae fragmenta* (Ghent, 1996); Maria Besse, *Namenpaare an der Sprachgrenze. Eine lautchronologische Untersuchung zu zweisprachigen Ortsnamen im Norden und Süden der deutsch-französischen Sprachgrenze* (Tübingen, 1997), pp. 304–532; Maria Besse, 'Les doublets toponymiques le long de la frontière linguistique: méthodologie, chronologie phonétique, étude de cas. L'exemple de la Belgique', *Bulletin de la Commission royale de Toponymie et de Dialectologie* 72 (2000), 35–102; Maria Besse, 'Romanisch-germanische Sprachbeziehungen: Niederlande und Belgien', in *Reallexikon der Germanischen Altertumskunde* 25 (2003), 246–51; Wolfgang Haubrichs, 'Fränkische Lehnwörter, Ortsnamen und Personennamen im Nordosten der Gallia. Die "Germania Submersa" als Quelle der Sprach- und Siedlungsgeschichte', in *Die Franken und die Alemannen bis zur 'Schlacht bei Zülpich' (496/97)*, ed. Dieter Geuenich (Berlin, 1998), pp. 102–29.

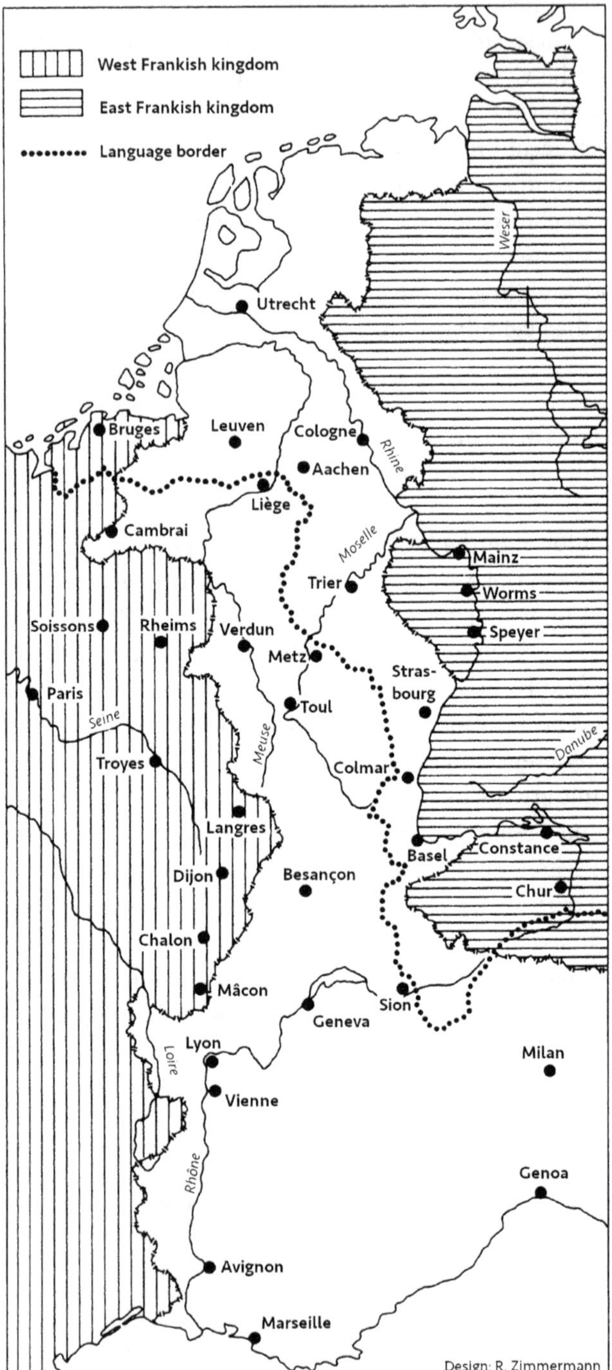

MAP 3.1 Lotharingia and the Romance-Germanic language border, with the political boundaries of the Treaty of Verdun (843)

northern, and central France (mostly limited to the far west of the fundamentally Romance-speaking two *Belgicae* provinces).[24] Toponyms and loanwords are only sometimes transmitted in contemporary documents. It is customary to reconstruct their etymological preforms and bases according to the methods of comparative historical linguistics and according to the principles of the phonetic chronology of the Romance and the Germanic languages. The starting point of reconstruction is always the fact that these words and names cannot be explained by the material and structure of the target language, and that they exhibit features implying borrowing in an earlier contact-situation with a foreign source-language. Reconstructed forms are marked by an asterisk (*).

According to the principles of phonetic chronology, the dating of the final integration of pre-Germanic toponyms and Latin borrowings into the Germanic languages of the incoming migrants must be determined by two criteria: first, do the toponyms or loanwords reflect recent early medieval Romance linguistic developments (*terminus post quem*)? Second, do the toponyms or loanwords already show recent linguistic developments of the Germanic target languages (*terminus ante quem*)? Among the toponymic relics along the Rhine *limes* between Cologne and Koblenz, it is hard to find Romance phonetic developments of the Merovingian period, such as the sonorization of voiceless stops or the palatalization of [ki, ke] > [tsi, tse].[25] Pre-Germanic [k] before [i, e] remains preserved, for example, in *Kehrig* south of Mayen in the eastern Eifel, twelfth century *Kirriche* < **Ciriacum* (derived from the personal name *Cirius* with the Gallo-Romance suffix *-acum*, which normally indicates a Roman *fundus*); or in the early loanword *Kirche* 'church' < Graecolatin **kyri(a)ka* 'house of the Lord'. The sonorization of [p] > [b], for instance, can be found in *Lövenich* southeast of Erkelenz, eleventh-century *Luvenich* < **Lubiniacu* < Latin **Lupîniacum* (Latin personal name *Lupînus*). Similarly, the early development of Romance [b] > [v] may be observed, as in *Rövenich* northwest of Euskirchen, 1140 *Rovenich* < **Rubîniacu* (Latin personal name *Rubînus*). The Romance phonetic substitution [gu] for Germanic [w], not easily pronounced by the former, and still today present in French or Italian lexemes such as *Guillaume* < *Willi-halm*, *guerra* < **werra* 'war', is to be seen in 770

24 Wolfgang Haubrichs, 'Sprache und Sprachzeugnisse der merowingischen Franken', in *Die Franken—Wegbereiter Europas. 5. bis 8. Jahrhundert n. Chr.*, eds Alfried Wieczorek, Patrick Périn, Karin von Welck, and Wilfried Menghin, 2 vols (Mainz, 1996), 1:559–73; Haubrichs, 'Fränkische Lehnwörter', pp. 106–12.

25 Cf. for the toponymic material Joachim Wirtz, *Die Verschiebung der germanischen p, t und k in den vor dem Jahre 1200 überlieferten Ortsnamen der Rheinlande* (Heidelberg, 1972); Haubrichs, 'Die verlorene Romanität', pp. 695–97.

in pago rigorinse,[26] eighth-century *in pago Riguerinse*, 770 *in pago rigorinse*[27] < **Riwarinse* < **Ripuarinse*, as it was written in a Rhenish centre (Lorsch). The evidence for long-lasting Romance continuity becomes more frequent in urban centres of the northern Rhineland: e.g. the loss of intervocalic [g] in 755 *Rigomo* < *Rigomago*, 773 *in regomensi marca* (Remagen);[28] or, as in French, the delabialization of Latin [kw] in Dutch *Aken*, 972 *Ahha* (*vulgari vocabulo Ahha nuncupatum*, 'called *Ahha* in the vernacular') < **Aka* < Latin *Aqua, Aquis*; or numerous other Romance anthroponyms and micro-toponyms.[29]

In order to date the beginnings of the integration of the remaining pre-Germanic names, the criterion of the Old High German sound shift must be considered, although this principle can only be used south of the border with Low Franconian (the 'Benrath line' near Düsseldorf), a dialect that did not undergo the sound shift.[30] For the Ripuarian dialect in the Cologne region, the sound shift is assuredly testified at the latest in the eighth century. All toponymic examples show the change of [k] > [χ] (in German written as <ch, h>) around the seventh or eighth century, e.g. **Lacîniacu* > 1135/42 *Lechenihc*, today *Lechenich* north of Euskirchen;[31] third century *Antunnaco* > 804 *Antiniche*, today *Andernach* on the Rhine.[32] But considering the earlier shift of [t] > [ts] (written as <z, tz, c>) in the sixth century, one notices a remarkable division: we find at the outer margins of the Rhenish centres, e.g. *Merzenich* near Düren, 1140 *Mercinich* < **Martîniacu*;[33] *Zons* near Dormagen, 1020 *Zu(o)nce*, 1057

26 *Fredegarii continuationes*, 42, ed. Bruno Krusch, MGH SS rer. Merov. 2 (Hanover, 1888), p. 186. Cf. in the same volume, *Virtutum s. Geretrudis continuatio*, 4, p. 473 (A.D. 782): *in terra Riguanense* < **-uarense*.

27 *Codex Laureshamensis*, ed. Karl Glöckner, 3 vols (Darmstadt, 1929–36), no. 11, 1:287–88. The document was *actum Rigimago* (Remagen) *seu Lauresham* (Lorsch) and written by a *presbyter* with a Latin name, *Saluius atque Thutearnus*.

28 Maurits Gysseling, *Toponymisch Woordenboek van België, Nederland, Luxemburg, Noord-Frankrijk en West-Duitsland (vóór 1226)*, 2 vols (Tongern, 1960), 2:833.

29 Gysseling, *Toponymisch Woordenboek*, 1:31.

30 For the Old High German sound shift, see Wolfgang Haubrichs, 'Lautverschiebung in Lothringen. Zur althochdeutschen Integration vorgermanischer Toponyme der historischen Sprachlandschaft zwischen Saar und Mosel', in *Althochdeutsch*, eds Rolf Bergmann, Heinrich Tiefenbach, and Lothar Voetz, 2 vols (Heidelberg, 1987), 2:1350–91; Wilhelm Braune and Frank Heidermanns, *Althochdeutsche Grammatik, I: Laut- und Formenlehre*, 16th ed. (Berlin, 2018), §§ 83–90.

31 Gysseling, *Toponymisch Woordenboek*, 1:599; Wirtz, *Die Verschiebung*, p. 115 (no. 62).

32 Gysseling, *Toponymisch Woordenboek*, 1:56–57; Wirtz, *Die Verschiebung*, p. 106 (no. 5).

33 Gysseling, *Toponymisch Woordenboek*, 1:691; Wirtz, *Die Verschiebung*, p. 118 (no. 78).

Zuonozo < **Tônatio*;[34] *Gürzenich* west of Düren, 1170 *Gurcenich* < **Curtîniacu*.[35] Quite the opposite is found near the Rhine and in the suburbs of the Roman centres. As evidence of Romance continuity, pre-Germanic [t] is preserved there, e.g. *Metternich* near Koblenz, 1184 *Metterich* < **Meteriacu*; Ober-*winter* near Remagen < Latin **vînitôriu* 'wine cellar'; and, as above, *Antunnaco*.[36]

One could point to further cases near Cologne and Jülich. The phonetic reception of Latin [v] corresponds to this picture of a relatively late integration on the Rhine *limes* and around Jülich (*Juliacum*). In the earlier period, Latin [v] was a bilabial sound and therefore substituted by Old High German [w], but after *c*.700, when the pronunciation of Latin [v] had probably changed, it came to be substituted by [f] (written also as <v> or <f>).[37] To the first period belong (e.g.) Königs-*winter* near Bonn and Ober-*winter* (see above). We meet cases of [f] only in a narrow circle around Cologne and Bonn, and near *Koblenz* < *Confluentes*, especially just to the south in the so-called 'Rheinengtal', e.g. *Virnich* southwest of Euskirchen, 1140 *Virnich* < **Verniacu*.[38]

The first Old High German phonetic change, which, after the shift of [k], prevailed across the whole region, is the 'umlaut', the vowel mutation of [a] before [i, j], e.g. in *Kerpen* west of Cologne, 870 *Kerpinna* < **Carpinea* 'plantation of hornbeams',[39] or (as mentioned above) *Merzenich* < **Martîniacu*. Thus, in the northern Rhineland, the era of bilingualism had come to its end at the latest in the first half of the eighth century, when the Old High German 'umlaut'—as seen in *gast*, 'guest', plural *gesti* (Modern German: *Gäste*)—was completed.

---

34 Gysseling, *Toponymisch Woordenboek*, 2:1104–5; Wirtz, *Die Verschiebung*, p. 40 (no. 17); Rudolf Schützeichel, 'Zons in Dormagen', in *Wortes anst, verbi gratia. Donum natalicium Gilbert A.R. de Smet*, eds Heinrich L. Cox, Valeer F. Vanacker, and Edward Verhofstadt (Leuven, 1986), pp. 439–48.

35 Gysseling, *Toponymisch Woordenboek*, 1:430; Wirtz, *Die Verschiebung*, p. 111 (no. 37).

36 Gysseling, *Toponymisch Woordenboek*, 1:694; Wirtz, *Die Verschiebung*, p. 118 (no. 82).

37 Cf. Monika Buchmüller-Pfaff, *Siedlungsnamen zwischen Spätantike und frühem Mittelalter. Die -(i)acum-Namen der römischen Provinz Belgica prima* (Tübingen, 1990), pp. 694–97; Wolfgang Kleiber and Max Pfister, *Aspekte und Probleme der römisch-germanischen Kontinuität. Sprachkontinuität an Mosel, Mittel- und Oberrhein sowie im Schwarzwald* (Stuttgart, 1992), pp. 79–80; Wolfgang Haubrichs, 'Galloromanische Kontinuität zwischen unterer Saar und Mosel. Problematik und Chancen einer Auswertung der Namenzeugnisse', in *Italica et Romanica. Festschrift für Max Pfister*, eds Günter Holtus, Johannes Kramer, and Wolfgang Schweickard (Tübingen, 1997), pp. 211–37, at 222.

38 Gysseling, *Toponymisch Woordenboek*, 2:1017; Wirtz, *Die Verschiebung*, p. 109 (no. 28).

39 Gysseling, *Toponymisch Woordenboek*, 1:559; Kleiber and Pfister, *Aspekte und Probleme*, p. 83. Cf. *Kerpen* near Trier: Wolfgang Jungandreas, *Historisches Lexikon der Siedlungs- und Flurnamen des Mosellandes* (Trier, 1962), p. 191.

In contrast with the northern regions, a noticeably smaller number of pre-Germanic place-names is preserved in the Middle Rhine region and Alsace between Bingen and the area around Colmar and Breisach. Antique sources unfortunately do not provide much more toponymic evidence.[40] Furthermore, the following toponyms all show the Old High German shift of [t] > [ts] and [p] > [f(f)], [pf] (dated sixth/seventh century):[41]

- Rhein-*zabern*, *c.*300 *Tabernis*, 1258 *Zabern*; likewise *Zabern*/Saverne (west of Strasbourg), fourth century *Tres Tabernas*;
- hydronym *Kinzig* (tributary of the Main), 796 *Kinzicha* < **Kintica*;
- *Mutzig* (west of Strasbourg), 1163 *Muzecha* < **Muttiacu*;
- *Zarten* (east of the Rhine near Freiburg) < second-century *Tarodounon*;
- *Pfortz* (near Germersheim), eighth-century *Porza* < Latin *portus* 'harbour';
- *Epfig* (near Barr, France, Bas-Rhin), 762 *Hepheka* < **Appiacu.*

The completed sound shift tells us that here on the Middle and Upper Rhine we must suppose a relatively early integration of the remaining Roman settlements. Oddly, pre-Germanic place-names often correspond to estates of the Merovingian and Carolingian royal *fiscus*, e.g. in the only compact zone of Romance continuity in northern Alsace (west of Strasbourg), around the royal *palatium* of *Marlenheim* < *Marilegium*, already mentioned in 589. In this area, one finds Romance names which are the result of Merovingian settlement,[42] e.g. *Neugartheim*, 1166 *Nougerthe* < **Nucarêtum* 'walnut tree planting', which do not show the shift of [k], but do feature the Romance sonorization of

---

40 Cf. Gerhard Rasch, *Antike geographische Namen nördlich der Alpen. Mit einem Beitrag von Hermann Reichert: Germanien in der Sicht des Ptolemaios*, ed. Stefan Zimmer, Reallexikon der Germanischen Altertumskunde—Ergänzungsbände 47 (Berlin, 2005).

41 Wolfgang Kleiber, 'Das moselromanische Substrat im Lichte der Toponymie und Dialektologie. Ein Bericht über neuere Forschungen', in *Zwischen den Sprachen. Siedlungs- und Flurnamen in germanisch-romanischen Grenzgebieten*, eds Wolfgang Haubrichs and Hans Ramge (Saarbrücken, 1983), pp. 153–92, at 169–72 and map nos 4–5; Haubrichs, 'Lautverschiebung in Lothringen', pp. 1368–70 and map no. 3; Albrecht Greule, 'Tarodunun—Zarten—Zähringen', in *Tarodunum/Zarten—Brigobannis/Hüfingen. Kelten, Galloromanen und frühe Alemannen in interdisziplinärer Sicht*, ed. Wolfgang Kleiber (Mainz, 2009), pp. 161–62; Wolfgang Haubrichs, 'Das frühmittelalterliche Elsass zwischen West und Ost: Merowingerzeitliche Siedlungsnamen und archaische Personennamen', in *Adel und Königtum im mittelalterlichen Schwaben. Festschrift für Thomas Zotz*, eds Andreas Bihrer, Mathias Kälble, and Heinz Krieg (Stuttgart, 2009), pp. 55–69, at 56–59.

42 For the Merovingian settlement around Marlenheim and Maursmünster/Marmoutier (*marca Aquilensis*), see Christa Jochum-Godglück, *Die orientierten Siedlungsnamen auf* -heim, -hausen, -hofen *und* -dorf *im frühdeutschen Sprachraum und ihr Verhältnis zur fränkischen Fiskalorganisation* (Frankfurt, 1995), pp. 573–95 and map on 577; Haubrichs, 'Das frühmittelalterliche Elsass', pp. 56–58.

[k] > [g].[43] To this we should add religious place-names of the type *dominus* + name of a saint, like *Dompfieter*, tenth-century *Domni Petri*, elsewhere only found in the Romance-speaking west.[44]

Otherwise, in the fertile *pagi* and 'Gaue' of the Middle Rhine, covered with earlier Merovingian and Carolingian Germanic settlement names composed with the elements *-heim* and *-ingen*, we can detect Romance continuity only in centres situated on the Rhine itself (*Antunnaco*/Andernach, *Baudobriga*/ Boppard, Bingen, *Magontia*/Mainz).[45] A continuous culture of inscriptions here reveals, in contrast to Cologne, bearers of Romance personal names until the seventh century and of Romanized Germanic names until the eighth.[46] Certainly it is no accident that we find the place-name *Finthen*, 1108 *Fundened* < *fontanêtu* 'source, font, spring', without the shift of [t], at the head of the Roman aqueduct of Mainz, called *Ageduth* (thirteenth century), derived from **ake-ductu* < Latin *aquae-ductu* with Romance sonorization.[47] At Wiesbaden (*Aquae Mattiacae*) and Worms (*Borbetomagus*), some fifth- and sixth-century inscriptions provide evidence of a strange (possibly Burgundian?) Romance-East Germanic mixed culture.[48] With the exception of a few surviving Roman centres, it can be assumed that along the Middle Rhine and in northern Alsace only a meagre and short-lived Romance continuity existed. The complexity of the cultural, linguistic, and ethnic conditions in the early Middle Ages,

---

43 Haubrichs, 'Das frühmittelalterliche Elsass', p. 57.

44 Haubrichs, 'Das frühmittelalterliche Elsass', p. 56. For the onomastic type *dominus* + saint's name, see Wolfgang Haubrichs, 'Die ekklesiogenen Siedlungsnamen des frühen Mittelalters als Zeugnisse der Christianisierung und der Kirchenorganisation im Raum zwischen Maas, Mosel und Saar', in *L'évangélisation des régions entre Meuse et Moselle et la fondation de l'abbaye d'Echternach* (*V*^{e}–*IX*^{e} *siècle*), ed. Michel Polfer (Luxembourg, 2000), pp. 215–44, at 220–29 and map on 226–27.

45 For the numerous Romance place-names and field-names in the 'Rheinengtal' between Bingen and Koblenz, see Manfred Halfer, *Die Flurnamen des oberen Rheintales. Ein Beitrag zur Sprachgeschichte des Westmitteldeutschen* (Stuttgart, 1988).

46 Winfried Schmitz, 'Zur Akkulturation von Romanen und Germanen im Rheinland. Eine Auswertung des inschriftlichen Materials', *Das Altertum* 43 (1997), 177–202; Winfried Schmitz, 'Spätantike und frühmittelalterliche Grabinschriften als Zeugnisse der Besiedlungs- und Sprachkontinuität in den germanischen und gallischen Provinzen', in *Germania inferior. Besiedlung, Gesellschaft und Wirtschaft an der Grenze der römisch-germanischen Welt*, ed. Thomas Grünewald (Berlin, 2001), pp. 261–305; Winfried Schmitz, 'Bedrohte Latinitas. Sprachliche Veränderungen auf spätantik-frühmittelalterlichen Grabinschriften aus dem Rhein-Mosel-Gebiet', in *Literacy in Ancient Everyday Life*, ed. Anne Kolb (Berlin, 2018), pp. 387–411; Wolfgang Haubrichs, 'VITALIS, REMICO, AUDULPIA—Romanische, germanische und romanisierte Personennamen in frühen Inschriften der Rhein- und Mosellande', *Rheinische Vierteljahrsblätter* 78 (2014), 1–37.

47 Kleiber and Pfister, *Aspekte und Probleme*, pp. 38–42.

48 Haubrichs, 'Ein namhaftes Volk', pp. 136–38.

however, is shown by the immense quantity of Germanic toponyms, which in many cases contain Romance and Romanized personal names, as well as by the place-names composed with the ethnonym *walaha* ('Romani'), wherever the settlers may have come from.[49]

The most densely-populated zone of Romance continuity within the parts of the Empire situated to the west of the Rhine is found along the river Moselle, between Koblenz and the area between Remich (Luxembourg) and Sierck (France, Moselle), in the lower valleys of its tributaries the Saar and Sauer, continuing down to the strong Romance centres of Metz and Toul in Lorraine.[50] The intensity and longevity of the so-called *Mosella Romana* is characterized by two factors: first, by the cultural radiance of the important *civitates* of Trier and Metz and of other late antique *castra* and *vici* which were often also ecclesiastical centres. These places preserved one of the most extensive cultures of Latin inscriptions and epitaphs.[51] Second, this region is characterized by the material culture of wine-growing along the Moselle and its tributaries, manifesting itself in a great number of loanwords drawn from the regional Latin viticultural jargon, e.g. *Gimme* 'bud, shoot' < Latin *gemma*; *pauern* 'to scoop must' < Latin *purare*, etc.[52] Given that a great number of the borrowings come from

49 Wolfgang Haubrichs, 'Kontinuität und Ansiedlung von Romanen am Ostrand der alten Gallia und östlich des Rheins: Sprachliche Indikatoren (500–900)', in *Walchen, Romani und Latini*, eds Pohl et al., pp. 59–85, at 66–68, 81–85.

50 Kleiber, 'Das moselromanische Substrat'; Kleiber and Pfister, *Aspekte und Probleme*, pp. 11–18; 43–51; 71–97; Monika Buchmüller, Wolfgang Haubrichs, and Rolf Spang, 'Namenkontinuität im frühen Mittelalter. Die nichtgermanischen Siedlungs- und Gewässernamen des Landes an der Saar', *Zeitschrift für die Geschichte der Saargegend* 34–35 (1986–87), 24–163; Haubrichs, 'Lautverschiebung in Lothringen', pp. 1372–91; Haubrichs, 'Kontinuität und Ansiedlung von Romanen', pp. 70–80; Wolfgang Haubrichs, 'La structuration linguistique de l'espace: du bilinguisme à l'émergence des frontières', in *De la mer du Nord à la Méditerrannée: Francia Media, une région au coeur de l'Europe (c. 840-c. 1050)*, eds Michèle Gaillard, Michel Margue, Alain Dierkens, and Hérold Pettiau (Luxembourg, 2011), pp. 41–68.

51 Schmitz, 'Zur Akkulturation von Romanen und Germanen'; Schmitz, 'Spätantike und frühmittelalterliche Grabinschriften'; Mark A. Handley, *Death, Society and Culture: Inscriptions and Epitaphs in Gaul and Spain, AD 300–750* (Oxford, 2003); Haubrichs, 'VITALIS, REMICO, AUDULPIA', pp. 7–10, 13–14; Haubrichs, 'Kontinuität und Ansiedlung von Romanen', pp. 62–67.

52 Rudolf Post, *Romanische Entlehnungen in den westmitteldeutschen Mundarten. Diatopische, diachrone und diastratische Untersuchungen zur sprachlichen Interferenz am Beispiel des landwirtschaftlichen Sachwortschatzes* (Wiesbaden, 1982); Rudolf Post, 'Galloromanische Reliktwortareale und Grenzentlehnungen im Pfälzischen', in *Sprache—Literatur—Kultur. Studien zu ihrer Geschichte im deutschen Süden und Westen. Festschrift für Wolfgang Kleiber*, eds Albrecht Greule and Uwe Ruberg (Stuttgart, 1989), pp. 161–74; Andreas Schorr, 'Zur Namengeografie galloromanischer Lehn- und Reliktwörter in Mikrotoponymen des

a general agrarian context, within which corresponding Germanic vernacular terms would have been available, this clearly indicates a long-term bilingualism. We must therefore conclude that here there was significant Romance continuity, comprising much more than viticulture.

The core of the *Mosella Romana* is occupied by a near-unbroken chain of pre-Germanic place-names, micro-toponyms, and hydronyms. An indication of their diversity can be seen in some examples from the surroundings of Trier: *Pellingen*, 973 *Pallinc* < Indo-European **pol-*, **pal-* 'to pour, humid, marsh' + Pre-Celtic suffix **-inkon*; *Krettnach*, 1147 *Cretenach* < personal name *Crit(t)ôn-* + Gallo-Romance suffix **-acum*; *Tawérn*, 1000 *Taberna* 'inn' (with preservation of the Latin accent); *Tarforst*, 1135 *Centarbers* < Romance **Cent arbors* 'hundred, many trees' (the last three without the shift of [t]).[53]

The entire Roman province of *Belgica Prima* (the later ecclesiastical province of Trier) in the early Middle Ages is characterized by a complex hotchpotch of bilingual zones of interference, Frankish linguistic islands in what will later become Old French-speaking districts, and, above all, numerous larger or smaller Romance islands in the future German-speaking (*theodisc*) districts. This is also affirmed by some inscriptions and texts from *Contrua*/Gondorf on the Moselle (seventh century), from Leutersdorf near Andernach, and finally from the monastery of Prüm (Eifel), all of which offer unambiguously Romance forms.[54] The integration of Frankish and Old High German could not have begun before the seventh century, because no pre-Germanic toponym features the sixth-century shift of [t] > [ts] (see above *Krettnach, Tawérn, Tarforst*). However, the shift of [k] > [χ] (seventh/eighth century) was always carried out (cf. above **-acum* > *-ach* in *Krettnach*; also in the loanword

---

Saar-Mosel-Raums', in *Interferenz-Onomastik. Namen in Grenz- und Begegnungsräumen in Geschichte und Gegenwart*, eds Wolfgang Haubrichs and Heinrich Tiefenbach (Saarbrücken, 2011), pp. 507–34; Stefan Barme, 'Von keifenden Hirschkäfern und ambrosischen Himbeeren: Notizen zu einigen moselromanischen Reliktwörtern', *Zeitschrift für romanische Philologie* 122 (2006), 363–79.

53 Jungandreas, *Historisches Lexikon*, pp. 792, 254, 1025; Haubrichs, 'Galloromanische Kontinuität', pp. 211–37.

54 Johannes Kramer, 'Zwischen Latein und Moselromanisch: Die Gondorfer Grabinschrift für Mauricius', *Zeitschrift für Papyrologie und Epigraphik* 118 (1997), 281–86; Géza Alföldy, 'Zur Grabinschrift des Giboaldus aus Leutesdorf, Kr. Neuwied', *Bonner Jahrbücher* 166 (1966), 444–45; Wolfgang Haubrichs and Max Pfister, 'Die Prümer Romania', in *Sprachgeschichte—Dialektologie—Onomastik—Volkskunde. Festschrift für Wolfgang Kleiber*, eds Rudolf Bentzinger, Damaris Nübling, and Rudolf Steffens (Stuttgart, 2001), pp. 171–95, at 173–74; Haubrichs, 'Kontinuität und Ansiedlung von Romanen', pp. 60–62; Stefan Barme, 'Latein—Vulgärlatein—Moselromanisch: Zur Sprache der frühchristlichen Grabinschriften im Raum Trier', *Zeitschrift für romanische Philologie* 124 (2008), 15–30.

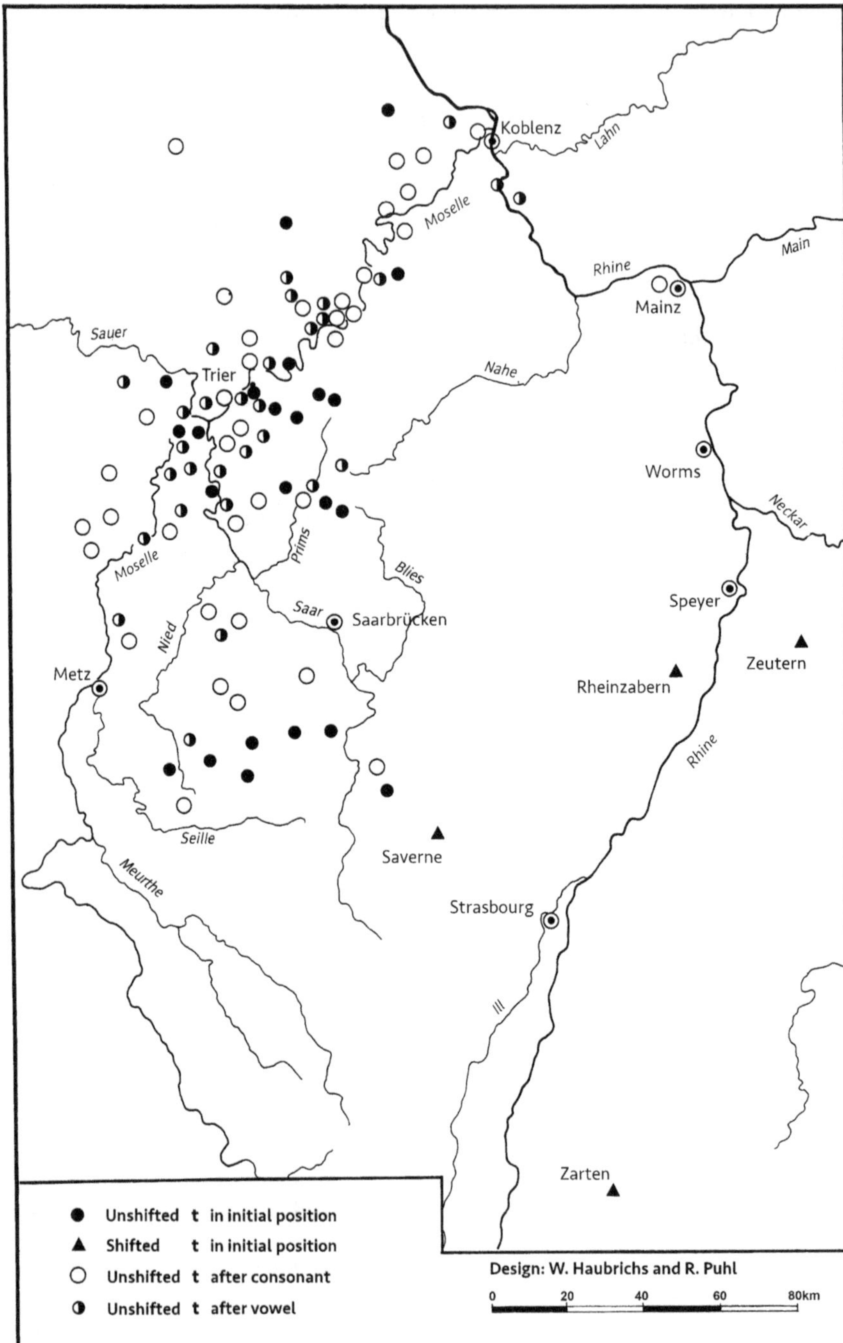

MAP 3.2 Distribution of pre-Germanic [t] between Rhine and Moselle

Macher < Latin *maceria* 'walls, stonework').[55] In the south of *Belgica Prima* this element of the sound shift even occurred before the Gallo-Romance palatalization of [ki, ke] > [tsi, tse], which can be seen in the Roman toponym of *Tarquimpol* (France, Moselle) < 1295 *Tachempach* with [χ] < fourth century *Decem pagi*.[56] The reception of regional Latin loanwords with preserved [ki, ke] also belongs to this period, such as *Kirkel* < *circulus* 'circle' or *Kermeter* < *coemeterium* 'cemetery'.[57] On the other hand, in the north of the province, that is, in the real *Mosella Romana*, the palatalization to [ts, tz] took priority: cf. the place-name *Detzem* near Trier < Latin (*ad*) *Decimas*; *Zerf* on the Hunsrück (district Trier) < 802 *Cervia* (*silva*) 'deer woods'.[58] This speaks once again for a long-lived Romance culture in the region.

As in the northern Rhineland, a second differentiation results from the fate of Latin [v], which early on was substituted by Old High German [w], but from the eighth century onwards replaced by [f].[59] On the margins of the *Mosella Romana* we find in the north *Wittlich* (Eifel) < **Vitelliacum*,[60] and in the south *Vic*-sur-Seille (France, Moselle), tenth century *Wich* < antique *Vicus Bodatius*;[61] but compare in the heart of the *Mosella Romana*, near Trier, *Filzen* < **Villicina*.[62]

A further example neatly illustrates how, with the help of phonetic chronology, we can determine the lifespan of linguistic islands. On the Hunsrück in the northern Saarland, Romance [eu] with loss of intervocalic [g] < [egu], as in *Tholey* (district Sankt Wendel), 634 (tenth-century copy) *Toleio, Taulegius, Teulegio* < **Têguleiu* 'brick building', was not affected by the Old High German sound change [eu] > [eo] > [io] > [ie] (eighth/ninth century).[63] In contrast, Romance [eu] > [au] > [o] developed there, so that we can suppose the existence of Romance speakers until the ninth century. Elsewhere, we have

55 Buchmüller, Haubrichs, and Spang, 'Namenkontinuität im frühen Mittelalter', pp. 74–75.

56 Haubrichs, 'Lautverschiebung in Lothringen', pp. 1380 (no. 59), 1382 (no. 73).

57 Haubrichs, 'Lautverschiebung in Lothringen', p. 1390.

58 Haubrichs, 'Lautverschiebung in Lothringen', p. 1389 (nos 128, 90); Haubrichs, 'Galloromanische Kontinuität', pp. 221, 231 (no. 141).

59 Cf. Haubrichs, 'Lautverschiebung in Lothringen', pp. 1390–91; Haubrichs, 'Galloromanische Kontinuität', p. 222. Cf. above, n. 37.

60 Buchmüller-Pfaff, *Siedlungsnamen zwischen Spätantike und frühem Mittelalter*, p. 507 (no. 843).

61 Haubrichs, 'Lautverschiebung in Lothringen', pp. 1381–82, n. 112, 1382 (no. 80): Moyenvic sixth/seventh century *Mediano vico*, 968 *Mediovic*, thirteenth century *Medwich*.

62 Haubrichs, 'Galloromanische Kontinuität', p. 229 (no. 103).

63 Max Pfister, 'Tholey und der saarländisch-lothringische Raum zwischen Romania und Germania', *Studien und Mitteilungen zur Geschichte des Benediktinerordens* 96 (1985), 282–98, at pp. 294–95; Haubrichs, 'Lautverschiebung in Lothringen', p. 1379.

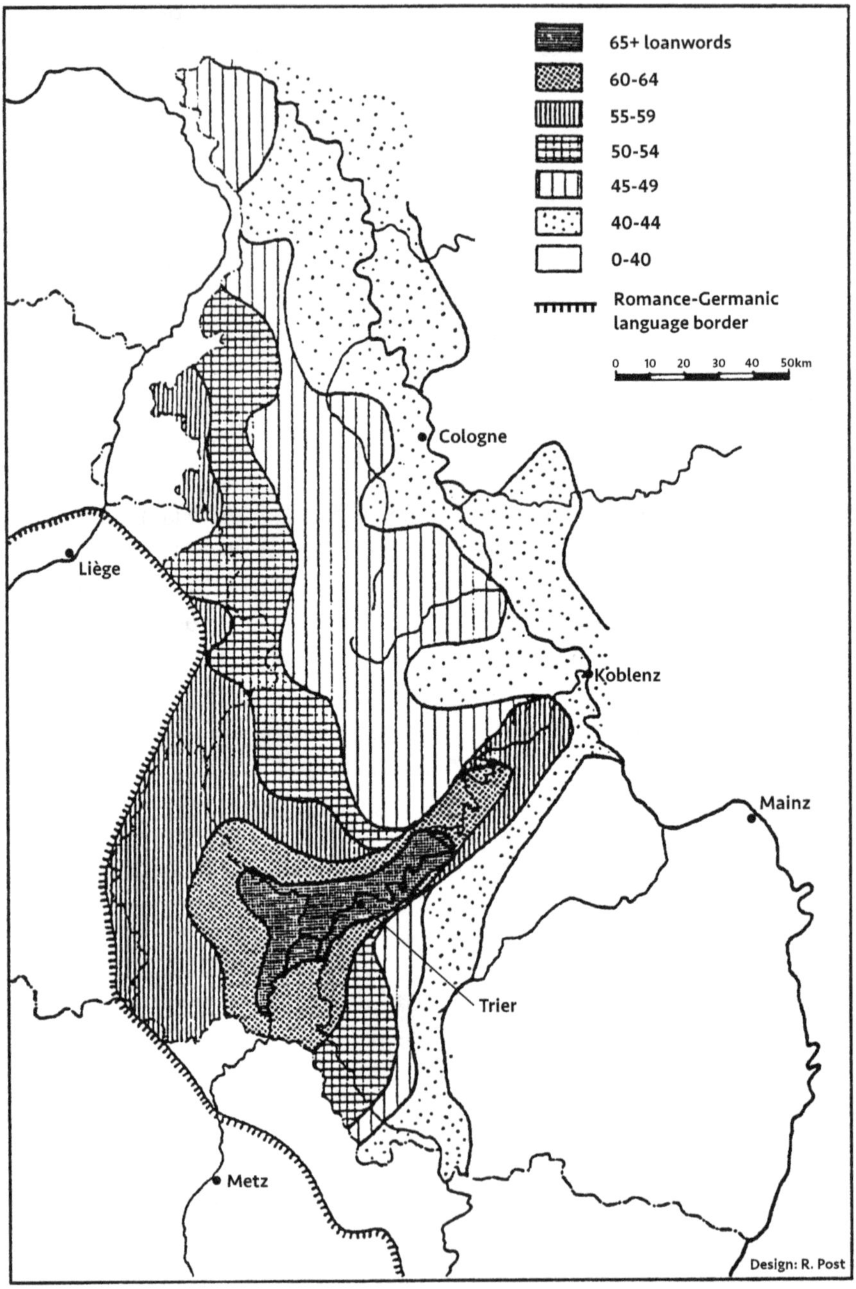

MAP 3.3 Areal distribution of Romance relic words between Rhine and Moselle

to reckon with the final integration of the outer Romance islands in the eighth century.[64]

The core of the *Mosella Romana* around Trier and Bernkastel on the Moselle preserved its pre-Germanic linguistic identity for much longer. Here we meet relics of unshifted [k] in older forms of place-names, e.g. Welsch-*billig* (district Trier), 981 *Billike* < **Billiacu*; also, *Nennig* (district Merzig) < **Nanniacu*, 924 *Nannec* and **Nanniei* with Romance development of the suffix *-iacu*.[65] Many place-names and field-names (*Flurnamen*) preserved the Latin 'paenultima'-accent: examples include *Tawérn* (district Trier) < *Tabérna* (see above); *Bonefánt* (Ediger near Cochem) < **(ad) bonum fóntem* 'at the good spring', etc.[66] A French sound change of the ninth and tenth centuries like the palatalization [á] > [é] is to be found in nuclei of the *Mosella Romana* around Cochem, Bernkastel, Trier, and on the lower reaches of the Saar.[67] Occasionally, even the eastern French diphthongization of long [é] > [ei] > [oi] > [o] (dated tenth/eleventh century) was achieved: e.g. 1065 *Faverota* < **Fabârêtu* 'bean planting'.[68] Thus, for the region between Bernkastel and Trier, we must suppose that the final integration of these areas as fully German-speaking occurred around the year 1000.[69]

At the same time, Frankish expansion into the far west of the Rhine-Meuse region created settlements and linguistic islands, often in hilly forests like the Ardennes, Argonnes (west of Verdun), and Vosges, and in many cases recognizable by clearing names like *Brabant*-sur-Meuse (France, Meuse), 1028 *Braiban* < **Brâka-banti* 'uncultivated area' (cf. *Brabant* in Belgium, *c.*743×50 *in Bracbante*); *Waly* (France, Meuse), 870 *Wasloi*, 916x17 *Waslogium* < **wasôn* 'wet meadow' + **lauha-*, Old High German *lôh* 'grove, glade'; or by Frankish hydronyms like *Flabas* near Damvillers (France, Meuse), tenth-century *Flabasium* < **flata-* 'flat, not deep' + **baki* 'brook'; *Le Thabas* near Foucaucourt (France, Meuse) < **thâhô* 'clay' + **baki*, etc.[70] Names of more specific types of settlement

64 Buchmüller, Haubrichs, and Spang, 'Namenkontinuität im frühen Mittelalter', pp. 105–39.

65 Buchmüller-Pfaff, *Siedlungsnamen zwischen Spätantike und frühem Mittelalter*, pp. 102–3 (no. 100), 373–74 (no. 585).

66 Wolfgang Kleiber, 'Probleme romanisch-germanischer Interferenz an der Mosel im Bereich der Prosodie von Eigennamen', *Namenkundliche Informationen* 47 (1985), 14–20; Haubrichs, 'Kontinuität und Ansiedlung von Romanen', pp. 78–80 and map 7.

67 Kleiber and Pfister, *Aspekte und Probleme*, pp. 78–79.

68 Kleiber and Pfister, *Aspekte und Probleme*, p. 73.

69 Cf. Kleiber and Pfister, *Aspekte und Probleme*, p. 90; Haubrichs, 'Kontinuität und Ansiedlung von Romanen', p. 80 and n. 82 (with bibliographic references).

70 Cf. Wolfgang Haubrichs, 'Germania submersa. Zu Fragen der Quantität und Dauer germanischer Siedlungsinseln im romanischen Lothringen und Südbelgien', in *Verborum Amor. Studien zur Geschichte und Kunst der deutschen Sprache. Festschrift für Stefan*

can be found near the language border in the region of Liège such as *Herstal*, 723 *Harastallio* < **Harja-stalja-* 'army camp',[71] or *Nivelles*, about 670 *Niuialcha* < **Niuwi-alha* 'new sanctuary'.[72] From a toponymic perspective, these Frankish settlement relics and interference zones are not well explored. But how far they once stretched can be seen by the example of the early monastic foundation of *Rebais*-en-Brie (France, Seine-et-Marne) in the Île-de-France: *c.*635 (forged) *quod vulgo appellatur Resbacis*, 637/38 *supra fluviolum Resbacem* < **Ris-baki* 'flowing (little) river'.[73] The **Ris-baki* must have existed before the monastery was founded.

The contact areas of northeastern Gaul are very clearly testified by an immense number of Frankish loanwords in Old French and Gallo-Romance dialects, as mentioned above.[74] The borrowings encompass nearly all areas of life: animals and birds (Old French *froiz* 'frogs' < **froska*; Old French *hairon* 'heron' < **haig(i)ron*, cf. Old High German *heigaro*; Old French *mulet* 'wood mouse' < **mul-* 'mole'; plants (Old French *hestre*, French *hêtre* 'young beech' < **haistru*; *escot* 'tree stump' < **skota* 'shoot'); the human body (Old Liègois *flancke*, French *flanc* 'hip' < **hlanka* 'hip, loin'); human characteristics (Old French *estout* 'bold, proud' < **stolt-* 'proud'); clothes and equipment (French

---

Sonderegger, eds Harald Burger, Alois M. Haas, and Peter von Matt (Berlin, 1992), pp. 633–66.

71 Gysseling, *Toponymisch Woordenboek*, 1:486; Haubrichs, 'Langobardisch-fränkische Ortsnamen', pp. 279–84.

72 Gysseling, *Toponymisch Woordenboek*, 2:743.

73 *Les privilèges de l'abbaye de Rebais-en-Brie*, eds Victor Leblond and Maurice Lecomte (Melun, 1910), no. 2, pp. 117–20; MGH DD Mer., no. 49, 1:127; dep. no 224, 2:594: '… super fluvium qui appellatur Resbacus …'. For bilingualism in Merovingian times, see Gabriella Almanza Ciotti, 'La situazione di bilinguismo negli *Historiarum libri decem* di Gregorio di Tours', in *Società multiculturali nei secoli V–IX. Scontri, convivenza, integrazione nel Mediterraneo occidentale*, ed. Marcello Rotili (Naples, 2001), pp. 55–61.

74 'Frankish' is linguistically defined as the language of the Franks, settling in what will later become the French-speaking regions of north, east, and central France, as well as Belgium ('West Frankish'); the Low Countries (the Netherlands), including Flemish Belgium and the lower Rhine ('Low Franconian' or 'Old Dutch'); the regions around Cologne and Trier ('Middle Franconian'); around Mainz, Worms, Speyer, and in eastern Lorraine ('Rhenish Franconian'); and, finally, the colonial regions east of the Rhine around the river Main ('East Franconian'). For the following list of West Frankish words, reconstructed from French borrowings, see Wolfgang Haubrichs and Max Pfister, 'Fränkisch (Frankish)', in *Wieser Encyclopaedia: Western European Languages*, eds Ulrich Ammon and Harald Haarmann (Klagenfurt, 2008), pp. 249–74, at 260–70. Etymologically, the lexical material is treated in Walther von Wartburg, *Französisches etymologisches Wörterbuch*, 25 vols (Basel, 1922–2002), vols 15–17 (words of Germanic origin).

froc 'dress, frock' < _*hrokka_; Old French _guant_, French _gant_ 'glove' < _*wanta_, cf. Latin seventh-century plural _wantos_ 'gloves'); tools (Old French _clenche_, Old Picard _clinke_ 'door-handle' < _*klenka, *klinka_; French _houe_ 'scratch plough' < _*hauwa_ 'hoe'); containers (Old Liègois _banste_, Old Flemish _bance_, Middle Dutch _banst_ 'big basket' < _*bansta_, already in the eighth-century Romance Reichenau Glosses, written at the monastery of Corbie, as plural _banstas_);[75] agriculture and farming (Old French _franc_ 'pigsty' < _*hranna_, already _hranne_ in the _Lex Salica_; French _herde_ 'herd, crowd' < _*herda_; Old Picard _gauffre_, French _gaufre_ 'honeycomb' < _*wâfla_ 'honeycomb, waffle'); architecture and buildings (Old French _hale_ 'covered market' < _*halla_ 'hall'; Middle French _hutte_ 'wooden hut' < _*hudda_, Old High German _hutta_); enclosures and settlements (French _haie_ 'hedge' < _*hagja_; Anglo-Norman _ham_ 'hamlet', frequently in toponyms of northeastern France < _*haima_ 'home, settlement'; Old Picard _hangar_ 'shed' < _*haim-gard_ 'enclosure beside the house'); hunting (Old French _beter_ 'to fight, to bite' < Germanic _*baitan_; Old French _algier_ 'spike' < _*âl-gêr_ 'eel-spear'); weapons and warfare, which are richly represented (Old French _bou_ 'bangle' < _*bauga_ 'ring', in the Reichenau Glosses _baucus: armilla_; Old French _gunfanun_ 'battle flag' < _*gund-fanon_; Old French _garçun_ 'servant, knight' < _*wrakkjon_ 'victim of persecution, exiled, warrior'); horse breeding and riding (Old French _estalon_ 'stallion' < _*stallon_; French _galoper_ 'to gallop' < Romance _*gual-lopa-_ < Germanic _*wala hlaupan_ 'to run well'); and, also richly represented from an early date, administration and law (Old French _mareschal_, French _maréchal_ 'marshal' < _*marah-skalk_ 'horse servant', already _mari-scalcus_ in the _Lex Salica_; Old Lorrain _eschavigne_ 'lay judge' < _*skapin_, Old High German _sceffin_; Old French _haschiere_ 'agony' < _harm-skara_ 'humiliating punishment', also in Carolingian capitularies; French _gage_, Old Liègois _wage_ < _*waddi_, Latin _wadium_ already in Merovingian _formulae_; Old French _manaie_ 'power, power of disposal' < _*man-haidu_ 'man-nature, bravery, courage').

Latin possessed terms and words for many of these several hundred Frankish loanwords in French, covering a diverse range of aspects of everyday life. The survival of most of the borrowings in Old French and its regional dialects can therefore only be explained by a vivid, intensive, and long-lasting state of multilingualism.

---

75 _Die Reichenauer Glossen_, ed. Hans-Wilhelm Klein, 2 vols (Munich, 1968–72), 2:149–50 (_cofinos: banstas_). The word _banstae_ (plural) is also used by Abbot Adalhard of Corbie in the early ninth century.

Regions of Basic Language Contact and Interference South of the Upper Rhine and the Danube

In the early Middle Ages, there was a further influential Romance-Germanic contact area directly to the south of Alsace and Lorraine, dominated by the *gens Alamannorum* and thus gradually Alemannized from the early sixth century. This area was bounded by the Franche-Comté around Besançon, the *Suisse romande* (Romandy) with the centres of Avenches, Yverdun, Lausanne, and Geneva, and finally in the east by the 'Raetoromania' (*Raetia Prima*) with its capital at Chur. The most important zone of continuity was formed by the so-called 'Baselromania', situated around the knee of the river Rhine.[76] Its core was the *civitas Basiliensium*, with the administrative and ecclesiastical centre of Basel together with the *castrum* of *Augusta Rauracorum* (Kaiseraugst, Aargau), where the continued presence of Romance-speaking people after 500 is demonstrated by archaeological finds and inscriptions containing Romanized Germanic personal names, e.g. sixth-/seventh-century *Baudoaldus* < **Baudo-walda*.[77] Although on a more limited scale, the 'Baselromania' should be considered alongside other nuclei of Roman continuity dominated by an urban centre such as Trier or Metz.[78] As there, the pre-Germanic names of small rivers have been handed down by *Romani* of the early Middle Ages, often preserved in place-names, e.g. *Sierenz* (France, Haut-Rhin), sixth-/seventh-century *SERENCIA*, 835 *Serencia* < Indo-European **Serantia*, having a direct parallel on the other side of the Rhine in the river name *Sirnitz*. As evidence for

76 Cf. *La région de Bâle et les rives du Rhin de l'Antiquité au Moyen Âge: aspects toponymiques et historiques*, eds Albrecht Greule, Rolf Max Kully, Wulf Müller, and Thomas Zotz (Stuttgart, 2013).

77 Cf. Max Martin, 'Das Fortleben der spätrömisch-romanischen Bevölkerung von Kaiseraugst und Umgebung im Frühmittelalter auf Grund der Orts- und Flurnamen', in *Provincialia. Festschrift für Rudolf Laur-Belart*, eds Elisabeth Schmid, Ludwig Berger, and Paul Bürgin (Basel, 1968), pp. 133–50; Max Martin, 'Die alten Kastellstädte und die germanische Besiedlung', in *Ur- und frühgeschichtliche Archäologie der Schweiz, VI: Das Frühmittelalter*, ed. Walter Drack (Basel, 1979), pp. 97–132, at 99, 102 and fig. 16 on p. 106; Max Martin, 'Die Romanen', in *Ur- und frühgeschichtliche Archäologie VI*, ed. Drack, pp. 11–20, at 15–20; Reto Marti, *Zwischen Römerzeit und Mittelalter. Forschungen zur frühmittelalterlichen Siedlungsgeschichte der Nordwestschweiz (4.–10. Jh.)* (Liestal, 2000); Wolfgang Haubrichs, 'Vorgermanische Toponymie am Oberrhein und im Basler Raum. Eine lautchronologische Auswertung', in *La région de Bâle*, eds Greule et al., pp. 143–47, at 145.

78 Haubrichs, 'Die verlorene Romanität', pp. 699–700; Haubrichs and Pfister, 'La Romania submersa', p. 231; Haubrichs, 'Vorgermanische Toponymie', pp. 145–46; Andres Kristol, 'La "Romania bâloise": la toponymie soleuroise permet-elle d'en savoir davantage?', in *La region de Bâle*, eds Greule et al., pp. 41–54.

Romance continuity, hydronyms are complemented by numerous settlement names, partly fixed on *castra* and other subcentres like *Magden* (Aargau), 371 *murum Magidunensem* < Celtic **Mago-dûnum.* Just as in the Cologne area and in the *Mosella Romana*, we must factor in a considerable number of -(*i*)*acum*-names, which signal ancient Roman *fundi*, e.g. *Lörrach* (Germany), 1102/3 *Lorrache* < **Lauriacum* (Latin personal name Laurius) and Merovingian church names such as *Dammer*-kirch/*Dannemarie* (France, Haut-Rhin), 823 *Domna Maria*. Some toponyms show still the Romance sonorization (e.g. [k] > [g] in *Nuglar* (Switzerland, canton Solothurn), 1147 *Nugerolo*, 1152 *Nugerols* < **Nucâriôlos* 'at the little walnut tree[s]'), also the Gallo-Romance palatalization of [ki, ke] and [ti + vowel] > [tsi, tse], e.g. *Ziefen* (canton of Basel-Country), 1226 *Civenne* < Celtic **Cebenna*. Furthermore, we must mention the frequent place- and field-names in the Basel region, derived from late loanwords, such as *prâtellu* 'small meadow', *campulu* 'piece of land', *calmen* 'uncultivated field, pastureland' (French *chaume*), *fontânas* and *fontellu* 'little spring'. In all these cases, the sound shift of the tenuis [t] (sixth century) is not performed, in contrast to the Middle Rhine and Alsace, e.g. also in *Altenach* (France, Haut-Rhin) < **Altânacu*. However, the shift of [k] (seventh/eighth century) is realized, as is the shift of [p] (seventh century): *Pfetterhausen* / French *Pérouse* (France, Haut-Rhin), 731/32 *Petrosa* 'stony river', 1241 *Pheter-husen* 'houses on the Petrosa'. While the final integration into Old High German was ongoing in this region in the seventh and eighth centuries, Romance may well have thrived for some time longer near the language border.

The earliest evidence for the Alemannization of German-speaking inner Switzerland comes from the generally sparse pre-Germanic toponyms, which show the first phase of the tenuis shift, that is, the change of [t] > [ts]: e.g. *Zürich*, eighth century *Ziurichi* < *Turicum*, in the high Alemannic 'Bündner German' *Turitg*; the hydronym *Zihl*, French *Thièle*, in the regional dialect *Toile* (which flows out of the Bielersee), 814 *Tela*, 1212 *Tila*, etc.[79] However, the shifted forms could also be exonyms brought in by the northern Alemannians for important toponyms or for landmarks.[80] In other regions around Lake Zürich and in foothills of the Alps, the pre-Germanic [t] was preserved, as in

79 Andres Kristol, 'Zürich', in *Lexikon der schweizerischen Gemeindenamen*, ed. Andres Kristol (Frauenfeld, 2005), pp. 992–93; Maria Besse, *Namenpaare an der Sprachgrenze. Eine lautchronologische Untersuchung zu zweisprachigen Ortsnamen im Norden und Süden der deutsch-französischen Sprachgrenze* (Tübingen, 1997), pp. 767–68; Haubrichs, 'Die verlorene Romanität', p. 700.

80 Wolfgang Haubrichs, 'Von Zirl bis Zürich. Exonyme und ihre Rolle bei der Germanisierung der nördlichen Alpenlandschaften', *Archivio per l'Alto Adige* 106–107 (2012–13), 421–34, at pp. 428–30.

the 'Baselromania' and in the *Mosella Romana*, e.g. *Kempraten* (canton Zürich) < 741 *Centoprata* 'hundred, many meadows'; *Tafers* (canton Fribourg), 1150 *Tabernae* 'the inns'.[81] In addition, we occasionally meet the Romance sonorization, as in Winterthur (canton Zürich), antique Celtic *Vitudurum* > **Vedodurum* > about 843 *Ventertura* (with Alemannic media shift [d] > [t]).[82] Here, we do not encounter the later shift of [p] that is normally carried out elsewhere. In contrast, the final shift of [k] (seventh/eighth century) is always performed in initial and medial position, as in the Basel region, as shown by many *-(i)acum-* and other names, e.g. *Cham* near Zug, 858 *Chama* < **Cama* (like *Cama* in the Rhaeto-Romanic valley of Calanca, canton Grisons); *Kirchet*, in the regional dialect *Chirchet* (canton Bern) < **Circâto* 'turn'.[83] To the south, in the valleys of the Alps, and to the west, along the later German-French language border, the Romance sonorization (also in initial position) was realized, just as in the 'Baselromania': e.g. *Alpiglen* (canton Bern) < **Alpicula*; *Gaster* west of Tuggen (canton Schwyz) < **Castra*.[84] The sonorization prevented the Alemannic shift of [k]. In this area, Latin endings were also preserved, like -s in *Tafers* < *Tabernas* (see above) and *Näfels* (canton Glarus), 1240 *Nevels* < Rhaetorom. **Navâlias* < **Novâlias* 'new land, clearing'.[85] Of course, these regions, showing the later phases of the tenuis shift, are also affected by the earlier Old High German media shift of [d] > [t], as in Winterthur (see above); *Thun* (canton Bern), seventh-century *lacus Dunensis* < Celtic **Dûnum*; *Solothurn* < antique Celtic *Salo-durum*.[86]

81 Peter Glatthard, *Ortsnamen zwischen Aare und Saane. Namengeographische und siedlungsgeschichtliche Untersuchungen im westschweizerdeutschen Sprachgrenzraum* (Bern, 1977), pp. 97, 122, 133; Stefan Sonderegger, 'Die Ausbildung der deutsch-romanischen Sprachgrenze in der Schweiz im Mittelalter', *Rheinische Vierteljahrsblätter* 31 (1966–67), 223–90, at pp. 262, 267; Stefan Sonderegger, 'Die Ortsnamen', in *Ur- und frühgeschichtliche Archäologie VI*, ed. Drack, pp. 75–96, at 82–85; Besse, *Namenpaare an der Sprachgrenze*, pp. 267–68 (no. 188); Haubrichs, 'Die verlorene Romanität', p. 700.

82 Gabrielle Schmid and Andres Kristol, 'Winterthur', in *Lexikon der schweizerischen Gemeindenamen*, ed. Kristol, pp. 971–72.

83 Andres Kristol, 'Cham' in *Lexikon der schweizerischen Gemeindenamen*, ed. Kristol, p. 228; Haubrichs, 'Die verlorene Romanität', p. 700.

84 Sonderegger, 'Die Ortsnamen', p. 83.

85 Gabrielle Schmid, 'Näfels', in *Lexikon der schweizerischen Gemeindenamen*, ed. Kristol, p. 636; Max Pfister, 'Ortsnamen in mehrsprachigen Ländern und Regionen: Romania submersa', in *Namenforschung*, eds Ernst Eichler, Gerold Hilty, Heinrich Löffler, Hugo Steger, and Ladislav Zgusta, Handbücher zur Sprach- und Kommunikationswissenschaft 11, 2 vols (Berlin, 1995–96), 2:1413–20, at p. 1418; Haubrichs, 'Die verlorene Romanität', p. 700.

86 Andres Kristol, 'Thun', in *Lexikon der schweizerischen Gemeindenamen*, ed. Kristol, p. 873; Gabrielle Schmid and Andres Kristol, 'Solothurn', in *Lexikon der schweizerischen*

For inner Switzerland, then, a first zone of Alemannization, in the sixth century at the latest, can be demonstrated only along the river Aare and in the area of the lower Lake Zürich. Further regions as far as Lake Lucerne and Lake Neuchâtel (especially in the main valleys) and the open landscapes of Aargau and Thurgau were affected before 700. In the eighth century we should add the lower Toggenburg (south of St Gall), the upper Lake Zürich, Lake Lucerne, and the Saane valley. Meanwhile, Romance language survived until the ninth century south and southeast of the integrated area in intermediate regions (Napf, Glarus, the 'Waldstaetten' Schwyz, Uri, Unterwalden, also places between Aare and Saane). However, in the face of numerous Alemannic toponyms south of these areas, we can conclude that there was a considerable degree of bilingualism in and around the Romance relic regions.[87]

In the west at this time, the language border became increasingly fixed, but preserved a broad bilingual edge, as attested by many double forms of place-names which do not yet show the Old High German 'umlaut' of the eighth and ninth centuries. In the south, we may catch initial fragments of the later language border above the Alpine valleys.

Loanwords of differing age[88] are further evidence of the complex conditions of the Swiss *Romania*, e.g. names of fish like *Barche* < **barca* with the Alemannic shift of [k] in the Bern lake district; cf. likewise in northeastern Switzerland *Chobel* < Romance **cubulum* 'cave, rock', but compare *Gubel*, sometimes *Gufel*, not shifted with Romance sonorization and thus retaining Romance [b] > [v].

On the Rhine *limes* and the southern shore of Lake Constance, the names of important Roman places were also handed down, e.g. *Koblenz* (Aargau) < *Confluentes* at the mouth of the Aare or *Constance* (Germany) < Latin *Constantia*; *Bregenz* (Austria), *c.*390 *Brecantia* < Celtic *Brigantia*.[89] In addition, near Arbon (Roman *Arbor Felix*) on Lake Constance, the phonetic substitution of Latin [v] by Old High German [f] (after 700) appears in *Feilen*, 1302 *Vailon* < **Vialia* 'Wege'. Furthermore, the shift of [t] (sixth century) is missing

Gemeindenamen, ed. Kristol, pp. 839–840; Sonderegger, 'Die Ortsnamen', p. 83; Besse, *Namenpaare an der Sprachgrenze*, pp. 680, 767, 641, 709, 711, 775.

87 Cf. Sonderegger, 'Die Ausbildung der deutsch-romanischen Sprachgrenze', pp. 260–83; Sonderegger, 'Die Ortsnamen', pp. 84–85, 92–95.

88 Hubert Klausmann and Thomas Krefeld, 'Romanische und rätoromanische Reliktwörter im Arlberggebiet', in *Raetia antiqua et moderna. Festschrift für W. Theodor Elwert*, eds Günter Holtus and Kurt Ringger (Tübingen, 1986), pp. 121–45; Thomas Krefeld, 'Reliktwort und Arealdistribution. Einige exemplarische Fälle aus dem Gebiet des Vorarlberger Sprachatlas', *Montfort* 45 (1993), 33–47; Haubrichs, 'Die verlorene Romanität', pp. 700–1.

89 *Deutsches Ortsnamenbuch*, ed. Manfred Niemeyer (Berlin, 2012), pp. 89, 328; Andres Kristol, 'Koblenz', in *Lexikon der schweizerischen Gemeindenamen*, ed. Kristol, p. 486.

in *Montlingen* (canton St Gall) < **monticulas* 'on the hills'. In contrast, all the pre-Germanic names show the shift of [k] (seventh/eighth century), e.g. on the Rhine *limes Küssnach* (Germany) < **Cassînacu*. So, north of the so-called 'Hirschensprung' near Gams on the Rhine, we must assume that the language of the *Romani*, as attested in the seventh century by the *Vita S. Galli*, survived only until the early eighth century, and certainly with a bilingual transition period.[90]

In the early medieval period, an extremely well-preserved Romance world extended south of the 'Hirschensprung' towards Chur, the centre of *Raetia Prima*, which even today finds expression in countless pre-Germanic toponyms and hydronyms (including numerous Latin lexemes contained in the names).[91] The incoming Alemannians clearly perceived the *Romanitas* of these areas of *Raetia Prima*, as is well documented by St Gall charters and anthroponyms.[92] They gave places names such as *Walgouwe* '*pagus* of Romance people' for Vorarlberg (*vallis Drusiana*), *Churwalaha* 'Raetia around Chur', and, on the other side of the mountain chain of the 'Churfirsten', *Walensee* 'lake of the *Romani*', *Walenstadt* 'shore of the *Romani*', etc. In the ninth century, however, there was a moderate penetration of Frankish language into the region, and, in the north, consequently, we must suppose a certain degree of bilingualism. *Walen* < Old High German *Walaha* was the Germanic group term (ethnonym) for the *Romani*.[93]

---

90 *Vita S. Galli vetustissima. Die älteste Lebensbeschreibung des Heiligen Gallus, Lateinisch/Deutsch*, ed. by the Stiftsbibliothek Sankt Gallen (St Gall, 2012). Cf. Sonderegger, 'Die Ortsnamen', p. 83; Thomas Anton Hammer, 'Die Orts- und Flurnamen des St. Galler Rheintals: Frühmittelalterliche Orts- und Flurnamen im Vorarlberger und St. Galler Rheintal', *Montfort* 42 (1990), 26–35; Philipp E. Egger-Perler, 'Namenschichtung und Besiedlungschronologie zwischen Konstanz und St. Gallen. Ein kontinuitätskritischer Beitrag der Toponomastik zur Siedlungsgeschichte des Frühmittelalters', *Thurgauer Beiträge zur Geschichte* 128 (1992), 5–306; Gerold Hilty, *Gallus und die Sprachgeschichte der Nordostschweiz* (St Gall, 2001), pp. 63–80, 167–79; Haubrichs 'Die verlorene Romanität', p. 701.

91 Hans Stricker, 'Sprachgeschichte des oberen Rheintals mit besonderer Berücksichtigung der romanischen Epoche und ihrer Überreste', *Werdenberger Jahrbuch* 5 (1991), 9–35; Hilty, *Gallus*, pp. 91–96, 125–32.

92 *Das Drusental. Der Walgau und das Vorderland im frühen Mittelalter*, ed. Peter Erhart (Nenzing, 2009); Bernhard Zeller, 'Über Romanen, Räter und Walchen im frühmittelalterlichen Churrätien', in *Walchen, Romani und Latini*, eds Pohl et al., pp. 153–62. See also Bernhard Zeller's contribution in this volume.

93 Thomas F. Schneider and Max Pfister, 'Romanen und ihre (Fremd-)Bezeichnungen im Mittelalter: Der Schweizer Raum und das angrenzende alemannische Gebiet', in *Walchen, Romani und Latini*, eds Pohl et al., pp. 127–52.

From the eighth century, the language border between the 'Rhaetoromania' proper and Alemannia was long-lasting, and only around 1200 was it pushed back in favour of German idioms. The conditions in Vorarlberg are quite comparable, for here we also find a persistent *Romanitas*, preserved until the high Middle Ages and often in a bilingual situation. An extensive vocabulary of Romance loanwords is found in the field-names and in the dialects of Vorarlberg and the Montafon (western Tyrol), to where these names spread principally via the inhabitants of the neighbouring Rhaeto-Romanic Engadin valley.[94]

The Roman provinces of *Raetia Secunda* and *Noricum Ripense* to the east, that is, the Danube regions of Bavaria and Austria and the Alpine *Romania* (Salzburg, Tyrol, South Tyrol), can be characterized here only briefly for reasons of space.[95] We meet traces of Romance continuity on the late Roman Danube *limes* only in the vicinity of *castra, castella*, and other fortifications. With the exception of the immediate surroundings of the *castrum* of Regensburg,[96] continuity here is concentrated at individual points. All toponyms already show the Old High German tenuis shift, e.g. [t] > [ts] in 425/30 *Batavis*, 754 *Bazzawe*, today *Passau*.[97] So, given also that Romance sonorization is lacking, we can fix at the latest the date of the final integration into the Bavarian language the end of the sixth century. But it is quite possible that Romance speakers existed

94 Karl Finsterwalder, 'Namen und Siedlung in der Silvretta', in Karl Finsterwalder, *Tiroler Ortsnamenkunde. Gesammelte Aufsätze und Arbeiten*, 3 vols (Innsbruck, 1990–95), 2:905–17 (originally published 1955); Guntram A. Plangg, *Die rätoromanischen Flurnamen des Brandnertales* (Innsbruck, 1962); Guntram A. Plangg, 'Flurnamen in St. Gallenkirch (Montafon)', *Bündner Monatsblatt* 1 (1992), 19–26.

95 Albrecht Greule, 'Kontinuität und Diskontinuität vorgermanischer Namen im Umfeld des Donau-Limes', *Regensburger Beiträge zur Regionalgeographie und Raumplanung* 10 (2005), 27–42; Peter Wiesinger, 'Die Zweite Lautverschiebung im Bairischen anhand der Ortsnamenintegrate. Eine lautchronologische Studie zur Sprach- und Siedlungsgeschichte in Bayern, Österreich und Südtirol', in *Interferenz-Onomastik*, eds Haubrichs and Tiefenbach, pp. 163–246; Peter Wiesinger, 'Die Romanen im frühmittelalterlichen bayerisch-österreichischen Raum aus namenkundlicher und sprachwissenschaftlicher Sicht', in *Walchen, Romani und Latini*, eds Pohl et al., pp. 87–112; Wolfgang Haubrichs, 'Baiovarii, Romani and Others. Language, Names and Groups South of the River Danube and in the Eastern Alps During the Early Middle Ages', in *The Baiuvarii and Thuringi. An Ethnographic Perspective*, eds Janine Fries-Knoblach, Heiko Steuer, and John Hines (Woodbridge, 2014), pp. 23–81; Peter Wiesinger and Albrecht Greule, *Baiern und Romanen. Zum Verhältnis der frühmittelalterlichen Ethnien aus der Sicht der Sprachwissenschaft und Namenforschung* (Tübingen, 2019).

96 Haubrichs, 'Baiovarii, Romani and Others', p. 46; Michael Prinz, *Regensburg—Straubing—Bogen. Studien zur mittelalterlichen Namenüberlieferung im ostbayerischen Donauraum* (Munich, 2007).

97 Wiesinger, 'Die Zweite Lautverschiebung', pp. 172 (no. 19), 192–94, 223.

here and there for a while longer, especially in the direction of the foothills of the Alps.

The situation was completely different in the Bavarian and Austrian Alpine regions, however. There, on the eastern side of the Inn river, in the pre-alpine foothills and in Upper Austria, pre-Germanic toponyms and place- or lake-names are sometimes composed with the ethnonym *Walchen* (*Romani*), e.g. 763 near the *Walchensee* (Germany, district Garmisch) the *pagus desertus Uualhogoi* ('*pagus* of the *Romani*'),[98] and near Salzburg 788 *Vicus Romaniscus* with *Walaho-wis* 'village of the *Romani*'.[99] A unique piece of evidence from the middle of the eighth century comes in the form of a charter (the so-called 'Rottachgau Fragment', perhaps the earliest extant Bavarian document) recording the sale of a clearing situated in the Rottachgau (an area south of Passau, east and west of the Inn), in a place named *Fonalva* < **Font-alba* 'clear fountain'.[100] This is certainly a Romance hydronym and later becomes the name of a village. Other pre-Germanic toponyms exist in the Rottachgau, such as *Gurten* (Austria, Innkreis), 763 *Curtana* < Romance **Curtina* 'small farm'. The names of the individuals acting in the charter are all of Romance provenance: *Floritus prepositus, Mai(o)ranus, Dominicus, Dominicans,* the *miles Vigilius,* and the *scriptor Quartinus*, thus clearly documenting the presence of *Romani* in the region. The centre of this 'Romania Norica' was the antique *civitas* of Salzburg-*Iuvavum*, where Romance language seems to have survived at least until the tenth century, and certainly since the later eighth century in a bilingual situation.[101] A similarly strong and enduring linguistic continuity appears in the Tyrolian Inn valley and in South Tyrol, where Bavarians began to settle from the late seventh century, albeit in a very different linguistic situation.[102]

98 Christa Jochum-Godglück, 'Walchensiedlungsnamen und ihre historische Aussagekraft', in *Die Anfänge Bayerns. Von Raetien und Noricum zur frühmittelalterlichen Baiovaria*, eds Hubert Fehr and Irmtraut Heitmeier (St Ottilien, 2012), pp. 197–218; Wiesinger, 'Die Romanen', pp. 105–6.

99 Ingo Reiffenstein, 'Namen im Sprachaustausch: Romanische Relikte im Salzburger Becken', in *Namenforschung*, eds Eichler et al., 2:997–1006; Wiesinger, 'Die Romanen', p. 105.

100 *Die Traditionen des Hochstifts Passau*, ed. Max Heuwieser (Munich, 1930), no. 1. Cf. Peter Wiesinger, 'Das Rottachgau-Fragment im Licht der Ortsnamenkunde', in *Walchen, Romani und Latini*, eds Pohl et al., pp. 113–25.

101 Reiffenstein, 'Romanische Relikte'; Haubrichs, 'Baiovarii, Romani and Others', pp. 49–51; Wolfgang Haubrichs, 'Romanische und bairische Personennamen im Salzburger Verbrüderungsbuch', in *Libri Vitae. Gebetsgedenken in der Gesellschaft des Frühen Mittelalters*, eds Dieter Geuenich and Uwe Ludwig (Cologne, 2015), pp. 405–39.

102 Finsterwalder, *Tiroler Ortsnamenkunde*; Peter Anreiter, 'Der Ostalpenraum im Spiegel vordeutscher Namen', *Namenkundliche Informationen* 79–80 (2001), pp. 89–123; Peter Anreiter, Christian Chapman and Gerhard Rampl, *Die Gemeindenamen Tirols. Herkunft und Bedeutung* (Innsbruck, 2009); Wiesinger, 'Die Zweite Lautverschiebung', pp. 195–200;

Many Romance loanwords also survived in South-Bavarian dialects.[103] Bearing in mind the adjacent regions of Ladinia, northern Italy, and 'Rhaetoromania', we must conclude that there were different types of bilingual zones here from the eighth century until the later Middle Ages.

The Multilingualism of the Upper Classes

With the exceptions of the *Mosella Romana* and the Noric *Romania* in the Alps (stretching from Salzburg to Tyrol), and of small strips around the later Romance-Germanic linguistic border, multilingualism in the former Roman territories west of the Rhine and south of the Upper Danube had essentially died out by the end of the eighth century. Certainly, this gradual linguistic dissociation had severe consequences for the Carolingian Empire, signifying not only great social change, but also changes in communication, especially as the last vestiges of Langobardic language in northern and central Italy disappeared at the end of the eighth century. The disparate regions of the Carolingian Empire began to become more monolingual. In addition, the Empire was reorganized, eventually splitting decisively into three constituent *regna*, a process that began in 843 with the Treaty of Verdun: the western *regnum Francorum*, including Aquitaine, leading eventually to France; the *regnum orientalium Francorum*, which gradually came to incorporate regions west of the Rhine including Lotharingia, the Rhineland, Alsace, and parts of Switzerland, and, to the east of the Rhine, Swabia (Alemannia), Bavaria, Thuringia, and Saxony; and finally the *regnum Italiae*. These divisions were not based on language, but certainly had a strong impact on the subsequent linguistic development and separation of central Europe.

From the Carolingian period onwards, second languages—*theodisca lingua* for Romance speakers, and the *rustica Romana lingua* (distinct from standardized Latin) for speakers of Germanic idioms—had to be learned artificially through schooling. Yet following Charlemagne's *divisio imperii* of 806, knowledge of foreign languages remained important for the aristocratic elites of the Empire, some of whom came from the east, such as the Rhenish Robertines (the later Capetians), the Welfs from Bavaria and Swabia, the Etichonids from

---

Haubrichs, 'Baiovarii, Romani and Others', pp. 51–55; Haubrichs, 'Die verlorene Romanität', pp. 702–4; Haubrichs, 'Von Zirl bis Zürich', pp. 428–29.

103 Karl Finsterwalder, 'Romanische Vulgärsprache in Rätien und Norikum von der römischen Kaiserzeit bis zur Karolingerepoche', in Finsterwalder, *Tiroler Ortsnamenkunde*, 1:33–64 (originally published 1966); Peter Anreiter, 'Die Besiedlung Nordtirols im Spiegel der Namen', *Onoma* 33 (1996–97), 98–113; Wiesinger, 'Die Romanen', pp. 107–10.

Alsace, Archbishop Fulk of Rheims (883–900), who came from a family with East Frankish roots, and many others.[104] The importance of language is acutely shown by several letters of Lupus, abbot of Ferrières (near Orléans), son of a Bavarian-Romance mixed family.[105] Between 829 and 836, Lupus studied and worked in the famous monastic school of Fulda under Abbot Hrabanus Maurus, where in those years the Old High German translation of the gospel harmony of Tatian was composed.[106] Lupus also seems to have concerned himself with the *lingua germanica*.[107] As abbot of Ferrières (837–after 862), Lupus, considered by Emmanuel von Severus to be the 'most important philologist of the ninth century',[108] stressed the value of the *lingua germanica* for the Romance-speaking West Frankish upper class. His ties with the eastern Franks were not cut by the Treaty of Verdun: connections continued to run between the Lotharingian monasteries of St-Maximin (Trier) and Prüm, two abbeys situated in the *Mosella Romana* whose leading personnel often came from the west, from Anjou, Orléans, Ferrières, and Sens.[109] When in 844 the Fulda monks Hatto and Rathari travelled to Ferrières, they naturally took the route via Prüm. In the same year, Lupus sent his nephew and two other young noblemen to Abbot Markward of Prüm, his relative, for the purpose of learning 'German': 'Filium Guagonis, nepotem meum vestrumque propinquum, et cum

---

104 Cf. Ernst Hellgardt, 'Zur Mehrsprachigkeit im Karolingerreich. Bemerkungen aus Anlass von Rosamond McKittericks Buch "The Carolingians and the Written Word"', *Beiträge zur Geschichte der deutschen Sprache und Literatur* 118 (1996), 1–48, at pp. 15–17, 20–24, 38–46; Wolfgang Haubrichs, *Die Anfänge: Versuche volkssprachiger Schriftlichkeit im frühen Mittelalter (ca. 700–1050/60). Geschichte der deutschen Literatur von den Anfängen bis zum Beginn der Neuzeit, I: Von den Anfängen bis zum hohen Mittelalter*, 2nd ed. (Tübingen, 1995) pp. 157–59; Philippe Depreux, 'Le comte Haganon, favori de Charles le Simple, et l'aristocratie d'entre Loire et Rhin', in *De la mer du Nord à la Méditerannée*, eds Gaillard et al., pp. 381–93.

105 Emmanuel von Severus, *Lupus von Ferrières* (Münster, 1940), pp. 18–183; Hubert Mordek, 'Lupus von Ferrières', in *Lexikon des Mittelalters*, 9 vols (Munich, 1980–98), 6:15–16.

106 Bernhard Bischoff, 'Paläographische Fragen deutscher Denkmäler der Karolingerzeit', *Frühmittelalterliche Studien* 5 (1971), 101–34, at pp. 105–106; Haubrichs, *Die Anfänge*, pp. 211–15; Achim Masser, 'Tatian', in *Althochdeutsche und altsächsische Literatur*, ed. Rolf Bergmann (Berlin, 2013), pp. 459–66.

107 Wolfgang Haubrichs and Max Pfister, *"In Francia fui". Studien zu den romanisch-germanischen Interferenzen und zur Grundsprache der althochdeutschen "Pariser (Altdeutschen) Gespräche" nebst einer Edition des Textes* (Stuttgart, 1989), p. 8; Hellgardt, 'Zur Mehrsprachigkeit im Karolingerreich', pp. 31–35.

108 Von Severus, *Lupus von Ferrières*, p. 170.

109 Wolfgang Haubrichs, *Die Kultur der Abtei Prüm zur Karolingerzeit. Studien zur Heimat des althochdeutschen Georgsliedes* (Bonn, 1979), pp. 60–67; Haubrichs and Pfister, *"In Francia fui"*, pp. 8–10; Bernd Isphording, *Prüm. Studien zur Geschichte der Abtei von ihrer Gründung bis zum Tod Kaiser Lothars I. (721–855)* (Mainz, 2005), pp. 165–82, 257–60.

eo duos alios puerulos nobiles et quandoque, si Deus vult, nostro monasterio suo servitio profuturos propter Germanicae linguae nanciscendam scientiam, vestra sanctitate mittere cupio, qui tres duobus tantummodo paedagogis contenti sint'.[110] We thus learn that at Prüm there were special *paedagogi*, teachers, for learning the *theodisc* language. Three years later, when the pupils returned to Ferrières in the company of a Prüm monk, Lupus commented with satisfaction: '... linguae vestrae pueros nostros fecistis participes, cujus usum hoc tempore pernecessarium nemo nisi nimis tardus ignorat' ('... that you let our young men participate in your language; nobody, unless completely sluggish in mind, can deny that even today the use of this language is absolutely necessary').[111]

It is certainly not coincidental that short readers and manuals for language acquisition have survived from the ninth century. They offer insight into the rudimentary learning of Old High German, that is, the *theodisca lingua*, by *Romani*. These texts served the practical purpose of communication in the cases of voyages and elementary conversations, and normally contain a short glossary and example sentences for everyday use. During the first quarter of the ninth century in Bavaria, the so-called 'Kassel Glosses' were recorded (Kassel, Landesbibliothek, 4° Ms. Theol. 24).[112] This *libellus* features a glossary translating the Vulgar Latin or Romance terms for parts of the body, domestic animals, lodging, dressing, and tools into Bavarian. It also includes a collection of conversation fragments in the form of questions and answers, which offer idiomatic expressions and sentences in order to help a Romance speaker navigate some challenges of everyday life: *wer pist du?* ('who are you?'); *wanna quimis?* ('where do you come from?'). Instructions for services are also present: *skir min fahs!* ('cut my hair!'); *skir minan part!* ('trim my beard!'). Notably, the Kassel Glosses contain a Latin-Romance vocabulary which obviously possesses a regional accent, indicating closeness with 'Rhaetoromania', Ladinia, and northern Italy, as for instance with *Ordig(l)as* 'toes' < Latin *articulos*, Italian *artiglio* 'claw'; *Putel* 'bowels' < Latin *butellus*, Italian *budella*; *Fidelli* 'calfs', written in German manner with <f> < Latin *vitellum*, Italian *vitello*; *Troia* 'sow' < Italian *troja*; *Aucas* 'geese' < Latin **avica*, Italian *oca*; *pulcins* 'chick' < Latin *pullicênu*, Italian *pulcino*; *Piz* 'crest, peak' < Late Latin *pizzu*, Italian *pizzo*, Veneto, Rhaeto-Romanic *piz*; *Saccuras* 'axes' < Late Latin *secure*, Italian

110 *Loup de Ferrières, Correspondance*, ed. and trans. Léon Levillain, 2 vols (Paris, 1927–35), no. 35, 1:155.

111 *Loup de Ferrières, Correspondance*, no. 70, 2:7–8.

112 Elias Steinmeyer and Eduard Sievers, *Die althochdeutschen Glossen*, 5 vols (Berlin, 1879–1922), 4:411–12. Cf. Stefanie Stricker, 'Kasseler Glossen', in *Althochdeutsche und altsächsische Literatur*, ed. Bergmann, pp. 225–27.

scure; *Manneiras* 'long axes, halberds' < Latin *manuâria*, Italian *mannaja*; *-tutti* 'all' < Late Latin *tôttu*, Italian *tutto*, etc.

The Kassel reader is also famous for a mnemonic sentence, formulated in both a substandard Latin and in Bavarian, which was to be given to pupils to learn:

Stulti sunt Romani,
Sapienti sunt Paioari,
Modica est sapientia in Romana,
Plus habent stultitia quam sapientia.

Tole sint Uualha,
spahe sint Peigira,
luzic ist spahi in Uualhum,
mera hapent tolaheiti denne spahi.

('The *Romani* are stupid,
the Bavarians are wise.
Wisdom is sparse with the *Romani*,
they have more stupidity than wisdom.')

The mnemonic sentence functions in the glossary as an example given under the heading *stultus*. It provides rather stark evidence for the coexistence of *Baioarii* and *Romani* in the contact areas south of the Danube and in the eastern Alps, relations between whom were clearly not always easy. But the sentence and its translation also testify to the existence of Romance-speaking people in the knowledge and in the life of the Bavarians.[113]

From Romance-speaking West Francia, we have an even more complex example that is characteristic of the bilingualism Lupus of Ferrières strived for. Around the year 900, the so-called 'Pariser (Altdeutsche) Gespräche' ('Paris [or Old German] conversations') were copied from an older redaction into the margins of a glossary manuscript, most likely written some years before in Burgundy or Provence.[114] The origin of this manuscript, which was later broken up (one leaf is now in Vatican, Biblioteca Apostolica Vaticana, Reg. lat. 566, while the rest is in Paris, Bibliothèque nationale, lat. 7641A), is not

113 Cf. Herbert Penzl, '"Stulti sunt Romani". Zum Unterricht im Bairischen des 9. Jahrhunderts', *Wirkendes Wort* 35 (1985), 241–48.

114 Haubrichs and Pfister, *"In Francia fui"*, pp. 6–11; Wolfgang Haubrichs, 'Pariser Gespräche', in *Althochdeutsche und altsächsische Literatur*, ed. Bergmann, pp. 347–50.

completely clear. Apparently, the codex was in a library of the Orléans region in the sixteenth century. This was a reader produced for acquisition of Old High German, collecting the 'Pariser Gespräche' together with some excerpts from the Fulda translation of the 'Tatian' and a list of place-names, and was recorded by a single hand in 'a script of pronounced French origin', according to Bernhard Bischoff.[115] The place-name list contains the names of nearby villages from the *pagus* of Sens, the ecclesiastical province of which included the diocese of Orléans. The monastery of Ferrières, where the famous abbot Lupus worked, was situated in the diocese of Sens. The distinctive Romance orthography of the text, e.g. <gu> for Germanic [w], for this period points to an area stretching from northern Burgundy up to Sens, Orléans, and Paris.[116] Numerous writing mistakes, corrections, miscorrections, and the frequent disregard of word boundaries reveal that the writer understood his text only very poorly. The underlying Old High German seems to have had its origin in a Middle Franconian dialect (the area of Trier, Koblenz, and Cologne) or in a bordering West Frankish idiom. The Latin lemmata and sentences are heavily interspersed with Romance forms and vocabulary.[117]

Like the Kassel Glosses, the 'Pariser Gespräche' begin with an Old High German-Latin glossary of body parts. There follows a 'phrasebook' that arranges its bilingual sample sentences and idiomatic expressions in the familiar manner of question and answer: 'Gueliche lande cumen ger . id est . de qua patria?' ('From which country have you come? …')—'E guas mer in gene francia . id est . in francia fui' ('I was in Francia …')—'Guaez ger da daden . id est . quid fecisti ibi?' ('What did you do there? …')—'Enbez mer dar . id est . disnavi me ibi' ('I dined there …'). The combination of these Old High German sentences with items of spoken Latin language is absolutely unique in texts of this time, and this manuscript points toward linguistic developments not otherwise observable for another century or two. This proves that one function of the text was communication in everyday speech.

While the 'Pariser Gespräche' do not offer a continuous thematic coherence, they nevertheless contain passages of varying complexity that deal with common questions concerning travel and the special interests of warriors, noblemen, and servants: e.g. 'Esconae cane(h)t . bellus uasallus' ('a fine vassal …')—'Isnel canet . uelox uasallus' ('a brave vassal …')—'Ubele canet, en mine terue . id est . malus uassallus' ('a nasty vassal …')—'Guer is(t) tin erro . id est . ubi e(st) senior tuus?' ('Where is your lord? …'). In addition, swear

115 Bischoff, 'Paläographische Fragen', p. 133.

116 Haubrichs and Pfister, *"In Francia fui"*, pp. 10–11, 23–31.

117 Haubrichs and Pfister, *"In Francia fui"*, pp. 73–82; Haubrichs, 'Pariser Gespräche', p. 349.

words and curses appear: 'Undes ars in tine naso . id est . canis culu in tuo naso' ('a dog's ass in your nose!'). This in fact reflects something that became a popular French insult and remained in use until very recently.

The third part, the excerpts from the Old High German 'Tatian' together with insertions of sentences composed of 'Tatian' vocabulary, also revolves around topics of drinking, hospitality, and sword-fighting. An atmosphere of feud reigns throughout the text. As we have already seen, vassals were judged by their quality and bravery. One must take care of more than one horse. One's armament contains shield, spear, sword, gauntlets, bar, and knife. One spends the night 'in the house of the count' ('in garaben (h)us . ad mansionem comitis'). One drinks *bonum vinum, got guin* ('a good wine'). As Stefan Sonderegger commented, 'It is a little travelling handbook, made for a special purpose', i.e. for a Romance-speaking nobleman or one of his vassals, 'a book communicating vocabulary and sentence patterns for body parts, dressing, services in the guesthouse, acquaintance and conversation with strangers, dealings with servants, riding, and weapons'.[118] The 'Pariser Gespräche' show that multilingualism was a desirable skill.

In the ninth and tenth centuries, bilingualism and multilingualism among elites was relatively frequent.[119] This can be demonstrated in the first place by a particularly exciting piece of evidence. Soon after 881, in northern France, near the language border, a single bi- or trilingual scribe recorded in excellent orthography two poems, one in *theodisc* (Old High German), the other in Romance (Old French), thus revealing his linguistic double competence (Valenciennes, Bibliothèque municipale, codex 150).[120] He wrote down an Old High German panegyric on the West Frankish king Louis III (the *Ludwigslied*), who was victorious over the Vikings at Saucourt, and an Old French hymn on the holy Eulalia (the *Chanson de S. Eulalie*).[121] Certainly, these texts were

118 Stefan Sonderegger, 'Altdeutsche Gespräche', in *Die deutsche Literatur des Mittelalters. Verfasserlexikon*, 13 vols, 2nd ed. (Berlin, 1978–2007), 1:284–86, at p. 286. Cf. Herbert Penzl, '"Gimer min ros": How German was Taught in the Ninth and Eleventh Centuries', *German Quarterly* 57 (1984), 394–400.

119 Hellgardt, 'Zur Mehrsprachigkeit im Karolingerreich', pp. 24–27.

120 Bischoff, 'Paläographische Fragen', p. 132; Haubrichs, *Die Anfänge*, pp. 137–46; Wolfgang Haubrichs, 'Volkssprache und volkssprachige Literaturen im lotharingischen Zwischenreich (9.-11. Jh.)', in *Lotharingia. Une région au centre de l'Europe autour de l'an Mil*, eds Hans-Walter Herrmann and Reinhard Schneider (Saarbrücken, 1995), pp. 181–244, at 227–37; Matthias Herweg, *Ludwigslied, De Heinrico, Annolied: die deutschen Zeitdichtungen des frühen Mittelalters im Spiegel ihrer wissenschaftlichen Rezeption und Erforschung* (Wiesbaden, 2002), pp. 19–180; Matthias Herweg, 'Ludwigslied', in *Althochdeutsche und altsächsische Literatur*, ed. Bergmann, pp. 241–52.

121 Louise Gnädinger, 'Eulalie, Chanson de Sainte', in *Lexikon des Mittelalters*, 4:93–94.

addressed to listeners in the entourage of the western king, who evidently could be expected to have understood both languages. The idiom of the *Ludwigslied*, called *rithmus teutonicus* ('song in the Germanic language of the people'), can be identified as essentially Rhenish Franconian, but it also contains some northern features and a rather archaic vocabulary, indicating western influence.[122] All these aspects may be understood as components of an elevated West Frankish language spoken at court and by the nobility. We should consider also various elements of Romance orthography in the text, such as the unorganic <h> in *hiu* instead of *iu* (personal pronoun accusative 'you'), or <tz> as a spelling in the light of the shifted dental fricative, e.g. *lietz* instead of the normal Old High German *liez* (preterite 'let'). So, from a linguistic perspective, the assumption that the scribe of these texts worked in an area of strong contacts between Romance and Frankish speakers is well justified.

The author of the *Ludwigslied* wrote in celebration of Louis' victory, but he also sought to justify the king's rule theologically and politically, so we should probably locate him in the court circle or even in the king's clerical staff of counsellors. He wrote in order to show solidarity with a knowing public, for whom Louis' victory over the pagan Northmen needed to be interpreted and commemorated. The deixis of the text tells us that author, public, and king are present *hier in Vrankon* ('here among the western Franks'). The multilingual audience of the two songs has been rightly searched for 'in the circle of the personal followers of Louis III',[123] as his chancellor Gauzlin was also abbot of Saint-Amand and thus head of the monastery where the manuscript of the songs was kept. The above-mentioned Fulk, who before becoming archbishop of Rheims in 883 was abbot of Saint-Bertin by 878 at the latest, was also part of the king's *comitatus*.

As Ernst Hellgardt put it, 'In the neighbouring regions of the linguistic borders and among the high nobility of the ninth century, multilingualism was quite natural'.[124] Already in the seventh and eighth century we hear of multi-

122 Cf. e.g. the word *êre-grehti*, 'grace, *maiestas domini*', literally an archaic compound of *êre* 'honour' and *girehti* 'justice': Wolfgang Haubrichs, 'Die Missionierung der Wörter. Vorbonifatianische und nachbonifatianische Strukturen der theodisken Kirchensprachen', in *Bonifatius—Leben und Nachwirken. Die Gestaltung des christlichen Europa im Frühmittelalter*, eds Franz J. Felten and Lutz E. von Padberg (Mainz, 2007), pp. 121–42.

123 Klaus J. Mattheier, 'Historisches und Figuratives im althochdeutschen Ludwigslied', in *Philologische Untersuchungen: gewidmet Elfriede Stutz zum 65. Geburtstag*, ed. Alfred Ebenbauer (Vienna, 1984), pp. 270–88, at 277.

124 Hellgardt, 'Zur Mehrsprachigkeit im Karolingerreich', p. 27. Cf. Paul Christopherson, 'The Spoken Word in International Contacts in Carolingian Europe', *NOWELE: North-Western European Language Evolution* 20 (1992), 53–64; Stephan Müller, 'Sprachkonflikte? Mehrsprachigkeit, Verständigungsroutinen und der Beginn der volkssprachigen Schriftlichkeit

lingual bishops such as Eligius and Mummolinus of Noyon and Amandus of Maastricht (who also founded the abbey of Saint-Amand), all of whom were of southern origin. At the end of the eighth century, Paul the Deacon reported in his *Liber de episcopis Mettensibus* that Archbishop Chrodegang of Metz (*c.*742–66), who came from a noble Frankish family of *Hasbania* (Hesbaye/Haspengau, Belgium), was 'eloquio facundissimus, tam patrio quamque etiam latino sermone imbutus'.[125] The *rustica romana lingua*, the Romance language, is not mentioned, perhaps because Latin and Gallo-Romance in early Carolingian times were not strictly separated. Concerning Adalhard, a cousin of Charlemagne and influential courtier who later became abbot of Corbie (780–826) and founder of the Saxon monastery of Corvey, his *confrater* Paschasius Radbertus tells us of his eloquence in three languages: '… Quem si vulgo audisses, dulcifluus emanabat: si vero idem barbara, quam theutiscam dicunt, lingua loqueretur praeeminebat claritatis eloquio; quod si Latine, iam ulterius prae aviditate dulcoris non erat spiritus'.[126] The panegyrical biographer praises the eloquence of Adalhard in the vulgar Romance language (*vulgo*), in the *theudisca* or *barbara lingua*, that is in a Germanic language, and finally in Latin. In the tenth century, multilingualism is still testified among the higher West Frankish strata. In his *Annales*, the chronicler Flodoard of Rheims describes how at the great synod of Ingelheim in 948, presided over by the western and eastern Frankish rulers Louis IV (936–54) and Otto I (936–73), a letter was read aloud and translated 'propter reges juxta teutiscam linguam'.[127] The kings first and foremost understood the *theodisc* language, but not (or only weakly) the Latin of the *epistola*. As for Louis IV, who spent his whole youth in Wessex at the court of his uncle, King Æthelstan, one can assume that he also understood and spoke Old English.

We should not forget the inverse of this situation: in the eastern part of the Frankish world, magnates and *optimates* also perceived the *utilitas* of the knowledge of the Romance language beyond classical or standard Latin. The Saxon chronicler Widukind of Corvey relates that Otto I did not benefit

im deutschen Frühmittelalter', *Jahrbuch für Germanistische Sprachgeschichte* 7 (2016), 116–32.

125 Paul the Deacon, *Gesta episcoporum Mettensium*, ed. Georg H. Pertz, MGH SS 2 (Hanover, 1829), pp. 267–68.

126 Paschasius Radbertus, *De vita S. Adalhardi*, ed. J.-P. Migne, *Patrologia Latina* 120 (Paris, 1852), cols 1507–56, at cols 1546 C and 1553 A; Paschasius Radbertus, *Vita Adalhardi*, ed. Georg H. Pertz, MGH SS 2 (Hanover, 1829), p. 542.

127 Flodoard, *Annales*, s.a. 948, ed. Philippe Lauer, *Les Annales de Flodoard* (Paris, 1905), pp. 112–13. See Willy Sanders, 'Imperator ore iucundo saxonizans', *Zeitschrift für deutsches Altertum* 98 (1969), 13–28, at p. 25.

from any special education and therefore did not speak Latin, but did speak Romance and Slavonic: 'Preterea Romana lingua Sclavonicaque loqui sit; sed rarum est, quo earum uti dignetur'.[128] Ekkehard IV, in his *Casus sancti Galli* reports a Romance formula of greeting that was apparently a linguistic quirk of Otto, who perhaps used it to dazzle his court. One morning in Speyer on the Rhine (*c.*971), he apparently greeted his *aequivocus* and grandson Otto, the later duke of Swabia (973–83), in a strange manner: '... arridens ei "bôn mân" habere romanisce dixit'.[129] Speyer, incidentally, was a city that had always been open to cultural influences from the west. Finally, Widukind reported for the year 939 that the royal army included a number of magnates and 'milites, qui Gallica lingua ex parte loqui sciebant', meaning that they spoke the Romance language in a passable manner.[130]

Conclusions

The examination of linguistic acts and changes does not reveal the impact of short-term political and historical surface processes. It does, however, allow us to discern basic social and cultural processes of the *longue durée*. In this chapter, a linguistic examination of names and loanwords found in charters, inscriptions, and other texts has been attempted in order to understand two long-term processes: first, the transformation of predominantly Latin-speaking regions of the Roman Empire into zones of Romance language, which over several centuries linguistically integrated immigrants from the Germanic East. Second, it has sought to characterize the inverse of this: the transformation of Latin-speaking regions near the *limites* of the Roman Empire into *theodisc* zones, which, similarly, over the centuries absorbed Romance islands and relic areas.

With some justification, we can therefore speak of two types of linguistic integration in the early Middle Ages. Contact and bilingual interference areas lying between the eventual monolingual regions disappeared around the end of the eighth century, with the exceptions of the *Mosella Romana*, still partly bilingual in the tenth century, and of the Alpine *Romania* around Salzburg and in Tyrol, which continued for even longer. In addition to these basic processes, which led to a near-total loss of bilingualism, we can detect a multilingualism

128 Widukind, *Res gestae Saxonicae*, II.36, ed. Paul Hirsch, MGH SS rer. Germ. 60, 5th ed. (Hanover, 1935), p. 96.

129 Ekkehard IV, *Casus sancti Galli*, 132, ed. Hans F. Haefele (Darmstadt, 1980), p. 254.

130 Widukind, *Res gestae Saxonicae*, II.17, p. 82.

among the upper strata of Frankish society that was steered by political and economic interests. As long as a basic multilingualism was regarded as natural in the contact areas, the knowledge of more than one language would hardly be perceptible in texts, however sparingly these have been handed down. Only from the eighth century, and especially in the ninth and tenth centuries, was multilingualism consciously strived for and thus registered as a desired individual ability.[131]

Bibliography

Primary Sources

Die althochdeutschen Glossen, eds Elias von Steinmeyer and Eduard Sievers, 5 vols (Berlin, 1879–1922).

Cassiodori Senatoris Variae, ed. Theodor Mommsen, MGH Auct. ant. 12 (Berlin, 1894).

Codex Laureshamensis, ed. Karl Glöckner, 3 vols (Darmstadt, 1929–36).

Ekkehard IV, *Casus sancti Galli*, ed. Hans F. Haefele (Darmstadt, 1980).

Flodoard of Rheims, *Annales*, ed. Philippe Lauer, *Les Annales de Flodoard* (Paris, 1905).

Fredegarii continuationes, ed. Bruno Krusch, MGH SS rer. Merov. 2 (Hanover, 1888), pp. 1–193.

Loup de Ferrières, Correspondance, ed. and trans. Léon Levillain, 2 vols (Paris, 1927–35).

Paschasius Radbertus, *Vita Adalhardi*, ed. Georg H. Pertz, MGH SS 2 (Hanover, 1829), pp. 524–32.

Paul the Deacon, *Gesta episcoporum Mettensium*, ed. Georg H. Pertz, MGH SS 2 (Hanover, 1829), pp. 260–68.

Paul the Deacon, *Historia Langobardorum*, ed. Georg Waitz, MGH SS rer. Germ. 48 (Hanover, 1878).

Les privilèges de l'abbaye de Rebais-en-Brie, eds Victor Leblond and Maurice Lecomte (Melun, 1910).

Die Reichenauer Glossen, ed. Hans-Wilhelm Klein, 2 vols (Munich, 1968–72).

Die Traditionen des Hochstifts Passau, ed. Max Heuwieser (Munich, 1930).

Vita sanctae Geretrudis, ed. Bruno Krusch, MGH SS rer. Merov. 2 (Hanover, 1888), pp. 447–74.

Vita s. Galli vetustissima. Die älteste Lebensbeschreibung des Heiligen Gallus, Lateinisch/ Deutsch, ed. by the Stiftsbibliothek Sankt Gallen (St Gall, 2012).

Widukind of Corvey, *Res gestae Saxonicae*, ed. Paul Hirsch, MGH SS rer. Germ. 60, 5th ed. (Hanover, 1935).

131 I would like to thank the editors for valuable advice and for linguistic and factual revision.

Secondary Sources

Albano Leoni, Federico, 'Bilinguismo e coscienza del bilinguismo nell'Italia longobarda', in *Italia linguistica: Idee, storia, strutture*, eds Federico Albano Leoni, Daniele Gambarara, Franco Lo Piparo, and Raffaele Simone (Bologna, 1983), pp. 133–48.

Alföldy, Géza, 'Zur Grabinschrift des Giboaldus aus Leutesdorf, Kr. Neuwied', *Bonner Jahrbücher* 166 (1966), 444–45.

Almanza Ciotti, Gabriela, 'La situazione di bilinguismo negli *Historiarum libri decem* di Gregorio di Tours', in *Società multiculturali nei secoli V–IX: Scontri, convivenza, integrazione nel mediterraneo occidentale*, ed. Marcello Rotili (Naples, 2001), pp. 55–61.

Anreiter, Peter, 'Die Besiedlung Nordtirols im Spiegel der Namen', *Onoma* 33 (1996/97), 98–113.

Anreiter, Peter, 'Der Ostalpenraum im Spiegel vordeutscher Namen', *Namenkundliche Informationen* 79/80 (2001), pp. 89–123.

Anreiter, Peter, Chapman, Christian, and Rampl, Gerhard, *Die Gemeindenamen Tirols. Herkunft und Bedeutung* (Innsbruck, 2009).

Auer, Anita and De Vaan, Michiel (eds), *The Gothic Palimpsest from Bologna. Philological and Linguistic Studies*, Cahiers de l'ILSL 50 (Lausanne, 2016).

Ausenda, Giorgio, Delogu, Paolo, and Wickham, Chris (eds), *The Langobards Before the Frankish Conquest: An Ethnographic Perspective* (Woodbridge, 2009).

Azzara, Claudio, *I Longobardi* (Bologna, 2015).

Barme, Stefan, 'Latein—Vulgärlatein—Moselromanisch: Zur Sprache der frühchristlichen Grabinschriften im Raum Trier', *Zeitschrift für romanische Philologie* 124 (2008), 15–30.

Barme, Stefan, 'Von keifenden Hirschkäfern und ambrosischen Himbeeren: Notizen zu einigen moselromanischen Reliktwörtern', *Zeitschrift für romanische Philologie* 122 (2006), 363–79.

Belli, Federico, 'Etnici e nomi di luogo di origine germanica in Italia', in *A Torino. Atti del XII Convegno Internazionale di Onomastica e Letteratura*, eds Daniela Cacia and Chiara Colli Tibaldi (Alessandria, 2008), pp. 309–38.

Besse, Maria, 'Les doublets toponymiques le long de la frontière linguistique: méthodologie, chronologie phonétique, étude de cas. L'exemple de la Belgique', *Bulletin de la Commission royale de Toponymie et de Dialectologie* 72 (2000), 35–102.

Besse, Maria, *Namenpaare an der Sprachgrenze. Eine lautchronologische Untersuchung zu zweisprachigen Ortsnamen im Norden und Süden der deutsch-französischen Sprachgrenze* (Tübingen, 1997).

Besse, Maria, 'Romanisch-germanische Sprachbeziehungen: Niederlande und Belgien', in *Reallexikon der Germanischen Altertumskunde* 25 (2003), 246–51.

Bischoff, Bernhard, 'Paläographische Fragen deutscher Denkmäler der Karolingerzeit', *Frühmittelalterliche Studien* 5 (1971), 101–34.

Braune, Wilhelm and Heidermanns, Frank, *Gotische Grammatik. Mit Lesestücken und Wörterverzeichnis*, 20th ed. (Tübingen, 2004).

Braune, Wilhelm and Heidermanns, Frank, *Althochdeutsche Grammatik, I: Laut- und Formenlehre*, 16th ed. (Berlin, 2018).

Brown, T. S., *Gentlemen and Officers: Imperial Administration and Aristocratic Power in Byzantine Italy A.D. 554–800* (Rome, 1984).

Buchmüller, Monika, Haubrichs, Wolfgang, and Spang, Rolf, 'Namenkontinuität im frühen Mittelalter. Die nichtgermanischen Siedlungs- und Gewässernamen des Landes an der Saar', *Zeitschrift für die Geschichte der Saargegend* 34/35 (1986/87), 24–163.

Buchmüller-Pfaff, Monika, *Siedlungsnamen zwischen Spätantike und frühem Mittelalter. Die -(i)acum-Namen der römischen Provinz Belgica prima* (Tübingen, 1990).

Christopherson, Paul, 'The Spoken Word in International Contacts in Carolingian Europe', *NOWELE: North-Western European Language Evolution* 20 (1992), 53–64.

Delogu, Paolo, 'Il regno longobardo', in *Longobardi e Bizantini*, eds Paolo Delogu, André Guillou, and Gherardo Ortalli, Storia d'Italia 2 (Turin, 1980), pp. 1–216.

Depreux, Philippe, 'Le comte Haganon, favori de Charles le Simple, et l'aristocratie d'entre Loire et Rhin', in *De la mer du Nord à la Méditerrannée: Francia Media, une région au coeur de l'Europe (c. 840–c. 1050)*, eds Michèle Gaillard, Michel Margue, Alain Dierkens, and Hérold Pettiau (Luxembourg, 2011), pp. 381–93.

Dietz, Klaus, 'Benennungen von Romanen und Kelten (und ihrer Sprache) im frühmittelalterlichen England', in *Walchen, Romani und Latini. Variationen einer nachrömischen Gruppenbezeichnung zwischen Britannien und dem Balkan*, eds Walter Pohl, Ingrid Hartl, and Wolfgang Haubrichs (Vienna, 2017), pp. 163–76.

Dietz, Klaus, Besse, Maria, Haubrichs, Wolfgang, Sonderegger, Stefan, Wiesinger, Peter, and Pitz, Martina, 'Romanisch-Germanische Sprachbeziehungen', in *Reallexikon der Germanischen Altertumskunde* 25 (2003), pp. 242–304.

Egger-Perler, Philipp E., 'Namenschichtung und Besiedlungschronologie zwischen Konstanz und St. Gallen. Ein kontinuitätskritischer Beitrag der Toponomastik zur Siedlungsgeschichte des Frühmittelalters', *Thurgauer Beiträge zur Geschichte* 128 (1992), 5–306.

Erhart, Peter (ed.), *Das Drusental. Der Walgau und das Vorderland im frühen Mittelalter* (Nenzing, 2009).

Falluomini, Carla, *The Gothic Version of the Gospels and Pauline Epistles: Cultural Background, Transmission and Character* (Berlin, 2015).

Falluomini, Carla, 'Zum gotischen Fragment aus Bologna', *Zeitschrift für deutsches Altertum* 143 (2014), 281–305.

Falluomini, Carla, 'Zum gotischen Fragment aus Bologna II: Berichtigungen und neue Lesungen', *Zeitschrift für deutsches Altertum* 146 (2017), 284–94.

Falluomini, Carla (ed.), *I Longobardi in Italia: lingua e cultura* (Alessandria, 2015).

Finsterwalder, Karl, 'Namen und Siedlung in der Silvretta', in Karl Finsterwalder, *Tiroler Ortsnamenkunde. Gesammelte Aufsätze und Arbeiten*, 3 vols (Innsbruck, 1990–95), 2:905–17.

Finsterwalder, Karl, 'Romanische Vulgärsprache in Rätien und Norikum von der römischen Kaiserzeit bis zur Karolingerepoche', in Karl Finsterwalder, *Tiroler Ortsnamenkunde. Gesammelte Aufsätze und Arbeiten*, 3 vols (Innsbruck, 1990–95), 1:33–64.

Francovich Onesti, Nicoletta, *I nomi degli Ostrogoti* (Florence, 2007).

Francovich Onesti, Nicoletta, 'Toponimi di origine germanica della Val di Cornia', *A.I.O.N. Filologia Germanica* 30/31 (1987/88), 7–42.

Francovich Onesti, Nicoletta, *Vestigia longobarde in Italia (568–774). Lessico e antroponimia* (Rome, 1999)

Gasparri, Stefano, *Italia longobarda. Il regno, i Franchi, il papato* (Bari, 2012).

Gasparri, Stefano (ed.), *Il regno dei Longobardi in Italia. Archeologia, società, istituzioni* (Spoleto, 2004).

Glatthard, Peter, *Ortsnamen zwischen Aare und Saane. Namengeographische und siedlungsgeschichtliche Untersuchungen im westschweizerdeutschen Sprachgrenzraum* (Bern, 1977).

Gnädinger, Louise, 'Eulalie, Chanson de Sainte', in *Lexikon des Mittelalters*, 9 vols (Munich, 1980–98), 4:93–94.

Greule, Albrecht, 'Kontinuität und Diskontinuität vorgermanischer Namen im Umfeld des Donau-Limes', *Regensburger Beiträge zur Regionalgeographie und Raumplanung* 10 (2005), 27–42.

Greule, Albrecht, 'Tarodunun—Zarten—Zähringen', in *Tarodunum/Zarten—Brigobannis/Hüfingen. Kelten, Galloromanen und frühe Alemannen in interdisziplinärer Sicht*, ed. Wolfgang Kleiber (Mainz, 2009), pp. 161–62.

Greule, Albrecht, Kully, Rolf Max, Müller, Wulf, and Zotz, Thomas (eds), *La région de Bâle et les rives du Rhin de l'Antiquité au Moyen Âge: aspects toponymiques et historiques* (Stuttgart, 2013).

Gysseling, Maurits, *Toponymisch Woordenboek van België, Nederland, Luxemburg, Noord-Frankrijk en West-Duitsland (vóór 1226)*, 2 vols (Tongern, 1960).

Heather, Peter, *The Goths* (Oxford 1996).

Heather, Peter, 'Theoderic, King of the Goths', *EME* 4 (1995), 145–73.

Halfer, Manfred, *Die Flurnamen des oberen Rheintales. Ein Beitrag zur Sprachgeschichte des Westmitteldeutschen* (Stuttgart, 1988).

Hammer, Thomas Anton, 'Die Orts- und Flurnamen des St. Galler Rheintals: Frühmittelalterliche Orts- und Flurnamen im Vorarlberger und St. Galler Rheintal', *Montfort* 42 (1990), 26–35.

Handley, Mark A., *Death, Society and Culture: Inscriptions and Epitaphs in Gaul and Spain, AD 300–750* (Oxford, 2003).

Haubrichs, Wolfgang, *Die Anfänge: Versuche volkssprachiger Schriftlichkeit im frühen Mittelalter (ca. 700–1050/60). Geschichte der deutschen Literatur von den Anfängen bis zum Beginn der Neuzeit, I: Von den Anfängen bis zum hohen Mittelalter*, 2nd ed. (Tübingen, 1995).

Haubrichs, Wolfgang, 'Akkulturation und Distanz. Germanische und romanische Personennamen im *regnum* der Burgunden', in *Völker, Reiche und Namen im frühen Mittelalter*, eds Matthias Becher and Stefanie Dick, Mittelalterstudien 22 (Munich, 2010), pp. 191–222.

Haubrichs, Wolfgang, 'Baiovarii, Romani and Others. Language, Names and Groups South of the River Danube and in the Eastern Alps During the Early Middle Ages', in *The Baiuvarii and Thuringi. An Ethnographic Perspective*, eds Janine Fries-Knoblach, Heiko Steuer, and John Hines (Woodbridge, 2014), pp. 23–81.

Haubrichs, Wolfgang, 'The Early Medieval Naming-World of Ravenna, Eastern Romagna and the Pentapolis', in *Ravenna: Its Role in Earlier Medieval Change and Exchange*, eds Judith Herrin and Jinty Nelson (London, 2016), pp. 253–95.

Haubrichs, Wolfgang, 'Die ekklesiogenen Siedlungsnamen des frühen Mittelalters als Zeugnisse der Christianisierung und der Kirchenorganisation im Raum zwischen Maas, Mosel und Saar', in *L'évangélisation des régions entre Meuse et Moselle et la fondation de l'abbaye d'Echternach (V^e^–IXe siècle)*, ed. Michel Polfer (Luxembourg, 2000), pp. 215–44.

Haubrichs, Wolfgang, 'Ethnisch signifikante und andere sprechende Namen im wisigotischen Spanien und im gotischen Italien', in *Sprache—Rhetorik—Translation. Festschrift für Alberto Gil*, eds Vahram Atayan and Ursula Wienen, Rhethos 3 (Frankfurt, 2012), pp. 41–54.

Haubrichs, Wolfgang, 'Fränkische Lehnwörter, Ortsnamen und Personennamen im Nordosten der Gallia. Die "Germania Submersa" als Quelle der Sprach- und Siedlungsgeschichte', in *Die Franken und die Alemannen bis zur 'Schlacht bei Zülpich' (496/97)*, ed. Dieter Geuenich (Berlin, 1998), pp. 102–29.

Haubrichs, Wolfgang, 'Das frühmittelalterliche Elsass zwischen West und Ost: Merowingerzeitliche Siedlungsnamen und archaische Personennamen', in *Adel und Königtum im mittelalterlichen Schwaben. Festschrift für Thomas Zotz*, eds Andreas Bihrer, Mathias Kälble and Heinz Krieg (Stuttgart, 2009), pp. 55–69.

Haubrichs, Wolfgang, 'Galloromanische Kontinuität zwischen unterer Saar und Mosel. Problematik und Chancen einer Auswertung der Namenzeugnisse', in *Italica et Romanica. Festschrift für Max Pfister*, eds Günter Holtus, Johannes Kramer, and Wolfgang Schweickard (Tübingen, 1997), pp. 211–37.

Haubrichs, Wolfgang, 'Germania submersa. Zu Fragen der Quantität und Dauer germanischer Siedlungsinseln im romanischen Lothringen und Südbelgien', in *Verborum Amor. Studien zur Geschichte und Kunst der deutschen Sprache. Festschrift für Stefan*

Sonderegger, eds Harald Burger, Alois M. Haas, and Peter von Matt (Berlin, 1992), pp. 633–66.

Haubrichs, Wolfgang, 'Kontinuität und Ansiedlung von Romanen am Ostrand der alten Gallia und östlich des Rheins: Sprachliche Indikatoren (500–900)', in *Walchen, Romani und Latini. Variationen einer nachrömischen Gruppenbezeichnung zwischen Britannien und dem Balkan*, eds Walter Pohl, Ingrid Hartl, and Wolfgang Haubrichs (Vienna, 2017), pp. 59–85.

Haubrichs, Wolfgang, *Die Kultur der Abtei Prüm zur Karolingerzeit. Studien zur Heimat des althochdeutschen Georgsliedes* (Bonn, 1979).

Haubrichs, Wolfgang, 'Langobardic Personal Names: Given Names and Name-giving Among the Langobards', in *The Langobards Before the Frankish Conquest: An Ethnographic Perspective*, eds Giorgio Ausenda, Paolo Delogu, and Chris Wickham (Woodbridge, 2009), pp. 195–236.

Haubrichs, Wolfgang, 'Langobardisch-fränkische Ortsnamen in Oberitalien: Zu den toponymischen Typen *Stuttgart, Gamundio* und *Herstall / Wardstall*', *Namenkundliche Informationen* 109/110 (2017), pp. 269–90.

Haubrichs, Wolfgang, 'Lautverschiebung in Lothringen. Zur althochdeutschen Integration vorgermanischer Toponyme der historischen Sprachlandschaft zwischen Saar und Mosel', in *Althochdeutsch*, eds Rolf Bergmann, Heinrich Tiefenbach, and Lothar Voetz, 2 vols (Heidelberg, 1987), 2:1350–91.

Haubrichs, Wolfgang, 'Die Missionierung der Wörter. Vorbonifatianische und nachbonifatianische Strukturen der theodisken Kirchensprachen', in *Bonifatius—Leben und Nachwirken. Die Gestaltung des christlichen Europa im Frühmittelalter*, eds Franz J. Felten and Lutz E. von Padberg (Mainz, 2007), pp. 121–42.

Haubrichs, Wolfgang, 'Ein namhaftes Volk—Burgundische Namen und Sprache des 5. und 6. Jahrhunderts', in *Die Burgunder. Ethnogenese und Assimilation eines Volkes*, ed. Volker Gallé (Worms, 2008), pp. 135–84.

Haubrichs, Wolfgang, 'Nescio latine! Volkssprache und Latein im Konflikt zwischen Arianern und Katholiken im wandalischen Afrika nach der Historia persecutionis des Victor von Vita', in *Geschichtsvorstellungen. Bilder, Texte und Begriffe aus dem Mittelalter. Festschrift für Hans-Werner Goetz*, eds Steffen Patzold, Anja Rathmann-Lutz, and Volker Scior (Cologne, 2012), pp. 15–42.

Haubrichs, Wolfgang, 'Pariser Gespräche', in *Althochdeutsche und altsächsische Literatur*, ed. Rolf Bergmann (Berlin, 2013), pp. 347–50.

Haubrichs, Wolfgang, 'Romanische und bairische Personennamen im Salzburger Verbrüderungsbuch', in *Libri Vitae. Gebetsgedenken in der Gesellschaft des Frühen Mittelalters*, eds Dieter Geuenich and Uwe Ludwig (Cologne, 2015), pp. 405–39.

Haubrichs, Wolfgang, 'Sprache und Schriftlichkeit im langobardischen Italien—Das Zeugnis von Namen, Wörtern und Entlehnungen', *Filologia Germanica—Germanic Philology* 2 (2010), 133–201.

Haubrichs, Wolfgang, 'Sprache und Sprachzeugnisse der merowingischen Franken', in *Die Franken—Wegbereiter Europas. 5. bis 8. Jahrhundert n. Chr.*, eds Alfried Wieczorek, Patrick Périn, Karin von Welck, and Wilfried Menghin, 2 vols (Mainz, 1996), 1:559–73.

Haubrichs, Wolfgang, 'Sprachliche Integration, Sprachinseln und Sprachgrenzbildung im Bereich der östlichen Gallia. Das Beispiel der Burgunden und der Franken', in *Von der Spätantike zum frühen Mittelalter: Kontinuitäten und Brüche, Konzeptionen und Befunde*, eds Theo Kölzer and Rudolf Schieffer, Vorträge und Forschungen 70 (Ostfildern, 2009), pp. 61–100.

Haubrichs, Wolfgang, 'La structuration linguistique de l'espace: du bilinguisme à l'émergence des frontières', in *De la mer du Nord à la Méditerrannée: Francia Media, une région au coeur de l'Europe (c. 840–c. 1050)*, eds Michèle Gaillard, Michel Margue, Alain Dierkens, and Hérold Pettiau (Luxembourg, 2011), pp. 41–68.

Haubrichs, Wolfgang, 'Die verlorene Romanität im deutschen Sprachraum', in *Romanische Sprachgeschichte. Ein internationales Handbuch zur Geschichte der romanischen Sprachen*, eds Gerhard Ernst, Martin-Dietrich Gleßgen, Christian Schmitt, and Wolfgang Schweickard, 3 vols (Berlin, 2003), 1:695–709.

Haubrichs, Wolfgang, 'VITALIS, REMICO, AUDULPIA—Romanische, germanische und romanisierte Personennamen in frühen Inschriften der Rhein- und Mosellande', *Rheinische Vierteljahrsblätter* 78 (2014), 1–37.

Haubrichs, Wolfgang, 'Volkssprache und volkssprachige Literaturen im lotharingischen Zwischenreich (9.-11. Jh.)', in *Lotharingia. Une région au centre de l'Europe autour de l'an Mil*, eds Hans-Walter Herrmann and Reinhard Schneider (Saarbrücken, 1995), pp. 181–244.

Haubrichs, Wolfgang, 'Von Zirl bis Zürich. Exonyme und ihre Rolle bei der Germanisierung der nördlichen Alpenlandschaften', *Archivio per l'Alto Adige* 106/107 (2012/13), 421–34.

Haubrichs, Wolfgang, 'Vorgermanische Toponymie am Oberrhein und im Basler Raum. Eine lautchronologische Auswertung', in *La région de Bâle et les rives du Rhin de l'Antiquité au Moyen Âge: aspects toponymiques et historiques*, eds Albrecht Greule, Rolf Max Kully, Wulf Müller, and Thomas Zotz (Stuttgart, 2013), pp. 143–47.

Haubrichs, Wolfgang and Pfister, Max, 'Fränkisch (Frankish)', in *Wieser Encyclopaedia: Western European Languages*, eds Ulrich Ammon and Harald Haarmann (Klagenfurt, 2008), pp. 249–74.

Haubrichs, Wolfgang and Pfister, Max, *"In Francia fui". Studien zu den romanisch-germanischen Interferenzen und zur Grundsprache der althochdeutschen "Pariser (Altdeutschen) Gespräche" nebst einer Edition des Textes* (Stuttgart, 1989).

Haubrichs, Wolfgang and Pfister, Max, 'Die Prümer Romania', in *Sprachgeschichte—Dialektologie—Onomastik—Volkskunde. Festschrift für Wolfgang Kleiber*, eds Rudolf Bentzinger, Damaris Nübling, and Rudolf Steffens (Stuttgart, 2001), pp. 171–95.

Haubrichs, Wolfgang and Pfister, Max, 'La Romania submersa dans les pays de langue allemande', in *Manuel des langues romanes*, eds Andre Klump, Johannes Kramer, and Aline Willems (Berlin, 2014), pp. 225–244.

Hellgardt, Ernst, 'Zur Mehrsprachigkeit im Karolingerreich. Bemerkungen aus Anlass von Rosamond McKittericks Buch "The Carolingians and the Written Word"', *Beiträge zur Geschichte der deutschen Sprache und Literatur* 118 (1996), 1–48.

Herweg, Matthias, 'Ludwigslied', in *Althochdeutsche und altsächsische Literatur*, ed. Rolf Bergmann (Berlin, 2013), pp. 241–52.

Herweg, Matthias, *Ludwigslied, De Heinrico, Annolied: die deutschen Zeitdichtungen des frühen Mittelalters im Spiegel ihrer wissenschaftlichen Rezeption und Erforschung* (Wiesbaden, 2002).

Higham, Nick (ed.), *The Britons in Anglo-Saxon England* (Woodbridge, 2007).

Hilty, Gerold, *Gallus und die Sprachgeschichte der Nordostschweiz* (St Gall, 2001).

Isphording, Bernd, *Prüm. Studien zur Geschichte der Abtei von ihrer Gründung bis zum Tod Kaiser Lothars I. (721–855)* (Mainz, 2005).

Jarnut, Jörg, *Geschichte der Langobarden* (Stuttgart, 1982), translated into Italian as *Storia dei Longobardi* (Turin, 1995).

Jochum-Godglück, Christa, *Die orientierten Siedlungsnamen auf* -heim, -hausen, -hofen *und* -dorf *im frühdeutschen Sprachraum und ihr Verhältnis zur fränkischen Fiskalorganisation* (Frankfurt, 1995).

Jochum-Godglück, Christa, 'Walchensiedlungsnamen und ihre historische Aussagekraft', in *Die Anfänge Bayerns. Von Raetien und Noricum zur frühmittelalterlichen Baiovaria*, eds Hubert Fehr and Irmtraut Heitmeier (St Ottilien, 2012), pp. 197–218.

Jungandreas, Wolfang, *Historisches Lexikon der Siedlungs- und Flurnamen des Mosellandes* (Trier, 1962).

Klausmann, Hubert and Krefeld, Thomas, 'Romanische und rätoromanische Reliktwörter im Arlberggebiet', in *Raetia antiqua et moderna. Festschrift für W. Theodor Elwert*, eds Günter Holtus and Kurt Ringger (Tübingen, 1986), pp. 121–45.

Kleiber, Wolfgang, 'Das moselromanische Substrat im Lichte der Toponymie und Dialektologie. Ein Bericht über neuere Forschungen', in *Zwischen den Sprachen. Siedlungs- und Flurnamen in germanisch-romanischen Grenzgebieten*, eds Wolfgang Haubrichs and Hans Ramge (Saarbrücken, 1983), pp. 153–92.

Kleiber, Wolfgang, 'Probleme romanisch-germanischer Interferenz an der Mosel im Bereich der Prosodie von Eigennamen', *Namenkundliche Informationen* 47 (1985), 14–20.

Kleiber, Wolfgang and Pfister, Max, *Aspekte und Probleme der römisch-germanischen Kontinuität. Sprachkontinuität an Mosel, Mittel- und Oberrhein sowie im Schwarzwald* (Stuttgart, 1992).

Korobov, Maksim, and Vinogradov, Andrey, 'Gotische Graffito-Inschriften aus der Bergkrim', *Zeitschrift für deutsches Altertum* 145 (2016), 141–57.

Kramer, Johannes, 'Zwischen Latein und Moselromanisch: Die Gondorfer Grabinschrift für Mauricius', *Zeitschrift für Papyrologie und Epigraphik* 118 (1997), 281–86.

Krefeld, Thomas, 'Reliktwort und Arealdistribution. Einige exemplarische Fälle aus dem Gebiet des Vorarlberger Sprachatlas', *Montfort* 45 (1993), 33–47.

Kristol, Andres, 'Cham' in *Lexikon der schweizerischen Gemeindenamen*, ed. Andres Kristol (Frauenfeld, 2005), p. 228.

Kristol, Andres, 'Koblenz', in *Lexikon der schweizerischen Gemeindenamen*, ed. Andres Kristol (Frauenfeld, 2005), p. 486.

Kristol, Andres, 'La "Romania bâloise": la toponymie soleuroise permet-elle d'en savoir davantage?', in *La région de Bâle et les rives du Rhin de l'Antiquité au Moyen Âge: aspects toponymiques et historiques*, eds Albrecht Greule, Rolf Max Kully, Wulf Müller, and Thomas Zotz (Stuttgart, 2013), pp. 41–54.

Kristol, Andres, 'Thun', in *Lexikon der schweizerischen Gemeindenamen*, ed. Andres Kristol (Frauenfeld, 2005), p. 873.

Kristol, Andres, 'Zürich', in *Lexikon der schweizerischen Gemeindenamen*, ed. Andres Kristol (Frauenfeld, 2005), pp. 992–93.

Marti, Reto, *Zwischen Römerzeit und Mittelalter. Forschungen zur frühmittelalterlichen Siedlungsgeschichte der Nordwestschweiz (4.–10. Jh.)* (Liestal, 2000).

Martin, Max, 'Die alten Kastellstädte und die germanische Besiedlung', in *Ur- und frühgeschichtliche Archäologie der Schweiz, VI: Das Frühmittelalter*, ed. Walter Drack (Basel, 1979), pp. 97–132.

Martin, Max, 'Die Romanen', in *Ur- und frühgeschichtliche Archäologie der Schweiz, VI: Das Frühmittelalter*, ed. Walter Drack (Basel, 1979), pp. 11–20.

Martin, Max, 'Das Fortleben der spätrömisch-romanischen Bevölkerung von Kaiseraugst und Umgebung im Frühmittelalter auf Grund der Orts- und Flurnamen', in *Provincialia. Festschrift für Rudolf Laur-Belart*, eds Elisabeth Schmid, Ludwig Berger, and Paul Bürgin (Basel, 1968), pp. 133–50.

Masser, Achim, 'Tatian', in *Althochdeutsche und altsächsische Literatur*, ed. Rolf Bergmann (Berlin, 2013), pp. 459–66.

Mattheier, Klaus J., 'Historisches und Figuratives im althochdeutschen Ludwigslied', in *Philologische Untersuchungen* (Vienna, 1984), pp. 270–88.

Merrills, Andy and Miles, Richard, *The Vandals* (Chichester, 2010).

Mordek, Hubert, 'Lupus von Ferrières', in *Lexikon des Mittelalters*, 9 vols (Munich, 1980–98), 6:15–16.

Morlicchio, Elda (ed.), *Lessico Etimologico Italiano (LEI). Germanismi, Vol. I* (Wiesbaden, 2015).

Müller, Stephan, 'Sprachkonflikte? Mehrsprachigkeit, Verständigungsroutinen und der Beginn der volkssprachigen Schriftlichkeit im deutschen Frühmittelalter', *Jahrbuch für Germanistische Sprachgeschichte* 7 (2016), 116–32.

Niemeyer, Manfred (ed.), *Deutsches Ortsnamenbuch* (Berlin, 2012).

Penzl, Herbert, '"Gimer min ros": How German was Taught in the Ninth and Eleventh Centuries', *German Quarterly* 57 (1984), 394–400.

Penzl, Herbert, '"Stulti sunt Romani". Zum Unterricht im Bairischen des 9. Jahrhunderts', *Wirkendes Wort* 35 (1985), 241–48.

Pfister, Max, 'Ortsnamen in mehrsprachigen Ländern und Regionen: Romania submersa', in *Namenforschung*, eds Ernst Eichler, Gerold Hilty, Heinrich Löffler, Hugo Steger, and Ladislav Zgusta, Handbücher zur Sprach- und Kommunikationswissenschaft 11, 2 vols (Berlin, 1995–96), 2:1413–20.

Pfister, Max, 'Tholey und der saarländisch-lothringische Raum zwischen Romania und Germania', *Studien und Mitteilungen zur Geschichte des Benediktinerordens* 96 (1985), 282–98.

Piel, Joseph M. and Kremer, Dieter, *Hispano-gotisches Namenbuch: Der Niederschlag des Westgotischen in den alten und heutigen Personen- und Ortsnamen der iberischen Halbinsel* (Heidelberg, 1976).

Plangg, Guntram A., 'Flurnamen in St. Gallenkirch (Montafon)', *Bündner Monatsblatt* 1 (1992), 19–26.

Plangg, Guntram A., *Die rätoromanischen Flurnamen des Brandnertales* (Innsbruck, 1962).

Post, Rudolf, 'Galloromanische Reliktwortareale und Grenzentlehnungen im Pfälzischen', in *Sprache—Literatur—Kultur. Studien zu ihrer Geschichte im deutschen Süden und Westen. Festschrift für Wolfgang Kleiber*, eds Albrecht Greule and Uwe Ruberg (Stuttgart, 1989), pp. 161–74.

Post, Rudolf, *Romanische Entlehnungen in den westmitteldeutschen Mundarten. Diatopische, diachrone und diastratische Untersuchungen zur sprachlichen Interferenz am Beispiel des landwirtschaftlichen Sachwortschatzes* (Wiesbaden, 1982).

Pohl, Walter and Erhart, Peter (eds), *Die Langobarden. Herrschaft und Identität* (Vienna, 2005).

Prinz, Michael, *Regensburg—Straubing—Bogen. Studien zur mittelalterlichen Namenüberlieferung im ostbayerischen Donauraum* (Munich, 2007).

Rasch, Gerhard, *Antike geographische Namen nördlich der Alpen. Mit einem Beitrag von Hermann Reichert: Germanien in der Sicht des Ptolemaios*, ed. Stefan Zimmer, Reallexikon der Germanischen Altertumskunde—Ergänzungsbände 47 (Berlin, 2005).

Reichert, Hermann, 'Die Bildungsweise der frühen germanischen Personennamen', in *Linguistica et Philologica. Gedenkschrift für Björn Collinder*, eds Otto Gschwantler, Karoly Redei, Hermann Reichert, and Helmut Birkhan (Vienna, 1984), pp. 355–67.

Reichert, Hermann, 'Sprache und Namen der Wandalen in Afrika', in *Namen des Frühmittelalters als sprachliche Zeugnisse und als Geschichtsquellen*, eds Albrecht Greule and Matthias Springer (Berlin, 2009), pp. 43–120.

Reiffenstein, Ingo, 'Namen im Sprachaustausch: Romanische Relikte im Salzburger Becken', in *Namenforschung*, eds Ernst Eichler, Gerold Hilty, Heinrich Löffler, Hugo Steger, and Ladislav Zgusta, Handbücher zur Sprach- und Kommunikationswissenschaft 11, 2 vols (Berlin, 1995–96), 2:997–1006.

Sanders, Willy, 'Imperator ore iucundo saxonizans', *Zeitschrift für deutsches Altertum* 98 (1969), 13–28.

Schmid, Gabrielle, 'Näfels', in *Lexikon der schweizerischen Gemeindenamen*, ed. Andres Kristol (Frauenfeld, 2005), p. 636.

Schmid, Gabrielle and Kristol, Andres, 'Solothurn', in *Lexikon der schweizerischen Gemeindenamen*, ed. Andres Kristol (Frauenfeld, 2005), pp. 839–40.

Schmid, Gabrielle and Kristol, Andres, 'Winterthur', in *Lexikon der schweizerischen Gemeindenamen*, ed. Andres Kristol (Frauenfeld, 2005), pp. 971–72.

Schmitz, Winfried, 'Bedrohte Latinitas. Sprachliche Veränderungen auf spätantik-frühmittelalterlichen Grabinschriften aus dem Rhein-Mosel-Gebiet', in *Literacy in Ancient Everyday Life*, ed. Anne Kolb (Berlin, 2018), pp. 387–411.

Schmitz, Winfried, 'Spätantike und frühmittelalterliche Grabinschriften als Zeugnisse der Besiedlungs- und Sprachkontinuität in den germanischen und gallischen Provinzen', in *Germania inferior. Besiedlung, Gesellschaft und Wirtschaft an der Grenze der römisch-germanischen Welt*, ed. Thomas Grünewald (Berlin, 2001), pp. 261–305.

Schmitz, Winfried, 'Zur Akkulturation von Romanen und Germanen im Rheinland. Eine Auswertung des inschriftlichen Materials', *Das Altertum* 43 (1997), 177–202.

Schneider, Thomas F. and Pfister, Max, 'Romanen und ihre (Fremd-)Bezeichnungen im Mittelalter: Der Schweizer Raum und das angrenzende alemannische Gebiet', in *Walchen, Romani und Latini. Variationen einer nachrömischen Gruppenbezeichnung zwischen Britannien und dem Balkan*, eds Walter Pohl, Ingrid Hartl, and Wolfgang Haubrichs (Vienna, 2017), pp. 127–52.

Schorr, Andreas, 'Zur Namengeografie galloromanischer Lehn- und Reliktwörter in Mikrotoponymen des Saar-Mosel-Raums', in *Interferenz-Onomastik. Namen in Grenz- und Begegnungsräumen in Geschichte und Gegenwart*, eds Wolfgang Haubrichs and Heinrich Tiefenbach (Saarbrücken, 2011), pp. 507–34.

Schützeichel, Rudolf, 'Zons in Dormagen', in *Wortes anst, verbi gratia. Donum natalicium Gilbert A.R. de Smet*, eds Heinrich L. Cox, Valeer F. Vanacker, and Edward Verhofstadt (Leuven, 1986), pp. 439–48.

Severus, Emmanuel von, *Lupus von Ferrières* (Münster, 1940).

Sonderegger, Stefan, 'Altdeutsche Gespräche', in *Die deutsche Literatur des Mittelalters. Verfasserlexikon*, 13 vols, 2nd ed. (Berlin, 1978–2007), 1:284–86.

Sonderegger, Stefan, 'Die Ausbildung der deutsch-romanischen Sprachgrenze in der Schweiz im Mittelalter', *Rheinische Vierteljahrsblätter* 31 (1966/67), 223–90.

Sonderegger, Stefan, 'Die Ortsnamen', in *Ur- und frühgeschichtliche Archäologie der Schweiz, VI: Das Frühmittelalter*, ed. Walter Drack (Basel, 1979), pp. 75–96.

Stricker, Hans, 'Sprachgeschichte des oberen Rheintals mit besonderer Berücksichtigung der romanischen Epoche und ihrer Überreste', *Werdenberger Jahrbuch* 5 (1991), 9–35.

Stricker, Stefanie, 'Kasseler Glossen', in *Althochdeutsche und altsächsische Literatur*, ed. Rolf Bergmann (Berlin, 2013), pp. 225–27.

Stutz, Elfriede, *Gotische Literaturdenkmäler* (Stuttgart, 1966).

Tjäder, Jan-Olof, 'Der Codex argenteus in Uppsala und der Buchmeister Viliaric in Ravenna', in *Studia Gotica. Die eisenzeitlichen Verbindungen zwischen Schweden und Südosteuropa*, ed. Ulf Erik Hagberg (Stockholm, 1972), pp. 144–64.

van Durme, Luc, *Galloromaniae Neerlandicae submersae fragmenta* (Ghent, 1996).

Vössing, Konrad, *Das Königreich der Vandalen. Geiserichs Herrschaft und das Imperium Romanum* (Darmstadt, 2014).

Wartburg, Walther von, *Französisches etymologisches Wörterbuch*, 25 vols (Basel, 1922–2002).

Wiemer, Hans-Ulrich, *Theoderich der Große. König der Goten—Herrscher der Römer* (Munich, 2018).

Wiesinger, Peter, 'Die Romanen im frühmittelalterlichen bayerisch-österreichischen Raum aus namenkundlicher und sprachwissenschaftlicher Sicht', in *Walchen, Romani und Latini. Variationen einer nachrömischen Gruppenbezeichnung zwischen Britannien und dem Balkan*, eds Walter Pohl, Ingrid Hartl, and Wolfgang Haubrichs (Vienna, 2017), pp. 87–112.

Wiesinger, Peter, 'Das Rottachgau-Fragment im Licht der Ortsnamenkunde', in *Walchen, Romani und Latini. Variationen einer nachrömischen Gruppenbezeichnung zwischen Britannien und dem Balkan*, eds Walter Pohl, Ingrid Hartl, and Wolfgang Haubrichs (Vienna, 2017), pp. 113–25.

Wiesinger, Peter, 'Die Zweite Lautverschiebung im Bairischen anhand der Ortsnamenintegrate. Eine lautchronologische Studie zur Sprach- und Siedlungsgeschichte in Bayern, Österreich und Südtirol', in *Interferenz-Onomastik. Namen in Grenz- und Begegnungsräumen in Geschichte und Gegenwart*, eds Wolfgang Haubrichs and Heinrich Tiefenbach (Saarbrücken, 2011), pp. 163–246.

Wiesinger, Peter and Greule, Albrecht, *Baiern und Romanen. Zum Verhältnis der frühmittelalterlichen Ethnien aus der Sicht der Sprachwissenschaft und Namenforschung* (Tübingen, 2019).

Wirtz, Joachim, *Die Verschiebung der germanischen p, t und k in den vor dem Jahre 1200 überlieferten Ortsnamen der Rheinlande* (Heidelberg, 1972).

Woolf, Alex, 'The Britons: From Romans to Barbarians', in *Regna and Gentes. The Relationship between Late Antique and Early Medieval Peoples and Kingdoms in the*

Transformation of the Roman World, eds Hans-Werner Goetz, Jörg Jarnut, and Walter Pohl (Leiden, 2003), pp. 345–80.

Zeller, Bernhard, 'Über Romanen, Räter und Walchen im frühmittelalterlichen Churrätien', in *Walchen, Romani und Latini. Variationen einer nachrömischen Gruppenbezeichnung zwischen Britannien und dem Balkan*, eds Walter Pohl, Ingrid Hartl, and Wolfgang Haubrichs (Vienna, 2017), pp. 153–62.

CHAPTER 4

Germanic Names, Vernacular Sounds, and Latin Spellings in Early Anglo-Saxon and Alemannic Charters

Annina Seiler

The present paper investigates the orthography of vernacular elements in two sets of late seventh- and eighth-century documents, namely single-sheet charters from Anglo-Saxon England and charters and charter drafts from the Alemannic monastery of St Gall. The two sets are very different in many respects; similar factors, however, appear to be at work with regard to orthography. At a time of incipient vernacular literacy, the spelling of Old English and Old High German was by no means standardized. As a result, both sets of charters display a relatively high degree of graphemic variability in the spelling of vernacular elements. Moreover, variation appears to have been triggered by the same factors: alternative spellings for the same sounds align on a continuum from more Latinate to more 'vernacular' spellings and the distribution of different graphs correlates with different sections of the charters. In a subtle shift from linguistic association to social distinction, the same spelling variants can also be used to differentiate between more and less important charter witnesses. While these early charters are generally written in Latin, their orthographic switches foreshadow the code-switching of later charters. The differences between the Anglo-Saxon and the Alemannic groups hint at the later divergent developments in the use—or non-use—of the vernacular in their respective documentary culture.

The material analysed in this chapter comprises the personal and place-names included in two groups of charters dating to the earliest period of vernacular writing in England and on the continent. The first group consists of 25 original single-sheet charters from Anglo-Saxon England dating to the late seventh and eighth centuries. These charters are mostly royal diplomas recording grants of property to religious communities. They provide a date and they name the people involved in the transaction, the properties in question, as well as the witnesses present at the royal assembly at which the transaction took place (though the scribes themselves remain anonymous). As the charters are written almost entirely in Latin, personal and place-names are the only Old English elements included. Despite the frequently occurring formula + *signum manus* [*name*] ('+ mark of the hand of …') to introduce the witnesses' names,

 | DOI:10.1163/9789004432338_005

neither crosses nor names are usually autographs.[1] The charters included in the analysis are the earliest extant Anglo-Saxon original charters together with a few early copies. They are grants by Kentish, Mercian, and Saxon kings or notables and have come down to us from various Southumbrian archives. The oldest charters come from Christ Church, Canterbury and date from 679 onwards; original charters issued by Mercian kings and in Mercian scripts survive from 736 onwards, while the earliest West Saxon charter is dated to 778.[2] As there are no surviving original charters from any northern archive earlier than the tenth century, Northumbria is not represented in this material.[3]

The second group is much larger: representing original private charters from the Alemannic monastery of St Gall, it comprises 125 originals surviving from the eighth century. These charters mostly record donations of land to St Gall and have been preserved in the abbey archives since the early Middle Ages. One of the reasons why such a large body of charters has survived lies in the fact that St Gall did not produce a cartulary. A considerable number of the St Gall charters preserve so-called *Vorakte*, or charter drafts, listing the most important information about the recorded transaction.[4] These details usually include the vernacular elements that we also find in the charters. Scribes apparently took notes during or right after the transaction, but only drew up the final charter when they were back in the scriptorium. For reasons that may have been practical, but could also have been connected to the legal act itself, the drafts were written on the dorse of the sheet of parchment on which the charter was afterwards copied out.[5] As a result of this procedure, two types of

1 On the *subscriptiones* in early Anglo-Saxon charters see Anton Scharer, *Die angelsächsischen Königsurkunden im 7. und 8. Jahrhundert* (Vienna, 1982), pp. 53–56.

2 The analysis will include the following charters: S 8 (*CantCC* 2), S 19 (*CantCC* 5), S 21 (*CantCC* 6), S 23 (*CantCC* 10), S 24 (*CantCC* 11), S 31 (*CantCC* 14), S 35 (*Roch* 9), S 56 (BCS 187, from Worcester), S 59 (BCS 203, from Worcester), S 65 (*CantCC* 9), S 89 (BCS 154, from Worcester), S 96 (*Malm* 49), S 106 (*CantCC* 16a), S 114 (BCS 230, from Evesham), S 123 (*CantCC* 22), S 128 (*CantCC* 24), S 139 (BCS 274, from Worcester), S 153 (*CantCC* 26), S 155 (*CantCC* 29), S 264 (BCS 225, possibly from Bedwyn), S 1184 (*Sel* 11), 1186a (*CantCC* 16b), S 1171 (BCS 81, from Barking), S 1428b (*LondStP* Appendix I), and S 1861 (BCS 364, uncertain archive).

3 See D. A. Woodman, *Charters of Northern Houses*, Anglo-Saxon Charters 16 (Oxford, 2012), pp. 1–6. Charters were issued in Northumbria from early on, but they have not been preserved; the earliest surviving Northumbrian charter is a grant of King Æthelstan to the church of St Peter at York issued in 934 (ibid., pp. 9–10, 16–19, 86–97).

4 See *Die Vorakte der älteren St. Galler Urkunden. Mit einer Beilage: Zum Konzeptwesen Karolingischer Privaturkunden*, ed. Albert Bruckner, Urkundenbuch der Abtei St. Gallen, Ergänzungsheft 1 (St Gall, 1931); *ChLA* 2, pp. xiii, xvi–xvii. For a comparison with endorsements on Anglo-Saxon charters see Gallagher and Wiles, this volume.

5 Bruckner (*ChLA* 2, p. xii) suggested that the sheet of parchment was placed on the piece of land to be transferred and then handed to the notary. For a discussion of various possible

writing by the same scribe have come down to us: an ephemeral draft, which became redundant once the charter had been written out fully, and the final version, which represented the permanent record of the transaction. Most of the St Gall charters are dated and the scribes are named, thus containing ideal material for linguistic analysis. For the present study the following sets of charters have been selected for analysis: all eighth-century records which also transmit a charter draft (32 charters in total, dating from the middle of the eighth century to 800);[6] all original charters written by two of the most prolific eighth-century scribes, namely Waldo (14 original charters, *c.*773–82)[7] and Mauvo (nine original charters, *c.*792–800).[8] This selection allows for insights into the graphemic differences between the drafts and the charters, while the

scenarios see Rosamond McKitterick, *The Carolingians and the Written Word* (Cambridge, 1989), pp. 94–98.

6 The analysis is based on the editions and facsimile in *ChLA* 1 and 2, and the *Chartularium Sangallense, I (700–840)*, ed. Peter Erhart with the collaboration of Karl Heidecker and Bernhard Zeller (St Gall, 2013), as well as the edition of the charter drafts in *Vorakte*, ed. Bruckner. The following charters with charter drafts are included in the analysis: W 17 (= *ChLA* 1, no. 50), W 42 (= *ChLA* 1, no. 63), W 63 (= *ChLA* 1, no. 76), W 70 (= *ChLA* 1, no. 81), W 77 (= *ChLA* 1, no. 78), W 82 (= *ChLA* 1, no. 88), W 83 (= *ChLA* 1, no. 89), W 84 (= *ChLA* 1, no. 86), W 85 (= *ChLA* 1, no. 91), W 88 (= *ChLA* 1, no. 94), W 94 (= *ChLA* 1, no. 90), W 98 (= *ChLA* 1, no. 99) (with *Vorakt* [hereafter VA] by a different scribe), W 102 (= *ChLA* 2, no. 113), W 103 (= *ChLA* 1, no. 108), W 105 (= *ChLA* 2, no. 110), W 108 (= *ChLA* 1, no. 107), W 114 (= *ChLA* 2, no. 116), W 116 (= *ChLA* 2, no. 118), W 120 (= *ChLA* 2, no. 122), W 122 (= *ChLA* 2, no. 120), W 124 (= *ChLA* 2, no. 109), W 136 (= *ChLA* 2, no. 130), W 143 (= *ChLA* 2, no. 138), W 144 (= *ChLA* 2, no. 139), W 145 (= *ChLA* 2, no. 140), W 147 (= *ChLA* 2, no. 142), W 148 (= *ChLA* 2, no. 143), W 153 (= *ChLA* 2, no. 135), W 154 (= *ChLA* 2, no. 147), W 156 (= *ChLA* 2, no. 145), W 159 (= *ChLA* 2, no. 148), and W 161 (= *ChLA* 2, no. 150).

7 Waldo's original charters are W 25 (= *ChLA* 2, no. 167), W 57 (= *ChLA* 1, no. 71), W 62 (= *ChLA* 1, no. 74), W 63 (= *ChLA* 1, no. 76) (+VA), W 64 (= *ChLA* 1, no. 77), W 76 (= *ChLA* 1, no. 75) (+VA), W 77 (= *ChLA* 1, no. 78) (+VA), W 80 (= *ChLA* 1, no. 85), W 83 (= *ChLA* 1, no. 89) (+VA), W 84 (= *ChLA* 1, no. 86) (+VA), W 88 (= *ChLA* 1, no. 94), (+VA), W 89 (= *ChLA* 1, no. 95), W 95 (= *ChLA* 1, no. 96), and W 96 (= *ChLA* 1, no. 97) (+VA?). On Waldo see Peter Erhart, 'Waldo', in *Historisches Lexikon der Schweiz* (2013), http://www.hls-dhs-dss.ch/textes/d/D13044.php; Bernhard Zeller, 'Urkunden und Urkundenschreiber des Klosters St Gallen bis ca. 840', in *Die Privaturkunden der Karolingerzeit*, eds Peter Erhart, Karl Heidecker, and Bernhard Zeller (Dietikon-Zürich, 2009), pp. 173–82, at 176–79; Franz Perret, 'Diakon Waldo und die Anfänge des Stiftsarchives St. Gallen vor 1200 Jahren', in *Festgabe für Paul Staerkle zu seinem achtzigsten Geburtstag am 26. März 1972* (St Gall, 1972), pp. 17–26.

8 Mauvo's charters are W 131 (= *ChLA* 2, no. 126), W 132 (= *ChLA* 2, no. 127), W 133 (= *ChLA* 2, no. 128), W 135 (= *ChLA* 2, no. 132), W 143 (= *ChLA* 2, no. 140) (+VA), W 146 (= *ChLA* 2, no. 141), W 153 (= *ChLA* 2, no. 135) (+VA), W 155 (= *ChLA* 2, no. 149), and W 160 (= *ChLA* 2, no. 152); cf. Zeller, 'Urkunden', p. 179; W 117. Not much seems to be known about Mauvo; see Paul Staerkle, *Die Rückvermerke der ältern St.Galler Urkunden* (St Gall, 1966), p. 38.

additional focus on the charters written by Waldo and Mauvo makes it possible to study the spelling practices of two particular scribes.

The two groups of documents are very different in so far as the early Anglo-Saxon charters are royal diplomas from various regions in England, whereas the St Gall records represent the private charters of a single archive. Yet, they are comparable in several respects: both groups of charters are essentially in Latin with vernacular elements occurring only in the shape of place and personal names; these names are among the earliest written records of Old English and Old High German respectively. Furthermore, as I will argue in this paper, the charters are comparable in terms of the strategies employed by the scribes in dealing with vernacular names and they yield a similar type of graphemic variation. As a result, the two groups provide insights into writing practices on different scales. While the Anglo-Saxon charters allow us to trace a diachronic development with spellings becoming increasingly sophisticated, the St Gall charters provide a micro-perspective on spelling variation and on the spelling choices of individual scribes. The year 800 has been chosen as a cut-off point. This is, of course, an arbitrary date; however, for both Old English and Old High German, vernacular literacy reached a first peak in the course of the ninth century,[9] with the eighth-century material thus representing the stage leading up to this phase.

Scripting the Vernacular

Latin charters with Old English or Old High German included only in the shape of names may seem poor material for a study of the spelling of vernacular languages. However, this type of evidence is in fact typical of the period that witnessed the emergence of the Germanic vernaculars as written languages. The earliest attestations of these languages consist of names in inscriptions and charters, various types of glosses, as well as short texts, such as the Old High German *Lord's Prayer* in the *Abrogans* manuscript, the Old Saxon *Baptismal Vow* or the Old English *Cædmon's Hymn*.[10] Such 'texts' consist just

9 On the development of literacy in Old English, see, for example, Daniel Donoghue, 'Early Old English (up to 899)', in *A Companion to the History of the English Language*, eds Haruko Momma and Michael Matto (Chichester, 2008), pp. 156–64; on early Old High German, see Stefan Sonderegger, *Althochdeutsche Sprache und Literatur. Eine Einführung in das älteste Deutsch: Darstellung und Grammatik* (Berlin, 2003), p. 15.

10 For an overview of the earliest written attestations of non-Romance vernacular languages see Stefan Sonderegger, 'Sprachgeschichtliche Aspekte der europäischen Christianisierung', in *Sprachgeschichte: Ein Handbuch zur Geschichte der deutschen Sprache und ihrer*

of small units, ranging in length from single-word items to no more than a few sentences. Moreover, such vernacular elements are normally embedded in an extensive Latin context. Names are generally the prototypical case for the first words to be written in a vernacular language since, semantically speaking, they have reference rather than meaning and are thus untranslatable.[11] Of course, most Germanic names were semantically transparent: personal names, like Old English *Æðelðryð* (i.e. 'noble' + 'strength'), or place-names, like Old English *Berepeg* (i.e. 'barley' + 'way') or Old High German *Fiscbahc* (i.e. 'fish' and 'brook'), derive from the common lexicon and follow the rules of vernacular grammar. When it comes to place-names, the distinction between appellative toponyms and proper names is moot; at what point exactly *berepeg* ceased to be understood as 'the path by/along the barley field' and came to denote one particular road cannot be decided.[12] In any case, while there are instances of toponyms translated into Latin,[13] the large majority are not, which points to their status as names in the mental grammar of the scribes as well as to their main function in charters, that is, to identify a certain piece of land

Erforschung, eds Werner Besch, Anne Betten, Oskar Reichmann, and Stefan Sonderegger, Handbücher zur Sprach- und Kommunikationswissenschaft 2.2, 2nd ed. (Berlin, 2000), pp. 1030–61, at 1041–44. On the emergence of Old English, see Julia Crick, 'English Vernacular Script', in *The Cambridge History of the Book in Britain*, I, *c.400–1100*, ed. Richard Gameson (Cambridge, 2012), pp. 174–86.

11 For an in-depth discussion of the properties of names and their referential-semantic status see Willy Van Langendonck, *Theory and Typology of Proper Names*, Trends in Linguistics: Studies and Monographs 168 (Berlin, 2007). On the issue of meaning versus reference of Old English names see Fran Colman, 'First Catch Your Name ...: On Names and Word Classes, Especially in Old English', *English Studies* 96 (2015), 310–36. On the historical-linguistic processes affecting names see *Namen und Wörter: Theoretische Grenzen—Übergänge im Sprachwandel*, eds Rolf Bergmann and Stefanie Stricker, Germanistische Bibliothek 64 (Heidelberg, 2018).

12 A modern-day example of a name that is still semantically transparent is provided by the place-name *Newcastle*; cf. Colman, 'First Catch Your Name', p. 321.

13 For example, the name of the city of Bath occurs in Latin translation in S 210 (BCS 509, A.D. 864), though it is immediately followed by its Old English equivalent: 'Scripta est autem huius donationis cartula in illo famoso urbe qui nominatur et calidum balneum. þæt is æt þæm hatum baðum' ('This charter of donation was written in the famous city that is called hot bath. That is at the hot baths'). I am grateful to Francesca Tinti for bringing this example to my attention. Similar cases are also cited by Schendl for the name of Worcester, which is usually referred to as *Weogorna ceastre* in Old English, but which occurs also in such Latinized versions as *in Wiogornensi monasterio, in ciuitate Weogernensi, Weogornensis aecclesiae*, as well as in mixed forms; see Herbert Schendl, 'Beyond Boundaries: Code-Switching in the Leases of Oswald of Worcester', in *Code-Switching in Early English*, eds Herbert Schendl and Laura Wright, Topics in English Linguistics 76 (Berlin, 2011), pp. 47–94, at 66–67.

unambiguously, which necessitated the use of a name according to local usage.[14] While the semantics of names recedes into the background, other features of their linguistic affiliation remain prominent, most importantly their phonology and morphology. It is the phonology of names which triggers the scripting of the vernacular languages in question—long before more extensive vernacular texts are written.

The emergence of a vernacular language in writing tends to comprise two levels of development: an *extensive* development, which refers to an increasing use of the vernacular in terms of the number and diversity of text types and communicative functions, and an *intensive* development, which involves the development of language structures necessary for successful written communication.[15] The very first step in the creation of a written language in terms of its intensive development is the scripting of the language—the process of putting it into writing—and involves the adoption and adaptation of a script. In alphabetic writing systems, this process necessitates the establishment of letter-sound correlations. In other words, characters have to be found to represent the sounds of the language. In most cases, establishing correspondences between Latin letters and Germanic sounds was unproblematic; however, Old English and Old High German had some sounds for which the alphabet did not provide any characters. The most important cases among the consonants are the phonemes /þ, ð/ as in Modern English ***th**orn*, ***th**ere*, /w/ as in Modern English ***w**ater* or the /χ/ sound of Modern German *ni**ch**t* ('not'), *Na**ch**t* ('night'). Theoretically, the scribes had the following options to solve such spelling problems (illustrated with Old English and Old High German spellings for Germanic */þ/):[16]

i) use a Latin character that represents a similar sound (<d>)
ii) use a combination of two (or more) characters (e.g. <th>[17] or <dh>)

14 On the importance of local knowledge for boundary clauses see Nicholas Howe, *Writing the Map of Anglo-Saxon England: Essays in Cultural Geography* (London, 2008), at pp. 33–46.

15 On extensive and intensive development see Wulf Oesterreicher, 'Verschriftung und Verschriftlichung im Kontext medialer und konzeptioneller Schriftlichkeit', in *Schriftlichkeit im frühen Mittelalter*, ed. Ursula Schaefer, ScriptOralia 53 (Tübingen, 1993), pp. 267–92, at 276–77.

16 Following linguistic conventions, phonemes are placed between slashes /…/ and graphs between angle brackets <…> throughout this paper.

17 The digraph <th> was initially used in Latin to transcribe the Greek letter theta in Greek loanwords; the digraph thus came to denote a 'special' kind of *t*-sound, which had the potential of being reinterpreted as a fricative in Germanic (and Irish) contexts. The fact that theta later came to denote a fricative sound in Greek may have reinforced the use of

iii) use a Latin character with a diacritic (<ð>)
iv) use a symbol from another script (<þ>, from the runic character ᚦ)
v) use a Latin character that is otherwise not necessary for that language (e.g. <z> for /þ/)
vi) invent a new symbol (e.g. the zeta-like symbol invented, according to Gregory of Tours, by King Chilperic)[18]

It is quite clear that the choices of the scribes with respect to these options were limited by various factors, most notably by the conventions of the Latin alphabet and by Latin orthographic rules. For example, it was inconceivable to use a character for a completely different sound than the one it denoted in Latin, as this would have made a text incomprehensible. For similar reasons, inventing new characters was not a popular option. According to Gregory of Tours, the Frankish king Chilperic tried to do that; yet, it was clearly not a successful venture, since no trace of Chilperic's characters has survived, apart from the passage in which Gregory comments on the king's invention.

Looking at the options favoured among the attested West Germanic languages, it becomes apparent that, overall, texts in Old High German (as well as Old Saxon and the extant traces of West Frankish) favoured letter combinations consisting of digraphs like <th>, <uu>, <ch>, but also complicated trigraphs such as <ouu> or <hch>. Throughout the Old High German period, spelling remains relatively variable and there is little tendency towards standardization. Old English orthography, on the other hand, eventually went for the two runic characters *thorn* and *wyn* and for the modified character *eth*, which consisted of an Insular rounded <d> with a stroke across the ascender. In the earliest Anglo-Saxon sources, however, this system is not yet in place, and there is significant diachronic and diatopic variation.

<th> for /þ/ in the West. On the other hand, the letter <h>, with its doubtful sound value in Latin, was an ideal candidate to turn into a diacritic of sorts. See Annina Seiler, 'Writing the Germanic Languages: The Early History of the Digraphs <th>, <ch> and <uu>', in *Writing Europe, 500–1450: Texts and Contexts*, eds Aidan Conti, Orietta Da Rold, and Philip Shaw (Cambridge, 2015), pp. 101–21.

18 Gregory of Tours, *Libri historiarum decem*, V.44, eds Bruno Krusch and Wilhelm Levison, MGH SS rer. Merov. 1.1 (Hanover, 1951), p. 254; cf. Seiler, 'Writing the Germanic Languages', p. 114; Norbert Wagner, 'König Chilperichs Buchstaben und andere Graphien', *Sprachwissenschaft* 1 (1976), 434–52.

The Orthography of Early Anglo-Saxon Charters

As I have discussed in detail in a previous study, Old English consonant spelling before 800 falls into three types.[19] The first type uses spelling solution i) and employs graphs like <u>, <d> or <c> to represent the sounds /w/, /þ/ and /χ/; the second type favours spelling solution ii), a combination of two characters like <uu>, <th>, <ch>; the third group combines solutions iii) and iv) and uses the graphs <ð> and <ƿ> for /þ/ and /w/ (and <h> for the velar fricative /χ/). In the course of the eighth century, there is clearly a diachronic development from type i) to type ii) and then to type iii/iv). It needs to be pointed out that the spellings for different sounds do not all change at the same time; this results in overlaps and transitional stages among the three groups.[20]

In the Anglo-Saxon charter corpus examined here, the spellings of the first type are represented only in a very small number of early Kentish charters: the two seventh-century charters S 8 (*CantCC* 2) and S 19 (*CantCC* 5), as well as S 1428b (*LondStP* App. 1), a letter from Bishop Wealdhere of London to Archbishop Berhtwald, written in 704 or 705.[21] The names of the witnesses in S 8, all listed in the genitive, illustrate the system: ***U**elhisci, Ae**d**ilmaeri, Gumber**c**ti*. S 19 (A.D. 697 or 712) already uses the second type of spelling for the velar fricative in *Beri**ch**tualdus* (and <h> in *Ui**h**tredus*) but is consistent in its use of type i) graphs when it comes to the representation of /w/ and /þ/. Outside the charter evidence, type i) graphs are employed in the early manuscripts of Bede's *Ecclesiastical History*.[22] We find the following forms in the first two verses of *Cædmon's Hymn*:[23] ***u**ard* 'guardian', *mae**c**ti* 'might', *modgi**d**anc*

19 Annina Seiler, *The Scripting of the Germanic Languages: A Comparative Study of 'Spelling Difficulties' in Old English, Old High German and Old Saxon*, Medienwandel—Medienwechsel—Medienwissen 30 (Zürich, 2014). The summary provided here is a highly abbreviated account and focuses only on the most frequently attested sound positions.

20 For example, the transition from <c> to <ch> and eventually to <h> to represent the velar fricative /χ/ in words like *Beorhtwald* happens much earlier than the shift from <u> to <uu> to <ƿ>; for details see Seiler, *The Scripting of the Germanic Languages*, pp. 204–10.

21 On the basis of the script, Bruckner (*ChLA* 3, no. 185) considered the document to be an eighth-century copy; Susan Kelly, however, has more recently reassessed it as original: Kelly, *LondStP*, p. 223.

22 The earliest manuscripts are the Moore Bede (Cambridge, University Library, Kk. 5. 16) and the Saint Petersburg Bede (Saint Petersburg, National Library of Russia, lat. Q. v. I. 18), traditionally dated to 737 and 746, respectively; for a summary of the discussion on the dates see Robert D. Fulk, *A History of Old English Metre* (Philadelphia, 1992), pp. 426–28.

23 *The Manuscripts of Cædmon's Hymn and Bede's Death Song: With a Critical Text of the Epistola Cuthberti de obitu Bedæ*, ed. Elliott van Kirk Dobbie (New York, 1937).

'thoughts', and hundreds of examples in the Old English names embedded in Latin texts.

The second type of spellings using digraphs is attested in Mercian and Kentish charters from the middle of the eighth century. The appearance of this spelling system coincides with Mercian political ascendancy.[24] The transition from the first to the second type is illustrated by two related charters, S 19, mentioned above, and S 21 (*CantCC* 6). The former is a donation of land to the church of St Mary's in Lyminge by King Wihtred of Kent of the year 697 or 712. The latter charter is probably an eighth-century copy of the former;[25] it is almost identical, except that the territory donated to St Mary's has been slightly extended—it now also includes Romney Marsh. In addition to that, most of the type i) spellings have been changed into type ii), for example, *uihtredus* (S 19) > *uuihtredus* (S 21), *aedilburgae* (S 19) > *aethilburgae* (S 21). Charter S 19 already includes the digraph <ch> for the velar fricative; this graph has been changed to <h>, for example, in *berichtualdus* (S 19) > *berhtuualdus* (S 21). Some of the forms, of course, remain unchanged, as is the case for *Cantuariorum*, the place-name *Bereueg*, the names of the witnesses *Enfridi*, *Aedilfridi*, *Aehcha* etc. The combination of the digraphs <uu> and <th> with <h> rather than <ch> for the velar fricative, as shown in S 21, is, in fact, the most commonly represented system: it occurs in S 23 (*CantCC* 10), S 89 (BCS 154), S 56 (BCS 187), S 114 (BCS 230, which also includes one example of <þ>), S 24 (*CantCC* 11, A.D. 741, and including one instance of <ð>), S 96 (*Malm* 49, probably a slightly later copy of a charter of 757), and possibly also in S 35 (*Roch* 9), in which /þ/ is not attested. The digraph <ch> seems to have been in use only for a very short period of time: <uu>, <th> as well as <ch> are attested in the first transaction recorded in S 1184 (*Sel* 11a, A.D. 780); however, <ð> also occurs in this charter. The Kentish charter S 31 (*CantCC* 14, *c.*748×762) uses these three digraphs in the personal names *Uuihtbrordis*, *Aethelnothes* (two witnesses), and *Heaberhcto* (the recipient); interestingly enough this last name contains the inverse letter combination <hc>, rather than <ch>. The digraph <hc> (in combination with <uu> and <th>) can elsewhere be found in the Mercian charter S 56 (A.D. 759) alongside <h>. Overall <hc> is very rare but it also occurs in some of the St Gall charters. My impression is that those spellings indicate that the digraph <ch> was falling out of use: the scribes seem to have used the more modern spelling <h>, but then proceeded to correct it immediately by adding the <c> after the <h>. Outside the charter evidence, digraphs are used in the Epinal glossary

24 *Mercia: An Anglo-Saxon Kingdom in Europe*, eds Michelle P. Brown and Carol A. Farr (London, 2001).

25 Brooks and Kelly, *CantCC*, pp. 294–96.

(Mercian, *c.*700),[26] for example, in the form ***uuaeterthruch*** 'water-pipe', glossing Latin *ca*[*ta*]*ractis*, with all three digraphs in one word.

The specifically vernacular graphs <ƿ> and <ð> make an appearance in the last third of the eighth century. However, it is only at the very end of the century that both characters appear together in the same documents, as is the case, for example, in S 155 (*CantCC* 29, A.D. 799). Most of the other charters use either <ð> and <uu>, or <ƿ> and <th> or <d>.[27] Outside the charter evidence, the use of <ƿ> and <ð> is the norm in texts from the ninth century, for example, in the interlinear gloss to the Vespasian Psalter (London, British Library, Cotton Vespasian A.i) and it also characterizes the early West Saxon texts produced at Alfred the Great's court.[28] The rune <þ>, though used occasionally in the earliest sources, becomes more widespread only in the texts of the tenth and eleventh century.

Apart from the clearly diatopic and diachronic distribution of early Old English spellings, there is another factor which influences graphemic variation. This aspect has to do with the fact that the different spelling variants are not completely interchangeable. The alternative graphs convey different cultural associations—though they are equally capable of representing the sounds in question. The associations of graphs are connected to their spheres of use: single graphs were already employed for the representation of Germanic names in classical Latin sources (cf. Caesar's *Cimbri, Uolcae* etc.). The digraphs can be traced to West Frankish spelling practice, since they are widely used in charters and coins of the Merovingian era (e.g. ***Chilperic, Uuandeberctus, Theuderico***).[29] This means that the two types of spellings represent different 'Latins', as it were, namely, classical and contemporary continental Latin. It is probably no coincidence that the oldest extant Kentish charters, dating from the late seventh century, use the classical Latin spellings for Germanic names: they were written at a time when Theodore of Tarsus was archbishop

26 *Old English Glosses in the Épinal-Erfurt Glossary*, ed. Joseph D. Pheifer (Oxford, 1974).

27 The graphs <uu>, <ð>, and <h> are found in S 59 (BCS 203) and in the second transaction recorded in S 1184 (*Sel* 11b); <ƿ> and <d> are used in S 106 (*CantCC* 16a). In S 155, *wyn* and *eth* are the majority variants, but there is also occasional use of <u> and <th>.

28 On early West Saxon see Donoghue, 'Early Old English'.

29 The digraph <th> is already part of the classical tradition, originating from Latin transliterations of Greek <θ>, and widely used in the spelling of foreign names of diverse origin; cf. Hermann Reichert, *Lexikon der altgermanischen Namen*, Thesaurus Palaeogermanicus 1 (Vienna, 1987), p. xxiii. See also Seiler, 'Writing the Germanic Languages', pp. 115–20; Christopher Wells, 'An Orthographic Approach to Early Frankish Personal Names', *Transactions of the Philological Society* 71 (1972), 101–64. On connections between the Continent and Anglo-Saxon England, see Joanna Story, *Carolingian Connections: Anglo-Saxon England and Carolingian Francia, c. 750–870* (Aldershot, 2003).

of Canterbury (668–90)—though it should be noted that none of the surviving Kentish charters are from Canterbury itself.[30] Frank M. Stenton and others have highlighted the probable impact of Theodore on charter production and record keeping;[31] this may also have extended to spelling and would certainly have included graphs used for foreign names in classical Latin.[32] That Bede also chose to use the same graphs is hardly surprising, given his extensive classical learning. The Merovingian digraphs, however, quickly supplanted those spellings, which may have had a somewhat archaic ring already by *c*.700. Apart from that, single graphs were not ideal for representing the Old English sound system unambiguously, since all those graphs also stood for the phonemes they commonly denoted in Latin. The characters *wyn* and *eth* (and later *thorn*), on the other hand, have clear vernacular connotations. The two runic characters were taken over from the script common to all Germanic peoples and *eth* was created to represent the dental fricative /þ/, a specifically Germanic sound. The presence of these graphs signals immediately that a text is written in Old English rather than in Latin.

In texts from the later Anglo-Saxon period this distinction is systematically deployed, insofar as <uu> and <th> are reserved for the spelling of Old English elements in Latin texts, whereas *wyn*, *thorn*, and/or *eth* are used in Old English sources. The names are thus orthographically adapted for their respective linguistic environments. The system of visually distinguishing languages is reinforced when Caroline minuscule is increasingly used for Latin writing in the mid-tenth century, while Insular script is retained for Old English.[33]

30 Brooks and Kelly, *CantCC*, pp. 2–3, 42–43.

31 Frank M. Stenton, *Anglo-Saxon England* (Oxford, 1955), pp. 134–35; see also Scharer, *Königsurkunden*, pp. 56–77; Bernhard Bischoff and Michael Lapidge, *Biblical Commentaries from the Canterbury School of Theodore and Hadrian*, Cambridge Studies in Anglo-Saxon England 10 (Cambridge, 1994), pp. 138–39; Jane Stevenson, *The 'Laterculus Malalianus' and the School of Archbishop Theodore*, Cambridge Studies in Anglo-Saxon England 14 (Cambridge, 1995), pp. 101–2. Ben Snook, 'Who Introduced Charters into England? The Case for Theodore and Hadrian', in *Textus Roffensis: Law, Language, and Libraries in Early Medieval England*, eds Bruce O'Brien and Barbara Bombi, Studies in the Early Middle Ages 30 (Turnhout, 2015), pp. 257–89, has reanalysed the debate, making a strong argument for Theodore as the person responsible for introducing charters in Anglo-Saxon England.

32 Carl Darling Buck argued that Theodore was responsible for the introduction of <y> into Old English orthography; see his 'The Letter Y', *The Manly Anniversary Studies in Language and Literature* (Chicago, 1923), pp. 340–50.

33 See N. R. Ker, *Catalogue of Manuscripts Containing Anglo-Saxon* (Oxford, 1957), pp. xxv–xxvi; Helmut Gneuss, 'The Origin of Standard Old English and Æthelwold's School at Winchester', *ASE* 1 (1972), 63–83, at pp. 81–82; Bernhard Bischoff, *Paläographie des römischen Altertums und des abendländischen Mittelalters* (Berlin, 1986), p. 125; David

Language, script and orthography are usually correlated but, as Michael Benskin has pointed out in a discussion of the spelling variation in S 1008 (KCD 781, A.D. 1045), '[t]he distinction between what counts as O[ld] E[nglish] and what counts as Latin is sometimes very fine'.[34] In charters, even small-scale language-switching is often accompanied by script-switching. This may result in an intricate interplay of language, script, and spelling.[35]

A typical example, S 1405 (A.D. 1058, from Worcester), shall serve to illustrate some of the implications of such switches.[36] The main body of this eleventh-century charter is written in Latin; the script used is Caroline minuscule interspersed with some capital and uncial letter forms to highlight certain elements (such as the name of the donor). The boundary clause, on the other hand, is in Old English and is written in Insular minuscule. The spelling in both sections is in accordance with the language used: the Old English section employs *wyn*, and *eth* or *thorn* for /w/ and /þ/, whereas in the Latin section, the place-name *Sanctae uuigornensis Aecclesiae* is spelled with 'Latinate' <uu>, and Bishop Ealdred's name (which does not include any of the sounds with alternative spellings) is Latinized as *Ealdredus*. At first glance, the distinction between the main charter text and the boundary clause appears clear-cut; yet, a closer look at *uuigornensis* reveals that *g*, *r* and *s* are Insular in form (flat-topped *g*, long *r* and *s*). The place-name NORÐTUN, on the other hand, includes the 'Germanic' character *eth*, though it uses rustic capitals as script.[37] Thus script, spelling, and language are not always pointing in the same direction. However, the use of some vernacular features—be it in script or in spelling—subtly distinguishes Anglo-Saxon place-names from the surrounding Latin text and flags their ultimate linguistic affiliation.

In the witness-list, the relationship between language, script, and spelling is even more complex: the language is Latin, yet Insular *g* is used in the word *ego*

N. Dumville, *English Caroline Script and Monastic History: Studies in Benedictinism, A.D. 950–1030* (Woodbridge, 1993); Crick, 'English Vernacular Script', pp. 180–81.

34 Michael Benskin, 'The Letters <þ> and <y> in Later Middle English, and Some Related Matters', *Journal of the Society of Archivists* 7 (1982), 13–30, at p. 19.

35 For a discussion of the correlation between language and script see Robert Gallagher and Francesca Tinti, 'Latin, Old English and Documentary Practice at Worcester from Wærferth to Oswald', *ASE* 46 (2019 for 2017), 271–325, at p. 286, who attribute some code-switching to multi-stage production of charters.

36 This is London, British Library, Add. Ch. 19801. For an image and an account of the different scripts employed, see Michelle P. Brown, *A Guide to Western Historical Scripts from Antiquity to 1600*, 2nd ed. (Toronto, 1993), pp. 21–22. The charter is also available online at http://www.bl.uk/manuscripts/FullDisplay.aspx?ref=Add_Ch_19801. To date it has been edited only in John Earle, *A Handbook of the Land-Charters and Other Saxon Documents* (Oxford, 1888), pp. 247–48.

37 On <ð> in Latin texts see Benskin, 'The Letters <þ> and <y>', p. 19.

throughout. The line including the name of King Edward continues in Caroline script, and the king's name is spelled *Eaduueard* in capitals and with 'Latinate' double-*u*. The same script is used for the second line naming Bishop *Ealdredus*. All subsequent witnesses, though, are added in Insular script and the names display the vernacular spellings *wyn* <ƿ> or *eth* <ð> (e.g. *Aegelƿig, Ƿulfstan, Norðman*, etc.). So, despite the use of the Latin language throughout the witness-list, its lower part can to some extent be described as more 'vernacular'. However, the distinction implied by these features is ultimately as much social as it is linguistic. Clearly, script and spelling were used to establish a visual hierarchy among the names of the attesters. If Latin is equated with 'more formal', then it makes sense to use the more 'Latin' features for the names of the king and bishop and the less 'Latin' style for the other, less prominent witnesses.

The systematic use of script, spelling and language in the Worcester document is very elaborate. Earlier Anglo-Saxon charters, on the other hand, are not as sophisticated, both because they employ just the Insular script and because orthographic conventions were then less firmly established. Some spelling switches can nevertheless be observed. Interestingly enough, the factors triggering graphemic choices seem to be the same as those in the Worcester charter. First of all, the spelling of personal names differs according to the section of the charter in which the names are found, with the more 'modern' spelling in the witness-list, while the main body of the charter text employs more 'conservative' spellings. In S 65 (*CantCC* 9, A.D. 704), for example, the name of the above-mentioned Bishop Wealdhere, the recipient of the grant, is spelled ***Uualdhario*** with <uu> in the charter text (l. 6) but ***Ƿaldhario*** with initial *wyn* in the witness-list (in middle of the first line of the witness-list; see Figure 4.1). Or, in S 1184 (*Sel* 11, A.D. 780), the form ***Suthsaxorum*** in the main text contrasts with <ð> in various personal names in the witness-list.[38] Some charters also seem to employ consciously archaizing forms in the main text. S 1171 (BCS 81, dated A.D. 685×693) uses the forms *Ho*[*d*]*ilredus* and *Hedil*[*b*]*urge* with unorganic <h-> for *Æðelred* and *Æðelburg*, respectively.[39]

38 This charter includes a confirmation by Offa of Mercia, which also uses <ð> in the name *Suðsax*[*orum*]; however, the confirmation is a later addition (A.D. 787×796), which may well explain the spelling difference. A facsimile of this charter (Chichester, West Sussex Record Office, Cap. I/17/2) is available in *ChLA* 4, no. 236, and in *Facsimiles of Anglo-Saxon Charters*, ed. Simon Keynes, Anglo-Saxon Charters Supplementary Volume 1 (London, 1991), no. 2.

39 The witness-list attests the spelling *Oedelraedus*; however, since this is probably a later addition to the charter, the name forms cannot be directly compared. For a discussion of the absence of i-mutation and other archaizing features in early Kentish charters (for example the form *Hlotharius* in S 8), see John Hines, 'The Writing of English in Kent: Contexts and Influences from the Sixth to the Ninth Century', *NOWELE: North-Western European Language Evolution* 50–51 (2007), 63–92, at pp. 76–79.

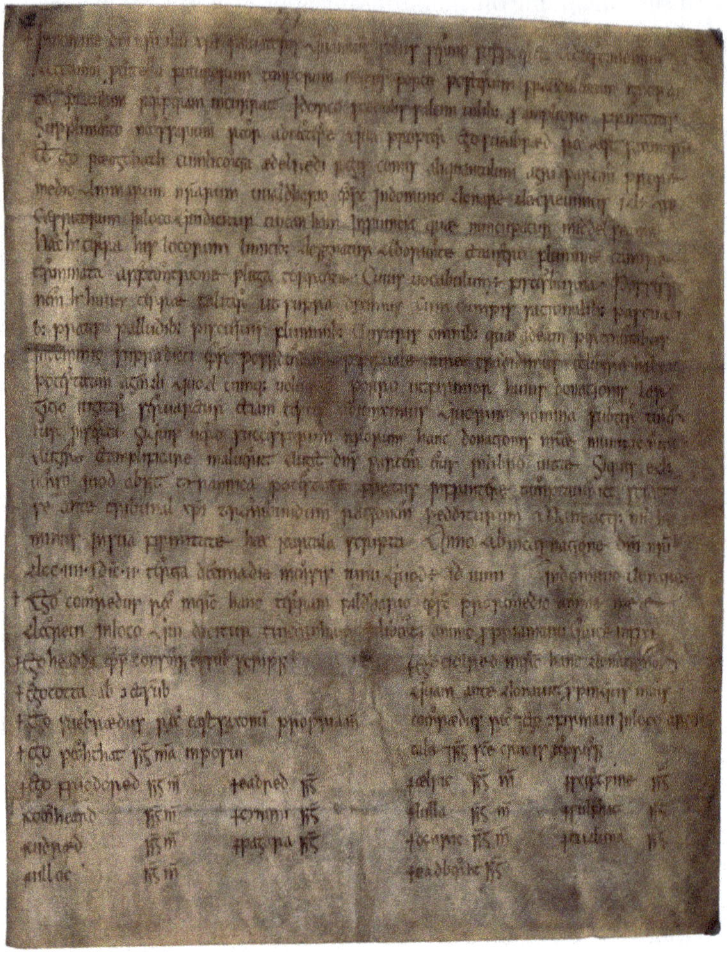

FIGURE 4.1 The face of London, British Library, Cotton Augustus ii.82 (S 65)

Furthermore, and this is again very similar to the eleventh-century Worcester charter, the choice of particular graphs as well as the presence or absence of Latin inflections within the witness-list seems to be triggered by the social status of the referent. People of higher social status are distinguished by a higher degree of Latinate features in the spelling of their names, as, for example, in the witness-list of S 1186a (*CantCC* 16b, A.D. 799x801), in which the digraph <th> in the archbishop's name contrasts with <ð> in the names of other witnesses, i.e. *Aethelheardus … archiepiscopus* but *Haðoberht episcopus, Tiðferð episcopus, Folðred abbas, Aeðelmund* etc.

Case endings also provide very interesting clues, as they establish a connection with the wider linguistic system in which the names are anchored by the scribes.[40] Three types of endings can be distinguished:

- Latinizing case endings, e.g. nominative *-us*, genitive *-i*, dative *-o*, but also consonantal endings, like the genitive form *Offani* for the name of King Offa of Mercia;
- Old English case endings, such as the strong genitive singular forms in *-es* (as in nouns like *stan, stanes*; *wine, wines*) or weak oblique forms in *-an* (as in nouns like *nama, naman*);
- Zero endings, which correspond to Old English nominative forms (but which also occur in genitive positions, for example, in the formula + *signum manus* [*X*] in the witness-lists).

Yet, it is not always possible to identify endings unequivocally as belonging to one or the other language, as Hilmer Ström has pointed out in a discussion of names in Bede's *Ecclesiastical History*: 'In several cases the endings admit of being explained both as Latin and as O[ld] E[nglish], making it very difficult to determine what particular form is meant [...].'[41]

Among the *c.*420 personal names in Anglo-Saxon charters from before the year 800, the last category, zero endings, covers a little more than half of all instances. Latinized forms make up almost 40 per cent of the names, while explicitly Old English inflectional endings are found in *c.*10 per cent. However, the distribution of the different forms is not at all equal across different sections of the charters. In the main body of the charter text, more than two thirds of all personal names have Latin inflectional endings; in the witness-lists, on the other hand, only about one third are Latinized (see Figure 4.2). Explicitly vernacular inflectional endings are rare in both the charter text and the witness-list (the difference in distribution between the sections is not statistically significant).

If we look at the Latinized forms within witness-lists, it is usually the names of the first two witnesses which display such forms, while the others have Old English or zero endings. Two connected factors may be responsible for the different treatment of those names. First, they are normally embedded in a longer Latin context, including the title (*rex*, *episcopus*, *abbas*, etc.) of the

40 On this topic see Fran Colman, *The Grammar of Names in Anglo-Saxon England: The Linguistics and Culture of the Old English Onomasticon* (Oxford, 2014), esp. pp. 73, 114–15, 121, 225, 231.

41 Hilmer Ström, *Old English Personal Names in Bede's History: An Etymological-Phonological Investigation*, Lund Studies in English 8 (Lund, 1939), p. 141.

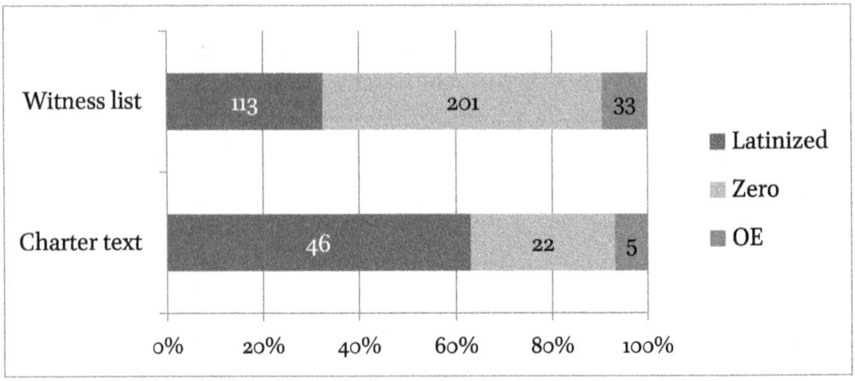

FIGURE 4.2 The Latinization of personal names in Anglo-Saxon charters before A.D. 800: charter text vs. witness-list

referent, while the names of lower witnesses occur within shorter subscription formulae, usually *signum manus* [*X*] or *ego* [*X*] *subscripsi*. Second, the first two witnesses are generally also the highest-ranking witnesses. S 31 (*CantCC* 14, A.D. 748×762) serves to illustrate how endings are typically distributed. In the main text of this Kentish charter, Latin case endings *-us, -o, -i* are consistently used for personal names. In the witness-list, the names of the king and the bishop are also Latinized (incidentally, both are called Eardwulf), but the names of the other, less exalted witnesses use English genitive forms in *-es*:[42]

+ Ego Eardulf**us** rex Cantiae praefatam donationem meam per propriam manum signo sanctae crucis roboraui.
+ Ego Earduulf**us** Hrofensis ecclesiae episcopus . consentiens subscripsi.
+ Signum manus Folcuuin**is**.
+ Signum manus Byrnham**es**.
+ Signum manus . Uuihtbrord**is**.
+ Signum manus Uuealhhun**es**.
+ Signum manus Aethelnoth**es**.

42 The ending *-is* (rather than *-es*) in *-uuinis* and *-brordis* may be attributed to different factors. In the *i*-stem *wini* the vowel may be due to analogy based on nominative forms in *-i* (Eduard Sievers and Karl Brunner, *Altenglische Grammatik*, 3rd ed. (Tübingen, 1965), p. 213; see also Ivar Dahl, *Substantival Inflexion in Early Old English: Vocalic Stems*, Lund Studies in English 7 (Lund, 1938), pp. 160–61). However, the ending *-is* can also be interpreted as a Latin genitive of the consonantal or *i*-declension. Given that Old English names are normally Latinized as *o*- or *a*-stems, it is also possible that the forms should be interpreted as contaminations of Latin genitives in *-i* and Old English genitives in *-es*.

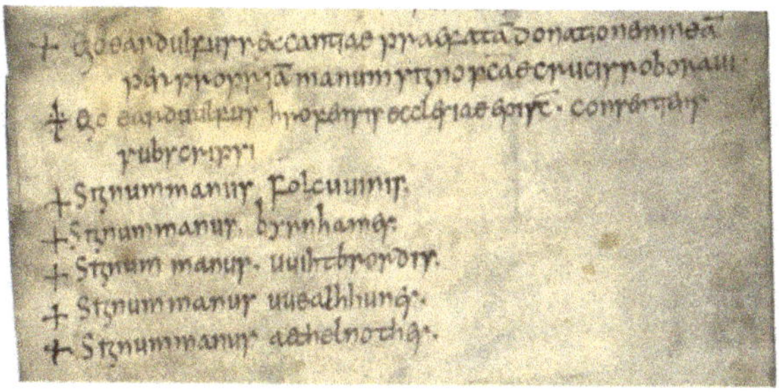

FIGURE 4.3
The witness-list of London, British Library, Stowe Charter 3 (S 31)

In addition to this linguistic distinction, the crosses of king and bishop are decorated with dots, while the ordinary witnesses have simple crosses (see Figure 4.3).

Although the very earliest charters favour Latin endings for most, or many witnesses (as in S 8, S 19, and S 21), the pattern described for S 31 is more widespread. S 264 (BCS 225, A.D. 778), for example, has Latinized *Aðelmodus episcopus* and *Egcbaldus episcopus*, but Old English genitives for other witnesses, i.e. *Scillinges, Aeðelnoðes, Colbrehtes, Aeðelmundes,* [...]*ferdes*. S 35 (*Roch* 9), S 123 (*CantCC* 22), and S 128 (*CantCC* 24)—all three with Archbishop Jænberht of Canterbury consenting to and witnessing the charter—use Latinized forms for the archbishop's name, but mostly zero endings for other names.[43] Meanwhile, S 65 (*CantCC* 9, a reliable slightly later copy of a charter dated 704) spells the names of Kings Coenred of Mercia and Swæfred of Essex with *-us* in the witness-list (i.e. as *Coenredus* and *Suebrædus*), while all the other names have zero ending. S 89 (BCS 154) has *Uuilfridus episcopus* and *Athilbaldo rege*, against other non-Latinized endings, including the name of King *Aetdilbalt* in the nominative.

When considering the development of the use of Old English in charters, it is also clear that personal names and place-names are not treated in the same way. It is often the case that we find more modern—or 'vernacular'— spellings in place-names. S 8 (*CantCC* 2, A.D. 679), for example, has *Uuestan.ae* (i.e. the 'western meadow') with <uu> against single <u> for /w/ in personal names, or S 114 (BCS 230, A.D. 779) uses *wyn* in the place-name *Ƿinesburg*, but <uu> elsewhere. Old English inflectional endings also occur much more frequently in place-names. Many Anglo-Saxon place-names consist of a personal name in the genitive and a toponymic appellative, e.g. *Godmundes leah* (S 114) 'Godmund's meadow'. While Old English genitive endings, in particular strong endings in *-es*, are quite rare among Old English personal names, these

43 The name of King Offa, appearing in the nominative case in S 123 and 128, is ambiguous: like all *n*-stems, it is inflected in Latin according to the pattern *-a, -anis*. On Old English *n*-stems see, for example, Alistair Campbell, *Old English Grammar* (Oxford, 1959), § 615.

same endings, as well as weak genitives in *-an*, are commonly used in place-names of the type just described. Examples are *Pleghelmes tun*, *Meguines paed* (S 19, *CantCC* 5; with Latin genitives or blank forms elsewhere), *Tuican hom*, *Tuiccanham*, *Fiscesburna* (S 65, *CantCC* 9), *Haganan treae* (S 123, *CantCC* 22), *Seleberhtes cert* (S 155, *CantCC* 29; with mostly Latinized endings for personal names within the same charter), *Biscopes uuic* (S 24, *CantCC* 11), *Godmundes leah*, *Þinesburg* (S 114, BCS 230; generally Latinized endings for personal names), *Cymenes denn* etc., *Peadan stigele* etc. (S 264, BCS 225), *Uuidmundesfelt* etc. (S 1171, BCS 81). However, the more vernacular treatment seems to apply only to local place-names. Supra-regional names, such as the demonym *Cantuarii*, *-orum*, 'the inhabitants of Kent' (and, by extension, the region in which they live), are spelled with the single graphs typical of the very earliest phase of vernacular writing in the late seventh century—despite the fact that this name not only has a Germanic etymology, but is also morphologically transparent.[44] Given their consistent rendering, they should probably be considered as Old English loanwords in Latin.

The Orthography of Early St Gall Charters

In comparison with contemporary Anglo-Saxon charters, the St Gall charters, deriving from a single archive, constitute a relatively homogenous set. Nevertheless, there is a considerable amount of spelling variation in the representation of Old High German names. This may be due to the fact that early St Gall charters are generally characterized by a certain 'individuality and variability'.[45] Yet, as I mentioned earlier, variability is typical of Old High German orthography throughout the period. Old High German spelling does not converge towards a more uniform written language as happens in Old English. Rather, the scripting of Old High German consists of isolated efforts at different times and places. The features that are common to all Old High German writing are the result of a shared background and similar circumstances of scribes rather than of a sustained development of Old High German orthography. All scribes are first of all writers of Latin and, when they attempt to put the vernacular language into writing, they make similar use of

44 The second element is OE *wara/-u* 'inhabitant', which is widely attested in Old English and which forms various compounds, such as *ceaster-wara* 'townspeople' or *eorþ-waru* 'earth-dwellers' (see *Dictionary of Old English: A to I Online*, s.vv., available at https://tapor.library.utoronto.ca/doe/). For a discussion of *-varii* names cf. Ludwig Rübekeil, *Diachrone Studien zur Kontaktzone zwischen Kelten und Germanen* (Vienna, 2002), pp. 304–411.

45 Zeller, 'Urkunden und Urkundenschreiber', p. 173.

the options provided by the Latin alphabet and Latin orthography. This leads to orthographic parallels in Old High German writing through a kind of 'invisible hand' process. Similar spellings are not however necessarily the result of a shared development. This becomes apparent from the fact that the specific rules with which certain graphs are applied differ from text to text: scribes employ different letter combinations, they distinguish different sound positions, and their graphemic systems are not equally rigorous.[46]

The sounds that presented challenges to the scribes were not quite the same ones as in Anglo-Saxon England since Old English and Old High German diverged in their phonological development. In Old High German a number of spelling difficulties were caused by the Second Consonant Shift, which led to the creation of new affricates and fricatives, most notably /k(h), h(h)/ and /tz, z(z)/. This sound change made the guttural and the dental series particularly 'crowded' and thus difficult to represent in writing. For the St Gall material, the sound change referred to as *Medienverschiebung* (i.e. devoicing of the voiced stops /b d g/ > /p t k/) resulted in additional orthographic insecurity. On the other hand, some spellings, like the use of <uu> for /w/ and of <z> for /tz, z(z)/ appear to be a given already at the beginning of the period.[47] Based on digraphs used for the representation of Germanic names in Merovingian Francia, Old High German scribes also experimented with the use of <h> as a diacritic, which resulted in the creation of numerous graphs like <gh>, <dh>, <hc>, or even trigraphs like <hch> (e.g. *Prampa**hch***, W 105, = *ChLA* 2, no. 110).[48] By contrast, Anglo-Saxon scribes appear to have been less eager to use letter combinations that are not found in Latin orthography. Old High German scribes also had to contend with developments in early Romance, which affected the letter-sound correlation of the Latin alphabet: <c> and <g>, for example, could no longer be used to represent /k/ and /g/ before palatal vowels due to Romance palatalization and assibilation of those sounds in this context, whereas it seems that Anglo-Saxons retained the 'classical' pronunciation of Latin until fairly late. To represent Old High German, non-assibilated /k/,

46 For more details on Old High German orthography, see Seiler, *The Scripting of the Germanic Languages*, pp. 210–15.

47 Cf. Friedrich Wilkens, *Zum hochalemannischen Konsonantismus der althochdeutschen Zeit. Beiträge zur Lautlehre und Orthographie des ältesten Hochalemannischen, auf Grundlage der deutschen Eigennamen in den Sanct Galler Urkunden (bis zum Jahre 825)* (Leipzig, 1891), p. vii. The digraph <uu> is clearly a Merovingian spelling (see above); the use of <z> is more difficult to explain but is probably connected to rare uses of <z> in medieval Latin and possibly motivated by descriptions of the sound value of <z> by Latin grammarians (cf. Seiler, *The Scripting of the Germanic Languages*, pp. 196–97).

48 On <ch> and <gh> in West Frankish names from Merovingian sources see Wells, 'An Orthographic Approach', pp. 120–42.

scribes resorted to the letter <k>, which was adopted into vernacular orthography in a slow process that never replaced <c> completely. In the early material, <ch> is one of the alternative solutions for representing the sound /k/ when it occurs before palatal vowels. This digraph, as well as <k> and some other graphs, is used in the names contained in charters from St Gall.

Despite the overall heterogeneous appearance of Old High German orthography, it is important to note that individual scribes were often highly consistent in the use of their spelling solutions. This is the case, for instance, in the three larger eighth-century vernacular sources, the *Vocabularius sancti Galli*, the *Abrogans* glossary, and the Old High German translation of Isidore of Seville's *De fide catholica*.[49] The high degree of consistency displayed by these texts suggests that their scribes made conscious efforts to represent their vernacular languages. Divergent orthographic practices of different scribes account for some spelling variation in the St Gall charter material. Germanic */þ/ (> German /d/), for example, is represented by the graphs <th>, <dh>, <d>, <t>, but not all of them are used by all scribes.[50] Of the two scribes whose charters I have analysed in detail, Waldo employed mainly <d> and <th> alongside <t>, while Mauvo favoured <dh>, as well as <d>. For Germanic */g/ (> Upper German /k/), both scribes wrote <g> or <c>, but only Waldo used the digraph <gh>.[51] Mauvo clearly preferred <g> to represent this sound, but also employed <k> and <c> fairly frequently. The function of both <gh> (Waldo) and <k> (Mauvo) is most likely to counteract mispronunciation due to Romance assibilation: the two graphs are used before palatal vowels as against <g, c> before velar vowels.

Similar to the graphemic variation found in the Anglo-Saxon charters, different spellings in the St Gall material occur in distinct sections of the documents. However, in the St Gall charters it is not so much a difference between the dispositive section and the witness-list as it is between the entire charter and the surviving original drafts (*Vorakte*). Stefan Sonderegger, in a seminal study of the language of the St Gall charter drafts, has shown that the name forms transmitted in the drafts are often phonologically more advanced than the forms in the charters themselves, for example, in the representation of

49 See Seiler, *The Scripting of the Germanic Languages*, pp. 222–28.

50 For more details see Rudolf Henning, *Über die Sanctgallischen Sprachdenkmäler bis zum Tode Karls des Grossen* (Strasbourg, 1874), pp. 127–28; Wilkens, *Zum hochalemannischen Konsonantismus*, §§ 119–31.

51 For details on spellings for Germanic */g/ in the St Gall charters see Henning, *Sprachdenkmäler*, pp. 136–41; Wilkens, *Zum hochalemannischen Konsonantismus*, §§ 101–18 and §§ 26–29 (on Mauvo). On Waldo see note 7 above and Bernhard Zeller (this volume).

Medienverschiebung or of primary umlaut (/a/ > /e/).[52] The following examples illustrate the switch from <t> to <d> in the two charters by Mauvo which preserve a *Vorakt* (VA):

> *Ermenolt* (VA) vs. *Ermenoldi* (W 143, = *ChLA* 2, no. 138)
> *Erchenhart* (VA) vs. *Erchanhardi* (W 143, = *ChLA* 2, no. 138)
> *Isanhart* (VA) vs. *Isanhardi* (W 153, = *ChLA* 2, no. 135; see Figure 4.4)

This peculiar pattern implies that the scribes regularly backtracked on the sound change /d/ > /t/ when writing the final copy of the charter and chose to employ an archaizing form of the names. There are altogether *c.*30 instances of reversed *Medienverschiebung* from the drafts to the final copies of the charters dating to the eighth century (and many more from the ninth),[53] but only some six instances in which the change goes in the opposite direction (i.e. draft form without *Medienverschiebung* / charter form with *Medienverschiebung*).[54] Sonderegger describes the phonologically more advanced forms of the charter drafts as transmitting 'real, spoken Old High German, which was directly heard when written down' and which 'differs considerably from the strongly Latinized and polished form of the final copy of the charters'.[55] In other words, the scribes adhered to different norms of scripting in the charter drafts and the charter proper. The forms in the drafts more closely represent the spoken language of the scribes, or possibly their informants, while the charter forms are

---

52 Stefan Sonderegger, 'Das Althochdeutsche der Vorakte der älteren St Galler Urkunden. Ein Beitrag zum Problem der Urkundensprache in althochdeutscher Zeit', *Zeitschrift für Mundartforschung* 28 (1961), 251–86.

53 Sonderegger provides a tabular overview of those cases ('Das Althochdeutsche der Vorakte', pp. 275–78); the following instances should be added to the list (with VA forms listed first): *Crimperto—Crinberto* (W 70, = *ChLA* 1, no. 81), *Nantkeri—Nandgeri* (W102, = *ChLA* 2, no. 113), *Cozperto—Gausberto* (W 114, = *ChLA* 2, no. 116); included in Sonderegger's table, but VA form misspelled as *Gozperto*), *Uualdperto—Uualdberto* (W 116, = *ChLA* 2, no. 118), *Ratolt—Ratoldi, Uuolfhart—Uuolfhardi* (W 120, = *ChLA* 2, no. 122), *Isanhart—Isanhardi* (W 153, = *ChLA* 2, no. 135).

54 The six instances are (again VA forms listed first): *Roberti—Rodperti* (W 102, = *ChLA* 2, no. 113), *Cosperdi—Cozberto, Amalperd—Amalberto, Erinperd—Erinperto* (W 124, = *ChLA* 2, no. 109), *Heribrando—Hariprando, Ercanbaldo—Ercanpoldo* (W 144, = *ChLA* 2, no. 139).

55 My translation of the German original: 'echtes, gesprochenes, bei der Aufzeichnung unmittelbar gehörtes Althochdeutsch [...] das von der in der Urkundenreinschrift geglätteten und oft stark latinisierten Sprachform ganz erheblich abweicht' (Sonderegger, 'Das Althochdeutsche der Vorakte', p. 252). See also Stefan Sonderegger, 'Reflexe gesprochener Sprache im Althochdeutschen', in *Sprachgeschichte*, eds Besch et al., pp. 1231–40, at 1235.

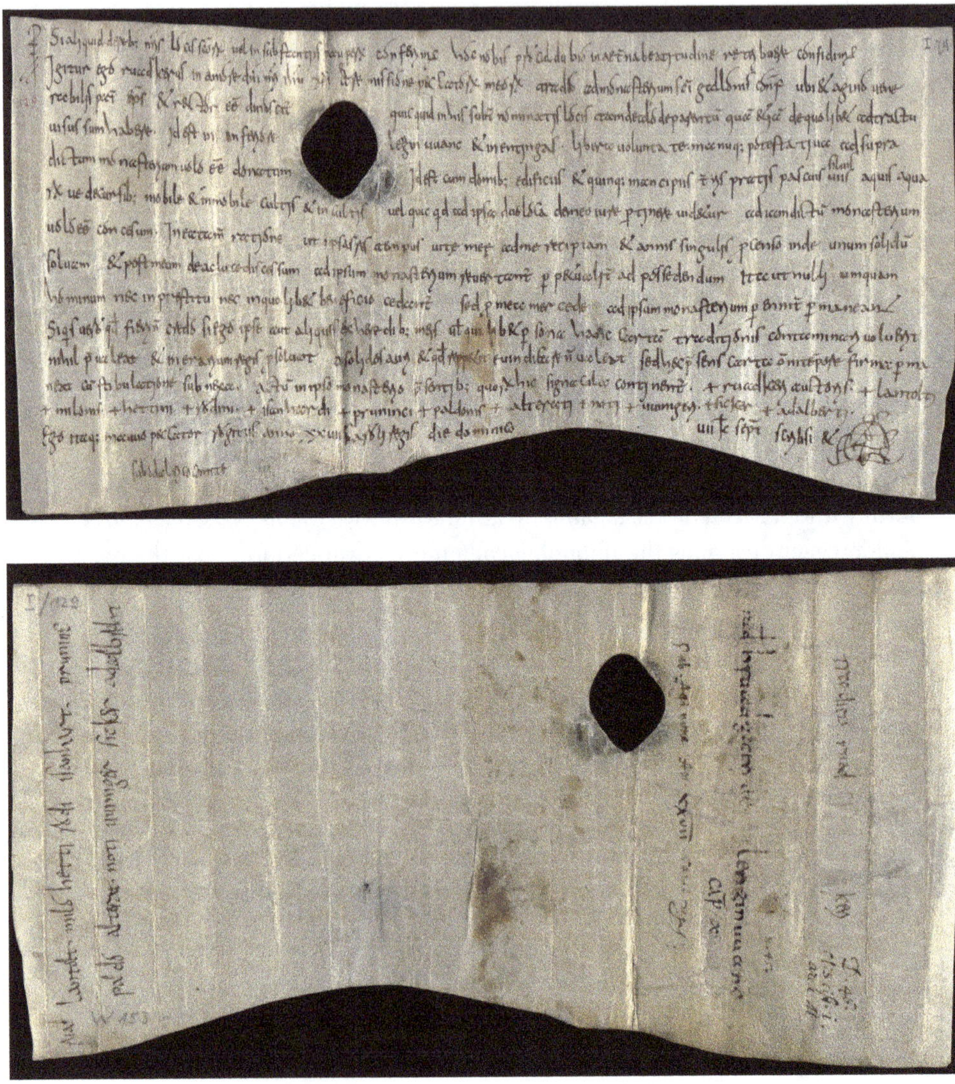

FIGURE 4.4 The face and dorse of St Gall, Stiftsarchiv I 129 (= W 153 and *Vorakt*; by Mauvo)

influenced by accepted orthographic conventions, following Frankish spelling practice to represent German sounds and Latinized inflections.

That matters are not always straightforward becomes apparent from forms like *Amalperd* (VA) and the corresponding *Amalberto* (witness-list, W 124, = *ChLA* 2, no. 109), in which *p* is reversed to *b*, but *d* shifted to *t*. The draft spelling is clearly not an exact representation of Upper German phonology, since *-pert* would be the expected form for the second element. Such mixed forms occur very frequently in the charter material. They imply that the draft forms are not, as it were, phonetic transcriptions but less norm-driven written representations which tolerate a degree of vagueness.[56] The distinction may be due to the different contexts in which the respective forms were written down—the drafts presumably represent the notes that a scribe took during the transaction, while the charter was copied out in the scriptorium. More importantly, the status of the text and its intended audience also play a role. In the draft the scribe was essentially writing to himself, and the *Vorakt* had fulfilled its function once the scribe had completed the final charter. The charter, on the other hand, is an official document preserving the deed and its concomitant details for posterity.

While many of the changes from draft to charter have phonological implications, others are only—or mainly—orthographic in nature. These changes seem to be concerned with achieving a more 'correct' written representation of the same sound. Yet, what counted as an appropriate written form seems to have been highly individual. Apart from adding Latin case endings (see below), a frequent change consists in replacing single consonant graphs with digraphs.[57] One example of this change is found in Waldo's charters. In the charters, he clearly preferred <gh> as a representation of /g/ before palatal vowels, rather than <g>; in the drafts, on the other hand, he seems to have been perfectly happy to employ <g>. The following instances are cases in which Waldo used <g> in the *Vorakt* or the dorsal note (i.e. the archival mark providing a brief summary of the transaction), but employed <gh> in the charter:[58]

> *agn* (VA) vs. *aghine* (witness-list, W 63, = *ChLA* 1, no. 76; see Figure 4.5)
> *sigihari* (dorsal note) vs. *sighiharius* (dispositive section), *sighiheri* (witness-list, W 63, = *ChLA* 1, no. 76)
> *sigimunt* (VA) vs. *sighimundum* (dispositive section, W 83, = *ChLA* 1, no. 89)

---

56 Abbreviated name forms are also tolerated in the charter drafts, e.g. *marc.* for *marcus* (W 17, = *ChLA* 1, no. 50), *agn* for *aghine*, *deotgr* for *theotgaeri*, *t* for *teotberti*, *uualdbr* for *uualdberti* (W 63, = *ChLA* 1, no. 76), *ruad* for *ruadingo* (W 82, = *ChLA* 2, no. 88), etc.

57 Other changes are, for example, the addition of inorganic <h> (e.g. *hisinberto, hamulberto, hanshelmmi, himmane, hiutone*) or the alternation of different forms of the same name element, such as *coz/gaus* or *preht/berht* (very common in Mauvo's charters). The first two features are probably owed to Raetian scribes; cf. Stefan Sonderegger, 'Althochdeutsche Namen in den rätischen Privaturkunden von St Gallen vor 800', in *Festschrift für Paul Zinsli*, eds Maria Bindschedler, Rudolf Hotzenköcherle, and Werner Kohlschmidt (Bern, 1971), pp. 145–60; and Bernhard Zeller (this volume).

58 Another example is Waldo's use of <hc> for the fricative out of Germanic */k/, which occurs more often in the charter forms than in the drafts. For more details on Waldo's digraphs see Annina Seiler, 'Die Urkunden des Schreibers Waldo: eine graphematische Analyse', *Sprachwissenschaft* 38 (2013), pp. 123–46. On dorsal notes see Staerkle, *Die Rückvermerke*.

More examples based on all eighth-century charters with preserved drafts are provided in Table 4.1 below. The spelling changes include <u> to <uu>, <d> or <t> to <th>, <g> to <gh>, <c> and <h> to <ch> or <hc> as well as some others.

There are very few instances in which the change operates in the other direction, i.e. where digraphs are replaced by simpler spellings, for example in *palduuuino* (VA) vs. *baldoino* (witness-list) or *uuitucauuuo* (VA) vs. *uuidogaugio* (witness-list); both examples come from the same charter (W 114, = *ChLA* 2,

TABLE 4.1 The alternation of single graphs and digraphs in consonant spellings of eighth-century St Gall charters and charter drafts

Wartmann 1 nos	Date / scribe (based on ChLA II)	Charter draft	Charter
17	s. viii^{med} Marcus	*stefani, ualgear, uuahiscinga*	*stephanis, uualgaero, uualahischinga*
63	775 Waldo	*agn* VA, *sigihari* ND	*aghine, sighiharius, sighiheri*
77	775 Waldo	*esgibach* ND	*esghibach*
83	778 Waldo	*sigimunt*	*sighimundum*
84	778 Waldo	*fiscbah, baturih*	*fiscbahc, baturihc*
95	781/82 Waldo	*emdrudis*	*emthrudis* (*emdrudis* WL)
96	781/82 Waldo	*deotgr*	*theotgaeri*
96	781/82 Waldo	*otger* VA, ND	*otgaer*[a]
102	785 Berahtcoz	*danho*	*danchoni*
105	786 Folcram	*ricardo*	*rihcardo*
114	787 Theoderam	*deotuni*	*theutone*
114	787 Theoderam	*adalger*	*adalghero*
116	788 Engilbert	*heripret*	*heripreth*
120	789 Waringis	*uuolfgeri*	*uuolfgaeri*
122	789 Salomon	*mahhelm*	*mahcelm*
124	790 Ratinh	*uuitigauuo ecgichard*	*uuitigauuuo ecchiardo*
145	797 Rihbert	*sigaperti*	*sichiperti*
147	797 Bertilo	*trodberti*	*thrudberti*
161	800 Arnolt	*herhanpret*	*erhcanpret*

a The use of the digraph <ae> is included among the consonant graphs because it is used only after <g> so that this character is not placed before a front vowel; its function is the same as that of <gh>, i.e. to counteract Romance assibilation.

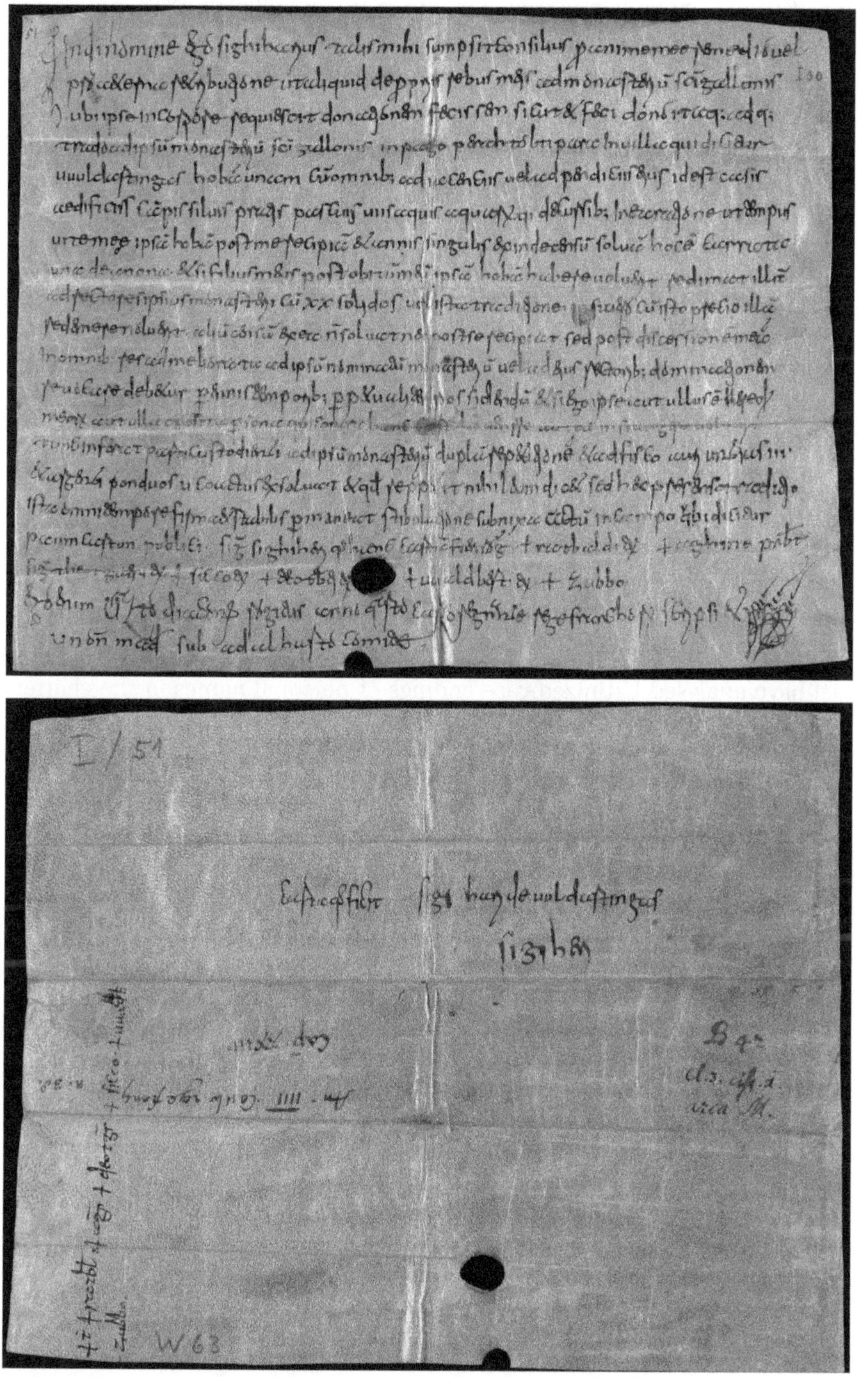

FIGURE 4.5 The face and dorse of St Gall, Stiftsarchiv I 51 (= W 63 and *Vorakt*; by Waldo)

no. 116) and use graphemic strategies which are modelled on West Frankish or Romance orthographic models.[59]

The replacement of single graphs by digraphs is often accompanied by the addition of Latin case endings—as we can see from some of the examples in Table 4.1 above. Sonderegger provides overall counts for the Latinization of personal names in the 104 drafts and corresponding charters produced between 750 and 907.[60] From his figures, we can deduce that in a large majority of instances (*c.*60 per cent) both drafts and charters have Old High German (i.e. non-Latinized) forms. For slightly more than ten per cent of all names, drafts and charters display Latin case endings. About 25 per cent of charter forms are Latinized against non-Latinized names in the drafts. And there are a handful of instances (*c.*2 per cent) in which charter forms are not Latinized, but the draft forms are. Sonderegger's figures show that, while most names are used in their Old High German form, there is a very clear tendency towards Latinization from the drafts to the charters. His study does not offer any details about the diachronic distribution of forms; Wilkens, however, states that completely Latinized forms (like *Audemaro* for *Otmar*, *Teutegaeri* for *Theotger*) appear predominantly in the earliest period, while Latin endings are common throughout.[61]

I have analysed Latinized case endings of personal names in the charters written by Waldo and Mauvo, distinguishing not only between draft and charter, but also looking at the differences between the main text of the charter (dispositive section and dating clause) and the witness-list. In addition, I have taken into account the forms from dorsal notes, if written by Waldo or Mauvo. The distribution of Latinized endings is visualized in Figure 4.6 below. Name forms are categorized as 'Latinized', 'ambiguous', and 'non-Latinized'. The 'ambiguous' category includes nominatives of *n*-stems ending in *-o* (e.g. *Uualdo, Mauuo, Hato*) and of short names in *-i* (e.g. *Sighi, Tuni*). In contrast to the Anglo-Saxon charters, there are no explicitly Old High German case endings in personal names.

The overall distribution pattern is fairly similar for the two scribes: in line with Sonderegger's findings, both scribes use Latin endings most frequently in

59 <oino> is the typical West Frankish rendering of Old High German *wini* 'friend' used as a second element in names; <gaug-> is the conventional (Romance) spelling for all place-names ending in Old High German *gewi* 'district, area' (cf. Wilkens, *Zum hochalemannischen Konsonantismus*, p. 19).

60 Sonderegger, 'Das Althochdeutsche der Vorakte', p. 255.

61 Wilkens, *Zum hochalemannischen Konsonantismus*, p. 18.

the main texts of charters and non-Latinized forms most often in the charter drafts. The forms in the witness-lists are somewhere in-between.[62] Concerning dorsal notes, the figures suggest that the proportion of Latinized forms is higher there than in the witness-lists, but not as high as in the charter text; however, as the overall number of names attested in dorsal notes is low, this observation should be taken with caution.

Waldo clearly displays a stronger tendency towards using Latinized forms. In the dispositive sections of his charters, only six names in total are not Latinized; in the drafts about a quarter of all forms have unambiguously Latinized endings. Mauvo's figure for Latinized forms in the main charter text is between 10–20 per cent lower than Waldo's—depending on how the ambiguous endings are taken into account. In his two charter drafts, he uses no clearly Latinized endings at all. In contrast, in the witness-list Mauvo's percentage of Latinized forms is slightly higher than Waldo's. In some of Waldo's charters, the name of the grantor is more formally styled in the dispositive section than in the witness-list. Examples are: *Emthrudis*—*Emdrudis* (W 76, = *ChLA* 1, no. 75), *Otgaer*—*Otger* (W 96, = *ChLA* 1, no. 97), *Sighiharius*—*Sighiheri* (W 63, = *ChLA* 1, no. 76), *Hrambertus*—*Hrambert* (W 84, = *ChLA* 1, no. 86), *Cundhohus*—*Cundhoh* (W 74). Mauvo, on the other hand, sometimes uses Latin endings for the names of the grantors/first witness in the witness-list (W 132, = *ChLA* 2, no. 127; W 133, = *ChLA* 2, no. 128; and W 146, = *ChLA* 2, no. 141) or displays a gradual transition from Latinized endings to non-Latinized ones as the witness-list grows in length (W 135, = *ChLA* 2, no. 132).

As Friedrich Wilkens already pointed out, Latinized forms are particularly frequent among the names of people of higher status, such as Abbot Grimald, Count Odalric, or Charlemagne, who are usually styled *Grimaldus*, *Odalricus*,

62 The problems related to the Latinization of Germanic personal names is addressed in a ninth-century formulary from St Gall, which prescribes genitive for the name of the abbot but advises using the nominative case for other witnesses 'when the oblique cases are too short in nature or do not fit a Latin declension class': 'Scribe nomina eorum per nominativum casum, quia obliqui aut nimium ex sua proprietate decidunt aut Latine declinationi non congruent' (*Formulae Merowingici et Karolini Aevi*, ed. Karl Zeumer, MGH Leges Formulae Merowingici et Karolini aevi 1 (Hanover, 1886), p. 404, no. 11, ll. 22–24). While the passage does not explicitly say so, the discussion implies that the use of nominative case entails zero endings as in the mono-thematic names *Hato* and *Sighi* cited above. On the St Gall formulary see Alice Rio, *Legal Practice and the Written Word in the Early Middle Ages: Frankish Formulae, c. 500–1000*, Cambridge Studies in Medieval Life and Thought, Fourth Series, 75 (Cambridge, 2009), pp. 152–58.

a. Charters of Waldo

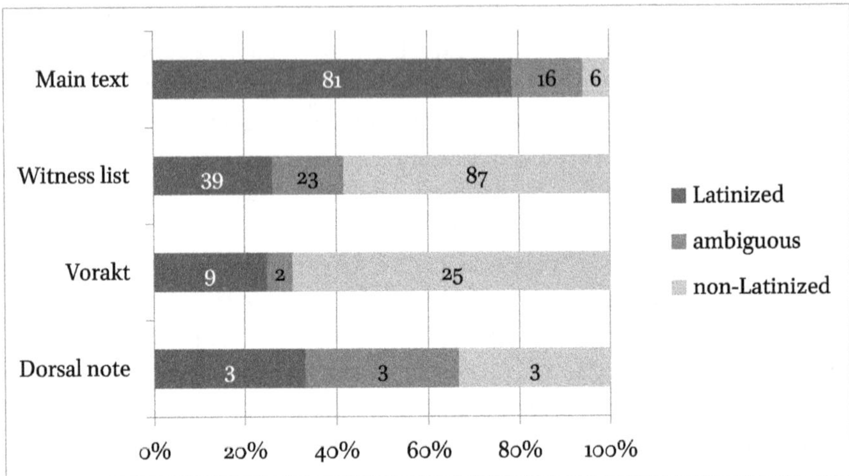

b. Charters of Mauvo

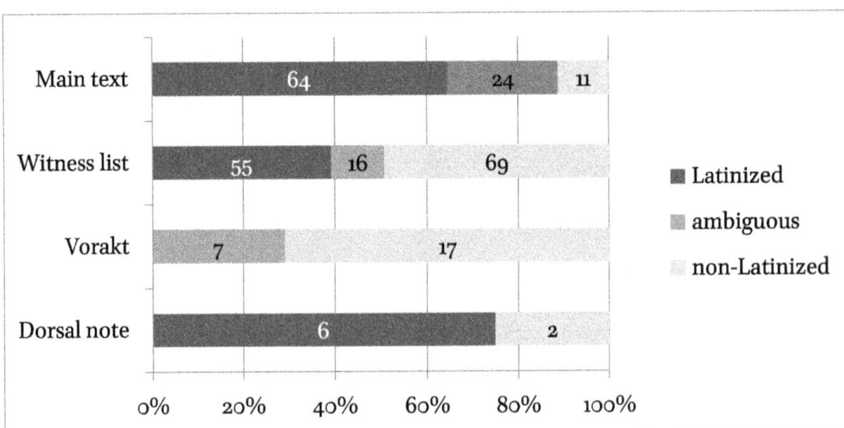

FIGURE 4.6 Latinized vs. non-Latinized endings of personal names in the charters of Waldo and Mauvo

Carolus, etc.[63] It is difficult to confirm or refute this statement on the basis of the charters of Waldo and Mauvo since these notable people are mentioned mostly in the dispositive section or the dating clause, in which Latinized forms dominate anyway.

A phenomenon that has been observed in the Anglo-Saxon charters is also attested in the early St Gall material, namely that place-names are treated in

63 Wilkens, *Zum hochalemannischen Konsonantismus*, pp. 18–19.

a more 'vernacular' way than personal names. This is most notable in the use of Old High German genitive endings *-es* (strong declension) or *-in* (weak declension) in place-names of the type 'X's place / houses / field', as is the case for *Uurmheresuilari* (W 77, = *ChLA* 1, no. 78), *Puzinesuillare* (W 132, = *ChLA* 2, no. 127), *Zillinhusir, Maginhusir*,[64] *Hesilinuanc* (W 135, = *ChLA* 2, no. 132). On the other hand, just a few place-names are Latinized, for example, *Amulpertiuuilari* (W 103, = *ChLA* 1, no. 108, VA and charter). This contrasts strongly with the treatment of personal names; as has been mentioned, no unambiguously Old High German case endings are attested among the personal names in Waldo's and Mauvo's charters. Though place-names, on the whole, are less frequently Latinized, there is again a difference between the draft forms and the charter forms, with more vernacular features being attested in the drafts—similar to what has been observed for personal names.[65]

Conclusions

A comparison of the spelling variation found in the charter material from Anglo-Saxon England and the abbey of St Gall from before 800 yields the following results: first of all, the degree of variability found in both sets of charters is relatively high. It is particularly striking that variants can be found within charters written by the same scribes and, moreover, within a single document. This is in marked contrast with other sources that survive in contemporary manuscripts, whose spelling systems are sometimes highly idiosyncratic but usually very consistent. In typological terms, the graphs found in the charter material fall into three groups. There are single graphs, which work on the principle of sound approximation; then there are digraphs, in which one character functions like a diacritic; and finally, there are the specialized Old English graphs *eth* <ð> and *wyn* <ƿ>, as well as the typically Old High German letters <z> and <k>. The variation observed consists of alternating graphs from different typological stages used in the spellings of the same names or sounds. In one way, the synchronic spelling variation attested in the charters reflects the diachronic development of Old English and Old High German orthography.

64 The plural ending of the second element *-husir* (sg. *hus* 'house'), analogically adopted from the *s*-stems, is also Old High German. On the declension class, see Wilhelm Braune and Ingo Reiffenstein, *Althochdeutsche Grammatik I: Laut- und Formenlehre*, 15th ed. (Tübingen, 2004), § 197.

65 See also Sonderegger, 'Das Althochdeutsche der Vorakte', pp. 262–64.

Spelling variants in the charters are distributed according to very specific patterns, which suggests that different spellings fulfil specific functions. Graphemic variation in non-standardized writing systems is often functional in unexpected ways. Or, as Jürgen Macha puts it, spellings become 'meaningful in more ways than just the dimension of "correct"-"incorrect"', as is the case in modern fully standardized orthographies, which usually allow for only one single way to represent a certain word.[66] Macha distinguishes culturally marked and culturally unmarked graphs, and introduces the concept of 'programmatic spellings' to describe those graphs that demonstrate a writer's connection with a certain social group. In Macha's material from seventeenth-century Germany, some graphs may, for example, highlight a writer's sympathies for the Catholic south. A similar—modern—example of programmatic graphs is discussed by Mark Sebba. He describes how the letter <k> is deployed in the Basque Country as an 'icon for "otherness" from Spanish':

> The points of difference between the two orthographies can be appropriated to iconize the two languages in a binary opposition. Jacqueline Urla shows how this enables Basques who are involved in radical youth culture to engage in a practice of 'parodic spellings of Spanish words' [...] where Spanish words are made to 'look like' Basque through the subversive use of <k> where the conventional Spanish spelling would use <c> or <qu>.[67]

The examples provided by Jaqueline Urla for this practice are *ke txorrada* for *que chorrada*, *la martxa* for *la marcha*, or *rok radikal basko*;[68] the words themselves are Spanish, but they appear to be Basque since they follow the graphemic conventions of that language rather than Spanish.

---

66 My translation of the German original: 'Dem Fehlen orthographischer Einheitlichkeit [...] entspricht andererseits der Effekt, daß Schreibvarianten für weitaus mehr Belange Aussagekraft besitzen bzw. erlangen können als nur für die Dimension "richtig"-"falsch".' Jürgen Macha, 'Schreibvariationen und ihr regional-kultureller Hintergrund: Rheinland und Westfalen im 17. Jahrhundert', in *Regionale Sprachgeschichte*, eds Walter Besch and Hans Joachim Solms, Zeitschrift für deutsche Philologie 117, Sonderheft (Berlin, 1998), pp. 50–66, at 51–52, 56–57.

67 Mark Sebba, 'Orthography as Social Action: Scripts, Spelling, Identity and Power', in *Orthography as Social Action: Scripts, Spelling, Identity and Power*, eds Alexandra Jaffe, Jannis Androutsopoulos, Mark Sebba, and Sally Johnson (Berlin, 2012), pp. 1–19, at 7–8.

68 Jacqueline Urla, 'Outlaw Language: Creating Alternative Public Spheres in Basque Free Radio', *Pragmatics* 5.2 (1995), 245–61, at p. 256.

This situation can be compared, *mutatis mutandis*, with what happens in the early Anglo-Saxon and St Gall charters. The digraphs are clearly culturally marked spellings in the sense that they imply (Merovingian) Latinity while those graphs that are only—or mainly—used for Old English or Old High German have vernacular connotations. By using Latinate spellings, vernacular names in the charters are associated with Latin. On the other hand, if typically vernacular graphs are employed, the Old English or Old High German nature of the names is foregrounded. Thus, spelling can be used to either highlight or downplay the vernacular character of the names. Incidentally, as in Basque, the letter <k> is one of the distinctive elements of Old High German orthography—though it is by no means 'subversive'.

That spellings are used to differentiate intentionally Latin items from intentionally vernacular ones is supported by the fact that this kind of spelling variation correlates with the presence or absence of Latin case endings. While names fall outside the normal system of languages, inflectional endings anchor an item within a particular linguistic system. In the Anglo-Saxon material, there often is a distinction between the names in the dispositive section and those in the witness-list: the former are treated as Latin items, while the latter are characterized by Old English features, both in terms of spelling and inflectional morphology. This kind of variation separates different sections of the charters. At the same time, it can signal social distinction when strongly Latinized forms highlight the names of secular or ecclesiastical dignitaries. This also applies to the witness-lists, in which the first two witnesses are often more formally styled with Latin case endings and Latinate orthography, whereas other names display zero endings. Zero endings correspond to Old English nominative forms but they are often found in positions in which other cases (usually genitive in the witness-list) would be expected. A handful of witness-lists in the early Anglo-Saxon charters introduce Old English genitive endings in the formula *Signum manus* [*X*] for the 'lower' names. This use is particularly striking since, despite the Latin context, these names are identified as Old English. On the other hand, Old English case endings regularly occur in place-names, which are often genitive compounds, again in combination with more 'vernacular' orthographic features. Considering the implications of the distribution of Latinate and vernacular features, I would like to argue that names that are marked as vernacular in their spelling represent instances of incipient code-switching, despite the fact that we are only dealing with proper nouns. In a study on code-switching in the leases of Oswald of Worcester, Herbert Schendl does not consider bare names as code-switching, unless they are part of an Old

English prepositional phrase.[69] In my view, the visual evidence tells a different story: those names for which specifically Old English spellings are used are clearly highlighted as vernacular forms and thus are distinguished from the names which, by contrast, are treated as Latin items. In a way, spelling takes the place of the 'phonological and phonetic clues' associated with code-switching in spoken language.[70]

In the Old High German material, patterns within charters are more difficult to recognize. There are some similarities to the Anglo-Saxon material, in particular with respect to the distribution of Latinized and zero endings in order both to distinguish different sections of the charters and to highlight the names of more important people (e.g. the grantor or the other notables mentioned). However, the most significant distinction is the one between the surviving drafts and the charters, rather than between different sections within the charters. As Sonderegger demonstrated, the charter drafts represent a language that is phonologically closer to the Upper German dialect that must have been spoken in St Gall at the time, while the name forms in the charters display archaizing features. Furthermore, there are purely orthographic differences; one change is the introduction of digraph spellings in the charter forms as opposed to single graphs in the corresponding names in the drafts. This suggests that the scribes used different registers for the drafts and for the charters: the names in all sections of the charters are treated as Latin and only the drafts are intentionally vernacular. The picture provided by the distribution of Latin case endings is less clear-cut: while the charter drafts are again very strongly marked as vernacular, the witness-lists also display a significant number of zero endings and are thus closer to the

69 'Single Old English names in a Latin context […] have not been classified as switches', but '[p]repositional forms of vernacular place-names of the type qui dicitur *æt uptune* […] are classified as code-switches'; Schendl, 'Beyond Boundaries', p. 54. On code-switching in Anglo-Saxon charters, see further Francesca Tinti, 'Writing Latin and Old English in Tenth-Century England: Patterns, Formulae and Language Choice in the Leases of Oswald of Worcester', in *Writing Kingship and Power in Anglo-Saxon England*, eds Rory Naismith and David Woodman (Cambridge, 2018), pp. 303–27; and Gallagher and Tinti, 'Latin, Old English and Documentary Practice'. See further Herbert Schendl, 'Multilingualism, Code-Switching, and Language Contact in Historical Sociolinguistics', in *The Handbook of Historical Sociolinguistics*, eds Juan Manuel Hernándes-Campoy and Juan Camilo Conde-Silvestre, Blackwell Handbooks in Linguistics 36 (Malden, MA, 2012), pp. 520–33, section 3.2.

70 Päivi Pahta, 'Code-Switching in English of the Middle Ages', in *The Oxford Handbook of the History of English*, eds Terttu Nevalainen and Elizabeth Closs Traugott (Oxford, 2012), pp. 528–37.

register used in the drafts. The more vernacular treatment of these forms may have been triggered by the predominance of vernacular items as well as by the formulaic nature of the Latin context in this section of the charter. Yet, judging from the performance of the two scribes Waldo and Mauvo, Latinization is about ten percent higher in the St Gall charters than it is in Anglo-Saxon charters; furthermore, no Old High German inflectional endings occur in personal names. The fact that there is no extensive spelling switch within the charters themselves may be significant insofar as Latin is used throughout the Old High German period in the St Gall charters, despite the fact that the abbey became one of the main centres of Old High German textual production.

Bibliography

Primary Sources

Cartularium Saxonicum: A Collection of Charters Relating to Anglo-Saxon History, ed. Walter de Gray Birch, 3 vols (London, 1885–99).

Chartae latinae antiquiores, eds Albert Bruckner et al., 118 vols (Olten et al., 1954–2019).

Charters of Christ Church Canterbury, eds N. P. Brooks and S. E. Kelly, Anglo-Saxon Charters 17–18 (Oxford, 2013).

Charters of Malmesbury Abbey, ed. S. E. Kelly, Anglo-Saxon Charters XI (Oxford, 2005).

Charters of Northern Houses, ed. D. A. Woodman, Anglo-Saxon Charters 16 (Oxford, 2012).

Charters of Rochester, ed. A. Campbell, Anglo-Saxon Charters I (Oxford, 1973).

Charters of Selsey, ed. S. E. Kelly, Anglo-Saxon Charters VI (Oxford, 1998).

Charters of St Paul's, London, ed. S. E. Kelly, Anglo-Saxon Charters X (Oxford, 2004).

Chartularium Sangallense, I (700–840), ed. Peter Erhart with the collaboration of Karl Heidecker and Bernhard Zeller (St Gall, 2013).

Earle, John, *A Handbook of the Land-Charters and Other Saxon Documents* (Oxford, 1888).

Facsimiles of Anglo-Saxon Charters, ed. Simon Keynes, Anglo-Saxon Charters Supplementary Volume 1 (London, 1991).

Formulae Merowingici et Karolini Aevi, ed. Karl Zeumer, MGH Leges Formulae Merowingici et Karolini aevi 1 (Hanover, 1886).

Gregory of Tours, *Libri historiarum decem*, eds Bruno Krusch and Wilhelm Levison, MGH SS rer. Merov. 1.1 (Hanover, 1951).

The Manuscripts of Cædmon's Hymn and Bede's Death Song: With a Critical Text of the Epistola Cuthberti de obitu Bedæ, ed. Elliott van Kirk Dobbie (New York, 1937).

Die Vorakte der älteren St. Galler Urkunden. Mit einer Beilage: Zum Konzeptwesen Karolingischer Privaturkunden, ed. Albert Bruckner, Urkundenbuch der Abtei St. Gallen, Ergänzungsheft 1 (St Gall, 1931).

Secondary Sources

Benskin, Michael, 'The Letters <þ> and <y> in Later Middle English, and Some Related Matters', *Journal of the Society of Archivists* 7 (1982), 13–30.

Bergmann, Rolf and Stricker, Stefanie (eds), *Namen und Wörter: Theoretische Grenzen—Übergänge im Sprachwandel*, Germanistische Bibliothek 64 (Heidelberg, 2018).

Bischoff, Bernhard, *Paläographie des römischen Altertums und des abendländischen Mittelalters* (Berlin, 1986).

Bischoff, Bernhard and Lapidge, Michael, *Biblical Commentaries from the Canterbury School of Theodore and Hadrian*, Cambridge Studies in Anglo-Saxon England 10 (Cambridge, 1994).

Braune, Wilhelm and Reiffenstein, Ingo, *Althochdeutsche Grammatik I: Laut- und Formenlehre*, 15th ed. (Tübingen, 2004).

Brown, Michelle P., *A Guide to Western Historical Scripts from Antiquity to 1600*, 2nd ed. (Toronto, 1993).

Brown, Michelle P. and Farr, Carol A. (eds), *Mercia: An Anglo-Saxon Kingdom in Europe* (London, 2001).

Buck, Carl Darling, 'The Letter Y', *The Manly Anniversary Studies in Language and Literature* (Chicago, 1923), pp. 340–50.

Campbell, Alistair, *Old English Grammar* (Oxford, 1959).

Colman, Fran, 'First Catch Your Name ...: On Names and Word Classes, Especially in Old English', *English Studies* 96 (2015), 310–36.

Colman, Fran, *The Grammar of Names in Anglo-Saxon England: The Linguistics and Culture of the Old English Onomasticon* (Oxford, 2014).

Crick, Julia, 'English Vernacular Script', in *The Cambridge History of the Book in Britain, I, c.400–1100*, ed. Richard Gameson (Cambridge, 2012), pp. 174–86.

Dahl, Ivar, *Substantival Inflexion in Early Old English: Vocalic Stems*, Lund Studies in English 7 (Lund, 1938).

Donoghue, Daniel, 'Early Old English (up to 899)', in *A Companion to the History of the English Language*, eds Haruko Momma and Michael Matto (Chichester, 2008), pp. 156–64.

Dumville, David N., *English Caroline Script and Monastic History: Studies in Benedictinism, A.D. 950–1030* (Woodbridge, 1993).

Fulk, Robert D., *A History of Old English Metre* (Philadelphia, 1992).

Gallagher, Robert and Tinti, Francesca, 'Latin, Old English and Documentary Practice at Worcester from Wærferth to Oswald', *ASE* 46 (2019 for 2017), 271–325.

Gneuss, Helmut, 'The Origin of Standard Old English and Æthelwold's School at Winchester', *ASE* 1 (1972), 63–83.

Henning, Rudolf, *Über die Sanctgallischen Sprachdenkmäler bis zum Tode Karls des Grossen* (Strasbourg, 1874).

Hines, John, 'The Writing of English in Kent: Contexts and Influences from the Sixth to the Ninth Century', *NOWELE: North-Western European Language Evolution* 50–51 (2007), 63–92.

Howe, Nicholas, *Writing the Map of Anglo-Saxon England: Essays in Cultural Geography* (London, 2008).

Ker, N. R., *Catalogue of Manuscripts Containing Anglo-Saxon* (Oxford, 1957).

Macha, Jürgen, 'Schreibvariationen und ihr regional-kultureller Hintergrund: Rheinland und Westfalen im 17. Jahrhundert', in *Regionale Sprachgeschichte*, eds Walter Besch and Hans Joachim Solms, Zeitschrift für deutsche Philologie 117, Sonderheft (Berlin, 1998), pp. 50–66.

McKitterick, Rosamond, *The Carolingians and the Written Word* (Cambridge, 1989).

Oesterreicher, Wulf, 'Verschriftung und Verschriftlichung im Kontext medialer und konzeptioneller Schriftlichkeit', in *Schriftlichkeit im frühen Mittelalter*, ed. Ursula Schaefer, ScriptOralia 53 (Tübingen, 1993), pp. 267–92.

Pahta, Päivi, 'Code-Switching in English of the Middle Ages', in *The Oxford Handbook of the History of English*, eds Terttu Nevalainen and Elizabeth Closs Traugott (Oxford, 2012), pp. 528–37.

Perret, Franz, 'Diakon Waldo und die Anfänge des Stiftsarchives St. Gallen vor 1200 Jahren', in *Festgabe für Paul Staerkle zu seinem achtzigsten Geburtstag am 26. März 1972* (St Gall, 1972), pp. 17–26.

Pheifer, Joseph D. (ed.), *Old English Glosses in the Épinal-Erfurt Glossary* (Oxford, 1974).

Reichert, Hermann, *Lexikon der altgermanischen Namen*, Thesaurus Palaeogermanicus 1 (Vienna, 1987).

Rio, Alice, *Legal Practice and the Written Word in the Early Middle Ages: Frankish Formulae, c. 500–1000*, Cambridge Studies in Medieval Life and Thought, Fourth Series, 75 (Cambridge, 2009).

Rübekeil, Ludwig, *Diachrone Studien zur Kontaktzone zwischen Kelten und Germanen* (Vienna, 2002).

Sawyer, P. H, *Anglo-Saxon Charters: An Annotated List and Bibliography* (London, 1968); revised as the Electronic Sawyer, www.esawyer.org.uk.

Scharer, Anton, *Die angelsächsischen Königsurkunden im 7. und 8. Jahrhundert* (Vienna, 1982).

Schendl, Herbert, 'Beyond Boundaries: Code-Switching in the Leases of Oswald of Worcester', in *Code-Switching in Early English*, eds Herbert Schendl and Laura Wright, Topics in English Linguistics 76 (Berlin, 2011), pp. 47–94.

Schendl, Herbert, 'Multilingualism, Code-Switching, and Language Contact in Historical Sociolinguistics', in *The Handbook of Historical Sociolinguistics*, eds Juan Manuel Hernándes-Campoy and Juan Camilo Conde-Silvestre, Blackwell Handbooks in Linguistics 36 (Malden, MA, 2012), pp. 520–33.

Sebba, Mark, 'Orthography as Social Action: Scripts, Spelling, Identity and Power', in *Orthography as Social Action: Scripts, Spelling, Identity and Power*, eds Alexandra Jaffe, Jannis Androutsopoulos, Mark Sebba, and Sally Johnson (Berlin, 2012).

Seiler, Annina, *The Scripting of the Germanic Languages: A Comparative Study of 'Spelling Difficulties' in Old English, Old High German and Old Saxon*, Medienwandel—Medienwechsel—Medienwissen 30 (Zürich, 2014).

Seiler, Annina, 'Die Urkunden des Schreibers Waldo: eine graphematische Analyse', *Sprachwissenschaft* 38 (2013), pp. 123–46.

Seiler, Annina, 'Writing the Germanic Languages: The Early History of the Digraphs <th>, <ch> and <uu>', in *Writing Europe, 500–1450: Texts and Contexts*, eds Aidan Conti, Orietta Da Rold, and Philip Shaw (Cambridge, 2015), pp. 101–21.

Sievers, Eduard and Brunner, Karl, *Altenglische Grammatik*, 3rd ed. (Tübingen, 1965).

Snook, Ben, 'Who Introduced Charters into England? The Case for Theodore and Hadrian', in *Textus Roffensis: Law, Language, and Libraries in Early Medieval England*, eds Bruce O'Brien and Barbara Bombi, Studies in the Early Middle Ages 30 (Turnhout, 2015), pp. 257–89.

Sonderegger, Stefan, 'Althochdeutsche Namen in den rätischen Privaturkunden von St Gallen vor 800', in *Festschrift für Paul Zinsli*, eds Maria Bindschedler, Rudolf Hotzenköcherle, and Werner Kohlschmidt (Bern, 1971), pp. 145–60.

Sonderegger, Stefan, *Althochdeutsche Sprache und Literatur. Eine Einführung in das älteste Deutsch: Darstellung und Grammatik* (Berlin, 2003).

Sonderegger, Stefan, 'Das Althochdeutsche der Vorakte der älteren St Galler Urkunden. Ein Beitrag zum Problem der Urkundensprache in althochdeutscher Zeit', *Zeitschrift für Mundartforschung* 28 (1961), 251–86.

Sonderegger, Stefan, 'Reflexe gesprochener Sprache im Althochdeutschen', in *Sprachgeschichte: Ein Handbuch zur Geschichte der deutschen Sprache und ihrer Erforschung*, eds Werner Besch, Anne Betten, Oskar Reichmann, and Stefan Sonderegger, Handbücher zur Sprach- und Kommunikationswissenschaft 2.2, 2nd ed. (Berlin, 2000), pp. 1231–40.

Sonderegger, Stefan, 'Sprachgeschichtliche Aspekte der europäischen Christianisierung', in *Sprachgeschichte: Ein Handbuch zur Geschichte der deutschen Sprache und ihrer Erforschung*, eds Werner Besch, Anne Betten, Oskar Reichmann, and Stefan Sonderegger, Handbücher zur Sprach- und Kommunikationswissenschaft 2.2, 2nd ed. (Berlin, 2000), pp. 1030–61.

Staerkle, Paul, *Die Rückvermerke der ältern St.Galler Urkunden* (St Gall, 1966).

Stenton, Frank M., *Anglo-Saxon England* (Oxford, 1955).

Stevenson, Jane, *The 'Laterculus Malalianus' and the School of Archbishop Theodore*, Cambridge Studies in Anglo-Saxon England 14 (Cambridge, 1995).

Story, Joanna, *Carolingian Connections: Anglo-Saxon England and Carolingian Francia, c. 750–870* (Aldershot, 2003).

Ström, Hilmer, *Old English Personal Names in Bede's History: An Etymological-Phonological Investigation*, Lund Studies in English 8 (Lund, 1939).

Tinti, Francesca, 'Writing Latin and Old English in Tenth-Century England: Patterns, Formulae and Language Choice in the Leases of Oswald of Worcester', in *Writing Kingship and Power in Anglo-Saxon England*, eds Rory Naismith and David Woodman (Cambridge, 2018), pp. 303–27.

Urla, Jacqueline, 'Outlaw Language: Creating Alternative Public Spheres in Basque Free Radio', *Pragmatics* 5.2 (1995), 245–61.

Van Langendonck, Willy, *Theory and Typology of Proper Names*, Trends in Linguistics: Studies and Monographs 168 (Berlin, 2007).

Wagner, Norbert, 'König Chilperichs Buchstaben und andere Graphien', *Sprachwissenschaft* 1 (1976), 434–52.

Wartmann, Hermann (ed.), *Urkundenbuch der Abtei Sanct Gallen*, 3 vols (Zürich, 1863–82).

Wells, Christopher, 'An Orthographic Approach to Early Frankish Personal Names', *Transactions of the Philological Society* 71 (1972), 101–64.

Wilkens, Friedrich, *Zum hochalemannischen Konsonantismus der althochdeutschen Zeit. Beiträge zur Lautlehre und Orthographie des ältesten Hochalemannischen, auf Grundlage der deutschen Eigennamen in den Sanct Galler Urkunden (bis zum Jahre 825)* (Leipzig, 1891).

Zeller, Bernhard, 'Urkunden und Urkundenschreiber des Klosters St Gallen bis ca. 840', in *Die Privaturkunden der Karolingerzeit*, eds Peter Erhart, Karl Heidecker, and Bernhard Zeller (Dietikon-Zürich, 2009), pp. 173–82.

Online Sources

Dictionary of Old English: A to I Online, https://tapor.library.utoronto.ca/doe/

Erhart, Peter, 'Waldo', in *Historisches Lexikon der Schweiz* (2013), http://www.hls-dhs-dss.ch/textes/d/D13044.php

CHAPTER 5

Language, Formulae, and Carolingian Reforms: The Case of the Alemannic Charters from St Gall

Bernhard Zeller

Introduction

More than 800 early medieval charters dating from before the year 1000 are still today preserved in original or contemporary single-sheet copies in the archive of the former abbey of St Gall. It is an extraordinary and, for the regions north of the Alps, unique collection of original charters. Apart from about seventy Carolingian royal or imperial charters, these documents are all so-called 'private' charters.[1] The documents were issued by all kinds of people, including aristocrats and important clerics, as well as peasant-proprietors and local priests.[2] Usually these charters deal with the conveyance of property and document legal transactions such as gifts, leases, exchanges, and sales of land. Sometimes they also record ownership disputes.[3] The St Gall charters

1 Even today, a good portion of the early medieval St Gall charters are still only available in the trustworthy but long since improved edition of Hermann Wartmann from the late nineteenth century: W. Ground-breaking for further studies was the facsimile edition of the roughly 130 original eighth-century private charters from St Gall organized by Albert Bruckner and Robert Marichal in the 1950s within the series of the *Chartae latinae antiquiores*: *ChLA* 1 and 2. During the last decade, the St Gall charters from the ninth century were published in facsimile within the second series of the *ChLA*: *ChLA* 100–111. Based on this new facsimile edition, the St Gall charters are now being reedited within the series of the *Chartularium Sangallensis*. In 2013 the first volume of the *Chartularium* (comprising the charters up to 840) was published: *Chartularium Sangallense, I (700–840)*, ed. Peter Erhart with the collaboration of Karl Heidecker and Bernhard Zeller (St Gall, 2013).

2 See, with further bibliographical references, Gesine Jordan, 'Wer war der Tradent? Methodische Überlegungen zur sozialgeschichtlichen Untersuchung von Privaturkunden des frühen Mittelalters, besonders der St. Galler Urkunden', in *Tätigkeitsfelder und Erfahrungshorizonte des ländlichen Menschen in der frühmittelalterlichen Grundherrschaft (bis ca. 1000). Festschrift Dieter Hägermann zum 65. Geburtstag*, ed. Brigitte Kasten, Vierteljahrschrift für Sozial- und Wirtschaftsgeschichte, Beihefte 184 (Munich, 2006), pp. 155–74.

3 Hans-Werner Goetz, 'Beobachtungen zur Grundherrschaftsentwicklung der Abtei St. Gallen vom 8. zum 9. Jahrhundert', in *Strukturen der Grundherrschaft im frühen Mittelalter*, ed. Werner Rösener, Veröffentlichungen des Max-Planck-Instituts für Geschichte 92 (Göttingen, 1989), pp. 197–246.

 | DOI:10.1163/9789004432338_006

provide material for a variety of questions, offering valuable information about the legal, economic, and social history of a large area encompassing modern Switzerland, southern Germany, and western Austria.[4] They also help elucidate the social and daily life of the early Middle Ages and sometimes allow us to reconstruct social groups and networks.[5] That the charters are originals is, however, of particular importance for auxiliary historical fields, especially diplomatics. The fact that they are preserved as single sheets of parchment provides invaluable insights into their redaction, production, later use, and conservation, as well as into the development of scripts and the spread of literacy.[6] The 'originality' of these precisely dated documents is also important from a philological point of view, because originals provide contemporary, unmodified spellings of words.

Most of the St Gall charters concern the monastery itself. They range in date from the early eighth century, when the monastery was founded, up to the late tenth century, when charter production in the monastery ceased. Geographically, most of these documents cover vast parts of early medieval Alemannia and the diocese of Constance. In addition, there is a group of roughly fifty documents arising from the neighbouring province of *Raetia* (*Curiensis*).[7] Many of these Raetian documents record transactions in which the monastery of St Gall was not directly implicated, but which can be associated with the career of Folcwin, a minor sub-comital official, active around 820. They seem to have made up part of an early medieval lay archive that came to St Gall long after the charters' redaction, probably in the late ninth century, though perhaps only in the tenth, when Raetia had already been

4 Goetz, 'Beobachtungen'; Hans-Werner Goetz, 'Die "private" Grundherrschaft des frühen Mittelalters im Spiegel der St. Galler Traditionsurkunden', in *Tätigkeitsfelder und Erfahrungshorizonte*, ed. Kasten, pp. 111–37; Karl Heidecker, 'Charters as Texts and as Objects in Judicial Actions: The Example of the Carolingian Private Charters of St Gall', in *Medieval Legal Process: Physical, Spoken and Written Performance in the Middle Ages*, eds Paul S. Barnwell and Marco Mostert (Turnhout, 2011), pp. 39–53.

5 Rolf Sprandel, *Das Kloster St. Gallen in der Verfassung des karolingischen Reiches* (Freiburg im Breisgau, 1958).

6 Rosamond McKitterick, *The Carolingians and the Written Word* (Cambridge, 1989), pp. 77–134; Rosamond McKitterick, 'Schriftlichkeit im Spiegel der frühen Urkunden St. Gallens', in *Das Kloster St. Gallen im Mittelalter. Die kulturelle Blüte vom 8. bis zum 12. Jahrhundert*, ed. Peter Ochsenbein (Darmstadt, 1999), pp. 69–82.

7 For a survey see Michael Borgolte, 'Kommentar zu Ausstellungsdaten, Actum- und Güterorten der älteren St. Galler Urkunden (Wartmann I und II mit Nachträgen in III und IV)', in *Subsidia Sangallensia I. Materialien und Untersuchungen zu den Verbrüderungsbüchern und zu den älteren Urkunden des Stiftsarchivs St. Gallen*, eds Michael Borgolte, Dieter Geuenich, and Karl Schmid, St. Galler Kultur und Geschichte 16 (St Gall, 1986), pp. 323–475.

absorbed into Alemannia and when, as other charters show, the abbey of St Gall had expanded its domain into this region.[8]

Alemannia and Raetia

It is important to keep in mind that Alemannia and Raetia were two distinct regions in the early Middle Ages. They had their own histories, their own institutional and legal traditions, and their own cultures.[9] Until the Carolingian takeover in the first half of the eighth century, Alemannia had been ruled by dukes who were tributaries of the Frankish kings but remained largely self-governing. The political heart of the duchy lay in southern Alemannia, around Lake Constance, at the ecclesiastical centres of the bishopric of Constance and the important Benedictine abbey of Reichenau (founded only in 724).[10] Raetia, on the other hand, was the 'successor state' of the later Roman province of *Raetia Prima*. At least from the seventh century onwards, this predominantly Alpine territory with its political centre at Chur was governed by members of the powerful Victorid (Zaccon) family, who had ties to the Merovingian dynasty in Gaul and under whose control secular and ecclesiastical power (i.e. the offices of bishop and *praeses*) were combined.[11] Whereas the bishopric of Constance was always oriented towards the Frankish-Burgundian church, Chur was at first a suffragan of the archbishop of Milan in northern Italy, and became subordinate to the archbishopric of Mainz only in the ninth century.

---

8 Peter Erhart and Julia Kleindinst, *Urkundenlandschaft Rätien*, Forschungen zur Geschichte des Mittelalters 7 (Vienna, 2004); Katherine Bullimore, 'Folcwin of Rankweil: The World of a Carolingian Local Official', *EME* 13 (2005), 43–77; Matthew Innes, 'Archives, Documents and Landowners in Carolingian Francia', in *Documentary Culture and the Laity in the Early Middle Ages*, eds Warren C. Brown, Marios Costambeys, Matthew Innes, and Adam J. Kosto (Cambridge, 2013), pp. 152–88, at 165–66.

9 See, with further bibliographical references, Herwig Wolfram, *Salzburg, Bayern, Österreich. Die Conversio Bagoariorum et Carantanorum und die Quellen ihrer Zeit*, Mitteilungen des Instituts für Österreichische Geschichtsforschung, Ergänzungsband 31 (Vienna, 1995), pp. 86–87, 103–23; Alfons Zettler, *Geschichte des Herzogtums Schwaben* (Stuttgart, 2003); Reinhold Kaiser, *Churrätien im frühen Mittelalter*, 2nd ed. (Basel, 2008); *Wandel und Konstanz zwischen Bodensee und Lombardei zur Zeit Karls des Großen*, ed. Hans Rudolf Sennhauser, Acta Müstair 3 (Zürich, 2013); Innes, 'Archives, Documents and Landowners', p. 172.

10 Zettler, *Geschichte des Herzogtums Schwaben*, pp. 41–47.

11 Kaiser, *Churrätien im frühen Mittelalter*, pp. 27–55.

The different political and cultural traditions and orientations of Alemannia and Raetia can be also traced in the St Gall charter material.[12]

Palaeographers distinguish 'Alemannic' minuscule from 'Raetian' minuscule, and have stressed that the former was influenced by western, Merovingian scripts, whereas the distinctive letter forms of the latter reveal that the script descended directly from late Roman cursive.[13] Similarly, diplomatic studies differentiate between Frankish-Alemannic charters on the one hand and Raetian charters on the other, while also emphasizing parallels between Frankish and Alemannic formulae and between Raetian charters and documents from northern Italy.[14] The St Gall charters also reflect an ethno-linguistic difference between Alemannia and Raetia. This becomes obvious when one looks at the different names of people and places in the charters, but this diversity is also recognizable in the Latin language of the documents.[15] Indeed, in contrast to Alemannia, early medieval Raetia was an alpine 'island of *romanitas*'.[16] In the tenth century, people from Raetia still spoke *romanice* and may have had problems with the use and pronunciation of the *lingua theodisca*.[17]

12 Zettler, *Geschichte des Herzogtums Schwaben*, pp. 44–47; Kaiser, *Churrätien im frühen Mittelalter*, pp. 96–103.

13 See, with further bibliographical references, McKitterick, *The Carolingians and the Written Word*, p. 85; Peter Erhart and Bernhard Zeller, 'Rätien und Alemannien. Schriftformen im Vergleich', in *Wandel und Konstanz zwischen Bodensee und Lombardei*, pp. 299–318; Natalie Maag, *Alemannische Minuskel (744–846 n. Chr.). Frühe Schriftkultur im Bodenseeraum und Voralpenland*, Quellen und Untersuchungen zur lateinischen Philologie des Mittelalters 18 (Stuttgart, 2014).

14 See, with further bibliographical references, Heinrich Fichtenau, *Das Urkundenwesen in Österreich vom 8. bis zum frühen 13. Jahrhundert*, Mitteilungen des Instituts für Österreichische Geschichtsforschung, Ergänzungsband 23 (Vienna, 1971), pp. 67–72; Peter Erhart, 'Erratische Blöcke am Alpennordrand? Die rätischen Urkunden und ihre Überlieferung', Bernhard Zeller, 'Urkunden und Urkundenschreiber des Klosters St. Gallen bis ca. 840', and Karl Heidecker, 'Urkunden schreiben im alemannischen Umfeld des Klosters St. Gallen', all in *Die Privaturkunden der Karolingerzeit*, eds Peter Erhart, Karl Heidecker, and Bernhard Zeller (Dietikon-Zürich, 2009), at pp. 161–71, 173–82 and 183–91 respectively.

15 Robert von Planta, 'Die Sprache der rätoromanischen Urkunden des 8.–10. Jahrhunderts', in *Regesten von Vorarlberg und Liechtenstein bis zum Jahre 1260*, ed. Adolf Helbok, Quellen zur Geschichte Vorarlbergs und Liechtensteins 1 (Innsbruck, 1920/25), pp. 62–108. With regard to names of people and places mentioned in charters from Raetia see, for example, Simone M. Berchtold, 'Orts- und Flurnamen', and Wolfgang Haubrichs, 'Die Personennamen', both in *Das Drusental. Der Walgau und das Vorderland im früheren Mittelalter*, ed. Peter Erhart, Elementa Walgau 7 (Nenzing, 2009), at pp. 139–58 and 161–65 respectively. See also the chapter of Wolfgang Haubrichs in this volume.

16 Innes, 'Archives, Documents and Landowners', p. 172.

17 See below, n. 23.

St Gall

Although it is important to stress these fundamental differences between Alemannia and Raetia, it is also clear that, as Rosamond McKitterick put it, 'we cannot think in terms of hermetically sealed communities'.[18] Especially in the case of the monastery of St Gall, situated in the Alemannic Thurgau, we can observe closer and long-term contacts with the neighbouring province of Raetia. Indeed, Gallus, the eponymous founder of the hermitage in the seventh century, already had a disciple of Raetian origin.[19] Otmar, who at the beginning of the eighth century founded a monastery proper on the site of the former hermitage, was of Alemannic origin, but had been educated at Chur in Raetia.[20] Furthermore, as the names in the monastic profession book (*Liber promissionum*) suggest, there were a significant number of Raetians among the earliest members of the new monastery.[21] In the 750s, there were still relatives of the bishop of Chur living in the St Gall community.[22]

This close connection between St Gall and Raetia, especially Chur, loosened during the course of the eighth century, particularly when Abbot Otmar was deposed in 759 and his monastery was subjected to the control of the bishops of Constance. However, connections to neighbouring Raetia remained and were further transformed when Raetia was politically absorbed into Alemannia during the ninth century. In fact, several episodes in the continuation of Ekkehard IV's *Casus sancti Galli* show that even in the tenth and eleventh centuries some St Gall monks, and probably also some of the monastery's servants, came from Raetia.[23] In any case, there were St Gall monks in the tenth century who were evidently to a certain degree bilingual. A prime example is the famous bathtub anecdote Ekkehard recounts involving his namesake, Ekkehard I, who lived in the first half of the tenth century. According to this account, one day, a traveller from West Francia (*Gallum genere*) came to St Gall. He pretended to be lame and demanded to be treated by the monks. Ekkehard's servant had

18 McKitterick, *Carolingians*, p. 83.

19 Wetti, *Vita sancti Galli*, 25, ed. Bruno Krusch, MGH SS rer. Merov. 4 (Hanover and Leipzig, 1902) pp. 256–80, at 270; Walahfrid, *Vita sancti Galli*, I, 25, ed. Bruno Krusch, MGH SS rer. Merov. 4 (Hanover and Leipzig, 1902) pp. 280–337, at 302–3.

20 Walahfrid, *Vita sancti Otmari*, 1, ed. Ildefons von Arx, in MGH SS 2 (Hanover, 1829), pp. 41–47, at 41.

21 *Liber promissionum sancti Galli*, ed. Paul Piper, MGH Necr. Supplement (Berlin, 1884), pp. 111–33, at 111; Max Schär, 'Sankt Galler Mönche unter Abt Otmar 720–760', *Studien und Mitteilungen zur Geschichte des Benediktinerordens und seiner Zweige* 120 (2009), 9–32.

22 Walahfrid, *Vita sancti Galli*, II.17, ed. Krusch, pp. 324–25.

23 Ekkehard IV, *Casus sancti Galli*, 72, 88, ed. Hans F. Haefele, Ausgewählte Quellen zur deutschen Geschichte des Mittelalters 10, 3rd ed. (Darmstadt, 1991), pp. 150, 180–82.

to carry the guest to the bathroom. Unfortunately, the guest was quite fat, but after some difficulty the servant got him into the tub. There, the guest immediately protested that the water was too hot and said *rustice*: 'Cald, cald est!', which, as Ekkehard explains, in German sounds like 'it is cold' ('quoniam id teutonum lingua "frigidum est" sonat'). The servant responded, 'Calefaciam', and poured more hot water into the tub. At this point, the guest cried out, 'cum clamore horrido: "Ei mi! Cald est, cald est!"' ('Have mercy on me, it is hot, it is hot!'). But the servant's answer was the same: 'Si adhuc frigidum est ... tibi illud caleficabo' ('If it is still cold, I will heat it for you'), and again he poured hot water into the tub. At this point, the guest forgot about his paralysis, jumped out of the water, and ran out of the bath. After the incident, Ekkehard scolded both the servant and the bather, each in his own language (*teutonice et romanice*).[24] Ekkehard I was thus bilingual, but the story also suggests that the servant had at least a passive knowledge of Romance language. As Anna Grotans has pointed out, the readers of the *Casus sancti Galli* would have also understood the joke, 'which means that they understood the Latin context in which it was told as well as the Romance and the German quotes'.[25]

Although there can be no doubt that early medieval St Gall remained in close contact with the neighbouring Romance-speaking region of Raetia, it is important to stress that from the beginning the monastery was situated in and primarily oriented towards Alemannia. In the eighth and ninth centuries, almost all benefactors were of Alemannic origin and almost all the monastery's properties were located in Alemannia. Furthermore, the charter model that was applied for the documentation of these donations to St Gall was essentially Frankish-Alemannic. Only in a few very early charters can one detect the influence of a different, Raetian 'matrix'. Several of these charters were written by and in the name of the St Gall monk Silvester, who was very probably of Raetian origin.[26]

The Charter Scribes, Their Educational Background, and Their Charters

Right from the start, St Gall monks such as Silvester were drawing up charters for their monastery, but a scriptorium in the proper sense (that is, a place

24 Ekkehard IV, *Casus sancti Galli*, 88, ed. Haefele, pp. 180–82.

25 Anna A. Grotans, *Reading in Medieval St. Gall*, Cambridge Studies in Palaeography and Codicology 13 (Cambridge, 2006), p. 123.

26 W 5, W 6 (= *ChLA* 2, no. 161, pp. 104–5), W 40 (= *ChLA* 2, no. 156, pp. 94–95).

not only of scribal activity, but also of scribal training) emerged only later.[27] Furthermore, as has been known for some time, a large number of the scribes who wrote charters were also engaged in the production of codices. In other words, there was no strict differentiation in the abbey between scribes for charters and for other manuscripts.[28] From the later eighth century onwards, and especially during the ninth century, when St Gall finally became independent of episcopal dominion, the percentage of monks involved in writing rose sharply.[29] The emergence of this effective scriptorium also implies the professionalization of writing in the abbey, a development that is also documented at other locations in this period.[30] The consequences of this professionalization are noticeable in many respects, both in the internal and the external characteristics of the charters. The graphic symbols of the charters were modified (simplified, in fact), while the script gradually changed from Alemannic to Caroline minuscule. The formulae and, as we shall see below, the language of the charters were also affected.

Beyond the monastic sphere, there is also a relatively rich and interesting body of documentary evidence for the activities of non-monastic scribes, at least until the early ninth century. Most of these scribes were secular clerics, primarily priests, who lived and operated in regions where they and their families came from and where they held possessions. Furthermore, they remained in close contact with their often wealthy kin groups and continued to act in their families' interests, not least when it came to dealing with land.[31] It is very probable that in most of these cases the duties and functions of these clerics were centred on pastoral care. The charters, however, give virtually no information about this core activity. Several priests seem to have exercised different

27 Rupert Schaab, *Mönch in St. Gallen. Zur inneren Geschichte eines frühmittelalterlichen Klosters*, Vorträge und Forschungen, Sonderband 47 (Ostfildern, 2003), pp. 122–26, 157–68.

28 Albert Bruckner, *Scriptoria Medii Aevi Helvetica. Denkmäler schweizerischer Schreibkunst des Mittelalters, vols 2–3: Schreibschulen der Diözese Konstanz* (*St. Gallen 1–2*) (Geneva, 1936–38); Beat von Scarpatetti, 'Das St. Galler Scriptorium', in *Das Kloster St. Gallen im Mittelalter. Die kulturelle Blüte vom 8. bis zum 12. Jahrhundert*, ed. Peter Ochsenbein (Darmstadt, 1999), pp. 31–67.

29 Heidecker, 'Urkunden schreiben'; Bernhard Zeller, 'Local Priests in Early Medieval Alamannia: The Charter Evidence', in *Men in the Middle. Local Priests in Early Medieval Europe*, eds Steffen Patzold and Carine van Rhijn, Ergänzungsbände zum Reallexikon der Germanischen Altertumskunde 93 (Berlin, 2016), pp. 32–49.

30 David Ganz, '*Temptabat et scribere*: Vom Schreiben in der Karolingerzeit', in *Schriftkultur und Reichsverwaltung unter den Karolingern*, ed. Rudolf Schieffer, Abhandlungen der Rheinisch-Westfälischen Akademie der Wissenschaften 97 (Opladen, 1996), pp. 13–33, at 16–20.

31 Zeller, 'Local Priests', pp. 31–37.

(and sometimes probably only additional) functions, as their zone of activity was not of a local but of a regional character. Some of them seem to have been connected to office-holders or noble families rather than to specific churches.[32]

As has previously been stressed by McKitterick, the charter evidence requires us to be flexible in defining the function and position of such clerics.[33] What becomes apparent, however, is that secular priests and clerics, acting both locally and regionally, played an important role in day-to-day literacy, that is, in the documentation of legal transactions.[34] It is usually assumed that secular clerics received their education in the schools of episcopal churches and monasteries. Indeed, several narrative sources from St Gall, such as Notker the Stammerer's *Gesta Karoli* and the above-mentioned continuation of the *Casus sancti Galli* by Ekkehard IV, indicate that this may often have been the case.[35] However, it is possible that such schooling formed only the second phase of training. There are also indications that future clerics could gain basic skills in literacy at a local level, probably in local schools which were organized and run by local priests and which are occasionally mentioned in council proceedings and episcopal statutes.[36] Interestingly, there is great diversity and range among the external features of charters drawn up by non-monastic clerics, such as the quality, adaptation, and format of the parchment, as well as their graphic symbols and scripts. This suggests that many of these clerics had not learned to write in a proper school attached to a big ecclesiastical institution. In fact, these documents often diverge remarkably from charters written by St Gall monks.[37] The internal features of several non-monastic charters also suggest the possibility of local training. Especially from the ninth century onwards, the formulae of these charters differ from those used by the St Gall monks. In several parts of early medieval Alemannia, we can even detect a local transmission of

32 Zeller, 'Local Priests', pp. 39–40.

33 McKitterick, *The Carolingians and the Written Word*, p. 120.

34 Heidecker, 'Urkunden schreiben'.

35 Christoph Dette, 'Schüler im frühen und hohen Mittelalter. Die St. Galler Klosterschule des 9. und 10. Jahrhunderts', *Studien und Mitteilungen zur Geschichte des Benediktinerordens und seiner Zweige* 105 (1994), 7–64, at 19–27; Grotans, *Reading in Medieval St. Gall*, pp. 53–67; Schaab, *Mönch in St. Gallen*, pp. 157–58.

36 Carine van Rhijn, *Shepherds of the Lord: Priests and Episcopal Statutes in the Carolingian Period*, Cultural Encounters in Late Antiquity and the Middle Ages 6 (Turnhout, 2007), p. 176.

37 See, for example, W 15 (= *ChLA* 1, no. 45, pp. 44–45), W 29 (= *ChLA* 2, no. 165, pp. 110–111), W 37 (= *ChLA* 2, no. 166, pp. 112–113), W 68 (= *ChLA* 1, no. 70, pp. 74–75), W 129 (= *ChLA* 2, no. 124, pp. 32–33), W 138 (= *ChLA* 2, no. 134, pp. 52–53), W 161 (= *ChLA* 2, no. 150, pp. 84–85), W 170 (= *ChLA* 2, no. 153, pp. 90–91).

certain formulae and thus reconstruct traces of local 'traditions of writing'.[38] Yet there is a problem of transmission: in the course of the ninth century, the hitherto rich documentary evidence for local scribes from outside the abbey gradually disappears. Among other factors, this was the result of efforts by the monks of St Gall themselves, who increasingly monopolized the production of charters relating to their abbey. Therefore, the following observations on the language of the St Gall charters will concentrate on those written in the eighth and early ninth centuries.

The Latin Language of the Early Alemannic Charters from St Gall

Especially in charters of the eighth century, and predominantly in those documents written by non-monastic scribes, we find variants of a Latin language which might be defined as 'scarcely regulated' early medieval Latin, characterized by a more or less pronounced unsteadiness and fuzziness with regard to orthography, morphology, and syntax (see Appendix 1).[39] While many of its features and particularities can be traced back to Roman times, they are far more typical of the early medieval period. They can be found concentrated in texts such as law-codes, charters, saints' lives, and sermons from seventh-century Gaul. Thus, this kind of Latin has often been called 'Merovingian Latin'.[40] Research has shown that its characteristics were often the result of a profound influence and interference of spoken language.[41] In early medieval Gaul, as in many other places, spoken 'vulgar' Latin was in transition to what we would

38 See Bernhard Zeller, *Diplomatische Studien zu den St. Galler Privaturkunden des frühen Mittelalters (ca. 720–980)* (forthcoming).

39 See also the chapter of Annina Seiler in this volume.

40 Einar Löfstedt, *Late Latin* (Oslo, 1959), p. 3; Dag Norberg, *Syntaktische Forschungen auf dem Gebiete des Spätlateins und des frühen Mittellateins* (Uppsala and Leipzig, 1943), p. 20; Peter Stotz, *Handbuch zur lateinischen Sprache des Mittelalters*. Handbuch der Altertumswissenschaft, 5 vols (München, 1996–2000), 1:87–93; Cf. József Herman, *Vulgar Latin*, trans. Roger Wright (University Park, PA, 2000), pp. 30–38; Reinhard Kiesler, *Einführung in die Problematik des Vulgärlateins* (Tübingen, 2006), pp. 42–44. Against an oversimplified opposition between 'decadent' Merovingian Latin and 'restored' Carolingian Latin, see Marc van Uytfanghe, 'The Consciousness of a Linguistic Dichotomy (Latin-Romance) in Carolingian Gaul: The Contradictions of the Sources and of their Interpretation', in *Latin and the Romance Languages in the Early Middle Ages*, ed. Roger Wright (London, 1991), pp. 114–29, at 122–23.

41 See, with further bibliographical references, Michel Banniard, 'The Transition from Latin to the Romance Languages', in *The Cambridge History of the Romance Languages, Volume 2: Contexts*, eds Martin Maiden, John Charles Smith, and Adam Ledgeway (Cambridge, 2013), pp. 57–106, at 76.

today refer to as the Romance languages. This emerging Romance vernacular interfered with written Latin.[42] Fundamentally, this interference led to one of two things happening: either authors accepted the usage belonging to their daily speech, or they fell into error by trying to avoid these features.[43] More recent sociolinguistic research, however, has demonstrated rather that the relationship between written Latin and the vernacular was more complex and that there were different levels and strata between the *sermo altus* and the *sermo rusticus*.[44]

At St Gall, situated in the border-region between Alemannia and Raetia, Latin was also affected by the interference of the spoken vernacular: on the one hand, of 'vulgar' Latin in transition to early Romance, and, on the other, of regional variations of Old High German. Thus, we are faced with a more complex set of linguistic relationships,[45] and it is sometimes hard to decide whether the 'scarcely regulated' Latin found in the St Gall charter material reflects 'changes in the spoken language and a shift to forms closer to early Romance' or is rather 'due to scribes having to learn Latin as a foreign or dead language, of which they had an increasingly poor command'.[46]

Furthermore, it is important to stress that not all of the linguistic evidence in the St Gall charters necessarily or directly reflects the Latinity of individual scribes. As charters offer rather formalized texts and as these documents were usually composed according to common formulae, some of the characteristic linguistic forms may have been transmitted and 'imported' via the Frankish

42 Concerning the problematic definition of 'vulgar' Latin, see Marc van Uytfanghe, 'Histoire du Latin, protohistoire des langues romanes et histoire de la communication. A propos d'un receuil d'études, et avec quelques observations préliminaires sur le débat intellectuel entre pensée structurale et pensée historique', *Francia* 11 (1983), 579–613; Herman, *Vulgar Latin*, pp. 1–8; Kiesler, *Einführung in die Problematik*, pp. 7–14. See also Paul Fouracre and Richard A. Gerberding, *Late Merovingian France: History and Hagiography, 640–720* (Manchester, 1996), p. 60.

43 Dag Norberg, *Manuel pratique de latin médiéval*, Connaissance des langues 4 (Paris, 1968), p. 29; English translation by R. H. Johnson: http://homepages.wmich.edu/~johnsorh/MedievalLatin/Norberg/.

44 See Michel Banniard, 'Niveaux de competence langagière chez les élites', in *La culture du Haut Moyen Âge, une question d'élites?*, eds François Bougard, Régine Le Jan, and Rosamond McKitterick, Collection Haut Moyen Âge 7 (Turnhout, 2009), pp. 39–61, who identified five separate but overlapping levels. See also Michel Banniard, 'Acrolecte et identité culturelle en Francia carolingienne (VIIIe–IXe s.)', in *Sprache und Identität im frühen Mittelalter*, eds Walter Pohl and Bernhard Zeller, Forschungen zur Geschichte des Mittelalters 20 (Vienna, 2012), pp. 109–20.

45 See McKitterick, *The Carolingians and the Written Word*, p. 21.

46 Alice Rio, *Legal Practice and the Written Word in the Early Middle Ages: Frankish Formulae, c.500–1000* (Cambridge, 2009), p. 15.

charter model and certain formulae attached to it.[47] For instance, in the St Gall charters, several features of a 'scarcely regulated' Latin usually arise only or primarily in certain formulaic contexts. This is the case, for example, with some syntactic constructions such as *pro* + accusative (e.g. *pro remedium/salutem animae meae*) and with defect formulations (e.g. *contra hanc cartula*). In addition, certain morphological variations (e.g. *contenere* instead of *continere*) and even orthographical variants (e.g. *adque* instead of *atque*) mainly appear within particular formulae.

We can undoubtedly demonstrate the influence of a 'vulgar' Latin or early Romance vernacular in the three charters issued in the name of the St Gall monk Silvester, probably all in the 730s.[48] These charters were actually drawn up in collaboration with at least four scribes. They were written in Raetian minuscule, but according to a rather fixed set of mainly Frankish formulae, which nevertheless demonstrates some influence of diplomatic traditions from the neighbouring province of Raetia.[49] In the text of the charters we can consistently detect the substitution of *u* with *o*, *p* with *b*, *t* with *d*, and *c* with *g*.[50] Thus, we find forms such as *aud* instead of *aut*, *diagonus* instead of *diaconus*, *ebistola* instead of *epistula*, *fudurus* instead of *futurus*, *logo* instead of *loco*, and *obiris* instead of *operis* (see Appendix 2a). As these characteristic spellings of the formulae and words vary in the documents, it seems clear that they were not just slavishly copied from a supposed 'Silvester-template', which, in any case, seems to have been composed already in a Latin closer to what we might call early Romance. Rather, the formulae were individually adapted and adjusted by the scribes in the course of writing.

To a far lesser extent, we can detect linguistic features that point towards the interference of an emerging Romance vernacular in the charters of other early St Gall monks such as Peter, Marcus, and Liutfrit. In their charters, we can observe a general fuzziness concerning grammatical standards and orthography. In addition, we also come across hyperurbanisms and simple errors.[51] The best examples of this kind of 'scarcely regulated', 'rustic' Latin, however, come from charters drawn up not by St Gall monks, but by non-monastic scribes,

47 On the influence of older formulae on charters see Norberg, *Syntaktische Forschungen*, p. 17.

48 W 5, W 6 (= *ChLA* 2, no. 161, pp. 104–105), and W 40 (= *ChLA* 2, no. 156, pp. 94–95). However, only W 5 provides a complete date (27 June 735).

49 For comparison with what Raetian charters might have looked like in this period see W 8 and W 9 (= *ChLA* 1, nos 40 and 44, pp. 38–39 and pp. 44–45).

50 See also Seiler, this volume.

51 W 16, W 17 (= *ChLA* 1, no. 50, pp. 50–51), W 18 (= *ChLA* 2, no. 163, pp. 106–107), W 19 (= *ChLA* 1, no. 46, pp. 46–47), W 20 (= *ChLA* 1, no. 48, pp. 48–49), W 73, W 94 (= *ChLA* 1, no. 90, pp. 110–111).

especially those from the Thurgau, Zürichgau, and southern Breisgau regions, that is, from areas which were contact zones between 'vulgar' Latin or early Romance-speaking and German(ic)-speaking communities (see Appendix 1).

Striking examples of this linguistic *rusticitas* can be found in the charters of the clerics Adam and Vunolf, who, in the Thurgau region during the 760s, drew up several documents by proxy (*ad vicem*) of the *cancellarius* Waringis.[52] When writing in the name or on behalf of Waringis, Adam, Vunolf, and several other monastic and non-monastic scribes usually used the same set of formulae which we can identify almost exclusively in charters explicitly related to Waringis. These 'Waringis formulae' (see Appendix 2b), which show parallels to western, Frankish-Alsatian formulae, were used over a period of almost forty years. It is therefore hard to imagine that this would have been possible without the existence of a written template.[53]

Interestingly, the execution of the formulae in the 'Waringis charters' differs greatly. In contrast to the documents written by Adam and Vunolf in a remarkably 'rustic' Latin, those charters drawn up by St Gall monks such as Waldo and Mauvo appear in a better, smoother Latin. Yet even the stylistically similar documents of Adam and Vunolf differ significantly with regard to orthography. This implies that, like the scribes in Silvester's circle, the scribes of the Waringis charters also adapted and adjusted their model text when they drew up documents for this *cancellarius*.

Considering the striking variety in the rendering of these formulae, it is hard to believe that all these scribes referred to a single template brought along by Waringis. However, Waringis' close connection to the formulae argues against the existence of several slightly different templates. A possible solution to this problem could be that Waringis sometimes dictated to the scribes, who wrote by his proxy. Consequently, the orthographic differences would be the result of diverse, individual written realizations of a recited Latin text by scribes with rather different educational backgrounds. If this were the case, the Waringis charters would attest to the Latin spoken during these proceedings.[54]

52 W 118 (= *ChLA* 2, no. 117, pp. 18–19), W 129 (= *ChLA* 2, no. 124, pp. 32–33), W 138 (= *ChLA* 2, no. 134, pp. 52–53).

53 There is a further indication of this: in one of the charters drawn up in the presence of Waringis and according to 'his' formulae (W 71 = *ChLA* 118, no. 17, pp. 46–47), we find the passage 'et ad fisco auri solidos **tot** et argenti pondera XII'. It seems clear that this passage refers to a written model text and that the placeholder *tot* ('as much') was not substituted but rather mistakenly left in the actual charter.

54 On this possibility see Mark Mersiowsky, *Die Urkunde in der Karolingerzeit. Originale, Urkundenpraxis und politische Kommunikation*, MGH Schriften 60, 2 vols (Wiesbaden, 2015), 2:835–37, with further references.

Carolingian Reforms and the Latinity of the St Gall Charters

Adam's and Vunolf's charters allow us sympathize with Dag Norberg, who claimed that by the year 700 Latin had become 'completely chaotic'. Yet the use of such a language in private charters also proves that, at least among lower levels of society, this type of Latin was considered acceptable and effective for the purposes of communication and administration. Of course, Norberg and others might be right that by the mid-eighth century such Latin was 'no longer adequate to serve as a means of communication in the administration or in the religious and educational life' of a growing, multiethnic, and multilingual realm. For these pragmatic reasons, as well as for religious and 'ideological' motivations, the Latin language was a key aspect of the Carolingian reforms.[55]

Efforts to improve education and Latin standards began around the middle of the eighth century, and we can also detect amendments in the St Gall charters which were drawn up by monastic scribes from the 760s onwards. While King Pippin had generated important impulses, these reforms accelerated significantly under his son Charlemagne.[56] Reform 'manifestos', such as the *Admonitio generalis* and the *Epistola de litteris colendis*, focused among other things on the improvement of the Latin language through the study of Latin grammar and literature.[57] Consequently, they also required the establishment and reorganization of episcopal and monastic schools, where *pueri* (and among them also future clerics) should learn how to read and write 'correctly'. Bishops functioned as important agents and middlemen, and were to a great extent responsible for the implementation of the Carolingian reforms and of royal orders in general in their dioceses.[58] Especially in the times of Charlemagne and Louis the Pious, bishops promulgated episcopal statutes,

55 Norberg, *Manuel pratique*, p. 31; English translation by Johnson: http://homepages.wmich.edu/~johnsorh/MedievalLatin/Norberg/.

56 Indeed the first results of such efforts are already tangible in the 770s. In a study from the 1930s, Mario A. Pei compared the language of two groups of charters of roughly equal extent, one dating from 700–17, the other from 750–70. Pei could demonstrate a considerable improvement in spelling. See Mario A. Pei, *The Language of the Eighth-Century Texts in Northern France. A Study of the Original Documents in the Collection of Tardif and other Sources* (New York, 1932).

57 Löfstedt, *Late Latin*, pp. 3–4; Michel Banniard, 'Language and Communication in Carolingian Europe', in *The New Cambridge Medieval History, Volume II: c.700–c.900*, ed. Rosamond McKitterick (Cambridge, 1995), pp. 695–708.

58 Carine van Rhijn, 'Priests and the Carolingian Reforms: The Bottlenecks of Local *correctio*', in *Texts and Identities in the Early Middle Ages*, eds Richard Corradini, Rob Meens, Christina Pössel, and Philip Shaw, Forschungen zur Geschichte des Mittelalters 13 (Vienna, 2006), pp. 219–37, at 221.

which were a 'key component of the Frankish reform program'.[59] These texts transmitted to priests a new conception of priesthood and outlined what they should be, what they should know, and how they should live. Priests should not only lead decent lives, but should also be better trained in order to be able to do their work properly.[60]

From the bishops of Constance, no such episcopal statutes have survived. In the late eighth century, however, two formulae collections were produced, the so-called *Formulae Augienses Collectio A* and the *Formulae Augienses Collectio B*. These two collections of model documents for private charters were very probably compiled in the monastery of Reichenau, where at this time the former St Gall monk Waldo was abbot and the monastic school was headed by Haito, from 801/2 also bishop of Basel.[61] Already in the 790s we can trace the reception and use of several formulae of these collections outside of Reichenau, in the charters of St Gall scribes as well as those of other non-monastic scribes. The reflection of these formulae in the charters of both scribal groups, St Gall monks and local clerics of the diocese of Constance, might point towards an episcopal initiative behind their distribution and dissemination. The rather fragmentary and patchy application of these formulae in actual charters might suggest that they were used for teaching and that different scribes and scribal groups developed them further or integrated them with pre-existing formulae. Either way, these formulae played a role in the formal standardization and, to a certain extent, in the linguistic improvement of private charters from the later eighth century onwards. Of course, these processes worked faster in the up-and-coming monastic scriptorium of St Gall than outside the monastery. Yet standards also improved in the sphere of local priests. After 810 there is only scarce evidence for constructions such as *pro remedium/salutem animae meae*, *ad ipsa/ipso ecclesia/monasterio/sancto* and *contra hanc donatione/firmitate/traditione/vinditione*. Likewise, the hitherto widespread alternative spellings became extremely rare and in many places even vanished. The phonetic and orthographic fuzziness concerning *e/i*, *o/u*, *c/g*, *d/t*, and *b/p* ceased, and the

59 Jennifer R. Davis, *Charlemagne's Practice of Empire* (Cambridge, 2015), p. 211.

60 van Rhijn, 'Priests and the Carolingian Reforms', p. 222.

61 After having become bishop of Basel, in 814 Haito succeeded Waldo as abbot of the monastery of Reichenau. Probably in 812 Haito composed twenty-five *capitula* directed at the priests of his diocese. See, with further bibliographical references: Haito, *Capitula*, ed. Peter Brommer, MGH Capit. episc. 1 (Hanover, 1984), pp. 203–19. Concerning Waldo, see Donald A. Bullough, '"Baiuli" in the Carolingian "regnum Langobardorum" and the Career of Abbot Waldo (d. 813)', *EHR* 77 (1962), 625–37; and Zettler, *Geschichte des Herzogtums Schwaben*, pp. 64–66. Concerning the *Formulae Augienses Collectio A* and the *Formulae Augienses Collectio B*, see Rio, *Legal Practice*, pp. 144–50, with further bibliographical references.

former loss of *h* in the initial sound of a word was emendated. What remained throughout the ninth century was the exchangeability of *ae*, *ę*, and *e*, as well as of *oe* and *e*, and, to a certain extent, also of *c*(*i*) and *t*(*i*) (see Appendix 1).

Refugia of elements and features of the older pre-reform Latinity seem to have been the Thurgau, the Zürichgau, and the Breisgau, that is to say, once again, the contact zones with 'vulgar' Latin or early Romance-speaking areas. In this context, it is also important to observe that in contrast to the situation of Alemannia, things changed only slightly in the charters of neighbouring Raetia. This resistance of elements of a 'pre-reform' Latinity in Raetia might testify to the limits of Carolingian reform, but it might also indicate that a gap was opening between 'reformed' Latin and the vulgar *sermo rusticus*.[62] If the Latin of the Raetian charters was not just due to an 'uncontrolled' linguistic background of the scribes, it might be interpreted as a deliberate choice. If this is true, it was very probably adopted for the audience involved in the legal transaction.[63] In the German(ic)-speaking parts of Alemannia, the emergence, adoption, and application of the reformed, 'Carolingian' Latin did not have the same impact and consequences as in the emerging Romance-speaking world. Nevertheless, a growing interest in the *theodisca* ('popular') *lingua* from the late eighth century must be seen in connection with the reform of Latin and an increasing awareness of the vernacular.

Old High German Vernacular in St Gall Charters

Most of the St Gall charter scribes were Alemans. Their native language was a High Germanic dialect, which according to philologists was spoken and

62 According to Roger Wright, *Late Latin and Early Romance in Spain and Carolingian France* (Liverpool, 1982), the Carolingian 'Renaissance' and the renewal of Latin actually led to an 'invention of Medieval Latin' and the creation of a large gap between a Latin vernacular (the emerging Romance languages) on the one hand and reformed Latin on the other. See also Roger Wright, 'The Conceptual Distinction Between Latin and Romance: Invention or Evolution?', in *Latin and the Romance Languages*, ed. Wright, pp. 103–13, at 109–10. Other scholars have indicated a longer organic connection between written and spoken languages. See, with further bibliographical references, Dag Norberg, 'À quelle époque a-t-on cessé de parler latin en Gaule?', *Annales* 21 (1966), 346–56; Michael Richter, 'À quelle époque a-t-on cessé de parler latin en Gaule? À propos d'une question mal posée', *Annales* 38 (1983), 439–48; van Uytfanghe, 'The Consciousness of a Linguistic Dichotomy', pp. 120–22; McKitterick, *The Carolingians and the Written Word*, pp. 8–12; Herman, *Vulgar Latin*, pp. 114–16; Banniard, 'Language and Communication', p. 700.

63 However, it must be stressed that this adoption of the written word was never intended as a complete assimilation of the spoken language. See Stotz, *Handbuch zur lateinischen Sprache*, 1:66.

written from *c*.750 to *c*.1050. Early medieval codices from St Gall provide some of the earliest documented interest in the vernacular. Even if the two famous St Gall glossaries, the *Abrogans* (St Gall, Stiftsbibliothek, Cod. Sang. 911) and the *Vocabularius sancti Galli* (Stiftsbibliothek, Cod. Sang. 913), were neither composed nor written at St Gall (as is held), these manuscripts could probably already be found in the monastic library in the eighth century. Roughly at the same time, in the 780s or 790s, St Gall scribes added 180 Old High German glosses to the letters of Paul in Stiftsbibliothek, Cod. Sang. 70, a codex that had been written by the St Gall monk Winithar, probably in the 760s. A little later, around 800, monks glossed the Latin text of the rule of St Benedict in Stiftsbibliothek, Cod. Sang. 916 with an Old High German translation. Whereas initially the St Gall monks glossed biblical, patristic, hagiographic, and liturgical manuscripts, they later also commented on grammatical treatises such as Donatus and Priscian, as well as philosophical and poetic works of Boethius, Prudentius, and others. Furthermore, in the ninth century the St Gall monks Hartmut and Werinbert were in close contact with Otfrid of Wissembourg, a pioneer of Old High German literature. Other monks such as Ratpert composed the first oeuvres in Old High German.[64]

On the whole, these few examples make it clear that there was a continuous interest in Old High German in St Gall in Carolingian times. Philologists have also drawn attention to the vernacular words used in the St Gall charter material. Already in the 1950s Stefan Sonderegger had compiled a list of all words of Germanic origin in charters deriving from Switzerland up to the year 1100. He counted sixty-two different words, which, in comparison with the aforementioned manuscripts, is relatively modest.[65] Of these sixty-two words of Germanic origin, many already appear in a Latinized form and for a long time had been in use not only in Alemannia, but also in other regions of

64 Stefan Sonderegger, *Althochdeutsch in St. Gallen: Ergebnisse und Probleme der althochdeutschen Sprachüberlieferung in St. Gallen vom 8. bis zum 12. Jahrhundert* (St Gall, 1970), pp. 28–29, 32–33, 49–52, 64–71; Stefan Sonderegger, 'Althochdeutsch in St. Gallen', in *Das Kloster St. Gallen im Mittelalter. Die kulturelle Blüte vom 8. bis zum 12. Jahrhundert*, ed. Peter Ochsenbein (Stuttgart, 1999), pp. 205–22, at 212–13. Concerning Hartmut, Werinbert, and their connections to Otfrid, see Wolfgang Haubrichs, 'Otfrids St. Galler "Studienfreunde"', *Amsterdamer Beiträge zur älteren Germanistik* 4 (1973), 49–112, at pp. 68–74; Wolfgang Haubrichs, 'Nekrologische Notizen zu Otfrid von Weißenburg. Prosopographische Studien zum sozialen Umfeld und zur Rezeption des Evangelienbuchs', in *Adelsherrschaft und Literatur*, ed. Horst Wenzel, Beiträge zur älteren Deutschen Literaturgeschichte 6 (Bern, 1980), pp. 7–113, at 27–29, 69–70; Schaab, *Mönch in St. Gallen*, pp. 76–77, 89 with nn. 234, 251, 386.

65 Stefan Sonderegger, 'Zu den althochdeutschen Sachwörtern in den lateinischen Urkunden der Schweiz', in *Archivalia et Historica. Arbeiten aus dem Gebiet der Geschichte und des Archivwesens. Festschrift für Anton Largiadèr* (Zürich, 1958), pp. 203–18.

the Frankish world, and sometimes even beyond. Most of these words concern agriculture and landed property, but also Carolingian statehood and its institutions, including such terms as *alodis* ('allod', 'property'), *friskinga* ('suckling pig', 'suckling lamb'), *huoba* ('oxgang', 'homestead'), *iuchum* ('yoke', measure of land), *salicus* ('Salic', i.e. pertaining to a demesne), *mallus* ('judicial assembly'), *scultaizus* ('subordinate officer' or 'local official'), and *wergild* ('wergeld', a man's legal value).[66]

Apart from these kinds of relatively common words of Germanic or Frankish origin, there is little evidence for a substantial use of Old High German vernacular in the St Gall charters. Furthermore, most of the words in question occur only once. Again, the respective terms tend to concern agriculture and landed property, as in the cases of *chuuiltiuuerch* ('night work'), *frehta* ('tribute'), or *hovastatt* ('farmstead'). Some other words pertain to law, such as *furiskiozzo* ('advocate'), *suonbuoch* ('legal document'), and *suuâscara* ('own share'). Other words describe certain textiles, e.g. *rufia* ('rough blanket') or *smoccho* ('linen shirt').[67] With the exception of the verb *brachare* ('to plug'), all of the vernacular words we come across in the St Gall charter material are nouns. There is no evidence of adjectives or adverbs. The nouns tend to explain, specify, and complement the Latin expression of the charter.[68] Indeed, in some cases, the vernacular expressions are introduced by phrases such as *quod Alamanni dicunt*, *qui dicitur*, and *quod tiutiscae nominamus*.[69] In this respect, we can observe analogous words and phrasings in the Alemannic law-code, the *Lex Alamannorum*, from the first half of the eighth century. In this text, we find roughly fifteen vernacular words, most of them specifying the Latin description of a crime or offense. More often than in the charters, the vernacular expression is introduced by the

66 Other words of this group were predominantly used in Alemannia and Bavaria, namely certain measuring and monetary units such as *maldra* and *saiga*. Still others are attested repeatedly in several parts of the Frankish world, but only rarely in St Gall charters, e.g. *anzing(a)* (measure of land), *baro* ('man'), or *feltrum* ('felt blanket'). For philological comment on these words, cf. Sonderegger, 'Zu den althochdeutschen Sachwörtern'; Vincenz Schwab, *Volkssprachige Wörter in Pactus und Lex Alamannorum*, Bamberger interdisziplinäre Mittelalterstudien 11 (Bamberg, 2017), pp. 216–547.

67 For philological comment on these words cf. Sonderegger, 'Zu den althochdeutschen Sachwörtern'; Schwab, *Volkssprachige Wörter*, pp. 216–547.

68 Sonderegger, 'Althochdeutsch in St. Gallen', p. 213; Sonderegger, 'Zu den althochdeutschen Sachwörtern', p. 218.

69 W 228 (= *ChLA* 101, no. 25, pp. 89–93): *quod Alamanni chwiltiwerch dicunt*; W 621 (= *ChLA* 108, no. 53, pp. 148–149): *quod tiutiscae suonbuoch nominamus*. Sonderegger, 'Althochdeutsch in St. Gallen', p. 213. See also W 506 (= *ChLA* 106, no. 55, pp. 138–139): *altero vero autem lineam, qui dicitur smoccho*; W 561 (= *ChLA* 107, no. 58, pp. 144–145): *curtis, id est hovistat*. See the chapter of Roberts and Tinti in this volume on similar 'flagged switches'.

phrase *quod Alamanni dicunt* which 'flagged' the introduction of vernacular terms.[70] As the manuscript evidence shows, in early medieval Alemannia and St Gall the vernacular was an ever-present language of preaching, teaching, and learning.[71] Why, then, is there not more evidence for Old High German words in the St Gall charters? There are several possible and rather pragmatic answers to this question. Apart from formal traditions, most of the St Gall charters document fairly common legal transactions such as donations, *precariae*, and property exchanges. Especially in those charters that document *precariae* (by which possession of the transferred property did not pass to the monastery; rather, the church simply became the landlord), these properties were often not specified or characterized. Most of these charters merely state that the donor transferred all or some of his property in a certain *pagus* and a certain village or place to the monastery. Instead of a proper description, the transferred goods were usually only indicated in the form of a highly standardized and thus rather unspecific appurtenance formula. Consequently, in most of these cases we are missing an accurate localization of the transferred goods. Boundary descriptions of transferred properties comparable to those of Anglo-Saxon charters, are rare, and, in contrast to the documents of neighbouring Raetia and many other parts of western Europe, the neighbours of adjacent properties are not mentioned either.[72] In this respect, the St Gall charters represent a rather simplified variation of the Frankish private charter. However, this model was evidently sufficient for most of the legal transactions that were documented. It seems that there was generally little need to explain and specify things, because the transactions were of a fairly standard

70 Raffaele De Rosa, *Quod Alamanni dicunt. I manoscritti della 'Lex Alamannorum' e il loro lessico antico alto tedesco* (Padova, 2001); Wolfgang Haubrichs, '*Quod Alamanni dicunt*: volkssprachliche Wörter in der *Lex Alamannorum*', in *Recht und Kultur im frühmittelalterlichen Alemannien: Rechtsgeschichte, Archäologie und Geschichte des 7. und 8. Jahrhunderts*, ed. Sebastian Brather, Ergänzungsbände zum Reallexikon der Germanischen Altertumskunde 102 (Berlin, 2017), pp. 169–209, who on 203 also underlines that the main function of the vernacular words is the specification of the Latin text. On the meaning of '*quod vulgo vocant*' in Romance-speaking Gaul, see van Uytfanghe, 'The Consciousness of a Linguistic Dichotomy', pp. 118–119; Katrien Heene, 'Audire, Legere, Vulgo: An Attempt to Define Public Use and Comprehensibility of Carolingian Hagiography', in *Latin and the Romance Languages*, ed. Wright, pp. 146–63, at 151–53. See also Tinti and Roberts, this volume.

71 Grotans, *Reading in Medieval St. Gall*, p. 118.

72 Edward Roberts, 'Boundary Clauses and the Use of the Vernacular in Eastern Frankish Charters, *c*.750–*c*.900', *Historical Research* 91 (2018), 580–604, at 583.

type. Furthermore, all kinds of local people were involved in these legal transactions: office holders, local priests, monastic advocates, and witnesses.[73]

Conclusions

When investigating the remarkable St Gall charter material, it is crucial to distinguish between the majority of charters from primarily German(ic)-speaking Alemannia and the special batch of about fifty charters from the neighbouring 'vulgar' Latin or early Romance-speaking province of Raetia. In addition, a distinction between monastic scribes (St Gall monks) and non-monastic scribes (often local clerics) should be made. This also holds true for questions concerning the formulae and languages used in the charters. Examining the Latin charter language in the Alemannic material, we can observe a strong improvement in line with the standards of the Carolingian reform movement from the 780s onwards. The pace of this improvement was quicker in the blossoming monastic scriptorium, but it is also visible among non-monastic scribes (who are, moreover, scarcely attested after 830).

Especially in contact zones of the German(ic)-speaking and the emerging Romance-speaking worlds, such as the Thurgau and the Zürichgau, as well as the southern Breisgau and the area around Basel, we can observe that only certain elements of a 'scarcely regulated', 'Merovingian' Latinity were more pronounced and can be traced over a longer period. In the charters from Raetia, by contrast, we do not see major changes to the 'vulgar' Latin charter language in the ninth and tenth centuries. This resistance of elements of a 'pre-reform' Latinity in Raetia testifies to a gap opening between 'reformed' Latin and the vulgar *sermo rusticus*, but suggests also that the use of a Latin that was closer to the vernacular was a deliberate choice. Additionally, in Alemannia we can detect a growing interest in the *theodisca lingua* from the late eighth century onwards. Not least in St Gall, the vernacular was ever-present and its importance is demonstrated by numerous manuscripts. However, there is relatively little evidence for Old High German words in the charter material. Apart from formal traditions, this lack might also be explained by the rather boilerplate legal content of these documents.[74]

73 Roberts, 'Boundary Clauses', pp. 593–94.

74 I am grateful to the editors for the original invitation to speak in Vitoria-Gasteiz and to contribute to this volume.

Appendix 1: Recurrent 'pre-Carolingian' Formulae and Spellings in St Gall charters from Alemannia[75]

abere/abire instead of ***habere***

W 13 (s. viii², 1/43, MS?), W 14 (751, NS, Lanthar, Breisgau), W 15 (752, 1/45, NS, Bero, Basel-Augst), W 29 (761, 2/165, NS/NS?, Waringis, [Thurgau]), W 22 (758, 1/53, NS?, ?), W 31 (761, 1/58, MS?, Pertcauz), W 32 (760×782, 1/54, NS*, Hartker), W 35 (762, NS, Waringis, Thurgau), W 37 (761/62, 2/166, NS/NS?, Waringis, Thurgau), W 69 (773/76, 1/80, MS, Adalrich), W 78 (775/78, 1/84, NS, Lanthar, Breisgau), W 94 (781, 1/90, MS, Liutfrit), W 98 (782?, 1/99, MS, Wincencius), W 108 (784?, 1/107, NS, Salomon, Baar), W 124 (789/90, 2/109, NS, Ratinh, Baar), W II Anh. 1 (780×790, NS, Rodolt), W 138 (795, 2/134, NS, Vunolf, Thurgau), W 140 (795, NS, Starcho, Aargau), W 144 (797, 2/139, NS, Caganhart, Nibelgau), W 161 (800, 2/150, NS, Arnolt, Breisgau), W 179 (804, 100/12, NS, Hadarich, Breisgau), W 189+II Anh. 2 (805/6, 100/20, NS, Emicho, Baar), W 195 (807, 100/26, NS, Huzo, Breisgau), W 257 (821, 111/19, NS, Hratbert, Breisgau), W 283 (823/24, 102/22, NS, Christian, Zürichgau), W 300 (826, 102/40, NS, Christian, Zürichgau), W 425 (853/54, 105/27, MS/MS, Irminfrid/Albarih?).

ad (ipsa) casa Dei

W 10 (743×746, 2/159, NS, Hiring, Zürichgau), W 39 (762/63, 1/60, MS/MS, Winithar/?), W 90 (779, 2/168, NS*, Alboin), W 115 (788/91, NS, Sigoald, Breisgau).

ad ipsa ecclesia

W 12 (743×747, 1/41, NS, Silvester, Zürichgau), W 16 (752, MS, Marcus, S), W 17 (719×759, 1/50, MS, Marcus), W 19 (754, 1/46, MS, Liutfrit), W 20 (755?, 1/48, NS/MS, Lazarus/ Liutfrit), W 29 (761, 2/165, NS/NS?, Waringis, [Thurgau]), W 36 (762, 1/55, MS, Autwin), W 70 (773, 1/81, NS, Hupert, Baar), W 100 (783, 1/105, MS, Wano), W 139 (795/96?, 2/131, NS, Audadcar, Baar), W 291 (825, 102/30, NS, Atto, Basel-Augst).

---

75 Explanation of the data-sets: W[artmann] number (date, *ChLA* volume/number, scribe, and, in the case of non-monastic scribes, the pagus/region of the *actum* location).
Abbreviations:
MS = monastic scribe
NS = non-monastic scribe
NS* = scribes not attested as monks, but writing at St Gall or in the service of the bishops of Constance and abbots of St Gall
MS/MS (e.g. Irminfrid/Albarih?): charter in which an individual is mentioned as the nominal scribe, but another scribe has executed it (e.g. Irminfrid is named as monastic scribe, but the charter was probably written by another monastic scribe, Albarih).

ad ipso (sacro/sancto) loco

W 15 (752, 1/45, NS, Bero, Basel-Augst), W 23 (758, 1/51, MS, Theotbald), W 31 (761, 1/58, MS?, Pertcauz), W 35 (762, NS, Waringis, Thurgau), W 37 (761/62, 2/166, NS/NS?, Waringis, Thurgau), W 78 (775/78, 1/84, NS, Lanthar, Breisgau), W 129 (791, 2/124, NS/NS, Waringis/Adam, Thurgau), W 138 (795, 2/134, NS, Vunolf, Thurgau), W 170a (801/2, 2/153, NS, Wanilo, Baar), W 170b (801/2, 2/170, NS, Wanilo, Baar), W 182 (803/5, 100/15, NS, Baldcoz, Thurgau).

ad (ipso) monasterio

W 37 (761/62, 2/166, NS/NS?, Waringis, Thurgau), W 52 (769, NS, Moathelm, Argengau), W 71 (774?, MS, Waldo), W 108 (784?, 1/107, NS, Salomon, Baar), W 134 (792/95, NS?, ?), W 182 (803/5, 100/15, NS, Baldcoz, Thurgau).

adque instead of *atque*

(Instances in approx. 40–50 charters) W 10 (743–46, 2/159, NS, Hiring, Zürichgau)—W 179 (804, 100/12, NS, Hadarich, Breisgau).
Thereafter: W 201 (809, 100/34, NS, Bernegar, Zürichgau), W 206 (812, 100/42, NS, Bernegar, Zürichgau), W 283 (823/24, 102/22, NS, Christian, Zürichgau), W 291 (825, 102/30, NS, Atto, Basel-Augst), W 300 (826, 102/40, NS, Christian, Zürichgau), W 301 (826, 102/41, NS, Christian, Zürichgau), W. II Anh. 26 (839, 111/20, NS, ?, Thurgau).

a(n)c instead of *ha(n)c*

W 22 (758, 1/53, NS?, ?), W 35 (762, NS, Waringis, Thurgau), W 37 (761/62, 2/166, NS/NS?, Waringis, Thurgau), W 40 ([736]?, 2/156, MS+MS), W 116 (788, 2/118, MS?, Engilbert), W 138 (795, 2/134, NS, Vunolf, Thurgau), W 153 (795/98, 2/135, MS, Mauvo), W 159 (799/802, 2/148, NS/MS-MS, Lanto, Baar?), W 161 (800, 2/150, NS, Arnolt, Breisgau), W 164 (801/2, 100/2, NS, Radmund, Bregenz), W 179 (804, 100/12, NS, Hadarich, Breisgau), W 186 (800x806?, 100/17, NS/MS, Scrutolf/Mauvo), W 283 (823/24, 102/22, NS, Christian, Zürichgau), W 300 (826, 102/40, NS, Christian, Zürichgau), W 301 (826, 102/41, NS, Christian, Zürichgau), W 322 (828/29, 103/12, MS, Rihpreht), W 374 (838/39, 104/19, MS, Theothart), W 376 (838, 104/14, NS, Baar).

contenere instead of *continere*

(Instances in more than 100 charters) W 11 (743×747, 2/160, NS, Silvester, Zürichgau) / W 43 (763/64, 1/61, MS)—W 216 (812×816, 101/9, MS).
Thereafter: W 283 (823/24, 102/22, NS, Christian, Zürichgau), W 291 (825, 102/30, NS, Atto, Basel-Augst), W 299 (826, 102/39, MS/MS, Bernwig/Watto), W 300 (826, 102/40, NS, Christian, Zürichgau), W 301 (826, 102/41, NS, Christian, Zürichgau), W 313 (828, NS, Hratbert, Breisgau), W 566 (860, 106/15, NS, Paldene, Zürichgau).

contra hanc donatione/firmitate/traditione/vinditione

W 14 (751, NS, Lanthar, Breisgau), W 15 (752, 1/45, NS, Bero, Basel-Augst), W 16 (752, MS, Marcus), W 18 (754?, 2/163, MS, Liutfrit), W 19 (754, 1/46, MS, Liutfrit), W 23 (758, 1/51, MS, Theotbald), W 31 (761, 1/58, MS?, Pertcauz), W 35 (762, NS, Waringis, Thurgau), W 68 (772/73, 1/70, NS+NS, Lanthar+?, Breisgau), W 71 (774?, MS, Waldo), W 81 (775×779, 1/87, NS, Laurentius, Baar), W 102 (785/86, 2/113, NS, Berahtcoz, Baar), W 105 (786, 2/110, NS, Folcram, Breisgau), W 107 (786/89, 2/112, NS*, Jacobus), W 111 (787/90, 2/115, NS*, Bobosinnus, Hegau), W 139 (795/96?, 2/131, NS, Audadcar, Baar), W 161 (800, 2/150, NS, Arnolt, Breisgau), W 166 (802/3, NS, 100/21, Hetti, Baar), W 175 (802/3, 100/22, NS, Hetti, Baar), W 205 (811, 100/41, NS, [Bernegar], Zürichgau), W 206 (812, 100/42, NS, Bernegar, Zürichgau), W 240 (819, 101/38, NS, Hiltiger, Baar), W 272 (822, 102/11, MS+MS, Bernwig+?), W 291 (825, 102/30, NS, Atto, Basel-Augst).

ec **instead of** ***hec***

W 6 ([736], 2/161, MS+MS, Silvester+?), W 40 ([736]?, 2/156, MS+MS), W 283 (823/24, 102/22, NS, Christian, Zürichgau), W 300 (826, 102/40, NS, Christian, Zürichgau), W 301 (826, 102/41, NS, Christian, Zürichgau).

eredes **instead of** ***heredes***

W 22 (758, 1/53, NS?, ?), W 25+II Anh. 1 (773×782, 2/167, MS+MS, Waldo+?), W 31 (761, 1/58, MS?, Pertcauz), W 40 ([736]?, 2/156, MS+MS), W 102 (785/86, 2/113, NS, Berahtcoz, Baar), W 105 (786, 2/110, NS, Folcram, Breisgau), W 108 (784?, 1/107, NS, Salomon, Baar), W 116 (788, 2/118, MS?, Engilbert), W 129 (791, 2/124, NS/NS, Waringis/Adam, Thurgau), W 137 (794/97, NS, Adalhard, Argengau), W 144 (797, 2/139, NS, Caganhart, Nibelgau), W 145 (797, 2/140, NS, Rihbert, Baar), W 275 (819?, O, 102/14, NS, Ato, Thurgau), W 283 (823/24, 102/22, NS, Christian, Zürichgau), W 300 (826, 102/40, NS, Christian, Zürichgau), W 301 (826, 102/41, NS, Christian, Zürichgau), W 315 (828, 103/5, MS, Amalger/?), W 316 (828, 103/6, NS/MS, Huzo/?), W II Anh. 26 (839, 111/20, NS).

fiere/-o **instead of** ***fieri***

W 17 (719×759, 1/50, MS, Marcus), W 35 (762, NS, Waringis, Thurgau), W 68 (772/73, 1/70, NS+NS, Lanthar+?, Breisgau), W 78 (775/78, 1/84, NS, Lanthar, Breisgau), W 81 (775×779, 1/87, NS, Laurentius, Baar), W 85 (779/82, 1/91, NS*, Wolvinus), W 105 (786, 2/110, NS, Folcram, Breisgau).

(h)abire **instead of** ***habere***

W 14 (751, NS, Lanthar, Breisgau), W 15 (752, 1/45, NS, Bero, Basel-Augst), W 23 (758, 1/51, MS, Theotbald), W 24 (754/59, MS?, Silvester), W 29 (761, 2/165, NS/NS?, Waringis, [Thurgau]), W 31 (761, 1/58, MS?, Pertcauz), W 68 (772/73, 1/70, NS+NS, Lanthar+?,

Breisgau), W 78 (775/78, 1/84, NS, Lanthar, Breisgau), W 94 (781, 1/90, MS, Liutfrit), W 105 (786, 2/110, NS, Folcram, Breisgau), W 112 (787?, NS, Theutpert, Thurgau), W 129 (791, 2/124, NS/NS, Waringis/Adam, Thurgau), W 138 (795, 2/134, NS, Vunolf, Thurgau), W 170a (801/2, 2/153, NS, Wanilo, Baar).

ic instead of ***hic***

W 6 ([736], 2/161, MS+MS, Silvester+?), W 37 (761/62, 2/166, NS/NS?, Waringis, Thurgau), W 40 ([736]?, 2/156, MS+MS), W 102 (785/86, 2/113, NS, Berahtcoz, Baar), W 118 (794, 2/117, NS, Adam, Thurgau), W 138 (795, 2/134, NS, Vunolf, Thurgau), W 283 (823/24, 102/22, NS, Christian, Zürichgau), W 300 (826, 102/40, NS, Christian, Zürichgau), W 301 (826, 102/41, NS, Christian, Zürichgau).

intecrum instead of ***integrum***

W 16 (752, MS, Marcus), W 138 (795, 2/134, NS, Vunolf, Thurgau), W 144 (797, 2/139, NS, Caganhart, Nibelgau), W 148 (797, 2/143, NS, Bernegar, Zürichgau), W 163 (802, 100/1, NS, Bernegar, Zürichgau), W 167 (802?, 100/3, NS, Ysanbert, Breisgau), W 201 (809, 100/34, NS, Bernegar, Zürichgau), W 206 (812, 100/42, NS, Bernegar, Zürichgau).

(per)mania(n)t instead of ***(per)manea(n)t***

W 6 ([736], 2/161, MS+MS, Silvester+?), W 14 (751, NS, Lanthar, Breisgau), W 15 (752, 1/45, NS, Bero, Basel-Augst), W 16 (752, MS, Marcus), W 20 (755?, 1/48, NS/MS, Lazarus/Liutfrit), W 37 (761/62, 2/166, NS/NS?, Waringis, Thurgau), W 40 ([736]?, 2/156, MS+MS), W 51 (767×768, 1/66, NS, ?, Baar?), W 73 (777?, MS, Liutfrit), W 78 (775/78, 1/84, NS, Lanthar, Breisgau), W 81 (775×779, 1/87, NS, Laurentius, Baar), W 94 (781, 1/90, MS, Liutfrit), W 105 (786, 2/110, NS, Folcram, Breisgau), W 138 (795, 2/134, NS, Vunolf, Thurgau), W 161 (800, 2/150, NS, Arnolt, Breisgau).

monastirium instead of ***monasterium***

W 18 (754?, 2/163, MS, Liutfrit), W 19 (754, 1/46, MS, Liutfrit), W 23 (758, 1/51, MS, Theotbald), W 26 (760, 1/56, MS?, Ilteri), W 27 (761?, 1/52, MS, Autwin), W 30 (761, 1/57, MS, Winithar), W 36 (762, 1/55, MS, Autwin), W 38 (763, 1/59, NS/MS, Maginrat, Breisgau), W 43 (763/64, 1/61, MS), W 81 (775×779, 1/87, NS, Laurentius, Baar), W 83 (778, 1/89, MS, Waldo), W 94 (781, 1/90, MS, Liutfrit).

noncopante/-i or ***noncobante/-i*** instead of ***nuncupante***

W 6 ([736], 2/161, MS+MS, Silvester+?), W 26 (760, 1/56, MS?, Ilteri), W 29 (761, 2/165, NS/NS?, Waringis, [Thurgau]), W 40 ([736]?, 2/156, MS+MS), W 94 (781, 1/90, MS, Liutfrit), W 167 (802?, 100/3, NS, Ysanbert, Breisgau), W 257 (821, 111/19, NS, Hratbert, Breisgau).

onor instead of ***honor***

W 15 (752, 1/45, NS, Bero, Basel-Augst), W 22 (758, 1/53, NS?, ?), W 70 (773, 1/81, NS, Hupert, Baar), W 105 (786, 2/110, NS, Folcram, Breisgau), W 138 (795, 2/134, NS, Vunolf, Thurgau), W 144 (797, 2/139, NS, Caganhart, Nibelgau), W 397 (838/45, 104/40, NS, Ramming, Breisgau), W 565 ([860], 106/14, NS, Paldene, Zürichgau), W 566 (860, 106/15, NS, Paldene, Zürichgau).

pacus instead of ***pagus***

W 15 (752, 1/45, NS, Bero, Basel-Augst), W 29 (761, 2/165, NS/NS?, Waringis, [Thurgau]), W 37 (761/62, 2/166, NS/NS?, Waringis, Thurgau), W 70 (773, 1/81, NS, Hupert, Baar) (*pace*), W 99 (783/86, 1/104, NS*, Ratfrid), W 102 (785/786, 2/113, NS, Berahtcoz, Baar), W 105 (786, 2/110, NS, Folcram, Breisgau), W 138 (795, 2/134, NS, Vunolf, Thurgau), W 144 (797, 2/139, NS, Caganhart, Nibelgau), W 161 (800, 2/150, NS, Arnolt, Breisgau).

prespiter instead of ***presbiter***

W 32 (760×782, 1/54, NS*, Hartker), W 87 (779, 1/92, NS, Maio, Linzgau), W 116 (788, 2/118, MS?, Engilbert) (*brespiter*), W 140 (795, NS, Starcho, Aargau), W 144 (797, 2/139, NS, Caganhart, Nibelgau), W 282 (824, 102/21, NS/MS, Cunzo/?), W 341 (832, 103/31, MS, Engilger), W 422 (853, 105/10, MS, Iso), W 522 (867, 107/16, NS, Walthere, Zürichgau), W 658 (887, 109/40, NS, Erchinpert, Thurgau), W 751 (910?, MS, Thioto), W 752 (910?, MS, Thioto), W 795 (941/942, NS, Wichinger, ?).

pro remedium animae meae

(Instances in approx. 30–40 charters) W 6 ([736], 2/161, MS+MS, Silvester+?)—W 701 (895, 110/26, NS, Nordpert, Thurgau).

pro salutem animae meae

W 11 (743×747, 2/160, NS, Silvester, Zürichgau) / W 12 (743×747, 1/41, NS, Silvester, Zürichgau), W 25+II Anh. 1 (773–82, 2/167, MS+MS, Waldo+?), W 60 (774, 1/73, NS*, Matheus), W 69 (773/76, 1/80, MS, Adalrich), W 126 (791/95?, NS/MS?, Plidolf/Mauvo?), W 191 (808?, 100/30, MS, Mano).

puplice/-i instead of ***publice***

(Instances in approx. 30–40 charters) W 15 (752, 1/45, NS, Bero, Basel-Augst)-W 211 (813/14, 100/46, NS, Maio, Linzgau) (corrected).

Thereafter: W 291 (825, 102/30, NS, Atto, Basel-Augst), W 561 (872, 107/58, MS, Liuto), W 669 (889, 109/51, NS, Salacho, Thurgau), W 684 (892, 110/6, NS, Vuoto, Baar).

rep(p)edere/rep(p)editio instead of *rep(p)etere/rep(p)etitio*

W 25+II Anh. 1 (773×782, 2/167, MS+MS, Waldo+?), W 33 (762?, 2/164, MS, Autwin), W 37 (761/62, 2/166, NS/NS?, Waringis, Thurgau), W 67 (772/76, 1/79, MS, Adalrich), W 85 (779/82, 1/91, NS*, Wolvinus), W 102 (785/86, 2/113, NS, Berahtcoz, Baar), W 103 (786, 1/108, NS-MS?, Reginbald), W 110 (786/89, 2/114, MS?, Lanbert, Breisgau), W 118 (794, 2/117, NS, Adam, Thurgau).

rocare instead of *rogare*

W 18 (754?, 2/163, MS, Liutfrit), W 19 (754, 1/46, MS, Liutfrit), W 20 (755?, 1/48, NS/MS, Lazarus/Liutfrit), W 22 (758, 1/53, NS?, ?), W 78 (775/78, 1/84, NS, Lanthar, Breisgau), W 102 (785/86, 2/113, NS, Berahtcoz, Baar), W 138 (795, 2/134, NS, Vunolf, Thurgau).

sagrus instead of *sacrus*

W 6 ([736], 2/161, MS+MS, Silvester+?), W 31 (761, 1/58, MS?, Pertcauz), W 35 (762, NS, Waringis, Thurgau), W 37 (761/62, 2/166, NS/NS?, Waringis, Thurgau), W 38 (763, 1/59, NS/MS, Maginrat, Breisgau), W 94 (781, 1/90, MS, Liutfrit), W 154 (798, 2/147, MS?, Bertilo), W 170a (801/2, 2/153, NS, Wanilo, Baar).

(sub)scribsi instead of *(sub)scripsi*

W 4 (721×736, MS, Peter), W 21 (756?, 1/49, NS, Arnulf, Alsatia), W 42 (764?, 1/63, NS, Werdo, Baar), W 128 (785×808, 1/102, NS-MS?/MS, Angilbert), W 136 (793, 2/130, NS/MS, Heriolt/Mauvo), W 143 (797, 2/138, MS, Mauvo), W 146 (797, 2/141, MS, Mauvo), W 147 (797, 2/142, MS?, Bertilo), W 151 (798, 2/144, NS*, Pertigar), W 153 (795/798, 2/135, MS, Mauvo), W 155 (800?, 2/149, MS, Mauvo), W 156 (798/99, 2/145, NS, Deodolt, Argengau), W 160 (800?, 2/152, MS, Mauvo), W 172 (802, 100/7, NS/MS, Ratinh/Mauvo), W 176 (797/98, 2/146, NS/MS, Pertigar/Mauvo), W 186 (800×806?, 100/17, NS/MS, Scrutolf/Mauvo), W 199 (809?, 100/32, NS/MS, Oto/Mauvo), W 246 (819/20, 101/43, MS, Wolfcoz), W 283 (823/24, 102/22, NS, Christian, Zürichgau), W 300 (826, 102/40, NS, Christian, Zürichgau), W 301 (826, 102/41, NS, Christian, Zürichgau), W 375 (838, 104/13, MS, Rihpret), W 383 (840/41, 104/26, MS, Wolfcoz), W 462 (858, 105/49, MS, Bernwig), W 469 (858/59, 106/12, MS, Nandcrim), W 481 (861, 106/22, MS, Bernwig), W 579 (874, 108/6, MS, Ecco), W 581 (868/69, 107/44, NS, Amalpert, Baar), W II Anh. 3 (900, 104/25, NS, Hitto, Thurgau).

sigla/segla instead of *sicla*

W 17 (719×759, 1/50, MS, Marcus), W 18 (754?, 2/163, MS, Liutfrit), W 32 (760–82, 1/54, NS*, Hartker), W 33 (762?, 2/164, MS, Autwin), W 73 (777?, MS, Liutfrit), W 87 (779, 1/92, NS, Maio, Linzgau), W 94 (781, 1/90, MS, Liutfrit), W 110 (786/89, 2/114, MS?, Lanbert,

Breisgau), W 142 (796, 2/136, MS?+NS, ?+Adam, Thurgau), W 148 (797, 2/143, NS, Bernegar, Zürichgau), W 163 (802, 100/1, NS, Bernegar, Zürichgau).

stibulatio instead of ***stipulatio***
(Instances in approx. 90–100 charters) W 10 (743×746, 2/159, NS, Hiring, Zürichgau)—W 219 (101/7, MS, Amalger).
Thereafter: W 240 (819, 101/38, NS, Hiltiger, Baar), W 257 (821, 111/19, NS, Hratbert, Breisgau), W 283 (823/24, 102/22, NS, Christian, Zürichgau), W 291 (825, 102/30, NS, Atto, Basel), W 300 (826, 102/40, NS, Christian, Zürichgau), W 301 (826, 102/41, NS, Christian, Zürichgau), W 397 (838/45, 104/40, NS, Ramming, Breisgau), W 400 (852, 105/44, MS, Fartman) (corrected), W 487+II Anh. 7 (855/61, 106/28, NS, Zezzo, Breisgau), W 559 (872?, 107/56, MS, Winidhere).

Appendix 2a: The (original) 'Silvester charters'[76]

W 6 ([736], 2/161, MS+MS, Silvester+?): 'In Christi nomine. Ego quidam Petto cogitavi Dei induidum vel divina retributionem vel pecadis meis veniam promirere, et ut mihi in fuduro mercis boni **obiris adcrescat**. Propterea vernacula terre **iuris** mei in logo **noncubantem**, quod dicitur Clata … cum agrus, cum pradus, cum silvis, cum aquis …'

W 40 ([736?], 2/156, MS+MS): 'In Christi nomine. Ego quidam Appo cogitavi Dei induidum vel divinam retributionem, ut mihi in fuduro mercis boni **oberis adgrescat**, et adgrevit mihi Dei volontas, ut terra **iures** mei in logo **noncobantem**, quo dicitur … cum pradus, cum agris, cum omni acesibus …'

W 6 ([736], 2/161, MS+MS, Silvester+?): 'Si quis vero, quod fudurum ese non gredo, si ego **ebse** aud ullus de eridibus **meis** vel ulla suposita persona, qui contra **hanc** donationem veneret aud agere temtaveret, solvat in fesco aurum libras II et argentum **pondira** V et quod **pedet** vendicare non valeat, sed presens ec ebistola omni tempore firma et inlisa permaniat cum extibulationem **supnixa**.'

W 40 ([736?], 2/156, MS+MS): 'Si quis autem, quod fudurum ese non gredo, si ego **epse** aut ullus de eredes **meus** vel aliquid suposita persona, qui contra **anc** donationem veneret aut ve[ne]re temtaveret, inprimis Dei ira ingorat, et a communionis corpuris Christi extranius sit, et solvat in fesco aurum libras duas et argentum **pondera** quinque, et quod **pedit** vendicare non valiat, sed presens ec gartola homni tempore ferma et inlisa permaniat cum extibulationem **supnixxa**.'

76 These texts fundamentally follow the edition of Wartmann, but take into account the newer editions found in *ChLA*.

Appendix 2b: The 'Waringis-formulae' in their Orthographic Variants (original charters only)

W 37 (761/62, 2/166, NS/NS?, Waringis): '**Sagrosancto** sancta eclesia sancti Gallune, qui est constructa **in paco** Durgauia, ubi **ipsic** in corpore **requiiscit** et Iohannis abbas **ad** presens rector eclesia esse videntur. Ego **in Dei nomen** Winibertus cogitans Dei [intuitum], ut **aliquit rem mea ad ipso sagro loco pro remedium animi mei** condonare **dibere**, quod et ita feci'.

W 129 (791, 2/124, NS/NS, Waringis/Adam): '**In Dei nomine** Adaloldus. Decrevit mihi voluntas, ut **aliquid de rem meam pro remedium animę meę** ad monisterium sancti Galloni, ubi **ipse** in corpore **requiescit** et Werdo abbas **et** presens esse videntur, condonare **debere**, quod et ita feci'.

W 131 (792, 2/126, MS, Mauvo v. Waringis): '**Sacrosancto** sancta ecclesia sancti Gallonis, ubi **ipse** in corpore **requiescit**, que est constructa in pago Arbunense, ubi Werdo abbas presens esse videtur. Ego **in Dei nomine** Wolfgaer cogitans Dei intuitum vel ęternam retributionem vel pro remedium anime meę aliquid de re mea **ad ipsum sacrum loco** condonare deberem, quod et ita feci'.

W 132 (792, 791, 2/127, MS, Mauvo v. Waringis): '**Sacrosancto** sancta ecclesia sancti Gallonis confessoris, ubi in corpore **requiescit** et Werdo abbas **ad** presens esse videtur. Ego **in Dei nomine** Rihpaldus clericus cogitans Dei intuitum vel ęternam retributionem vel pro remedium animę meę, ut aliquid de re mea **ad ipsum sacrum locum** condonare deberem, quod et ita feci'.

W 138 (795, 2/134, NS, Vunolf a. Waringis): '**Sacrosancto** sancta eclesia, qui est constructa **in paco** Arbonninse in onore sancte Callone, **ube ipsic** in corpore [**re**]**quiissis**. Ego in Dei nomen Vunolf cliricus **tecrevit** mih[i] voluntas, **quo aliquit te rem mea pro remmedium animi mei** ad ipso sacro loco **contonare tepere**, quod et ita feci'.

W 37 (761/62, 2/166, NS/NS?, Waringis): '**oc est in paco** ... quicquid ibidem visus sum **abere, mancipies, pecunies, casas, casalis,** campis, pratis, silvis, aquis aquarumque decursibus, omnia ex integro de meo iure **ad ipso monasterio** sancti Gallune post opito meo trado adque transfundo ...'

W 129 (791, 2/124, NS/NS, Waringis/Adam): '**hoc est in pago** ... quicquid ibidem visus sum **habere, mancipiis, pecuniis, casis, casalis,** campis, pratis, silvis, aquis aquarumque decursibus, ad integrum a die presente **ad ipso sacro** loco trado adque transfundo dominatione ...'

W 131 (792, 2/126, MS, Mauvo v. Waringis): '**hoc est in pago** ... quicquid ibidem ... id est casas, casales, campis, pratis, silvis, aquis aquarumque decursibus, omnia ex integro a die presente **ad ipsum sacrum locum** trado atque transfundo dominationem ...'

W 132 (792, 2/127, MS, Mauvo v. Waringis): '**hoc est in pago** ... cum ipsis mancipiis et cum casas et pecuniis et casales, campis, pratis, silvis, aquis aquarumque decursibus, omnia ex integro **ad ipsum sacrum locum** trado atque transfundo'

W 138 (795, 2/134, NS, Vunolf a. Waringis): '**oc est in baco** … quidquid ibidem visus sum **abere, casas, casalis**, campis, pratis, silvis, aquis **aquerumque tecursibus, omnia ex intecro te me iore a tie presente in dominacione sancti Callone** …'

W 37 (761/62, 2/166, NS/NS?, Waringis): 'Si quis ego **aut eridis** mei aut ulla oposita **persuna**, qui contra **anc tradicione ista** venire **timtaverit** aut agere **presumserit**, tunc inferat parti custodiente **dubla repedi[ti]one** et a fisco auri uncia quinque et argenti punduras duas, et **nichilhominus** presens tradicio istic firma et **stabelis permaniat** stibulatione **subnixsa**.'

W 129 (791, 2/124, NS/NS, Waringis/Adam): 'Si quis ego **aut eredis** mei aut ulla oposita **persona**, qui **contra hanc tradicionem istam** venire **tentaverit** aut agere **presumpserit**, tunc inferat parti custodiente **dupla repeticione** et a fisco auri uncias tres et argento pondoras duas, et **nihilhominus** presens tradicio istic omni tempore firma et **stabilis permaneat** stibulacione **subnexa**.'

W 131 (792, 2/126, MS, Mauvo v. Waringis): 'Si quis ego **aut heredes** mei aut ulla **opposita persona** contra **hanc tradicionem istam** venire **temptaverit** aut agere **presumserit**, tunc **inferat parte custodiente duplam repetitionem** et a fisco auri untias III et argenti **pondera** dua, et **nihilominus presens tradicio** omni tempore firma et **stabilis permaneat stibulatione subnexa**.'

W 138 (795, 2/134, NS, Vunolf a. Waringis): 'Si quis ego **aud** ullus te generacione mea aud ullo **oposita persona**, qui contra **anc t[r]adicione ista** venire **t[e]nctaverit aud** ea agere **presumserit**, tunc **inferat parte cusdodiente tubla rebidicione** et ad **visco auri uncias tuas** et argenti pondera una, et nihhilominus **present tradicio isdic** omni tempore firma et **stapilis permaniad stibulacione subnexsa**.'

W 118 (794, 2/117, NS, Adam a. Waringis): ' … ut nec ego nec heredis mei nec nulla **oposita persona** de ipsa commutacione nihil dicere nec **repedire non dibiamus**, sed commutacio istic omni tempore firma et stabilis permaneat stibulacione subnexa.'

W 132 (792, 2/127, MS, Mauvo v. Waringis [NS]): ' … ut nec ego nec nullus de generatione mea nec nulla **opposita persona** de ipsa tradicione nihil dicere nec **repetire non debeamus** … et nihilominus presens tradicio istic omni tempore firma et stabilis permaneat stibulatione subnexa.'

W 37 (761/62, 2/166, NS/NS?, Waringis): 'Actum in villa Wila **puplici** presentibus **cor ic** signacula contenuntur. Signum + Winiberto **auture**, qui **anc tradicione ista firi rogavit**'.

W 118 (794, 2/117, NS, Adam a. Waringis [NS]): 'Actum in villa Elihcauia **puplici**, presentibus **quorum ic** signacula contenuntur. Signum + Werinberto **auctore**, qui **hanc** commutationem **istam fieri rogavit**'.

W 129 (791, 2/124, NS/NS, Waringis/Adam): 'Actum in villa Wangas **puplici**, presentibus **quorum hic** signacula contenuntur. Signum + Adaloldi **auctore**, qui **hanc tradicionem istam fieri rogavit**'.

W 131 (792, 2/126, MS, Mauvo v. Waringis): 'Actum in monasterio sancti Gallonis **publice**, presentibus **quorum hic** signacula continentur. Signum Wolfger **auctoris**, qui **hanc tradicionem fieri rogavit**'.

W 132 (792, 2/127, MS, Mauvo v. Waringis): 'Actum in villa Puzinesvillare **publice**, presentibus **quorum hic** signacula continentur. Signum Rihpaldi clerici **auctoris**, qui **hanc traditionem fieri rogavit**'.

W 138 (795, 2/134, NS, Vunolf a. Waringis): 'Actum in villa Tecerscai **puplici**, presentibus **corum ic** sincnacula continuntur. Sinum Vunolf cliricus **auctore**, qui **anc tradicione ista viro rocavit**'.

Bibliography

Primary Sources

Chartae latinae antiquiores, eds Albert Bruckner et al., 118 vols (Olten et al., 1954–2019).

Chartularium Sangallense, I (700–840), ed. Peter Erhart with the collaboration of Karl Heidecker and Bernhard Zeller (St Gall, 2013).

Ekkehard IV, *Casus sancti Galli*, ed. Hans F. Haefele, Ausgewählte Quellen zur deutschen Geschichte des Mittelalters 10, 3rd ed. (Darmstadt, 1991).

Haito, *Capitula*, ed. Peter Brommer, MGH Capit. episc. 1 (Hanover, 1984), pp. 203–19.

Liber promissionum sancti Galli, ed. Paul Piper, MGH Necr. Supplement (Berlin, 1884), pp. 111–33.

Urkundenbuch der Abtei Sanct Gallen, ed. Hermann Wartmann, 3 vols (Zürich, 1863–82).

Walahfrid, *Vita sancti Galli*, ed. Bruno Krusch, MGH SS rer. Merov. 4 (Hanover and Leipzig, 1902) pp. 280–337.

Walahfrid, *Vita sancti Otmari*, 1, ed. Ildefons von Arx, in MGH SS 2 (Hanover, 1829), pp. 41–47.

Wetti, *Vita sancti Galli*, ed. Bruno Krusch, MGH SS rer. Merov. 4 (Hanover and Leipzig, 1902) pp. 256–80.

Secondary Sources

Banniard, Michel, 'Acrolecte et identité culturelle en Francia carolingienne (VIIIe–IXe s.)', in *Sprache und Identität im frühen Mittelalter*, eds Walter Pohl and Bernhard Zeller, Forschungen zur Geschichte des Mittelalters 20 (Vienna, 2012), pp. 109–20.

Banniard, Michel, 'Language and Communication in Carolingian Europe', in *The New Cambridge Medieval History, Volume II: c.700–c.900*, ed. Rosamond McKitterick (Cambridge, 1995), pp. 695–708.

Banniard, Michel, 'Niveaux de competence langagière chez les élites', in *La culture du Haut Moyen Âge, une question d'élites?*, eds François Bougard, Régine Le Jan, and Rosamond McKitterick, Collection Haut Moyen Âge 7 (Turnhout, 2009), pp. 39–61.

Banniard, Michel, 'The Transition from Latin to the Romance Languages', in *The Cambridge History of the Romance Languages, Volume 2: Contexts*, eds Martin Maiden, John Charles Smith, and Adam Ledgeway (Cambridge, 2013), pp. 57–106.

Berchtold, Simone M., 'Orts- und Flurnamen', in *Das Drusental. Der Walgau und das Vorderland im früheren Mittelalter*, ed. Peter Erhart, Elementa Walgau 7 (Nenzing, 2009), pp. 139–58.

Borgolte, Michael, 'Kommentar zu Ausstellungsdaten, Actum- und Güterorten der älteren St. Galler Urkunden (Wartmann I und II mit Nachträgen in III und IV)', in *Subsidia Sangallensia I. Materialien und Untersuchungen zu den Verbrüderungsbüchern und zu den älteren Urkunden des Stiftsarchivs St. Gallen*, eds Michael Borgolte, Dieter Geuenich, and Karl Schmid, St. Galler Kultur und Geschichte 16 (St Gall, 1986), pp. 323–475.

Bruckner, Albert, *Scriptoria Medii Aevi Helvetica. Denkmäler schweizerischer Schreibkunst des Mittelalters, vols 2–3: Schreibschulen der Diözese Konstanz (St. Gallen 1–2)* (Geneva, 1936–38).

Bullimore, Katherine, 'Folcwin of Rankweil: The World of a Carolingian Local Official', *EME* 13 (2005), 43–77.

Bullough, Donald A., '"Baiuli" in the Carolingian "regnum Langobardorum" and the Career of Abbot Waldo (d. 813)', *EHR* 77 (1962), 625–37.

Davis, Jennifer R., *Charlemagne's Practice of Empire* (Cambridge, 2015).

De Rosa, Raffaele, *Quod Alamanni dicunt. I manoscritti della 'Lex Alamannorum' e il loro lessico antico alto tedesco* (Padova, 2001).

Dette, Christoph, 'Schüler im frühen und hohen Mittelalter. Die St. Galler Klosterschule des 9. und 10. Jahrhunderts', *Studien und Mitteilungen zur Geschichte des Benediktinerordens und seiner Zweige* 105 (1994), 7–64.

Erhart, Peter, 'Erratische Blöcke am Alpennordrand? Die rätischen Urkunden und ihre Überlieferung', in *Die Privaturkunden der Karolingerzeit*, eds Peter Erhart, Karl Heidecker, and Bernhard Zeller (Dietikon-Zürich, 2009), pp. 161–71.

Erhart, Peter and Kleindinst, Julia, *Urkundenlandschaft Rätien*, Forschungen zur Geschichte des Mittelalters 7 (Vienna, 2004).

Erhart, Peter and Zeller, Bernhard, 'Rätien und Alemannien. Schriftformen im Vergleich', in *Wandel und Konstanz zwischen Bodensee und Lombardei zur Zeit Karls des Großen*, ed. Hans Rudolf Sennhauser, Acta Müstair 3 (Zürich, 2013), pp. 299–318.

Fichtenau, Heinrich, *Das Urkundenwesen in Österreich vom 8. bis zum frühen 13. Jahrhundert*, Mitteilungen des Instituts für Österreichische Geschichtsforschung, Ergänzungsband 23 (Vienna, 1971).

Fouracre, Paul and Gerberding, Richard A., *Late Merovingian France: History and Hagiography, 640–720* (Manchester, 1996).

Ganz, David, '*Temptabat et scribere*: Vom Schreiben in der Karolingerzeit', in *Schriftkultur und Reichsverwaltung unter den Karolingern*, ed. Rudolf Schieffer, Abhandlungen der Rheinisch-Westfälischen Akademie der Wissenschaften 97 (Opladen, 1996), pp. 13–33.

Goetz, Hans-Werner, 'Beobachtungen zur Grundherrschaftsentwicklung der Abtei St. Gallen vom 8. zum 9. Jahrhundert', in *Strukturen der Grundherrschaft im frühen Mittelalter*, ed. Werner Rösener, Veröffentlichungen des Max-Planck-Instituts für Geschichte 92 (Göttingen, 1989), pp. 197–246.

Goetz, Hans-Werner, 'Die "private" Grundherrschaft des frühen Mittelalters im Spiegel der St. Galler Traditionsurkunden', in *Tätigkeitsfelder und Erfahrungshorizonte des ländlichen Menschen in der frühmittelalterlichen Grundherrschaft (bis ca. 1000). Festschrift Dieter Hägermann zum 65. Geburtstag*, ed. Brigitte Kasten, Vierteljahrschrift für Sozial- und Wirtschaftsgeschichte, Beihefte 184 (Munich, 2006), pp. 111–37.

Grotans, Anna A., *Reading in Medieval St. Gall*, Cambridge Studies in Palaeography and Codicology 13 (Cambridge, 2006).

Haubrichs, Wolfgang, 'Nekrologische Notizen zu Otfrid von Weißenburg. Prosopographische Studien zum sozialen Umfeld und zur Rezeption des Evangelienbuchs', in *Adelsherrschaft und Literatur*, ed. Horst Wenzel, Beiträge zur älteren Deutschen Literaturgeschichte 6 (Bern, 1980), pp. 7–113.

Haubrichs, Wolfgang, 'Otfrids St. Galler "Studienfreunde"', *Amsterdamer Beiträge zur älteren Germanistik* 4 (1973), 49–112.

Haubrichs, Wolfgang, 'Die Personennamen', in *Das Drusental. Der Walgau und das Vorderland im früheren Mittelalter*, ed. Peter Erhart, Elementa Walgau 7 (Nenzing, 2009), pp. 161–65.

Haubrichs, Wolfgang, '*Quod Alamanni dicunt*: volkssprachliche Wörter in der *Lex Alamannorum*', in *Recht und Kultur im frühmittelalterlichen Alemannien: Rechtsgeschichte, Archäologie und Geschichte des 7. und 8. Jahrhunderts*, ed. Sebastian Brather, Ergänzungsbände zum Reallexikon der Germanischen Altertumskunde 102 (Berlin, 2017), pp. 169–209.

Heene, Katrien, 'Audire, Legere, Vulgo: An Attempt to Define Public Use and Comprehensibility of Carolingian Hagiography', in *Latin and the Romance Languages in the Early Middle Ages*, ed. Roger Wright (London, 1991), pp. 146–63.

Heidecker, Karl, 'Charters as Texts and as Objects in Judicial Actions: The Example of the Carolingian Private Charters of St Gall', in *Medieval Legal Process: Physical, Spoken and Written Performance in the Middle Ages*, eds Paul S. Barnwell and Marco Mostert (Turnhout, 2011), pp. 39–53.

Heidecker, Karl, 'Urkunden schreiben im alemannischen Umfeld des Klosters St. Gallen', in *Die Privaturkunden der Karolingerzeit*, eds Peter Erhart, Karl Heidecker, and Bernhard Zeller (Dietikon-Zürich, 2009), pp. 183–91.

Herman, József, *Vulgar Latin*, trans. Roger Wright (University Park, PA, 2000).

Innes, Matthew, 'Archives, Documents and Landowners in Carolingian Francia', in *Documentary Culture and the Laity in the Early Middle Ages*, eds Warren C. Brown, Marios Costambeys, Matthew Innes, and Adam J. Kosto (Cambridge, 2013), pp. 152–88.

Jordan, Gesine, 'Wer war der Tradent? Methodische Überlegungen zur sozialgeschichtlichen Untersuchung von Privaturkunden des frühen Mittelalters, besonders der St. Galler Urkunden', in *Tätigkeitsfelder und Erfahrungshorizonte des ländlichen Menschen in der frühmittelalterlichen Grundherrschaft (bis ca. 1000). Festschrift Dieter Hägermann zum 65. Geburtstag*, ed. Brigitte Kasten, Vierteljahrschrift für Sozial- und Wirtschaftsgeschichte, Beihefte 184 (Munich, 2006) pp. 155–74.

Kaiser, Reinhold, *Churrätien im frühen Mittelalter*, 2nd ed. (Basel, 2008).

Kiesler, Reinhard, *Einführung in die Problematik des Vulgärlateins* (Tübingen, 2006).

Löfstedt, Einar, *Late Latin* (Oslo, 1959).

Maag, Natalie, *Alemannische Minuskel (744–846 n. Chr.). Frühe Schriftkultur im Bodenseeraum und Voralpenland*, Quellen und Untersuchungen zur lateinischen Philologie des Mittelalters 18 (Stuttgart, 2014).

McKitterick, Rosamond, *The Carolingians and the Written Word* (Cambridge, 1989).

McKitterick, Rosamond, 'Schriftlichkeit im Spiegel der frühen Urkunden St. Gallens', in *Das Kloster St. Gallen im Mittelalter. Die kulturelle Blüte vom 8. bis zum 12. Jahrhundert*, ed. Peter Ochsenbein (Darmstadt, 1999), pp. 69–82.

Mersiowsky, Mark, *Die Urkunde in der Karolingerzeit. Originale, Urkundenpraxis und politische Kommunikation*, MGH Schriften 60, 2 vols (Wiesbaden, 2015).

Norberg, Dag, 'À quelle époque a-t-on cessé de parler latin en Gaule?', *Annales* 21 (1966), 346–56.

Norberg, Dag, *Manuel pratique de latin médiéval*, Connaissance des langues 4 (Paris, 1968); English translation by R. H. Johnson: http://homepages.wmich.edu/~johnsorh/MedievalLatin/Norberg/.

Norberg, Dag, *Syntaktische Forschungen auf dem Gebiete des Spätlateins und des frühen Mittellateins* (Uppsala and Leipzig, 1943).

Pei, Mario A., *The Language of the Eighth-Century Texts in Northern France. A Study of the Original Documents in the Collection of Tardif and other Sources* (New York, 1932).

Planta, Robert von, 'Die Sprache der rätoromanischen Urkunden des 8.-10. Jahrhunderts', in *Regesten von Vorarlberg und Liechtenstein bis zum Jahre 1260*, ed. Adolf Helbok, Quellen zur Geschichte Vorarlbergs und Liechtensteins 1 (Innsbruck, 1920/25), pp. 62–108.

Richter, Michael, 'À quelle époque a-t-on cessé de parler latin en Gaule? À propos d'une question mal posée', *Annales* 38 (1983), 439–48.

Rio, Alice, *Legal Practice and the Written Word in the Early Middle Ages: Frankish Formulae, c.500–1000* (Cambridge, 2009).

Roberts, Edward, 'Boundary Clauses and the Use of the Vernacular in Eastern Frankish Charters, *c.*750-*c.*900', *Historical Research* 91 (2018), 580–604.

Scarpatetti, Beat von, 'Das St. Galler Scriptorium', in *Das Kloster St. Gallen im Mittelalter. Die kulturelle Blüte vom 8. bis zum 12. Jahrhundert*, ed. Peter Ochsenbein (Darmstadt, 1999), pp. 31–67.

Schaab, Rupert, *Mönch in St. Gallen. Zur inneren Geschichte eines frühmittelalterlichen Klosters*, Vorträge und Forschungen, Sonderband 47 (Ostfildern, 2003).

Schär, Max, 'Sankt Galler Mönche unter Abt Otmar 720–760', *Studien und Mitteilungen zur Geschichte des Benediktinerordens und seiner Zweige* 120 (2009), 9–32.

Schwab, Vincenz, *Volkssprachige Wörter in Pactus und Lex Alamannorum*, Bamberger interdisziplinäre Mittelalterstudien 11 (Bamberg, 2017).

Sennhauser, Hans Rudolf (ed.), *Wandel und Konstanz zwischen Bodensee und Lombardei zur Zeit Karls des Großen*, Acta Müstair 3 (Zürich, 2013).

Sonderegger, Stefan, 'Althochdeutsch in St. Gallen', in *Das Kloster St. Gallen im Mittelalter. Die kulturelle Blüte vom 8. bis zum 12. Jahrhundert*, ed. Peter Ochsenbein (Stuttgart, 1999), pp. 205–22.

Sonderegger, Stefan, *Althochdeutsch in St. Gallen: Ergebnisse und Probleme der althochdeutschen Sprachüberlieferung in St. Gallen vom 8. bis zum 12. Jahrhundert* (St Gall, 1970).

Sonderegger, Stefan, 'Zu den althochdeutschen Sachwörtern in den lateinischen Urkunden der Schweiz', in *Archivalia et Historica. Arbeiten aus dem Gebiet der Geschichte und des Archivwesens. Festschrift für Anton Largiadèr* (Zürich, 1958), pp. 203–18.

Sprandel, Rolf, *Das Kloster St. Gallen in der Verfassung des karolingischen Reiches* (Freiburg im Breisgau, 1958).

Stotz, Peter, *Handbuch zur lateinischen Sprache des Mittelalters*. Handbuch der Altertumswissenschaft, 5 vols (München, 1996–2000).

van Rhijn, Carine, '*Priests and the Carolingian Reforms: The Bottlenecks of Local correctio*', in *Texts and Identities in the Early Middle Ages*, eds Richard Corradini, Rob Meens, Christina Pössel, and Philip Shaw, Forschungen zur Geschichte des Mittelalters 13 (Vienna, 2006), pp. 219–37.

van Rhijn, Carine, *Shepherds of the Lord: Priests and Episcopal Statutes in the Carolingian Period*, Cultural Encounters in Late Antiquity and the Middle Ages 6 (Turnhout, 2007).

van Uytfanghe, Marc, 'The Consciousness of a Linguistic Dichotomy (Latin-Romance) in Carolingian Gaul: The Contradictions of the Sources and of their Interpretation', in *Latin and the Romance Languages in the Early Middle Ages*, ed. Roger Wright (London, 1991), pp. 114–29.

van Uytfanghe, Marc, 'Histoire du Latin, protohistoire des langues romanes et histoire de la communication. A propos d'un receuil d'études, et avec quelques observations préliminaires sur le débat intellectuel entre pensée structurale et pensée historique', *Francia* 11 (1983), 579–613.

Wolfram, Herwig, *Salzburg, Bayern, Österreich. Die Conversio Bagoariorum et Carantanorum und die Quellen ihrer Zeit*, Mitteilungen des Instituts für Österreichische Geschichtsforschung, Ergänzungsband 31 (Vienna, 1995).

Wright, Roger, 'The Conceptual Distinction Between Latin and Romance: Invention or Evolution?', in *Latin and the Romance Languages in the Early Middle Ages*, ed. Roger Wright (London, 1991), pp. 103–13.

Wright, Roger, *Late Latin and Early Romance in Spain and Carolingian France* (Liverpool, 1982).

Zeller, Bernhard, *Diplomatische Studien zu den St. Galler Privaturkunden des frühen Mittelalters (ca. 720–980)* (forthcoming).

Zeller, Bernhard, 'Local Priests in Early Medieval Alamannia: The Charter Evidence', in *Men in the Middle. Local Priests in Early Medieval Europe*, eds Steffen Patzold and Carine van Rhijn, Ergänzungsbände zum Reallexikon der Germanischen Altertumskunde 93 (Berlin, 2016), pp. 32–49.

Zeller, Bernhard, 'Urkunden und Urkundenschreiber des Klosters St. Gallen bis ca. 840', in *Die Privaturkunden der Karolingerzeit*, eds Peter Erhart, Karl Heidecker, and Bernhard Zeller (Dietikon-Zürich, 2009), pp. 173–82.

Zettler, Alfons, *Geschichte des Herzogtums Schwaben* (Stuttgart, 2003).

CHAPTER 6

Signalling Language Choice in Anglo-Saxon and Frankish Charters, *c*.700–*c*.900

Edward Roberts and Francesca Tinti

Charters have long been at the heart of research on the use of the written word in early medieval Europe. However, the role of vernacular languages in the documentary cultures of Germanic-speaking societies has tended to be overlooked. This is less true in studies of Anglo-Saxon England, where the vernacular gradually became much more conspicuous in virtually all aspects of written culture.[1] By contrast, the documentary evidence from eastern Francia presents different challenges: Old High German and Old Saxon, unlike Old English, never became widely used administrative languages, and Latin remained the near-universal language of written documents well into the thirteenth century.[2] Nevertheless, some illuminating evidence for the

1 For growing scholarly awareness of the significant linguistic features of Anglo-Saxon charters, see the classic studies by Susan Kelly, 'Anglo-Saxon Lay Society and the Written Word', and Simon Keynes, 'Royal Government and the Written Word in Late Anglo-Saxon England', both in *The Uses of Literacy in Early Mediaeval Europe*, ed. Rosamond McKitterick (Cambridge, 1990), pp. 36–62 and 226–57, with the more recent Kathryn A. Lowe, 'Lay Literacy in Anglo-Saxon England and the Development of the Chirograph', in *Anglo-Saxon Manuscripts and Their Heritage*, eds Philip Pulsiano and Elaine M. Treharne (Aldershot, 1998), pp. 161–204; Herbert Schendl, 'Beyond Boundaries: Code-Switching in the Leases of Oswald of Worcester', in *Code-Switching in Early English*, eds Herbert Schendl and Laura Wright, Topics in English Linguistics 76 (Berlin, 2011), pp. 47–94; Robert Gallagher, 'The Vernacular in Anglo-Saxon Charters: Expansion and Innovation in Ninth-Century England', *Historical Research* 91 (2018), 205–35; Francesca Tinti, 'Writing Latin and Old English in Tenth-Century England: Patterns, Formulae and Language Choice in the Leases of Oswald of Worcester', in *Writing, Kinship and Power in Anglo-Saxon England*, eds Rory Naismith and David A. Woodman (Cambridge, 2018), pp. 303–27; and Robert Gallagher and Francesca Tinti, 'Latin, Old English and Documentary Practice at Worcester from Wærferth to Oswald', *ASE* 46 (2019 for 2017), 271–325. See also Francesca Tinti's introduction to this volume for traditional historiographical interpretations of Anglo-Saxon written linguistic practices as an exceptional case in early medieval western Europe.

2 Continental charters as a whole engaged with the vernacular much later than those from England: Thomas Brunner, 'Le passage aux langues vernaculaires dans les actes de la pratique en Occident', *Le Moyen Age* 115 (2009), 29–72.

 | DOI:10.1163/9789004432338_007

use of the vernacular in the Frankish East can be picked out from this Latin corpus.[3] Charters from outside the Romance-language area offer ideal material for investigating interactions between the spoken word and the written word in the early Middle Ages. In these regions, it is reasonable to suppose that the vernacular was the predominant language spoken during legal proceedings, as suggested by, among other things, the presence of vernacular elements in the *Vorakte* of the St Gall charters or the need to translate Latin documents into Old English at public assemblies, as is occasionally mentioned in Anglo-Saxon sources.[4] Thus, even charters written more or less entirely in Latin—which is to say the majority from England in the late seventh to ninth centuries and virtually all those from continental Western Europe in the same period—offer an underexploited resource for historical sociolinguists. The actors involved in these proceedings and the scribes who recorded them had two languages available to them during the process of a transaction and its documentation. The linguistic choices they made in such contexts rested on a variety of conditions, including local custom, the practices of individual scriptoria, the availability of models such as formularies, and personal preference.[5]

The documentary corpora of Anglo-Saxon England and eastern Carolingian Francia in the period *c.*700 to *c.*900 form the basis of this chapter. There are excellent grounds for considering these two regions in comparison: for one, they share a linguistic and cultural Germanic heritage. In addition, substantial early medieval documentary collections have survived in both areas. We argue that Anglo-Saxon and eastern Frankish charters of this period attest to several notable developments in the consciousness of language-use and

3 See for instance Patrick J. Geary, 'Land, Language and Memory in Europe, 700–1100', *Transactions of the Royal Historical Society*, 6th series, 9 (1999), 169–84; Rolf Bergmann, 'Pragmatische Voraussetzungen althochdeutscher Texte: Die Grenzbeschreibungen', *Jahrbuch für Germanistische Sprachgeschichte* 3 (2012), 57–74; Edward Roberts, 'Boundary Clauses and the Use of the Vernacular in Eastern Frankish Charters, *c.*750–*c.*900', *Historical Research* 91 (2018), 580–604.

4 For instance, papal letters were translated into the vernacular at the synod of *Clofesho* in 747: Kelly, 'Anglo-Saxon Lay Society', pp. 56–57. See in general Patrick J. Geary, *Language and Power in the Early Middle Ages* (Waltham, MA, 2013), pp. 63–68. On *Vorakte*, see Stefan Sonderegger, 'Das Althochdeutsche der Vorakte der älteren St. Galler Urkunden. Ein Beitrag zum Problem der Urkundensprache in althochdeutscher Zeit', *Zeitschrift für Mundartforschung* 28 (1961), 251–86; and Annina Seiler in this volume.

5 Kelly 'Anglo-Saxon Lay Society'; Lowe, 'Lay Literacy'; Alice Rio, *Legal Practice and the Written Word in the Early Middle Ages: Frankish Formulae,* c.*500*–c.*1000* (Cambridge, 2009), pp. 9–40; Nicholas Brooks, 'Latin and Old English in Ninth-Century Canterbury', in *Spoken and Written Language: Relations between Latin and the Vernacular Languages in the Earlier Middle Ages*, eds Mary Garrison, Arpad P. Orbán, and Marco Mostert (Turnhout, 2013), pp. 113–31; Tinti, 'Writing Latin and Old English'.

its application in documentary contexts in both territories. Our analysis focuses on what linguists refer to as 'code-switching', the alternating use of two languages in a single utterance or text.[6] We identify and investigate the different types of code-switching that can be observed in Anglo-Saxon and East Frankish charters, ranging from seamless, un-signalled shifts between languages to clearly demarcated translations or clarifications, which were often indicated by phrases such as *quod vulgo dicitur* or *qui nominatur nostra propria lingua*. These latter phenomena are sometimes referred to as 'flagged switches'.[7] Furthermore, we examine instances of explicit linguistic consciousness in charters, most notably through references to the *theodisca* (usually continental Germanic language) and *saxonica* languages (usually Old English). The invocation of the vernacular as a language that could be described as 'ours', 'theirs', or 'of the people', or explicitly termed as, for example, 'Saxon' suggests that language came to be identified with groups, peoples, and places in new ways in the late eighth and ninth centuries.[8] Latin's status as the standard language of written administration in both England and Francia has usually led scholars to suppose that Old English or Old High German elements were included in charters simply to facilitate communication in societies with minimal or partial Latin literacy. We suggest that the vernacular rather could be invoked quite deliberately as a means of engendering social inclusion or exclusion, and that it usually conveyed intention and meaning far beyond simple clarification or translation.

Charters and Languages in England and Francia

Anglo-Saxon and Frankish charters derived from a common Roman diplomatic tradition. Across continental western Europe, there is demonstrable continuity between late Roman and early medieval documentary practices. In England, however, there seems to have been a fissure in the use of written documents following the end of Roman Britain and the arrival of Christianity

6 For definitions, see Charlotte Hoffmann, *An Introduction to Bilingualism* (London, 1991), pp. 109–17; and for historically-situated discussion, see J. N. Adams, *Bilingualism and the Latin Language* (Cambridge, 2003), pp. 18–29.

7 Suzanne Romaine, *Bilingualism*, 2nd ed. (Oxford, 1995), p. 153; Adams, *Bilingualism and the Latin Language*, pp. 318–19.

8 On the issue of how language can (though does not necessarily) express identity, see *Sprache und Identität im frühen Mittelalter*, eds Walter Pohl and Bernhard Zeller (Vienna, 2012). Charter evidence, however, is seldom drawn on in this volume.

around the turn of the seventh century.[9] Although it is not clear exactly when charters were reintroduced in England, they may have been modelled on late Roman private deeds rather than on Merovingian charters, as might be expected owing to Frankish influence in the kingdom of Kent. Documentary practices were probably transmitted by missionaries sent from Rome, with Augustine (597–609) and Theodore (668–90) of Canterbury being the most likely candidates.[10] But whereas 'barbarian' rulers on the continent inherited and continued to employ a variety of documentary forms and notarial practices, in England a single charter template was adopted and used more or less indiscriminately for land grants made by kings, other laymen, and ecclesiastics. Thus, whereas in Francia charters issued by rulers were formulaically and visually distinct from those issued by bishops, abbots, dukes, counts, and others (so-called 'private' charters), in England it is not possible to detect such significant differences in the diplomatic structure of the earlier records.[11] While there are good reasons to treat the classical diplomatic categories of 'public' and 'private' documents with caution, the distinction this draws between royal

9 On documentary continuities in early medieval Europe, see *Documentary Culture and the Laity in the Early Middle Ages*, eds Warren C. Brown, Marios Costambeys, Matthew Innes, and Adam Kosto (Cambridge, 2013).

10 Wilhelm Levison, *England and the Continent in the Eighth Century* (Oxford, 1946), pp. 224–33; Pierre Chaplais, 'Who Introduced Charters into England? The Case for Augustine', *Journal of the Society of Archivists* 3.10 (1969), 526–42; Kelly, 'Anglo-Saxon Lay Society', pp. 40–43; Ben Snook, 'Who Introduced Charters into England? The Case for Theodore', in *Textus Roffensis: Law, Language and Libraries in Early Medieval England*, eds Bruce O'Brien and Barbara Bombi (Turnhout, 2015), pp. 257–89. On the evidence for Merovingian overlordship of Kent, see Ian Wood, *The Merovingian Kingdoms, 450–751* (Harlow, 1994), pp. 176–80. On the study of Anglo-Saxon charters, see Nicholas Brooks, 'Anglo-Saxon Charters: Recent Work', in his *Anglo-Saxon Myths: State and Church 400–1066* (London, 2000), pp. 181–215; Simon Keynes, 'Anglo-Saxon Charters: Lost and Found', in *Myth, Rulership, Church and Charters: Essays in Honour of Nicholas Brooks*, eds Julia Barrow and Andrew Wareham (Aldershot, 2008), pp. 45–66. For Augustine's death date see Richard Shaw, 'When did Augustine of Canterbury Die?', *Journal of Ecclesiastical History* 67 (2016), 473–91.

11 Albert Bruckner, 'Zur Diplomatik der älteren angelsächsischen Urkunde', *Archivalische Zeitschrift* 61 (1965), 11–45; and his introduction to *ChLA* 4, pp. xiii–xxiii. See also Snook, 'Who Introduced Charters into England?', p. 267. On the relationship between Carolingian-era royal diplomas and private charters, see Mark Mersiowsky, 'Y-a-t-il une influence des actes royaux sur les actes privés du IXe siècle?', in *Les actes comme expression du pouvoir au Haut Moyen Âge. Actes de la Table Ronde de Nancy, 26–27 novembre 1999*, eds Marie-José Gasse-Grandjean and Benoît-Michel Tock (Turnhout, 2003), pp. 139–78; and Mark Mersiowsky, *Die Urkunde in der Karolingerzeit. Originale, Urkundenpraxis und politische Kommunikation*, 2 vols, MGH Schriften 60 (Wiesbaden, 2015), 1:413–18 and *passim*.

and non-royal documents is helpful for the present comparison (and need not imply anything about the legitimacy of the issuing authority).[12] In this respect, the proportional differences of surviving royal versus private charters from England and East Francia are striking: in the period 700–900, there are about 300 substantially authentic extant charters from Anglo-Saxon England, the great majority of which are royal diplomas (including both 'original' single-sheets and later copies).[13] In contrast, for the same period in eastern Francia (that is, the Germanic-speaking lands which, after 843, roughly constituted the kingdom of Louis the German), there are well over 8,000 extant charters, of which only about 700 were issued by kings.[14]

The preponderance of private charters from East Francia owes much to the archival innovation of the cartulary around 800, which ensured the survival of thousands of records at monasteries such as Fulda, Lorsch, Mondsee, and Wissembourg and episcopal churches such as Freising, Regensburg, and Passau. In Anglo-Saxon England, by contrast, there are no extant cartularies predating the eleventh century.[15] Consequently, a far higher proportion of Anglo-Saxon charters survive as original single-sheet documents—about 80 of the roughly 300 known to have been issued between 700 and 900. Most of these single-sheets come from Christ Church, Canterbury.[16] Royal charters also predominate among extant original single-sheet Frankish documents, with the notable exception of the more than 700 original charters from St Gall.[17]

12 See in general *Documentary Culture*, eds Brown et al., pp. 11–12; Mersiowsky, *Die Urkunde in der Karolingerzeit*, 1:278–80.

13 See *The Languages of Anglo-Saxon Charters Database*: http://www.ehu.eus/lasc.

14 On the problems of 'originality' and 'authenticity', see Kelly, 'Anglo-Saxon Lay Society', pp. 42–43. For East Frankish numbers, see Fred Schwind, 'Beobachtungen zur inneren Struktur des Dorfes in karolingischer Zeit', in *Das Dorf der Eisenzeit und des frühen Mittelalters. Siedlungsform, wirtschaftliche Funktion, soziale Struktur*, ed. Herbert Jankuhn (Göttingen, 1977), pp. 444–93, at 445–49.

15 Hans Hummer, 'The Production and Preservation of Documents in Francia: The Evidence of Cartularies', in *Documentary Culture*, eds Brown et al., pp. 189–230; G. R. C. Davis, *Medieval Cartularies of Great Britain and Ireland*, revised by Claire Breay, Julian Harrison, and David M. Smith (London, 2010), pp. xv, 217–18; Francesca Tinti, *Sustaining Belief: The Church of Worcester from c.870 to c.1100* (Farnham, 2010), pp. 85–125.

16 On Anglo-Saxon private charters before 900, see Anton Scharer, 'Das angelsächsische Urkundenwesen (7.–9. Jahrhundert)', in *Die Privaturkunden der Karolingerzeit*, eds Peter Erhart, Karl Heidecker, and Bernhard Zeller (Dietikon-Zürich, 2009), pp. 229–36; Simon Keynes, 'Angelsächsische Urkunden (7.–9. Jahrhundert)', in *Mensch und Schrift im frühen Mittelalter*, eds Peter Erhart and Lorenz Hollenstein (St Gall, 2006), pp. 97–109; Brooks and Kelly, *CantCC*, pp. 40–50. See also Gallagher and Wiles, this volume, for a catalogue of single sheets.

17 Mersiowsky, *Die Urkunde in der Karolingerzeit*, 1:54–64. On the St Gall archive, see Peter Erhart, '*Carta ista amalfitana est et nescitur legere*: The Charters of Cava dei Tirenni and

In this same period in Anglo-Saxon England, the granting of charters seems generally to have been less frequent and more usually associated with secular rulers, although the initiative most likely came from the Church. Certainly at this time, Anglo-Saxon charters were written by their beneficiaries, implying that clerical elites were well aware of the utility of documents from very early on. The proliferation of councils and assemblies in the eighth and ninth centuries probably provided a venue for the clerical promotion of documentary practices.[18] From the beginning, however, Anglo-Saxon charters lacked several characteristics of their continental counterparts, such as the scribe's name, authentication mechanisms, and formulaic features that distinguished royal and non-royal documents. These idiosyncrasies suggest that an incipient documentary culture was encouraged by clerics with some knowledge of late Roman diplomatic conventions, but that adherence to such norms either proved impractical or was deemed to have limited benefit.[19] One also has to bear in mind that, as mentioned above, charters were reintroduced in Anglo-Saxon society by churchmen following a notable documentary hiatus,[20] and that because they possessed a markedly religious character and were issued less frequently than on the continent, they were probably revered as special, possibly sacred objects.

These aspects of Anglo-Saxon documentary practice represent important contrasts with charters produced in other regions of the former western Roman Empire, which more directly imitated Roman examples.[21] Even though

St Gall and Their Evidence for Early Archival Practice', *Gazette du livre médiéval* 50 (2007), 27–39; Matthew Innes, 'Archives, Documents and Landowners in Carolingian Francia', in *Documentary Culture*, eds Brown et al., pp. 152–88.

18 Simon Keynes, 'Church Councils, Royal Assemblies, and Anglo-Saxon Royal Diplomas', in *Kingship, Legislation and Power in Anglo-Saxon England*, eds Gale R. Owen-Crocker and Brian W. Schneider (Woodbridge, 2013), pp. 17–182.

19 Kelly, 'Anglo-Saxon Lay Society', pp. 42–45; Charles Insley, 'Archives and Lay Documentary Practice in the Anglo-Saxon World', in *Documentary Culture*, eds Brown et al., pp. 336–62, at 341–42.

20 For the possibility that Celtic-speaking communities in Britain were using charters earlier than the Anglo-Saxons, see Wendy Davies, 'The Latin Charter-Tradition in Western Britain, Brittany and Ireland in the Early Mediaeval Period', in *Ireland in Early Medieval Europe: Studies in Memory of Kathleen Hughes*, eds Dorothy Whitelock, Rosamond McKitterick, and David Dumville (Cambridge, 1982), pp. 258–80.

21 Patrick Wormald, '*Lex scripta* and *verbum regis*: Legislation and Germanic Kingship from Euric to Cnut', in *Early Medieval Kingship*, eds P. H. Sawyer and I. N. Wood (Leeds, 1977), pp. 105–38; Peter Classen, 'Fortleben und Wandel spätrömischen Urkundenwesens im frühen Mittelalter', in *Recht und Schrift im Mittelalter*, ed. Peter Classen (Sigmaringen, 1977), pp. 13–54, with discussion of the language of late Roman charters at pp. 25–28; Rosamond McKitterick, *The Carolingians and the Written Word* (Cambridge, 1989), pp. 77–134; and

such peoples as the Alemanni and the Bavarians, like the Anglo-Saxons, spoke Germanic and needed to be Christianized, their occupation of the more Romanized provinces of Germania Superior and Raetia arguably led to stronger continuities of earlier legal traditions. This is probably explicable by these groups' geographical proximity to Rome, their close links with more thoroughly Romanized regions to the west and south, and their subjection to the Franks.[22] The greater geographical isolation of Britain may also account for the more frequent recourse to the vernacular in Anglo-Saxon charters.[23] In this regard, law-codes offer a well-known, instructive parallel, with those from England having been written in Old English, and those from other post-Roman kingdoms in Latin.[24] There has been considerable debate about why Romano-British culture and Brittonic language were so comprehensively overthrown by the arrival of the Anglo-Saxons, whereas Latin continued to thrive in Gaul, Spain, and Italy long after the arrival of the Franks, Goths, and Lombards.[25] In the case of Frankish Gaul, it is relatively clear that the Merovingian elites became

---

the chapters of *Documentary Culture*, eds Brown et al., especially Warren C. Brown, 'The *gesta municipalia* and the Public Validation of Documents in Frankish Europe', pp. 95–124.

22 For comparative views on the emergence of post-Roman peoples and polities, see *Regna and Gentes: The Relationship between Late Antique and Early Medieval Peoples and Kingdoms in the Transformation of the Roman World*, eds Hans-Werner Goetz, Jörg Jarnut, and Walter Pohl (Leiden, 2003). On linguistic developments among the Alemanni and Bavarians, see Wolfgang Haubrichs and Max Pfister, 'La *Romania submersa* dans les pays de langue allemande', in *Manuel des langues romanes*, eds Andre Klump, Johannes Kramer, and Aline Willems (Berlin, 2014), pp. 224–44; and Wolfgang Haubrichs, 'Baiovarii, Romani and Others. Language, Names and Groups South of the River Danube and in the Eastern Alps during the Early Middle Ages', in *The Baiuvarii and Thuringi: An Ethnographic Perspective*, eds Janine Fries-Knoblach, Heiko Steuer, and John Hines (Woodbridge, 2014), pp. 23–81.

23 Julia M. H. Smith, 'Writing in Britain and Ireland, c. 400 to c. 800', in *The Cambridge History of Early Medieval English Literature*, ed. Claire A. Lees (Cambridge, 2013), pp. 19–49, at 48; Andy Orchard, 'Latin and the Vernacular Languages: The Creation of a Bilingual Textual Culture', in *After Rome*, ed. Thomas Charles-Edwards (Oxford, 2003), pp. 191–219.

24 Wormald, '*Lex scripta* and *verbum regis*', p. 115; Nicholas Brooks, 'The Laws of King Æthelberht of Kent: Preservation, Content, and Composition', in *Textus Roffensis*, eds O'Brien and Bombi, pp. 105–36, at 125–30. Note, however, the fragmentary vernacular translations of Latin legislation on the continent: Rolf Bergmann, *Althochdeutsche und altsächsische Literatur* (Berlin, 2013), pp. 236–38, 467–69.

25 See for instance, Hans-Werner Goetz, '*Gens*, Kings and Kingdoms: The Franks', and Alex Woolf, 'The Britons: From Romans to Barbarians', both in *Regna and Gentes*, eds Goetz et al., pp. 307–44 and 345–80 respectively; *Britons in Anglo-Saxon England*, ed. Nick Higham (Woodbridge, 2007), especially the contributions of Nick Higham, 'Historical Narrative as Cultural Politics: Rome, "British-ness" and "English-ness"', pp. 68–79, Alex Woolf, 'Apartheid and Economics in Anglo-Saxon England', pp. 115–29, and Richard Coates, 'Invisible Britons: The View from Linguistics', pp. 172–91.

bilingual, having adopted Latin while retaining their West Germanic vernacular ('Frankish' or 'Old Frankish'). Thus, Charibert (d. 567) was acclaimed in Paris by 'barbarians' (Franks) and Romans 'in different tongues', that is, in their own languages, while Chilperic (d. 584) thought it prudent to introduce four new characters into the alphabet, evidently in an attempt to aid Germanic literacy.[26] Whereas Old English emerged as a common language of the newly established Anglo-Saxon kingdoms (albeit with several dialects), a large part of Merovingian Francia was bilingual. In the eighth century, Frankish language died out in Gaul, having never fully developed as a written language, and the West Franks seem to have become monolingual Romance speakers.[27]

The dramatic expansion of the Frankish realm under the Carolingians helped ensure that it remained a polity in which multiple languages coexisted. Germanic persisted as a spoken language on the eastern margins of the Merovingian world in Frisia and Thuringia, but the Carolingian conquests of Alemannia, Bavaria, and Saxony brought a far greater Germanic-speaking territory under direct Frankish control.[28] While Latin clearly remained intelligible and functional among imperial elites, there has been much discussion about the extent to which people in different parts of the Empire could also

---

26 For these stories, see, respectively, Venantius Fortunatus, *Opera poetica*, VI.2, ed. Friedrich Leo, MGH Auct. ant. 4.1 (Berlin, 1881), p. 131; Gregory of Tours, *Libri historiarum decem*, V.44, eds Bruno Krusch and Wilhelm Levison, MGH SS rer. Merov. 1.1 (Hanover, 1951), p. 254.

27 For Old English dialects, see Peter R. Kitson, 'The Nature of Old English Dialect Distributions, Mainly as Exhibited in Charter Boundaries: Part 1, Vocabulary', in *Medieval Dialectology*, ed. Jacek Fisiak, Trends in Linguistics, Studies and Monographs 79 (Berlin, 1995), pp. 43–135. On Frankish, see Wolfgang Haubrichs and Max Pfister, 'Fränkisch (Frankish)', in *Wieser Enzyklopädie. Sprachen des europäischen Westens. Erster Band* (Klagenfurt, 2008), pp. 249–74; and on the evidence for Merovingian bilingual areas, see Wolfgang Haubrichs, 'Sprache und Sprachzeugnisse der merowingischen Franken', in *Die Franken—Wegbereiter Europas. 5. bis 8. Jahrhundert n. Chr.*, eds Alfried Wieczorek, Patrick Périn, Karin von Welck, and Wilfried Menghin, 2 vols (Mainz, 1996), 1:559–73; Wolfgang Haubrichs, 'Germania submersa. Zu Fragen der Quantität und Dauer germanischer Siedlungsinseln im romanischen Lothringen und Südbelgien', in *Verborum Amor. Studien zur Geschichte und Kunst der deutschen Sprache. Festschrift für Stefan Sonderegger zum 65. Geburtstag*, eds Harald Burger, Alois M. Haas, and Peter von Matt (Berlin, 1992), pp. 633–66; Michel Banniard, 'Germanophonie, latinophonie et accès à la *Schriftlichkeit* (V^e^–VIIIe siècle)', in *Akkulturation. Probleme einer germanisch-romanischen Kultursynthese in Spätantike und frühem Mittelalter*, eds Dieter Hägermann, Wolfgang Haubrichs, and Jörg Jarnut (Berlin, 2004), pp. 340–58.

28 For an overview, see Marios Costambeys, Matthew Innes, and Simon MacLean, *The Carolingian World* (Cambridge, 2011), pp. 31–79.

understand each other's spoken native Romance or Germanic vernaculars.[29] The Carolingians' encouragement of regular and correct Latin, the language of the Bible and of the Roman Empire, was ideal for governing a vast, multi-ethnic polity, but may also have inhibited the spread of written German in administrative or legal contexts.[30]

The allure of tradition partly explains why private charters tended to be formulaically and linguistically uniform across Frankish Europe.[31] Furthermore, the consistency of royal diplomas owes something to the fact that, under Charlemagne and Louis the Pious, there was a single political centre where the royal chancery honed a documentary format that reflected the imperial, sacred character of Carolingian kingship. Carolingian diplomas were clearly intended as official documents produced by royal notaries who carefully followed protocols of appearance, language, and validation.[32] In England, by contrast, there were multiple kingdoms and multiple agencies issuing royal diplomas. In the eighth century the political situation was dominated by the kings of Mercia, who managed to extend their control over other polities, such as the kingdoms of the Hwicce and the South Saxons; their rulers continued to issue charters, although styling themselves as subkings and, later, ealdormen.

29 McKitterick, *The Carolingians and the Written Word*, pp. 7–8, 21–22; Michel Banniard, 'Language and Communication in Carolingian Europe', in *The New Cambridge Medieval History, Volume II*: c.700–c.900, ed. Rosamond McKitterick (Cambridge, 1995), pp. 695–708; Wolfgang Haubrichs and Max Pfister, 'Die Prümer Romania', in *Sprachgeschichte—Dialektologie—Onomastik—Volkskunde. Beiträge zum Kolloquium am 3./4. Dezember 1999 an der Johannes Gutenberg-Universität Mainz. Wolfgang Kleiber zum 70. Geburtstag*, eds Rudolf Bentzinger, Damaris Nübling, and Rudolf Steffens (Stuttgart, 2001), pp. 169–95; Ernst Hellgardt, 'Zur Mehrsprachigkeit im Karolingerreich. Bemerkungen aus Anlaß von Rosamond McKittericks Buch "The Carolingians and the Written Word"', *Beiträge zur Geschichte der deutschen Sprache und Literatur* 118 (1996), 1–48; Hans J. Hummer, *Politics and Power in Early Medieval Europe: Alsace and the Frankish Realm, 600–1000* (Cambridge, 2005), pp. 130–54; Jens Schneider, *Auf der Suche nach dem verlorenen Reich: Lotharingien im 9. und 10. Jahrhundert* (Cologne, 2010), pp. 283–423. See further Haubrichs, this volume.

30 McKitterick, *The Carolingians and the Written Word*, pp. 7–22; Janet L. Nelson, 'Literacy in Carolingian Government', in *The Uses of Literacy*, ed. McKitterick, pp. 258–96; Mayke de Jong, 'Some Reflections on Mandarin Language', in *East and West: Modes of Communication. Proceedings of the First Plenary Conference at Merida*, eds Evangelos Chrysos and Ian Wood (Leiden, 1999), pp. 61–69.

31 Paul Fouracre, 'Cultural Conformity and Social Conservatism in Early Medieval Europe', *History Workshop Journal* 33 (1992), 152–61, at pp. 155–56; and, more generally, *Die Privaturkunden der Karolingerzeit*, eds Erhart et al.

32 Rosamond McKitterick, *Charlemagne: The Formation of a European Identity* (Cambridge, 2008), pp. 199–204; Geoffrey Koziol, *The Politics of Memory and Identity in Carolingian Royal Diplomas: The West Frankish Kingdom (840–987)* (Turnhout, 2012), pp. 52–62; Mersiowsky, *Die Urkunde in der Karolingerzeit*, 1:64–115.

The kingdom of Kent offered more resistance to Mercian expansion in the second half of the eighth century, though by 798 it was firmly under Mercian control. Wessex, by contrast, never really suffered from Mercian encroachment, and, by the late ninth century, was the only kingdom that had managed to survive intact in the aftermath of Scandinavian attacks and settlement.[33] Over the period under consideration charters were issued in the name of rulers from all the above-mentioned polities, but they were still normally produced in ecclesiastical scriptoria rather than royal chanceries, and very often by the beneficiaries themselves. Wessex represents an exception in this respect, where extant ninth-century charters bear witness to the emergence of a centralized system of documentary production, thus anticipating some of the features which characterize the much better attested tenth-century royal writing office.[34] It is important to bear in mind, however, that, as mentioned above, the overwhelming majority of single-sheet charters from before *c.*900 come from Christ Church, Canterbury. These documents are generally agreed to indicate composition in ecclesiastical scriptoria, even at the end of our period, when Kent was firmly under the control of Wessex, as the emergence of a West Saxon diplomatic tradition did not affect the charters that the ninth-century kings issued as rulers of Kent.[35]

The use of charters and language thus varied in accordance with the prevailing political and social conditions of the Anglo-Saxon and eastern Frankish kingdoms. Ultimately, however, we are dealing with two societies in which, by the middle of the eighth century, individuals and institutions placed similar value in the written word and were beginning to contemplate whether their vernacular could be used in documentary contexts.

---

33 Simon Keynes, 'England, 700–900', in *The New Cambridge Medieval History II*, ed. McKitterick, pp. 18–42.

34 Simon Keynes, 'The West Saxon Charters of King Æthelwulf and his Sons', *EHR* 109 (1994), 1109–49. For the debate on the Anglo-Saxon royal chancery, see, classically, Richard Drögereit, 'Gab es eine angelsächsische Königskanzlei?', *Archiv für Urkundenforschung* 13 (1935), 335–436; Pierre Chaplais, 'The Origin and Authenticity of the Royal Anglo-Saxon Diploma', *Journal of the Society of Archivists* 3.2 (1965), 48–61; Simon Keynes, *The Diplomas of King Æthelred 'the Unready', 978–1016: A Study in Their Use as Historical Evidence* (Cambridge, 1980), pp. 14–153; with the summary of Brooks, 'Anglo-Saxon Charters', pp. 188–89, 207–9. See also Kelly, *Abing*, pp. lxxii–cxxxi. For a more recent and detailed treatment of historiographical developments in the study of Anglo-Saxon royal diplomas from the late nineteenth century to the present day, see Keynes, 'Church Councils', pp. 42–102.

35 Nicholas Brooks, *The Early History of the Church of Canterbury: Christ Church from 597 to 1066* (London, 1984), pp. 168–70, 327–30; Simon Keynes, 'The Control of Kent in the Ninth Century', *EME* 2 (1993), 111–31; Keynes, 'West Saxon Charters'; Brooks and Kelly, *CantCC*, pp. 112–35.

Using the Vernacular in Charters: from Technical Terms to Boundary Clauses

There are two general contexts for the appearance of the vernacular in early medieval charters. The first of these is the employment of vernacular technical terms. This was relatively common in Francia, where Frankish terms for specific rights, procedures, obligations, and types of property had long been Latinized and used in charters and normative legal texts.[36] Germanic words such as *alodis, marca, bannus, mallus, mundiburdium,* and *wadium* were very common. Less common vernacular terms were also normally Latinized and invoked, for example, to denote payments (e.g., *stofa*, an annual royal levy), social groups (e.g., *barscalci*, 'free men'), secular offices (e.g., *furiskeozus*, 'advocate'), properties (e.g., *hluz* or *hluzzum*, 'lot', that is, a portion of property), and more.[37] The describing, surveying, and transacting of property frequently provided circumstances for the invocation of vernacular terms. Thus, for example, an 819 charter from Regensburg records a survey of the *marca* of Cham undertaken by Bishop Baturich and local notables, describing the perambulation with a unique Old High German noun: 'Haec sunt nomina eorum, qui audierunt rationem istam et cauallicauerunt illam commarcam et fuerunt in ista pireisa …'[38] The witness list of a Fulda charter of 824 states that 'isti sunt testes qui hoc audierunt et uiderunt giuueridam …'[39] An original St Gall charter of 837 records a grant of property made out of the donor's *swascara*, his

36 Ruth Schmidt-Wiegand, 'Stammesrecht und Volkssprache in karolingischer Zeit', in *Aspekte der Nationenbildung im Mittelalter*, eds Helmut Beumann and Werner Schröder (Sigmaringen, 1978), pp. 171–203; D. H. Green, *Language and History in the Early Germanic World* (Cambridge, 1998), pp. 182–200.

37 *Stofa*: MGH D Lothar II, no. 6, pp. 391–92 (Metz, A.D. 856); *barscalci*: *Die Traditionen des Hochstifts Freising*, ed. Theodor Bitterauf, 2 vols, Quellen und Erörterungen zur bayerischen und deutschen Geschichte, N. F. 4–5 (Munich, 1905), no. 523b, 1:450 (A.D. 825); *furiskeozus*: W 300 (= *ChLA* 102, no. 40, pp. 96–97, A.D. 826); *hluz*: see *Traditionen Freising*, no. 326, 1:279 (A.D. 814); no. 534, 1:456 (A.D. 826); no. 537, 1:458 (A.D. 826); no. 538, 1:458–59 (A.D. 826). For Lombard parallels, see Stoffella in this volume.

38 *Die Traditionen des Hochstifts Regensburg und des Klosters S. Emmeram*, ed. Josef Widemann, Quellen und Erörterungen zur bayerischen Geschichte, N. F. 8 (Darmstadt, 1969), no. 16, pp. 15–17: 'These are the names of those who heard this verdict and rode [around] the *commarca* and were in this *pireisa* ("riding")'. See Reinhard Bauer, *Die ältesten Grenzbeschreibungen in Bayern und ihre Aussagen für Namenkunde und Geschichte* (Munich, 1988), pp. 129–39; Michael Prinz, 'Vergessene Wörter—frühe volkssprachige Lexik in lateinischen Traditionsurkunden', *Jahrbuch für germanistische Sprachgeschichte* 1 (2010), 292–322, at pp. 300–1.

39 *Codex diplomaticus Fuldensis*, ed. Ernst Friedrich Johann Dronke (Kassel, 1850), no. 448, p. 198: 'These are the witnesses who heard this and saw the *giuuerida* ("investiture")'.

special right or privilege over a portion of land ('... et in meam suuascaram accepi ...').[40] In virtually all these cases, etymologically vernacular words were declined as Latin nouns and thus effectively treated as loanwords, and scribes did not signal any shift from Latin to Germanic language.

By contrast, vernacular technical terms were rarely Latinized in this way in Anglo-Saxon charters. In England, it was more common for a scribe to give a Latin approximation for an Old English term, as in the cases of *hid* ('hide'), often rendered as *mansus* or *manens*, and *sulung*, often given as *aratrum*. If a charter required an Old English word, it usually followed a Latin word and was introduced with a clarifying statement such as *id est* or *quod dicimus*.[41] We discuss such 'flagging' of vernacular language in more detail below; here it is sufficient to note simply that Anglo-Saxon documents seldom incorporate Latinized vernacular technical terms. This contrast with Frankish charters suggests an interesting difference in the ways Latin and the vernacular were approached in our two societies: in the period under investigation Anglo-Saxon scribes seem to have been less willing than their East Frankish counterparts to shoehorn Germanic words into an overarching Latin syntax and morphology.[42]

The second context in which one often finds vernacular language in a charter is the boundary clause and, more generally, topographical descriptions. This applies especially to Anglo-Saxon England, but it is also true to some extent of Frankish charters. Previous work on the use of the vernacular in early medieval documents has often focused on such descriptions of landscape,

40 W 360 (= *ChLA* 104, no. 1, pp. 15–17).

41 E.g. S 178 (*CantCC* 51, p. 553, A.D. 815): 'Liberata quoque terra ista ab omnibus saecularium seruitutibus permaneat . exceptis his arcis et pontis constructionibus et expeditione ac singulare prętium ad penam . *id est angylde* . aliqua uero foras nihil persoluat' (emphasis ours).

42 On this point see also David Trotter, 'A Polyglot Glossary of the Twelfth Century', in *De Mot en Mot: Aspects of Medieval Linguistics*, eds Stewart Gregory and D. A. Trotter (Cardiff, 1997), pp. 81–91, at 89: 'when Anglo-Saxons wrote English they wrote English, and when they wrote Latin they wrote Latin. They did not contaminate their Latin with English [...]. But from the very beginning of Norman traditions in England one encounters scores and hundreds of English words in Latin forms in hundreds of documents'. A search through the database of the *Dictionary of Medieval Latin from British Sources* has produced a list of *c*.800 words whose etymology is certainly or possibly related to Old English terms. Interestingly, however, the great majority of these Latinized originally vernacular words only appear in post-Conquest texts, with the earliest attestations often coming from Domesday Book or the *Quadripartitus*, i.e. the extensive Latin translation of Anglo-Saxon legislation compiled in the early twelfth century. The impression that eighth- and ninth-century Anglo-Saxon charters did not include Latinized vernacular words would thus seem to be confirmed. We thank Dr Richard Ashdowne for sharing the list with us and for drawing our attention to David Trotter's remark.

which is where the vast majority of vernacular language in Anglo-Saxon and East Frankish charters before *c.*900 appears.[43] Much of this research has been conducted from philological perspectives examining the early development of English and German, especially in relation to the study of place-names.[44] However, more remains to be said about such boundary descriptions from a sociolinguistic point of view, that is, in terms of what this evidence can tell us about the interaction between Latin and the vernacular in the overall process of oral property transactions and their documentation. Anglo-Saxon boundary clauses furnish many examples of 'intra-sentential' code-switching. One of the earliest examples of a mixed-language boundary description is contained in an original diploma of Wihtred of Kent from 697×712.[45] From a later period there is an original private charter of *c.*853×859 from Canterbury recording a purchase of land by a certain Plegred which delineates its boundary in a mixture of Latin and Old English.[46] Although most of the original single-sheet diplomas providing examples of such mixed-language topographical descriptions come from Christ Church Canterbury, due to the above-mentioned circumstances of

43 For England, see Michael Reed, 'Anglo-Saxon Charter-Boundaries', in *Discovering Past Landscapes*, ed. Michael Reed (London, 1984), pp. 261–306; Peter Kitson, 'Quantifying Qualifiers in Anglo-Saxon Charter Boundaries', *Folia Lingusitica Historica* 14 (1993), 29–82; Kathryn A. Lowe, 'The Development of the Anglo-Saxon Boundary Clause', *Nomina* 21 (1998), 63–100; Nicholas Howe, *Writing the Map of Anglo-Saxon England: Essays in Cultural Geography* (New Haven, CT, 2008), pp. 32–38. For East Francia, see Bauer, *Die ältesten Grenzbeschreibungen*; Geary, 'Land, Language and Memory'; Roberts, 'Boundary Clauses'. On the issues of vernacular place-names and properhood, see below, text corresponding to nn. 53–56. On the growth of vernacular usage in ninth-century England, see Brooks, 'Latin and Old English'; and Gallagher, 'The Vernacular in Anglo-Saxon Charters'.

44 See, for instance, *Ortsname und Urkunde. Frühmittelalterliche Ortsnamenüberlieferung*, ed. Rudolf Schützeichel (Heidelberg, 1990). For more recent approaches on Anglo-Saxon place-names, building on the developments of landscape history, see the essays in *Place-Names, Language and the Anglo-Saxon Landscape*, eds Nicholas J. Higham and Martin J. Ryan (Woodbridge, 2011).

45 S 19 (*CantCC* 5, p. 286): '… conferre bassilicae beatae Mariae genitricis Dei quae sita est in loco qui dicitur Limingae terram .iiii. aratrorum quae dicitur Pleghelmestun . cum omnibus ad eandem terram pertinentibus iuxta notissimos terminos id est bereueg . et meguines paed et stretleg …'. It should be noted that in this early single-sheet charter the description of the bounds is contained within the body of the main text of the charter rather than being supplied after the main text, as would become customary in later Anglo-Saxon diplomas.

46 S 1196 (*CantCC* 85, p. 747): 'Ego Plegred aliquam terre unculam emi \et/ Eðelmode duci sexcentis denariis hoc est an healf tun que ante pertinebat to Ƿilburgepellan ðet land healf 7 healfne tun hiis terminibus circumcincta Ab oriente cyniges heipeg A meritie stret to Scufeling forde Ab occidente Stur Ab aquilone cyninges land 7 halfne per una prata on burgpara medam suðepeardum 7 an norðepeardum burgparamedam healfmed 7 meahselog an cyninges strete …'.

archival preservation, similar cases of intra-sentential code-switching can be found in many other boundary clauses contained in generally reliable copies of late seventh-, eighth-, and ninth-century charters from such diverse archives as Barking, Muchelney, Glastonbury, Wells, Worcester, Evesham, Rochester, and Abingdon.[47] In addition to these early occurrences of the vernacular in boundary clauses and in other references to the landscape, one could highlight several other cases of code-switching, which, from the early decades of the ninth century, begin to appear in Anglo-Saxon charters for purposes other than geographical descriptions.[48] Such recourse to the vernacular in Anglo-Saxon charters has traditionally been viewed either as evidence of poor Latinity or as an attempt to render key aspects of transactions comprehensible to lay audiences. More recent studies, however, have argued that the diversity and irregularity of this linguistic interplay indicates that such code-switching could arise from an array of scribal or authorial choices made in relation to different audiences.[49] While early Anglo-Saxon charters were rather uniform, by the ninth century, documents were being produced in different ways in different scriptoria and kingdoms; there was no single documentary form or linguistic protocol. Thus, one occasionally finds apparently anomalous charters such as the surviving original grant of King Berhtwulf of Mercia to his thegn Forthred, issued in 844×845 and written almost entirely in Old English.[50]

In Carolingian Francia, as outlined above, documents tended to conform more to formularies and a narrower set of diplomatic standards, and royal charters drew legitimation from newly fixed chancery practices. Historical and political circumstances thus militated against the use of the vernacular in the documents of Germanic-speaking eastern Francia. Boundary clauses were not formulaic or common on the continent. Nevertheless, there are a number of mixed-language boundary descriptions from this region which display remarkable similarities to those from England. Moreover, they provide rare examples

47 See for instance S 1171 (Barking, A.D. 685×693), S 244 (Muchelney, A.D. 702), S 1410 (Glastonbury, A.D. 744), S 262 (Wells, A.D. 766), S 109 (Worcester, A.D. 775 or 777), S 114 (Evesham, A.D. 779, original or contemporary copy), S 129 (Rochester, A.D. 788), and S 268 (Abingdon, A.D. 801).

48 Gallagher, 'The Vernacular in Anglo-Saxon Charters'.

49 For older arguments, see especially N. P. Brooks, 'England in the Ninth Century: The Crucible of Defeat', *Transactions of the Royal Historical Society*, Fifth Series, 29 (1979), 1–20; Kelly, 'Anglo-Saxon Lay Society'; but cf. more recent works such as Brooks, 'Latin and Old English', pp. 115–16; Lowe, 'Lay Literacy'; Helen Gittos, 'The Audience for Old English Texts: Ælfric, Rhetoric and "the Edification of the Simple"', *ASE* 43 (2014), 231–66; Tinti, 'Writing Latin and Old English'; Gallagher, 'The Vernacular in Anglo-Saxon Charters'; Gallagher and Tinti, 'Latin, Old English and Documentary Practice'.

50 S 204 (*CantCC* 75).

of non-Latinized vernacular language being used in East Frankish charters. For instance, there is a single-sheet charter of 777 from the monastery of Fulda describing the investiture and boundaries of the estate of Hammelburg, which had been granted by Charlemagne earlier that year. The prose switches between Latin and Old High German without any indication that different languages were being used, and there is no attempt to Latinize the Germanic vocabulary.[51] A Fulda charter of 801 (surviving only in an early modern copy) describes a grant of newly cleared land belonging to the *villa* of Burghaun made by a group of landowners to the monastery, providing the boundary in a similar mixture of Latin and German words and phrases.[52] Although the quantity of vernacular language in Frankish documents is far smaller than in those of Anglo-Saxon England, these continental boundary descriptions nevertheless constitute important examples of 'un-signalled' code-switching and furnish crucial evidence for the interplay between Latin and the Germanic vernacular. Having examined the more usual vernacular contexts of technical terms and landscape descriptions, let us now turn to a different and more explicit type of evidence for linguistic awareness in this same corpus.

Language Consciousness

Some charters provide clearer evidence for attentiveness to language, as when scribes and draftsmen employed certain phrasings to 'flag' language switches.

51 *ChLA* 12, no. 542, pp. 72–73 (which also includes a facsimile): '… Et descriptus est atque consignatus idem locus undique his terminis, postquam iuraverunt nobiliores terrae illius, ut edicerent veritatem de ipsius fisci quantitate: primum de Salu iuxta Teitenbah in caput suum, de capite Teitenbah in Scaranuirst, de Scaranuirste in caput Staranbah, de capite Staranbah in Scuntra, de Scuntra in Nendichenueld, deinde in thie teofun gruoba, inde in Ennesfirst then uuestaron, inde in Perenfirst, inde in orientale caput Lutibah, inde in Lutibrunnon, inde in obanentig Uuinessol, inde in obanentig Uuinestal, inde in then burguueg, inde in Otitales houbit, deinde in thie michilun buochun, inde in Blenchibrunnon, inde ubar Sala in thaz marchoug, inde in then matten uueg, inde in thie teofun clingun, inde in Hunzesbah in Eltingesbrunnon, inde in mittan Eichinaberg, inde in Hiltifridesburg, inde in thaz steinina houg, inde in then lintinon seo, inde in theo teofun clingun unzi themo brunnen, inde in ein sol, inde in ein steininaz hog, inde in Steinfirst, inde in Sala in then elm.' See Bauer, *Die ältesten Grenzbeschreibungen*, pp. 3–27; Geary, 'Land, Language and Memory', pp. 177–79; Bergmann, 'Pragmatische Voraussetzungen'.

52 *Urkundenbuch des Klosters Fulda*, ed. Edmund E. Stengel (Marburg, 1956–58), no. 275, pp. 397–400: '… a Tunibach sursum vel sursum Tunibach usque ad Treuiches eichi, deinde sursum in Bramfirst, deinde in Caltenbahhes haubit, deinde in Ruhunbah, deinde in des kuninges uueg per ambos hagon, inde in Suuarzahafurt, deinde in daz smala eihahi, deinde after dero firsti in Rinacha haubit, deinde iterum in Tunibach …'

These phrases varied according to several different factors, including local practice, adherence to available formularies, and personal preferences. Some patterns can however be identified in the bodies of materials considered here. As mentioned above, the introduction of vernacular terms in otherwise mostly Latin texts is particularly frequent when dealing with topographical elements. In the great majority of cases such switches occur in order to introduce place-names through the use of phrases such as *in loco qui dicitur* or *terra quae appellatur*. These phrases appear in charters issued all over Western Europe, but, on account of their generic character, they do not demonstrate a specific awareness on the part of the scribe or draftsman of the linguistic nature of the words which follow them. Caution is needed however, since place-names normally originate as descriptions of features of the landscape and are directly related to the way in which a local community speaks of such topographical features.[53] Moreover, we are no longer in a position to establish whether the terms which follow phrases like the above-mentioned ones still had semantic meaning when the charters that contain them were issued. In other words, we cannot ascertain whether terms that function as place-names were already employed just as labels or, by contrast, whether local users could still relate their meaning to the features to which they originally, as common nouns or phrases, referred.[54] For example, in an eighth-century charter issued by Ealdwulf, king of the East Saxons, in favour of a *comes* named Hunlaf, one of the places where the land granted was located is referred to as 'loco qui dicitur Stanmere'.[55] The latter term means 'stony pool', but we do not know whether the pool which gave origin to this way of calling the place was still there when the charter was issued, or whether local inhabitants would have been thinking of it when

53 See Hubertus Menke, *Das Namengut der frühen karolingischen Königsurkunden* (Heidelberg, 1980), pp. 341–44. For similar issues in French documents from a slightly later period, see Michel Parisse, '*Quod vulgo dicitur*: la latinisation des noms communs dans les chartes', *Médiévales* 42 (2002), 45–54, at pp. 45–6.

54 For a detailed treatment see Richard Coates, 'Singular Definite Expressions with a Unique Denotatum and the Limits of Properhood', *Linguistics* 38.6 (2000), 1161–74, and, by the same author, 'A Strictly Millian Approach to the Definition of the Proper Name', *Mind and Language* 24 (2009), 433–44; Bergmann, 'Pragmatische Voraussetzungen', pp. 63–69. See also Kate Wiles, 'The Treatment of Charter Bounds by the Worcester Cartulary Scribes', *New Medieval Literatures* 13 (2011), 113–36; and Fran Colman, 'First, Catch Your Name … On Names and Word Classes, Especially in Old English', *English Studies* 96 (2015), 310–36 for a discussion focusing on Anglo-Saxon materials. On place-name morphology in Francia, see *Ortsname und Urkunde*, ed. Schützeichel.

55 S 50 (*CantCC* 17). This is the modern place-name Stanmer, still used to refer to the same location in Sussex. The charter only survives in a thirteenth-century copy and, though its most recent editors consider it untrustworthy in this received form, they believe that it 'ultimately depends on an eighth-century document': Brooks and Kelly, *CantCC* 17, p. 370.

referring to this location.[56] Conversely, modern editing conventions require the employment of a capital initial letter when such place-names appear in documents, even though the original texts did not employ similarly unequivocal ways of signalling properhood. Such conventions tend to suggest to a modern reader's mind that those words were already functioning as labels when the charters containing them were produced, thus obfuscating the possibility that they could in fact retain semantic meaning.

This is relevant because, as mentioned above, terms which function as place-names, irrespective of whether they still conveyed semantic meaning, obviously originated at a local level among those who lived in or near the location itself. In Anglo-Saxon and East Frankish charters, such terms would thus almost invariably introduce Germanic words within a Latin text. When draftsmen flagged the inclusion of these terms with such relatively neutral phrases as the ones quoted above, it is not possible to ascertain whether they were aware of the code-switching they were introducing, whether they thought they were simply giving proper names, or whether they would have automatically recognized the semantic meaning of those words. Various factors would have determined one or the other possibility and, in fact, in many cases things may have been far from clear-cut, with vernacular phrases still preserving semantic force while also being on their way to becoming labels.[57]

In many other cases, however, draftsmen do provide hints in charters about their attitude to and awareness of the inclusion of vernacular Germanic single terms or strings of words. In England, place-names could be introduced through reference to local knowledgeable people with phrases such as *quam*

56 In those cases in which scribes provided a Latin rendering of a vernacular place-name, it would seem, by contrast, that there persisted a clear awareness of the geographical features to which the name itself referred. One such example is provided by a ninth-century charter from Worcester referring to the city of Bath as follows: 'in illo famoso urbe qui nominatur et calidum balneum, *þæt is æt þæm hatum baðum*' (emphasis ours): S 210 (BCS 509).

57 Not surprisingly a more acute awareness of place-names' semantic value is generally shown by foreigners or authors who are writing for a foreign audience. A case in point is undoubtedly Asser, the Welsh biographer of King Alfred the Great, who often spells out in his Latin account of the king's Life the meaning of the English place-names he mentions; e.g., 'in insula quae vocatur Sceapieg, quod interpretatur "insula ovium"' (ch. 3); 'in loco qui dicitur Aclea, id est "in campulo quercus"' (ch. 5). On several occasions he also provides the Old Welsh corresponding place-name: 'insula quae dicitur in Saxonica lingua Tenet, Britannico autem sermone Ruim' (ch. 9); 'ad alium locum qui dicitur Saxonice Exanceastre, Britannice autem Cairuuisc, Latine quoque civitas Exae' (ch. 49). For further significant examples see chs 37, 55, and 57. All quotations are from *Asser's Life of King Alfred together with the Annals of Saint Neots Erroneously Ascribed to Asser*, ed. William Henry Stevenson (Oxford, 1959).

solicolæ ... nominant, ubi ab incolis ... appellatur, or *quem ruricolae ... solent clamare*.[58] By referring to those who would have commonly called or described relevant locations through the vernacular words contained in the documents, draftsmen evoked a space inhabited by people who spoke a language markedly different from the Latin of the charters. In Anglo-Saxon documents, where these phrases are especially common, the term *vulgus* is also occasionally employed, as in the case of a charter of King Coenwulf of Mercia which refers to Tamworth, the place where the diploma was issued in 808, through the words 'Actum est in loco celeberrimo quae a uulgo uocatur Tomeworðig'.[59] Here the word *vulgus*, instead of denoting specifically the persons who lived in the locality as in the case of *solicolae* or *incolae*, conveys the more general meaning of 'common people', thus implying that in order to name Tamworth, it was necessary to employ the more commonly spoken vernacular in contrast to the Latin of the documents.

In continental charters, the language of the common people is frequently referred to with some variation of the phrase *quod vulgo dicitur*, in which *vulgo*, originally the ablative form of *vulgus*, functions as an adverb meaning 'commonly' or 'usually'.[60] The phrase has attracted the attention of historians and philologists, albeit largely in relation to the long-running debate on the divergence of Latin and Romance.[61] Studies have thus mostly focused on texts produced in Romance-speaking areas, only touching occasionally on the contemporary use of this phrase in eastern Frankish territories, where it usually signalled the introduction of Germanic terms and phrases in Latin documents.[62]

58 See for example S 258 (BCS 179, from Winchester, Old Minster; A.D. 749), S 161 (*CantCC* 37; A.D. 805), S 178 (*CantCC* 51; A.D. 815). The reference to *incolae* seems to be especially favoured at Canterbury in the early ninth century, whereas *solicolae* is attested at Worcester and Winchester. Interestingly, references to local inhabitants appear seldom to have occurred in eastern Francia.

59 S 163 (*CantCC* 40).

60 This adverbial usage is widely attested in antiquity: Frédérique Biville, '"Qui vulgo dicitur ..." Formes "vulgaires" de la creation lexicale en Latin', in *Latin vulgaire, latin tardif IV. Actes du 4ᵉ colloque international sur le latin vulgaire et tardif, Caen, 2–5 septembre 1994*, ed. Louis Callebat (Hildesheim, 1995), pp. 193–203; Rosanna Sornicola, '"Vulgo dicitur": Vulgarisms in Legal Latin', *Journal of Latin Linguistics* 12 (2013), 269–99, at pp. 274–77, 281–2.

61 Marc van Uytfanghe, 'Les expressions du type *quod vulgo vocant* dans des textes latins antérieurs au Concile de Tours et aux Serments de Strasbourg: témoignages lexicologiques et sociolinguistiques de la "langue rustique romaine"?', *Zeitschrift für romanische Philologie* 105 (1989), 28–49, with further bibliography; Parisse, 'Quod vulgo dicitur'.

62 An exception is *Quod vulgo dicitur. Studien zum Altniederländischen*, eds W. Pijnenburg, A. Quak, and T. Schoonheim (Amsterdam, 2003), although despite the volume's title, the only contribution that deals with this expression in any detail is Dirk P. Blok,

The occurrences of *quod vulgo dicitur* (or similar variants) in charters from the Frankish East are particularly noteworthy, as the presence of the adverb *vulgo* bridges the written Latin of the documents and the Germanic vernacular spoken language. Moreover, the phrase is not simply or solely employed to introduce topographical terms (although this was often the case at Freising),[63] but occurs especially in contexts in which scribes introduced vernacular terms after having first given their meaning in Latin. In other words, phrases containing the adverb *vulgo* are often employed to introduce translations from Latin to the Germanic vernacular. A Lorsch charter of 770 provides one such example when tracing the perimeter of a large tract of woodland, which was marked by tree-notching: 'ipsa incisio arborum in ipsa die facta fuit, que uulgo lachus appellatur siue diuisio'.[64] In a Freising charter of 793 recording a donation of property around Donauwörth by Count Helmoin, the phrase *quod vulgo dicitur* is used to provide a vernacular translation of a portion of the boundary clause contained in the document: '... exinde tendit in iusu iuxta rivolum usque ad magnum rubum quod vulgo dicitur nidar pi deru lahhun za deru mihilun eihi ...'.[65] In these and other similar cases, scribes were clearly conscious of their code-switching, relying on the adverb *vulgo* to express a change from the usual, expected Latin to their native tongue.[66] The phrase in Helmoin's charter, however, is particularly striking, given the scarcity of vernacular usage in Frankish documents, and we are compelled to ask what may have prompted the interruption. The political background to Helmoin's donation is relatively

---

'Altniederländisches in lateinischen Dokumenten, 800–ca. 1250', pp. 169–82, who notes that such phrases seem to have become common in the Low Countries in the Carolingian period: pp. 174–81.

63 See, e.g., *Traditionen Freising*, no. 34, 1:61–62; no. 100, 1:117–18; no. 197, 1:187–90; no. 199, 1:191–92; no. 273, 1:240–41; no. 405, 1:349; no. 434a, 1:371–72; no. 437, 1:376; no. 475, 1:406–7; no. 560, 1:481–82; no. 575, 1:492; no. 576, 1:493–94. See further Bauer, *Die ältesten Grenzbeschreibungen*, pp. 274–76.

64 *Codex Laureshamensis*, ed. Karl Glöckner, 3 vols (Darmstadt, 1929–36), no. 10, 1:286–87: 'a tree-notch was made on that same day, which in the vernacular is called a *lachus*, or "division"'. For tree-marking, see also for instance MGH D Louis the Pious, no. 378, pp. 942–45; *Traditionen Regensburg*, no. 59, pp. 59–60.

65 *Traditionen Freising*, no. 166a, 1:161–64: 'from there it extends downwards along the stream up to the big oak tree which is commonly [or 'in the vernacular'] called *nidar pi deru lahhun za deru mihilun eihi* ("down by the stream to the great oak tree")'. See Bauer, *Die ältesten Grenzbeschreibungen*, pp. 166–73.

66 See for example *Cartulaire de l'abbaye de Gorze*, ed. A. d'Herbomez (Paris, 1898), no. 11, pp. 24–28: 'vineas quoque sepire, quod vulgo dicitur manuerc arare' (as well as two other instances in the same charter); *Traditionen Freising*, no. 326, 1:279: 'territorium quod vulgo dicitur einan hluz'; MGH D Louis the German, no. 124, pp. 174–75: 'ut eis liceret habere plenam legem, quae vulgo dicitur phaath'.

clear: in 788, Charlemagne deposed Tassilo III, the last Agilolfing duke of Bavaria, and stayed there in 791–93 to oversee the integration of the region into his kingdom. Helmoin, a prominent member of the Agilolfing family, was consequently subjected to the Carolingian takeover. As the charter recounts, the land in question had been appropriated for the fisc by royal commissioners. Charlemagne, however, intervened and restored the property to Helmoin on the condition that he donate it to the church of Freising. As part of the re-investment of the land, its boundary was perambulated, and it is here that the vernacular statement was made. This portion of the property, most likely an inheritance of particular significance, was commemorated in the count's own language, perhaps as an assertion of his family identity in the face of this foreign imposition and the enforced alienation of the land.[67]

Anglo-Saxon draftsmen, by contrast, did not employ the phrase *quod vulgo dicitur*, but found other ways to flag the use of Old English in their Latin charters. In this same period—the late eighth and early ninth century—it is possible to observe the appearance of two new, much more explicit, language-flagging features in Anglo-Saxon charters: the naming of the vernacular language as 'Saxon' and the use of phrases containing a first-person plural verb, such as *quem nos vocamus*. Alternatively, but clearly to the same effect, we also find the first-person possessive adjective *nostra* in phrases like *qui nominatur nostra propria lingua*. Both features can be found in a charter from Abingdon dated 801, preserved in an early thirteenth-century cartulary.[68] This was issued by Beorhtric, king of the West Saxons in favour of a *princeps* named Lulla. The land transacted is said to have been located 'ubi nota appellatione Saxonice Eastun dicitur', while the bounds refer to a 'sharp stone' through the words 'iuxta uno acerbo lapidum quem nos stancestil uocamus'. The use of the word *saxonice* makes explicit the necessary switch to the vernacular to introduce

67 Janet L. Nelson, 'The Language of Charters and Charter-related Documents in the Reign of Charlemagne', lecture delivered at Universidad del País Vasco, Vitoria-Gasteiz, 8 February 2016, video available online: https://ehutb.ehu.es/video/58c6703af82b2b990f8b457a. For the Bavarian context, see Janet L. Nelson, 'Staging Integration in Bavaria, 791–793', in *Neue Wege der Frühmittelalterforschung: Bilanz und Perspektiven*, eds Walter Pohl, Maximilian Diesenberger, and Bernhard Zeller (Vienna, 2018), pp. 225–38; and on the identification of individuals and groups with particular properties, see Geary, 'Land, Language and Memory'.

68 S 268 (*Abing* 7). Although earlier scholars had cast some doubts on the authenticity of this document, its latest editor—Susan Kelly—has identified features which point towards its likely authenticity, particularly in the boundary clause: *Abing* 7, p. 34. The earliest occurrence of *saxonice* can be found in a record from the Worcester archive dated 796 and preserved in an early eleventh-century cartulary; S 148 (BCS 278): 'in celebri monasterio quod Saxonice nominatur æt Baðum'.

the place-name *Eastun* (i.e. Crux Easton, Hants.). This represents an important development from the more neutral ways in which place-names were provided in the examples examined above. In this case the scribe is not simply reporting the name of a place; he is also explicitly saying that in order to do so he needs to change language, and that the code he is introducing is the vernacular 'Saxon' language. Here, then, the vernacular is given a precise name and identity, and is thus provided with status and recognition. The flagging in the boundary clause takes things even further: although the name of the language is not repeated there, the use of the first-person plural *nos … uocamus* generates a process through which both the scribe and his audience can identify with the vernacular word *stancestil*. The function of this flagging phrase is similar to that performed by the words *quod vulgo dicitur* in continental sources, in that in both cases we are witnessing the insertion of a vernacular translation of text previously provided in Latin. Thanks to the use of the first person in Beorhtric's charter, however, the Old English word is marked up as a portion of the text which—the scribe can guarantee—will be recognizable by all those with access to the charter, either through direct reading or by hearing it read out.[69]

The earliest charter surviving in its original form in which the same mechanism can be identified is a diploma issued by King Coenwulf of Mercia in 811 in favour of Archbishop Wulfred of Canterbury.[70] While the place-names mentioned in this charter are introduced by phrases such as *ibi ab incolis … nuncupato*, or *quod … illic nominatur*, the urban tenements granted by the king to the archbishop, together with other landed properties in Kent, are described as 'duas possessiunculas et tertiam dimediam id est in nostra loquella ðridda half haga' ('two and a half small properties, that is, in our speech, two and a half tenements'). Old English works rather differently from Latin to express half numerals, as is shown by the pattern emerging from this example (ordinal number + *half* + noun).[71] The provision of an Old English translation for this technical aspect of the text can be at least in part attributed to the pragmatic nature of the information conveyed, which has often been cited to justify the presence of the vernacular in documentary sources. However, one

69 On charters as texts for reading either in public or private contexts and, more generally, on their performative nature, see D. H. Green, *Medieval Listening and Reading: The Primary Reception of German Literature, 800–1300* (Cambridge, 1994), pp. 99–101; Kelly, 'Anglo-Saxon Lay Society', pp. 56–57; Geary, 'Land, Language and Memory'; and Scott Thompson Smith, *Land and Book: Literature and Land Tenure in Anglo-Saxon England* (Toronto, 2012), pp. 22–69.

70 S 168 (*CantCC* 44).

71 See Alistair Campbell, *Old English Grammar* (Oxford, 1959, reprinted with corrections 1991), p. 285.

must also bear in mind that the reference to *nostra loquella* would have engendered in the draftsman and his audience the same process of identification with the language that has been observed in the case of Beorhtric's charter. There are numerous other examples in ninth-century Anglo-Saxon charters of vernacular terms inserted through references to 'our language' or the use of first-person plurals like *dicimus*, *vocamus* etc. As well as in documents from Canterbury and Abingdon, these occur in records from Worcester, Rochester, Malmesbury, and Winchester.[72] In several of these cases we can also observe in the same sentence the combination of a reference to 'us' and/or 'our language' with the explicit naming of the language as 'Saxon'. This is exemplified by a surviving single sheet from the Worcester cathedral archive, a diploma of King Wiglaf of Mercia, dated 836, granting privileges to the minster at Hanbury (Worcestershire).[73] Among the exemptions from worldly obligations granted, there is one described as 'difficultate illa quam nos Saxonice faestingmenn dicimus'. The Old English term *fæstingmen* would seem to indicate a category of people, probably royal agents, whom religious institutions such as that at Hanbury had the obligation to feed and entertain.[74] Furthermore, it is worth noting that references to the vernacular as the 'Saxon' language can be found in charters issued in Mercia, Kent, and Wessex between the late eighth century and the beginning of the tenth.[75] The term itself, which would seem to appear at the turn of the ninth century to refer to the Old English vernacular in charters

---

72 E.g. S 177 (*CantCC* 48), S 287 (*CantCC* 71), S 293 (*CantCC* 73), S 328 (*CantCC* 83), S 332 (*CantCC* 86), S 344 (*CantCC* 93), all from Canterbury, Christ Church; S 190 (BCS 416), S 193 (BCS 434), S 206 (BCS 487), S 207 (BCS 489), from Worcester; S 1271 (*Abing* 12), from Abingdon; S 299 (*Roch* 229), S 315 (*Roch* 23), from Rochester; S 356 (*Malm* 20), from Malmesbury; S 1277 (BCS 544), from Winchester, Old Minster.

73 S 190 (BCS 416).

74 See Kelly, *Abing* 12, pp. 58–59. The same reference to this exemption, including the explicit mention of the 'Saxon' language, can also be found in other ninth-century charters from Mercia and Kent: S 271 (*Roch* 18); S 193 (BCS 434) from Worcester; S 1271 (*Abing* 12). As observed in Gallagher, 'The Vernacular in Anglo-Saxon Charters', p. 209, *fæstingmen* is one of the earliest non-locative vernacular terms to appear in Anglo-Saxon charters.

75 These are, in chronological order, S 148 (BCS 278), S 268 (*Abing* 7), S 161 (*CantCC* 37, a slightly more complex case referring to *ritu Saxonica*; cf. S 169, *CantCC* 46), S 190 (BCS 416), S 287 (*CantCC* 71), S 193 (*Pet* Appendix 3), S 293 (*CantCC* 73), S 1271 (*Abing* 12), S 315 (*Roch* 23), S 207 (BCS 489), S 332 (*CantCC* 86), S 1284 (BCS 590), S 374 (BCS 564), S 372 (BCS 613), S 1286 (BCS 611). The remarkable paucity of surviving early charters from Northumbria does not allow one to ascertain whether the same term would have also been used in charters produced there: *Charters of Northern Houses*, ed. D. A. Woodman, Anglo-Saxon Charters 16 (Oxford, 2012), pp. 1–6. For the terms used by the Northumbrian Bede to define the vernacular English language, see Nicholas Brooks, *Bede and the English*, Jarrow Lecture 1999 (Jarrow, 2000), pp. 8–9, 15, and by the same author, 'English Identity from Bede to the Millennium', *Haskins Society Journal* 14 (2003), 33–51, at pp. 35–36.

from all the above-mentioned regions, is obviously associated with the ethnonym that had been most commonly used to define the Anglo-Saxons since the fifth century, i.e. *Saxones*. Bede famously departed from this usage preferring to adopt the term *Angli* and to speak in most cases of the *lingua Anglorum*, a choice which, as suggested by Jennifer O'Reilly, was probably meant to avoid possible negative associations with the word *saxum*, sometimes used to refer to the hardness of unconverted peoples.[76] Bede's choice, however, does not seem to have had an impact on surviving eighth- and ninth-century charters, though one wonders whether the resulting picture would be different if records from this period had also been preserved in Northumbria.[77] Such uniformity at this time is in any case striking, given that England still encompassed a number of different polities in various states of political and military turmoil, a process which would eventually lead to the expansion of the West Saxon kingdom and, in the first half of the tenth century, the creation of the kingdom of the English. In spite of the political divisions and the geographical distribution of Old English dialects, surviving charters attest to a clear notion of a shared vernacular language throughout all these territories.[78]

Continental charters, by contrast, present a different picture in this respect. For one, the use of first-person plural verbs, such as *dicimus* or *nominamus*, in order to introduce vernacular terms appears to have been restricted to private charters.[79] A Freising charter of 802, for instance, employs the phrases 'duo loca quod dicimus houasteti' and 'territorium quod dicimus kapreitta' to introduce vernacular terms indicating farmsteads (*houasteti*) and a field (*kapreitta*).[80] A Fulda charter of 817×818 uses the verb *dicimus* before a vernacular word whose meaning had first been given in Latin ('extra tres laboraturas siluae quas nos dicimus thriurothe').[81] In this case we can perceive the same translating function that has been observed for Anglo-Saxon documents employing vernacular technical terms whose meaning is first provided in Latin. An interesting

76 Jennifer O'Reilly, 'The Multitude of Isles and the Corner-stone: Topography, Exegesis, and the Identity of the *Angli* in Bede's *Historia ecclesiastica*', in *Anglo-Saxon Traces*, eds Jane Roberts and Leslie Webster, Essays in Anglo-Saxon Studies 4 (Tempe, AZ, 2011), pp. 201–27. Cf. Michael Richter, 'Bede's *Angli*: Angles or English?', *Peritia* 3 (1984), 99–114; Brooks, *Bede and the English*; Brooks, 'English Identity'.

77 Ninth-century Latin narrative texts also call the Old English vernacular 'Saxon', as is the case for Asser's *Life of King Alfred*, about which see above, n. 57.

78 Kitson, 'The Nature of Old English Dialect Distributions'.

79 Though cf. the use of a first-person verb in this way in Charlemagne's *Capitulare Italicum*, discussed below.

80 *Traditionen Freising*, no. 185, 1:177–78; see also no. 534a, 1:456; and, for a slightly later period, no. 1007, 1:760–61.

81 *Codex diplomaticus Fuldensis*, no. 354, p. 167. See also no. 332, p. 161 (*fahstat*).

contrast, however, is provided by an original single-sheet private charter of 817 from St Gall which introduces the vernacular term *chuuiltiuuerch* ('evening work') through the formula *quod Alamanni dicunt*.[82] This phrase also occurs in the *Lex Alamannorum* to signpost the use of specific Alemannic (i.e. Upper German) terms in the otherwise Latin text of the legislative code.[83] To understand the use of this phrase in the St Gall charter, which was written by a monastic scribe named Wolfcoz and records a donation of Count Chadaloh to the monastery, one should bear in mind that St Gall's domain covered both Romance- and Germanic-speaking areas (Raetia and Alemannia, respectively).[84] It is probably for this reason that an inclusive first-person plural verb (such as *dicimus*) could not be used here to refer to a specifically Germanic technical term such as *chuuiltiuuerch*. The word was instead signposted in this private charter through reference to the long-established ethnic identity of those who, in this region, were associated with that vernacular.

Moving from private to royal charters, one finds that first-person verbs and possessive adjectives rarely appear in eastern Frankish royal diplomas to signpost the use of vernacular terms.[85] By contrast, in diplomas dealing with territories which had been recently conquered by the Franks, it is possible to encounter third-person plural verbs and pronouns. One example is provided by an original single-sheet diploma of Charlemagne issued in 811, through which the emperor confirmed Count Bennit's ownership of land given to his father, Amalung the Saxon, for his fidelity: 'Praecipientes ergo iubemus, ut nullus fidelium nostrorum praesentium scilicet et futurorum praefatum Bennit vel heredes illius de hoc propriso, *quod in lingua eorum dicitur bivanc*, expoliare

82 W 228 (= *ChLA* 101, no. 25, pp. 89–93): 'puelle vero infra salam manentes tres opus ad vestrum et tres sibi faciant dies, et hoc quod Alamanni chuuiltiuuerch dicunt non faciant'. On the definition of this term, see Stefan Sonderegger, *Althochdeutsche Sprache und Literatur*, 3rd ed. (Berlin, 2003), p. 72.

83 See Wolfgang Haubrichs, '*Quod Alamanni dicunt*. Volkssprachliche Wörter in der *Lex Alamannorum*', in *Recht und Kultur im frühmittelalterlichen Alemannien. Rechtsgeschichte, Archäologie und Geschichte des 7. und 8. Jahrhunderts*, ed. Sebastian Brather (Berlin, 2017), pp. 169–209. On Old High German dialects, see Wolfgang Haubrichs, *Die Anfänge: Versuche volkssprachiger Schriftlichkeit im frühen Mittelalter* (*ca.* 700–1050/60). *Geschichte der deutschen Literatur von den Anfängen bis zum Beginn der Neuzeit, I: Von den Anfängen bis zum hohen Mittelalter*, 2nd ed. (Tübingen, 1995), pp. 23–26.

84 McKitterick, *The Carolingians and the Written Word*, pp. 81–90; *Urkundenlandschaft Rätien*, eds Peter Erhart and Julia Kleindinst (Vienna, 2004), pp. 70–74; Zeller, this volume.

85 MGH D Louis the German, no. 51, pp. 67–69, purportedly issued in 848, includes the phrase 'quod nos foravuerch vocamus', but this is an eleventh-century interpolation. *Foravuerch* is an Old Saxon term for 'outlying farm' or 'manor'; see Heinrich Tiefenbach, *Altsächsische Handwörterbuch* (Berlin, 2010), p. 101.

aut inquietare ullo quoque tempore praesumatis ... ' (emphasis ours).[86] The beneficiary of this diploma was a member of the Saxon elite, active in a territory which had experienced a relatively recent Frankish takeover. The charter presents us with an outsider perspective, or perhaps a top-down one, rather than the inclusive descriptions of the vernacular language encountered in the English charters. Charlemagne ruled over a vast territory, which, as discussed, was markedly more multilingual than ninth-century England, and in which a royal diploma could never unequivocally refer to 'our language' as English records do. Hence the need to signpost the use of vernacular terms through the phrase *quod in lingua eorum dicitur*, i.e., 'in their language' rather than 'our own'. Similar attitudes to the language of the Saxons emerge from the later diplomas of Louis the German, in which on occasion one finds the phrase *eorum lingua*. This is the case for two royal diplomas, issued respectively in 858 and 859, in favour of the female monastery at Herford, in Saxony, which signpost the employment of the vernacular term *lazi/lati* (= *lazzi*, 'semi-free people') through the phrase *quae/qui lingua eorum ... dicuntur*.[87] The dissociative effect obtained through the use of this phrase is probably a product of politico-linguistic circumstance: Old Saxon, as a Low German dialect, could be easily recognized as different from the Old High German dialects spoken by the inhabitants of the main territories in the eastern regions of the Frankish Empire.[88]

Such linguistic features should be kept in mind when considering the increasing use of the adjective *theodisca* to define the vernacular language in the diplomas issued by Louis the German for institutions located further south, that is, closer to the heart of his political base. In 837, he gave land located at

86 MGH D Charlemagne, no. 213, pp. 284–85; and cf. the identical use of this phrase in no. 218, pp. 290–92. On *bivanc* (= *bifang*, *bifangum*), see Sebastian Freudenberg, *Trado atque dono. Die frühmittelalterliche private Grundherrschaft in Ostfranken im Spiegel der Traditionsurkunden der Klöster Lorsch und Fulda (750 bis 900)* (Stuttgart, 2013), pp. 159–64.

87 MGH DD Louis the German, no. 93, pp. 134–35, and no. 95, pp. 137–38. On *lazzi*, see Eric J. Goldberg, *Struggle for Empire: Kingship and Conflict under Louis the German* (Ithaca, 2006), p. 110.

88 On *lingua eorum* as a phrase indicating the language of the Saxons in documentary sources, see Heinrich Tiefenbach, *Studien zu Wörtern volkssprachiger Herkunft in karolingischen Königsurkunden. Ein Beitrag zum Wortschatz der Diplome Lothars I. und Lothars II.* (Munich, 1973), p. 22, and Goldberg, *Struggle for Empire*, p. 179 n. 146. Cf. MGH D Arnulf, no. 69, pp. 103–4: 'quae secundum illorum linguam steora vel ostarstuopha vocatur'; with Tiefenbach, *Studien zu Wörtern*, pp. 89–92. For further examples of such differentiation of peoples through reference to language, see Hans-Werner Goetz, 'Lingua. Indizien und Grenzen einer Identität durch Sprache im frühen Mittelalter', in *Sprache und Identität*, eds Pohl and Zeller, pp. 61–74, at 69–72.

the confluence of the rivers Ybbs and Danube to the church of Salzburg, one of several grants in the southeast in favour of Bavarian ecclesiastical institutions. The relevant portion of the text reads 'ex utraque parte ipsius fluminis terminatur ab occidentale parte, quod Theodisca lingua wagreini dicitur'.[89] In another charter of the same year in favour of the Alemannic monastery of Kempten, the same phrase was employed to introduce the vernacular word *muta*, indicating a specific due from which the monastery was being exempted ('nullum theloneum neque quod lingua Theodisca muta vocatur').[90] The use of *lingua theodisca* in these contexts seems to be analogous to the references to the Saxon language in the English charters discussed above.

The adjective *theodisca* (in Old High German, *diutisk*, and whence *deutsch*) was derived from the unattested Proto-Germanic noun **þeudō-* ('people'), and so is a Latinization literally meaning 'of the people', thus suggesting interesting parallels with the Latin adjective *vulgaris*. It became the general term most commonly used in the Frankish world to refer to the vernacular Germanic tongue, often in opposition to the *lingua romana*, that is, the Romance vernacular. Interestingly, the earliest attested use of the term is found in a report prepared by George of Ostia for Pope Hadrian following the legatine councils held in England in 786.[91] To ensure full understanding of the council's canons at an assembly held in Mercia, George's decrees were read out 'tam latine quam theodiscę', meaning in this case that they were translated into English.[92]

89 MGH D Louis the German, no. 25, pp. 30–31; Goldberg, *Struggle for Empire*, pp. 79–80. *Wagreini* probably means 'ridge': Gerhard Köbler, *Althochdeutsches Wörterbuch*, 6th ed. (2014), http://www.koeblergerhard.de/ahdwbhin.html.

90 MGH D Louis the German, no. 24, pp. 29–30; Goldberg, *Struggle for Empire*, pp. 80–81. This charter survives in a twelfth-century cartulary, but a renewal of the privilege in 844 (MGH D Louis the German, no. 36, pp. 46–47), preserved in the original, repeats the phrase precisely.

91 Levison, *England and the Continent*, pp. 126–30; Heinz Thomas, 'Der Ursprung des Wortes Theodiscus', *Historische Zeitschrift* 247 (1988), 295–331; Wolfgang Haubrichs, 'Theodiscus, Deutsch und Germanisch—drei Ethnonyme, drei Forschungsbegriffe. Zur Frage der Instrumentalisierung und Wertbesetzung deutscher Sprach- und Volksbezeichnungen', in *Zur Geschichte der Gleichung 'germanisch-deutsch': Sprache und Namen, Geschichte und Institutionen*, eds Heinrich Beck, Dieter Geuenich, Heiko Steuer, and Dietrich Hakelberg (Berlin, 2004), pp. 199–227; and Wolfgang Haubrichs and Herwig Wolfram, 'Theodiscus', *Reallexikon der Germanischen Altertumskunde*, eds Heinrich Beck, Dieter Geuenich, and Heiko Steuer, 35 vols (Berlin, 1972–2008), 30:421–33.

92 Edited in Alcuin, *Epistolae*, ed. Ernst Dümmler, MGH Epp. 4 (Berlin, 1895), no. 3, p. 28. For general context, see Catherine Cubitt, *Anglo-Saxon Church Councils c.650–c.850* (London, 1995), pp. 152–90; and Joanna Story, *Carolingian Connections: Anglo-Saxon England and Carolingian Francia, c. 750–870* (Aldershot, 2003), pp. 55–92. The letter is transmitted in a late tenth-century manuscript alongside a canon law collection associated with

Theodisca next appears in the *Annales regni Francorum*, where in the entry for 788 the annalist reports that Tassilo, duke of the Bavarians, was summoned to Ingelheim by Charlemagne and tried for deserting King Pippin's army in 763. This was a crime, 'quod theodisca lingua harisliz dicitur'.[93] A very similar phrase concerning *harisliz* is found a few years later in Charlemagne's *Capitulare Italicum* of 801, although here the text implies that the *lingua theodisca* is the king's own: 'quod nos teudisca lingua dicimus herisliz'.[94] Here, then, the *lingua theodisca* has become the word of the king. The nature of these references to *harisliz* has led to the suggestions that the term *theodisca* was primarily used specifically to denote legal terminology, and that on the continent the *lingua theodisca* was a kind of 'high language' of the assembled, multi-ethnic Frankish army.[95] But, while *theodisca* could denote legal or military obligations (as was also the case in Louis the German's diplomas), it clearly possessed a broader meaning, as demonstrated by its appearance in the report of the Mercian synod of 786. Here, *theodisca* obviously refers to the language of those who were present. To a Romance-speaker such as George of Ostia, Old English would probably have sounded similar to continental Germanic speech. In fact, the adjective *theodiscus* can be found in relation to virtually all Germanic languages in this period.[96] Among the best-known occurrences are the decree of the 813 council of Tours requiring homilies to be translated (*transferre*) 'in rusticam Romanam linguam aut Thiotiscam', and the historian Nithard's account of the oaths sworn by Louis the German and Charles the Bald at Strasbourg

Archbishop Ruotger of Trier (916–31), but its textual integrity is not doubted; see Story, *Carolingian Connections*, p. 58.

93 *Annales regni Francorum*, s.a. 788, eds Georg Heinrich Pertz and Friedrich Kurze, MGH SS rer. Germ. 6 (Hanover, 1895), p. 80. For context, see McKitterick, *Charlemagne*, pp. 118–27.

94 *Capitulare Italicum*, ed. Alfred Boretius, MGH Capit. 1 (Hanover, 1883), no. 98, pp. 204–6, at 205; Jennifer R. Davis, *Charlemagne's Practice of Empire* (Cambridge, 2015), pp. 285–86.

95 Thomas, 'Der Ursprung des Wortes Theodiscus'; Heinz Thomas, 'Frenkisk. Zur Geschichte von theodiscus und teutonicus im Frankreich des 9. Jahrhunderts', *Beihefte der Francia* 22 (1990), 67–95; Hermann Jakobs, *Theodisk im Frankenreich* (Heidelberg, 1998), pp. 32–45; Hermann Jakobs, 'Diot und Sprache. Deutsch im Verband der Frankenreiche (8. bis frühes 11. Jahrhundert)', in *Nation und Sprache. Die Diskussion ihres Verhältnisses in Geschichte und Gegenwart*, ed. Andreas Gardt (Berlin, 2000), pp. 7–46; Ruth Schmidt-Wiegand, '*Quod theodisca lingua harisliz dicitur*. Das Zeugnis der Lorscher Annalen (788) im Kontext frühmittelalterlicher Rechtssprache', in *Grammatica Ianua Artium. Festschrift für Rolf Bergmann zum 60. Geburtstag*, eds Elvira Glaser and Michael Schlaefer (Heidelberg, 1997), pp. 85–91. On vernacular glossing of legal terms, cf. the Germanic glosses of the *Lex Salica* known as the 'Malberg glosses': Ruth Schmidt-Wiegand, 'Die Malbergischen Glossen, eine frühe Überlieferung germanischer Rechtssprache', in *Germanische Rest- und Trümmersprachen*, ed. Heinrich Beck (Berlin, 1989), pp. 157–74.

96 See Haubrichs and Wolfram, 'Theodiscus'.

in 842, spoken respectively in the 'romana' and 'teudisca' *linguae* so that each could be understood by the other's followers.[97] The use of the adjective *theodisca* in reference to the vernacular in Louis' diplomas should also be understood against the backdrop of a substantial linguistic and cultural programme which characterized Louis' rule of the eastern Frankish territories.[98] The central decades of the ninth century marked the golden age of Old High German literature. The production of vernacular translations and original compositions attest to the development of a new awareness of the possibilities offered by the Germanic vernacular as a written code, which may have also contributed to the appearance of this language's common designation in royal diplomas.

A generation later, in England, explorations of the possibilities offered by the vernacular were taken even further, as demonstrated by the ambitious cultural programme of King Alfred the Great (871–99), culminating in the translation into Old English of works such as Gregory the Great's *Regula pastoralis*, Boethius' *De consolatione philosophiae*, St Augustine's *Soliloquia*, and the first fifty Psalms.[99] In his preface to the translation of Gregory's work,

---

97 *Concilium Turonense*, ed. Albert Werminghoff, MGH Conc. 2.1 (Hanover, 1906), no. 38, pp. 286–93, at 288; Nithard, *Historiae*, III.5, ed. Philippe Lauer, *Nithard, Histoire des fils de Louis le Pieux* (Paris, 1926), p. 35. On the controversial meaning of *transferre* at the council of Tours, see Michel Banniard, *Viva voce. Communication écrite et communication orale du IVe au IXe siècle en Occident latin* (Paris, 1992), pp. 411–13; and Roger Wright, *Late Latin and Early Romance in Spain and Carolingian France* (Liverpool, 1982) pp. 118–22. On the evidence of glosses, see Ingo Reiffenstein, '*theodiscus* in den althochdeutschen Glossen', in *Grammatica Ianua Artium*, eds Glaser and Schlaefer, pp. 71–84.

98 Wolfgang Haubrichs, 'Die Praefatio des Heliand. Ein Zeugnis der Religions- und Bildungspolitik Ludwigs des Deutschen', *Niederdeutsches Jahrbuch* 89 (1966), 7–32; Wolfgang Haubrichs, 'Ludwig der Deutsche und die volkssprachige Literatur', in *Ludwig der Deutsche und seine Zeit*, ed. Wilfried Hartmann (Darmstadt, 2004), pp. 203–32; Dieter Geuenich, 'Die volkssprachige Überlieferung der Karolingerzeit aus der Sicht eines Historikers', *Deutsches Archiv* 39 (1983), 104–30, at pp. 121–30; Goldberg, *Struggle for Empire*, pp. 179–85; though cf. Hummer, *Politics and Power*, pp. 130–54. For other terms used for the Germanic vernacular in the ninth century, see Haubrichs and Wolfram, 'Theodiscus', pp. 425–27.

99 These are the five works of Old English prose that are traditionally associated with Alfred, even though it should be noted that the debate as to what the king himself penned is still lively, with some scholars doubting that he authored anything at all. Other vernacular works that date back to the same period and are considered as results of the Alfredian cultural programme are the Old English version of Orosius' *Histories against the Pagans*, Bishop Wærferth's translation of Gregory the Great's *Dialogues*, the first recension of the Anglo-Saxon Chronicle, and the Old English version of Bede's *Ecclesiastical History*. See *A Companion to Alfred the Great*, eds Nicole Guenther Discenza and Paul E. Szarmach, Brill's Companions to the Christian Tradition 58 (Leiden, 2014), especially the editors' introduction, and chs 4 and 10, by Janet M. Bately and Mary P. Richards respectively.

Alfred famously provides justification for his programme of vernacular translations by referring to such illustrious precedents as those of the Greeks and the Romans, whose example the king wanted to follow when deciding to 'turn into the language that we can all understand certain books, which are the most necessary for all men to know'.[100] Just a few years earlier, references to the Greeks and the Romans as precedents for the activity of translation also featured in Otfrid of Wissembourg's *Evangelienbuch*, a vernacular gospel harmony written in the 860s. In both an introductory Latin prose text addressed to Liutbert, archbishop of Mainz, and the first chapter of the work proper, Otfrid justified his use of the vernacular language through arguments similar to those also used by Alfred.[101] One therefore finds contemporary, parallel appeals to the political and cultural importance of the vernacular in both of the regions studied here.[102] This context further suggests that the more frequent and pointed references to language in Anglo-Saxon and Frankish charters of the late eighth to late ninth centuries may indeed represent a broader sensitivity to the ways in which the vernacular could be invoked as a strategy of identification.

Conclusion

In both England and the eastern Frankish territories the linguistic awareness emerging in the documentary sources explored here can be understood in relation to ambitious literary programmes in which the emerging vernaculars played unprecedented and substantial roles.[103] Looking beyond the well-known sources attesting to these programmes, however, charters take us deeper into society and offer a more expansive view thanks to their wide geographical distribution. Moreover, by their very nature, they provide glimpses of

100 *Alfred the Great, Asser's Life of King Alfred and Other Contemporary Sources*, trans. Simon Keynes and Michael Lapidge (London, 1983), p. 126. For the original Old English text see *King Alfred's West Saxon Version of Gregory's Pastoral Care*, ed. Henry Sweet, 2 vols, Early English Text Society Original Series 45 and 50 (London, 1871), reprinted 1958 with corrections and additions by N. R. Ker, p. 7.

101 On the possibility that Otfrid's work was known at Alfred's court see Malcolm Godden, 'Prefaces and Epilogues in the Old English *Pastoral Care*, and Their Carolingian Models', *Journal of English and Germanic Philology* 110 (2011), 441–73, at pp. 456–59. See also Geary, *Language and Power*, pp. 47–48.

102 On the use of the vernacular as an expression of political identity, see Jens Schneider, 'Langues germaniques', in *Les barbares*, ed. Bruno Dumézil (Paris, 2016), pp. 843–49 at 847.

103 See further Godden, 'Prefaces and Epilogues', pp. 455–59.

language-use in day-to-day contexts.[104] The analysis we have conducted here has shown quantitative and qualitative differences in the ways the vernacular could be invoked and harnessed in the documentary cultures of England and eastern Francia. In spite of those differences, however, charters from both regions demonstrate comparable interrelationships between Latin and vernacular languages while attesting to a growing linguistic consciousness on the part of draftsmen in the eighth and ninth centuries. They could usually choose whether to employ Latin or vernacular terms and phrases, or indeed both, and when draftsmen did introduce vernacular elements, they could flag such usage in a number of different ways. Such code-switching often reveals that the vernacular was employed deliberately, not merely as a substitute for poor Latinity. Establishing why this only occurred on certain occasions is an altogether more difficult question, however. The social and political settings in which charters were produced can only ever be partially reconstructed. But, as has been amply demonstrated in recent years, charters are not just passive witnesses to transfers of property rights; they are active attempts to assert and formalize social relationships.[105] Since charters are negotiated statements of co-operation, we may posit that donors also influenced their redaction, and this should be taken into consideration when asking why a vernacular term or statement appears in a particular context. In this light, the striking Old High German phrase in Count Helmoin's donation to Freising of 793 becomes what Patrick Geary has termed a 'strategy of representation', a defiant assertion of Helmoin's identification with his family property amidst the upheaval caused by the Carolingian conquest of Bavaria.[106] Similarly, the trend we have observed in Anglo-Saxon and Frankish charters of this period towards describing a vernacular tongue with possessive pronouns or in relation to the people who spoke it indicates a growing awareness of the instrumentality of language in contemporary documentary practices. Historians of post-Roman societies have generally agreed that language was not a determining factor in the formation of group or ethnic identities on the continent following the end of the Roman Empire.[107] We do not wish to

104 As noted by Alice Rio, charters may be more easily relied upon by historians because 'their context of production was the same as that of the actions they describe' and 'although they were not put in participants' own words, were at least verified by them': Rio, *Legal Practice*, pp. 10–11.

105 See especially Barbara H. Rosenwein, *To Be the Neighbor of Saint Peter: The Social Meaning of Cluny's Property, 909–1049* (Ithaca, NY, 1989); Matthew Innes, *State and Society in the Early Middle Ages: The Middle Rhine Valley, 400–1000* (Cambridge, 2000).

106 Geary, *Language and Power*, p. 66.

107 E.g. Walter Pohl, 'Telling the Difference: Signs of Ethnic Identity', in *Strategies of Distinction: The Construction of Ethnic Communities, 300–800*, eds Walter Pohl and Helmut Reimitz (Leiden, 1998), pp. 17–69, at 22–27; and the same author's comments in the introduction

suggest that the invocation of vernacular languages in our documents should be interpreted as part of a linear process in the creation of such identities, let alone in the definition of national character, as was often maintained in the late eighteenth and early nineteenth centuries.[108] We do, however, argue that, in the late eighth and ninth centuries, language was employed as a marker of social distinction, as attested by the numerous strategies through which it was signalled in Anglo-Saxon and eastern Frankish charters.[109]

Bibliography

Primary Sources

Alcuin, *Epistolae*, ed. Ernst Dümmler, MGH Epp. 4 (Berlin, 1895).

Alfred the Great, Asser's Life of King Alfred and Other Contemporary Sources, trans. Simon Keynes and Michael Lapidge (London, 1983).

Annales regni Francorum, eds Georg Heinrich Pertz and Friedrich Kurze, MGH SS rer. Germ. 6 (Hanover, 1895).

Asser's Life of King Alfred together with the Annals of Saint Neots Erroneously Ascribed to Asser, ed. William Henry Stevenson (Oxford, 1959).

Cartulaire de l'abbaye de Gorze, ed. A. d'Herbomez (Paris, 1898).

Capitularia regum Francorum, eds Alfred Boretius and Victor Krause, MGH Capit. 1 (Hanover, 1883).

Cartularium Saxonicum: A Collection of Charters Relating to Anglo-Saxon History, ed. Walter de Gray Birch, 3 vols (London, 1885–99).

Chartae latinae antiquiores, eds Albert Bruckner et al., 118 vols (Olten et al., 1954–2019).

Charters of Abingdon Abbey, ed. S. E. Kelly, Anglo-Saxon Charters VII–VIII (Oxford, 2000).

Charters of Christ Church Canterbury, eds N. P. Brooks and S. E. Kelly, Anglo-Saxon Charters 17–18 (Oxford, 2013).

---

to *Sprache und Identität*, eds Pohl and Zeller, pp. 9–22; Hans-Werner Goetz, '*Gentes et linguae*. Völker und Sprachen im Ostfränkisch-deutschen Reich in der Wahrnehmung der Zeitgenossen', in *Theodisca. Beiträge zur althochdeutschen und altniederdeutschen Sprache und Literatur in der Kultur des frühen Mittelalters*, eds Wolfgang Haubrichs, Ernst Hellgardt, Reiner Hildebrandt, Stephan Müller, and Klaus Ridder (Berlin, 2000), pp. 290–312.

108 On which see Geary, *Language and Power*, pp. 11–37.

109 For help provided on various aspects of this chapter we are grateful to Richard Ashdowne, Robert Gallagher, Wolfgang Haubrichs, Annina Seiler, and Elizabeth Tyler. This chapter is part of the activities conducted by the University of the Basque Country Research Group GIU17/006 within the research project HAR2017-86502-P funded by the Spanish Ministerio de Ciencia e Innovación.

Charters of Malmesbury Abbey, ed. S. E. Kelly, Anglo-Saxon Charters XI (Oxford, 2005).
Charters of Northern Houses, ed. D. A. Woodman, Anglo-Saxon Charters 16 (Oxford, 2012).
Charters of Rochester, ed. A. Campbell, Anglo-Saxon Charters I (Oxford, 1973).
Codex diplomaticus Fuldensis, ed. Ernst Friedrich Johann Dronke (Kassel, 1850).
Codex Laureshamensis, ed. Karl Glöckner, 3 vols (Darmstadt, 1929–36).
Concilia aevi Karolini, ed. Albert Werminghoff, MGH Conc. 2.1 (Hanover, 1906).
Gregory of Tours, *Libri historiarum decem*, eds Bruno Krusch and Wilhelm Levison, MGH SS rer. Merov. 1.1 (Hanover, 1951).
King Alfred's West Saxon Version of Gregory's Pastoral Care, ed. Henry Sweet, 2 vols, Early English Text Society Original Series 45 and 50 (London, 1871), reprinted 1958 with corrections and additions by N. R. Ker.
Nithard, Histoire des fils de Louis le Pieux, ed. Philippe Lauer (Paris, 1926).
Die Traditionen des Hochstifts Freising, ed. Theodor Bitterauf, 2 vols, Quellen und Erörterungen zur bayerischen und deutschen Geschichte, N.F. 4–5 (Munich, 1905).
Die Traditionen des Hochstifts Regensburg und des Klosters S. Emmeram, ed. Josef Widemann, Quellen und Erörterungen zur bayerischen Geschichte, N.F. 8 (Darmstadt, 1969).
Die Traditionen des Hochstifts Freising, ed. Theodor Bitterauf, 2 vols, Quellen und Erörterungen zur bayerischen und deutschen Geschichte, N.F. 4–5 (Munich, 1905).
Die Urkunden Arnolfs, ed. Paul Kehr, MGH Diplomata regum Germaniae ex stirpe Karolinorum 3 (Berlin, 1940).
Urkundenbuch der Abtei Sanct Gallen, ed. Hermann Wartmann, 3 vols (Zürich, 1863–82).
Urkundenbuch des Klosters Fulda, ed. Edmund E. Stengel (Marburg, 1956–58).
Urkundenlandschaft Rätien, eds Peter Erhart and Julia Kleindinst (Vienna, 2004).
Die Urkunden Lothars I. und Lothars II., ed. Theodor Schieffer, MGH Diplomata Karolinorum 3 (Berlin and Zürich, 1966).
Die Urkunden Ludwigs des Frommen, eds Theo Kolzer, Jens Peter Clausen, Daniel Eichler, Britta Mischke, Sarah Patt, and Susanne Zwierlein, MGH Diplomata Karolinorum 2 (Wiesbaden, 2016).
Die Urkunden Ludwigs des Deutschen, Karlmanns und Ludwigs der Jüngeren, ed. Paul Kehr, MGH Diplomata regum Germaniae ex stirpe Karolinorum 1 (Berlin, 1934).
Die Urkunden Pippins, Karlmanns und Karls des Grossen, ed. Engelbert Mühlbacher, MGH Diplomata Karolinorum 1 (Hanover, 1906).
Venantius Fortunatus, *Opera poetica*, ed. Friedrich Leo, MGH Auct. ant. 4.1 (Berlin, 1881).

Secondary Sources

Adams, J. N., *Bilingualism and the Latin Language* (Cambridge, 2003).
Banniard, Michel, '*Germanophonie, latinophonie et accès à la Schriftlichkeit* (V[e]–VIIIe siècle)', in *Akkulturation. Probleme einer germanisch-romanischen Kultursynthese in*

Spätantike und frühem Mittelalter, eds Dieter Hägermann, Wolfgang Haubrichs, and Jörg Jarnut (Berlin, 2004), pp. 340–58.

Banniard, Michel, 'Language and Communication in Carolingian Europe', in *The New Cambridge Medieval History, Volume II: c.700–c.900*, ed. Rosamond McKitterick (Cambridge, 1995), pp. 695–708.

Banniard, Michel, *Viva voce. Communication écrite et communication orale du IVe au IXe siècle en Occident latin* (Paris, 1992).

Bately, Janet M., 'Alfred as Author and Translator', in *A Companion to Alfred the Great*, eds Nicole Guenther Discenza and Paul E. Szarmach, Brill's Companions to the Christian Tradition 58 (Leiden, 2014), pp. 113–42.

Bauer, Reinhard, *Die ältesten Grenzbeschreibungen in Bayern und ihre Aussagen für Namenkunde und Geschichte* (Munich, 1988).

Bergmann, Rolf, *Althochdeutsche und altsächsische Literatur* (Berlin, 2013).

Bergmann, Rolf, 'Pragmatische Voraussetzungen althochdeutscher Texte: Die Grenzbeschreibungen', *Jahrbuch für Germanistische Sprachgeschichte* 3 (2012), 57–74.

Biville, Frédérique, '"Qui vulgo dicitur …" Formes "vulgaires" de la creation lexicale en Latin', in *Latin vulgaire, latin tardif IV. Actes du 4e colloque international sur le latin vulgaire et tardif, Caen, 2–5 septembre 1994*, ed. Louis Callebat (Hildesheim, 1995), pp. 193–203.

Blok, Dirk P., 'Altniederländisches in lateinischen Dokumenten, 800 - ca. 1250', in *Quod vulgo dicitur. Studien zum Altniederländischen*, eds W. Pijnenburg, A. Quak, and T. Schoonheim (Amsterdam, 2003), pp. 169–82.

Brooks, Nicholas, 'Anglo-Saxon Charters: Recent Work', in his *Anglo-Saxon Myths: State and Church 400–1066* (London, 2000), pp. 181–215.

Brooks, Nicholas, *Bede and the English*, Jarrow Lecture 1999 (Jarrow, 2000).

Brooks, Nicholas, *The Early History of the Church of Canterbury: Christ Church from 597 to 1066* (London, 1984).

Brooks, N. P., 'England in the Ninth Century: The Crucible of Defeat', *Transactions of the Royal Historical Society*, Fifth Series, 29 (1979), 1–20.

Brooks, Nicholas, 'English Identity from Bede to the Millennium', *Haskins Society Journal* 14 (2003), 33–51.

Brooks, Nicholas, 'Latin and Old English in Ninth-Century Canterbury', in *Spoken and Written Language: Relations between Latin and the Vernacular Languages in the Earlier Middle Ages*, eds Mary Garrison, Arpad P. Orbán, and Marco Mostert (Turnhout, 2013), pp. 113–31.

Brooks, Nicholas, 'The Laws of King Æthelberht of Kent: Preservation, Content, and Composition', in *Textus Roffensis: Law, Language and Libraries in Early Medieval England*, eds Bruce O'Brien and Barbara Bombi (Turnhout, 2015), pp. 105–36.

Brown, Warren C., 'The *gesta municipalia* and the Public Validation of Documents in Frankish Europe', in *Documentary Culture and the Laity in the Early Middle Ages*, eds Warren C. Brown, Marios Costambeys, Matthew Innes, and Adam Kosto (Cambridge, 2013), pp. 95–124.

Brown, Warren C., Costambeys, Marios, Innes, Matthew, and Kosto, Adam, *Documentary Culture and the Laity in the Early Middle Ages* (Cambridge, 2013).

Bruckner, Albert, 'Zur Diplomatik der älteren angelsächsischen Urkunde', *Archivalische Zeitschrift* 61 (1965), 11–45.

Brunner, Thomas, 'Le passage aux langues vernaculaires dans les actes de la pratique en Occident', *Le Moyen Age* 115 (2009), 29–72.

Campbell, Alistair, *Old English Grammar* (Oxford, 1959, reprinted with corrections 1991).

Chaplais, Pierre, 'The Origin and Authenticity of the Royal Anglo-Saxon Diploma', *Journal of the Society of Archivists* 3.2 (1965), 48–61.

Chaplais, Pierre, 'Who Introduced Charters into England? The Case for Augustine', *Journal of the Society of Archivists* 3.10 (1969), 526–42.

Classen, Peter, 'Fortleben und Wandel spätrömischen Urkundenwesens im frühen Mittelalter', in *Recht und Schrift im Mittelalter*, ed. Peter Classen (Sigmaringen, 1977), pp. 13–54.

Coates, Richard, 'Invisible Britons: The View from Linguistics', in *Britons in Anglo-Saxon England*, ed. Nick Higham (Woodbridge, 2007), pp. 172–91.

Coates, Richard, 'Singular Definite Expressions with a Unique Denotatum and the Limits of Properhood', *Linguistics* 38.6 (2000), 1161–74.

Coates, Richard, 'A Strictly Millian Approach to the Definition of the Proper Name', *Mind and Language* 24 (2009), 433–44.

Colman, Fran, 'First, Catch Your Name … On Names and Word Classes, Especially in Old English', *English Studies* 96 (2015), 310–36.

Costambeys, Marios, Innes, Matthew, and MacLean, Simon, *The Carolingian World* (Cambridge, 2011).

Cubitt, Catherine, *Anglo-Saxon Church Councils c.650–c.850* (London, 1995).

Davies, Wendy, 'The Latin Charter-Tradition in Western Britain, Brittany and Ireland in the Early Mediaeval Period', in *Ireland in Early Medieval Europe: Studies in Memory of Kathleen Hughes*, eds Dorothy Whitelock, Rosamond McKitterick, and David Dumville (Cambridge, 1982), pp. 258–80.

Davis, G. R. C., *Medieval Cartularies of Great Britain and Ireland*, revised by Claire Breay, Julian Harrison and David M. Smith (London, 2010).

Davis, Jennifer R., *Charlemagne's Practice of Empire* (Cambridge, 2015).

Discenza, Nicole Guenther and Szarmach, Paul E. (eds), *A Companion to Alfred the Great*, Brill's Companions to the Christian Tradition 58 (Leiden, 2014).

Drögereit, Richard, 'Gab es eine angelsächsische Königskanzlei?', *Archiv für Urkundenforschung* 13 (1935), 335–436.

Erhart, Peter, '*Carta ista amalfitana est et nescitur legere*: The Charters of Cava dei Tirenni and St Gall and Their Evidence for Early Archival Practice', *Gazette du livre médiéval* 50 (2007), 27–39.

Fouracre, Paul, 'Cultural Conformity and Social Conservatism in Early Medieval Europe', *History Workshop Journal* 33 (1992), 152–61.

Freudenberg, Sebastian, *Trado atque dono. Die frühmittelalterliche private Grundherrschaft in Ostfranken im Spiegel der Traditionsurkunden der Klöster Lorsch und Fulda (750 bis 900)* (Stuttgart, 2013).

Gallagher, Robert, 'The Vernacular in Anglo-Saxon Charters: Expansion and Innovation in Ninth-Century England', *Historical Research* 91 (2018), 205–35.

Gallagher, Robert and Tinti, Francesca, 'Latin, Old English and Documentary Practice at Worcester from Wærferth to Oswald', *ASE* 46 (2019 for 2017), 271–325.

Geary, Patrick J., 'Land, Language and Memory in Europe, 700–1100', *Transactions of the Royal Historical Society*, 6th series, 9 (1999), 169–84.

Geary, Patrick J., *Language and Power in the Early Middle Ages* (Waltham, MA, 2013).

Geuenich, Dieter, 'Die volkssprachige Überlieferung der Karolingerzeit aus der Sicht eines Historikers', *Deutsches Archiv* 39 (1983), 104–30.

Gittos, Helen, 'The Audience for Old English Texts: Ælfric, Rhetoric and "the Edification of the Simple"', *ASE* 43 (2014), 231–66.

Godden, Malcolm, 'Prefaces and Epilogues in the Old English *Pastoral Care*, and Their Carolingian Models', *Journal of English and Germanic Philology* 110 (2011), 441–73.

Goetz, Hans-Werner '*Gens*, Kings and Kingdoms: The Franks', in *Regna and Gentes: The Relationship between Late Antique and Early Medieval Peoples and Kingdoms in the Transformation of the Roman World*, eds Hans-Werner Goetz, Jörg Jarnut, and Walter Pohl (Leiden, 2003), pp. 307–44.

Goetz, Hans-Werner, '*Gentes et linguae*. Völker und Sprachen im Ostfränkisch-deutschen Reich in der Wahrnehmung der Zeitgenossen', in *Theodisca. Beiträge zur althochdeutschen und altniederdeutschen Sprache und Literatur in der Kultur des frühen Mittelalters*, eds Wolfgang Haubrichs, Ernst Hellgardt, Reiner Hildebrandt, Stephan Müller, and Klaus Ridder (Berlin, 2000), pp. 290–312.

Goetz, Hans-Werner, 'Lingua. Indizien und Grenzen einer Identität durch Sprache im frühen Mittelalter', in *Sprache und Identität im frühen Mittelalter*, eds Walter Pohl and Bernhard Zeller (Vienna, 2012), pp. 61–74.

Goetz, Hans-Werner, Jarnut, Jörg, and Pohl, Walter (eds), *Regna and Gentes: The Relationship between Late Antique and Early Medieval Peoples and Kingdoms in the Transformation of the Roman World* (Leiden, 2003).

Goldberg, Eric J., *Struggle for Empire: Kingship and Conflict under Louis the German* (Ithaca, 2006).

Green, D. H., *Language and History in the Early Germanic World* (Cambridge, 1998).

Green, D. H., *Medieval Listening and Reading: The Primary Reception of German Literature, 800–1300* (Cambridge, 1994).

Haubrichs, Wolfgang, *Die Anfänge: Versuche volkssprachiger Schriftlichkeit im frühen Mittelalter (ca. 700–1050/60). Geschichte der deutschen Literatur von den Anfängen bis zum Beginn der Neuzeit, I: Von den Anfängen bis zum hohen Mittelalter*, 2nd ed. (Tübingen, 1995).

Haubrichs, Wolfgang, 'Baiovarii, Romani and Others. Language, Names and Groups South of the River Danube and in the Eastern Alps during the Early Middle Ages', in *The Baiuvarii and Thuringi: An Ethnographic Perspective*, eds Janine Fries-Knoblach, Heiko Steuer, and John Hines (Woodbridge, 2014), pp. 23–81.

Haubrichs, Wolfgang, 'Germania submersa. Zu Fragen der Quantität und Dauer germanischer Siedlungsinseln im romanischen Lothringen und Südbelgien', in *Verborum Amor. Studien zur Geschichte und Kunst der deutschen Sprache. Festschrift für Stefan Sonderegger zum 65. Geburtstag*, eds Harald Burger, Alois M. Haas, and Peter von Matt (Berlin, 1992), pp. 633–66.

Haubrichs, Wolfgang, 'Ludwig der Deutsche und die volkssprachige Literatur', in *Ludwig der Deutsche und seine Zeit*, ed. Wilfried Hartmann (Darmstadt, 2004), pp. 203–32.

Haubrichs, Wolfgang, '*Quod Alamanni dicunt*. Volkssprachliche Wörter in der *Lex Alamannorum*', in *Recht und Kultur im frühmittelalterlichen Alemannien. Rechtsgeschichte, Archäologie und Geschichte des 7. und 8. Jahrhunderts*, ed. Sebastian Brather (Berlin, 2017), pp. 169–209.

Haubrichs, Wolfgang, 'Die Praefatio des Heliand. Ein Zeugnis der Religions- und Bildungspolitik Ludwigs des Deutschen', *Niederdeutsches Jahrbuch* 89 (1966), 7–32.

Haubrichs, Wolfgang, 'Sprache und Sprachzeugnisse der merowingischen Franken', in *Die Franken—Wegbereiter Europas. 5. bis 8. Jahrhundert n. Chr.*, eds Alfried Wieczorek, Patrick Périn, Karin von Welck, and Wilfried Menghin, 2 vols (Mainz, 1996), 1:559–73.

Haubrichs, Wolfgang, 'Theodiscus, Deutsch und Germanisch—drei Ethnonyme, drei Forschungsbegriffe. Zur Frage der Instrumentalisierung und Wertbesetzung deutscher Sprach- und Volksbezeichnungen', in *Zur Geschichte der Gleichung 'germanisch-deutsch'. Sprache und Namen, Geschichte und Institutionen*, eds Heinrich Beck, Dieter Geuenich, Heiko Steuer, and Dietrich Hakelberg (Berlin, 2004), pp. 199–227.

Haubrichs, Wolfgang and Pfister, Max, 'Fränkisch (Frankish)', in *Wieser Enzyklopädie. Sprachen des europäischen Westens. Erster Band* (Klagenfurt, 2008), pp. 249–74.

Haubrichs, Wolfgang and Pfister, Max, 'Die Prümer Romania', in *Sprachgeschichte—Dialektologie—Onomastik—Volkskunde. Beiträge zum Kolloquium am 3./4. Dezember*

1999 an der Johannes Gutenberg-Universität Mainz. Wolfgang Kleiber zum 70. Geburtstag, eds Rudolf Bentzinger, Damaris Nübling, and Rudolf Steffens (Stuttgart, 2001), pp. 169–95.

Haubrichs, Wolfgang and Pfister, Max, 'La *Romania submersa* dans les pays de langue allemande', in *Manuel des langues romanes*, eds Andre Klump, Johannes Kramer, and Aline Willems (Berlin, 2014), pp. 224–44.

Haubrichs, Wolfgang and Wolfram, Herwig, 'Theodiscus', *Reallexikon der Germanischen Altertumskunde*, eds Heinrich Beck, Dieter Geuenich, and Heiko Steuer, 35 vols (Berlin, 1972–2008), 30:421–33.

Hellgardt, Ernst, 'Zur Mehrsprachigkeit im Karolingerreich. Bemerkungen aus Anlaß von Rosamond McKittericks Buch "The Carolingians and the Written Word"', *Beiträge zur Geschichte der deutschen Sprache und Literatur* 118 (1996), 1–48.

Higham, Nick (ed.), *Britons in Anglo-Saxon England* (Woodbridge, 2007).

Higham, Nick, 'Historical Narrative as Cultural Politics: Rome, "British-ness" and "English-ness"', in *Britons in Anglo-Saxon England*, ed. Nick Higham (Woodbridge, 2007), pp. 68–79.

Higham, Nicholas J. and Ryan, Martin J. (eds), *Place-Names, Language and the Anglo-Saxon Landscape* (Woodbridge, 2011).

Hoffmann, Charlotte, *An Introduction to Bilingualism* (London, 1991).

Howe, Nicholas, *Writing the Map of Anglo-Saxon England: Essays in Cultural Geography* (New Haven, CT, 2008).

Hummer, Hans, 'The Production and Preservation of Documents in Francia: The Evidence of Cartularies', in *Documentary Culture and the Laity in the Early Middle Ages*, eds Warren C. Brown, Marios Costambeys, Matthew Innes, and Adam Kosto (Cambridge, 2013), pp. 189–230.

Hummer, Hans J., *Politics and Power in Early Medieval Europe: Alsace and the Frankish Realm, 600–1000* (Cambridge, 2005), pp. 130–54.

Innes, Matthew, 'Archives, Documents and Landowners in Carolingian Francia', in *Documentary Culture and the Laity in the Early Middle Ages*, eds Warren C. Brown, Marios Costambeys, Matthew Innes, and Adam Kosto (Cambridge, 2013), pp. 152–88.

Innes, Matthew, *State and Society in the Early Middle Ages: The Middle Rhine Valley, 400–1000* (Cambridge, 2000).

Insley, Charles, 'Archives and Lay Documentary Practice in the Anglo-Saxon World', in *Documentary Culture and the Laity in the Early Middle Ages*, eds Warren C. Brown, Marios Costambeys, Matthew Innes, and Adam Kosto (Cambridge, 2013), pp. 336–62.

Jakobs, Hermann, 'Diot und Sprache. Deutsch im Verband der Frankenreiche (8. bis frühes 11. Jahrhundert)', in *Nation und Sprache. Die Diskussion ihres Verhältnisses in Geschichte und Gegenwart*, ed. Andreas Gardt (Berlin, 2000), pp. 7–46.

Jakobs, Hermann, *Theodisk im Frankenreich* (Heidelberg, 1998).

de Jong, Mayke, 'Some Reflections on Mandarin Language', in *East and West: Modes of Communication. Proceedings of the First Plenary Conference at Merida*, eds Evangelos Chrysos and Ian Wood (Leiden, 1999), pp. 61–69.

Kelly, Susan, 'Anglo-Saxon Lay Society and the Written Word', in *The Uses of Literacy in Early Mediaeval Europe*, ed. Rosamond McKitterick (Cambridge, 1990), pp. 36–62.

Keynes, Simon, 'Angelsächsische Urkunden (7.–9. Jahrhundert)', in *Mensch und Schrift im frühen Mittelalter*, eds Peter Erhart and Lorenz Hollenstein (St Gall, 2006), pp. 97–109.

Keynes, Simon, 'Anglo-Saxon Charters: Lost and Found', in *Myth, Rulership, Church and Charters: Essays in Honour of Nicholas Brooks*, eds Julia Barrow and Andrew Wareham (Aldershot, 2008), pp. 45–66.

Keynes, Simon, 'Church Councils, Royal Assemblies, and Anglo-Saxon Royal Diplomas', in *Kingship, Legislation and Power in Anglo-Saxon England*, eds Gale R. Owen-Crocker and Brian W. Schneider (Woodbridge, 2013), pp. 17–182.

Keynes, Simon, 'The Control of Kent in the Ninth Century', *EME* 2 (1993), 111–31.

Keynes, Simon, *The Diplomas of King Æthelred 'the Unready', 978–1016: A Study in Their Use as Historical Evidence* (Cambridge, 1980).

Keynes, Simon, 'England, 700–900', in *The New Cambridge Medieval History, Volume II: c.700–c.900*, ed. Rosamond McKitterick (Cambridge, 1995), pp. 18–42.

Keynes, Simon, 'Royal Government and the Written Word in Late Anglo-Saxon England', in *The Uses of Literacy in Early Mediaeval Europe*, ed. Rosamond McKitterick (Cambridge, 1990), pp. 226–57.

Keynes, Simon, 'The West Saxon Charters of King Æthelwulf and his Sons', *EHR* 109 (1994), 1109–49.

Kitson, Peter R., 'The Nature of Old English Dialect Distributions, Mainly as Exhibited in Charter Boundaries: Part 1, Vocabulary', in *Medieval Dialectology*, ed. Jacek Fisiak, Trends in Linguistics, Studies and Monographs 79 (Berlin, 1995), pp. 43–135.

Kitson, Peter, 'Quantifying Qualifiers in Anglo-Saxon Charter Boundaries', *Folia Lingusitica Historica* 14 (1993), 29–82.

Koziol, Geoffrey. *The Politics of Memory and Identity in Carolingian Royal Diplomas: The West Frankish Kingdom (840–987)* (Turnhout, 2012).

Levison, Wilhelm, *England and the Continent in the Eighth Century* (Oxford, 1946).

Lowe, Kathryn A., 'The Development of the Anglo-Saxon Boundary Clause', *Nomina* 21 (1998), 63–100.

Lowe, Kathryn A., 'Lay Literacy in Anglo-Saxon England and the Development of the Chirograph', in *Anglo-Saxon Manuscripts and Their Heritage*, eds Philip Pulsiano and Elaine M. Treharne (Aldershot, 1998), pp. 161–204.

McKitterick, Rosamond, *The Carolingians and the Written Word* (Cambridge, 1989).

McKitterick, Rosamond, *Charlemagne: The Formation of a European Identity* (Cambridge, 2008).

Menke, Hubertus, *Das Namengut der frühen karolingischen Königsurkunden* (Heidelberg, 1980).

Mersiowsky, Mark, *Die Urkunde in der Karolingerzeit. Originale, Urkundenpraxis und politische Kommunikation*, 2 vols, MGH Schriften 60 (Wiesbaden, 2015).

Mersiowsky, Mark, 'Y-a-t-il une influence des actes royaux sur les actes privés du IXe siècle?', in *Les actes comme expression du pouvoir au Haut Moyen Âge. Actes de la Table Ronde de Nancy, 26–27 novembre 1999*, eds Marie-José Gasse-Grandjean and Benoît-Michel Tock (Turnhout, 2003), pp. 139–78.

Nelson, Janet L., 'Literacy in Carolingian Government', in *The Uses of Literacy in Early Mediaeval Europe*, ed. Rosamond McKitterick (Cambridge, 1990), pp. 258–96.

Nelson, Janet L., 'Staging Integration in Bavaria, 791–793', in *Neue Wege der Frühmittelalterforschung: Bilanz und Perspektiven*, eds Walter Pohl, Maximilian Diesenberger, and Bernhard Zeller (Vienna, 2018), pp. 225–38.

Orchard, Andy, 'Latin and the Vernacular Languages: The Creation of a Bilingual Textual Culture', in *After Rome*, ed. Thomas Charles-Edwards (Oxford, 2003), pp. 191–219.

O'Reilly, Jennifer, 'The Multitude of Isles and the Corner-stone: Topography, Exegesis, and the Identity of the *Angli* in Bede's *Historia ecclesiastica*', in *Anglo-Saxon Traces*, eds Jane Roberts and Leslie Webster, Essays in Anglo-Saxon Studies 4 (Tempe, AZ, 2011), pp. 201–27.

Parisse, Michel, '*Quod vulgo dicitur*: la latinisation des noms communs dans les chartes', *Médiévales* 42 (2002), 45–54.

Pijnenburg, W., Quak, A., and Schoonheim, T., *Quod vulgo dicitur. Studien zum Altniederländischen* (Amsterdam, 2003).

Pohl, Walter, 'Telling the Difference: Signs of Ethnic Identity', in *Strategies of Distinction: The Construction of Ethnic Communities, 300–800*, eds Walter Pohl and Helmut Reimitz (Leiden, 1998), pp. 17–69.

Pohl, Walter, 'Sprache und Identität: Einleitung', in *Sprache und Identität im frühen Mittelalter*, eds Walter Pohl and Bernhard Zeller (Vienna, 2012), pp. 9–22.

Pohl, Walter and Zeller, Bernhard (eds), *Sprache und Identität im frühen Mittelalter* (Vienna, 2012).

Prinz, Michael, 'Vergessene Wörter—frühe volkssprachige Lexik in lateinischen Traditionsurkunden', *Jahrbuch für germanistische Sprachgeschichte* 1 (2010), 292–322.

Reed, Michael, 'Anglo-Saxon Charter-Boundaries', in *Discovering Past Landscapes*, ed. Michael Reed (London, 1984), pp. 261–306.

Reiffenstein, Ingo, '*theodiscus* in den althochdeutschen Glossen', in *Grammatica Ianua Artium. Festschrift für Rolf Bergmann zum 60. Geburtstag*, eds Elvira Glaser and Michael Schlaefer (Heidelberg, 1997), pp. 71–84.

Richards, Mary P., 'The Laws of Alfred and Ine', in *A Companion to Alfred the Great*, eds Nicole Guenther Discenza and Paul E. Szarmach, Brill's Companions to the Christian Tradition 58 (Leiden, 2014), pp. 282–309.

Richter, Michael, 'Bede's *Angli*: Angles or English?', *Peritia* 3 (1984), 99–114.

Rio, Alice, *Legal Practice and the Written Word in the Early Middle Ages: Frankish Formulae, c.500–c.1000* (Cambridge, 2009).

Roberts, Edward, 'Boundary Clauses and the Use of the Vernacular in Eastern Frankish Charters, c.750–c.900', *Historical Research* 91 (2018), 580–604.

Romaine, Suzanne, *Bilingualism*, 2nd ed. (Oxford, 1995).

Rosenwein, Barbara H., *To Be the Neighbor of Saint Peter: The Social Meaning of Cluny's Property, 909–1049* (Ithaca, NY, 1989).

Sawyer, P. H., *Anglo-Saxon Charters: An Annotated List and Bibliography* (London, 1968); revised as the Electronic Sawyer, www.esawyer.org.uk.

Scharer, Anton, 'Das angelsächsische Urkundenwesen (7.-9. Jahrhundert)', in *Die Privaturkunden der Karolingerzeit*, eds Peter Erhart, Karl Heidecker, and Bernhard Zeller (Dietikon-Zürich, 2009), pp. 229–36.

Schendl, Herbert, 'Beyond Boundaries: Code-Switching in the Leases of Oswald of Worcester', in *Code-Switching in Early English*, eds Herbert Schendl and Laura Wright, Topics in English Linguistics 76 (Berlin, 2011), pp. 47–94.

Schmidt-Wiegand, Ruth, 'Die Malbergischen Glossen, eine frühe Überlieferung germanischer Rechtssprache', in *Germanische Rest- und Trümmersprachen*, ed. Heinrich Beck (Berlin, 1989), pp. 157–74.

Schmidt-Wiegand, Ruth, '*Quod theodisca lingua harisliz dicitur*. Das Zeugnis der Lorscher Annalen (788) im Kontext frühmittelalterlicher Rechtssprache', in *Grammatica Ianua Artium. Festschrift für Rolf Bergmann zum 60. Geburtstag*, eds Elvira Glaser and Michael Schlaefer (Heidelberg, 1997), pp. 85–91.

Schmidt-Wiegand, Ruth, 'Stammesrecht und Volkssprache in karolingischer Zeit', in *Aspekte der Nationenbildung im Mittelalter*, eds Helmut Beumann and Werner Schröder (Sigmaringen, 1978), pp. 171–203.

Schneider, Jens, *Auf der Suche nach dem verlorenen Reich: Lotharingien im 9. und 10. Jahrhundert* (Cologne, 2010).

Schneider, Jens, 'Langues germaniques', in *Les barbares*, ed. Bruno Dumézil (Paris, 2016), pp. 843–49.

Schützeichel, Rudolf (ed.), *Ortsname und Urkunde. Frühmittelalterliche Ortsnamenüberlieferung* (Heidelberg, 1990).

Schwind, Fred, 'Beobachtungen zur inneren Struktur des Dorfes in karolingischer Zeit', in *Das Dorf der Eisenzeit und des frühen Mittelalters. Siedlungsform, wirtschaftliche Funktion, soziale Struktur*, ed. Herbert Jankuhn (Göttingen, 1977), pp. 444–93.

Shaw, Richard, 'When did Augustine of Canterbury Die?', *Journal of Ecclesiastical History* 67 (2016), 473–91.

Smith, Julia M. H., 'Writing in Britain and Ireland, c. 400 to c. 800', in *The Cambridge History of Early Medieval English Literature*, ed. Claire A. Lees (Cambridge, 2013), pp. 19–49.

Smith, Scott Thompson, *Land and Book: Literature and Land Tenure in Anglo-Saxon England* (Toronto, 2012).

Snook, Ben, 'Who Introduced Charters into England? The Case for Theodore', in *Textus Roffensis: Law, Language and Libraries in Early Medieval England*, eds Bruce O'Brien and Barbara Bombi (Turnhout, 2015), pp. 257–89.

Sonderegger, Stefan, 'Das Althochdeutsche der Vorakte der älteren St. Galler Urkunden. Ein Beitrag zum Problem der Urkundensprache in althochdeutscher Zeit', *Zeitschrift für Mundartforschung* 28 (1961), 251–86.

Sonderegger, Stefan, *Althochdeutsche Sprache und Literatur*, 3rd ed. (Berlin, 2003).

Sornicola, Rosanna, '"Vulgo dicitur": Vulgarisms in Legal Latin', *Journal of Latin Linguistics* 12 (2013), 269–99.

Story, Joanna, *Carolingian Connections: Anglo-Saxon England and Carolingian Francia, c. 750–870* (Aldershot, 2003).

Thomas, Heinz, 'Frenkisk. Zur Geschichte von theodiscus und teutonicus im Frankreich des 9. Jahrhunderts', *Beihefte der Francia* 22 (1990), 67–95.

Thomas, Heinz, 'Der Ursprung des Wortes Theodiscus', *Historische Zeitschrift* 247 (1988), 295–331.

Tiefenbach, Heinrich, *Altsächsische Handwörterbuch* (Berlin, 2010).

Tiefenbach, Heinrich, *Studien zu Wörtern volkssprachiger Herkunft in karolingischen Königsurkunden. Ein Beitrag zum Wortschatz der Diplome Lothars I. und Lothars II.* (Munich, 1973).

Tinti, Francesca, *Sustaining Belief: The Church of Worcester from c.870 to c.1100* (Farnham, 2010).

Tinti, Francesca, 'Writing Latin and Old English in Tenth-Century England: Patterns, Formulae and Language Choice in the Leases of Oswald of Worcester', in *Writing, Kinship and Power in Anglo-Saxon England*, eds Rory Naismith and David A. Woodman (Cambridge, 2018), pp. 303–27.

Trotter, David, 'A Polyglot Glossary of the Twelfth Century', in *De Mot en Mot: Aspects of Medieval Linguistics*, eds Stewart Gregory and D. A. Trotter (Cardiff, 1997), pp. 81–91.

van Uytfanghe, Marc, 'Les expressions du type *quod vulgo vocant* dans des textes latins antérieurs au Concile de Tours et aux Serments de Strasbourg: témoignages lexicologiques et sociolinguistiques de la "langue rustique romaine"?', *Zeitschrift für romanische Philologie* 105 (1989), 28–49.

Wiles, Kate, 'The Treatment of Charter Bounds by the Worcester Cartulary Scribes', *New Medieval Literatures* 13 (2011), 113–36.

Wood, Ian, *The Merovingian Kingdoms, 450–751* (Harlow, 1994).

Woolf, Alex, 'Apartheid and Economics in Anglo-Saxon England', in *Britons in Anglo-Saxon England*, ed. Nick Higham (Woodbridge, 2007), pp. 115–29.

Woolf, Alex, 'The Britons: From Romans to Barbarians', in *Regna and Gentes: The Relationship between Late Antique and Early Medieval Peoples and Kingdoms in the Transformation of the Roman World* (Leiden, 2003), pp. 345–80.

Wormald, Patrick, '*Lex scripta* and *verbum regis*: Legislation and Germanic Kingship from Euric to Cnut', in *Early Medieval Kingship*, eds P. H. Sawyer and I. N. Wood (Leeds, 1977), pp. 105–38.

Wright, Roger, *Late Latin and Early Romance in Spain and Carolingian France* (Liverpool, 1982).

Online Sources

Köbler, Gerhard, *Althochdeutsches Wörterbuch*, 6th ed. (2014), http://www.koeblergerhard.de/ahdwbhin.html.

The Languages of Anglo-Saxon Charters Database, http://www.ehu.eus/lasc.

Nelson, Janet L., 'The Language of Charters and Charter-related Documents in the Reign of Charlemagne', lecture delivered at Universidad del País Vasco, Vitoria-Gasteiz, 8 February 2016, https://ehutb.ehu.es/video/58c6703af82b2b990f8b457a.

CHAPTER 7

The Endorsement Practices of Early Medieval England

Robert Gallagher and Kate Wiles

Relatively few Anglo-Saxon charters survive in their original forms. Instead, most specimens are extant only thanks to their later copying in cartularies, chronicles, gospel-books, and other contexts. As a result, little can be said for certain about the physical appearance of many of these documents, though it is thought that the vast majority would originally have been produced on unbound single pieces of parchment, sometimes in multiple copies. For those charters that do survive in their original single-sheet forms, their layout and materiality are especially valuable, providing us with otherwise hidden insights into stages of production, as well as the subsequent ways in which individuals engaged with the written record. One simple point that can be made here is that, in most cases, the majority of the charter text occupied a single side (the 'face') of the parchment. This is not to say, however, that the back ('dorse') of a charter was left bare—in fact, almost all surviving single sheets at some point in their lifetime acquired text on their dorses—and often it is here, through endorsements, that we find some of the most fruitful evidence for contemporary and subsequent engagement with charters, not least in terms of the linguistic dynamics of early medieval documentary culture.

As a group, such dorsal texts have received relatively little scholarly attention. This is somewhat apparent, for example, in the edition of charters in the ongoing British Academy Anglo-Saxon charter volumes, in which endorsements are normally printed within the manuscript apparatus rather than alongside the text of the face of the charter. As to discussions of dorsal texts, two of the most substantial and significant publications on the topic remain works of the 1930s—respectively by Richard Drögereit and Mary Prescott Parsons.[1] Both these and more recent contributions have been concerned primarily with

1 Richard Drögereit, 'Gab es eine angelsächsische Königskanzlei?', *Archiv für Urkundenforschung* 13 (1935), 335–436; M. P. Parsons, 'Some Scribal Memoranda for Anglo-Saxon Charters of the Eighth and Ninth Centuries', *Mitteilungen des Österreichischen Instituts für Geschichtsforschung*, Erg. Bd. 14 (1939), 1–32.

 | DOI:10.1163/9789004432338_008

two issues, namely the function of endorsements and, more specifically, the rise of an apparent standard endorsement formula in the mid-tenth century.[2] Important points have emerged from these publications, yet, with exceptions that are concerned with particular case studies, most of these discussions have focused almost exclusively on royal diplomas and on endorsements that were written during or soon after the production of the earliest text of the charter. In other words, at present no study exists that examines Anglo-Saxon endorsement practices in their totality, considering the 'standard' endorsement formula of the tenth century alongside examples that sit outside this convention, and including both endorsements written contemporaneously with the main text as well as those written much later. It is the aim of this chapter, therefore, to present an overview of the entirety of single-sheet evidence for endorsements. In doing so, we have three aims: first, to summarize the size and nature of the surviving single-sheet corpus—which, we hope, will also be of use to readers for the study of Anglo-Saxon charters more generally; second, to establish the form and typologies of endorsements within a chronological, geographic, and diplomatic framework; and third, to consider the phrasing and the varied uses of Latin and Old English within this material.

Before venturing forth, we must make clear what our working definition of an 'endorsement' is. Previous discussions of this topic have lacked explicit definitions, though distinctions have been drawn between 'scribal notes' and 'endorsements', the former presumed to have been composed before the writing of the main text of the charter and the latter after.[3] In a seminal piece, Parsons identified several dorsal texts on Anglo-Saxon charters as 'scribal notes',[4] though the physical evidence of the single sheets, which points to these texts having been added after folding, has led to the rejection of this interpretation and, indeed, of the idea that dorses routinely played a role in the composition of Anglo-Saxon charter prose.[5] Instead, it appears that the vast majority are

2 Drögereit, 'Gab es eine angelsächsische Königskanzlei?', pp. 431–32; Cyril Hart, 'The *Codex Wintoniensis* and the King's *Haligdom*', in *Land, Church and People: Essays Presented to Professor H. P. R. Finberg*, ed. Joan Thirsk (Reading, 1970), pp. 7–38, at Appendix I; Simon Keynes, *The Diplomas of King Æthelred 'the Unready', 978–1016: A Study in Their Use as Historical Evidence* (Cambridge, 1980), pp. 24–28; Simon Keynes, 'Church Councils, Royal Assemblies, and Anglo-Saxon Royal Diplomas', in *Kingship, Legislation and Power in Anglo-Saxon England*, eds Gale R. Owen-Crocker and Brian W. Schneider (Woodbridge, 2013), pp. 17–182, at 66 and 163–66; Susan D. Thompson, *Anglo-Saxon Royal Diplomas: A Palaeography* (Woodbridge, 2006), pp. 50–53.

3 Thompson, *Anglo-Saxon Royal Diplomas*, pp. 52–53.

4 Parsons, 'Some Scribal Memoranda'; see also Annina Seiler's contribution to this volume.

5 *CantCC*, pp. 119–20, 568, and 709; see also Keynes, *The Diplomas of King Æthelred*, p. 36, n. 66.

FIGURE 7.1 The dorse of London, British Library, Cotton Augustus ii.41 (S 594)

likely to have been written afterwards.[6] With this in mind, for us an endorsement on an Anglo-Saxon charter is any text that was composed with the intention that it was to be written on the dorse, regardless of how much available space there was on the face of the single sheet. In most cases, an 'endorsement' would remain visible if the sheet was partially or fully folded up, as was common practice for the transportation and storage of such documents. See, for instance, Figure 7.1, which is a diploma issued by King Eadwig in 956. This has accrued several layers of text on its dorse over the centuries, including one below the second horizontal fold by a tenth-century hand (which may well be the same hand as that of the face of the charter). In terms of both function and placement this tenth-century text is entirely typical of Anglo-Saxon endorsement practices, in that it summarizes the contents of the document and it is laid out so it could be read without completely unfolding the single sheet.[7]

6 The most conspicuous exceptions are those instances that may represent pen-trials. See below, n. 21, for details.

7 S 594 (*Abing* 54). The tenth-century endorsement reads as follows: 'Þis is þara .xv. hida boc æt middel / tune þe eadpig cing gebocode / ælfpine on ece yrfe :—' ('This is the book of 15 hides at Milton that King Eadwig granted to Ælfwine in perpetual inheritance'). Note that throughout this chapter, for brevity and ease of comprehension, we refer to single sheets by their related Sawyer numbers rather than shelfmarks; shelfmarks along with Sawyer numbers and details of editions are instead provided in the Appendix. Unless indicated otherwise, all cited single-sheet charters survive in only one pre-Conquest single-sheet context. Note also that all translations in this chapter are our own, unless otherwise stated.

Our definition means that we have excluded writing on the dorse that appears simply to be a continuation of the main text of the charter, i.e. when the scribe has run out of space on the face and is forced to 'spill over' onto the dorse. In many such cases, it is the witness-list that has been partially or fully copied out onto the dorse.[8] See at Figure 7.2, for example, how a single scribe began the witness-list to this diploma of King Offa on the face of the charter and continued on the dorse, though they evidently paid less attention to visual presentation once they had moved to the back of the single sheet.

A caveat here must be that a scribe may have carefully planned the physical spacing of the document so that the entire face is filled and that some elements would intentionally be copied out onto the dorse. Several specimens arguably fit this profile, though given the nature of their dorsal texts, in most cases it seems that the use of the dorse was a predominantly pragmatic decision.[9] We, on the other hand, are concerned primarily with those cases where the location of the text on the dorse appears to be an intrinsic part of its function. We have, however, been inclusive in terms of who wrote the endorsement and when it was written: we consider here endorsements written out by the main text scribe (presumably at the point of production, but after the writing of the main prose), as well as those added by any additional scribes of the pre-Conquest period.[10]

The Single-Sheet Corpus

To begin, we need to state what the corpus of material under consideration in this study comprises. With the understanding that the majority of Anglo-Saxon charters in their original forms were produced as single-sheet documents, we have limited our investigation to those charters that survive in what are likely to be pre-Conquest single-sheet forms. The reason for doing so is that later copies of Anglo-Saxon charters rarely state which parts of the text were originally on the face and which parts were on the dorse of the charter.[11] We may

8 See, for example, S 40, S 114, S 139, S 296, S 1171, S 1270.

9 See, for example, S 204, S 1347, and S 1508.

10 Note that there are a small number of dorsal texts referred to as endorsements specifically in British Academy editions that do not fit our working definition. See, for instance, the editions to S 287 and S 1186a: *CantCC* 71(*d*) and *CantCC* 16(*b*).

11 Exceptions exist; see, for example, the transcriptions of Worcester charters made by William Hopkins in the seventeenth century (now London, British Library, Harley 4660). Hopkins' transcripts were subsequently printed in G. Hickes and H. Wanley, *Antiquæ*

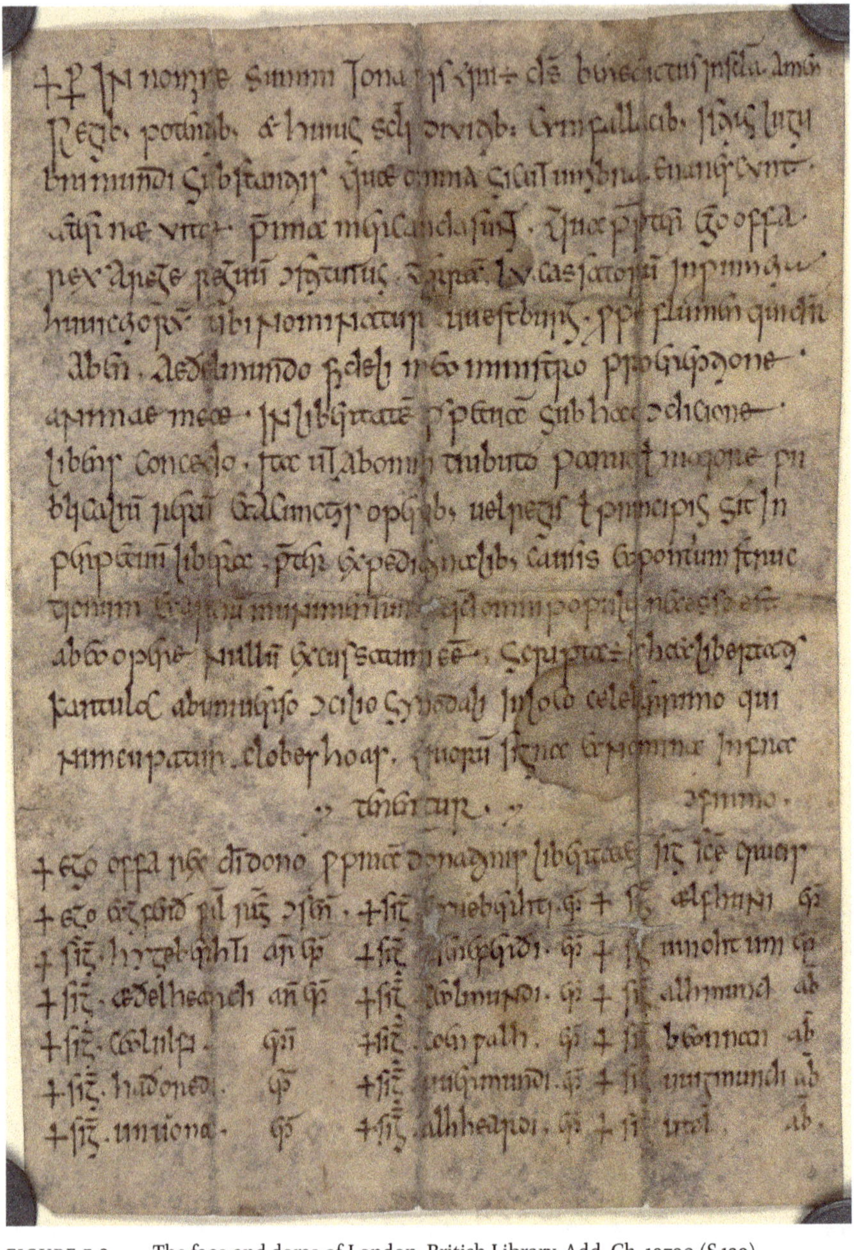

FIGURE 7.2 The face and dorse of London, British Library, Add. Ch. 19790 (S 139)
© THE BRITISH LIBRARY BOARD

suspect that certain elements of later copies may have once inhabited the dorse of a single sheet, especially when they echo the formulae of tenth- and eleventh-century endorsements (as will be discussed below).[12] But with the loss of palaeographic evidence that copying elicits, such material is of limited value to the present study, particularly when we are seeking to establish chronological, geographical, and typological frameworks for their development.

The charters that do survive in pre-Conquest single-sheet forms need to be divided into two groups: (1) those that are originals and are not, to the best of our knowledge, copied from an earlier single sheet; for those that contain a dating clause, it is likely that the surviving single sheet was produced at this time; (2) those that are non-contemporary, single-sheet copies of purportedly earlier charters. For the former, we have considered all examples that date to 1066 or earlier; while for the latter we have included all examples that are likely to have been produced before *c.*1050. This categorization is seemingly straightforward, yet there is a degree of uncertainty surrounding the statuses of several of these single sheets, whether they be originals, near-contemporary copies, or significantly later productions. In many cases a judgement must be made based on the palaeography of the charter—and for those documents that are evidently later copies, the date of their production almost always can only be approximate. It is for this reason that we have included non-contemporary single sheets only if they appear to have been produced before *c.*1050, although, perhaps inevitably, there are certain examples for which their date of production has been the subject of debate. We must stress that our assessment of the dating of any given single sheet has been guided by the views of previous scholarly authorities; in particular, works by Nicholas Brooks, Pierre Chaplais, Julia Crick, David Dumville, Susan Kelly, Simon Keynes, and Susan Thompson have been especially valuable.[13] The numbers that we provide should, there-

Literaturæ Septentrionalis Libri Duo (Oxford, 1703–5), 1:139–41, 142, and 169–76. See Simon Keynes, 'Anglo-Saxon Charters: Lost and Found', in *Myth, Rulership, Church and Charters: Essays in Honour of Nicholas Brooks*, eds Julia Barrow and Andrew Wareham (Aldershot, 2008), pp. 45–66, at 58–59.

12 See, for example, the treatment of formulaic endorsements as rubrics in the *Codex Wintoniensis* (London, British Library, Add. 15350) and their discussion in Hart, 'The *Codex Wintoniensis*', Appendix I.

13 First and foremost we are indebted to the work of the editors of the British Academy Anglo-Saxon Charters series, most notably Susan Kelly. Recent work by Julia Crick has also been invaluable: 'Script and the Sense of the Past in Anglo-Saxon England', in *Anglo-Saxon Traces*, eds Jane Roberts and Leslie Webster (Tempe, AZ, 2011), pp. 1–29; Julia Crick, 'Insular History? Forgery and the English Past in the Tenth Century', in *England and the Continent in the Tenth Century: Studies in Honour of Wilhelm Levison (1876–1947)*, eds

fore, be understood with the view that they may be subject to some change, depending on one's view of certain single sheets, but any such differences of opinion are unlikely to alter the overriding statistical patterns found within the corpus in a significant way.

It is with this in mind that we can state that we consider a total of 191 single sheets as possibly original pre-Conquest charters.[14] These are listed in Table 7.1 of the Appendix. Over 20 medieval archives are represented by these documents. By far the largest collection of originals comes from Christ Church, Canterbury (90 charters); the next most numerous are Worcester (20); Exeter (13); Winchester's Old Minster (eight); Westminster (eight); and Abingdon (seven). The majority of these charters, particularly those specimens from places other than Christ Church, are royal diplomas. As to chronological distribution, the surviving corpus is significantly weighted towards the later Anglo-Saxon period. No more than 20 survive from the seventh and eighth centuries; over 50 survive from the ninth century; over 60 from the tenth century; and over 50 from the eleventh century in the period up to 1066. In other words, there is a sharp increase in the number of extant originals when we move into the ninth century, while the period between 900 and 1066 accounts for close to 60 per cent of surviving originals.

Similar yet more extreme patterns of survival are to be found with non-contemporary single sheets, which are listed in Table 7.2 of the Appendix. We have included 50 such documents in our survey. With 24 specimens, the Christ Church archive again dominates, although at least nine other archives contain non-contemporary single sheets, the next most numerous being Winchester's Old Minster (six) and Rochester (five). Compared with originals,

---

David Rollason, Conrad Leyser, and Hannah Williams (Turnhout, 2010), pp. 515–44; Julia Crick, 'Historical Literacy in the Archive: Post-Conquest Imitative Copies of Pre-Conquest Charters and Some French Comparanda', in *The Long Twelfth-Century View of the Anglo-Saxon Past*, eds Martin Brett and David A. Woodman (Farnham, 2015), pp. 159–90. In addition to publications cited throughout this chapter, we are also indebted to the following: Pierre Chaplais, 'The Authenticity of the Royal Anglo-Saxon Diplomas of Exeter', *Historical Research* 39 (1966), 1–34; *Facsimiles of Anglo-Saxon Charters*, ed. Simon Keynes, Anglo-Saxon Charters Supplementary Volume 1 (Oxford, 1991); *DigiPal: Digital Resource and Database of Manuscripts, Palaeography and Diplomatic* (London, 2011–14), http://www.digipal.eu; Francesca Tinti, 'The Reuse of Charters at Worcester Between the Eighth and the Eleventh Century: A Case-Study', *Midland History* 37 (2012), 127–41. We are also grateful to Colleen Curran for her consultation on issues of palaeography and dating.

14 In compiling this corpus, we were aided greatly by the Electronic Sawyer database (http://www.esawyer.org.uk), as well as by Simon Keynes, 'A Classified List of Anglo-Saxon Charters on Single Sheets' (unpublished but available at https://pdfs.semanticscholar.org/1157/703a4e3199f8f13f566b47155cfb2d60f2e2.pdf).

an even greater proportion of these copies are royal diplomas—only seven represent other types of documentation—while the chronological distribution is even more skewed towards the tenth and eleventh centuries. In part, the chronological spread may be due to the fact that on the whole it is more challenging to differentiate between 'originals' and 'copies' among the extant single sheets of the seventh and eighth centuries: not only are there relatively few specimens, but the possible temporal distance between a seventh- or eighth-century copy and its purported origin can be no greater than a few decades (given that no one example claims to be from any earlier than the late seventh century). That said, no surviving single sheet from the seventh century is currently interpreted by scholars as a copy, while at the very most two (both from Christ Church) date to the eighth century. From the ninth century, we have perhaps 12 (of which, notably, four may come from the Rochester archive; the remaining eight derive from the Christ Church (seven) and Worcester (one) archives), while some 25 and 22 possibly date to the tenth and first half of the eleventh centuries respectively. The production of such non-contemporary single sheets has been the subject of recent work by Julia Crick, who has drawn attention to the 'imitative' palaeographic features of a considerable number of these documents, which betray a scribe's sense of a specifically 'insular', historicized tradition of scripts and diplomatic.[15] The possible reasons for the production of such charters are potentially numerous. It should be stressed here that while some are evidently outright forgeries, others may well be faithful copies of once-existing earlier charters; many may fall somewhere between the two—reworkings of earlier material, not necessarily with the intended exemplar to hand for guidance. Crick points out that many specimens are found in archives (including Christ Church, Exeter, and Rochester) that are known to have suffered serious trauma during the early medieval period and thus were perhaps created as replacements for damaged or destroyed earlier documentation, as several claim to be.[16] Others were clearly drawn up specifically in response to tenurial disputes and in this regard Crick stresses that the vast majority of non-contemporary single sheets, by dating to the tenth and eleventh centuries, come from a time when we know shire courts convened relatively regularly and were the venues for many litigation cases.[17] More generally, such single sheets, whether the work of individuals seeking to confirm a truth

15 Crick, 'Script and the Sense of the Past'; Crick, 'Insular History?'. See also Crick, 'Historical Literacy in the Archive'.

16 Crick, 'Script and the Sense of the Past', p. 25.

17 Crick, 'Script and the Sense of the Past', pp. 21–23 and 25.

or to deceive, unambiguously betray a concern to record and prove claims in writing.

The Distribution, Authorship, and Functions of Endorsements

In providing an overview of charter endorsements, two basic points can be stated from the outset. First, the majority—roughly 65 per cent—of surviving Anglo-Saxon single-sheet charters acquired an endorsement at some point during the pre-Conquest period. Second, the vast majority of endorsements serve a similar purpose: they summarize the contents of the charter in some capacity. In other words, most do not contain information that cannot be found in the main body of the document. There is, however, considerable variation in how an endorsement scribe might choose to do this, as is discussed further below. There are, furthermore, a relatively small number of single sheets that attracted later layers of writing on their dorses that do provide new details (not all of which, it should be noted, would be fully visible when the charter is folded). In many of these instances the writing on the dorse seems first and foremost to be a practical decision, simply because there was no room on the face, and they are not therefore, according to our definition, endorsements. Others including new information do, however, appear to have been added with the intention that they would be visible without the need to unfold the charter entirely and, as such, they have been considered as endorsements for the present study. Some of these endorsements appear on palaeographic grounds to have been added relatively soon after the initial production of the respective single sheets and either they provide new details regarding the original codified agreement,[18] or they confirm the details of the charter by a new party;[19] others record later transactions involving the exchange of the related lands into new hands.[20] Some single sheets also attracted additional words and passages for reasons that are not immediately apparent and are perhaps simply reflective of charter dorses as being convenient spaces for taking notes and

18 See, for example, S 230 (*CantCC* 3) and S 1215 (*CantCC* 128).

19 See, for example, the endorsement added to MSS A1 and A3 of S 1438 (*CantCC* 69), as recorded in the Appendix.

20 See, for example, S 717 (*CantCC* 126), S 1204 (*CantCC* 91), and S 1276 (*CantCC* 98).

trialling pens.[21] We have included these within our corpus, though it should be noted that they represent a relatively small number of examples.

What, then, is the chronology of endorsement practices in early medieval England? What are the earliest endorsements? And what further chronological developments can we detect within the corpus of endorsements? Here in some respects we must privilege the evidence of original single sheets, which on the whole provide far greater chronological precision than non-contemporary copies.

The first point to make is that relatively few surviving single-sheets originals from the seventh and eighth centuries received endorsements before the ninth century. This suggests that endorsing was not a widespread practice in early Anglo-Saxon documentary activity. From 20 originals that potentially date to these two earliest centuries, we have perhaps only five such early endorsements, representing documentary activity in multiple locales across southern England. Three of these endorsements simply comprise the vernacular names of geographic locations to which the charters relate.[22] The remaining two are, however, striking. One was added to a record of a late seventh-century land donation to Æthelburh, the abbess of Barking Abbey, made by Æthelred, a *parens* of the king of the East Saxons;[23] the other is found on the dorse of the famous letter of Wealdhere, bishop of London, to Berhtwald, archbishop of Canterbury.[24] The endorsements to both of these documents are in Latin and both contain gaps in their texts. These gaps appear to have been created in order to allow space for a wrapping-tie to hold the single sheet shut without

21 See the unconnected note on S 332, as discussed in Brooks and Kelly, *CantCC* 86, pp. 761–62; see also 'manus' added to S 963 (KCD 744); 'sal sapientiae' on S 1458 (*Roch* 34); possibly also 'regnante' on S 367 (*CantCC* 101). Here and throughout, dorsal texts are quoted from the authors' transcriptions rather than printed editions.

22 The three are found on S 31 (*CantCC* 14); two endorsements on S 1184 (*Sel* 11).

23 S 1171 (BCS 81). Note that opinion has varied regarding whether the single sheet is an original or an eighth-century copy; either way, the endorsement has been described as 'contemporary'. See, for example, Pierre Chaplais, who believed that the single sheet may well be an original: 'Some Early Anglo-Saxon Diplomas on Single Sheets: Originals or Copies?', *Journal of the Society of Archivists* 3 (1968), 315–36, at pp. 331–32; Kelly, *LondonStP*, pp. 222–23; cf. Bruckner, *ChLA* 3, no. 185.

24 S 1428b (*LondStP* Appendix I). This letter was composed in either 704 or 705. For further seminal discussion of the single sheet, see Pierre Chaplais, 'The Letter from Bishop Wealdhere of London to Archbishop Brihtwold of Canterbury: The Earliest Original "Letter Close" Extant in the West', in *Medieval Scribes, Manuscripts and Libraries: Essays Presented to N. R. Ker*, eds M. B. Parkes and Andrew G. Watson (London, 1978), pp. 3–23. We have included this letter within our study due to its inclusion in the Sawyer catalogue. Note that no other Anglo-Saxon document produced before the tenth century survives in its original form that is customarily considered to be an epistolary correspondence. For discussion of the remit of the Sawyer catalogue, see Kathryn A. Lowe, this volume.

FIGURE 7.3 The dorsal address via multispectral imaging of London, British Library, Cotton Augustus ii.18 (S 1428b)

obscuring the words of the endorsement. Such intentional gaps can be found in dorsal texts on several single sheets from subsequent centuries,[25] and while the endorsement on the charter for Abbess Æthelburh, like many later examples, simply summarizes the contents of the document, the dorsal text on the letter is more unusual. Although now faded, it is thought to be the work of the main scribe of the document and, as one can see in Figure 7.3, it reads as 'A UALDH . D[.] [.] b[...]tuald.'[26] In all likelihood this appears to be an address from Wealdhere to Berhtwald, added before the letter was sent on its journey to the archbishop. In this case, the use of an endorsement therefore reflects the fact that the intended recipient of the document was probably at some geographic distance from the scribe that produced it.

Aside from Wealdhere's letter, it is not until the early ninth century that we find single sheets wherein the text on the face and an endorsement are the work of a single scribe. Perhaps unsurprisingly, given the dominance of the

---

25 See, for example, S 316, S 328, and S 1547. For discussion, see Chaplais, 'The Letter from Bishop Wealdhere', pp. 15–17.

26 More of the text of the endorsement has been made more visible thanks to recent use of multispectral imaging. For details, see Rebecca Lawton, 'A Useless Letter?', *British Library Medieval Manuscripts Blog* (12 December 2018), https://blogs.bl.uk/digitisedmanuscripts/2018/12/a-useless-letter.html. See also Rebecca Lawton, 'Knowing Rome from Home: Reassessing Early Manuscript Witnesses of Papal Letters, Pilgrim Itineraries and Syllogae in England and Francia, c. 600–900' (unpublished PhD thesis, University of Leicester, 2019), chapter 2. For the endorsement being the work of the main scribe, see Chaplais, 'The Letter from Bishop Wealdhere', pp. 8 and 17.

Christ Church archive in the distribution of surviving single sheets, almost all of the earliest such specimens come from this archive. Potentially the earliest example is found on the original single sheet of a royal diploma of King Coenwulf that was issued in 808 to a *minister* called Eadwulf granting him an estate in Kent, the name of which forms the basis for the endorsement text ('CULINGA BOC'). While the text of the charter face was written in a pointed insular minuscule, the endorsement is entirely in majuscule letters, making comparison between the two difficult, especially in terms of dating.[27] An alternative contender for the earliest ninth-century example of an endorsement in the hand of the main scribe is that found on another single-sheet diploma of King Coenwulf, this time issued in 814 for a *comes* named Swithnoth, and preserved via the Worcester archive.[28] The endorsement reads '+ be cerT Suiðnoðes boec ∴ Regardless of which of these two examples is earlier, it is clear that the early ninth century was a formative period in the development of endorsement practices. Further instances are to be found from Canterbury in the 820s and the 830s, including specimens by those Christ Church scribes that Nicholas Brooks and Susan Kelly have identified as 'scribe 2', 'scribe 3', and 'scribe 4'.[29] What must be stressed, however, is that with these early examples, as with later single sheets, there were varying practices when it came to scribes endorsing their own charters—and often there are no immediately discernible patterns to explain such variance. Christ Church scribe 2, for example, drew up a single-sheet charter that they did not endorse just one year before they

27 S 163 (*CantCC* 40).

28 S 173 (BCS 343). This charter was evidently at Worcester in the eighteenth century, since it is included in London, British Library, Harley 4660, though its earlier history is unknown. It does not feature in any of Worcester's medieval cartularies, while in some respects it has closer affinities with Kentish diplomatic. Not only does the charter record a grant of land in Kent, but it contains references to *molina* ('mills') and *aratra* ('sulung') that are otherwise found only in Kentish charters; in addition, its sanction occurs only once elsewhere, in S 159 (*CantStA* 16), a royal diploma in the St Augustine's archive that purports to date to 804. One should also note the unusual position of the dating clause in S 173 near the beginning of the charter, a feature elsewhere found only in Kentish royal diplomas and synodal diplomatic; Thompson, *Anglo-Saxon Royal Diplomas*, p. 29 observes that dating clauses near the beginning are found in only four single-sheet royal diplomas (S 169, S 173, S 188, and S 35), of which all but S 173 are from Canterbury.

29 Christ Church 'scribe 2' produced and endorsed S 187 (*CantCC* 54); 'scribe 3' produced and endorsed S 188 (*CantCC* 60); 'scribe 4' produced and endorsed S 1268 (*CantCC* 62). For the identification of these hands, see Brooks and Kelly, *CantCC*, pp. 115–17. One might note here that the endorsement of 'scribe 2' contains the possessive pronoun *minra*. Given that the charter in question was a grant to Archbishop Wulfred, Brooks has thus suggested that 'scribe 2' may be Archbishop Wulfred himself. See Nicholas Brooks, *The Early History of the Church at Canterbury: Christ Church from 597 to 1066* (Leicester, 1984), p. 168.

produced and endorsed a second charter, yet these two documents are typologically extremely similar: both are royal diplomas of King Ceolwulf issued in favour of Archbishop Wulfred.[30] Further apparent variation can be seen, for example, in the early 930s with the two surviving original single sheets of 'Æthelstan A', only one of which is contemporaneously endorsed;[31] one can similarly find inconsistency with the products of 'Edgar A', and elsewhere.[32] Such variation should serve as a reminder that charters were produced in a variety of circumstances, for a variety of purposes, and that practices could vary accordingly.

The greatest relative consistency of scribes endorsing their own charters can be found in the second and third quarters of the tenth century. This is a period that scholars have already identified as exceptional in terms of diplomatic, since it is from these years that the evidence for the 'centralized' production of royal diplomas is at its strongest. Indeed, it is for this reason that Simon Keynes has recently described this fifty-year period as the 'golden age of the Anglo-Saxon royal diploma'.[33] The strength of the evidence comes in part from the fact that an exceptionally large number of original single-sheet diplomas survives from this period; but what must also be stressed is that these diplomas make up a particularly large proportion of the extant single-sheet originals from these decades. It is with this in mind that we may note that we have considered 44 single sheets from this period as possible originals, of which 33 appear to have been endorsed by their main scribe or a contemporary. Of these 44, 36 are royal diplomas, 29 of which palaeographically appear probably to have been endorsed at the point of production. In other words, the evidence suggests that endorsing was a relatively consistent part of the production process for royal scribes during these years.

A further pattern with endorsements likely to have been produced at the point of production can be detected in the eleventh century, a period from

30 These two diplomas are S 186 and S 187. The former does not have a contemporary endorsement.

31 S 416 (BCS 677) and S 425 (*CantCC* 106). S 425 does not contain any pre-Conquest endorsements whatsoever. For identification of the scribes, see Pierre Chaplais, 'The Origin and Authenticity of the Royal Anglo-Saxon Diploma', *Journal of the Society of Archivists* 3 (1965), 48–61, at pp. 59–60, reprinted in *Prisca Munimenta: Studies in Archival and Administrative History Presented to Dr A. E. J. Hollaender*, ed. Felicity Ranger (London, 1973), pp. 28–42, at 41–42.

32 Five surviving single-sheet diplomas have been identified as the work of the scribe 'Edgar A': S 687, S 690, S 703, S 706, and S 717 (see Keynes, 'Church Councils', p. 159). Of these, three were endorsed by 'Edgar A' (S 687, S 706, and S 717) and two were not (S 690 and S 703).

33 Keynes, 'Church Councils', p. 52.

which there is considerably more variety in the types of documents that are extant as single-sheet originals than in the tenth century. Most of these charters, other than royal diplomas, are predominantly in the vernacular. The originals with contemporary endorsements, however, with one possible exception,[34] can be accounted for in one of two ways: they are royal diplomas, or they are products of the Worcester scriptorium. There are 21 original single-sheet royal diplomas surviving from between 1000 and 1066, representing at least 11 different medieval archives, 16 of which possess endorsements that appear to have been added at the point of production.[35] None of these 21 eleventh-century diplomas has survived via the Worcester archive. There, instead, we have eleventh-century originals of seven episcopal leases,[36] one will,[37] one dispute memorandum,[38] and one royal writ.[39] Of these ten documents, seven received endorsements that palaeographically look to be the work either of the main scribe or a contemporary. Of those three that were not contemporaneously endorsed, one was issued on behalf of the abbot of Evesham and was thus perhaps not produced at Worcester;[40] one is a writ, also unlikely to have been produced by the Worcester scriptorium;[41] while the third is a lease issued on behalf of Bishop Brihtheah of Worcester in the 1030s.[42] The evidence thus points towards endorsing as a regular part of private charter production at Worcester during the pre-Conquest period of the eleventh century, if not before.[43] This sits in contrast to the small amount of evidence that we have for eleventh-century private charter production elsewhere: 15 private charter single-sheet originals can be

34 S 1503 (*CantCC* 142) MS A1.

35 Eleventh-century royal diplomas extant as original single sheets are as follows: S 898, S 905, S 916, S 922, S 950, S 956, S 961, S 963, S 971 MS 1, S 974, S 977, S 994, S 1003, S 1004, S 1005, S 1008, S 1019, S 1021, S 1028, S 1031, and S 1044. Note that two of these charters do not record permanent donations of land: S 905 is a royal lease, while S 1021 records Edward the Confessor's joining of two dioceses. Of these 21 charters, the following five do not have contemporary endorsements: S 977, S 994, S 1028, S 1031, and S 1044.

36 S 1385, S 1393, S 1394, S 1399, S 1405, S 1407, and S 1423.

37 S 1534 (*ASWills* 19).

38 S 1460 (*ASChart* 83).

39 S 1156 (*ASWrits* 115).

40 S 1423 (*ASChart* 81).

41 S 1156 (*ASWrits* 115). Note that no original single-sheet writ (of which there are seven surviving examples) was endorsed during the Anglo-Saxon period.

42 S 1399 (*ASChart* 87).

43 Three tenth-century single-sheet private charters survive from Worcester: S 1281, S 1326, and S 1347. Only the earliest of these, S 1281, dated to 904, appears to have been endorsed by its main scribe. For further comment on endorsement practices at Worcester, see Francesca Tinti, *Sustaining Belief: The Church of Worcester from c. 870 to c. 1100* (Farnham, 2010), pp. 83–84.

found collectively in the Bury St Edmunds, Christ Church or Exeter archives, none of which carries contemporary endorsements.[44]

Endorsements added by the main scribe of the charter, however, are unlikely to account for more than 40 per cent of endorsements that appear to have been added to original single sheets during the pre-Conquest period. What, then, can be said about other endorsements? These additions offer important insights into how single sheets may have been used and valued years and generations after their initial production. As we have already noted, a relatively small number of later dorsal notes record additional information, occasionally noting a change of ownership or providing details purportedly relating to the original agreement that are not found in the original charter; in both cases, the concern seems to be to pre-empt any future competing claims to the related estates. The majority of later endorsements, however, serve simply to summarize the content of the charter in some way and appear, therefore, to reflect moments when later generations were organizing older documentation. We see early hints of such activity with a document from the Evesham archive, as well as two records from Christ Church, Canterbury, all three of which are eighth-century single sheets that attracted endorsements, possibly in the ninth century, stating the names of estates to which the documents relate.[45] A handful of comparable examples date to the first half of the eleventh century from Christ Church, Exeter, Glastonbury, and Worcester; yet by far the greatest number of such endorsements appears to date to the tenth century. As is perhaps to be expected, given the dominance of this archive in terms of single sheets, most tenth-century examples come from Christ Church. This includes the work of a single mid-tenth-century scribe who added the name of the related estates to multiple single sheets previously without endorsements.[46] Further Canterbury examples will be discussed below.[47] Hints of comparable administrative activity can also be identified elsewhere, most notably at Rochester, whence we have four eighth- and ninth-century single sheets to which summarizing endorsements were added in the tenth century.[48]

44 From Bury St Edmunds we have single sheets of a will (S 1489) and private land grant (S 1225); from Christ Church we have single sheets of one episcopal lease (S 1390), two wills (S 1503 and S 1530), four memoranda (S 1467, S 1471, S 1472, S 1473), one episcopal land grant (S 1400), and one private land grant (S 1220); from Exeter we have single sheets of one will (S 1492) and two independent sets of bounds (S 1546b and S 1547).

45 The Evesham charter is S 114 (BCS 230) and the Christ Church, Canterbury charters are S 123 and 128 (*CantCC* 22 and 24).

46 Brooks and Kelly, *CantCC*, pp. 40–41.

47 See below, pp. 252–54.

48 S 35, S 88, S 165, and S 327. The single sheet of S 35 dates to the eighth century, while the three others date to the ninth century. Note that the endorsements added to S 35 and S 165

How do the non-contemporary single sheets fit into this picture? First it should be said that there are no clear chronological patterns for the endorsement of such material. This is perhaps not surprising, given that most non-contemporary single sheets date to either the tenth or eleventh centuries and, moreover, that the dating of these specimens can often only be approximate, based on their palaeographic features alone. Chronology aside, one may note that much like single-sheet originals, the vast majority of endorsements to non-contemporary copies summarize the contents of the charter.[49] As to numbers, we can say that while just over two-thirds (34) of the specimens considered here contain what appears to be a pre-Conquest endorsement of some sort, only 18 of these (all of which purport to be royal diplomas) are potentially the work of the main scribe. The evidence, therefore, points towards endorsing being of variable importance to the production of such later single-sheet copies, even between non-contemporary single sheets from the same archive,[50] but two patterns do emerge: first, a relatively large proportion of those non-contemporary copies that do not contain endorsements are private charters; and second, one archive where we do find consistency is the Old Minster, Winchester, where almost all (if not all) of the non-contemporary single sheets look to have been endorsed at the point of production.[51]

---

have the same simple formulation, comprising a cross + place-name + *boc*. Elsewhere in the Rochester archive, a more extensive version of this formulation was used to endorse the tenth-century single sheet of S 280 by its main scribe. A tenth-century summarizing endorsement can also be found on the ninth-century single sheet of S 88, though it does not share these formulaic elements; this is perhaps unsurprising, given that this charter does not relate to land tenure (and thus a reference to a named estate and the use of *boc* may not have been deemed appropriate). The hands of several of these endorsements (particularly those of S 35, S 165, and S 327) share similar characteristics and it is possible that those of S 165 and S 327 are the work of a single scribe; however, the small amount of text in each makes it difficult to draw firm palaeographic conclusions. Our thanks to Colleen Curran for her advice with this matter.

49 An interesting exception here is the endorsement to S 230 (*CantCC* 3), which, although simply summarizing the respective original agreement, provides information not found in the main text (Brooks and Kelly, *CantCC*, p. 273).

50 Contrasts can be seen, for instance, between later single sheets within the following archives: Christ Church, Canterbury, Exeter, Rochester, and Westminster.

51 Note that all of these Old Minster single sheets purport to be royal diplomas and all appear to have been produced in the eleventh century. It should also be noted here that in contrast to the observable endorsement patterns at eleventh-century Worcester in the production of new private charters, the only non-contemporary single sheet that appears to date to Worcester in the first half of the eleventh century, S 117, does not contain an

The Languages of Endorsements

What, then, can be said of the languages of endorsements? Most fundamentally, the vast majority of endorsements are in Old English. This is regardless of its form and function, or of the text genre, scribe, date, or centre of production of the charter and its endorsements; moreover, it is regardless of the language of the rest of the charter text. In light of this, the few instances of Latin or bilingual endorsements are particularly interesting. In what follows, the linguistic characteristics of endorsements will be addressed, summarizing the salient features of Old English endorsements written on single-sheet originals at the point of production and by later scribes; endorsements on non-contemporary single sheets will be then considered; finally, we will briefly discuss those single sheets with endorsements containing Latin.

Vernacular Endorsements Added to Original Single Sheets at the Point of Production

As noted above, beyond the letter of Bishop Wealdhere, the earliest single sheets to have been endorsed possibly by the main text scribe and thus probably at the point of production are two single-sheet diplomas of King Coenwulf of Mercia. Both of the related endorsements comprise short vernacular summaries of the charter content.[52] From here on, the practice of adding an Old English endorsement to a single sheet at the point of production varies across the ninth to eleventh centuries. The surviving corpus allows us to identify the development of a specific endorsement formula in the mid-tenth century, employed first and foremost by the scribes of royal diplomas. This formula counts for approximately half of the total vernacular endorsements produced at the point of production and it will be discussed in detail shortly. Beyond this formula, however, there is little consistency in the type of information conveyed, the vocabulary used, or the structure of Old English endorsements produced by the main scribe of a charter. A number of observations can nevertheless be made concerning the endorsements beyond this standardized formula.

First, of those documents which record the donation of an estate, the land is always identified in some manner in the endorsement, typically with a place-name, although in the case, for example, of one Canterbury single sheet dated to 823 it is described and located but not named: 'londboc minra ƿica 7 ðritiges

endorsement by the main scribe. This reinforces the impression, perhaps unsurprisingly, that the production of such non-contemporary copies sits outside the mainstream of documentary activity.

52 S 163 (*CantCC* 40) and S 173 (BCS 343). See above, p. 242.

æcra be norðan byrg'.[53] Elsewhere, on an early eleventh-century single-sheet diploma of King Æthelred, one finds the land contemporaneously described but not located: '+ Þis ẏs þæs hagan / bóc .'[54] The next most common piece of information to be included is, as might be expected, the beneficiary, although only seven beneficiaries are explicitly named in such endorsements—all being individuals rather than institutions—and there is no clear pattern that unites these seven examples, either in terms of place of origin, typology of text or status of beneficiary.[55] The anomaly here is a lease issued by Bishop Wærferth of Worcester in 904, the endorsement of which notes the beneficiary, but not the land: 'uulfsiges lond boc'.[56] This identification by beneficiary alone perhaps indicates that Wulfsige was unlikely to receive any further documents from Worcester (i.e. there was no need to differentiate between multiple charters given to this individual). That said, the lack of other surviving single sheets from Wærferth's episcopate makes it difficult to assess the significance of such unusual phrasing.[57]

Vernacular endorsements written at the point of production range in structure from simple noun phrases of place-names + *boc* (or similar element), as in '+ ƿESTUNES LANDBÓC.' or 'Boc to bere ƿicaN:—',[58] to presenting that same information in sentence form, as in '+ Þis ẏs þæs hagan / bóc .' or 'Her is stantunes boc'.[59] At the more complex end are endorsements which describe the details of the transaction, acting as summaries of the charter's contents: '+ þis is ƿeƿesiges boc þe eadmund / cing gebocode þam ƿiƿum æt ƿin / tan ceastre

53 'Landbook of my tenements (*wica*) and of thirty acres to the north of the city' (trans. *CantCC* 54, p. 568). This is the aforementioned S 187 produced by Christ Church 'scribe 2', who may well have been Archbishop Wulfred himself. For details, see above, n. 29.

54 'This is the book for the *hagan*/*agri*'. This endorsement is found on the single sheet of S 905 (*CantCC* 139).

55 Named beneficiaries range across reeve, *minister*, *comes*, kinsman, steward, and bishop (S 173, S 316, S 768, S 1204, S 1281, S 1393, and S 1407). On only three occasions, however, are the named beneficiaries accorded titles in the endorsements (S 768, S 1204, and S 1407), and there is no correlation between the beneficiary being named and what office they held.

56 S 1281 (*ASChart* 18).

57 For an overview of documentary activity and the documentary corpus from Wærferth's episcopate, see Robert Gallagher and Francesca Tinti, 'Latin, Old English and Documentary Practice at Worcester from Wærferth to Oswald', *ASE* 46 (2019 for 2017), 271–325, at pp. 278–98.

58 S 922 (*Burt* 32) and S 974 (*CantCC* 155).

59 S 905 (*CantCC* 139) and S 677 (*Bath* 31). Keynes labels the latter as an endorsement 'of a basic kind' ('Church Councils', p. 175). Thompson, *Anglo-Saxon Royal Diplomas*, p. 50 also gives a brief overview of endorsements of this type.

to scrud fultume / for his fæder saple.'[60] There is further variation between those endorsements which describe the physical object and those which describe the transaction detailed therein. This difference becomes apparent in the language used to describe the document. Perhaps the most unambiguous example here is the use of *geanboc*: 'Ƿpegra hida géan boc 7 anre gerde æt pest tune. þe ealdred / ge bocade baldpine his stiparde þreora manna dæg'.[61] *Geanboc* survives in several instances from the eleventh century and appears to be a word specific to Worcester diplomatic: it is found in this chirographic episcopal lease issued in 1053; in an antiquarian copy of a now-lost original episcopal lease from 1017;[62] and within the *Liber Wigorniensis* cartulary in passages introducing leases pertaining to various shires in which the church of Worcester possessed land.[63] The best translation for it might be 'duplicate charter', which, given its use on a chirograph, suggests it refers to the multiple copies rather than to reissues or later copies. Given that so many chirographs were produced at Worcester in the tenth and eleventh centuries, primarily for episcopal leasing,[64] it is perhaps unsurprising that such a specific word gained popularity there. Elsewhere, the most common document labels are *boc* and *landboc*. Their use is nearly equal across endorsements written on original single sheets at the point of production, although there is a preference for *boc*, concentrated in the period 940–60.[65] They do not only appear on royal diplomas, but can also be found in the endorsements of a few private charters and leases.[66] Other document labels include *gewrixle* and *gehpearf*, 'exchange',[67]

60 'This is the book for Pewsey that King Edmund gave [*gobocode*] the community at Winchester towards provision for clothes, for his father's soul', S 470 (*WinchNM* 12).

61 'The chirograph [*geanboc*] for two hides and one yardland at Weston, that Ealdred gave [*gebocade*] to Baldwin his steward for three lives', S 1407.

62 S 1384 (KCD 1313), now surviving in London, British Library, Harley 4660, fol. 9v.

63 For related discussion, see Tinti, *Sustaining Belief*, pp. 111 and 115.

64 Kathryn A. Lowe, 'Lay Literacy in Anglo-Saxon England and the Development of the Chirograph', in *Anglo-Saxon Manuscripts and Their Heritage*, eds Philip Pulsiano and Elaine M. Treharne (Aldershot, 1998), pp. 161–204, at 177; Tinti, *Sustaining Belief*, p. 12.

65 There are *c.*30 instances of *boc* and 23 of *landboc*, written in endorsements by the scribe of the main text, allowing for variation in identification of hands, across the corpus. See Keynes, *The Diplomas of King Æthelred*, p. 81, n. 162 for discussion of the use of these terms.

66 S 1215, S 1268, S 1281, and S 1393. For the restrictive use of *boc* to royal diplomas, see A. G. Kennedy, 'Disputes about *bocland*: The Forum for Their Adjudication', *ASE* 14 (1985), 175–95, at p. 175, n. 2.

67 S 552 (*Abing* 44) and S 1266 (*CantCC* 55) respectively.

læn, 'lease',[68] *talu*, 'tale; account',[69] *freols* and *friodom*, 'freedom; immunity',[70] *gewrit*, 'written document',[71] and *cwide*, 'will'.[72]

A point of contrast is offered by an endorsement to a mid-ninth-century record of a private land transaction, added by the main scribe of the charter. It makes no reference to the physical object of the charter, but instead summarizes its contents: '+ ciolulf sealde eanmunde / his mege ðisne tuun betpix eum / pið .cxx. in ęc ęrbe ęðeredes cyninges / friols 7 his hand seten 7 sęlen:'.[73] It is striking that there is no apparent chronological development of form or type here. Simple place-name + *boc* endorsements appear from the early ninth century to the mid-eleventh in a large number of archives; so, too, do more elaborately constructed formulae. The exception might be Christ Church, Canterbury, where on occasion scribes before the mid-ninth century applied endorsements at the point of production to royal diplomas. These endorsements are typically short and simple. After this date, different types of charters are endorsed at the point of production. These bring with them more variety in style and length, with no clear rules guiding their exact form and content. This variety continues to be seen beyond and alongside the standardized endorsement formula that emerges predominantly in royal diplomatic production in the mid-tenth century (discussed below).

Vernacular Endorsements Added Later to Originals

Some 100 Old English endorsements were added to original single-sheets by a scribe who is not that of the main text.[74] Such endorsements first appear

68 S 1417 (*WinchNM* 9).

69 S 1447 (BCS 1063).

70 S 1021 (*Councils and Synods with Other Documents relating to the English Church, I: A.D. 871–1204*, eds D. Whitelock, M. Brett, and C. N. L. Brooke (Oxford, 1981), no. 71) and S 190 (BCS 416).

71 S 1508 (*CantCC* 96). In this instance, *gewrit* refers to a will: 'Þis is ęlfredes ęrfe / geprit:'. ('This is the will for Alfred's property').

72 For example, S 1522 (*The Crawford Collection of Early Charters and Documents*, eds A. S. Napier and W. H. Stevenson (Oxford, 1895), no. 9) and S 1534 (*ASWills* 19). While some of these might be argued to refer to the physical single sheet, many fall into a grey area and more work needs to be done to determine the extent to which the physical object of a document stands for the information it records. This is potentially illuminating in terms of conceptions about typologies of text. Endorsements, if we think of them as labels, are a key corpus for exploring this.

73 'Ceolwulf gave this property (*tun*) between them to his kinsman, Eanmund, for 120 [pence] in (the) perpetual inheritance of King Æthelred's freedom and of his signature (*hondseten*) and grant (*selen*).' (S 1204, *CantCC* 91, pp. 782–88, at 786).

74 Thompson, *Anglo-Saxon Royal Diplomas*, pp. 50–53 differentiates these from inscriptions made at the point of production by calling them 'archive marks' as opposed to 'endorsements'.

in the eighth century, predating the practice of adding endorsements at the point of production—at least in the extant corpus—beyond, that is, the example of the letter of Bishop Wealdhere. The eighth century saw roughly four vernacular endorsements added to charters (a further two endorsements in Latin were also produced in this period; these are discussed below).[75] The first two endorsements of this date, both added to a charter issued by Oslac, the leader of the South Saxons, are of the place-names for land at Earnley, Sussex, and *Tielæsora*, the second of which was added after folding, while a subsequent eighth-century confirmation has made the first less visible.[76] Walter de Gray Birch suggests that the first endorsement was 'written accidentally upside-down'.[77] Perhaps this was a result of it being an unfamiliar practice, at this date, to endorse folded charters. The remaining eighth-century vernacular endorsements are both written by scribes contemporary with those of their main texts and, again, are simple non-Latinized place-names.[78]

As vernacular endorsements pick up pace through the ninth century and into the tenth, it is striking that, in contrast to the variety of endorsements written at the point of production, those added later tend to be much simpler and shorter, rarely giving more information than place-names. The majority of these are single place-names, reflecting a specific area of land being granted and using the names given in the main text. In a further 11 instances the endorsement prioritises a single place (or, in the case of one ninth-century single sheet, two)[79] out of several estates mentioned in the charter, and in three cases the place-names in the endorsements locate, rather than name, the land.[80] This overarching trend for simple labels might be a symptom of the process by which they are written: a scribe coming to a charter later might consider some details less important, or be less able or interested to extract them from the text.

75 Two endorsements were added to S 1184 in the eighth century; one to S 31; and one to S 65.

76 S 1184 (*Sel* 11). This is not necessarily first chronologically as such short scribal stints make dating imprecise. The endorsements read: 'Earnalēa 7 tieles ora' and 'Earnaleah / 7 teles ora' (both translate as 'Earnley and *Tielæsora*').

77 Walter de Gray Birch, *The Anglo-Saxon Charter of Oslac, Duke of the South Saxons, A.D. 780* (London, 1892), p. 4. See also H. L. Rogers, 'The Oldest West-Saxon Text?', *Review of English Studies*, New Series, 32 (1981), 257–66.

78 S 31 (*CantCC* 14), a grant of 1 *sulung* at Perhamstede from Eardwulf, king of Kent, to Abbot Heaberht and his *familia* at Reculver (A.D. 748×762) endorsed with '[Per]hamstede [...]'; and S 65 (*CantCC* 9), a grant of land at Twickenham from Swæfred, king of the East Saxons, and Pæogthath, *comes*, to Bishop Wealdhere in 704, with a confirmation by Ceolred from 709×716.

79 S 1436 (*CantCC* 59) MS A1.

80 Two of these are 'Norðstur', added to S 89 (BCS 154) in the ninth and eleventh centuries, which indicate that the land in question is located to the north of the River Stour (although further land is also included in the grant, at Brochyl in Morfe Forest, towards the River Severn).

Similarly, once a charter is with its intended holder, the most useful information would in many cases have been the place-name, for easy navigation of a collection. This can be illustrated by a series of acquisitions by Archbishop Wulfred (805–32) between 811 and 815, in which Wulfred brought together several small properties around Graveney, near Faversham, combining them 'within the fences of a single boundary' for easier administration.[81] There are several contemporary single-sheet charters attesting to this process, on three of which are endorsements identifying Graveney, dating from the ninth and tenth centuries.[82] The first of these is a grant from 811 of land at *Suithhunincg lond* at Graveney as well as two tenements in Canterbury, in exchange for 126 mancuses.[83] On the original single sheet, a hand possibly of the tenth century has marked 'grafen ea'.[84] The second document is a ninth-century single sheet for an exchange for two areas of land, one in Graveney and one at Cheriton, on the other side of Kent, from 812.[85] Here, again, a tenth-century endorsement has prioritized Graveney over any other details, reading: 'grauan ea'. Finally, there is a grant for one hide of land at *Seleberhting lond* to Wulfred in 815.[86] While Graveney is mentioned in the main text of the previous two charters, it does not appear here, yet a hand of the ninth century, possibly that

FIGURE 7.4
The Graveney endorsements of (clockwise from top left) London, British Library, Cotton Augustus ii.10 (S 168); Canterbury, Dean & Chapter, ChAnt C. 1278 (S 169), reproduced courtesy of the Chapter of Canterbury; London, British Library, Stowe Charter 12 (S 178)

81 'ut facilius elaborare ac desudare sua propria in illis potuissent quasi adunate unius termini intra septa conclusi', S 1264 (*CantCC* 43), trans. *CantCC*, pp. 153–54 and p. 556.

82 The documents relating to Graveney are: S 168, S 169, S 170, S 177, S 178, S 1203, and S 1414 (*CantCC*, pp. 153–54). The three endorsed with Graveney are S 168, S 169, and S 178.

83 S 168 (*CantCC* 44).

84 A second, later, hand of the tenth or eleventh century has added 'spiðhuning land . Grauanea.', perhaps to reinstate some specificity.

85 S 169 (*CantCC* 46).

86 S 178 (*CantCC* 51).

of the main text, has written 'GRAUENEA / HES BEC.' on the dorse, prioritising the archbishop's plan and archival holdings over the contents of the face.

These 'Graveney' endorsements are certainly the work of different hands, active at different times, but perhaps working with reference to each other: each is notable for being in a large, clear script, atypical for Anglo-Saxon endorsements, and for containing the same information, for administrative purposes. Visually, they look like an attempt at consistency. They are not concerned with the details of the original transaction or about the individual areas of land being bought or exchanged, but about the archbishop's organization of his holdings and documents. Evidence of this kind across the dorses of multiple charters is unique to the Christ Church archive, thanks to its exceptional number of surviving single sheets. As noted above, however, examples from beyond Canterbury suggest that other religious communities also used endorsements as a tool for organizing their documentary collections,[87] and it is entirely feasible that this particular process might have been replicated elsewhere as a useful archival practice, not dissimilar from the ordering and subdividing of holdings in a cartulary.[88]

In other cases the later addition of a vernacular endorsement could reflect a change in status of some aspect of the charter. The dorse of an original single-sheet diploma of Wihtred, king of Kent, to St Mary's Church in Lyminge of 4 *sulungs* at *Pleghelmestun* in Kent, issued in 697 or 712, is particularly illustrative of this.[89] There are three pre-Conquest endorsements, written around each other within one square of the grid of fold-marks. All are in hands of the tenth or eleventh century.[90] Two are entirely in the vernacular, while a third (discussed further below) is a mixture of Latin and Old English. Their probable order is:

1. 'delhames / boc' ('The book for Delham')
2. 'ðæs landes boc æt ber / picum' ('The landbook for Berwick')
3. 'Nunc pigelmignc / tun' ('now *Wieghelmestun*')[91]

87 See above, p. 245.

88 As in, for example, the organizational and ordering work conducted by Archbishop Wulfstan and the compilers of the *Liber Wigorniensis* cartulary, as delineated in Tinti, *Sustaining Belief*, pp. 85–125.

89 S 19 (*CantCC* 5).

90 These datings follow Brooks and Kelly, *CantCC*, pp. 286–87. Peter Sawyer, conversely, assigned them to the ninth century; see his *From Roman Britain to Norman England*, 2nd ed. (Oxford, 1998), pp. 152–53.

91 The third endorsement has been written in an apparent attempt to continue from the first, following directly on as if written to follow a line.

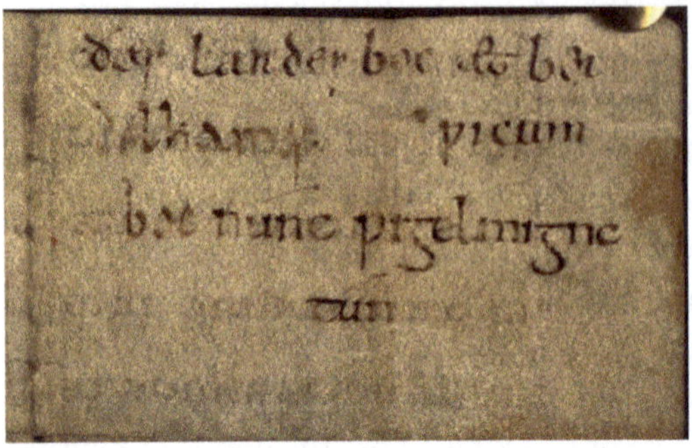

FIGURE 7.5
The endorsements of London, British Library, Stowe Charter 1 (S 19)

They represent a series of efforts to reflect changing names and ownerships: Delham was one name for the estate, as were *Pleghelmestun* and the name it had acquired by the ninth century, *Wieghelmestun*, potentially after the ninth-century Kentish landowner Wighelm; Berwick is the name of the estate to the east of that granted here.[92]

Many vernacular endorsements added later, however, do not update or add new information, but repeat information that was already written on the dorse, generally a place-name.[93] This seems to be the case on a charter from the Worcester archive that records a grant of lands located to the north of the River Stour (as discussed above).[94] Here, two scribes—one perhaps in the ninth century and the other perhaps in the eleventh century—have added 'norð stur' and 'Norðstur' to the dorse.[95] The first of these two is inverted, near the edge of the sheet, in a clear area of parchment away from a note pertaining to a second estate. This is perhaps the most prominent spot to add an endorsement for administrative or archival purposes if the sheet is unfolded. The second is written on what would have been the outside of the folded package.[96]

92 Sawyer, *From Roman Britain to Norman England*, pp. 152–53. See also S 21 (*CantCC* 6) and the discussion in G. Ward, 'The Wilmington Charter of A.D. 700', *Archaeologia Cantiana* 98 (1936), 11–28.

93 S 31, S 89, S 111, S 163, S 293, S 350, S 563, S 1184, and S 1269. Of these, Mary Parsons suggests that, in the cases of S 31, S 163, and S 1184, one of the two place-name endorsements is a contemporary archive mark and the other a scribal memorandum, noted before the charter's production; Parsons, 'Some Scribal Memoranda', pp. 13–32.

94 See above, p. 251, especially n. 80.

95 S 89 (BCS 154).

96 It is common for one of the endorsements to be written upside down (that is, in relation to each other as it is hard on an otherwise blank dorse to identify a top or bottom). In most of these cases, it appears that, after the charter had been folded a later scribe had added an identifying place-name on an outside surface.

In both cases, visibility is, understandably, an important consideration, particularly when dorses become crowded with extra text.

The 'þis is þara' Formula

These general observations provide useful context for the single most striking development in the phrasing of endorsements, a development that can be localized to the late 930s and 940s, when we see the emergence of a specific endorsement formula that was to become extremely widespread in the documentary practices of the later Anglo-Saxon period. In the words of Simon Keynes, this stock phrasing is 'as formulaic as any part of the formulation of the Latin text'.[97]

The earliest extant example of this formula in its fully formed state is a diploma of 943: a grant of 6 hides at *Miclan grafe* in Thanet from King Edmund to Ælfstan, his *minister* (Figure 7.6).[98] The endorsement was most likely written by the main scribe of the charter, named by Richard Drögereit as 'Æthelstan C'.[99] It reads as follows: 'Þis is þara VI sulunga boc / æt miclangrafe. Þe eadmund / cing gebocode . ælfstane his / þenge on ece yrfe .·.'[100] Each

FIGURE 7.6 The dorse of London, British Library, Stowe Charter 24 (S 512)

97 Keynes, 'Church Councils', p. 166.

98 S 512 (*CantCC* 112).

99 Drögereit, 'Gab es eine angelsächsische Königskanzlei?', p. 340. Similar formulae can be found endorsing the two surviving single sheets of 'Æthelstan C' (S 447 and S 449), which will be discussed below.

100 'This is the book of six *sulungs* at *Miclan grafe* that King Edmund gave to Ælfstan his thegn, in perpetual inheritance'.

endorsement of this type follows the same sequence of elements: '+ ÞIS IS ÞARA | LAND SIZE [hidage] | LOCATION OF LAND GRANTED [ÆT 'place-name'] | GRANTOR | BENEFICIARY | ON ECE YRFE'. These elements constitute the 'operative details' that are otherwise needed for a central agency to produce the dispositive section of a charter: 'the name and appropriate designation of the beneficiary; the assessment or hidage of the estate (in hides [*mansae*] or *sulungs*); and the name of the estate'.[101] In this formulaic endorsement, the elements of the charter have been condensed to their simplest form.[102] Meanwhile, the concluding phrase of the formula, 'on ece yrfe', reflects the inherent permanence of the grant; while this phrase does appear within the text of various charters, its use is not widespread outside of endorsements, appearing in perhaps only 20 charter texts from archives across the south of England.[103] Beyond the charter corpus, the phrase appears only once, in the Old English translation of the *Hexateuch*.[104] It is striking that,

101 Keynes, 'Church Councils', pp. 66 and 163–66.

102 At Exeter the relationship between endorsement and charter text is particularly apparent. In several charters from the late tenth century the information given in the boundary clause introduction is the same as that given in the *Þis is þara* formula. Take, for example, S 795 (BCS 1303), whose endorsement opens: 'ðis is ðara ðreora hida boc æt nẏmed' and whose bounds are introduced with the phrase: 'Þis is þæra þreora hida land gemære æt nymed', in which the only difference is between *boc* and *land gemære*. Similarities can be found between the endorsements and boundary introductions of all those Exeter charters that are endorsed with the *Þis is þæra* formula (S 795, S 830, S 890, S 963, S 971, and S 1019; S 1021 does not have bounds). In addition, S 1005 (*CantCC* 168), a grant of 1044 from Edward to his *minister* Ordgar of land at Elddin, should be considered here. It is now archived with Christ Church, Canterbury but comes from a West Country archive. The similarity between its endorsement, which opens: 'Ðys is þære anre gyrde land boc beniðan ELDDIN' and its bounds, which are introduced: 'Ðys is þære anre gyrde landgemæru beniðan Elddin', perhaps points to that archive being Exeter. In these instances, the scribes seem to be making an effort towards precision and exactness in their labelling of the land, giving details that are consistent between the body of the text and its endorsement.

103 These are: S 204, S 217, S 355, S 544, S 567, S 677, S 781, S 789, S 833, S 842, S 886, S 984, S 1121, S 1220, S 1443, S 1446, S 1458, S 1471, S 1539, and S 1603. It is striking that six of these are found in charters associated with Abingdon. This list is drawn from a proximity search of the *Dictionary of Old English Corpus*, compiled by Antonette diPaolo Healey with John Price Wilkin and Xin Xiang (Toronto, 2009) for *on ece yrfe* and *on ece erfe* and excludes any examples drawn from endorsements or cartulary rubrics. They appear with increasing frequency from the mid-ninth century onwards, although 11 survive only in cartulary copies (S 1603, from A.D. 685×689, only appears in the twelfth-century Abingdon cartulary and might be an outlier or the work of the cartulary scribe). To this list should be added S 1481f, a list of serfs copied into *Textus Roffensis*, which is drawn from S 1458; see David A. E. Pelteret, 'Two Old English Lists of Serfs', *Mediaeval Studies* 48 (1986), 470–513, at p. 493.

104 'Ne sylle ge ðæt land on ece yrfe for þa*m* ðe hit ys ^Godes^ 7 ge syndon utan cymene 7 mine tilian', corresponding to Leviticus 25:23. London, British Library, Cotton Claudius

across the endorsement corpus, *irfe* is consistently spelled in the West Saxon 'y-', regardless of place of production,[105] with only two instances of *erfe* appearing in endorsements of any type.[106] This near-total orthographic conformity is impressive. It adds weight to the argument for a centralized point of production from which these endorsements were disseminated, and it speaks to the enduring authority of the formula in its prototypical form.[107]

The appearance and development of this formulaic endorsement has been described by Richard Drögereit, Cyril Hart, and Simon Keynes, each with subtly different categorizations and subdivisions.[108] Drögereit, with the purpose of understanding why certain single sheets carry endorsements and others do not, identified a series of key endorsements on surviving original specimens that mark stages in the formula's development, namely a diploma of 'Æthelstan A' from 931;[109] a more detailed endorsement on a single sheet of 'Æthelstan C'

B.iv, fol. 110r. This manuscript was produced in the second quarter of the eleventh century, probably at St Augustine's, Canterbury (N. R. Ker, *Catalogue of Manuscripts Containing Anglo-Saxon* (Oxford, 1957), no. 142, pp. 178–79 and *The Old English Illustrated Heptateuch British Museum Cotton Claudius B. IV*, eds C. R. Dodwell and P. Clemoes (Copenhagen, 1974), p. 16). It is a compilation of the work of Ælfric and an anonymous scriptural translator(s). The portion of the *Hexateuch* containing Leviticus was the work of the anonymous translator(s), who followed on from Ælfric's translation work under the patronage of Æthelweard (d. *c*.998); see Mark Griffith, 'Ælfric's Preface to Genesis: Genre, Rhetoric and the Origins of the *ars dictaminis*', ASE 29 (2000), 215–34, at pp. 215–16. The choice of wording in this translation may be a reference to the expression of perpetual inheritance used in charter formulation. It is perhaps worth noting that Scott Thompson Smith draws a tacit connection between this verse and Anglo-Saxon land tenure by opening his chapter, 'Tenure in Translation', with it; Scott Thompson Smith, *Land and Book: Literature and Land Tenure in Anglo-Saxon England* (Toronto, 2012), p. 108.

105 We are grateful to the late E. C. Stanley for his observation here at the Joint Committee on Anglo-Saxon Charters' 22nd Annual Symposium, London, 11 September 2017.

106 S 768 (*Burt* 23) and S 898 (KCD 705). Neither of these endorsements are of the *Þis is þara* type, although the example in S 898 (*Councils and Synods*, eds Whitelock et al., no. 71, pp. 523–33) is perhaps an attempt by the scribe to emulate it (variations on the formula will be discussed below).

107 Indeed, the appearance of the phrase in the endorsement of S 1021 (*Councils and Synods*, eds Whitelock et al., no. 71), an Exeter production, which is not a royal diploma concerned with the creation of bookland but the record of King Edward joining the dioceses of Devon and Cornwall, shows its standardized nature. For the Exeter production, see Simon Keynes, 'Regenbald the Chancellor (*sic*)', *Anglo-Norman Studies* 10 (1988), 185–222, at p. 213, n. 47.

108 Drögereit, 'Gab es eine angelsächsische Königskanzlei?', pp. 431–32; Hart, 'The *Codex Wintoniensis*', Appendix I; Keynes, *The Diplomas of King Æthelred*, p. 24, n. 33 and p. 81, n. 162; Keynes, 'Church Councils', pp. 66 and 163–66. See also Thompson, *Anglo-Saxon Royal Diplomas*, pp. 50–51, for related palaeographic comments.

109 'þis is þæs landes boc æt hamme' (S 416, BCS 677).

written in 939;[110] and, finally, an original diploma of King Edmund, also written by 'Æthelstan C', in 943.[111] In doing so, he connects the form, production, and function of the endorsement to the context of centralized production, performance to the witan, and the status of the land in question. In contrast, Hart pointed to the mid-ninth-century reign of King Æthelwulf as the origin for this dorsal formulation. Much of Hart's analysis, somewhat problematically, focuses on the forms found in the rubrics copied into the twelfth-century *Codex Wintoniensis*, which Hart believed to be 'accurate copies of the endorsements on the original membranes of these landbooks, as they lay before the cartulary scribes'.[112] Furthermore, although Hart also considered endorsements on single sheets, he did not recognize that his two mid-ninth-century specimens were products of a single Canterbury scribe.[113] Nevertheless, Hart divided the development of this endorsement into five 'formulae', the later stages of which broadly follow the dates and phrases of progression identified by Drögereit. To this, Keynes has provided a revised model. Keynes identifies a series of groups of formulaic endorsement added to royal diplomas in the period 925–75, subdivided into four types in a successive chronology, which show a development of the formula as information is added to it in increments. The first three of these show the most significant development of the form and coincide with the three key endorsements identified by Drögereit:

- Type 1: 'This is the landbook at Place' (the earliest extant example of which is S 416)
- Type 2: 'This is Place's [land]book which King .N. booked to .N. in perpetual inheritance' (S 417)
- Type 3: 'This is the [land]book of oo hides at Place which King .N. booked to .N. in perpetual inheritance' (S 512)[114]

Keynes' Types add nuance to the formula described above. It is his 'Type 3' that correlates to the fully realized *Þis is þara* formula as we describe it above. The endorsements listed as Keynes' Type 2 roughly correspond to two groups

110 '+ Þis is meap ham[.]s land boc / þe . æþelstan cin[.] gebocode . / ealdulfe his þegne on ece yrfe .' (S 447, *CantCC* 107).

111 'Þis is þara VI sulunga boc / æt miclangrafe. Þe eadmund / cing gebocode . ælfstane his / þenge on ece yrfe .' (S 512, *CantCC* 112).

112 Hart, 'The *Codex Wintoniensis*', p. 21, n. 3. The evidence certainly corroborates this, allowing for any interpolations—intentional or otherwise—introduced by the cartulary scribes during the copying process. In his corpus, however, he also includes private charters (S 1266 and S 1268). Neither of these materially affects the chronology he describes.

113 Namely the single sheets of S 316 and 328, both of which were produced by Christ Church 'scribe 7' and both of which were probably also endorsed by this same scribe; see Brooks and Kelly, *CantCC*, pp. 724 and 736.

114 Keynes, 'Church Councils', p. 166.

of related but subtly different endorsements from the period 937–43, of which 'Æthelstan C' was the scribe of two, which Keynes earlier described in his *Diplomas*.[115] Not all of the endorsements from this group exactly match the *Þis is þara* formula—some lack the 'þara [land size]' and show variation in the later elements.[116] However, they are similar enough that the identification and inclusion of cartulary copies in Keynes' groups suggests that, while not the originator of the formula, 'Æthelstan C' was closely connected to the milieu in which it was first produced.[117] This milieu, as Drögereit originally suggested, appears to be royal assemblies, events at which multiple diplomas would often have been produced at the same time. Within this context, such a formulaic vernacular endorsement would have been invaluable as a means of ensuring that each beneficiary took the correct piece of folded parchment home.

About 40 royal diplomas on original single sheets are endorsed using variations of this formula at the point of production. Roughly another seven examples appear on later copies of diplomas, although only one of these exactly matches the formula's construction.[118] All of these might have been copied from lost originals, or, in the case of spurious documents, might be additions by the scribe in an effort to replicate the features of an authentic document of the mid-tenth century.[119] In total, there are some 47 instances across the corpus, ranging from the 930s until the end of the Anglo-Saxon period. The ubiquity of this formula becomes apparent when we consider that, in that same period, there are only 63 endorsements possibly added to original single sheets by the scribes of the main text.[120] Strikingly, there are no instances of endorsements of this type being added to an earlier single sheet by a later scribe.

115 Keynes, *The Diplomas of King Æthelred*, pp. 24–28.

116 S 467 (BCS 764) and S 470 (*WinchNM* 12), for example, give further information on the details of the transaction.

117 Keynes, *The Diplomas of King Æthelred*, pp. 24–28.

118 These are: S 43, S 443, S 540, S 587, S 702, S 738, and S 801. It is notable that of these seven, four are eleventh-century Winchester, Old Minster copies.

119 See, for example, S 43 (*Sel* 4), a late tenth-century copy of a Selsey grant, dated 775, but an undoubted forgery: Kelly, *Sel*, pp. xli and 25–29. Its endorsement reads: 'Þis is seo land boc þe nunna / cẏng gebocade eadberhte b / into hugubeorgū . xx. hida.' The endorsement here echoes contemporary practice rather than that of the supposed date of the text.

120 Allowing for some margin of variation for exact dating, the 'original' status of a single sheet, and the identification of scribal hands. If we expand the criteria to include rubrics in cartularies we can see that, particularly in *Codex Wintoniensis*, the formula was much more widespread than the initial figures suggest. It is also copied, post-Conquest, on eleventh-century copies of charters, such as S 623 (Burton-on-Trent, Burton-on-Trent Museum, Muniments 2), perhaps with the purpose of producing an 'authentic' appearance.

The importance of this formulaic construction, however, goes beyond centralized production at royal assemblies. Its appearance on such diplomas is apparently influential and it is adopted into wider documentary practice and used until the end of the Anglo-Saxon period. Endorsements which recognisably follow the *Þis is þara* formula appear in, for example, a mid-eleventh-century 'regional production', perhaps from St Petroc's, which found its way to Christ Church, Canterbury:[121] '+ þis is þære oþre healfan [...][122] / gẏrde landboc to tref hrigoni.7 to tref hrẏt / þe eadpeard cẏngc het gebocian eadulfe / his þegene on ece ẏrfe . —'.[123]

With the spread of this formula comes the inevitable introduction of variation. The choice between roman numerals or the Old English word to express the size of land is a matter of scribal preference, and the word used to measure the land (*hide*, *gyrd*, or *sulung*) appears to be dictated by the region in which the estate lies.[124] On occasion, the verb and beneficiary switch order. More significant, however, are adaptations of the formula to suit the specific requirements of individual charters, adaptations the scribe feels free to make without compromising the integrity of the formula, or endorsements that are echoing or mimicking a formula that has become so ubiquitous as to be perceived as the standard. For example, in the endorsement to a private charter of 968, added by the main scribe of the charter, we see the adoption of the formula beyond royal diplomas in a modified form in order to take into account an additional transaction following the initial grant: 'ðis is hyring ðænnes boc ðe eadpold / 7 æðelflæd geuðan. ælfpolde pið / his licpyrðan scætte'.[125] Meanwhile in a royal diploma of King Edgar, the endorsement reads: '+ Þis is ealra Þara landa freols Þe / eadgar cyning ge ed freolsade pulfrice / his Þegene on

121 S 1019 (KCD 787), dating to 1049. On its possible place of production, see O. J. Padel, *Cornish Place-Name Elements* (Cambridge, 1985), pp. 8–9.

122 Here is a character which looks like a half-formed <h>. It is unclear if this is an erasure or a scribal error.

123 'This is the landbook of the other half ... *gyrd* to Tregony and to Trerice that King Edward gave Eadulf his thegn, in perpetual inheritance'.

124 *Sulung* is used in the endorsements of S 512, S 497, and S 671, all of which refer to land in Kent. The first is the work of 'Æthelstan C', the second of 'Edmund C', the third is spurious, the first two of these suggesting that the use of the word is dictated by the local representatives at the transaction rather than a centralized scribe. *Gyrd* (one quarter of a hide) is more common than *sulung*, appearing in the endorsements of S 736, S 830, S 1004, S 1005, and S 1019. These all refer to land given in Dorset, Devon, and Cornwall and seem to be vernacular translations for *pertica* in the main text of the charters (and, in S 736, '3 virgae'). In the wider Anglo-Saxon corpus, *gyrd* appears in texts from the West Country from the late tenth century, as well as a few instances from Winchester and Worcester.

125 S 1215 (*CantCC* 128). 'This is the book for Herondon, which Eadwold and Æthelflæd granted Ælfwold in return for the appropriate sum'.

ece yrfe'.[126] Here we see the formula adapted to reflect the fact that the charter was recording a grant of privileges (*freols*) rather than bookland, yet it keeps enough elements—the opening phrase, the king's name as benefactor, the name and title of the beneficiary and the closing phrase *on ece yrfe*—to recognisably conform to its structure. Similarly, the endorsement to a diploma of King Æthelred reads: 'ÐIS IS ÞÆRALANDDABOCTOSUÞHAM7TO /^ 7TO hREODBURNAN: ^ / hLODBROCE: ÞE ÆÞELRED CẎNING / SEAL DELEOFƿINEEALDORMENON / ECEẎRFE:.'[127] Here, Æthelred is redistributing land after the previous owner, Wistan, forfeited it for murder. To reflect this, *gebocian* in the endorsement is replaced with *sellan*.

We might also consider the following endorsement added to a diploma of King Æthelred, seemingly by the main scribe of the single sheet: 'þis is þara .xxv. hida boc þe æþelred / cẏngc gebocode . ẏceantun . clofige / his þegne a on ^.ece.^ erfe .:'[128] Here, the elements (land location and benefactor name) have been transposed. The reason for this is unclear—human inconsistency, or perhaps unfamiliarity with the formula—but its appearance is worth noting in light of the overall regularity in the other instances.

Finally, one might note here that in the tenth, and increasingly in the eleventh, century, some endorsements not adhering to the *Þis is þara* formula also include more information than place-names and beneficiaries, perhaps in response to the spread and influence of this formula.[129] The tenth-century endorsement added to a Rochester grant of 860 (a probable ninth-century original), for example, gives the hidage, the location of the land, and the name and title of the beneficiary: '.lxxx. æcera boc . be eastan / porte 7 ðæs mersces . pær / mundes . biscopes .:'[130] These elements follow the order and contain much of the same information of the *Þis is þara* formula, excluding only the opening and closing phrases (*on ece erfe*) and the name of the grantor—in this case Æthelberht, king of Wessex.

126 S 687 (*Abing* 86). 'This is all the land freedoms that King Edgar re-enfranchised to Wulfric his thegn in perpetual inheritance'.

127 S 892 (*The Crawford Collection*, eds Napier and Stevenson, no. 8). 'This is the landbook to Southam and to Ladbroke ^and to Radbourne^ that King Æthelred sold to Ealdorman Leofwine in perpetual inheritance'.

128 S 898 (KCD 705). 'This is the book of 25 hides at Itchington that King Æthelred gave to Clofi his thegn, forever in all perpetuity'. This diplomas dates to 1001 and its single sheet derives from the Coventry archive.

129 This is alongside those mentioned above, which are emulating the formula.

130 S 327 (*Roch* 24). 'The book for 80 acres to the east of the port and of Bishop Wærmund's marsh'. For the probable date of this single sheet, see Brooks, *The Early History of the Church*, pp. 360–61, n. 70, 'Scribe 8'.

Later Copies: Main Scribe and Later

Around 31 later copies of charters were produced during the early medieval period that carry Old English endorsements, about half of which were added at the point of production by the main text scribe or by a contemporary. These endorsements were, bar two, produced in the tenth and eleventh centuries.[131] All but two are royal grants.[132] The endorsements follow contemporary practice, as seen in the chronology of endorsements to original single sheets: until the late ninth century, they are largely simple noun phrases, focusing on place-names (as place-name, or place-name + *boc*). While these continue to be produced in the eleventh century, there are also several endorsements of the *Þis is þara* type, as discussed above, which also shows later copies of charters were being endorsed in line with contemporary practice.[133]

Latin and Mixed

There is very little Latin in the corpus of pre-Conquest endorsements: 16 endorsements are entirely Latin and a further seven might be considered bilingual. They range in date from the eighth to the eleventh centuries (although most were produced in the tenth and eleventh centuries), and the majority are associated with Canterbury and Rochester.[134] Most examples are found on royal diplomas (chiefly new grants of land, although a number are confirmations); the remainder are on lay and ecclesiastical grants, on an ecclesiastical account of acquisitions, and on an episcopal letter.[135]

Endorsements containing Latin in some form are a varied group. Many are short notes of names—both personal and place—which echo the simplest types of vernacular endorsement. See, for example, the Latinized personal name in 'Cnuto Dreigtun', an endorsement added possibly at the point of

---

131 S 65 (*CantCC* 9) has an eighth/ninth-century endorsement; S 153 (*CantCC* 26) has a ninth-century endorsement. It is striking that the scribe of S 65, in producing the copy, made efforts to reproduce an earlier exemplar, mimicking aspects of its appearance (Brooks and Kelly, *CantCC*, p. 322). The presence of an endorsement is at odds with such efforts.

132 S 1171 (BCS 81) and S 1203 (*CantCC* 94) are both lay grants.

133 S 43, S 443, S 540, S 587, S 702, S 738, and S 801. Each of these is a non-original single sheet, endorsed either by the main scribe or, in the cases of S 540 and S 738, by a contemporary or near-contemporary scribe.

134 See, for example, S 20 (*CantCC* 7), a Canterbury production, which has a Latin endorsement by the scribe of the main text. Further endorsements containing Latin that were possibly added by the main scribe can be found on S 280, S 540, S 956, and S 1458.

135 Latin can be found in endorsements to the following lay and ecclesiastical grants: S 1171, S 1203, and S 1211. The ecclesiastical account of acquisitions is S 1458. The episcopal letter is the aforementioned letter of Bishop Wealdhere (S 1428b); for discussion, see above, p. 241.

production to a royal diploma issued by Cnut.[136] Other Latin endorsements, however, are more elaborate, comparable with the *Þis is þara* formula and containing the information that became typical of vernacular endorsements in the tenth and eleventh centuries.[137] Take, for instance, the early ninth-century single sheet supposedly recording an agreement of a synod at *Clofesho* of 742, which in its present form was forged by or for Wulfred, archbishop of Canterbury.[138] The endorsement, tucked into an unused square at the bottom, surrounded by the witness-list, reads 'Libertas eclesie Xpī / eþelbaldi regis merc̄ / cuþberti arc̄ ep',[139] summarizing the privileges outlined in the main text.

In many of these cases, the Latin endorsement fits comfortably within the expected typology of vernacular endorsements. That is, they express the same categories of information in similar constructions, either by naming places or agents of the transaction, describing the document type or by using more lengthy constructions. Others, however, do not conform so readily and can be somewhat surprising. Particularly unusual is the 'sal sapientiae' ('salt of wisdom') added to the dorse of a late tenth-century record of an acquisition of land by Archbishop Dunstan on behalf of the community at St Andrew's, Rochester.[140] This dorsal note looks to be contemporary with the production of the single sheet—it is possibly the work of the main scribe—though its relevance to the main text is not immediately apparent. 'Salt of wisdom' can otherwise be found in early medieval baptismal rites, given to catechumens before their anointing and variably interpreted as a means of cleansing and of protecting against future enemies.[141] This phrase was perhaps therefore added as a comparable blessing for the agreement recorded by the charter. Elsewhere, we have a grant of 40 hides at Ely from King Eadwig to Archbishop Oda, issued in 957.[142] This has a *Þis is þara* type endorsement by the scribe of the main text.

136 S 956 (*WinchNM* 33). The code-switching here could be compared with the most common type of code-switching seen in predominantly Latin charter texts, namely the inclusion of vernacular place-names. For discussion, see Robert Gallagher, 'The Vernacular in Anglo-Saxon Charters: Expansion and Innovation in Ninth-Century England', *Historical Research* 91 (2018), 205–35, at pp. 208–9. For more examples of such code-switching endorsements, see S 19 (*CantCC* 5) and S 646 (BCS 1347).

137 See, for example, S 88 (*Roch* 2) and S 801 (BCS 1312).

138 S 90 (*CantCC* 12). For its association with Archbishop Wulfred, see Brooks and Kelly, *CantCC*, pp. 341–46.

139 'The freedom to Christ Church of Æthelbald, king of the Mercians, [and] of Archbishop Cuthbert'.

140 S 1458 (*Roch* 34).

141 For the significant of the 'salt of wisdom' in relation to baptism, see Henry Ansgar Kelly, *The Devil at Baptism: Ritual, Theology, and Drama* (Ithaca and London, 1985), esp. pp. 112, 116 and 204–7. Our thanks to Carolyn Twomey for advice regarding this matter.

142 S 646 (BCS 1347). Brooks, *The Early History of the Church*, pp. 224 and 354, n. 55.

A later hand, possibly of the tenth century, has added 'DEEĐANDUNE' ('concerning Edington')—the royal *tun* of *Edington* being the meeting place at which the transaction took place.[143] There do not appear to be any other endorsements that name the meeting place. Similarly, one of the aforementioned tenth- or eleventh-century additions to the dorse of a diploma of Wihtred, king of Kent, notes a new name for the settlement being sold: 'Nunc pigelmignc / tun'.[144] Again, this does not add details of the transaction typically found in vernacular endorsements (beneficiary, donor, land-size or location, and so on), but is information that a later user considered important and relevant to the use of the charter.

Given the prevalence of Old English within the endorsement corpus, the question then arises as to why scribes on occasion chose to write in Latin. In the case of 'sal sapientiae', this may represent a familiar liturgical phrase that was in some way pertinent to the document. In other cases, mention of saints was an opportunity for Latinity; Francesca Tinti has, for example, noted code-switching in Oswald's leases when referring to saints in otherwise vernacular passages, perhaps as a reference to the invocation of saints in prayers.[145] The contemporary endorsement to an eleventh-century single sheet from Winchester's Old Minster of a purportedly tenth-century royal diploma, reads: 'þis is ðæs landes boc æt duntune . / ðe eadred cyngc ednypon gebocade / scæ trinitate . 7 scæ petre . 7 paule / iNg to ealdan mynstre : —'.[146] Here the scribe switches to Latin—*trinitate* in the ablative—in an otherwise vernacular endorsement. See, too, the small endorsement added to a single-sheet diploma of King Eadred in a hand of the eleventh century, which states: *sɔs ODO* ('s*anct*us Odo').[147]

143 P. H. Sawyer, 'The Royal tun in Pre-Conquest England', in *Ideal and Reality in Frankish and Anglo-Saxon Society*, eds Patrick Wormald, Donald Bullough, and Roger Collins (Oxford, 1983), pp. 273–300, at 293.

144 For more on this endorsement, see above, pp. 253–54.

145 Francesca Tinti, 'Writing Latin and Old English in Tenth-Century England', in *Writing, Kingship and Power in Anglo-Saxon England*, eds Rory Naismith and David A. Woodman (Oxford, 2017), pp. 303–27, at 325.

146 S 540 (BCS 862): 'This is the landbook for Downton that King Eadred granted again to within the Old Minster of the Holy Trinity and Saint[s] Peter and Paul'.

147 S 546 (*CantCC* 120). We are grateful to Colleen Curran for her guidance on dating here. The endorsement refers to Archbishop Oda of Canterbury, who along with his community was the beneficiary of this diploma. Note the spelling of his name, *Odo*, which is also found in the main body of the charter; Brooks and Kelly identify this as a continental form: *CantCC*, pp. 941–42. The addition of Oda's name to the dorse is perhaps to reinforce a saintly connection with the text after his canonization, to reaffirm saintly ownership and protection of the property—a 'saintly landlord'. The use of Latin in this context might reinforce the authority of this association. We are grateful to Alison Hudson

However, perhaps the most striking pattern in Latin endorsement practices is the fact that most surviving specimens are found on non-contemporary single sheets, sometimes added at the point of production. The use of Latin endorsements thus perhaps reflects a desire to confer authority on these later copies, or perhaps even a misguided attempt at archaizing. In this regard, a tenth-century single sheet from Canterbury is particularly emblematic. This forged document purports to record a seventh-century grant of 70 hides across Sussex, including at Pagham, to Bishop Wilfrid and a further ten to the community of St Andrew at *Wedringmutha*. It has two pre-Conquest endorsements.[148] The first is a typical single place-name ('+PACGAN HAMM'), written contemporaneously with the production of the sheet, perhaps by the main text scribe and perhaps taken from the scribe's model.[149] A second endorsement, probably also written in the tenth century, reads: '+ Uuilfridus episcop' / cartulam hanc . Multi / modasque et humilli / mas theodoro archiepis / copo in xpo salutes :.'[150] This records Wilfrid's supposed later gift of the charter to Archbishop Theodore and constitutes the first explicit mention of Pagham in connection with Canterbury, solidifying its claim on the estate.[151] This text may be an adaptation of an earlier fabrication; Susan Kelly suggests that the scribe inserted 'an immunity clause and a statement of powers permitting the beneficiary to alienate the land'.[152] It is this addition to which the endorsement refers. As with several previous examples, this endorsement adds further information not contained within the body of the charter. To do so in Latin, moreover, was perhaps to enhance the antiquated character of the document.

To sum up, the use of Latin in endorsements in the seventh and eighth centuries is consistent with the overall dominance of Latin in documentary production at that time. The appearance of Latin in endorsements produced later in the pre-Conquest period might in some instances indicate that a scribe was aiming to give an appearance of age.[153] While many of the Latin and

---

for useful discussion of the relationship between saints and monastic property in charters and for sharing her work with us at an unpublished stage. For the notion of 'undying landlords', see David Rollason, *Saints and Relics in Anglo-Saxon England* (Oxford, 1989), p. 196.

148 S 230 (*CantCC* 3).

149 Brooks and Kelly, *CantCC*, p. 273.

150 '+ Bishop Wilfred [gave] this charter and manifold and humble greetings in Christ to Archbishop Theodore'.

151 Brooks and Kelly, *CantCC*, p. 273; Kelly, *Sel*, p. 101.

152 Kelly, *Sel*, p. 103.

153 For similar attempts at archaizing using palaeographical rather than textual means, see Crick, 'Insular History?'; Crick, 'Script and the Sense of the Past'.

bilingual endorsements behave like typical vernacular endorsements, several other Latin endorsements function differently from the general vernacular types, adding extra information that is not strictly part of the original text; that is, they are typically not summaries of details of the transaction. Beyond this, however, there are few discernible trends.

Conclusion

In the present survey we have sought to demonstrate the most salient features of endorsement practices as they are attested by surviving Anglo-Saxon single-sheet charters. Further case studies could have been included in our discussion, and one could also extend this investigation to consider charters that do not survive in single-sheet forms. Any and all additional examples would only increase the considerable weight of evidence for the variety of ways with which scribes engaged with single sheets, both during their production and in later decades and centuries. What has been presented here is a framework for the chronology and nature of such activity, which, as we have seen, is overwhelmingly expressed in Old English. Indeed, it can be stated unambiguously that to a large extent endorsements are a vernacular phenomenon.

In several ways the history of endorsement practices mirrors wider developments in Anglo-Saxon documentary culture. Thus, while there is limited evidence for endorsing as an aspect of documentary activity in the seventh and eighth centuries—a period during which charters appear to have served a relatively limited number of functions—the practice of endorsing at the point of production emerges clearly in the early ninth century, a period in which we see new charter forms and expanded uses of the vernacular in documentary production more generally.[154] The development in the late 930s of standardized phrasing for such endorsements on royal diplomas, furthermore, comes from a decade when there is seemingly heightened interest in the performative value of such documents as 'instruments of royal government', at a time when

154 In focusing on the early ninth century for increased endorsing at the point of production, we must acknowledge the earlier evidence for the endorsing of letters by their main scribes, as represented by S 1428b.

evidence for centralized production of diplomatic at royal assemblies is at its very strongest.[155]

In terms of function, the vast majority of endorsements, whether the work of the original scribe or a later hand, serve to summarize the charter in some way. As we have seen, there is considerable variation in how a scribe might do this, and one is able to identify several instances when even a single scribe does not maintain the same endorsement practices across the production of different charters. There is a sense, therefore, of endorsements being not necessarily fundamental to the authentication of a document. Nor is text often added to the dorse of a single sheet unthinkingly, without relevance, a specific purpose or appropriate adaption of phrasing. On most occasions such texts distil the charter down to a feature that is salient to its use and value for an endorser and, by doing so, they conceal the complexities of the agreements that the documents record. Beyond the standardized formula that emerges in the late 930s, the majority summarize using the name of the land to which a charter relates, less often with the name of the benefactor, and very rarely with the name of a beneficiary—the latter of which would naturally be of less interest to most individuals, presumably being relevant on most occasions only if the single sheet was in the care of an individual who was contemporary with, but who was not, the beneficiary, especially if the agreement codified by the charter was not perpetual (such as a lease). Such summaries can, furthermore, offer insights into the conceptualizations of documents and the changing ways in which charters and the land to which they relate were managed over time. Thus, we have seen several endorsements that appear to attest to (modest) campaigns of archival organization; elsewhere we have evidence for the renaming of places within the landscape. What is perhaps their most consistent, collective feature, however, is their clear evidence for the continued importance of the single sheet over generations—emblematic of materiality as a crucial dimension of a documentary culture in which, perhaps not entirely unrelatedly, the evidence for cartulary production is late and restricted.

There remain several aspects to endorsements that, due to space, we have not addressed fully here. Perhaps most notably, we have said little about the visual features of endorsements, especially how their script, layout, and formality compare with text on the face of the single sheet. Here we will only say that there is indeed variation, particularly as regards to script choice and its relationship to language choice. Another area worthy of further consideration is the relationship endorsements may have with seals. It is certainly striking

155 Keynes, 'Church Councils', p. 62.

that those Anglo-Saxon charters most closely associated with seals, writs, were not endorsed. This is perhaps a reflection of their relatively ephemeral nature, yet it may also be productive to think further in terms of the roles that such elements played in the folding and conveyance of documents of various kinds. Finally, this material would certainly merit further analysis in the light of comparison with documentary practices elsewhere in early medieval Europe. For this, we will limit ourselves to saying that the most immediate place of comparison is probably the St Gall archive, famously furnished by a wealth of eighth-, ninth-, and tenth-century single-sheet charters, and that comparison with this archive primarily reminds us of what Anglo-Saxon endorsements are not. Although a considerable number of Anglo-Saxon examples suggest attempts at archival organization, probably on most occasions on a relatively small scale, none point towards comparably complex systems of administrative organization as do the Roman numerals found on many St Gall dorses.[156] Moreover, in contrast to the many working notes (*Vorakte*) found on the dorses of St Gall's single sheets,[157] almost no Anglo-Saxon endorsements appear to have been written before the main text of the charter. This at once reminds us of the gap inherent in the extant Anglo-Saxon charter corpus between composition and single-sheet production—a process that is largely unknown to us today but in which, evidently, the dorse of a single sheet did not play a role.[158]

156 Peter Erhart, '*Carta ista amalfitana est et nescitur legere*: The Charters of Cava dei Tirreni and St Gall and their Evidence for Early Medieval Archival Practice', *Gazette du livre médiéval* 50 (2007), 27–39, at p. 35. For a broader overview of endorsement practices at St Gall, see Paul Staerkle, *Die Rückvermerke der ältern St.Galler Urkunden* (St Gall, 1966).

157 Matthew Innes, 'Archives, Documents and Landowners in Carolingian Francia', in *Documentary Culture and the Laity in the Early Middle Ages*, eds Warren C. Brown, Marios Costambeys, Matthew Innes, and Adam Kosto (Cambridge, 2013), pp. 152–88, at 156–57. See also Mark Mersiowsky, *Die Urkunde in der Karolingerzeit. Originale, Urkundenpraxis und politische Kommunikation*, MGH Schriften 60, 2 vols (Wiesbaden, 2015), 2:846–49, and for more general comment on Carolingian archival practices, see 2:915–21. Also see Annina Seiler within this volume.

158 We would like to thank Edward Roberts and Francesca Tinti and the anonymous reviewers for invaluable feedback on an earlier version of this chapter. The completion of this chapter was assisted by a Leverhulme Trust Early Career Fellowship awarded to Robert Gallagher.

Appendix

Within this appendix we provide a list of all the single-sheet charters that we have included within our study, along with a summary of the endorsements added to these sheets of parchment during the Anglo-Saxon period. As summarized above, we have divided the single sheets into two groups, represented by the two tables within this appendix: (1) single sheets that are likely to be originals, i.e. they were produced at the time of the issuing of the charter; (2) single sheets that were produced after the purported date of issue. In the case of the second group, we have only included single sheets that are likely to have been produced before *c.*1050, given the uncertainties surrounding the exact date of production of many non-contemporary single sheets. Our dating, and indeed, all of the information we include in these tables, has been guided by earlier scholarship.[159] In both tables, each row represents an individual single sheet. We have ordered the entries in alphabetical order of archives in which the material has a known medieval provenance. Within each archive group, we have then listed the single sheets in chronological order of purported date of issue.

In Table 7.1 there are six columns. From left to right, the first four columns contain the following information: the modern shelfmark of the single sheet; the Sawyer number of the related charter text(s); the medieval archive and the modern edition of the charter text(s); the date of issue of the charter. As regards to the modern edition information, we include the details of only one critical edition, though in several cases the charter has been edited on multiple occasions. When available, we give precedence to the British Academy editions, which implicitly provide the name of the medieval archive; see the front of this volume for a list of abbreviations. Abbreviated references not found in this list are explained in footnotes.

The remaining two columns of Table 7.1 provide the endorsement information. In the left-hand side of the endorsement columns we include details of the date and language of endorsements. Each individual pre-Conquest endorsement is indicated by its own date; even if two endorsements both date to the same century, they are individually represented and separated from one another with a semi-colon (thus 's. x; s.x' indicates two separate tenth-century endorsements). Note that the dating of endorsements is based almost entirely on palaeographic features. In many cases our dating is no more specific than to a century, though for some specimens we have provided more accurate dates, having been guided by previous scholarship. More specific details of date can often be deduced from our comments in the right-hand column, in which

159 We are particularly indebted to the British Academy editions of Anglo-Saxon charters, as well as the following publications and resources: *Facsimiles of Anglo-Saxon Charters*, ed. Keynes; Crick, 'Insular History?'; Peter A. Stokes, *English Vernacular Minuscule from Æthelred to Cnut, circa 990–circa 1035* (Woodbridge, 2014); *DigiPal*.

we state whether the endorsement is possibly the work of the scribe of the main text of the charter. Much like in the left-hand column, the details for individual endorsements are separated by a semi-colon, and they are listed in the same order as in the left-hand column. Here it should be noted that the 'main texts' of some single sheets are evidently the work of multiple scribes, all of whom we consider to be 'main scribes'. Note also that we have stated that some endorsements look to be 'contemp.' (i.e. contemporary) with the 'main scribe'; in some of these cases, the endorsement may even be the work of the 'main scribe', possibly writing, for example, less calligraphically than on the face of the single sheet.

As to language, we indicate in the left-hand endorsement column with (L) those endorsements that are in Latin and with (M) those endorsements that are a mix of Latin and Old English; if the entry lacks either an (L) or (M), this means that the endorsement is in Old English.

TABLE 7.1 Possible original single-sheet charters

Shelfmark	Sawyer number	Archive and modern edition	Date	Date and languages of endorsement(s)	Endorsement(s) by main scribe(s)?
Dorchester, Dorset History Centre, D-FSI	736	Abbotsbury (BCS 1165)	965	s. x	Yes
Dorchester, Dorset History Centre, D-FSI	961	Abbotsbury (KCD 741)	1024	s. xi	Yes
Dorchester, Dorset History Centre, D-FSI	1004	Abbotsbury (KCD 772)	1044	s. xi; s. xi	Yes; No
Dorchester, Dorset History Centre, D-FSI	1602f	Abbotsbury (Keynes, p. 229)[a]	s. xi^{med}		
Dorchester, Dorset History Centre, D-FSI	[none]	Abbotsbury (*OSFacs* ii. Earl of Ilchester 5)	s. xi^{med}		
BL,[b] Cotton Augustus ii.44	552	*Abing* 44	949	s. x; s. x	Contemp.; Contemp.

a Keynes = Simon Keynes, 'The Lost Cartulary of Abbotsbury', *ASE* 18 (1989), 207–43.

b Note that in this appendix BL = London, British Library.

TABLE 7.1 Possible original single-sheet charters (*cont.*)

Shelfmark	Sawyer number	Archive and modern edition	Date	Date and languages of endorsement(s)	Endorsement(s) by main scribe(s)?
BL, Cotton Augustus ii.41	594	*Abing* 54	956	s. x	Contemp.
BL, Cotton Augustus ii.45	624	*Abing* 65	956	s. x	Yes
BL, Cotton Augustus ii.43	618	*Abing* 66	956	s. x	Contemp.
BL, Cotton Augustus ii.40	687	*Abing* 86	960	s. x	Yes
BL, Cotton Augustus ii.39	690	*Abing* 87	961		
BL, Cotton Augustus ii.38	876	*Abing* 124	993		
BL, Cotton Augustus ii.29	1171	Barking (BCS 81)	685×693	s. viii (L); s. x; s. x; unknown	Contemp.; No; No; No
Chelmsford, Essex Record Office, D/DP T 209	704	Buckfast (Rose-Troup 1929, pp. 250–53)[c]	962		
Stafford, William Salt Library, 84/2/41	768	*Burt* 23	968	s. x	Yes
Stafford, William Salt Library, 84/4/41	878	*Burt* 27	996		
Stafford, William Salt Library, 84/5/41	922	*Burt* 32	1009	s. xi	Possibly
BL, Harley Charter 43 C 3	703	Bury St Edmunds (BCS 1082)	962		

c Rose-Troup 1929 = Frances Rose-Troup, 'The New Edgar Charter and the South Hams', *Transactions of the Devonshire Association* 61 (1929), 249–80.

TABLE 7.1 Possible original single-sheet charters (*cont.*)

Shelfmark	Sawyer number	Archive and modern edition	Date	Date and languages of endorsement(s)	Endorsement(s) by main scribe(s)?
BL, Cotton Augustus ii.85	1489	Bury St Edmunds (*ASWills* 26)	1035×1040		
BL, Cotton Augustus ii.84	1225	Bury St Edmunds (*ASChart* 93)	*c.*1040		
BL, Cotton Augustus ii.80	1071	Bury St Edmunds (*ASWrits* 11)	1044×1065 (?1044)		
BL, Cotton Augustus ii.49	1084	Bury St Edmunds (*ASWrits* 24)	1065x1066		
BL, Cotton Augustus ii.2	8	*CantCC* 2	679		
BL, Stowe Charter 1	19	*CantCC* 5	697 or 712	s. x or xi; s. x or xi (M); s. x or xi	No; No; No
BL, Cotton Augustus ii.18	1428b	Christ Church, Canterbury (*LondStP* Appendix I)	704×705	s.viii (L)	Probably
BL, Cotton Augustus ii.91	23	*CantCC* 10	732	?s. x^2	No
BL, Cotton Augustus ii.101	24	*CantCC* 11	741	s. x or xi	No
BL, Stowe Charter 3	31	*CantCC* 14	748×762	s. viii; s. x or xi	Uncertain; No
BL, Cotton Augustus ii.26, 27	106; 1186a	*CantCC* 16	767, 799×801		
BL, Stowe Charter 5	123	*CantCC* 22	785	?s. ix/x	No

TABLE 7.1 Possible original single-sheet charters (*cont.*)

Shelfmark	Sawyer number	Archive and modern edition	Date	Date and languages of endorsement(s)	Endorsement(s) by main scribe(s)?
Canterbury, D&C, ChAnt M. 340	128	*CantCC* 24	788	s. ix or x	No
BL, Stowe Charter 7	155	*CantCC* 29	799	?s. x	No
BL, Cotton Augustus ii.61	1431a	*CantCC* 32	803		
Canterbury, D&C, ChAnt C. 1	1431b MS A	*CantCC* 33	803		
BL, Cotton Augustus ii.55	1259	*CantCC* 36	805		
BL, Stowe Charter 9	161	*CantCC* 37	805	s. x or xi	No
BL, Cotton Augustus ii.87	40	*CantCC* 38	805	s. x or xi	No
BL, Cotton Augustus ii.100	41 MS A	*CantCC* 39	805×807	s. x	No
BL, Stowe Charter 8	41 MS B; 1500	*CantCC* 39	805×807	s. xi	No
BL, Cotton Augustus ii.98	163	*CantCC* 40	808	s. ix; s. ix	Contemp.; Contemp.
BL, Cotton Augustus ii.47	1264	*CantCC* 43	811		
BL, Cotton Augustus ii.10	168 MS A	*CantCC* 44	811	?s. x; ?s. x/xi	No; No
Canterbury, D&C, ChAnt C. 1278	169	*CantCC* 46	812	s. x	No
BL, Cotton Augustus ii.74	177	*CantCC* 48	814	s. xi	No
BL, Stowe Charter 12	178	*CantCC* 51	815	s. ix	Contemp.
BL, Cotton Augustus ii.93	186	*CantCC* 53	822	s. x	No

TABLE 7.1 Possible original single-sheet charters (*cont.*)

Shelfmark	Sawyer number	Archive and modern edition	Date	Date and languages of endorsement(s)	Endorsement(s) by main scribe(s)?
BL, Cotton Augustus ii.75	187	*CantCC* 54	823	s. ix	Yes
BL, Stowe Charter 13	1266	*CantCC* 55	824	s. ix	No (perhaps contemp.)
BL, Stowe Charter 14	1434	*CantCC* 56	824	?s. x; s. x² or xi¹	No; No
BL, Cotton Augustus ii.78	1436 MS A1	*CantCC* 59	825 [? for *c.*827]	s. ix; s. x	No (perhaps contemp.); No
BL, Stowe Charter 15	1436 A2	*CantCC* 59	825 [? for *c.*827]	s. ix	No (perhaps contemp.)
BL, Cotton Augustus ii.94	188	*CantCC* 60	831	s. ix	Yes
BL, Cotton Augustus ii.72	1268	*CantCC* 62	825×832	s. ix	Yes
BL, Cotton Augustus ii.21	1438 A1	*CantCC* 69	838	?s. x	No
BL, Cotton Augustus ii.20	1438 A2	*CantCC* 69	838–9		
BL, Cotton Augustus ii.37	1438 A3	*CantCC* 69	839	s. ix; s. x	Yes; No
BL, Cotton Augustus ii.64	1482	*CantCC* 70	833×839, ?835	s. ix	Yes
BL, Stowe Charter 17	293	*CantCC* 73	843	s. x; s. x/xi	No; No
Canterbury, D&C, ChAnt C. 1280	204	*CantCC* 75	844×845		
BL, Stowe Charter 18	1194	*CantCC* 76	845	s. x or xi	No
BL, Cotton Augustus ii.60	296	*CantCC* 77	845	s. ix	No (perhaps contemp.)
BL, Cotton Augustus ii.42	1510	*CantCC* 78	845×853		

TABLE 7.1 Possible original single-sheet charters (*cont.*)

Shelfmark	Sawyer number	Archive and modern edition	Date	Date and languages of endorsement(s)	Endorsement(s) by main scribe(s)?
BL, Cotton Augustus ii.52	1195	*CantCC* 79	c.850		
BL, Cotton Augustus ii.71	316	*CantCC* 81	855	s. ix	Yes
BL, Cotton Augustus ii.66	328	*CantCC* 83	858	s. ix	Yes
BL, Cotton Augustus ii.92	1197	*CantCC* 84	843×863, ?843×859	s. ix	Yes
BL, Cotton Augustus ii.16	1196	*CantCC* 85	859 [? for *c.*853×858]	[one illegible word]	Uncertain
Canterbury, D&C, ChAnt M. 14	332	*CantCC* 86	863	s. x	No
Canterbury, D&C, ChAnt M. 369	1199	*CantCC* 87	858×865		
BL, Stowe Charter 16	1269	*CantCC* 88	863×867	s. ix; s. ix	No; Uncertain
BL, Cotton Augustus ii.95	338	*CantCC* 89	867	s. ix (M); [illegible text]	No; Uncertain
BL, Cotton Augustus ii.19	1200	*CantCC* 90	863×870, ?867×870		
BL, Cotton Augustus ii.17	1204	*CantCC* 91	888 [? for 867]	s. ix	Yes
BL, Cotton Augustus ii.76	214	*CantCC* 92	869		
BL, Stowe Charter 19	344	*CantCC* 93	873	s. ix	Yes
BL, Stowe Charter 20	1508	*CantCC* 96	871×889	s. ix	Yes
Canterbury, D&C, ChAnt H. 130	1276	*CantCC* 98	889	s. ix/x or x^{1}; s. x	No; No
Canterbury, D&C, ChAnt F. 150	350	*CantCC* 99	898	?s. x^{1}; ? s. x^{1}	No; No

TABLE 7.1 Possible original single-sheet charters (*cont.*)

Shelfmark	Sawyer number	Archive and modern edition	Date	Date and languages of endorsement(s)	Endorsement(s) by main scribe(s)?
BL, Stowe Charter 22	367	*CantCC* 101	903	s. x (L)	Uncertain
BL, Stowe Charter 23	1288	*CantCC* 102	['924' (for 905 or 920, probably 905)]		
Canterbury, D&C, ChAnt C. 1282	1445	*CantCC* 104	899×924	s. x	Contemp.
BL, Cotton Augustus ii.65	425	*CantCC* 106	934		
BL, Cotton Augustus ii.23	447	*CantCC* 107	939	s. x	Yes
BL, Cotton Augustus ii.62	464	*CantCC* 110	940	s. x	Yes
BL, Stowe Charter 24	512	*CantCC* 112	943	s. x	Contemp.
BL, Stowe Charter 25	497	*CantCC* 114	944	s. x	Yes
BL, Cotton Augustus ii.73	510	*CantCC* 115	946	s. x	Contemp.
BL, Cotton Augustus ii.83	528	*CantCC* 116	947	s. x	Yes
BL, Stowe Charter 26	535	*CantCC* 118	948		
Canterbury, D&C, ChAnt R. 14	546 MS A	*CantCC* 120	949	s. x; s. x/xi (M)	Contemp.?; No
BL, Stowe Charter 28	1211	*CantCC* 124	c.959	s. xi (L)	No
BL, Stowe Charter 29	717	*CantCC* 126	963	s. x; s. x/xi	Yes; No
BL, Stowe Charter 30	1215	*CantCC* 128	968	s. x	Yes
BL, Cotton Augustus ii.15	1454	*CantCC* 133	990×992		

TABLE 7.1 Possible original single-sheet charters (*cont.*)

Shelfmark	Sawyer number	Archive and modern edition	Date	Date and languages of endorsement(s)	Endorsement(s) by main scribe(s)?
Canterbury, D&C, ChAnt B. 1	939	*CantCC* 137	995×999		
BL, Stowe Charter 35	905	*CantCC* 139	1003 [for 1002]	s. xi	Yes
BL, Stowe Charter 37	1503 MS A1	*CantCC* 142	1014	s. xi	Contemp.?
Canterbury, D&C, ChAnt H. 68	1503 MS A2	*CantCC* 142	1014		
BL, Stowe Charter 38	950	*CantCC* 144	1018	s. xi	Yes
Canterbury, D&C, ChAnt S. 458	1220	*CantCC* 148	1013×1020 [?1013×1018]		
BL, Stowe Charter 41	974	*CantCC* 155	1035	s. xi	Yes
Canterbury, D&C, ChAnt R. 17	1390	*CantCC* 161	1020×1038		
BL, Cotton Augustus ii.90	1467	*CantCC* 164	after 1038×1040		
Canterbury, D&C, ChAnt C. 70	1530 A1	*CantCC* 166	1042×1043		
BL, Cotton Augustus ii.68	1044	*CantCC* 167	1042×1044		
BL, Cotton Augustus ii.59	1005	*CantCC* 168	1044	s. xi	Yes
Canterbury, D&C, ChAnt A. 207	1472	*CantCC* 169	1044×1045		
BL, Cotton Augustus ii.70	1471	*CantCC* 170	1045×1047		
BL, Cotton Augustus ii.35	1473	*CantCC* 171	1044×1048		
BL, Stowe Charter 42	1400	*CantCC* 172	1048×1050		

TABLE 7.1 Possible original single-sheet charters (*cont.*)

Shelfmark	Sawyer number	Archive and modern edition	Date	Date and languages of endorsement(s)	Endorsement(s) by main scribe(s)?
Canterbury, D&C, ChAnt C. 1281	1019	*CantCC* (ex Bodmin, St Petroc's) (KCD 787 (omits bounds))	1049	s. xi	Yes
BL, Campbell Charter xxi.5	1088	*CantCC* 179	1052×1066 [? for 1052]		
Oxford, Bodleian Library, Eng. hist. a. 2, no. VI	892	Coventry (Napier and Stevenson 8)[d]	998	s. x	Yes
BL, Cotton Augustus ii.22	898	Coventry (KCD 705)	1001	s. xi; s. xi	Yes; No
BL, Cotton Augustus ii.4	114	Evesham (BCS 230)	779	s. ix/x	No
BL, Cotton Augustus ii.63	495	Evesham (BCS 792)	944		
BL, Cotton Augustus ii.24	977	Evesham (KCD 736)	1021×1023	s. xi	No
Exeter, D&C, 2522	684	Exeter (BCS 1056)	960	s. x	Yes
London, The National Archives, PRO 30/26/11	795	Exeter (ex Crediton) (BCS 1303)	974	s. x; s. xi	Yes; No
Exeter, D&C, 2523	830	Exeter (ex Crediton) (Rose-Troup 1942)[e]	976	s. x	Yes

d Napier and Stevenson = *The Crawford Collection of Early Charters and Documents*, eds A. S. Napier and W. H. Stevenson (Oxford, 1895).

e Rose-Troup 1942 = F. Rose-Troup, 'Crediton Charters of the Tenth Century', *Transactions of the Devonshire Association* 74 (1942), 237–61, at pp. 255–56.

TABLE 7.1 Possible original single-sheet charters (*cont.*)

Shelfmark	Sawyer number	Archive and modern edition	Date	Date and languages of endorsement(s)	Endorsement(s) by main scribe(s)?
Oxford, Bodleian Library, Eng. hist. a. 2, no. XIV	1296	Exeter (ex Crediton,? ex St German's) (*Councils and Synods* 35.II)[f]	981×988		
Exeter, D&C, 2070	880	Exeter (ex Bodmin) (KCD 686)	994	s. x	No
BL, Stowe Charter 34	890	Exeter (ex Crediton) (*OSFacs* iii.35)	997	s. x	Yes
Oxford, Bodleian Library, Eng. hist. a. 2, no. XIII	1492	Exeter (ex Crediton) (Napier and Stevenson 10)	1008×1012		
BL, Cotton Augustus ii.69	963	Exeter (ex Crediton) (KCD 744)	1031	s. xi; ?s. xi (L); ?s. xi	Yes; No; No
Exeter, D&C, 2525	971 MS 1	Exeter/Christ Church, Canterbury (? ex Crediton) (Davidson, pp. 290–2)[g]	1031	s. xi; s. xi	Yes; No
Exeter, D&C, 2526	1003	Exeter (Davidson, pp. 292–5)	1044	s. xi	Yes

f *Councils and Synods* = *Councils and Synods with Other Documents relating to the English Church, I: A.D. 871–1204*, eds D. Whitelock, M. Brett, and C. N. L. Brooke (Oxford, 1981).

g Davidson = James B. Davidson, 'On Some Anglo-Saxon Charters at Exeter', *Journal of the British Archaeological Association* 39 (1883), 259–303.

TABLE 7.1 Possible original single-sheet charters (*cont.*)

Shelfmark	Sawyer number	Archive and modern edition	Date	Date and languages of endorsement(s)	Endorsement(s) by main scribe(s)?
Exeter, D&C, 2072	1021	Exeter (*Councils and Synods* 71)	1050	s. xi	Yes
Oxford, Bodleian Library, Eng. hist. a. 2, no. IIa	1546b	Exeter (ex Crediton) (Hooke, pp. 86–7)[h]	s. xi	s. xi; s. xi	No; No
Exeter, D&C, 2530	1547	Exeter (ex Crediton) (Hooke, p. 217)	s. xi	s. xi	No
Longleat, Marquess of Bath, Muniment 10565	563	*Glast* 44	955	?s. xi; ?s. xi	No; No
BL, Cotton Charters viii.27	221	Much Wenlock (BCS 587)	901	s. x	No
Taunton, Somerset Record Office, DD/SAS PR 502	884	Muchelney (Bates 4)[i]	995		
Paris, Archives nationales, Cartons de rois, K 19, no. 6	1105	Paris, Saint-Denis (*ASWrits* 55)	1053×1057		
Paris, Archives nationales, Cartons de rois, K 19, no. 6	1028	Paris, Saint-Denis (*ASWrits*, pp. 538-39)	1059		
Oxford, Bodleian Library, Eng. hist. a. 2, no. V	646	probably Ely (BCS 1347)	957	s. x; ?s. x (M)	Yes; No

h Hooke = *Pre-Conquest Charter Bounds of Devon and Cornwall*, ed. and trans. Della Hooke (Woodbridge, 1994).

i Bates = *Two Cartularies of the Benedictine Abbeys of Muchelney and Athelney in the County of Somerset*, ed. E. H. Bates (London, 1899).

TABLE 7.1 Possible original single-sheet charters (*cont.*)

Shelfmark	Sawyer number	Archive and modern edition	Date	Date and languages of endorsement(s)	Endorsement(s) by main scribe(s)?
Hereford, D. C., A. 4067	1270	probably Hertford (BCS 429)	840×852	?	No
BL, Cotton Charters viii.34	35	*Roch* 9	778	s. x	No
BL, Cotton Charters viii.32	331	*Roch* 25	862		
BL, Cotton Charters viii.33	671	*Roch* 29	955 for ?973	s. x	Contemp.
BL, Cotton Charters viii.14	864	*Roch* 30	987		
BL, Cotton Charters viii.20	1458	*Roch* 34	964×988	s. x (L); s. x	Contemp.; No
Chichester, West Sussex Record Office, Cap I/17/2	1184	*Sel* 11	780	s. viii; s. viii	No; No
Princeton, Scheide Library, MS.140	1497	*StAlb* 7	956×1002		
Oxford, , Eng. hist. a. 2, no. VII (25rv)	916	*StAlb* 12	1007	s. xi	Yes
BL, Cotton Charters viii.39	1861	Uncertain (Mercia?) [unedited]	796×821		
BL, Cotton Charters viii.4	264	Uncertain (Bedwyn?) (BCS 225)	778		
BL, Cotton Charters viii.3	96	Uncertain [Malmesbury ?] (BCS 181)	757	?s. x	No
BL, Harley Charter 43 C 7	1379	Uncertain (KCD 691)	995 (for 994)	s. xi	No

TABLE 7.1 Possible original single-sheet charters (*cont.*)

Shelfmark	Sawyer number	Archive and modern edition	Date	Date and languages of endorsement(s)	Endorsement(s) by main scribe(s)?
Burton-on-Trent, Burton-on-Trent Museum, Muniments 3	1863	Uncertain [unedited]	c.987		
BL, Cotton Charters viii.28	706	Uncertain (BCS 1083)	962	s. x	Yes
Wells, D. & C., Cathedral Charter I	677	*Wells* 31	958	s. x	Contemp.
London, Westminster Abbey, W. A. M. viii	1447	Westminster (BCS 1063)	968×988	s. x	Yes
BL, Stowe Charter 32	1451	Westminster (BCS 1290)	978		
BL, Stowe Charter 36	1487	Westminster (*ASWills* 13)	975×1016	s. xi	No
BL, Stowe Charter 33	1450 MS 1	Westminster (*OSFacs* iii.34)	986		
Oxford, Bodleian Library, Eng. hist. a. 2, no. XII	1522	Westminster (Napier and Stevenson 9)	998	s. xi	Yes
London, Westminster Abbey, W. A. M. xviii	1125	Westminster (*ASWrits* 81)	1049×1066		
Hertford, Hertfordshire Archives and Local Studies, DE/Lw/Z22/4	1031	Westminster (Barlow)[j]	1060		

j Barlow = Frank Barlow, *Edward the Confessor* (London, 1970), pp. 334–35.

TABLE 7.1 Possible original single-sheet charters (*cont.*)

Shelfmark	Sawyer number	Archive and modern edition	Date	Date and languages of endorsement(s)	Endorsement(s) by main scribe(s)?
London, Westminster Abbey, W. A. M. xii	1140	Westminster (*ASWrits* 96)	1062×1066		
Winchester, Winchester College Muniments, 12092	1417	*WinchNM* 9	924×933	s. x	Contemp.
Winchester, Winchester College Muniments, 12091	470	*WinchNM* 12	940	s. x	Yes
Winchester, Winchester College Muniments, 12093	956	*WinchNM* 33	1019	s. xi (M); s. xi (L)	Contemp.; No
BL, Cotton Charters viii.36	298	WinchOM (BCS 451)[k]	846	s. x	No
BL, Cotton Charters viii.16	416; 1533	WinchOM (BCS 677 and 679; *ASChart* 26)	931	s. x	Contemp.
BL, Cotton Charters viii.22	449	WinchOM (BCS 734)	939	s. x	Contemp.
BL, Cotton Charters viii.12	636	WinchOM (BCS 926)	956	s. x	Yes
Winchester, DC/A1/5	649	WinchOM (BCS 1003)	957	s. x	Yes
BL, Harley Charter 43 C 2	697	WinchOM (BCS 1072)	961	s. x; s. x/xi	Yes; No
BL, Harley Charter 43 C 8	994	WinchOM (KCD 763)	1042	s. xi	No

k WinchOM = Winchester, Old Minster. An edition of the charters of this archive is currently being prepared by Alexander R. Rumble.

TABLE 7.1 Possible original single-sheet charters (*cont.*)

Shelfmark	Sawyer number	Archive and modern edition	Date	Date and languages of endorsement(s)	Endorsement(s) by main scribe(s)?
BL, Cotton Charters viii.9	1008	WinchOM (KCD 781)	1045	s. xi	Yes
BL, Add. Ch. 19789	56	Worcester (BCS 187)	759	s. x	No
BL, Cotton Augustus ii.3	89	Worcester (BCS 154)	736	?s. ix; ?s. xi	No; No
BL, Add. Ch. 19790	139	Worcester (BCS 274)	793×796	s. xi	No
BL, Harley Charter 83 A 1	173	Worcester (BCS 343)	814	s. ix; ?s. ix	Yes; No
BL, Cotton Augustus ii.9	190	Worcester (BCS 416)	836	s. ix; s. ix; s. ix; ?s. ix	Contemp.; Contemp.; Contemp.; No
BL, Add. Ch. 19791	1281	Worcester (BCS 609)	904	s. x; s. x	Yes; No
BL, Add. Ch. 19793	772	Worcester (BCS 1229)	969	s. x	Yes
BL, Add. Ch. 19792	1326	Worcester (*ASChart* 46)	969	?s. x	No
BL, Cotton Augustus ii.6	786	Worcester (ex Pershore) (Stokes)[l]	972	s. x^2 (L)	Uncertain
BL, Add. Ch. 19794	1347	Worcester (Earle, pp. 207–9)[m]	984	?s. xi	No

l Stokes = Peter A. Stokes, 'King Edgar's Charter for Pershore (AD 972)', *ASE* 37 (2008), 31–78, at pp. 43–53.
m Earle = *A Hand-Book to the Land-Charters, and Other Saxonic Documents*, ed. John Earle (Oxford, 1888).

TABLE 7.1 Possible original single-sheet charters (*cont.*)

Shelfmark	Sawyer number	Archive and modern edition	Date	Date and languages of endorsement(s)	Endorsement(s) by main scribe(s)?
BL, Harley Charter 83 A 2	1534	Worcester (*ASWills* 19)	*c.*1000	s. xi	Contemp.
BL, Add. Ch. 19795	1385	Worcester (Earle, pp. 234–5)	1003× 1016	?s. xi	Contemp.
BL, Cotton Charters viii.37	1460	Worcester (*ASChart* 83)	*c.*1010× 1023	s. xi	Contemp.
BL, Add. Ch. 19796	1423	Worcester (*ASChart* 81)	1016× 1023		
BL, Add. Ch. 19798	1393	Worcester (Earle, pp. 239–40)	1038	s. xi	Yes
BL, Add. Ch. 19797	1399	Worcester (*ASChart* 87)	1033× 1038		
BL, Add. Ch. 19799	1394	Worcester (*ASChart* 94)	1042	s. xi	Yes
BL, Add. Ch. 19800	1407	Worcester	1053× 1056	s. xi	Yes
BL, Add. Ch. 19801	1405	Worcester (Earle, pp. 247–8)	1058	s. xi	Contemp.
BL, Add. Ch. 19802	1156	Worcester (*ASWrits* 115)	1062		

The structure and information of Table 7.2 is much the same as Table 7.1, with one important difference: the date of the charter text does not represent the date of the single sheet, thus we have included an additional column for the latter. Much like with endorsements, the dating of non-contemporary single sheets is to a large extent based on palaeographic features, thus the dates we provide are broad, and they are in many cases the dates given in the respective editions.

TABLE 7.2 Non-contemporary single-sheet charters

Shelfmark	Sawyer number	Medieval archive and modern edition	Purported date of issue	Date of single sheet	Date and languages of endorsement(s)	Endorsement by main scribe?
BL, Cotton Augustus ii.33	587	*Abing* 70	956	s. xi	s. xi	Yes
BL, Harley Charter 43 C 4	1486; 1494	Bury St Edmunds (*ASWills* 14 and 15)	962×991; 1000×1002	s. xi		
BL, Cotton Augustus ii.86	230	*CantCC* 3	680	s. x^{med} or x^2	s. x; s. x (L)	Uncertain; No
BL, Cotton Augustus ii.88	21	*CantCC* 6	697 or 712	s. viii	s. x or xi	No
Maidstone, Centre for Kentish Studies, MS U 140	20	*CantCC* 7	699	s. ix^1	s. ix (L)	Yes
BL, Stowe Charter 2	22	*CantCC* 8	699×716	s. xi^1		
BL, Cotton Augustus ii.82	65	*CantCC* 9	704	s. viii^2 or ix^1	s. viii or ix	No
Canterbury, D&C, ChAnt M. 363	90	*CantCC* 12	742	s. ix^1	s. x (L)	No
BL, Cotton Augustus ii.99	110	*CantCC* 19	774	s. x^{med}	s. xi	No
BL, Stowe Charter 4	111	*CantCC* 20	774	s. x^2 or x/xi	s. x^2 or x/xi; s. xi	Yes; No
BL, Stowe Charter 6	125	*CantCC* 23	786	?s. xi	?s. xi	No

TABLE 7.2 Non-contemporary single-sheet charters (*cont.*)

Shelfmark	Sawyer number	Medieval archive and modern edition	Purported date of issue	Date of single sheet	Date and languages of endorsement(s)	Endorsement by main scribe?
Canterbury, D&C, ChAnt C. 69	132	*CantCC* 25	790 [? for 795]	s. x	s. x	No
BL, Cotton Augustus ii.97	153	*CantCC* 26	798	s. ix^1	s. ix^1	Yes
BL, Cotton Augustus ii.96	156	*CantCC* 30	799	s. x^{ex} or xi		
Canterbury, D&C, ChAnt C. 196	1431b MS B	*CantCC* 33	803	s. xi^1		
BL, Cotton Augustus ii.79	1188	*CantCC* 42	*c*.798×810	s. ix^1	s. ix	No (but possibly contemp.)
BL, Stowe Charter 10	168 MS B	*CantCC* 44	811	s. x^2 or x/xi		
BL, Stowe Charter 11	175 MS B1	*CantCC* 49	814	s. x	s. x	Contemp.
BL, Cotton Augustus ii.77	175 MS B2	*CantCC* 49	814	?s. x^2	?s. x	No
Canterbury, D&C, ChAnt C. 1279	282	*CantCC* 61	845 [for *c*.825×832, ?830]	?s. x^{ex} or xi^1		
BL, Cotton Augustus ii.102	270	*CantCC* 65	733 [? for 833]	s. x^{med} or x^2	s. x	Possibly
BL Cotton Augustus ii.28	287	*CantCC* 71	839	s. ix^2		

TABLE 7.2 Non-contemporary single-sheet charters (*cont.*)

Shelfmark	Sawyer number	Medieval archive and modern edition	Purported date of issue	Date of single sheet	Date and languages of endorsement(s)	Endorsement by main scribe?
BL, Cotton Augustus ii.46	1862	*CantCC* 80	854	s. x^{med}		
BL, Cotton Augustus ii.89	1203	*CantCC* 94	875	s. ix/x	s. x; s. x/xi (L)	No; No
BL, Cotton Augustus ii.57	546 MS B	*CantCC* 120	949	s. x or xi	s. x or xi	No
BL, Cotton Augustus ii.34	1530 MS A2	*CantCC* 166	1042×1043	s. xi		
Oxford, Bodleian Library, Eng. hist. a. 2, no. III	405; 1387	Exeter (ex Crediton) (Napier and Stevenson, pp. 5–9)	930	s. x/xi		
BL, Cotton Augustus ii.31	421	Exeter (ex Crediton) (BCS 694)	933	s. x/xi	s. x/xi (L)	Yes
Longleat, Marquess of Bath, Muniment 10564	236	*Glast* 3	681	s. x	s. x	Yes
BL, Cotton Charters xvii.1	88	*Roch* 2	733	s. ix	s. x (L)	No
BL, Cotton Charters vi.4	266	*Roch* 11	761 (altered to 781)	s. ix/x		
BL, Cotton Charters viii.31	165	*Roch* 17	811	s. ix	s. x	No

TABLE 7.2 Non-contemporary single-sheet charters (*cont.*)

Shelfmark	Sawyer number	Medieval archive and modern edition	Purported date of issue	Date of single sheet	Date and languages of endorsement(s)	Endorsement by main scribe?
BL, Cotton Charters viii.30	280	*Roch* 19	838	s. x	s. x (M)	Yes
BL, Cotton Charters viii.29	327	*Roch* 24	?860	s. ix	s. x	No
Chichester, West Sussex Record Office, Cap I/17/1	43	*Sel* 4	775	s. x	s. x	Yes
BL, Cotton Charters viii.35	308	Uncertain (BCS 469)	854	s. xi	s. xi	Yes
BL, Add. 7138	1451a	Uncertain (St Augustine's, Canterbury?)	s. x^2	s. x^2		
BL, Cotton Charters viii.38	1539	Uncertain (Shaftesbury?) (*ASWills* 3)	c.950	s. xi		
London, Westminster Abbey, W. A. M. v	670	Westminster (BCS 1048)	951 for ?959	s. x		
London, Westminster Abbey, W. A. M. x	702	Westminster (BCS 1085)	962	s. x^{med}	s. x	Yes
London, Westminster Abbey, W. A. M. vii	753	Westminster (BCS 1198)	967	s. x^2		

TABLE 7.2 Non-contemporary single-sheet charters (*cont.*)

Shelfmark	Sawyer number	Medieval archive and modern edition	Purported date of issue	Date of single sheet	Date and languages of endorsement(s)	Endorsement by main scribe?
Edinburgh, University Library, Laing ch. 18	313	WinchOM (*ASChart* 8)	854	s. xi	s. xi	Contemp.
BL, Harley Charter 43 C 1	376	WinchOM (BCS 620)	909	s. x/xi	s. x/xi	Yes
BL, Cotton Charters viii.17	443	WinchOM (BCS 727)	938	s. xi	s. xi; ?	Yes; ?
BL, Cotton Charters viii.11	540	WinchOM (BCS 862)	948	s. xi	s. xi (M)	Contemp.
BL, Harley Charter 43 C 5	738	WinchOM (BCS 1176)	966	s. xi	s. xi	No (possibly contemp.)
BL, Harley Charter 43 C 6	801	WinchOM (BCS 1312)	975 [? for 974]	s. xi	s. xi; s. xi	Yes; No
BL, Add. Ch. 19788	67	Worcester (BCS 32)	624 [? for 674]	s. x	s. xi	No (possibly contemp.)
Worcester, Cathedral Muniments, B.1598	59	Worcester (BCS 203)	770	s. ix		
BL, Cotton Augustus ii.30	117	Worcester (BCS 234)	780	s. xi	s. xi; s. xi	No; No

Bibliography

Primary Sources

Anglo-Saxon Charters, ed. and trans. Agnes J. Robertson, 2nd ed. (Cambridge, 1956).

Anglo-Saxon Wills, ed. and trans. Dorothy Whitelock (Cambridge, 1930).

Anglo-Saxon Writs, ed. and trans. Florence E. Harmer (Manchester, 1952; 2nd ed. Stamford, 1989).

Cartularium Saxonicum: A Collection of Charters Relating to Anglo-Saxon History, ed. Walter de Gray Birch, 3 vols (London, 1885–99).

Chartae latinae antiquiores, eds Albert Bruckner et al., 118 vols (Olten et al., 1954–2019).

Charters of Abingdon Abbey, ed. S. E. Kelly, Anglo-Saxon Charters VII–VIII (Oxford, 2000).

Charters of Bath and Wells, ed. S. E. Kelly, Anglo-Saxon Charters 13 (Oxford, 2007).

Charters of Burton Abbey, ed. P. H. Sawyer, Anglo-Saxon Charters II (Oxford, 1979).

Charters of Christ Church Canterbury, eds N. P. Brooks and S. E. Kelly, Anglo-Saxon Charters 17–18 (Oxford, 2013).

Charters of Rochester, ed. A. Campbell, Anglo-Saxon Charters I (Oxford, 1973).

Charters of Selsey, ed. S. E. Kelly, Anglo-Saxon Charters VI (Oxford, 1998).

Charters of St Augustine's Abbey, Canterbury, ed. S. E. Kelly, Anglo-Saxon Charters IV (Oxford, 1995).

Charters of St Paul's, London, ed. S. E. Kelly, Anglo-Saxon Charters X (Oxford, 2004).

Charters of the New Minster, Winchester, ed. S. Miller, Anglo-Saxon Charters IX (Oxford, 2001).

Codex Diplomaticus Ævi Saxonici, ed. J. M. Kemble, 6 vols (London, 1839–48), paperback reprint, 6 vols (Cambridge, 2011).

Councils and Synods with Other Documents relating to the English Church, I: A.D. 871–1204, eds D. Whitelock, M. Brett, and C. N. L. Brooke (Oxford, 1981).

The Crawford Collection of Early Charters and Documents, eds A. S. Napier and W. H. Stevenson (Oxford, 1895).

Facsimiles of Anglo-Saxon Charters, ed. Simon Keynes, Anglo-Saxon Charters Supplementary Volume 1 (Oxford, 1991).

A Hand-Book to the Land-Charters, and Other Saxonic Documents, ed. John Earle (Oxford, 1888).

The Old English Illustrated Heptateuch British Museum Cotton Claudius B. IV, eds C. R. Dodwell and P. Clemoes (Copenhagen, 1974).

Pre-Conquest Charter Bounds of Devon and Cornwall, ed. and trans. Della Hooke (Woodbridge, 1994).

Two Cartularies of the Benedictine Abbeys of Muchelney and Athelney in the County of Somerset, ed. E. H. Bates (London, 1899).

Secondary Sources

Barlow, Frank, *Edward the Confessor* (London, 1970).

Birch, Walter de Gray, *The Anglo-Saxon Charter of Oslac, Duke of the South Saxons, A.D. 780* (London, 1892).

Brooks, Nicholas, *The Early History of the Church at Canterbury: Christ Church from 597 to 1066* (Leicester, 1984).

Chaplais, Pierre, 'The Authenticity of the Royal Anglo-Saxon Diplomas of Exeter', *Historical Research* 39 (1966), 1–34.

Chaplais, Pierre, 'The Letter from Bishop Wealdhere of London to Archbishop Brihtwold of Canterbury: The Earliest Original "Letter Close" Extant in the West', in *Medieval Scribes, Manuscripts and Libraries: Essays Presented to N. R. Ker*, eds M. B. Parkes and Andrew G. Watson (London, 1978), pp. 3–23.

Chaplais, Pierre, 'The Origin and Authenticity of the Royal Anglo-Saxon Diploma', *Journal of the Society of Archivists* 3 (1965), 48–61; reprinted in *Prisca Munimenta: Studies in Archival and Administrative History Presented to Dr A. E. J. Hollaender*, ed. Felicity Ranger (London, 1973), pp. 28–42.

Chaplais, Pierre, 'Some Early Anglo-Saxon Diplomas on Single Sheets: Originals or Copies?', *Journal of the Society of Archivists* 3 (1968), 315–36.

Crick, Julia, 'Historical Literacy in the Archive: Post-Conquest Imitative Copies of Pre-Conquest Charters and Some French Comparanda', in *The Long Twelfth-Century View of the Anglo-Saxon Past*, eds Martin Brett and David A. Woodman (Farnham, 2015), pp. 159–90.

Crick, Julia, 'Insular History? Forgery and the English Past in the Tenth Century', in *England and the Continent in the Tenth Century: Studies in Honour of Wilhelm Levison (1876–1947)*, eds David Rollason, Conrad Leyser, and Hannah Williams (Turnhout, 2010), pp. 515–44.

Crick, Julia, 'Script and the Sense of the Past in Anglo-Saxon England', in *Anglo-Saxon Traces*, eds Jane Roberts and Leslie Webster (Tempe, AZ, 2011), pp. 1–29.

Davidson, James B., 'On Some Anglo-Saxon Charters at Exeter', *Journal of the British Archaeological Association* 39 (1883), 259–303.

Drögereit, Richard, 'Gab es eine angelsächsische Königskanzlei?', *Archiv für Urkundenforschung* 13 (1935), 335–436.

Erhart, Peter, '*Carta ista amalfitana est et nescitur legere*: The Charters of Cava dei Tirreni and St Gall and their Evidence for Early Medieval Archival Practice', *Gazette du livre médiéval* 50 (2007), 27–39.

Gallagher, Robert, 'The Vernacular in Anglo-Saxon Charters: Expansion and Innovation in Ninth-Century England', *Historical Research* 91 (2018), 205–35.

Gallagher, Robert and Tinti, Francesca, 'Latin, Old English and Documentary Practice at Worcester from Wærferth to Oswald', *ASE* 46 (2019 for 2017), 271–325.

Griffith, Mark, 'Ælfric's Preface to Genesis: Genre, Rhetoric and the Origins of the *ars dictaminis*', ASE 29 (2000), 215–34.

Hart, Cyril, 'The *Codex Wintoniensis* and the King's *Haligdom*', in *Land, Church and People: Essays Presented to Professor H. P. R. Finberg*, ed. Joan Thirsk (Reading, 1970), pp. 7–38.

Hickes, G. and Wanley, H., *Antiquæ Literaturæ Septentrionalis Libri Duo* (Oxford, 1703–5).

Innes, Matthew, 'Archives, Documents and Landowners in Carolingian Francia', in *Documentary Culture and the Laity in the Early Middle Ages*, eds Warren C. Brown, Marios Costambeys, Matthew Innes, and Adam Kosto (Cambridge, 2013), pp. 152–88.

Kelly, Henry Ansgar, *The Devil at Baptism: Ritual, Theology, and Drama* (Ithaca and London, 1985).

Kennedy, A. G., 'Disputes about *bocland*: The Forum for Their Adjudication', ASE 14 (1985), 175–95.

Ker, N. R., *Catalogue of Manuscripts Containing Anglo-Saxon* (Oxford, 1957).

Keynes, Simon, 'Anglo-Saxon Charters: Lost and Found', in *Myth, Rulership, Church and Charters: Essays in Honour of Nicholas Brooks*, eds Julia Barrow and Andrew Wareham (Aldershot, 2008), pp. 45–66.

Keynes, Simon, 'Church Councils, Royal Assemblies, and Anglo-Saxon Royal Diplomas', in *Kingship, Legislation and Power in Anglo-Saxon England*, eds Gale R. Owen-Crocker and Brian W. Schneider (Woodbridge, 2013), pp. 1–182.

Keynes, Simon, *The Diplomas of King Æthelred 'the Unready', 978–1016: A Study in Their Use as Historical Evidence* (Cambridge, 1980).

Keynes, Simon, 'The Lost Cartulary of Abbotsbury', ASE 18 (1989), 207–43.

Keynes, Simon, 'Regenbald the Chancellor (*sic*)', *Anglo-Norman Studies* 10 (1988), 185–222.

Lawton, Rebecca, 'Knowing Rome from Home: Reassessing Early Manuscript Witnesses of Papal Letters, Pilgrim Itineraries and Syllogae in England and Francia, c. 600–900' (unpublished PhD thesis, University of Leicester, 2019).

Lowe, Kathryn A., 'Lay Literacy in Anglo-Saxon England and the Development of the Chirograph', in *Anglo-Saxon Manuscripts and Their Heritage*, eds Philip Pulsiano and Elaine M. Treharne (Aldershot, 1998), pp. 161–204.

Mersiowsky, Mark, *Die Urkunde in der Karolingerzeit. Originale, Urkundenpraxis und politische Kommunikation*, MGH Schriften 60, 2 vols (Wiesbaden, 2015).

Padel, O. J., *Cornish Place-Name Elements* (Cambridge, 1985).

Parsons, M. P., 'Some Scribal Memoranda for Anglo-Saxon Charters of the Eighth and Ninth Centuries', *Mitteilungen des Österreichischen Instituts für Geschichtsforschung*, Erg. Bd. 14 (1939), 1–32.

Pelteret, David A. E., 'Two Old English Lists of Serfs', *Mediaeval Studies* 48 (1986), 470–513.

Rogers, H. L., 'The Oldest West-Saxon Text?', *Review of English Studies*, New Series, 32 (1981), 257–66.

Rollason, David, *Saints and Relics in Anglo-Saxon England* (Oxford, 1989).

Rose-Troup, F., 'Crediton Charters of the Tenth Century', *Transactions of the Devonshire Association* 74 (1942), 237–61.

Rose-Troup, Frances 'The New Edgar Charter and the South Hams', *Transactions of the Devonshire Association* 61 (1929), 249–80.

Sawyer, P. H. *Anglo-Saxon Charters: An Annotated List and Bibliography* (London, 1968); revised as the Electronic Sawyer, www.esawyer.org.uk.

Sawyer, P. H., *From Roman Britain to Norman England*, 2nd ed. (Oxford, 1998).

Sawyer, P. H., 'The Royal tun in Pre-Conquest England', in *Ideal and Reality in Frankish and Anglo-Saxon Society*, eds Patrick Wormald, Donald Bullough, and Roger Collins (Oxford, 1983), pp. 273–300.

Smith, Scott Thompson, *Land and Book: Literature and Land Tenure in Anglo-Saxon England* (Toronto, 2012).

Staerkle, Paul, *Die Rückvermerke der ältern St.Galler Urkunden* (St Gall, 1966).

Stokes, Peter A., *English Vernacular Minuscule from Æthelred to Cnut, circa 990–circa 1035* (Woodbridge, 2014).

Stokes, Peter A., 'King Edgar's Charter for Pershore (AD 972)', *ASE* 37 (2008), 31–78.

Thompson, Susan D., *Anglo-Saxon Royal Diplomas: A Palaeography* (Woodbridge, 2006).

Tinti, Francesca, 'The Reuse of Charters at Worcester Between the Eighth and the Eleventh Century: A Case-Study', *Midland History* 37 (2012), 127–41.

Tinti, Francesca, *Sustaining Belief: The Church of Worcester from c. 870 to c. 1100* (Farnham, 2010).

Tinti, Francesca, 'Writing Latin and Old English in Tenth-Century England', in *Writing, Kingship and Power in Anglo-Saxon England*, eds Rory Naismith and David A. Woodman (Oxford, 2017), pp. 303–27.

Ward, G., 'The Wilmington Charter of A.D. 700', *Archaeologia Cantiana* 98 (1936), 11–28.

Online Sources

Dictionary of Old English Corpus, compiled by Antonette diPaolo Healey with John Price Wilkin and Xin Xiang (Toronto, 2009), https://www.doe.utoronto.ca/pages/index.html.

DigiPal: Digital Resource and Database of Manuscripts, Palaeography and Diplomatic (London, 2011–14), http://www.digipal.eu.

Keynes, Simon, 'A Classified List of Anglo-Saxon Charters on Single Sheets' (unpublished; available at https://pdfs.semanticscholar.org/1157/703a4e3199f8f13f566b4715 5cfb2d60f2e2.pdf.

Lawton, Rebecca, 'A Useless Letter?', *British Library Medieval Manuscripts Blog* (12 December 2018), https://blogs.bl.uk/digitisedmanuscripts/2018/12/a-useless -letter.html.

CHAPTER 8

Traces of Bilingualism in Early Medieval Northern Italy: The Evidence from Eighth- and Ninth-Century Private Charters

Marco Stoffella

This chapter investigates the scattered evidence for bilingualism in early medieval northern Italy on the basis of late Lombard and early Carolingian charters that have been preserved mostly as originals in ecclesiastical archives.[1] The cities of Milan, Piacenza, Verona, Lucca, and Siena hold the richest collections of early medieval charters in the northern part of the former Lombard kingdom, known as *Langobardia maior*, which consisted of the four provinces of *Austria*, *Neustria*, *Emilia*, and *Tuscia*.[2] Their content, scribes, and subscribers are here investigated in order to understand the mentality and the choices made by authors and scribes, who could be either lay people or clerics. This chapter thus examines the linguistic skills and possible bilingualism of these northern Italian writers. At the centre of this analysis are several procedures which attest to the survival and integration of Lombardic—a West Germanic language related to Alemannic—, Bavarian, and Frankish, which overlapped and partially assimilated the pre-existing Gothic language in the Italian peninsula during the era of Lombard rule (568–774).[3] The continued use of the language

1 François Bougard, *La justice dans le royaume d'Italie de la fin du VIIIe siècle au début du XIe siècle*, Bibliothèque des Ècoles françaises d'Athènes et de Rome 291 (Rome, 1995), pp. 79–108; Nicholas Everett, 'Lay Documents and Archives in Early Medieval Spain and Italy, *c.* 400–700', in *Documentary Culture and the Laity in the Early Middle Ages*, eds Warren C. Brown, Marios Costambeys, Matthew Innes, and Adam J. Kosto (Cambridge, 2013), pp. 63–94, at 93–94; Marios Costambeys, 'The Laity, the Clergy, the Scribes and Their Archives: The Documentary Record of Eighth- and Ninth-Century Italy', in *Documentary Culture*, eds Brown et al., pp. 231–58, at 232–42; Mark Mersiowsky, *Die Urkunde in der Karolingerzeit. Originale, Urkundenpraxis und politische Kommunikation*, 2 vols, MGH Schriften 60 (Wiesbaden, 2015), 1:360–61.

2 Stefano Gasparri, 'Il regno longobardo in Italia. Struttura e funzionamento di uno stato altomedievale', in *Langobardia*, eds Paolo Cammarosano and Stefano Gasparri (Udine, 1990), pp. 237–305; a revised version is in *Il regno dei Longobardi in Italia. Archeologia, società e istituzioni*, ed. Stefano Gasparri (Spoleto, 2004), pp. 1–92, at 72–81.

3 Carlo Battisti, 'L'elemento gotico nella toponomastica e nel lessico italiano', in *I Goti in Occidente. Problemi*, Settimane 3 (Spoleto, 1956), pp. 621–49, at 636; Maria Giovanna Arcamone, 'I Germani d'Italia: lingue e "documenti" linguistici', in *Magistra Barbaritas. I*

 | DOI:10.1163/9789004432338_009

is further documented in the subsequent Carolingian period, especially by toponyms and onomastics,[4] but also by formulae used by charter scribes.[5]

Northern Italy also experienced language change on account of the linguistic acculturation of the Lombards into late Latin/early Romance, especially during the eighth century.[6] In contrast with Germanic-speaking territories north of the Alps such as Francia, Alemannia, and Bavaria, Latin was more influential than the Germanic vernacular (i.e. the Lombard language), while early written Italo-Romance also began to emerge in this period.[7] Evidence for the latter phenomenon is substantial and is found scattered in a variety of different kinds of texts, including charters. The most famous example is the mid-eighth-century 'Veronese Riddle', from northern Italy, which was written in the upper margin of fol. 3r of the manuscript preserved today as

---

barbari in Italia, ed. Giovanni Pugliese Carratelli, Antica Madre. Collana di studi sull'Italia antica 7 (Milan, 1984), pp. 381–409; Piergiuseppe Scardigli, *Goti e Longobardi. Studi di filologia germanica* (Rome, 1987).

4 Arcamone, 'I Germani d'Italia', pp. 383–84; Maria Vollono, 'Plurilinguismo nell'Italia postlongobarda: considerazioni a proposito della presenza longobarda e franca e suoi riflessi linguistici', in *Il plurilinguismo in area germanica nel Medioevo: XXX Convegno Associazione Italiana di Filologia Germanica, Bari 4–6 giugno 2003*, ed. Lucia Sinisi (Bari, 2005), pp. 271–300; Elda Morlicchio, 'Dinamiche sociolinguistiche nell'Italia delle 'invasioni barbariche'', in *Archeologia e storia delle migrazioni. Europa, Italia, Mediterraneo fra tarda età romana e alto medioevo. Atti del Convegno internazionale di studi Cimitile-Santa Maria Capua Vetere, 17–18 giugno 2010*, eds Carlo Ebanista and Marcello Rotili, Giornate sulla Tarda Antichità e il Medioevo 3 (Cimitile, 2011), pp. 219–31.

5 Antonella Ghignoli, 'Koinè, influenze, importazioni transalpine nella documentazione 'privata' dei secoli VII–VIII: lo stato dell'arte', in *Le Alpi porta d'Europa. Scritture, uomini, idee da Giustiniano al Barbarossa. Atti del convegno di studio (Cividale del Friuli, 5–7 ottobre 2006)*, eds Laura Pani and Cesare Scalon (Spoleto, 2009), pp. 83–110; Antonella Ghignoli and François Bougard, 'Elementi romani nei documenti longobardi', in *L'héritage byzantin en Italie (VIIIe–XIIe siécle). I: La fabrique documentaire*, eds Jean-Marie Martin, Annick Peters-Custot, and Vivien Prigent, Collection de l'École française de Rome 449 (Rome, 2011), pp. 241–301.

6 Alberto Varvaro, 'Latin and the Making of the Romance Languages', in *The Cambridge History of the Romance Languages*, eds Martin Maiden, John C. Smith, and Adam Ledgeway, 2 vols (Cambridge, 2013), 2:6–56; Michel Banniard, 'The Transition from Latin to the Romance Languages', in *The Cambridge History of the Romance Languages*, eds Martin, Peters-Custot, and Bougard, 2:57–106; James Clackson, 'Latin as a Source for the Romance Languages', in *The Oxford Guide to the Romance Languages*, eds Adam Ledgeway and Martin Maiden (Oxford, 2016), pp. 3–13; Roger Wright, 'Latin and Romance in the Medieval Period. A Sociophilological Approach', in *The Oxford Guide to the Romance Languages*, eds Ledgeway and Maiden, pp. 14–23.

7 Serenella Baggio and Glauco Sanga, 'Sul volgare in età longobarda', in *Italia settentrionale: crocevia di idiomi romanzi. Atti del convegno di studi, Trento, 21–23 ottobre 1993*, eds Emanuele Banfi, Giovanni Bonfadini, Patrizia Cordin, and Maria Iliescu (Tübingen, 1995), pp. 247–60.

Verona, Biblioteca Capitolare, MS LXXXIX (84).[8] These singularities—that is, the stronger foundations of Latin in these territories and the emergence of written Italo-Romance—cannot be ignored and must briefly be considered together with the notion of Latin/Romance and Germanic bilingualism, since they were paralleled by the use of terms of Germanic origin that became embedded in local and regional tradition, albeit with important variants across different areas. In addition to the use of such Germanic terms in combination with expressions of early Italo-Romance origin, we must consider here the training of northern Italian scribes and notaries, as well as the influence of their social context.[9] Notaries were assigned a public function; they were not only scribes, but, as documented in several cases, also teachers of subsequent generations of scribes who were responsible for the implementation of graphic phenomena such as hypercorrect spellings in late Lombard and early Carolingian documents.[10]

In spite of changes brought about by the Carolingian takeover of 773–74, a framework of continuity in document production ensured a degree of cultural and linguistic uniformity across the former Lombard regions. Regional differences did nonetheless emerge.[11] According to the papal biographers of

8 *CLA* 5, no. 515. Serenella Baggio, Glauco Sanga, and Attilio Bartoli Langeli, 'Novità sull'Indovinello veronese', *Quaderni veneti* 21 (1995), 39–97; Armando Petrucci and Carlo Romeo, 'L'*Orazionale* visigotico di Verona: aggiunte avventizie, indovinello grafico, tagli maffeiani', *Scritture e civiltà* 22 (1998), 13–30; reprinted in and cited from Armando Petrucci, *Letteratura italiana: una storia attraverso la scrittura* (Rome, 2017), pp. 247–63, at 259–60.

9 Luigi Schiaparelli, 'Note diplomatiche sulle carte longobarde. I. I notai nell'età longobarda', *Archivio Storico Italiano* s. VII, 17 (1932), 3–34; reprinted in and cited from Luigi Schiaparelli, *Note di diplomatica (1896–1934)*, ed. Alessandro Pratesi (Turin, 1972), pp. 183–214, at 185; Attilio Bartoli Langeli, 'I documenti', in *Carte di famiglia. Strategie, rappresentazione e memoria del gruppo familiare di Totone di Campione (721–877)*, eds Stefano Gasparri and Cristina La Rocca (Rome, 2005), pp. 237–64; François Bougard, 'Notaires d'élite, notaires de l'élite dans le royaume d'Italie', in *La culture du haut Moyen Âge. Une question d'élites?*, eds François Bougard, Régine Le Jan, and Rosamond McKitterick, Haut Moyen Âge 7 (Turnhout, 2009), pp. 439–60.

10 Armando Petrucci, 'Scrittura e libro nella Tuscia altomedievale (secoli VIII–IX)', in *Lucca e la Tuscia nell'alto medioevo. Atti del 5° Congresso internazionale di studi sull'alto medioevo (Lucca, 3–7 ottobre 1971)* (Spoleto, 1973), pp. 627–43, at 628–36; Armando Petrucci, 'Il codice n. 490 della Biblioteca Capitolare di Lucca: un problema di storia della cultura medievale ancora da risolvere', *Actum Luce* 2 (1971), 159–75; reprinted without illustrations as 'Il codice e i documenti: scrivere a Lucca fra VIII e IX secolo' in Armando Petrucci and Carlo Romeo, « *Scriptores in urbibus* ». *Alfabetismo e cultura scritta nell'Italia altomedievale* (Bologna, 1992), pp. 77–108. Cf. also Figure 8.1, below.

11 Baggio and Sanga, 'Sul volgare in età longobarda', pp. 249, 258; Francesco Sabatini, *Riflessi linguistici della dominazione longobarda nell'Italia mediana e meridionale* (Florence,

the *Liber pontificalis*, the Frankish conquest was swift and smooth.[12] A feared large-scale insurrection did not take place,[13] as a revolt against Frankish rule was only attempted by Rodgaud, duke of Friuli, and by two other dukes from *Austria*, namely Gaido of Vicenza and Stabilinius of Treviso.[14] In winter 775–76 Charlemagne left the Saxon front in order to deal with the Italian situation, and in spring 776 he thwarted the uprising.[15] As the *Annales regni Francorum* report, Charlemagne subsequently placed his men only in the *civitates* which had taken part in the insurrection, without attempting to replace all Lombard dukes with Frankish counts.[16] Verona was among the first towns to be affected by these events through the imposition of counts and especially bishops of Alemannic provenance. The presence in northern and central Italy of high-ranking officers of Frankish, Alemannic, and Bavarian origin during the first 30 years of Carolingian rule inevitably raises issues about the linguistic interactions between these officials and the local population: to what extent would they have been able to communicate with the Lombard aristocracy?[17] This question requires a much more detailed treatment than is possible to

1963), p. 249. A revised version is now in *Aristocrazie e società fra transizione romano-germanica e alto medioevo. Atti del Convegno internazionale di studi (Cimitile-Santa Maria Capua Vetere, 14–15 giugno 2012)*, eds Carlo Ebanista and Marcello Rotili (San Vitaliano, Naples, 2015), pp. 353–441; Nicoletta Francovich Onesti, 'L'antroponimia longobarda della Toscana: caratteri e diffusione', *Rivista Italiana di Onomastica* 6 (2000), 357–74; reprinted in Nicoletta Francovich Onesti, *Le Regine dei Longobardi e altri saggi*, Proteo 72 (Rome, 2013), pp. 41–59, at 43–46.

12 *Le Liber Pontificalis. Texte, introduction et commentaire*, ed. Louis Duchesne, 2 vols (Paris, 1886–92), 1:486–99.

13 Paolo Cammarosano, *Nobili e re. L'Italia politica nell'alto medioevo* (Rome-Bari, 1998), pp. 102–3, 116–17.

14 Harald Krahwinkler, *Friaul im Frühmittelalter. Geschichte einer Region vom Ende des fünften bis zum Ende des zehnten Jahrhunderts*, Veröffentlichungen des Instituts für Österreichische Geschichtsforschung 30 (Vienna, 1992), pp. 119–43, at 119–26; Stefano Gasparri, 'Istituzioni e potere nel territorio friulano in età longobarda e carolingia', in *Paolo Diacono e il Friuli altomedievale (secc. VI–X), Atti del XIV Congresso internazionale di studi sull'alto medioevo, Cividale del Friuli—Bottenicco di Moimacco, 24–29 settembre 1999*, 2 vols (Spoleto, 2001), 1:105–28, at 111–12, 115–18; Marco Stoffella, 'Rodgaudo', in *Dizionario Biografico degli Italiani* (Rome, 1960-), 87:78–80.

15 Bernard S. Bachrach, *Charlemagne's Early Campaigns (768–777): A Diplomatic and Military Analysis*, History of Warfare 82 (Leiden, 2013), pp. 356–70, 456–68, 473–509.

16 *Annales regni francorum*, s.a. 776, ed. Friedrich Kurze, MGH SS rer. Germ. 6 (Hanover, 1895), pp. 43–45.

17 On these northern officials in general, see Eduard Hlawitschka, *Franken, Alemannen, Bayern und Burgunder in Oberitalien (774–962). Zum Verständnis der fränkischen Königsherrschaft in Italien*, Forschungen zur oberrheinischen Landesgeschichte 8 (Freiburg im Breisgau, 1960), pp. 23–52.

provide here, bearing in mind that the purview of these officers' activities encompassed territories both north and south of the Alps. A possible cultural contiguity between these regions, which has thus far not received proper attention, is suggested by Charlemagne's 806 plan for the division of his empire; if carried out, this would have led to a geographical and political unification of Alemannia, Bavaria, and Italy.[18] In addition to the promotion of Frankish officers southward across the Alps, in some regions the Carolingian administration ensured the continuation of careers which had already begun in the Lombard period. Dukes Ildeprand of Spoleto and Arichis II of Benevento are two examples of high-ranking officers who had been promoted by Desiderius and who were still holding office in the 780s.[19] This was also the case for Duke Allo of Lucca,[20] as well as of Duke Gudiprand of Florence, Duke Reginbald of Città di Castello, and Duke John of Persiceta.[21] It is very likely that there were other aristocrats, not attested in surviving sources, who were permitted to keep their offices after the Carolingian conquest. Thus, in spite of these sweeping political convulsions, there is good reason to suppose a degree of cultural and linguistic continuity between late Lombard and early Carolingian Italy.

After identifying episodes of linguistic interplay in eighth- and early ninth-century northern Italy, this chapter will address specific questions with regard to Tuscany, a region with distinctive political, documentary, and linguistic features. The second part of the chapter will thus focus on important collections of Tuscan documentary sources, through which some of these linguistic aspects will be examined and clarified. As a particularly significant case study, I shall focus on the use of *ferquidem*, a term of Germanic origin, in eighth-century Tuscan charters. Related forms of the same term are first attested in Rothari's law-code (643), where they appear five times. Later on, just one occurrence is found in Liutprand's laws (735).[22] Interestingly, however, the term

18 Brigitte Kasten, *Königssöhne und Königsherrschaft. Untersuchungen zur Teilhabe am Reich in der Merowinger- und Karolingerzeit*, MGH Schriften 44 (Hanover, 1997), pp. 154–60.

19 Stefano Gasparri, *Italia longobarda. Il regno, i Franchi, il papato* (Rome-Bari, 2012), pp. 124–25.

20 Speculation on the possible origins of the Lombard duke Allo can be found in Antonella Ghignoli, 'Su due famosi documenti pisani del secolo VIII', *Bullettino dell'Istituto Storico Italiano per il Medio Evo* 106 (2004), 1–69, at pp. 62–64.

21 Stefano Gasparri, *I duchi longobardi*, Studi Storici 109 (Rome, 1978), pp. 48–49, 57, 58, 60; Gasparri, *Italia longobarda*, p. 130.

22 *Le leggi dei Longobardi. Storia, memoria e diritto di un popolo germanico*, eds Claudio Azzara and Stefano Gasparri, Altomedioevo 4 (Rome, 2005), pp. 44, 54, 94, 96, 100, 234; Florus van der Rhee, *Die germanischen Wörter in der langobardischen Gesetzen* (Rotterdam, 1970), pp. 52–54; Ruth Schmidt-Wiegand, 'Die volkssprachige Wörter der Leges barbarorum', *Frühmittelalterliche Studien* 13 (1979), 56–87, at p. 84; Arcamone, 'I Germani d'Italia', p. 386;

appears repeatedly in formulae employed in Tuscan private documents, albeit with some peculiarities. As we shall see, *ferquidem* does not occur in the earliest Lombard charters, but is rather attested in Tuscan documents from the middle decades of the eighth century, at which time it also disappears from Lombard law-codes.[23] In the subsequent period, it was used as a formulaic word which, once it had been recognized and accepted by local scribes and notaries, became embedded in regional tradition.

A Brief *status quaestionis*

Scholars have not always agreed on how words of Germanic origin should be recognized, explained, or traced back to one tradition or another. There are, for instance, some terms which philologists and editors of sources have recognized as Germanic relics, but which have subsequently been interpreted in different ways. Before analysing more specific aspects of this problem, however, a brief synthesis of the more recent positions concerning debates over language-use in early medieval Italy will help frame the present study. Two main issues examined by scholars must be outlined: the ways through which the Germanic language spread and the conditions of its survival. Germanic language owes its presence in Italy to Lombard rule, and its use is attested especially by toponymic and onomastic evidence which can be traced in epigraphs and documents.[24]

Nicoletta Francovich Onesti, *Vestigia longobarde in Italia (568–774). Lessico e antroponimia*, Proteo 6 (Rome, 1999), pp. 79, 135.

23 The charters written before spring 774 and mentioned in this article have been edited in CDL 1–2. On Lombard documents, see Herbert Zielinski, 'Die Charta der Langobarden. Forschungsgeschichte und aktuelle Perspektiven', in *Die Privaturkunden der Karolingerzeit*, eds Peter Erhart, Karl Heidecker, and Bernhard Zeller (Dietikon-Zürich, 2009), pp. 47–56.

24 Carlo Alberto Mastrelli, 'La toponomastica lombarda di origine longobarda', in *I Longobardi e la Lombardia. Saggi* (Milan, 1978), pp. 35–46; Max Pfister, 'Langobardische Superstratwörter im Italienischen', *Jahrbuch für Internationale Germanistik* 11 (1979), 100–10; Maria Giovanna Arcamone, 'Antroponimia germanica nella toponomastica italiana', in *La toponomastica come fonte di conoscenza storica e linguistica. Atti del convegno della Società Italiana di Glottologia, Belluno, 31 marzo-2 aprile 1980*, ed. Edoardo Vineis (Pisa, 1981), pp. 29–45; Maria Giovanna Arcamone, 'Toponomastica italiana di origine longobarda', in *Scríbthair a ainm n-ogaim. Scritti in memoria di Enrico Campanile*, eds Riccardo Ambrosini, Maria Patrizia Bologna, Filippo Motta, and Chatia Orlandi, 2 vols (Pisa, 1997), 1:39–50; Maria Giovanna Arcamone, 'Die Verteilung der Ortsnamen langobardischen Ursprungs in den Regionen Italiens', in *Interferenz-Onomastik. Namen in Grenz- und Begegnungsräumen in Geschichte und Gegenwart. Saarbrücker Kolloquium des Arbeitskreises für Namenforschung vom 5.–7. Oktober 2006*, eds Wolfgang Haubrichs

In recent decades, scholars have repeatedly devoted attention to these problems and expressed different positions on bilingualism in the Lombard period, especially in the northern part of the peninsula. Federico Albano Leoni, Maria Giovanna Arcamone, Max Pfister, Nicoletta Francovich Onesti, Giovanna Princi Braccini, Nicholas Everett, Wolfgang Haubrichs, and many others have variously described the language as living or obsolete at different stages between the end of the sixth century and the middle of the eighth.[25] In particular, the question of precisely when the use of the Lombard language ended has been long discussed. For how long did the Lombards preserve their native Germanic language and when did they start to switch to late Latin/early Italo-Romance?

In a classic study, Ernesto Sestan held that bilingualism was restricted to the upper social strata, and that Germanic language-use progressively declined in favour of Latin within three or four generations. This process, he argued, was concluded at the latest by the mid-seventh century, when the

---

and Heinrich Tiefenbach, Veröffentlichungen der Kommission für Saarländische Landesgeschichte und Volksforschung 43 (Saarbrücken, 2010), pp. 65–78; Elda Morlicchio, *Antroponimia longobarda a Salerno nel IX secolo. I nomi del* Codex diplomaticus Cavensis (Naples, 1985); Maria Giovanna Arcamone, 'Die langobardischen Personennamen in Italien: Nomen und gens aus der Sicht der linguistischen Analyse', in *Nomen et gens. Zur historischen Aussagekraft frühmittelalterlicher Personennamen*, eds Dieter Geuenich, Wolfgang Haubrichs, and Jörg Jarnut, Ergänzungsbände zum Reallexikon der Germanischen Altertumskunde 16 (Berlin, 1997), pp. 157–75; Maria Giovanna Arcamone, 'L'onomastica personale nell'Europa occidentale fra IV e VIII secolo', in *Morfologie sociali e culturali in Europa tra tarda antichità e alto Medioevo*, Settimane 45 (Spoleto, 1998), pp. 585–618; Wolfgang Haubrichs, 'Langobardic Personal Names: Given Names and Name-Giving Among the Langobards', in *The Langobards from the Migration Period to the Eighth Century: An Ethnographic Perspective*, eds Giorgio Ausenda, Paolo Delogu, and Chris Wickham (Woodbrige, 2009), pp. 195–236.

25 Federico Albano Leoni, 'Bilinguismo e coscienza del bilinguismo nell'Italia longobarda', in *Italia linguistica: idee, storia, strutture*, eds Federico Albano Leoni, Daniele Gambarara, Franco Lo Piparo, and Raffaele Simone (Bologna, 1983), pp. 133–48; cf. Arcamone, 'I Germani d'Italia', pp. 383–86, where she never openly mentions the phenomenon of bilingualism during the Lombard period, but does refer to the Gothic language in the mid-sixth-century western Mediterranean as a sort of *lingua franca* that nearly everybody could speak or understand. Max Pfister, 'Germanisch und Romanisch', in *Lexikon der Romanistischen Linguistik*, eds Günter Holtus, Michael Metzeltin, and Christian Schmitt, 12 vols (Tübingen, 1998), 7:231–45; Francovich Onesti, *Vestigia longobarde*, pp. 48–49; Giovanna Princi Braccini, 'Vecchi e nuovi indizi sui tempi della morte della lingua dei Longobardi', *Archivio per l'Alto Adige* 93–94 (2000), 353–74; Nicholas Everett, *Literacy in Lombard Italy, c. 568–774* (Cambridge, 2003), pp. 100–62; Wolfgang Haubrichs, 'Amalgamierung und Identität. Langobardische Personennamen in Mythos und Herrschaft', in *Die Langobarden. Herrschaft und Identität*, eds Walter Pohl and Peter Erhart, Forschungen zur Geschichte des Mittelalters 9 (Vienna, 2005), pp. 67–99.

Lombards definitively became Catholic and spoken Latin became the everyday language.[26] As Stefano Gasparri has pointed out, however, Sestan's influential social and linguistic theories were based on his own preconceptions rather than on source analysis, thus reflecting the nationalistic historiography then prevailing in Italy.[27] Others, such as Albano Leoni and Max Pfister, nevertheless supposed that the Lombards abandoned their Germanic language within two or three generations, that is, between the beginning and middle of the seventh century at the latest.[28] Likewise, Nicoletta Francovich Onesti, though openly admitting that she had no proof for her assumptions, maintained that the Lombard language must have died out well before the end of the seventh century. Sharing some of the positions previously adopted by Sestan, she affirmed that the loss of the Germanic language came within just over a century of the Lombards' arrival in Italy, a period corresponding to four or five generations. Francovich Onesti thought it improbable that a Germanic language would still have been used by a Lombard minority living in a Latin-Roman environment after such a long period of time.[29] Gasparri has also expressed similar convictions, assuming that the Lombard language was no longer spoken by the beginning of the eighth century.[30]

In another recent treatment of bilingualism in Lombard Italy, Nicholas Everett has altogether denied its significance. Even while admitting that there was a persistence of Germanic language among the Lombards following their settlement in Italy, he concluded that 'a unified and diffused native Langobardic language may have never existed'.[31] Wolfgang Haubrichs has challenged Everett's arguments, maintaining that the Germanic Lombard language was still in use around the middle of the eighth century. For Haubrichs, even in the late eighth century, the Lombard language was not yet extinct, although it was increasingly restricted to use within families.[32] In contrast with other

26 Ernesto Sestan, 'La composizione etnica della società in rapporto allo svolgimento della civiltà in Italia nel secolo VII', in *Caratteri del secolo VII in Occidente*, Settimane 5 (Spoleto, 1958), pp. 649–77, at 667–75.

27 Stefano Gasparri, 'I Germani immaginari e la realtà del regno. Cinquant'anni di studi sui Longobardi', in *I Longobardi dei ducati di Spoleto e Benevento. Atti del 16° Congresso internazionale di studi sull'alto medioevo (Spoleto, 20–23 ottobre 2002—Benevento, 24–27 ottobre 2002)*, 2 vols (Spoleto, 2003), 1:3–28, at pp. 8–11.

28 Albano Leoni, 'Bilinguismo', p. 141; Pfister, 'Germanisch und Romanisch', p. 239.

29 Francovich Onesti, *Vestigia longobarde*, pp. 48–49.

30 Stefano Gasparri, 'Breve storia dei Longobardi', in *Paolo Diacono, Storia dei Longobardi*, eds Stefano Gasparri and Antonio Zanella (Milan, 2000), pp. 9–16, at 13.

31 Everett, *Literacy in Lombard Italy*, pp. 100–129, 322.

32 Wolfgang Haubrichs, 'Sprache und Schriftlichkeit im langobardischen Italien—Das Zeugnis von Namen, Wörtern und Entlehnungen. Ein Kommentar zu Nicholas Everett,

scholars, Haubrichs has convincingly identified several instances of bilingual interaction, such as the presence of the term *hidebohrit* (spelled *hidebohohlrit* and probably meaning 'the one elevated anew') next to Duke Ratchis's name in an otherwise entirely Latin inscription found on an altar in *Forum Iulii* (Cividale del Friuli) commissioned by the duke himself in the central decades of the eighth century.[33] A Lombard word inserted at the end of the inscription and associated with the name of Ratchis could have been understood only in a bilingual society.[34] Moreover, Haubrichs has shown that similar elements of linguistic interaction can be identified in the north of the Italian peninsula as late as the second half of the eighth century. On the basis of the phonetic evolution of certain names, Haubrichs has argued that late developments such as the shift of the Lombard diphthong *-ai-* to *-ei-* (as in the cases of Chei-perti and Gheiri-paldus, attested at Lucca in the second half of the eighth century) could only have taken place if the Germanic language was still alive and spoken.[35]

Literacy in Lombard Italy', *Filologia Germanica—Germanic Philology. I Germani e l'Italia. The Early Germanic Peoples and Italy* 2 (2010), 133–202; Wolfgang Haubrichs, 'Langobardic Personal Names', pp. 210, 221–22.

33 On the altar and its inscription see Silvia Lusuardi Siena and Paola Piva, 'Scultura decorativa e arredo liturgico a Cividale e in Friuli tra VIII e IX secolo', in *Paolo Diacono e il Friuli altomedievale (secc. VI–X). Atti del XV Congresso internazionale di studi sull'Alto Medioevo. Cividale del Friuli-Bottenicco di Moimacco 24–29 settembre 1999*, 2 vols (Spoleto, 2001), 2:493–594, at pp. 512–19, 551–52; Paola Piva and Silvia Lusuardi Siena, 'Da Pemmone a Paolino d'Aquileia: appunti sull'arredo liturgico e la scultura in Friuli tra VIII e IX sec.', *Hortus Artium Medievalium* 8 (2002), 295–323; Laura Chinellato, 'L'altare di Ratchis', in *L'VIII secolo: un secolo inquieto. Atti del Convegno Internazionale di Studi (Cividale del Friuli, 4–7 dicembre 2008)*, ed. Valentino Pace (Cividale del Friuli, 2010), pp. 83–91, 353–58 and tables III–V, a–b; Marco Stoffella, 'Pemmo, duca del Friuli', in *Dizionario Biografico degli Italiani*, 82:206–7; Marco Stoffella, 'Ratchis, re dei Longobardi', in *Dizionario Biografico degli Italiani*, 86:549–52.

34 Haubrichs, 'Langobardic Personal Names', pp. 206, 222; Francovich Onesti, *Vestigia longobarde*, pp. 96–97.

35 Wolfgang Haubrichs, 'I nomi dei Longobardi', in *I Longobardi in Italia. Lingua e cultura*, ed. Carla Falluomini, Bibliotheca Germanica. Studi e testi 37 (Alessandria, 2015), pp. 227–68, at 246–47; similar conclusions can be found in Nicoletta Francovich Onesti, 'Discontinuità e integrazione nel sistema onomastico dell'Italia tardoantica. L'incontro coi nomi germanici', in *Le trasformazioni del mondo romano e le grandi migrazioni. Nuovi popoli dall'Europa settentrionale e centro-orientale alle coste del Mediterraneo. Atti del Convegno internazionale di studi Cimitile-Santa Maria Capua Vetere, 16–17 giugno 2011*, eds Marcello Rotili and Carlo Ebanista, Giornate sulla Tarda Antichità e il Medioevo 4 (Cimitile, 2012), pp. 33–50, at 46 with n. 34.

The Issue of Bilingualism in Early Medieval Tuscany

Bilingualism in eighth-century Lombard Italy remains a contentious issue that cannot be resolved here. While I do not propose to offer lasting solutions to this important question, I would like to add further elements to the debate. I shall therefore keep myself at the margin of these discussions and embrace the position recently emphasized by Haubrichs, which I share on the basis of my own studies of the documents and society of Lombard and Carolingian Tuscany.[36] Following Haubrichs's recent results and pursuing several issues which have arisen from my work, I shall introduce evidence from northwestern Tuscany into these debates.

Broadly speaking, the territory of Lombard and early Carolingian Tuscany corresponds to late antique and early medieval *Tuscia*, one of the regions of the *Langobardia maior* that differed from the heartland of the Lombard kingdom, with its centre north of the Apennines.[37] At the same time, Tuscany was not a detached and distant duchy like Spoleto and Benevento, for it was connected to the Lombard capital of Pavia by the *strata Francigena* or *Romea*, the main road which passed through Piacenza, the Cisa pass, and Lucca en route to Rome.[38] In the seventh and eighth centuries, *Tuscia* also included the cities of Sovana, Viterbo, and Tuscania in the south, and Luni in the north west.[39] The

36 Marco Stoffella, 'Crisi e trasformazioni delle élites nella Toscana nord-occidentale nel secolo VIII: esempi a confronto', *Reti Medievali Rivista* 8 (2007), 1–49; Marco Stoffella, 'Le relazioni tra Baviera e Toscana tra VIII e IX secolo: appunti e considerazioni preliminari', *Mélanges de l'École française de Rome. Moyen-Âge* 120 (2008), 73–85; Marco Stoffella, 'Aristocracy and Rural Churches in the Territory of Lucca between Lombards and Carolingians: A Case Study', in *774: ipotesi su di una transizione*, ed. Stefano Gasparri, Seminari internazionali del Centro interuniversitario per la storia e l'archeologia dell'alto medioevo 1 (Turnhout, 2008), pp. 289–311; Marco Stoffella, 'In a Periphery of the Empire: Tuscany between the Lombards and the Carolingians', in *Charlemagne. Les temps, les espaces, les hommes. Construction et déconstruction d'un règne*, eds Rolf Grosse and Michel Sot, Haut Moyen Âge 34 (Turnhout, 2018), pp. 319–36; Bernhard Zeller, Charles West, Francesca Tinti, Marco Stoffella, Nicolas Schroeder, Carine van Rhijn, Steffen Patzold, Thomas Kohl, Wendy Davies, and Miriam Czock, *Neighbours and Strangers: Local Societies in Early Medieval Europe* (Manchester, 2020), pp. 70–71, 152–55, 170–73, 226–27.

37 Gasparri, 'Il regno longobardo in Italia', pp. 72–82.

38 Giuseppe Sergi, *Luoghi di strada nel medioevo. Fra il Po, il mare e le Alpi occidentali* (Turin, 1986). On the *Via Francigena* in Tuscany see Julius Jung, 'Das Itinerar des Erzbischofs Sigeric von Canterbury und die Straße von Rom über Siena nach Lucca', *Mitteilungen des Instituts für Österreichische Geschichtsforschung* 24 (1904), 3–90; Renato Stopani, *La via francigena in Toscana. Storia di una strada medievale* (Florence, 1984); *La via Francigena e altre strade della Toscana medievale*, ed. Stella Patitucci Uggeri, Quaderni di Archeologia medievale 7 (Florence, 2004); *La via Francigena in Toscana. Da Lucca alla Val d'Orcia*, ed. Massimo Dringoli (Pisa, 2016).

39 Paolo Cammarosano, *Storia dell'Italia medievale. Dal VI all'XI secolo* (Rome, 2001), pp. 75–77.

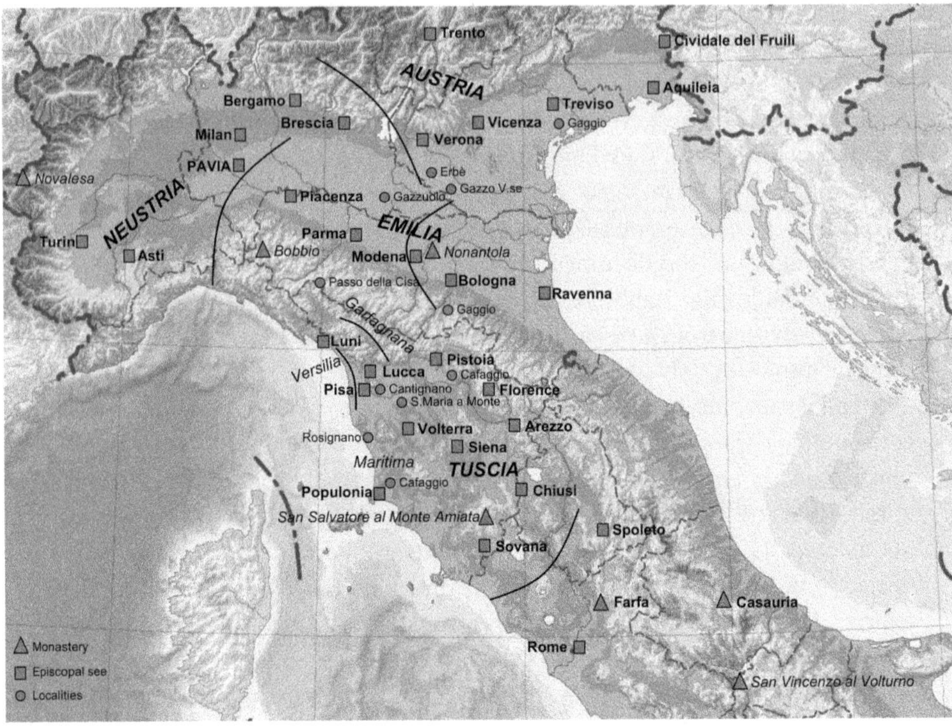

MAP 8.1 Northern Italy in the central decades of the eighth century

main centre of the northern part of the region was Lucca, the seat of a powerful *ducatus* and of a bishopric which controlled large areas such as Versilia, Garfagnana, and the western part of the Valdarno valley with its surroundings hills, as well as part of the *Maritima* to the south along the Tyrrhenian coast.[40] The city of Chiusi was also the seat of a *dux*, while the presence of a third *dux* in Florence is only sporadically attested at the beginning of the Carolingians' rule in Italy.[41] Other important administrative cities and bishoprics included Pisa, Volterra, Pistoia, Siena, Arezzo, Fiesole, and Populonia.[42]

Tuscany has tended to receive significant attention in discussions of Lombard toponyms and onomastics because of the important early medieval

40 Gasparri, 'Il regno longobardo in Italia', pp. 79–80; Pier Maria Conti, 'La Tuscia e i suoi ordinamenti territoriali nell'alto medioevo', in *Lucca e la Tuscia nell'alto medioevo. Atti del 5° Congresso internazionale di studi sull'alto medioevo (Lucca, 3–7 ottobre 1971)* (Spoleto, 1973), pp. 61–116; Hagen Keller, 'La marca di Tuscia fino all'anno mille', in *Lucca e la Tuscia*, pp. 117–40.

41 Gasparri, *I duchi longobardi*, pp. 46, 57, 60, 94, 98.

42 Cammarosano, *Storia dell'Italia medievale*, pp. 75–77.

archives preserved in its northern and southern parts—respectively, in the areas of Lucca and Pisa, and of Monte Amiata and Chiusi—which have allowed scholars to conduct research over a long period of time from the beginning of the eighth century onwards.[43] Based on the linguistic peculiarities of northern Italy, a scholarly consensus has emerged that there was an evolutionary divide between the territories of the Po valley and those south of the Apennines. Even today, Tuscany is strongly characterized by its dialect; its early medieval territory coincides almost exactly with its modern boundaries in which six different areas have been described, one of them coinciding with western Tuscany.[44] This is a unique case in the Italian peninsula, since it is a neatly defined linguistic territory, characterized by several common traits that can be found across the whole region but stand in contrast to the northern Italian dialects and to the central-southern linguistic group.[45] This uniqueness also encompasses Germanisms and especially toponyms of Lombard origin, with different results between the Po valley and the other parts of northern and central Italy, including Tuscany (linguists traditionally further distinguish between the western and eastern parts of northern Italy).

In order to give weight to these statements, we should recall how some toponyms of Lombard origin such as *braida/praida* (open flatlands or suburban fields) and its variants are diffused only in northern Italy, mainly in the Po valley. The Lombard word *gahagium*, meaning 'enclosed land' or 'preserve', is attested today in northern Italy and in the Po valley in the forms of *Gazzo, Gazzuolo.* In eighth-century Tuscan charters, the variants of *cahagio, caagio, cagio*, and *cafagio* are attested; they survive nowadays in the forms of *Cafaggio* or *Gaggio* across the whole region.[46] Some words of Germanic origin, therefore,

---

43 On the recent new edition of Lucca's oldest charters, see Francesco Magistrale, 'Le pergamene dell'Archivio Arcivescovile di Lucca (secoli VIII–IX): l'esperienza delle *Chartae Latinae antiquiores*', in *Il patrimonio documentario della chiesa di Lucca. Prospettive di ricerca. Atti del Convegno internazionale di studi (Lucca, Archivio arcivescovile, 14–15 novembre 2008)*, eds Sergio Pagano and Pierantonio Piatti, Toscana Sacra 2 (Florence, 2010), pp. 73–92; *CAAPi* 1; Wilhelm Kurze, *Codex Diplomaticus Amiatinus. Urkundenbuch der Abtei S. Salvatore am Monteamiata von den Anfängen bis zum Regierungsantritt Papst Innozenz III. (736–1198)*, 4 vols (Tübingen, 1974–98).

44 Giovan Battista Pellegrini, *Carta dei dialetti d'Italia* (Pisa, 1977), p. 30.

45 Giacomo Devoto and Gabriella Giacomelli, *I dialetti delle regioni d'Italia* (Florence, 1972), pp. 64–71.

46 Paul Aebischer, 'Les dérivés italiens du langobard "gahagi" et leur répartition d'après les chartes médiévales', *Zeitschrift für romanische Philologie* 63 (1938), 51–62; Nicoletta Francovich Onesti, 'Indizi di sviluppi romanzi nelle voci germaniche e nei nomi propri', *Filologia Germanica—Germanic Philology. I Germani e l'Italia. The Early Germanic Peoples and Italy* 2 (2010), 67–101, at pp. 89–91; reprinted in Francovich Onesti, *Le Regine dei Longobardi*, pp. 141–74, at 166–67.

survive exclusively in the Po valley, where the tendency towards lenition or voicing of consonants is registered, while others represent variants north and south of the Apennines or are attested only in Tuscany. In the latter region the preservation of voiceless consonants, even with regard to Lombard imports, was common.[47] This is the case with *Teupasciu*, a hydronym used in both the northern and southern parts of the region in the mid-eighth century; coming from Germanic *_Theud-bachiō_ < -_bakiō_ (brook), it indicated a public brook or a royal property. Its form reveals an advanced stage of Romance acculturation, since the shift [k] > [x] at this stage had already taken place, with [x] being substituted with a sibilant, spelled <sc>, <ss>, <s>.[48] A diffusion restricted to Tuscany can also be seen for the measure term *scaffilo/iscaffilo*.[49]

While the study of Tuscan Lombard place-names relies on a long scholarly tradition,[50] that of Lombard onomastics, though not as well established, has proved to be more productive. Recent studies have revisited the discussions on nomenclature and onomastics with special attention to Tuscan documents and to the issue of bilingualism.[51] Local linguistic peculiarities seem to emerge most clearly in personal names, especially those of Lombard origin, which, in the eighth century, were still a good majority. Some of these particular linguistic features can be attributed to regional Romance trends, such as the frequent use of certain suffixes. Others were linked to local developments of Lombard sounds and phonemes or, at least, to their graphic rendering and to scribal

---

47 Maria Giovanna Arcamone, 'La toponomastica del Monte Amiata: la componente longobarda e l'etimo di Amiata (e del lucchese Meati)', in *L'Amiata nel Medioevo. Atti del convegno internazionale di studi (Abbadia San Salvatore, 29 maggio-1 giugno 1986)*, eds Wilhelm Kurze and Mario Ascheri (Rome, 1989), pp. 261–88.

48 Haubrichs, 'Langobardic Personal Names', p. 211.

49 Francovich Onesti, *Vestigia longobarde*, p. 115.

50 Carlo Alberto Mastrelli, 'L'elemento germanico nella toponomastica toscana', in *Lucca e la Tuscia*, pp. 645–71; Maria Giovanna Arcamone, 'Chinzica: toponimo pisano di origine longobarda', *Bollettino Storico Pisano* 47 (1978), 205–46; Arcamone, 'La toponomastica del Monte Amiata'; Maria Giovanna Arcamone, 'L'eredità longobarda nell'odierna toponomastica pistoiese', in *L'eredità longobarda*, Studi storici pistoiesi 5 (Rome, 2014), pp. 39–62; Nicoletta Francovich Onesti, 'Toponimi di origine germanica della Val di Cornia', *AION—Filologia Germanica* 30–31 (1987–88), 7–42.

51 Maria Giovanna Arcamone, 'L'antroponimia germanica a Pisa durante l'età longobarda', *Filologia e critica. Studi in onore di Vittorio Santoli*, eds Paolo Chiarini, Carlo Alberto Mastrelli, Piergiuseppe Scardigli, and Luciano Zangari, Studi di filologia tedesca 6–7, 2 vols (Rome, 1976), 1:133–58; Maria Giovanna Arcamone, 'Antroponimia e storia: problemi di metodo sulla base del *Codex Diplomaticus Amiatinus*', in *Antroponimia e storia nell'Italia centrale (Atti del Convegno di Gabicce Mare, 18 sett. 1993)*, ed. Ettore Baldetti, Proposte e Ricerche 33 (1994), pp. 123–31; Francovich Onesti, 'L'antroponimia longobarda della Toscana'; Haubrichs, 'Langobardic Personal Names'; Haubrichs, 'I nomi dei Longobardi'.

habits.[52] Moreover, the reliance upon inherited traditions of name-giving during the Lombard and the early Carolingian period allows us to evaluate the extent to which language and names were regarded as signs of self-confidence and identity, and, consequently, how long the Lombards were able to preserve their own language.

Onomastic analysis of original documents has shown that the Lombard language underwent both phases of the so-called High German sound shift, especially the first phase with the shift of the voiceless, the tenuis.[53] The shift of voiced plosives, the mediae [d], [b], [g] > [t], [p], [k], was in progress towards the end of the seventh century and the first decades of the eighth century, whereas the tenuis shift had already begun by the end of the sixth century, appearing especially in the early Italo-Romance Latin of the Lombard documents from Tuscany. Interestingly, the tenuis shift also began in the sixth century in the High German dialects spoken by the Alamans and the Bavarians, while the medial shift began later. These elements indicate that there were remarkable similarities between the Lombard language and those spoken by the two other related *gentes*, a correspondence that may have been strengthened through political and cultural ties involving not only the Lombard court, but also Tuscany during the eighth and ninth centuries.[54] Finally, the appearance of medial shifting in late seventh- and early eighth-century Tuscan Lombard documents indicates that the Lombard language was still alive at this time.[55]

As elsewhere in northern Italy, a number of vernacular linguistic features are detectable in eighth-century Latin documents from Tuscany, although they do not yet display clear dialectal developments.[56] When did Romance linguistic acculturation of the originally Germanic-speaking population

52 Stefan Sonderegger, 'Prinzipien germanischer Personennamengebung', in *Nomen et gens*, eds Geuenich et al., pp. 1–29; Haubrichs, 'Langobardic Personal Names', p. 196.

53 Wilhelm Bruckner, *Die Sprache der Langobarden* (Strasbourg, 1895; reprinted Berlin, 1969), pp. 147–49, 157–59, 167–69; Walther Mitzka, 'Das Langobardische und die althochdeutsche Dialektgeographie', *Zeitschrift für Mundartforschung* 20 (1951), 1–7; Florus van der Rhee, 'Die hochdeutsche Lautverschiebung in den langobardischen Gesetzen. Datierung, Umfang, orthographische Wiedergabe', *Neophilologus* 60 (1976), 397–411; Giulia Petracco Sicardi, 'La seconda mutazione consonantica negli antroponimi di origine longobarda', in *Studi di filologia germanica e letteratura tedesca in onore di Nicola Accolti Gil Vitale*, eds Giancarlo Bolognese and Giorgio Sichel (Florence, 1977), pp. 7–20; Francovich Onesti, *Vestigia longobarde*, pp. 142–43, 149.

54 Stoffella, 'Le relazioni tra Baviera e Toscana', pp. 82–85.

55 Haubrichs, 'Langobardic Personal Names', pp. 211–12.

56 Robert L. Politzer and Frieda N. Politzer, *Romance Trends in 7th and 8th Century Latin Documents* (Chapel Hill, NC, 1953).

become an irreversible process? As linguistic artefacts, personal names have once again offered an answer: the increase of Romance elements shows that this development accelerated after the middle of the eighth century when the two anthroponomical German and late-Latin traditions were interwoven, suggesting that a much wider exchange between the two languages and their onomastic traditions was taking place.[57] Haubrichs has suggested that these phenomena must not be overlooked, since the existence of a bilingual Lombardic-Romance society emerges even when a Romance *supernomen* is added to a Germanic name, or vice-versa.[58] Therefore, we cannot speak of a complete decline and replacement of the Lombard language by the various dialects of early Italo-Romance, especially if we consider the treatment of Germanic [h] (which disappears at the beginning of words, or is substituted with another spirant, as in the case of [f] in the middle of words), the development of the Lombard-Old High German sound changes (such as medial shifts, or [ai] > [ei]), and the continued creative use of Germanic name-giving principles. All these factors suggest that there was a knowledge of the language and its rules even at such a late date.[59] Moreover, when interpreting developments in the eighth century, we need to pay attention to this basic socio-onomastic structure. As Francovich Onesti has shown, Romance baptismal names in Tuscany, including names with Romance suffixes and hybrid names, are primarily found among the lower and middle classes. The upper middle classes—*arimanni*, *viri honesti*, *exercitales*—and the aristocracy, by contrast, avoided suffixed names and mostly followed Lombard tradition, indicating bilingual situations through a mixed name-giving tradition.[60] All this also shows that to a certain extent Romance-speaking people of the upper and middle classes adopted the traditions of the Lombards and utilized them fruitfully, with a shared basic understanding of the rules of the Lombard language. Eighth-century Tuscan society, therefore, did not uniformly move towards Romance linguistic acculturation, and even in the later part of the eighth century, the Lombard language was not entirely dead.[61]

57 Francovich Onesti, 'L'antroponimia longobarda', pp. 43–44.
58 Haubrichs, 'Langobardic Personal Names', pp. 206, 210.
59 Francovich Onesti, 'Discontinuità e integrazione', p. 46; Haubrichs, 'Langobardic Personal Names', p. 220.
60 Francovich Onesti, 'L'antroponimia longobarda', pp. 50–51.
61 Haubrichs, 'Langobardic Personal Names', pp. 216–17.

Archaisms and Novelties

Together with the transformations that characterize Tuscany and differentiate the region from the Po valley, it has been observed that a kind of archaizing revival of traditional Lombard terms in official documents occurred when the Carolingians were reinforcing their rule over Italy and Tuscany at the beginning of the ninth century.[62] For instance, the use in the *notitiae placiti* of terms such as *arimanni*—a word of Germanic origin rarely found in documents written during the period of Lombard rule—is striking, especially in comparison with the homologous and more diffused *viri devoti* or *exercitales* (i.e. free men who were required to join the king's army).[63] In the same period, the use of early Italo-Romance words and expressions emerged, as can be found in the formulae and texts of private charters, or in the dorsal notes of late eighth- and early ninth-century parchments.[64] These phenomena are best understood, however, as aspects of texts that derive to a greater extent from the spontaneity of their scribes and from closeness to oral depositions, as for instance in the reports of judicial disputes, namely *brevia* and *notitiae placiti*.[65] François Bougard has characterized these early Carolingian Italian texts as rather lively, for the different parties' arguments are often narrated in the first person.[66] Nevertheless, Chris Wickham, while sharing Bougard's impressions for the period up to about the year 880, has underlined how the repetition of the same sentences by different individuals, actors or witnesses, demonstrates that beneath the apparent oral spontaneity of direct speech, one must recognize the use of formularies.[67]

62 Stefano Gasparri, '« *Nobiles et credentes omines liberi arimanni* ». Linguaggio sociale e tradizioni longobarde nel regno italico', *Bullettino dell'Istituto Italiano per il Medio Evo e Archivio Muratoriano* 105 (2003), 25–51, at pp. 29–30; Stoffella, 'In a Periphery of the Empire', pp. 321–24.

63 Giovanni Tabacco, *I liberi del re nell'Italia carolingia e postcarolingia* (Spoleto, 1966); Gasparri, '« *Nobiles et credentes omines liberi arimanni* »', pp. 28–29, 38–42; Andrea Castagnetti, *Arimanni e distinzione sociale nelle sepolture* (Verona, 2015).

64 Ross Balzaretti, 'Spoken Narratives in Ninth-Century Milanese Court Records', in *Narrative and History in the Early Medieval West*, eds Elizabeth M. Tyler and Ross Balzaretti (Turnhout, 2006), pp. 11–37.

65 Attilio Bartoli Langeli, 'Sui "brevi" italiani altomedievali', *Bullettino dell'Istituto storico italiano per il Medio Evo*, 105 (2003), 1–23, at p. 16; Attilio Bartoli Langeli, 'Forma langobardica. La lingua dei documenti italiani altomedievali (secoli VIII–IX)', in *Scrittura memoria degli uomini. Atti della giornata di studio in ricordo di Giuliana Cannataro* (Bari, 2006), pp. 17–34.

66 Bougard, *La justice dans le royaume d'Italie*, pp. 109–37.

67 Chris Wickham, 'Land Disputes and Their Social Framework in Lombard-Carolingian Italy, 700–900', in *The Settlement of Disputes in Early Medieval Europe*, eds Wendy Davies

It is, however, unquestionable that in *notitiae placiti* we find the first evidence of Italo-Romance. I refer here not to the famous Capua *placitum* of 960,[68] but to earlier texts such as *placita* held in Tuscany during the late eighth and early ninth century.[69] A *placitum* debated in Lucca in 822 is particularly revealing: it concerns a dispute between a cleric, Guntelmus, and two brothers, named Natale and Auripert, who contended some estates of the episcopal church of Santa Maria a Monte in the Arno valley, of which Guntelmus was rector. In this document, the deposition in favour of the church given by a certain Popo is striking. He stated: 'Sappo res illas [...] essere sancte Marie'.[70] It is clear that this sentence treads a fine line between late Latin and Italo-Romance, a mixture that can also be observed in other charters, as in the earlier example 'accepit ego Pettu da te presbitero Aloin',[71] or in the less formal apparatus of dorsal notes: 'libello da Sundriperto homo lucense'.[72] The inclusion of Romance elements suggests the relatively spontaneous use of certain depositions written in the *notitiae placiti*, as well as a lack of filtering by scribes concerning what was really said. At the same time, these features attest to the progressive use of Romance elements in everyday speech.[73] Professional scribes adopted these elements, which therefore emerge even in judicial reports.[74] To provide a further example, mention should be made of a *notitia placiti* or *notitia iudicati* written in Pisa in 796 by the notary Istaipert/Staipert, which records depositions concerning the servile status of three men who were bound to the cathedral church of Pisa: 'Iscio Ascausulu pater istorum Rotranduli, Aspertuli clerici et Perticausuli infra trigintas annos esset servus sancte Marie et quando

and Paul Fouracre (Cambridge, 1986), pp. 105–24; reprinted in Chris Wickham, *Land and Power. Studies in Italian and European Social History, 400–1200* (London, 1994), pp. 229–56.

68 Glauco Sanga, 'Il volgare nei placiti cassinesi: vecchie questioni e nuove acquisizioni', *Rivista Italiana di Dialettologia. Lingue dialetti società* 18 (1994), 8–30; Baggio and Sanga, 'Sul volgare in età longobarda', p. 253.

69 Marco Stoffella, 'Condizionamenti politici e sociali nelle procedure di risoluzione dei conflitti nella Toscana occidentale tra età longobarda e carolingia', *Studi Medievali* 3rd ser., 59 (2018), 35–61.

70 *ChLA* 75, no. 8, pp. 36–40 (Lucca, April 822), at 38, l. 32.

71 *CDL* 1, no. 68, pp. 212–13 (at the church of St Peter in the territory of Lucca, January 739), at 212.

72 *CAAPi* 1, no. 18, pp. 47–49 (Pisa, December 827), at 47. On dorsal notes see also Seiler, and Gallagher and Wiles in this volume.

73 Alessandro Pratesi, *Genesi e forme del documento medievale*, 2nd ed. (Rome, 1987), pp. 90–92.

74 Gasparri, '« *Nobiles et credentes omines liberi arimanni* »', pp. 42–43.

Rincualdo battedit ipsum Anscausulu …'.[75] Staipert introduced vernacular elements taken from everyday language. At the same time, however, he employed some uncommon words of Germanic origin which I shall return to in the last part of this chapter. In sum, contemporary use of articulate language shows how Tuscan notaries were able to manage complex and multi-layered linguistic competences.[76]

It would be misleading, nevertheless, to overemphasize the importance of Tuscany as the region where Italo-Romance first emerged. As we have already seen, this was a regional context where, during the second half of the eighth century, bilingualism was still relatively common among the upper middle classes and perhaps also among scribes. Moreover, insisting on late-Latin or on Romance elements could take us too far in the wrong direction, for both the emergence of vernacularisms and the revival of certain terms of Germanic origin must be appreciated in contemporary written sources. This is the case with the 'Veronese Riddle', as mentioned above; according to recent reassessments of its place of composition and its inclusion of Romance elements, this pen trial should be placed at the *scriptorium* of the cathedral church of Verona around the middle of the eighth century.[77] Interestingly, in 846, a century later in the same territory of Verona, the notary Garibert creatively blended Germanic, late Latin, and Italo-Romance nouns when he wrote down a will dictated by Engelbert of Erbè, son of the deceased Grimoald, an aristocrat of Lombard origin.[78] Garibert explicitly listed various precious objects that

75 *CAAPi* 1, no. 14, pp. 36–39 (Pisa, 5 June 796), at 37: 'I know that Ascausulus, father of these men, i.e. Rotrandulus, Anspertulus the cleric, and Perticausulus, was for thirty years a *servus* of [the church of] St Mary, and when Rincualdus beat the same Ascausulus …'

76 Bartoli Langeli, 'Forma langobardica', pp. 17–24.

77 Scevola Mariotti, 'Sull'« indovinello veronese »', in *Letterature comparate. Problemi di metodo. Studi in onore di Ettore Paratore*, 4 vols (Bologna, 1981) 2:987–96; Serenella Baggio and Glauco Sanga, 'Un'ipotesi sintattica per l'Indovinello veronese—Il bue e l'indovinello. Commento al più antico testo italiano finora noto', *Rivista italiana di dialettologia* 16 (1992), 9–27; Aurelio Roncaglia, 'L'indovinello veronese-friulano, i suoi « latinismi » e la « legge Tobler-Mussafia »', in *Omaggio a Gianfranco Folena*, 3 vols (Padua, 1993), 1:49–59; Ricarda Liver, 'Ecrire au Moyen Age. A propos d'une nouvelle interprétation de l'« indovinello veronese »', in *Mélanges de philologie et de littérature médiévales offerts à Michel Burger*, eds Jacqueline Cerquiglini-Toulet and Olivier Collet, Publications romanes et françaises 208 (Geneva, 1994), pp. 203–13; Mauro Braccini, 'Singolarità e affiliazioni nel cosiddetto « Indovinello veronese »', *Studi di filologia italiana* 69 (2011), 5–52.

78 *ChLA* 60, no. 25, pp. 109–17 (Erbè, 28 May 846). Cf. Andrea Castagnetti, 'La distribuzione geografica dei possessi di un grande proprietario veronese del secolo IX: Engelberto del fu Grimoaldo', *Rivista di storia dell'agricoltura* 9 (1969), 15–26; Andrea Castagnetti, 'Le

reflected the social status of their owner.[79] The linguistic skills of the Veronese notary also emerged in this part of the document.[80] Among the many items that Garibert listed, some were described making use of words of probable Lombard origin, such as *sperones*, *blaiones*, or *vuintingas*:

> Similiter volo ut deveninat in ipsos rogatores meos baugos duos,[81] balcio uno, forfele argenteo uno, sperones argenteos duos,[82] betramo aureo uno, curtina una, spata una, coclare argentea una, busece argentea una, facitergio uno, blaiones duos,[83] mapa uno, orecio uno, camisio uno cum vuintingas,[84] vestido caterno uno, vueta una, camisile uno, mudandas

aristocrazie della *Langobardia* nelle città e nei territori rurali', in *Città e campagna nei secoli altomedievali*, Settimane 54 (Spoleto, 2009), pp. 539–619, at 606–10.

79 François Bougard, 'Tesori e mobilia italiani nell'alto medioevo', in *Tesori. Forme di acculturazione della ricchezza nell'alto medioevo*, eds Sauro Gelichi and Cristina La Rocca, Altomedioevo 3 (Rome, 2004), pp. 69–122, at 86–88; Tiziana Franco, 'Con gli occhi di Raterio: note sulla cultura artistica veronese di X secolo', in *La più antica veduta di Verona. Iconografia rateriana. L'archetipo e l'immagine tramandata. Atti del seminario di studi (Museo di Castelvecchio, 6 maggio 2011)* (Verona, 2012), pp. 167–81, at 169–70. On the will see also Stefano Gasparri, 'I testamenti nell'Italia settentrionale fra VIII e IX secolo', in *Sauver son âme et se perpétuer. Trasmission du patrimoine et mémoire au haut moyen âge*, eds François Bougard and Cristina La Rocca, Collection de l'École Française de Rome 351 (Rome, 2005), pp. 97–113, at 85–87. On *rogatores* mentioned in this will and in other late Lombard and Carolingian documents see Marco Stoffella, 'Competizione e collaborazione nelle esecuzioni testamentarie dell'Italia carolingia', in *Coopétition. Rivaliser, coopérer dans les sociétés du haut Moyen Âge (500–1100)*, eds Régine Le Jan, Geneviève Bührer-Thierry, and Stefano Gasparri, Haut Moyen Âge 31 (Turnhout, 2018), pp. 185–213, at 190–91.

80 Massimiliano Bassetti, 'Novità lessicali nel latino dei documenti privati del Veneto medievale (secoli X–XII)', *Bulletin du Cange* 74 (2016), 239–60, at p. 253.

81 *Bauga, baugus* (armring) is also a term of Germanic origin, with corresponding forms attested in Old High German, Old English, and Old Norse; Wolfgang Haubrichs, personal communication.

82 Francovich Onesti, *Vestigia longobarde*, p. 120; this is a loanword from Germanic **sperôn* = spur, which became common in medieval Latin and Italo-Romance. It is attested in Tuscany in the Lombard period, as is the case for the *sporuni argentei* which can be found in CDL 2, no. 295, pp. 440–44 (Pisa, 768×?774); for a more recent edition (with different dating) and further discussion of the same document see below at nn. 87–88. See also Friedrich Kluge and Elmar Seebold, *Etymologisches Wörterbuch der deutschen Sprache*, 25th ed. (Berlin, 2011), p. 870, and Manlio Cortelazzo, Paolo Zolli, *Il nuovo etimologico. DELI. Dizionario etimologico della lingua italiana*, 2nd ed. (Bologna, 1999), p. 1584.

83 Sabatini, 'Riflessi linguistici', p. 420, where he supposes an origin from Lombard language: **blahjo*/**plahjo* = sheet.

84 Silvia Bellocchio, 'Sulle tracce di due lemmi germanici: Widimo e Windangassia', in *I longobardi in Italia*, pp. 333–47, at 341–44.

> duas, culcedra una, plumacio uno, caballos duos, pario ereo uno, urciolo ereo uno, cordereses duo, corios de cervos duos.[85]

According to Francesco Sabatini, the word *blaiones*, a term of Germanic origin, is rare and is primarily limited to central and southern Italy.[86] It is striking, therefore, that, as in this case, Verona notaries of the mid-ninth century were still able to correctly use specific Lombard terms, alternating between them and late Latin and early Italo-Romance words. We should also remember that during the second half of the eighth century words of Germanic origin for spurs and other objects were used in the Tuscan city of Pisa;[87] here, they appear among the precious items listed in the very last part of the famous *breve de moniminas* which once belonged to the *ancilla Dei* Ghittia.[88]

Another correspondence that linguistically binds northeastern Italy and northwestern Tuscany is the use of the Germanic word *vuintingas*, which was one of the terms used by Garibert in Verona and which has recently been studied by Silvia Bellocchio.[89] She has argued that this word should be associated with the term *windangassia*, which appears in an original *charta repromissionis* issued in Lucca on 10 March 846—interestingly, precisely the same year Engelbert dictated his will in the territory of Verona.[90] However, in the Lucchese document, which was issued by the notary Rachifonsus, active in the central decades of the ninth century,[91] only clothes and textiles were mentioned: 'uno vestito caprino texto in siricho cum vuindangassia et uno tapp[ite…]tum', where the words *cum vuindangassia* were added by the

---

85 *ChLA* 60, no. 25, pp. 109–17 (Erbè, 28 May 846), at 112, ll. 42–44: 'Similarly I want the executors [of my will] to have my two armillas, one belt, one silver knife, two silver spurs, a gold *betramo*, one blanket, one sword, one silver spoon, one silver *busece*, one napkin, two sheets, one tablecloth, one *orecio*, a tunic with a strip of tissue, one *caterno* dress, one garment, one shirt, two underpants, one pillow case, one pillow, two horses, one copper pot, one copper jar, two goatskins, two deerskins'.

86 Sabatini, 'Riflessi linguistici', p. 420.

87 *CAAPi* 1, no. 10, pp. 25–31 ([Pisa], [*post* 1 March 763 (*ante* 1 March 769?)]), at 29: '[…] uno baltio cum banda et fibila de argento inaurato […] sporuni argentei'.

88 Pier Silverio Leicht, 'L'archivio di Alahis', in *Studi di storia e diritto in onore di Enrico Besta per il suo XL anno del suo insegnamento*, 4 vols (Milan, 1937), 2:29–36; reprinted in Pier Silverio Leicht, *Scritti vari di storia del diritto italiano*, 2 vols (Milan, 1948), 2.1:233–39; Gasparri, 'Il regno longobardo in Italia', pp. 64–65; Bartoli Langeli, 'Sui 'brevi' italiani altomedievali'; Antonella Ghignoli, 'Su due famosi documenti pisani'.

89 Bellocchio, 'Sulle tracce di due lemmi germanici', pp. 341–44.

90 *ChLA* 79, no. 5, pp. 28–30 (Lucca, 10 March 846).

91 Rachifonsus *notarius* is one of the notaries who can be linked to the school of Gaudentius. See Figure 8.1.

same Rachifonsus in the space between the lines.[92] The editor of the relevant *Chartae latinae antiquiores* volume has interpreted the Germanic term as an unknown item of clothing, but Bellocchio has suggested that its meaning is connected to the Lombard verb **windan* (to wrap, to ring), probably meaning a strip of tissue that was usually wrapped, and which eventually referred to leggings.[93] Even if the recent edition of this charter has not been able to interpret the meaning of this very specific and uncommon word of Germanic origin correctly, it has at least emended an error introduced by Daniele Bertini in his 1836 edition of the Lucca documents.[94] Its misunderstanding has for a long time led to mistaken and extravagant deductions about the production of organdie in early medieval Lucca.[95]

Returning to the issue of bilingualism, we can observe here the problem of how words of Germanic origin have been or are recognized and explained, and how they are traced back to one tradition or another. The example of *windangassia/vuintingas*, which in its northern Tuscan variant has been incorrectly recognized and poorly explained for nearly two centuries, also raises the related matter of the variants and neologisms that early medieval notaries may have used in the charters they wrote. In some cases, they may even have transformed or modified words of Germanic origin. This is the case, for instance, with *Hermentrudi sculdarissi*, a well-off woman recorded in a Veronese document of 841, who has only recently been recognized as female.[96] Teudelabus, the *clericus et notarius* who wrote this deed of sale, introduced a neologism which described Hirmindrut through the modified masculine Lombard term of *sculdhais/sculdassius*.[97] Editors and commentators have long misread and misinterpreted both the world *sculdarissi* and Hirmindrut's gender,[98] denying

92 *ChLA* 79, no. 5, pp. 28–30 (Lucca, 10 March 846), at 28, l. 8: 'a goatskin dress adorned with wrapped silk and one carpet/tapestry [...]'.

93 Bellocchio, 'Sulle tracce di due lemmi germanici', p. 344.

94 *Memorie e Documenti per servire all'Istoria del Ducato di Lucca*, IV, ed. Daniele Bertini, 2 vols (Lucca, 1818–36), 2:40.

95 Bellocchio, 'Sulle tracce di due lemmi germanici', p. 341.

96 Hailey J. LaVoy, 'Hirmindrut Sculdarissa: A Ninth-Century Woman's Original Letter and its Implications', *The Journal of Medieval Latin* 25 (2015), 29–50. This mistake does not appear in Mark Mersiowsky, 'Preserved by Destruction: Carolingian Original Letters and CLM 6333', in *Early Medieval Palimpsests*, ed. George Declercq, Bibliologia 26 (Turnhout, 2007), pp. 73–97. For the diffusion of the name Hirmindrut in Lombard Italy and for the meaning of the Lombard word *sculdahis*, see Francovich Onesti, *Vestigia longobarde*, pp. 191 and 118–19.

97 Bassetti, 'Novità lessicali nel latino', pp. 248–52.

98 *Codice diplomatico veronese* I. *Dalla caduta dell'Impero romano alla fine del periodo carolingio*, ed. Vittorio Fainelli, Monumenti storici pubblicati dalla r. Deputazione di storia patria per le Venezie, 1 (Venice, 1940), pp. 232–35; *ChLA* 59, no. 15, pp. 75–79 (*Vico Saltesanus*,

the possibility that the masculine Lombard title of *sculdahis* could be declined into the feminine gender and thus given to a woman.[99]

Many other words of Germanic origin were frequently used in Pisa from the beginning of the eighth century, carrying on into the eleventh century and beyond. In addition to the examples mentioned above, this is also the case with words such as *allodium* (land held in full proprietorial right), *anagrip* (kidnapping of a woman), *barbano* (uncle), *frea* (free woman), *gastaldo/castaldionem* (royal officer), *launehil/launeghil/launeschilt* (counter-gift), *morgincap/moriincap* (morning gift), *mundium* (legal guardianship), *mundualda/mundualdus* (the person who gives guardianship), *vadia/guadia* (any formal promise signified by the offer of an object), *salam* (hall),[100] and *vuarigangus* (foreigner seeking asylum).[101]

Ferquidem

The word *ferquidem* (and related forms) began to be used in the formulae of Tuscan private charters around the mid-eighth century. By focusing on how, why, and when notaries used this term in charters written in Pisa and Lucca between the second half of the eighth and the first half of the ninth century, in the last section of this chapter I shall try to cast some further light on issues related to bilingualism in early medieval Tuscany. Following the studies of Maria Giovanna Arcamone,[102] Nicoletta Francovich Onesti has recently reasserted that the adjective *ferquido* should be recognized as a Lombard word whose original meaning was 'aforesaid': *fer-quide* <**kweden*.[103] This definition agrees with an earlier one of Arcamone, who in 1969 stated that *ferquido* (ablative),

---

23 January 841), at 78, ll. 5–6, where Francesca Santoni in 2001 wrongly interpreted the gender of the purchaser, talking of an *Ermentrudo sculdascio*. The same mistake is also in Giulia Ammannati, 'Una lettera veronese del secolo IX', *Scrittura e civiltà* 25 (2001), 377–83.

99 Bassetti, 'Novità lessicali nel latino', pp. 251–53.

100 Maria Giovanna Arcamone, 'Glossario', in *Carte dell'Archivio Capitolare di Pisa*, 4 (1101–1120), ed. Matilde Tirelli Carli, Thesaurus Ecclesiarum Italiae VII, 4 (Rome, 1969), pp. 264–72; Maria Vollono, 'Methodik und Probleme bei der Erforschung des Langobardischen am Beispiel einiger juristischen Fachbegriffe: mundoald, launegild, sculdhais', in *Die Langobarden*, eds Pohl and Erhart, pp. 477–503.

101 Maria Giovanna Arcamone, 'Glossario delle parole di origine germanica', in *Carte dell'Archivio Capitolare di Pisa*, 3 (1076–1100), ed. Matilde Tirelli Carli, Thesaurus Ecclesiarum Italiae VII, 3 (Rome, 1977), pp. 237–46, at 244–45.

102 Arcamone, 'Glossario', p. 267.

103 Francovich Onesti, *Vestigia longobarde*, pp. 79–80.

ferquidem (accusative), _ferquidis_ (plural ablative) should be translated as 'already said', 'corresponding', or 'of the same value'. According to Arcamone, these forms go back to an unattested nominative case *_ferquidus_ or *_ferquidis_. As mentioned above, the term was frequently used in early medieval Latin texts, beginning with the Edict of King Rothari, through the forms _ferquido_, _ferquidum_, etc., which can be interepreted as Latinizations of a compound formed by <*_kwetha-_ 'to say' (past participle *_kwethan-_), *_kwithan-_ ('said') and the prefix <*_fara-_ 'before'. Subsequently, the term can be found in the charter formulae _in ferquido loco, in ferquidem loco, in ferquidis locis_, etc. According to Arcamone, these forms are diffused only across Italy, which is what confirms their undoubtedly Lombard origin.[104] A century ago, however, Leo Wiener offered a rather different explanation about the origins of this word, illustrating the numerous uses of _ferquidem_ in Tuscan documents. He saw it as the result of a Latin corruption which may have occurred in Visigothic Spain, whence it could have been imported into Lombard Italy via Tuscany and Pisa, its main port on the Tyrrhenian sea.[105]

Wiener's interpretation today has been completely overturned, for both international and Italian research traditions now place the term _ferquidem_ (and related forms) among those linguistic elements whose origins are Lombard.[106] In Rothari's law-code of 643, where versions of the term are first attested, Latin glosses reading _id est simile_ are also provided to explain its meaning.[107] The mechanism, therefore, is the same as that employed for other Germanic terms for which the legislator thought it was necessary to provide further explanations; in the same edict, for instance, we find: 'de haistan, id est furorem'; 'de gamahalos, id est confabulatus', and others.[108] A form of the same term appears just once in the laws of King Liutprand of 735, but its meaning in this instance is not completely clear.[109] After 735, the word disappears from Lombard legal

104 Arcamone, 'Glossario', p. 267.

105 Leo Wiener, _Commentary to the Germanic Laws and Mediaeval Documents_ (Cambridge, 1915), pp. 1–10.

106 van der Rhee, _Die germanischen Wörter_, pp. 52–54.

107 _Le leggi dei Longobardi_, eds Azzara and Gasparri, p. 44 (_Edictum Rothari_, 147): 'damnum conponat ferquido, id est simile'; p. 54 (_Edictum Rothari_, 175): 'si ausus non fuerit iurare, quod compositum sit, reddat ei ferquido, id est simile, quales in illa diae fuit, quando donatum est'; p. 94 (_Edictum Rothari_, 330): 'nam si post ipsum iactaverit et eum occiderit, reddat ferquido, id est similem'; p. 96 (_Edictum Rothari_, 337): 'recepiat ipsum, qui laesus factus est, et reddat ei ferquido, id est simile'; p. 100 (_Edictum Rothari_, 349): 'nisi si minus fuerint de decim et occiderit, reddat ferquido, id est simile'.

108 _Le leggi dei Longobardi_, eds Azzara and Gasparri, p. 78 (_Edictum Rothari_, 277), p. 96 (_Edictum Rothari_, 362); Haubrichs, 'Sprache und Schriftlichkeit', pp. 133–201.

109 _Le leggi dei Longobardi_, eds Azzara and Gasparri, p. 234 (_Liutprandi leges_, 151): 'reddat ille, qui occisit, ipsos porcus ferquidus'.

texts and reappears soon after in charters issued mainly in western Tuscany, in the area that was politically influenced by Lucca and its elites; interestingly, Jan-Olof Tjäder has also underlined the presence of the expression *in ferquide/ ferquidem loco* in a document issued at Farfa in 763.[110] If in the central decades of the eighth century *ferquidem* was sporadically used as an alternative to the Latin word *eodem*, in the second part of the eighth century this Lombard word became recurrent in the area of Lucca within a formula used in final clauses of sales or exchanges written by both lay and ecclesiastic scribes (see Figure 8.1).

TABLE 8.1 Occurrences of *ferquidem* in early medieval Tuscan private charters (720–90)

Date and place	Edition	Writer	Formula
January 739, S. Pietro, Lucca	*ChLA* 31, no. 915, pp. 2–4	*Teuderad amicus noster*	*in aferquede loco*
744×745, S. Donato *in Fasqua*, Volterra	*ChLA* 31, no. 922, pp. 28–31	*Altipert amicus meus*	*in ferquede loco*
July 747, Lucca	*ChLA* 31, no. 929, pp. 54–55	*Teutpert vir devotus*	*in ferquidem locum*
June 752, Lucca	*ChLA* 31, no. 935, pp. 78–79	*Teutpert vir devotus*	*in ferquido locum*
September 752, Lucca	*ChLA* 31, no. 936, pp. 80–81	*Raspert amicus meus*	*in ferquede loco*
25 March 753, Lucca	*ChLA* 32, no. 937, pp. 3–5	*Osprandus subdiaconum*	*ferquidem talem res*
31 March 759, Lucca	*ChLA* 32, no. 951, pp. 62–63	*Teutpert*	*in ferquidem locum*
June 759, Lucca	*ChLA* 32, no. 952, pp. 64–65	*Prandulo*	*in ferquide locum*
May 760, Paterno, Val di Cornia (GR)	*ChLA* 32, no. 959, pp. 88–89	*Autelmu diaconus amicus meus*	*in ferquide locum*
January 761, Lucca	*ChLA* 33, no. 962, pp. 7–10	*Georgius*	*in ferquidem locum*
May 764, Lucca	*ChLA* 33, no. 980, pp. 88–90	*Rachipert*	*in ferquide locum*

110 *ChLA* 26, no. 810, pp. 69–73 (Cantignano, July 783), at 72, n. 7.

TABLE 8.1 Occurrences of *ferquidem* in early medieval (*cont.*)

Date and place	Edition	Writer	Formula
24 August 765, Lucca	*ChLA* 34, no. 987, pp. 14–15	*Osprandus diaconus*	*in ferquide locum*
September 767, Lucca	*ChLA* 34, no. 998, pp. 50–51	*Ghisprand*	*ferquidem in ferquidem loco*
2 July 768, Lucca	*ChLA* 34, no. 1002, pp. 66–67	*Prandulo*	*in ferquidem loco*
11 July 769, Lucca	*ChLA* 34, no. 1007, pp. 82–85	*Osprandus diaconus*	*in ferquidem loco*
30 December 769, Lucca	*CDL* 2, no. 236, pp. 301–2	*Osprandus diaconus*	*in ferquidem loco*
1, 5, or 13 June 770, Lucca	*ChLA* 35, no. 1014, pp. 19–21	*Austripertus clericus*	*in ferquide loco*
1 September 770, Lucca	*ChLA* 35, no. 1016, pp. 26–28	*Austripertus clericus*	*in ferquide loco*
30 March 772, Lucca	*ChLA* 35, no. 1030, pp. 81–83	*Austripertus presbiter*	*in ferquide loco*
May 772, S. Giuliano, Lucca	*ChLA* 35, no. 1034, pp. 94–97	*Firmiteu scriptor*	*ferquidem*
10 February 773, *Ursiano*, Lunata (LU)	*ChLA* 36, no. 1039, pp. 2–3	*Rachiprandus clericus*	*in ferquide loco*
19 April 773, Lucca	*ChLA* 36, no. 1041, pp. 6–7	*Rachiprandus clericus*	*in ferquide loco*
June 773, Lucca	*ChLA* 36, no. 1044, pp. 13–15	*Prandulo*	*ferquidem et in ferquidem loco*
16 July 774, Lucca	*ChLA* 36, no. 1047, pp. 22–23	*Gheipertus clericus*	*in ferquide loco*
July 774, Lucca	*ChLA* 36, no. 1048, pp. 25–27	*Petru*	*in ferquidem locum*
27 December 774, Lucca	*ChLA* 36, no. 1051, pp. 32–33	*Gheipertus clericus*	*ferquidem, in ferquide loco*
4 March 775, Lucca	*ChLA* 36, no. 1052, pp. 34–35	*Rachiprandus clericus*	*in ferquide loco*
9 July 775, Lucca	*ChLA* 36, no. 1053, pp. 36–37	*Rachiprandus clericus*	*ferquide, in ferquide loco*
26 May 776, Lucca	*ChLA* 36, no. 1056, pp. 42–43	*Rachiprandu*	*in ferquidem loco*
August 776, Pisa	*ChLA* 26, no. 810, pp. 64–67	*Istaipertu notarius*	*ferquide*

TABLE 8.1 Occurrences of *ferquidem* in early medieval (*cont.*)

Date and place	Edition	Writer	Formula
December 776, *Monaciaticum* (LU)	*ChLA* 36, no. 1058, pp. 42–49	*Gunprandu*	*ferquidem et in ferquidem locum*
March 777, Lucca	*ChLA* 36, no. 1060, pp. 52–53	*Prandulfus notarius*	*in ferquidem loco*
24 July 777, *Valeriana* (LU)	*ChLA* 36, no. 1063, pp. 63–65	*Filippus subdiaconus*	*in ferquidem loco*
16 March 778, Lucca	*ChLA* 36, no. 1065, pp. 69–75	*Filippus subdiaconus*	*in ferquidem loco*
March 778, S. Regolo in Gualdo (GR)	*ChLA* 36, no. 1067, pp. 83–85	*Austripert clericus*	*in ferquidem loco*
25 February 779, Triana (LU)	*ChLA* 37, no. 1069, pp. 3–7	*Rachiprandus presbiter*	*in ferquide loco*
June 779, Lucca	*ChLA* 37, no. 1070, pp. 9–11	*Teudipert*	*ferquide et in ferquide*
December 779, Lucca	*ChLA* 37, no. 1071, pp. 13–15	*Ratfonsus*	*ferquidem in ferquidem locum*
12 April 780, Lucca	*ChLA* 37, no. 1072, pp. 17–19	*David*	*in ferquidem loco*
23 July 780, Santarlascio (LU)	*ChLA* 37, no. 1074, pp. 23–25	*Rachipaldus*	*in ferquidem loco*
April 782, Lucca	*ChLA* 37, no. 1080, pp. 38–43	*Teudipert*	*ferquide et in ferquide*
August 782, Lucca	*ChLA* 37, no. 1084, pp. 38–61	*Ratfonsus*	*ferquide[m] in ferquidem locum*
July 783, Cantignano (LU)	*ChLA* 26, no. 811, pp. 69–73	*Teudipert*	*in ferquide loco*
10 October 783, Lucca	*ChLA* 37, no. 1088, pp. 72–76	*Teudipert*	*in ferquidem loco*
1 July 785, Lucca	*ChLA* 38, no. 1096, pp. 3–5	*Filippus presbiter*	*in ferquide loco*
28 August 785, Lucca	*ChLA* 38, no. 1097, pp. 6–7	*Gumpertus subdiaconus*	*in ferquidem loco*
August 786, S. Maria di Gello (PI)	*ChLA* 38, no. 1105, pp. 35–37	*Dominicus notarius*	*in ferquidem loco*
September 787, Lucca	*ChLA* 38, no. 1112, pp. 56–57	*Gumpertus subdiaconus*	*in ferquidem loco*
4 January 788, Lucca	*ChLA* 38, no. 1117, pp. 69–71	*Filippus presbiter*	*in ferquide loco*

TABLE 8.1 Occurrences of *ferquidem* in early medieval (*cont.*)

Date and place	Edition	Writer	Formula
May 788, S. Pietro di Capannoli (PI)	*ChLA* 38, no. 1120, pp. 76–77	*Austrualdus subdiaconus*	*in ferquide loco*
18 August 788, Lucca	*ChLA* 38, no. 1122, pp. 82–85	*Gumpertus subdiaconus*	*in ferquidem loco*
16 December 788, Lucca	*ChLA* 38, no. 1123, pp. 86–87	*Gumpertus subdiaconus*	*in ferquidem loco*
9 June 789, Lucca	*ChLA* 38, no. 1124, pp. 88–91	*Ermimari subdiaconus*	*ferquide in ferquidem locum*
23 June 789, Lucca	*ChLA* 38, no. 1125, pp. 92–95	*Saxo clericus*	*in ferquidem loco*
7 August 790, Lucca	*ChLA* 39, no. 1128, pp. 14–15	*Gumpertus presbiter*	*in ferquidem loco*

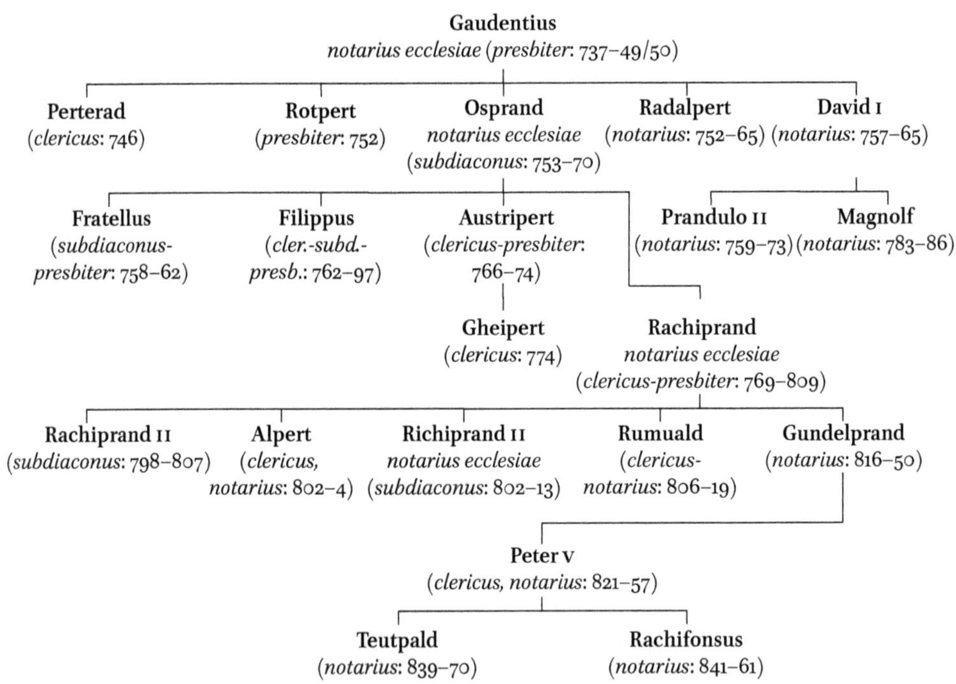

FIGURE 8.1 A revised version of the school of the *presbiter* Gaudentius. Adapted from Armando Petrucci, 'Il codice e i documenti: scrivere a Lucca fra VIII e IX secolo', in Armando Petrucci and Carlo Romeo, «*Scriptores in urbibus*». *Alfabetismo e cultura scritta nell'Italia altomedievale* (Bologna, 1992), pp. 77–108, at 108, with *ChLA* 30–40 and 72–87

In Lucca, the term is attested for the first time in 739, when the lay scribe Teuderad used the expression *in aferquede loco* in a deed of sale he issued in the countryside for his *amicus* Petto, *vir devotus*.[111] Unfortunately, this is the only preserved charter written by Teuderad, so we cannot say if the expression *in aferquede loco* was normally used by him, nor whether he had begun using it in previous decades. Interestingly, his Lucchese contemporary, the *notarius ecclesiae* and *presbiter* Gaudentius, who has been recognized as the master of the school at the cathedral church of Lucca (see Figure 8.1), was using a similar final clause.[112] However, he avoided the Germanic word that was glossed in the Lombard laws and that Teuderad used in 739, preferring the equivalent Latin expression *in eodem loco*.[113] Given that Gaudentius did not use the term, it is unclear how it spread in Lucca. A turning point might be represented by the activity of the lay scribe Teutpert, who in the first part of his career never used this Lombard word[114] but around the mid-eighth century began to employ it in his charters (see Table 8.1). Together with other lay writers such as Teuderad, Altipert, and Raspert, for all of whom we only have scanty evidence, Teutpert could have influenced the local tradition and helped spread the use of *ferquidem* (and related forms) in Lucca. In fact, Teutpert may have been one of the initators of this local use, as by the mid-eighth century he must already have been an influential scribe. His importance is confirmed by the fact that in 752 he was asked to issue a sale which involved two very distinguished brothers, Bishop Vualtprand of Lucca (737–54), who lost his life after joining the

111 *ChLA* 26, no. 915, pp. 2–4 (the church of St Peter in the territory of Lucca, January 739), at 2, l. 26: '… reprometto adque spondeo me esset conpunere in duppla meliorata terrula, de quo agitor, sub stemationem, in aferquede loco; et cartula uenditionis in sua manea fermitatem'.

112 Luigi Schiaparelli, *Il codice 490 della Biblioteca Capitolare di Lucca e la scuola scrittoria lucchese (sec. VIII–IX). Contributi allo studio della minuscola precarolina in Italia*, Studi e Testi 36 (Rome, 1924), p. 68; Petrucci, 'Scrittura e libro', pp. 79–81.

113 *ChLA* 31, no. 919, pp. 16–18 (Lucca, 739×740), at 16, ll. 14–15: 'ego uel meis heridis, conpuna tibi uel ad tuis heridis in dupplo, res meliorata de quod agitor, in eodem loco'.

114 *ChLA* 31, no. 918, pp. 14–51 (Lucca, April 740), at 14: 'spundeo ego Baruncio cum meus heridis cunpunere tiui Gundualdi et ad tuos heridis, de quod superium legitor, in dupra, meliorata terra unde agitor'; *ChLA* 31, no. 921, pp. 24–27 (Lucca, October 742), at 26: 'cunpuna ego Mauro unam cum meus heridis tibi Crispine vel ad tuos heridis, de quod superius legitor, in dupla, bona condicionem in melioratam terra et vineam et serbus unde hic agitor, sum stimationem quales tunc fueret'.

army of King Aistulf,[115] and his brother Perprand, *vir clarissimus*;[116] they were both sons of Vualtpert, the Lombard duke of Lucca.[117] The portion of property placed in southern Tuscany and alienated by Perprand in 752 was a *sala sundriale*, a typically Lombard definition for an estate with a demesne which, in the ninth century, would come to be described in Tuscan charters as a *curtis dominicata*.

It is difficult to be more precise about the diffusion in Lucca of the word *ferquidem* and its variants, since we lack the evidence concerning lay professional scribes who probably issued charters mainly for lay elites rather than ecclesiastical institutions. As a matter of fact, the existing Lucca charters have been preserved within the archiepiscopal archive, so they mainly represent the interests of Lucchese archbishops and clerics.[118] All these reasons could therefore explain why in Lucca the use of *ferquidem* in final clauses, which began during the central decades of the eighth century among lay scribes, was not shared at the cathedral school by its master, Gaudentius. It did, however, affect some of his most influential pupils, such as Osprand, attested in the first stage of his career as subdeacon, but shortly afterwards promoted to deacon (compare Table 8.1 with Figure 8.1).

Interestingly, in the nearby city of Pisa the diffusion of this Lombard term was very limited. Its first mention can be traced back to the year 776, when the lay notary Istaipert/Staipert did not invoke the formula *in ferquide/ferquidem loco*, but instead employed the word in a different sentence with an apparently correct understanding of its meaning: 'Et si ea vovis da omnem hominem defendere non potueremus, alia tanta terra sub extimatjionem ferquide tale tivi aut ad tuos heredes ego aut meus heredes restaurare deveamus'.[119] Istaipert/

---

115 Hansmartin Schwarzmaier, *Lucca und das Reich bis zum Ende des 11. Jahrhunderts. Studien zur Sozialstruktur einer Herzogstadt in der Toskana*, Bibliothek des Deutschen Historischen Instituts in Rom 41 (Tübingen, 1972), pp. 74–78; Stoffella, 'Crisi e trasformazioni', p. 23 and n. 136.

116 *ChLA* 31, no. 935, pp. 78–79 (Lucca, June 752).

117 Schwarzmaier, *Lucca und das Reich*, pp. 159–61.

118 Anne Mailloux, 'Modalités de constitution du patrimoine épiscopal de Lucques, VIIIe–Xe siècle', in *Les transferts patrimoniaux en Europe occidentale, VIIIe–X^{e} siécle (I): Actes de la table ronde de Rome (Rome 6, 7 et 8 mai 1999)*, ed. François Bougard, Mélanges de l'École Française de Rome, Moyen Âge 111 (2000), pp. 701–23; Schwarzmaier, *Lucca und das Reich*, pp. 9–12; Bougard, *La justice dans le royaume d'Italie*, pp. 97–98; Costambeys, 'The Laity, the Clergy', pp. 239–41; Mersiowsky, *Die Urkunde in der Karolingerzeit*, pp. 360–61.

119 *CAAPi* 1, no. 12, pp. 31–33 (Pisa, August 776). Cf. *ChLA* 26, no. 809, pp. 64–67 (Pisa, August 776): 'and if we will not be able to defend you and your rights from everybody, then I or my heirs will have to refund you or your heirs with the same amount of land after an estimate, as already said'.

Staipert is the same scribe of the above-mentioned *notitia iudicati* written in Pisa in 796, in which he used the vernacular term *battedit*. In the *notitia* of 796 he also spelled his name in two different ways, *Istaipertu/Staipertu*, and employed the variant *iscio* instead of *scio* within the text of the judicial report.[120] In fact, in early medieval Tuscan anthroponyms, we find examples in Lombard names as well as in Latin ones of prothesis of a front vowel, *e-* or *i-*, before [s] followed by a consonant, as in the case of Istaipert/Staipert.

The next example in chronological order is a charter now preserved in Pisa. It was written in 783 by a lay scribe named Teudipert in Cantignano, a locality in the countryside between Lucca and Pisa. In this act, Perprand, son of the deceased Vualtpert, gave to his daughter Ololia a *curtis* in Rosignano, an important fiscal centre south of Pisa and Livorno.[121] Not only did Teudipert use the phrase *in ferquide loco*, but he interestingly also used a Frankish term, *curtis*, which was not yet common in Tuscany. On the other hand, he also employed many Lombard words which typically identified aristocratic estates, such as *sala*,[122] *sundrio*,[123] and *cafagio*:[124] 'sala una ubi dicitur ad Monte, una cum sundrio de vinea ante se seo et ipso oliveto in ipso monte seo et cafagio meo in ipso loco Rasiniano'.[125] Moreover, in the same document he referred to unfree and semi-free people, using for the latter the Lombard terms *aldionibus et aldiane*. In addition, Perprand declared that he was following the *lex Langobardorum* and its traditions, by relying on the *launechild* (the counter-gift prescribed in the Edict of King Rothari which had to be given when someone received a gift): 'Et adcepi a te launichildi legibus meis Langubardorum, sicut edicti contenet autorita, uno pario manicias'.[126] The conscious repetition of

120 *CAAPi* 1, no. 14, p. 37.

121 *CAAPi* 1, no. 13, pp. 33–35 (Cantignano, Lucca, July 783). See also *ChLA* 26, no. 810, pp. 69–73 (Cantignano, July 783): 'ut sit conponituri ipsi heredis meis tibi vel ad tuis heredis omne ipse case et res vel homenis, omnia in duplum in ferquide locum su extimatione quales tunc fuere'. Ololia is a Romance form of Eulalia; Wolfgang Haubrichs, personal communication.

122 Francovich Onesti, *Vestigia longobarde*, pp. 113–14.

123 Francovich Onesti, *Vestigia longobarde*, p. 122.

124 Francovich Onesti, *Vestigia longobarde*, pp. 87–88.

125 *CAAPi* 1, no. 13, pp. 33–35 (Cantignano, Lucca, July 783), at 34: 'a hall placed in the locality named Monte, with its demesne vineyard opposite it, and the same olive yard on the same mountain and my part of fenced wood in the same locality of Rosignano (Livorno)'.

126 *CAAPi* 1, no. 13, p. 34: 'and I received from you the *launechild* (counter-gift), owed to me according to the laws of the Lombard laws, just as the authority of the Edict holds, a pair of gloves'. *Le leggi dei Longobardi*, eds Azzara and Gasparri, p. 54 (*Edictum Rothari*, 175): 'De Launegild. Si quis rem suam cuicumque donaverat, et postea qui donavit launegild requisiverit, tunc ille, […] qui accepit, aut heredes eius, si ausus non fuerit iurare, quod conpositum sit, reddat ei ferquido, id est similem, quales in illa diae fuit, quando

these traditional Lombard terms, the explicit reference to Lombard law, and the use of other, recently adopted words such as *curtis* must lead us to conclude that this gift-giving act was written for a Lombard aristocrat connected with the territories of Pisa and Lucca and their administration. 'Perprandu filio bone memorie Vualperti', the donor in the transaction recorded in the charter, who signed it with an imposing and trembling writing, probably on account of his old age, can be identified with Perprand, son of the above-mentioned Lombard Duke Vualtpert, who was by then deceased.[127] Attested in 752 together with his brother Vualtprand,[128] Perprand is mentioned again in 754 alongside another brother, Pertifuns.[129] As in the previously discussed case regarding Teutpert and the use of *ferquidem* in 752, the commissioning of this document by the son of a Lombard duke could explain the abundant use of terms that are strictly connected with Lombard tradition. At the same time, they testify to the adapting skills of professional scribes who lived during the early Carolingian period, assisting Lombard aristocrats and adopting linguistic codes close to their patrons' traditions while also introducing updated and more politically relevant terminologies.[130] Even though this charter is today found in the archiepiscopal archive of Pisa, it is most probable that the scribe Teudipert worked for aristocrats and well-off inhabitants in Lucca's territory, especially since two earlier documents written by him have survived in the Lucchese archiepiscopal archive (see Table 8.1).[131] Interestingly, he used the word *ferquide* once, in a document issued in 779 which, however, has been transmitted as a contemporary copy.[132] In 782, Teudipert used the word *ferquidem* twice in the same document, including once in association with the word *locus*.[133] Finally, he used a

donatum est; et si iuraverit, sit exsolutus'. See Chris Wickham, 'Compulsory Gift Exchange in Lombard Italy, 650–1150', in *The Languages of Gift in the Early Middle Ages*, eds Wendy Davies and Paul Fouracre (Cambridge, 2010), pp. 193–216.

127 Schwarzmaier, *Lucca und das Reich*, pp. 159–61.

128 *ChLA* 31, no. 935, pp. 78–79 (Lucca, June 752). This is one of the three documents written by Teutpert in which he used the expression *in ferquido loco*.

129 *ChLA* 32, no. 939, pp. 8–10 (Lucca, 754). See Stoffella, 'Crisi e trasformazioni', pp. 6–7 with n. 138; Haubrichs, 'Langobardic Personal Names', pp. 214, 231 and appendix 6.2.

130 Similar uses of typically Lombard terms are in *ChLA* 37, no. 1069, pp. 3–7 (Triana, Lucca, 25 February 779); *ChLA* 37, no. 1084, pp. 38–61 (August 782, Lucca); *ChLA* 39, no. 1128, pp. 14–15 (Lucca, 7 August 790).

131 *ChLA* 37, no. 1070, pp. 9–11 (Lucca, June 779); *ChLA* 37, no. 1080, pp. 38–43 (Lucca, April 782). See Castagnetti, *Arimanni e distinzione sociale*, pp. 58–59 and n. 61.

132 *ChLA* 37, no. 1070, p. 10, ll. 22–25: 'defensare non potuerimus spondimus vobis conponere ipsa suprascripta res et homenis in duplum ferquide et in ferquide cum suextimatione quales tunc fuere'.

133 *ChLA* 37, no. 1080, p. 39, ll. 39–40: 'Omnia ipsa res vel homenis in triplum ferquide et in ferquide locus qualis tunt fueris unde agitor'.

similar formula in 783, though on this occasion he slightly altered it, preferring the phrase *ferquide locum*.[134] Teudipert's case is particularly significant as it opens an important window on those lay writers who were certainly active in the Lucca territory, but whose work is only attested by an exiguous number of surviving charters. Differently from those who were educated at the cathedral church and carried out their work there in the interest of parties closely related to the diocesan see, Teudipert appears to have written charters especially for the Lombard higher aristocracy. The disappearance of lay archives, and with them the evidence for actors who were not directly tied to episcopal interests, makes it impossible to provide more information on the education and scribal activities of writers such as Teudipert. For this reason, it is difficult to establish the extent to which such writers may have chosen to make use of terms deriving from Lombard cultural tradition. In other words, it may be because of the modalities of documentary preservation that we only catch glimpses or traces of possible bilingualism through the employment of terms that we tend to describe as archaizing, but may in fact reflect the demands or preferences of the local lay aristocracies.

Conclusions

In Pisa, the term *ferquidem* and related forms spread relatively late, during the ninth century, normally as part of the formula *in ferquidem loco*. However, alternative formulae were used, as in the case of the *notarius* Garoin, who in a sale written in 816 used the analogous phrase 'in consimili loco'.[135] When was it first used in northwestern Tuscany? Looking at its earliest occurrences, we can observe that in Lucca this term began to be employed frequently in the second half of the eighth century. As we have seen, however, the way in which the word *ferquidem* and the phrase *in ferquide/ferquidem loco/locum* were used changed over time. Moreover, its use was not obligatory. Quite the opposite: the large quantity of extant original charters from the archiepiscopal archive of Lucca allow us to deduce that scribes in late Lombard and early Carolingian Lucca could have used the phrase *in ferquide/ferquidem loco/locum*, but a large number of them ignored it.

In this respect, the most interesting case study is the lay scribe Teutpert, who defined himself as a *vir devotus*. He was the author of six charters written

134 *ChLA* 26, no. 810, p. 72: 'in duplum in ferquide locum'.

135 *ChLA* 58, no. 2, pp. 19–23 (*Curtole*, January 816).

in Lucca between 740 and 768.[136] In the first two, written in 740 and 742,[137] he avoided the use of *ferquidem*.[138] Teutpert began using the expression *in ferquido/ferquidem loco/locum* in three other documents written between 747 and 759.[139] These occurrences do not necessarily mean that once a scribe or notary came to Lucca and introduced the phrase into his formulary, he was then required to use it every time. When in 768 the same Teutpert issued a will in which some executors were chosen, he did not use that phrase.[140] A further counter-example is given by Altipert, who issued two documents in the middle of the eighth century. In 744 he used the words *in ferquede loco*,[141] while two years later, in a sale written in 746, he did not employ them, even though he could have done so given the typology of the act.[142]

In the following decades, we can see that there was a high degree of arbitrariness among scribes and notaries when using *in ferquidem locum*. If we take the roughly 300 documents issued in Lucca, Pisa, Volterra, Siena, Arezzo, and Florence between 720 and 790, this expression appears 55 times: never in Siena, Arezzo, or Florence, once in Volterra, once in Pisa, and in all other instances in Lucca and the areas directly subjected to it. We must further specify that 32 of the 55 occurrences can be ascribed to only eight scribes, three lay (Teutpert, Prandulo, and Teudipert) and five clerical (Osprand, Austripert, Rachiprand, Filippus, and Gumpert). They all used the phrase *in ferquidem locum* and its variants rather arbitrarily. Moreover, five of them can be recognized in the genealogical scheme of the cathedral school of Lucca that was elaborated some decades ago by Armando Petrucci and which I have partially modified (see Figure 8.1).[143]

136 A document written in Lucca in 768 has to be attributed to the same *vir devotus* Teutpert. In this contemporary copy, in which we cannot recognize Teutpert's handwriting, he ended the text with his typical and uncommon formula: 'Ego Teutpert pos tradita supplevi et dedi'. Cf. *ChLA* 26, no. 1000, pp. 55–61 (Lucca, 19 February 768).

137 CDL 1, no. 74, pp. 222–23 (Lucca, April 740); no. 80, pp. 234–35 (Lucca, October 742).

138 *ChLA* 31, no. 918, pp. 14–15 (Lucca, April 740), at 14. This also includes a description of Teutpert's handwriting. See also *ChLA* 31, no. 921, pp. 24–27 (Lucca, October 742).

139 CDL 1, no. 91, pp. 264–65 (Lucca, July 747); cf. *ChLA* 31, no. 929, pp. 54–55 (Lucca, July 747); CDL 1, no. 105, pp. 301–2 (Lucca, June 752); cf. *ChLA* 31, no. 935, pp. 78–79 (Lucca, June 752); CDL 2, no. 134, pp. 24–25 (Lucca, 31 March 759); cf. *ChLA* 32, no. 951, pp. 62–63 (Lucca, 31 March 759).

140 *ChLA* 26, pp. 55–61 (Lucca, 19 February 768). On executors in northern early medieval Italy see Stoffella, 'Competizione e collaborazione nelle esecuzioni testamentarie', pp. 199–214.

141 CDL 1, no. 84, pp. 249–50 (S. Donato in Fasqua, in the territory of Volterra, 744×745); cf. *ChLA* 31, no. 922, pp. 28–31 (in the territory of Volterra [after 744×745]), at 30, l. 20.

142 CDL 1, no. 87, pp. 255–56 (*Massa*, in the territory of Lucca, 16 December 746); cf. *ChLA* 31, no. 925, pp. 38–41 (Massa Marittima, 16 December 746).

143 Petrucci, 'Scrittura e libro', p. 108.

Observing Petrucci's scheme, we can easily understand why these terms emerged at Lucca between the eighth and the first half of the ninth century. The leading position of the *subdiaconus* and *diaconus* Osprand, a direct pupil of the master Gaudentius, who in turn was the master of Ostripert and Rachiprand—attested as clerics and priests—must have contributed significantly to the definition and diffusion of the formula. Its spread must have been reinforced in the following decades thanks to other pupils active within the same context, becoming even more common during the later Carolingian period. We still need to understand why this archaic tradition emerged and, above all, why this happened only in Lucca and the surrounding areas in connection with Lucca, such as the *Maritima*, Pisa, and the area of Volterra. It is highly probable that this was not a learned invention of the master Gaudentius: in the documents he issued, we do not find any form of *ferquidem*, nor the formula *in ferquidem loco*.

The deacon Osprand, the most influential scribe at Lucca in the final decades of Lombard rule, may have learned the word from law-codes or from other contemporary scribes, since he used the term *ferquidem* for the first time in 753 with the meaning of *id est*.[144] Interestingly, Osprand used this Germanism when issuing a charter for two sons of Duke Vualtpert of Lucca; the previous year, Teutpert also used the expression *in ferquido loco* when he issued a document for the members of the same Lombard ducal family.[145] Though it is a less convincing hypothesis, Osprand may have learned to use it as a scribe of authenticated copies of older documents in which the expression had been used. In any case, we should not forget that when the lay scribe Teuderad used the word for the first time in Lucca in 739, he did so through the formula *in aferquede loco*.[146]

We have no further conclusive elements at the moment. I would therefore suggest that in mid- to late-eighth-century Lucca those who wrote documents had skills that enabled them to understand and conscientiously use different linguistic registers, which included not only terms taken from late Latin or Italo-Romance, but also from the Lombard tradition. They also knew that it was possible to re-employ terms with an archaic nuance but which, at least initially, must have had a mixed nature that enabled writers to decide whether or not they should use the word *ferquidem* and/or related phrases. This situation changed in favour of a progressive linguistic homogenization, when formulae

144 *ChLA* 32, no. 937, pp. 3–5 (Lucca, 25 March 753), at 4, l. 29: 'spundeo tibi esse restauratur ferquidem talem res de quod superius legitur'.

145 *ChLA* 31, no. 935, pp. 78–79. Cf. Stoffella, 'Crisi e trasformazioni', pp. 16–17 and n. 96.

146 *ChLA* 31, no. 915, pp. 2–4.

crystallized. In Pisa, *ferquidem* was apparently used for the first time immediately after the fall of the Lombard kingdom. However, it was employed irregularly until the central decades of the ninth century, at which point it became more common in formulae used by notaries in their charters. Once it entered into local tradition, both *ferquidem* and the phrase *in ferquidem loco* became part of the formulae and, therefore, frequently used by notaries between the tenth and twelfth centuries, especially in Lucca but also in Pisa.

In conclusion, can the use of *ferquidem* in Tuscan documents be read as evidence for the continuity of a spoken bilingualism in early medieval northern Italy? The above discussion of the term's usage seems to allow for a cautiously positive answer, especially if we take into account the scanty evidence from the central decades of the eighth century. The exploration of how this term began to be used by charter scribes in the northwestern part of Tuscany, however, has also shown how this tradition came to be adopted by some notaries and embedded in the charters' formulae already in the last decades of the eighth century, crystallizing in the ninth century and beyond. This phenomenon should not be seen as a singularity, but rather assessed as part of a wider sociolinguistic framework in which bilingualism, especially among political and cultural elites, must be considered a factor. It would therefore seem that in the second half of eighth century the Lombard language was not yet extinct, although it was increasingly restricted to use within elite families. These are, however, only scattered traces of bilingualism, and it is to be hoped that further multidisciplinary investigation on these materials, encompassing palaeographical, philological, and historical analysis, will cast further light on their significance, as it would seem that eighth-century Tuscan society did not uniformly move towards Romance linguistic acculturation. The survival of such Germanic elements could therefore also partially explain why at the very beginning of the ninth century, when the Carolingians were reinforcing their rule over Italy, we can observe a revival of traditional Lombard terminology in official documents, as was the case for *arimanni*, employed in a kind of archaizing fashion.[147]

147 Gasparri, '« *Nobiles et credentes omines liberi arimanni* »'; Stefano Gasparri, 'The Fall of the Lombard Kingdom: Facts, Memory and Propaganda', in *774: ipotesi su di una transizione*, ed. Gasparri, pp. 41–65. This chapter was partially written at the Friedrich Meinecke Institut, Freie Universität, Berlin. I thank the Deutsche Akademische Austauschdients and Stefan Esders for their support and hospitality. I am also grateful to Wolfgang Haubrichs for reading and commenting on an earlier version; any remaining errors are my own responsibility.

Bibliography

Primary Sources

Annales regni francorum, ed. Friedrich Kurze, MGH SS rer. Germ. 6 (Hanover, 1895).

Carte dell'Archivio Arcivescovile di Pisa, Fondo arcivescovile. 1. 720–1100, ed. Antonella Ghignoli, *2. 1101–1150*, ed. Silio P. P. Scalfati, *3. 1151–1200*, ed. Silio P. P. Scalfati, Biblioteca del « Bollettino Storico Pisano », Fonti, 11, 3 vols (Pisa, 2006).

Chartae latinae antiquiores, eds Albert Bruckner et al., 118 vols (Olten et al., 1954–2019).

Codice diplomatico Longobardo, eds Luigi Schiaparelli et al., 5 vols (Rome, 1929–2003).

Codice diplomatico veronese I. Dalla caduta dell'Impero romano alla fine del periodo carolingio, ed. Vittorio Fainelli, Monumenti storici pubblicati dalla r. Deputazione di storia patria per le Venezie, 1 (Venice, 1940).

Codices latini antiquiores. A Palaeographical Guide to Latin Manuscripts prior to the Ninth Century, ed. Elias Avery Lowe, 11 vols + supplement (Oxford, 1935–71).

Kurze, Wilhelm, *Codex Diplomaticus Amiatinus. Urkundenbuch der Abtei S. Salvatore am Monteamiata von den Anfängen bis zum Regierungsantritt Papst Innozenz III. (736–1198)*, 4 vols (Tübingen, 1974–98).

Le leggi dei Longobardi. Storia, memoria e diritto di un popolo germanico, eds Claudio Azzara and Stefano Gasparri, Altomedioevo 4 (Rome, 2005).

Le Liber Pontificalis. Texte, introduction et commentaire, ed. Louis Duchesne, 2 vols (Paris, 1886–92).

Memorie e Documenti per servire all'Istoria del Ducato di Lucca, IV, ed. Daniele Bertini, 2 vols (Lucca, 1818–36).

Secondary Sources

Aebischer, Paul, 'Les dérivés italiens du langobard "gahagi" et leur répartition d'après les chartes médiévales', *Zeitschrift für romanische Philologie* 63 (1938), 51–62.

Ammannati, Giulia, 'Una lettera veronese del secolo IX', *Scrittura e civiltà* 25 (2001), 377–83.

Arcamone, Maria Giovanna, 'Antroponimia e storia: problemi di metodo sulla base del *Codex Diplomaticus Amiatinus*', in *Antroponimia e storia nell'Italia centrale (Atti del Convegno di Gabicce Mare, 18 sett. 1993)*, ed. Ettore Baldetti, Proposte e Ricerche 33 (1994), pp. 123–31.

Arcamone, Maria Giovanna, 'L'antroponimia germanica a Pisa durante l'età longobarda', *Filologia e critica. Studi in onore di Vittorio Santoli*, eds Paolo Chiarini, Carlo Alberto Mastrelli, Piergiuseppe Scardigli, and Luciano Zangari, Studi di filologia tedesca 6–7, 2 vols (Rome, 1976), 1:133–58.

Arcamone, Maria Giovanna, 'Antroponimia germanica nella toponomastica italiana', in *La toponomastica come fonte di conoscenza storica e linguistica. Atti del convegno della Società Italiana di Glottologia, Belluno, 31 marzo–2 aprile 1980*, ed. Edoardo Vineis (Pisa, 1981), pp. 29–45.

Arcamone, Maria Giovanna, 'Chinzica: toponimo pisano di origine longobarda', *Bollettino Storico Pisano* 47 (1978), 205–46.

Arcamone, Maria Giovanna, 'I Germani d'Italia: lingue e "documenti" linguistici', in *Magistra Barbaritas. I barbari in Italia*, ed. Giovanni Pugliese Carratelli, Antica Madre. Collana di studi sull'Italia antica 7 (Milan, 1984), pp. 381–409.

Arcamone, Maria Giovanna, 'Glossario', in *Carte dell'Archivio Capitolare di Pisa*, 4 (1101–1120), ed. Matilde Tirelli Carli, Thesaurus Ecclesiarum Italiae VII, 4 (Rome, 1969), pp. 264–72.

Arcamone, Maria Giovanna 'Glossario delle parole di origine germanica', in *Carte dell'Archivio Capitolare di Pisa*, 3 (1076–1100), ed. Matilde Tirelli Carli, Thesaurus Ecclesiarum Italiae VII, 3 (Rome, 1977), pp. 237–46.

Arcamone, Maria Giovanna, 'Die langobardischen Personennamen in Italien: Nomen und gens aus der Sicht der linguistischen Analyse', in *Nomen et gens. Zur historischen Aussagekraft frühmittelalterlicher Personennamen*, eds Dieter Geuenich, Wolfgang Haubrichs, and Jörg Jarnut, Ergänzungsbände zum Reallexikon der Germanischen Altertumskunde 16 (Berlin, 1997), pp. 157–75.

Arcamone, Maria Giovanna, 'L'eredità longobarda nell'odierna toponomastica pistoiese', in *L'eredità longobarda*, Studi storici pistoiesi 5 (Rome, 2014), pp. 39–62.

Arcamone, Maria Giovanna, 'L'onomastica personale nell'Europa occidentale fra IV e VIII secolo', in *Morfologie sociali e culturali in Europa tra tarda antichità e alto Medioevo*, Settimane 45 (Spoleto, 1998), pp. 585–618.

Arcamone, Maria Giovanna, 'La toponomastica del Monte Amiata: la componente longobarda e l'etimo di Amiata (e del lucchese Meati)', in *L'Amiata nel Medioevo. Atti del convegno internazionale di studi (Abbadia San Salvatore, 29 maggio-1 giugno 1986)*, eds Wilhelm Kurze and Mario Ascheri (Rome, 1989), pp. 261–88.

Arcamone, Maria Giovanna, 'Toponomastica italiana di origine longobarda', in *Scríbthair a ainm n-ogaim. Scritti in memoria di Enrico Campanile*, eds Riccardo Ambrosini, Maria Patrizia Bologna, Filippo Motta, and Chatia Orlandi, 2 vols (Pisa, 1997), 1:39–50.

Arcamone, Maria Giovanna, 'Die Verteilung der Ortsnamen langobardischen Ursprungs in den Regionen Italiens', in *Interferenz-Onomastik. Namen in Grenz- und Begegnungsräumen in Geschichte und Gegenwart. Saarbrücker Kolloquium des Arbeitskreises für Namenforschung vom 5.-7. Oktober 2006*, eds Wolfgang Haubrichs and Heinrich Tiefenbach, Veröffentlichungen der Kommission für Saarländische Landesgeschichte und Volksforschung 43 (Saarbrücken, 2010), pp. 65–78.

Bachrach, Bernard S., *Charlemagne's Early Campaigns (768–777): A Diplomatic and Military Analysis*, History of Warfare 82 (Leiden, 2013).

Baggio, Serenella and Sanga, Glauco 'Un'ipotesi sintattica per l'Indovinello veronese—Il bue e l'indovinello. Commento al più antico testo italiano finora noto', *Rivista italiana di dialettologia* 16 (1992), 9–27.

Baggio, Serenella and Sanga, Glauco, 'Sul volgare in età longobarda', in *Italia settentrionale: crocevia di idiomi romanzi. Atti del convegno di studi, Trento, 21–23 ottobre 1993*, eds Emanuele Banfi, Giovanni Bonfadini, Patrizia Cordin, and Maria Iliescu (Tübingen, 1995), pp. 247–60.

Baggio, Serenella, Sanga, Glauco, and Bartoli Langeli, Attilio 'Novità sull'Indovinello veronese', *Quaderni veneti* 21 (1995), 39–97.

Balzaretti, Ross, 'Spoken Narratives in Ninth-Century Milanese Court Records', in *Narrative and History in the Early Medieval West*, eds Elizabeth M. Tyler and Ross Balzaretti (Turnhout, 2006), pp. 11–37.

Banniard, Michel, 'The Transition from Latin to the Romance Languages', in *The Cambridge History of the Romance Languages*, eds Martin Maiden, John C. Smith, and Adam Ledgeway, 2 vols (Cambridge, 2013), 2:57–106.

Bartoli Langeli, Attilio, 'I documenti', in *Carte di famiglia. Strategie, rappresentazione e memoria del gruppo familiare di Totone di Campione (721–877)*, eds Stefano Gasparri and Cristina La Rocca (Rome, 2005), pp. 237–64.

Bartoli Langeli, Attilio, 'Forma langobardica. La lingua dei documenti italiani altomedievali (secoli VIII–XI)', in *Scrittura memoria degli uomini. Atti della giornata di studio in ricordo di Giuliana Cannataro* (Bari, 2006), pp. 17–34.

Bartoli Langeli, Attilio, 'Sui "brevi" italiani altomedievali', *Bullettino dell'Istituto storico italiano per il Medio Evo*, 105 (2003), 1–23.

Bassetti, Massimiliano, 'Novità lessicali nel latino dei documenti privati del Veneto medievale (secoli X–XII)', *Bulletin du Cange* 74 (2016), 239–60.

Battisti, Carlo, 'L'elemento gotico nella toponomastica e nel lessico italiano', in *I Goti in Occidente. Problemi*, Settimane 3 (Spoleto, 1956), pp. 621–49.

Bellocchio, Silvia, 'Sulle tracce di due lemmi germanici: Widimo e Windangassia', in *I Longobardi in Italia. Lingua e cultura*, ed. Carla Falluomini, Bibliotheca Germanica. Studi e testi 37 (Alessandria, 2015), pp. 333–47.

Bougard, François, *La justice dans le royaume d'Italie de la fin du VIIIe siècle au début du XIe siècle*, Bibliothèque des Ècoles françaises d'Athènes et de Rome 291 (Rome, 1995).

Bougard, François, 'Notaires d'élite, notaires de l'élite dans le royaume d'Italie', in *La culture du haut Moyen Âge. Une question d'élites?*, eds François Bougard, Régine Le Jan, and Rosamond McKitterick, Haut Moyen Âge 7 (Turnhout, 2009), pp. 439–60.

Bougard, François, 'Tesori e mobilia italiani nell'alto medioevo', in *Tesori. Forme di acculturazione della ricchezza nell'alto medioevo*, eds Sauro Gelichi and Cristina La Rocca, Altomedioevo 3 (Rome, 2004), pp. 69–122.

Braccini, Mauro, 'Singolarità e affiliazioni nel cosiddetto « Indovinello veronese »', *Studi di filologia italiana* 69 (2011), 5–52.

Bruckner, Wilhelm, *Die Sprache der Langobarden* (Strasbourg, 1895; reprinted Berlin, 1969).

Cammarosano, Paolo, *Nobili e re. L'Italia politica nell'alto medioevo* (Rome-Bari, 1998).

Cammarosano, Paolo, *Storia dell'Italia medievale. Dal VI all'XI secolo* (Rome, 2001).

Castagnetti, Andrea, *Arimanni e distinzione sociale nelle sepolture* (Verona, 2015).

Castagnetti, Andrea, 'Le aristocrazie della *Langobardia* nelle città e nei territori rurali', in *Città e campagna nei secoli altomedievali*, Settimane 54 (Spoleto, 2009), pp. 539–619.

Castagnetti, Andrea, 'La distribuzione geografica dei possessi di un grande proprietario veronese del secolo IX: Engelberto del fu Grimoaldo', *Rivista di storia dell'agricoltura* 9 (1969), 15–26.

Chinellato, Laura, 'L'altare di Ratchis', in *L'VIII secolo: un secolo inquieto. Atti del Convegno Internazionale di Studi (Cividale del Friuli, 4–7 dicembre 2008)*, ed. Valentino Pace (Cividale del Friuli, 2010), pp. 83–91.

Clackson, James, 'Latin as a Source for the Romance Languages', in *The Oxford Guide to the Romance Languages*, eds Adam Ledgeway and Martin Maiden (Oxford, 2016), pp. 3–13.

Conti, Pier Maria, 'La Tuscia e i suoi ordinamenti territoriali nell'alto medioevo', in *Lucca e la Tuscia nell'alto medioevo. Atti del 5° Congresso internazionale di studi sull'alto medioevo (Lucca, 3–7 ottobre 1971)* (Spoleto, 1973), pp. 61–116.

Cortelazzo, Manlio, Zolli, Paolo, *Il nuovo etimologico. DELI. Dizionario etimologico della lingua italiana*, 2nd ed. (Bologna, 1999).

Costambeys, Marios, 'The Laity, the Clergy, the Scribes and Their Archives: The Documentary Record of Eighth- and Ninth-Century Italy', *Documentary Culture and the Laity in the Early Middle Ages*, eds Warren C. Brown, Marios Costambeys, Matthew Innes, and Adam J. Kosto (Cambridge, 2013), pp. 231–58.

Devoto, Giacomo and Giacomelli, Gabriella, *I dialetti delle regioni d'Italia* (Florence, 1972).

Dringoli, Massimo (ed.), *La via Francigena in Toscana. Da Lucca alla Val d'Orcia* (Pisa, 2016).

Everett, Nicholas, 'Lay Documents and Archives in Early Medieval Spain and Italy, *c.* 400–700', in *Documentary Culture and the Laity in the Early Middle Ages*, eds Warren C. Brown, Marios Costambeys, Matthew Innes, and Adam J. Kosto (Cambridge, 2013), pp. 63–94.

Franco, Tiziana, 'Con gli occhi di Raterio: note sulla cultura artistica veronese di X secolo', in *La più antica veduta di Verona. Iconografia rateriana. L'archetipo e l'immagine tramandata. Atti del seminario di studi (Museo di Castelvecchio, 6 maggio 2011)* (Verona, 2012), pp. 167–81.

Francovich Onesti, Nicoletta, 'L'antroponimia longobarda della Toscana: caratteri e diffusione', *Rivista Italiana di Onomastica* 6 (2000), 357–74; reprinted in Nicoletta Francovich Onesti, *Le Regine dei Longobardi e altri saggi*, Proteo 72 (Rome, 2013), pp. 41–59.

Francovich Onesti, Nicoletta, 'Discontinuità e integrazione nel sistema onomastico dell'Italia tardoantica. L'incontro coi nomi germanici', in *Le trasformazioni del mondo romano e le grandi migrazioni. Nuovi popoli dall'Europa settentrionale e centro-orientale alle coste del Mediterraneo. Atti del Convegno internazionale di studi Cimitile-Santa Maria Capua Vetere, 16–17 giugno 2011*, eds Marcello Rotili and Carlo Ebanista, Giornate sulla Tarda Antichità e il Medioevo 4 (Cimitile, 2012), pp. 33–50.

Francovich Onesti, Nicoletta, 'Indizi di sviluppi romanzi nelle voci germaniche e nei nomi propri', *Filologia Germanica—Germanic Philology. I Germani e l'Italia. The Early Germanic Peoples and Italy* 2 (2010), 67–101; reprinted in Nicoletta Francovich Onesti, *Le Regine dei Longobardi e altri saggi*, Proteo 72 (Rome, 2013), pp. 141–74.

Francovich Onesti, Nicoletta, 'Toponimi di origine germanica della Val di Cornia', *AION—Filologia Germanica* 30–31 (1987–88), 7–42.

Francovich Onesti, Nicoletta, *Vestigia longobarde in Italia (568–774). Lessico e antroponimia*, Proteo 6 (Rome, 1999).

Gasparri, Stefano, 'Breve storia dei Longobardi', in *Paolo Diacono, Storia dei Longobardi*, eds Stefano Gasparri and Antonio Zanella (Milan, 2000), pp. 9–16.

Gasparri, Stefano, *I duchi longobardi*, Studi Storici 109 (Rome, 1978).

Gasparri, Stefano, 'The Fall of the Lombard Kingdom: Facts, Memory and Propaganda', in *774: ipotesi su di una transizione*, ed. Stefano Gasparri, Seminari internazionali del Centro interuniversitario per la storia e l'archeologia dell'alto medioevo 1 (Turnhout, 2008), pp. 41–65.

Gasparri, Stefano, 'I Germani immaginari e la realtà del regno. Cinquant'anni di studi sui Longobardi', in *I Longobardi dei ducati di Spoleto e Benevento. Atti del 16° Congresso internazionale di studi sull'alto medioevo (Spoleto, 20–23 ottobre 2002-Benevento, 24–27 ottobre 2002)*, 2 vols (Spoleto, 2003), 1:3–28.

Gasparri, Stefano, 'Istituzioni e potere nel territorio friulano in età longobarda e carolingia', in *Paolo Diacono e il Friuli altomedievale (secc. VI–X), Atti del XIV Congresso internazionale di studi sull'alto medioevo, Cividale del Friuli—Bottenicco di Moimacco, 24–29 settembre 1999*, 2 vols (Spoleto, 2001), 1:105–28.

Gasparri, Stefano, *Italia longobarda. Il regno, i Franchi, il papato* (Rome-Bari, 2012).

Gasparri, Stefano, '« *Nobiles et credentes omines liberi arimanni* ». Linguaggio sociale e tradizioni longobarde nel regno italico', *Bullettino dell'Istituto Italiano per il Medio Evo e Archivio Muratoriano* 105 (2003), 25–51.

Gasparri, Stefano, 'Il regno longobardo in Italia. Struttura e funzionamento di uno stato altomedievale', in *Langobardia*, eds Paolo Cammarosano and Stefano Gasparri (Udine, 1990), pp. 237–305 (revised version in *Il regno dei Longobardi in Italia. Archeologia, società e istituzioni*, ed. Stefano Gasparri (Spoleto, 2004), pp. 1–92).

Gasparri, Stefano, 'I testamenti nell'Italia settentrionale fra VIII e IX secolo', in *Sauver son âme et se perpétuer. Trasmission du patrimoine et mémoire au haut moyen âge*, eds François Bougard and Cristina La Rocca, Collection de l'École Française de Rome 351 (Rome, 2005), pp. 97–113.

Ghignoli, Antonella, 'Koinè, influenze, importazioni transalpine nella documentazione 'privata' dei secoli VII–VIII: lo stato dell'arte', in *Le Alpi porta d'Europa. Scritture, uomini, idee da Giustiniano al Barbarossa. Atti del convegno di studio (Cividale del Friuli, 5–7 ottobre 2006)*, eds Laura Pani and Cesare Scalon (Spoleto, 2009), pp. 83–110.

Ghignoli, Antonella, 'Su due famosi documenti pisani del secolo VIII', *Bullettino dell'Istituto Storico Italiano per il Medio Evo* 106 (2004), 1–69.

Ghignoli, Antonella and Bougard, François, 'Elementi romani nei documenti longobardi', in *L'héritage byzantin en Italie (VIIIe–XIIe siécle). I: La fabrique documentaire*, eds Jean-Marie Martin, Annick Peters-Custot, and Vivien Prigent, Collection de l'Ècole française de Rome 449 (Rome, 2011), pp. 241–30.

Haubrichs, Wolfgang, 'Amalgamierung und Identität. Langobardische Personennamen in Mythos und Herrschaft', in *Die Langobarden. Herrschaft und Identität*, eds Walter Pohl and Peter Erhart, Forschungen zur Geschichte des Mittelalters 9 (Vienna, 2005), pp. 67–99.

Haubrichs, Wolfgang, 'Langobardic Personal Names: Given Names and Name-Giving Among the Langobards', in *The Langobards from the Migration Period to the Eighth Century: An Ethnographic Perspective*, eds Giorgio Ausenda, Paolo Delogu, and Chris Wickham (Woodbrige, 2009), pp. 195–236.

Haubrichs, Wolfgang, 'I nomi dei Longobardi', in *I Longobardi in Italia. Lingua e cultura*, ed. Carla Falluomini, Bibliotheca Germanica. Studi e testi 37 (Alessandria, 2015), pp. 227–68.

Haubrichs, Wolfgang, 'Sprache und Schriftlichkeit im langobardischen Italien—Das Zeugnis von Namen, Wörtern und Entlehnungen. Ein Kommentar zu Nicholas Everett, Literacy in Lombard Italy', *Filologia Germanica—Germanic Philology. I Germani e l'Italia. The Early Germanic Peoples and Italy* 2 (2010), 133–202.

Hlawitschka, Eduard, *Franken, Alemannen, Bayern und Burgunder in Oberitalien (774–962). Zum Verständnis der fränkischen Königsherrschaft in Italien*, Forschungen zur oberrheinischen Landesgeschichte 8 (Freiburg im Breisgau, 1960).

Jung, Julius, 'Das Itinerar des Erzbischofs Sigeric von Canterbury und die Straße von Rom über Siena nach Lucca', *Mitteilungen des Instituts für Österreichische Geschichtsforschung* 24 (1904), 3–90.

Kasten, Brigitte, *Königssöhne und Königsherrschaft. Untersuchungen zur Teilhabe am Reich in der Merowinger- und Karolingerzeit*, MGH Schriften 44 (Hanover, 1997).

Keller, Hagen, 'La marca di Tuscia fino all'anno mille', in *Lucca e la Tuscia nell'alto medioevo. Atti del 5° Congresso internazionale di studi sull'alto medioevo (Lucca, 3–7 ottobre 1971)* (Spoleto, 1973), pp. 117–40.

Kluge, Friedrich and Seebold, Elmar, *Etymologisches Wörterbuch der deutschen Sprache*, 25th ed. (Berlin, 2011).

Krahwinkler, Harald, *Friaul im Frühmittelalter. Geschichte einer Region vom Ende des fünften bis zum Ende des zehnten Jahrhunderts*, Veröffentlichungen des Instituts für Österreichische Geschichtsforschung 30 (Vienna, 1992), pp. 119–43.

LaVoy, Hailey J., 'Hirmindrut Sculdarissa: A Ninth-Century Woman's Original Letter and its Implications', *The Journal of Medieval Latin* 25 (2015), 29–50.

Leicht, Pier Silverio, 'L'archivio di Alahis', in *Studi di storia e diritto in onore di Enrico Besta per il suo XL anno del suo insegnamento*, 4 vols (Milan, 1937), 2:29–36; reprinted in Pier Silverio Leicht, *Scritti vari di storia del diritto italiano*, 2 vols (Milan, 1948), 2.1:233–39.

Leoni, Federico Albano, 'Bilinguismo e coscienza del bilinguismo nell'Italia longobarda', in *Italia linguistica: idee, storia, strutture*, eds Federico Albano Leoni, Daniele Gambarara, Franco Lo Piparo, and Raffaele Simone (Bologna, 1983), pp. 133–48.

Liver, Ricarda, 'Ecrire au Moyen Age. A propos d'une nouvelle interprétation de l'« indovinello veronese »', in *Mélanges de philologie et de littérature médiévales offerts à Michel Burger*, eds Jacqueline Cerquiglini-Toulet and Olivier Collet, Publications romanes et françaises 208 (Geneva, 1994), pp. 203–13.

Lusuardi Siena, Silvia and Piva, Paola, 'Scultura decorativa e arredo liturgico a Cividale e in Friuli tra VIII e IX secolo', in *Paolo Diacono e il Friuli altomedievale (secc. VI–X). Atti del XV Congresso internazionale di studi sull'Alto Medioevo. Cividale del Friuli-Bottenicco di Moimacco 24–29 settembre 1999*, 2 vols (Spoleto, 2001), 2:493–594.

Magistrale, Francesco, 'Le pergamene dell'Archivio Arcivescovile di Lucca (secoli VIII–IX): l'esperienza delle *Chartae Latinae antiquiores*', in *Il patrimonio documentario della chiesa di Lucca. Prospettive di ricerca. Atti del Convegno internazionale di studi (Lucca, Archivio arcivescovile, 14–15 novembre 2008)*, eds Sergio Pagano and Pierantonio Piatti, Toscana Sacra 2 (Florence, 2010), pp. 73–92.

Mailloux, Anne, 'Modalités de constitution du patrimoine épiscopal de Lucques, VIIIe–Xe siècle', in *Les transferts patrimoniaux en Europe occidentale, VIIIe–X^e siécle (I): Actes de la table ronde de Rome (Rome 6, 7 et 8 mai 1999)*, ed. François Bougard, Mélanges de l'École Française de Rome, Moyen Âge 111 (2000), pp. 701–23.

Mariotti, Scevola, 'Sull'« indovinello veronese »', in *Letterature comparate. Problemi di metodo. Studi in onore di Ettore Paratore*, 4 vols (Bologna, 1981) 2:987–96.

Mastrelli, Carlo Alberto, 'L'elemento germanico nella toponomastica toscana', in *Lucca e la Tuscia nell'alto medioevo. Atti del 5° Congresso internazionale di studi sull'alto medioevo (Lucca, 3–7 ottobre 1971)* (Spoleto, 1973), pp. 645–71.

Mastrelli, Carlo Alberto, 'La toponomastica lombarda di origine longobarda', in *I Longobardi e la Lombardia. Saggi* (Milan, 1978), pp. 35–46.

Mersiowsky, Mark, 'Preserved by Destruction: Carolingian Original Letters and CLM 6333', in *Early Medieval Palimpsests*, ed. George Declercq, Bibliologia 26 (Turnhout, 2007), pp. 73–97.

Mersiowsky, Mark, *Die Urkunde in der Karolingerzeit. Originale, Urkundenpraxis und politische Kommunikation*, 2 vols, MGH Schriften 60 (Wiesbaden, 2015).

Mitzka, Walther, 'Das Langobardische und die althochdeutsche Dialektgeographie', *Zeitschrift für Mundartforschung* 20 (1951), 1–7.

Morlicchio, Elda, *Antroponimia longobarda a Salerno nel IX secolo. I nomi del Codex diplomaticus Cavensis* (Naples, 1985).

Morlicchio, Elda, 'Dinamiche sociolinguistiche nell'Italia delle 'invasioni barbariche'', in *Archeologia e storia delle migrazioni. Europa, Italia, Mediterraneo fra tarda età romana e alto medioevo. Atti del Convegno internazionale di studi Cimitile-Santa Maria Capua Vetere, 17–18 giugno 2010*, eds Carlo Ebanista and Marcello Rotili, Giornate sulla Tarda Antichità e il Medioevo 3 (Cimitile, 2011), pp. 219–31.

Patitucci Uggeri, Stella (ed.), *La via Francigena e altre strade della Toscana medievale*, Quaderni di Archeologia medievale 7 (Florence, 2004).

Pellegrini, Giovan Battista, *Carta dei dialetti d'Italia* (Pisa, 1977).

Petracco Sicardi, Giulia, 'La seconda mutazione consonantica negli antroponimi di origine longobarda', in *Studi di filologia germanica e letteratura tedesca in onore di Nicola Accolti Gil Vitale*, eds Giancarlo Bolognese and Giorgio Sichel (Florence, 1977), pp. 7–20.

Petrucci, Armando, 'Il codice n. 490 della Biblioteca Capitolare di Lucca: un problema di storia della cultura medievale ancora da risolvere', *Actum Luce* 2 (1971), 159–75; reprinted without illustrations as 'Il codice e i documenti: scrivere a Lucca fra VIII e IX secolo' in Armando Petrucci and Carlo Romeo, « *Scriptores in urbibus* ». *Alfabetismo e cultura scritta nell'Italia altomedievale* (Bologna, 1992), pp. 77–108.

Petrucci, Armando, 'Scrittura e libro nella Tuscia altomedievale (secoli VIII–IX)', in *Lucca e la Tuscia nell'alto medioevo. Atti del 5° Congresso internazionale di studi sull'alto medioevo (Lucca, 3–7 ottobre 1971)* (Spoleto, 1973), pp. 627–43.

Petrucci, Armando and Romeo, Carlo, 'L'*Orazionale* visigotico di Verona: aggiunte avventizie, indovinello grafico, tagli maffeiani', *Scritture e civiltà* 22 (1998), 13–30; reprinted in Armando Petrucci, *Letteratura italiana: una storia attraverso la scrittura* (Rome, 2017), pp. 247–63.

Pfister, Max, 'Germanisch und Romanisch', in *Lexikon der Romanistischen Linguistik*, eds Günter Holtus, Michael Metzeltin, and Christian Schmitt, 12 vols (Tübingen, 1998), 7:231–45.

Pfister, Max, 'Langobardische Superstratwörter im Italienischen', *Jahrbuch für Internationale Germanistik* 11 (1979), 100–10.

Piva, Paola and Lusuardi Siena, Silvia, 'Da Pemmone a Paolino d'Aquileia: appunti sull'arredo liturgico e la scultura in Friuli tra VIII e IX sec.', *Hortus Artium Medievalium* 8 (2002), 295–323.

Politzer, Robert L. and Politzer, Frieda N., *Romance Trends in 7th and 8th Century Latin Documents* (Chapel Hill, NC, 1953).

Pratesi, Alessandro, *Genesi e forme del documento medievale*, 2nd ed. (Rome, 1987).

Princi Braccini, Giovanna, 'Vecchi e nuovi indizi sui tempi della morte della lingua dei Longobardi', *Archivio per l'Alto Adige* 93–94 (2000), 353–74.

van der Rhee, Florus, *Die germanischen Wörter in der langobardischen Gesetzen* (Rotterdam, 1970).

van der Rhee, Florus, 'Die hochdeutsche Lautverschiebung in den langobardischen Gesetzen. Datierung, Umfang, orthographische Wiedergabe', *Neophilologus* 60 (1976), 397–411.

Roncaglia, Aurelio, 'L'indovinello veronese-friulano, i suoi « latinismi » e la « legge Tobler-Mussafia »', in *Omaggio a Gianfranco Folena*, 3 vols (Padua, 1993), 1:49–59.

Sabatini, Francesco, *Riflessi linguistici della dominazione longobarda nell'Italia mediana e meridionale* (Florence, 1963); revised version reprinted in *Aristocrazie e società fra transizione romano-germanica e alto medioevo. Atti del Convegno internazionale di studi (Cimitile-Santa Maria Capua Vetere, 14–15 giugno 2012)*, eds Carlo Ebanista and Marcello Rotili (San Vitaliano, Naples, 2015), pp. 353–441.

Sanga, Glauco, 'Il volgare nei placiti cassinesi: vecchie questioni e nuove acquisizioni', *Rivista Italiana di Dialettologia. Lingue dialetti società* 18 (1994), 8–30.

Scardigli, Piergiuseppe, *Goti e Longobardi. Studi di filologia germanica* (Rome, 1987).

Schiaparelli, Luigi, *Il codice 490 della Biblioteca Capitolare di Lucca e la scuola scrittoria lucchese (sec. VIII–IX). Contributi allo studio della minuscola precarolina in Italia*, Studi e Testi 36 (Rome, 1924).

Schiaparelli, Luigi, 'Note diplomatiche sulle carte longobarde. I. I notai nell'età longobarda', *Archivio Storico Italiano* s. VII, 17 (1932), 3–34; reprinted in Luigi Schiaparelli, *Note di diplomatica (1896–1934)*, ed. Alessandro Pratesi (Turin, 1972), pp. 183–214.

Schmidt-Wiegand, Ruth, 'Die volkssprachige Wörter der Leges barbarorum', *Frühmittelalterliche Studien* 13 (1979), 56–87.

Schwarzmaier, Hansmartin, *Lucca und das Reich bis zum Ende des 11. Jahrhunderts. Studien zur Sozialstruktur einer Herzogstadt in der Toskana*, Bibliothek des Deutschen Historischen Instituts in Rom 41 (Tübingen, 1972).

Sergi, Giuseppe, *Luoghi di strada nel medioevo. Fra il Po, il mare e le Alpi occidentali* (Turin, 1986).

Sestan, Ernesto 'La composizione etnica della società in rapporto allo svolgimento della civiltà in Italia nel secolo VII', in *Caratteri del secolo VII in Occidente*, Settimane 5 (Spoleto, 1958), pp. 649–77.

Sonderegger, Stefan, 'Prinzipien germanischer Personennamengebung', in *Nomen et gens. Zur historischen Aussagekraft frühmittelalterlicher Personennamen*, eds Dieter Geuenich, Wolfgang Haubrichs, and Jörg Jarnut, Ergänzungsbände zum Reallexikon der Germanischen Altertumskunde 16 (Berlin, 1997), pp. 1–29.

Stoffella, Marco, 'Aristocracy and Rural Churches in the Territory of Lucca between Lombards and Carolingians: A Case Study', in *774: ipotesi su di una transizione*, ed. Stefano Gasparri, Seminari internazionali del Centro interuniversitario per la storia e l'archeologia dell'alto medioevo 1 (Turnhout, 2008), pp. 289–311.

Stoffella, Marco, 'Competizione e collaborazione nelle esecuzioni testamentarie dell'Italia carolingia', in *Coopétition. Rivaliser, coopérer dans les sociétés du haut Moyen Âge (500–1100)*, eds Régine Le Jan, Geneviève Bührer-Thierry, and Stefano Gasparri, Haut Moyen Âge 31 (Turnhout, 2018), pp. 185–213.

Stoffella, Marco, 'Condizionamenti politici e sociali nelle procedure di risoluzione dei conflitti nella Toscana occidentale tra età longobarda e carolingia', *Studi Medievali* 3rd ser., 59 (2018), 35–61.

Stoffella, Marco, 'Crisi e trasformazioni delle élites nella Toscana nord-occidentale nel secolo VIII: esempi a confronto', *Reti Medievali Rivista* 8 (2007), 1–49.

Stoffella, Marco, 'In a Periphery of the Empire: Tuscany between the Lombards and the Carolingians', in *Charlemagne. Les temps, les espaces, les hommes. Construction et déconstruction d'un règne*, eds Rolf Grosse and Michel Sot, Haut Moyen Âge 34 (Turnhout, 2018), pp. 319–36.

Stoffella, Marco, 'Pemmo, duca del Friuli', in *Dizionario Biografico degli Italiani* (Rome, 1960–), 82:206–7.

Stoffella, Marco, 'Ratchis, re dei Longobardi', in *Dizionario Biografico degli Italiani* (Rome, 1960–), 86:549–52.

Stoffella, Marco, 'Le relazioni tra Baviera e Toscana tra VIII e IX secolo: appunti e considerazioni preliminari', *Mélanges de l'École française de Rome. Moyen-Âge* 120 (2008), 73–85.

Stoffella, Marco, 'Rodgaudo', in *Dizionario Biografico degli Italiani* (Rome, 1960–), 87:78–80.

Stopani, Renato, *La via francigena in Toscana. Storia di una strada medievale* (Florence, 1984).

Tabacco, Giovanni, *I liberi del re nell'Italia carolingia e postcarolingia* (Spoleto, 1966).

Varvaro, Alberto, 'Latin and the Making of the Romance Languages', in *The Cambridge History of the Romance Languages*, eds Martin Maiden, John C. Smith, and Adam Ledgeway, 2 vols (Cambridge, 2013), 2:6–56.

Vollono, Maria, 'Methodik und Probleme bei der Erforschung des Langobardischen am Beispiel einiger juristischen Fachbegriffe: mundoald, launegild, sculdhais', in *Die Langobarden. Herrschaft und Identität*, eds Walter Pohl and Peter Erhart, Forschungen zur Geschichte des Mittelalters 9 (Vienna, 2005), pp. 477–503.

Vollono, Maria, 'Plurilinguismo nell'Italia postlongobarda: considerazioni a proposito della presenza longobarda e franca e suoi riflessi linguistici', in *Il plurilinguismo in area germanica nel Medioevo: XXX Convegno Associazione Italiana di Filologia Germanica, Bari 4–6 giugno 2003*, ed. Lucia Sinisi (Bari, 2005), pp. 271–300.

Wickham, Chris, 'Compulsory Gift Exchange in Lombard Italy, 650–1150', in *The Languages of Gift in the Early Middle Ages*, eds Wendy Davies and Paul Fouracre (Cambridge, 2010), pp. 193–216.

Wickham, Chris, 'Land Disputes and Their Social Framework in Lombard-Carolingian Italy, 700–900', in *The Settlement of Disputes in Early Medieval Europe*, eds Wendy Davies and Paul Fouracre (Cambridge, 1986), pp. 105–24; reprinted in Chris Wickham, *Land and Power. Studies in Italian and European Social History, 400–1200* (London, 1994), pp. 229–56.

Wiener, Leo, *Commentary to the Germanic Laws and Mediaeval Documents* (Cambridge, 1915).

Wright, Roger, 'Latin and Romance in the Medieval Period. A Sociophilological Approach', in *The Oxford Guide to the Romance Languages*, eds Adam Ledgeway and Martin Maiden (Oxford, 2016), pp. 14–23.

Zeller, Bernhard, West Charles, Tinti, Francesca, Stoffella Marco, Schroeder Nicolas, van Rhijn, Carine, Patzold, Steffen, Kohl, Thomas, Davies, Wendy, and Czock, Miriam, *Neighbours and Strangers: Local Societies in Early Medieval Europe* (Manchester, 2020).

Zielinski, Herbert, 'Die Charta der Langobarden. Forschungsgeschichte und aktuelle Perspektiven', in *Die Privaturkunden der Karolingerzeit*, eds Peter Erhart, Karl Heidecker, and Bernhard Zeller (Dietikon-Zürich, 2009), pp. 47–56

CHAPTER 9

Languages of Boundaries and Boundaries of Language in Cornish Charters

Charles Insley

The relationship between Latin and Old English in Anglo-Saxon documentary culture is one that has attracted some long overdue attention over the last few years.[1] Many of the assumptions previously held by scholars as to the rationale for language choice in documents, such as the supposed contrast between secular/profane (Old English) and spiritual (Latin) have been reassessed. Inevitably, perhaps, the relationship between Latin and the vernacular has proved to be far more complex than hitherto has been thought.[2] A range of imperatives governed the choice of language or languages for a document, including audience, local scribal traditions, as well as issues around identity. By the later tenth century, code-switching in texts was often signalled by the use of different scripts, with English Square Minuscule generally reserved for Old English and Caroline Minuscule-derived scripts deployed for Latin.[3]

What has attracted less attention has been the relationship in documentary use between the Insular vernaculars.[4] In part, this is a function of the division

1 For an overview see Nicholas Brooks, 'Latin and Old English in Ninth-Century Canterbury', in *Spoken and Written Language: Relations between Latin and the Vernacular Languages in the Earlier Middle Ages*, eds Mary Garrison, Arpad P. Orbán, and Marco Mostert (Turnhout, 2013), pp. 113–31; Rebecca Stephenson, 'Byrthferth's *Enchiridion* and the Effectiveness of Hermeneutic Latin', in *Conceptualizing Multilingualism in England c.800–c.1250*, ed. Elizabeth M. Tyler (Turnhout, 2011), pp. 121–44. See Francesca Tinti, 'Writing Latin and Old English in Tenth-Century England: Patterns, Formulae and Language Choice in the Leases of Oswald of Worcester', in *Writing, Kingship and Power in Anglo-Saxon England*, eds Rory Naismith and David A. Woodman (Cambridge, 2018), pp. 303–27 for a discussion of bilingualism in the documentary practice of Worcester cathedral.

2 Susan Kelly, 'Anglo-Saxon Lay Society and the Written Word', in *The Uses of Literacy in Early Medieval Europe*, ed. Rosamond McKitterick (Cambridge, 1990), pp. 36–62; Robert Gallagher, 'The Vernacular in Anglo-Saxon Charters: Expansion and Innovation in Ninth-Century England', *Historical Research* 91 (2018), 205–35; Tinti, 'Writing Latin and Old English', p. 327.

3 David N. Dumville, *English Caroline Script and Monastic History: Studies in Benedictinism, A.D. 950–1030* (Woodbridge, 1993), pp. 153–55; David N. Dumville, 'English Square Minuscule Script: The Background and Earliest Phases', *ASE* 16 (1987), 147–79.

4 Although see Helen Fulton, 'Negotiating Welshness: Multilingualism in Wales Before and After 1066', in *Conceptualizing Multilingualism*, ed. Tyler, pp. 145–70; and Julia Crick,

 | DOI:10.1163/9789004432338_010

of Insular history and literature into the separate fields of 'Celtic' and 'Anglo-Saxon' studies, itself a reflection of divergent philological and linguistic histories. Old English and the other Insular vernacular languages belong to different language families and the amount of demonstrable contact between them seems to have been relatively limited, unlike, let us say, Old English and Old Norse.[5] It is extremely unusual, for instance, to see both Old English and Celtic vernaculars occurring in the same documentary context. The one area where the dialogue between the Insular vernaculars has received some attention is the field of place-name studies. One can point to the studies of place-name scholars and local historians who have worked on the Anglo-Welsh border, where settlement, identity, and the formation of place-names existed in a highly complex and fluid relationship across time and space.[6] We could point, for instance, to the Middle Saxon place-names of north-east Wales, recorded in Domesday Book as part of Cheshire beyond the Dee, which were subsequently Cymricized in the twelfth and thirteenth centuries.[7] The south-western peninsula of Britain—the modern English counties of Devon and Cornwall—is another area where the Insular vernaculars can be seen in dialogue, and in similar documentary contexts. Cornwall, in particular, was and is a Celtic-speaking part of Britain, with a Brittonic Celtic vernacular closely related to Old Welsh. By *c.*800, according to Peter Schrijver, it is possible to distinguish between very early West British (that which becomes Old Welsh) and very early South-West British (which becomes later Cornish and Breton), but such differences were very slight and certainly not enough to impede mutual intelligibility.[8] Any distinction between Cornish and Breton forms of South-West British is not readily apparent until the eleventh century at the earliest.[9] The Anglo-Saxon charters from the south west—in particular those from Cornwall—form the focus of the following discussion.[10]

'The English and the Irish from Cnut to John: Speculation on a Linguistic Interface', in *Conceptualizing Multilingualism*, ed. Tyler, pp. 217–38.

5 Matthew Townend, *Language and History in Viking Age England: Linguistic Relations between Speakers of Old Norse and Old English* (Turnhout, 2002), at pp. 181–212.

6 C. P. Lewis, 'Welsh Territories and Welsh Identities in Late Anglo-Saxon England', in *Britons in Anglo-Saxon England*, ed. N. J. Higham (Woodbridge, 2007), pp. 130–43.

7 Lewis, 'Welsh Territories', p. 143; Richard Morgan, 'Place-Names in the Northern Marches of Wales', in *A Commodity of Good Names: Essays in Honour of Margaret Gelling*, eds Oliver Padel and David Parsons (Donnington, 2008), pp. 204–16.

8 P. Schrijver, 'Old British', in *Brythonic Celtic—Britannisches Keltisch. From Medieval British to Modern Breton*, ed. Elmar Ternas (Bremen, 2011), pp. 1–84, at 4.

9 Schrijver, 'Old British', p. 4.

10 See Appendix 1 for a list of charters.

What follows will briefly introduce the history—or rather, the gaps in the history—of the south west in the period up to *c*.1100, before moving on to a discussion of the charters and what light they shed on the relationship between Latin, Old English, and Cornish. The final part of this discussion will, based on the evidence of the charters, offer some more general observations about Cornish society—or, at least, the documentary culture of this society—in the two centuries before the Norman Conquest, the period covered by the charter evidence.

The history of south-western Britain between the end of the Roman period—roughly 400—and the eleventh century is poorly understood, in large part a function of very poor documentary survival and patchy archaeological evidence.[11] In terms of geography and settlement, the south-western peninsula is dominated by two central upland zones, Dartmoor and Bodmin Moor. Consequently, settlement until the post-medieval period was largely confined to the areas north and south of these zones, along the river valleys that drain into the English and Bristol Channels. There does seem to have been some measure of settlement dislocation in the late Roman/Romano-British period, and the distinctive Iron Age enclosures known as 'rounds' (*ker* in Cornish) seem to have been abandoned.[12] In many cases, settlement centres did not move very far, suggesting that land use may have remained the same—and possibly estate structures—but that human habitation moved into unenclosed sites. Quite what the political structures were that followed Roman rule (as far as we can talk of 'Roman' rule in the far south west) is almost completely obscure, although the first *vita* of St Samson of Dol points to organized, structured lordship in Cornwall during the lifetime of the saint, in the early sixth century.[13]

11 For a general overview see Sam Turner, *Making a Christian Landscape. The Countryside in Early Medieval Cornwall, Devon and Wessex* (Exeter, 2006); less recent are Susan Pearce, *The Kingdom of Dumnonia. Studies in History and Tradition in South-Western Britain* (Padstow, 1978); Malcolm Todd, *The South-West to AD 1000* (London, 1987). See also Duncan Probert, 'Church and Landscape: A Study in Social Transition in South-Western Britain, A.D. c.400 to c.1200' (unpublished PhD thesis, University of Birmingham, 2002). For early church history see Susan Pearce, *The Early Church in Western Britain and Ireland* (Oxford, 1982); Lynette Olson, *Early Monasteries in Cornwall* (Woodbridge, 1993); Karen Jankulak, *The Medieval Cult and Relics of St Petroc* (Woodbridge, 2001); Nicholas Orme, *The Saints of Cornwall* (Oxford, 2002).

12 Turner, *Making a Christian Landscape*, pp. 72–75.

13 *La vie ancienne de Saint Samson de Dol. Texte édité, traduit et commenté*, I, 46, ed. and trans. Pierre Flobert (Paris, 1997), pp. 212–15; Duncan Probert, 'New Light on Aldhelm's Letter to King Gerent of Dumnonia', in *Aldhelm and Sherborne. Essays to Celebrate the Founding of the Bishopric*, ed. Katherine Barker with Nicholas Brooks (Oxford, 2010), pp. 110–28, at 122–23.

It may be that political power in early medieval Cornwall was in part based on the ability of political figures to broker Mediterranean trade; there are a number of sites in Cornwall, as well as in south-east Wales (e.g. Dinas Powys) which suggest that the later fifth and sixth centuries saw a significant amount of Mediterranean trade entering Britain via the south west.[14]

How far there was an existing ecclesiastical structure in the south west is also not clear, although again Samson's *vita* points to a functioning church in the south west in the sixth century, while part of Gildas' condemnation of Constantine, the 'tyrant of Dumnonia' (presumably roughly contemporaneous with St Samson) was that amongst his many crimes was the murder of two boys whilst clothed in the robe of an abbot, suggesting parallels with the world of king-abbots that we can glimpse in parts of early medieval Ireland, such as the Cashel branch of the Eóghanachta dynasty in the ninth century.[15] Charles Thomas argued in the early 1970s for *Lann-* place-names indicating early enclosed churchyards and cemeteries, perhaps as early as the fifth or sixth centuries.[16] Current scholarship is perhaps more measured, and *Lann-* place-names are no longer seen as indicative of early ecclesiastical settlements, although most *Lann-* place-names seem to have been in existence by the twelfth century.[17] A telling example might be an ecclesiastical community attested both in St Samson's *vita* and in a tenth-century charter; modern Lanow, in St Kew.[18] Although in the tenth-century charter (of which more later) the community is referred to as *Landochou*, the church [enclosure] of St *Dochou*, in Samson's *vita* it is only referred to as *Docco*; the community was clearly there, since Samson visited it, but it seems not to have been associated

14 Ewan Campbell, *Continental and Mediterranean Imports into Atlantic Britain and Ireland, AD 400–800* (York, 2007); Andrew Seaman, 'Dinas Powys in Context: Settlement and Society in Post-Roman Wales', *Studia Celtica* 67 (2013), 1–23, at pp. 18–19.

15 Gildas, *De excidio et conquestu Britanniae*, 28, ed. and trans. Michael Winterbottom, *Gildas: The Ruin of Britain and Other Works* (Chichester, 1978), pp. 29–30; Edel Bhreathnach, *Ireland in the Medieval World AD 400–1000* (Dublin, 2013), p. 189; Matthew Stout, *Early Medieval Ireland 431–1169* (Dublin, 2017), pp. 136–39.

16 Charles Thomas, *The Early Christian Archaeology of North Britain* (Oxford, 1971), pp. 49–51. For a survey of models of church development in western Britain see Turner, *Making a Christian Landscape*, pp. 5–14.

17 Turner, *Making a Christian Landscape*, pp. 6–8; David Petts, 'Cemeteries and Boundaries in Western Britain', in *Burial in Early Medieval England and Wales*, eds Andrew Reynolds and Sam Lucy (Leeds, 2002), pp. 24–46; Oliver Padel, *Cornish Place-Name Elements* (Nottingham, 1985), pp. 142–44.

18 S 810 (ed. W. M. M. Picken, 'The "Landochou" Charter', in W. G. Hoskins, *The Westward Expansion of Wessex* (Leicester, 1960), pp. 36–44); see below, pp. 361–65.

at that point with a *Lann*-type enclosed space.[19] Most of what appears to have been early post-Roman settlements in Cornwall seem to have been marked by place-names using the elements *tre-* and *bod-*, which Oliver Padel translates respectively as 'estate' and 'dwelling'.[20] Distinguishing the two on the ground is difficult, but it seems that *tre-* settlements were both more prestigious and more likely to be associated with churches by the twelfth century.[21]

In the broadest terms, a contrast can be drawn between the far south west—to the west of the River Tamar, where the majority of the modern place-names are Cornish (and ultimately Brittonic) in origin, and the area to the east of the Tamar, including the upper part of the valley of the Tamar itself, where a significant majority of place-names is ultimately derived from Old English.[22] Even for those place-names in Devon and Somerset whose ultimate origin is a Brittonic language, it is often the case that the place-name as it survives has been filtered through an English speech community and English speech patterns.[23] This division conforms to a large extent to the modern boundaries between the counties of Devon (east of the Tamar) and Cornwall (to the west); this is not an exact correspondence, however, since very many of the place-names in the very eastern part of Cornwall, in Stratton and East Wivelshire hundreds, are also derived from Old English forms. Nonetheless, the general absence of pre-English toponyms in Devon by the eleventh century is surely indicative of a significant early linguistic boundary.[24]

How one is to read this pattern is not at all clear. For previous generations of historians, one could see the extent of English place-names in the south west as the evidence on the ground of the westward expansion of the kingdom of Wessex as it is recorded in the late ninth-century 'common stock' of the

19 *La vie ancienne de Saint Samson*, I, 45, ed. and trans. Flobert, p. 212; Jonathon Wooding, 'The Representation of Early British Monasticism and *Peregrinatio* in *Vita Prima S. Samsoni*', in *St Samson of Dol and the Earliest History of Brittany, Cornwall and Wales*, ed. Lynette Olson (Woodbridge, 2017), pp. 137–62, at 154; Olson, *Early Monasteries*, pp. 81–82; Oliver Padel, 'Two New Pre-Conquest Charters for Cornwall', *Journal of Cornish Studies* 6 (1978), 20–27.

20 O. J. Padel, 'Place-Names and the Saxon Conquest of Britain and Cornwall', in *Britons in Anglo-Saxon England*, ed. Higham, pp. 215–30, at 215–21.

21 Padel, 'Place-Names and the Saxon Conquest', p. 217.

22 Padel, 'Place-Names and the Saxon Conquest', pp. 218–19.

23 For example, see Duncan Probert, 'Mapping Early Medieval Language Change in South-West England', in *Britons in Anglo-Saxon England*, ed. Higham, pp. 231–44, at 233–34.

24 Probert, 'Mapping Early Medieval Language Change', p. 233, citing O. J. Padel, 'Cornwall as a Border Area', *Nomina* 6 (1982), 18–22.

Anglo-Saxon Chronicle.[25] Inevitably, the situation is far more complicated than this. The Anglo-Saxon Chronicle is far from a perfect guide to events in the early Anglo-Saxon period, not least in the picture it constructs of hostility between the Anglo-Saxons and their Brittonic neighbours. This is not to say that there was not extensive warfare between the Anglo-Saxons and the British, but that there was also a whole range of contacts between the two communities, many of which were not violent. We are on firmer ground by the time we get to the tenth century, the period for which Cornwall starts to be represented in surviving documentary sources. The society and landscape that we can see by the time of Domesday Book (A.D. 1086) are firmly under English control, with administrative structures that look, superficially at least, much like those of the rest of southern England. Yet they are also very distinctive, with an ecclesiastical and parochial structure that may have had more in common with Wales than the rest of southern England, and where many of the inhabitants were probably not English speakers.[26] Some of the socio-economic processes that created the landscape of southern England in Domesday Book—manorialization, settlement nucleation—also seem to have been different in Cornwall.[27]

There are two main, interrelated questions that interest historians of the far south west. First, what sort of society emerged in the post-Roman centuries, and what sort of socio-economic processes were at play? How, in other words, do we get to the Cornwall of Domesday Book? And second, what was the impact of English settlement and lordship on the far south west? The following discussion will not answer these questions, except tangentially, but thinking about the issues of language use in charters does arguably help us towards a fuller understanding of Cornish society in the immediately pre-Conquest period.

Returning to the question of interaction between Anglo-Saxons and Britons, it is worth highlighting the evidence for more peaceful encounters, even in the early Anglo-Saxon period. Most historians would accept that Anglo-Saxon settlement in Devon—the transformation of eastern Dumnonia into *Defenascire*—was a process under way in the eighth century, but we should not forget that even earlier, Winfrith, the future St Boniface, began his religious career at Exeter in the late seventh century in a church ruled by an abbot with

---

25 For example, William Hoskins, *The Westward Expansion of Wessex* (Leicester, 1960); H. P. R. Finberg, 'Sherborne, Glastonbury, and the Expansion of Wessex', in H. P. R. Finberg, *Lucerna: Studies of Some Problems in the Early History of England* (London, 1964), pp. 95–115.

26 Padel, 'Place-Names and the Saxon Conquest', p. 222.

27 Turner, *Making a Christian Landscape*, pp. 118–30.

an Anglo-Saxon name, Wulfheard.[28] The works of Boniface's slightly earlier contemporary, Aldhelm, also make it clear that for ecclesiastics, at least, contacts between the Anglo-Saxons and the British of the south west were probably more common than we might think.[29] Britons were a clearly identifiable group within Wessex in the eighth century: the presence of Britons in the law-code issued by the early eighth-century West Saxon king Ine is well known, as is the fact that they were also legally disadvantaged, having lower wergild than a Saxon of equivalent rank.[30] Whether we should see this as a form of legal apartheid, as Martin Grimmer and Alex Woolf have argued, is not the focus of this discussion, but it is worth noting that those Britons who fell under the aegis of Ine's laws were of all ranks and status, not simply servile, and Ine's code also envisaged royal servants who were Britons.[31]

Two of Aldhelm's surviving works make explicit reference to the Britons of the south west; the *Carmen rhythmicum* and his letter to Gerent, king of Dumnonia.[32] Others—notably Duncan Probert—have explored these texts in more detail, but there are a couple of points to be drawn out here. First is that in the *Carmen*, Aldhelm describes being caught in a storm whilst travelling through 'bare' Cornubia towards Dumnonia; unless we dismiss this journey as part of Aldhelm's poetic artifice, then it suggests that West Saxon ecclesiastics might journey through and expect hospitality in the British south west. Second is that the *Carmen* draws a distinction between Dumnonia and Cornubia. The nature of this distinction, whether Cornubia was an entirely separate entity from Dumnonia, is less clear. The general supposition is that the kingdom of Dumnonia—first recorded in Gildas' polemical *De excidio et conquestu Britanniae* of the late fifth, or more likely mid-sixth, century—is that Dumnonia covered the

28 Willibald, *Vita Bonifatii*, 1, ed. Wilhelm Levison, MGH SS rer. Germ. 57 (Hanover, 1905), pp. 1–58, at 6; Probert, 'New Light on Aldhelm's Letter', pp. 124–25.

29 Probert, 'New Light on Aldhelm's Letter'.

30 Ine, cc. 23.3, 24.2, 32, 33, 46.1, *Die Gesetze der Angelsachsen*, ed. Felix Lieberman, 3 vols (Halle, 1903–11), 1:89–123; *The Laws of the Earliest English Kings*, ed. Frederick Attenborough (Cambridge, 1922), pp. 36–61; *English Historical Documents. I: c.500–1042*, ed. Dorothy Whitelock, 2nd ed. (London, 1979), pp. 398–407; Patrick Wormald, *The Making of English Law: King Alfred to the Twelfth Century. I: Legislation and its Limits* (Oxford, 1999), pp. 103–6; Louis M. Alexander, 'The Legal Status of Native Britons in Late Seventh-Century Wessex as Reflected by the Law Code of Ine', *Haskins Society Journal* 7 (1995), 31–38.

31 Martin Grimmer, 'Britons in Early Wessex: The Evidence of the Law Code of Ine', in *Britons in Anglo-Saxon England*, ed. Higham, pp. 102–14; Alex Woolf, 'Apartheid Economics in Anglo-Saxon England', in *Britons in Anglo-Saxon England*, ed. Higham, pp. 115–29, at 127–29.

32 *Aldhelmi Opera*, ed. Rudolf Ehwald, MGH Auct. ant. 15 (Berlin, 1919), pp. 480–86 (letter to King Gerent) and 523–28 (*Carmen*).

whole of the south-western peninsula including Cornwall, so we should perhaps regard Cornwall/Cornubia as a sub-unit of the Dumnonian kingdom, at least until the ninth century.[33]

Aldhelm's letter to King Gerent, probably written when Aldhelm was bishop of Sherborne in the early eighth century, also tells us something about early medieval Cornwall. The letter concerns the religious observances of the British of the south west, part of the wider disjuncture between Roman and Insular religious practice in the seventh and eighth centuries. Aldhelm urges Gerent to encourage his subjects to follow the canonical position on Easter and the monastic (i.e. Petrine) tonsure, contrasting this with the unwillingness of the British of *Demetia* (Dyfed in south-west Wales) to adopt right practice.[34] This letter presupposes two things. First, that Gerent was in a position to do something about this, but also that Aldhelm as bishop of Sherborne had, or at least claimed, some sort of loosely defined oversight of pastoral care and discipline in the far south west, perhaps indicating that by the early eighth century the Cornish were under some sort of—however loose or ephemeral—West Saxon overlordship, at least in ecclesiastical terms.

This relationship between the Cornish and the bishops of Sherborne is supported by two further pieces of evidence. Two fourteenth-century lists, one copied into the Sherborne Missal (London, British Library, Add. 74236), assert that a King Gerent gave an estate at *Macor* (modern Maker) to Sherborne at some point before *c.*710.[35] Given the absence of any other kings of that name known from the south west, this is almost certainly the same figure as that in Aldhelm's letter. The pastoral responsibility of the bishops of Sherborne for the Cornish—or, at least, their claim to it—is highlighted in two tenth-century accounts of the early history of the south-western sees, one in English, one in Latin. Both are concerned with the division of the enormous diocese of Sherborne in around 909 or 910, with the creation of the bishoprics of Wells and Crediton, and the subsequent division of Crediton in around 930 to create a separate Cornish diocese at St Germans.[36] Although there are differences between the two accounts, both agree that Ecgberht, king of the West Saxons between 802 and 839, gave three estates in Cornwall—Pawton,

33 Gildas, *De excidio et conquestu Britanniae*, 28, ed. and trans. Winterbottom, pp. 29–30.

34 Probert, 'New Light on Aldhelm's Letter', pp. 115–19.

35 O'Donovan, *Sherb*, pp. xx–xxxi and xxxvii–li; Heather Edwards, *The Charters of the Early West-Saxon Kingdom* (Oxford, 1988), pp. 243–53; Probert, 'New Light on Aldhelm's Letter', p. 125.

36 S 1296 and S 1451a (*Councils and Synods with Other Documents relating to the English Church, I: A.D. 871–1204*, eds D. Whitelock, M. Brett, and C. N. L. Brooke (Oxford, 1981), no. 35 (i) and (ii)).

Cællincg/Cællwic, and Lawhitton—to the bishop to enable him to minister to the Cornish and emend their errors. This is, perhaps, a hint that the customs of the native church in Cornwall sat uneasily with those of the increasingly dominant Anglo-Saxon clerical establishment.[37]

Further ecclesiastical contacts between the Cornish and the West Saxons can be seen in the ninth century in the surviving undated profession of obedience of Bishop Kenstec to Archbishop Ceolnoth of Canterbury (r. 833–70).[38] Kenstec was bishop of a place called *Dinuurin*, which has plausibly been identified with an early enclosed site near Bodmin; Bodmin priory itself was dedicated to St Guron (early Cornish *Uuron*).[39] It is tempting to see Kenstec's profession as part of the extension of West Saxon overlordship over the far south west; Ecgberht had fought two battles against the Cornish in the 830s, including against a combined force of Britons and Norse at Hingston Down in 838.[40] Kenstec's profession may have followed in the wake of this defeat, as may have the grant to Sherborne of Pawton, Lawhitton, and *Cællincg/Cællwic*. Nonetheless, this is only a possibility. Kenstec's profession can be dated no more closely than at some point during Ceolnoth's very long pontificate, and it is not impossible that his profession was as much to do with ecclesiastical politics within Cornwall as external factors. An analogous event might be the profession of Patrick, bishop of Dublin, to Archbishop Lanfranc in 1074, which was as much about internal wranglings within the Irish church, in particular the primacy of Armagh, as it was about the reality of Canterbury's claims to metropolitan status across Britain and Ireland.[41] A late tenth-century charter issued in the name of Æthelred II for Bishop Ealdred of St Germans has a reference to the 'rule' or 'governance' of St Petroc (*regimen sancti Petroci*) being placed under the authority of the Bishop of St Germans.[42] Lynette Olsen has argued that this referred to the episcopal authority associated with St Petroc's community being granted or confirmed to Bishop Ealdred, in turn suggesting that rivalry between competing episcopal jurisdictions within Cornwall

37 It is not clear where *Cællincg/Cællwic* was. It may be modern Callington, but William Picken suggests Kelly, in Egloshayle: W. M. M. Picken, 'Callington and Kelliwic', *Devon and Cornwall Notes and Queries* 27 (1956–58), 225–26.

38 *Canterbury Professions*, ed. Michael Richter (Torquay, 1973), p. 27.

39 Lynette Olson, 'Introduction', in *St Samson of Dol*, ed. Olson, pp. 1–18, at 12–13; Olson, *Early Monasteries*, pp. 52–56 and 63.

40 *The Anglo-Saxon Chronicle: A Revised Translation*, eds Dorothy Whitelock, David Douglas, and Susie Tucker (London, 1961), A, *s.a.* 838.

41 Clare Downham, *Medieval Ireland* (Cambridge, 2018), p. 146.

42 S 880 (KCD 686).

provides us with as much context for Kenstec's earlier profession as West Saxon military campaigns.[43]

What does seem to emerge from the evidence is that by the ninth century, and quite possibly earlier, Cornwall was under some sort of loose West Saxon overlordship, but it also had its own kings and lords and a powerful and largely independent church. In the tenth century, however, this Anglo-Saxon overlordship became much tighter and more structured. The last Cornish king who appears in the evidence drowned in 877 and, while an identifiably native elite seems to have flourished well into the twelfth century, they were under English royal lordship.[44] We can see one manifestation of this in the manumissions entered as marginal notes into the Bodmin Gospels. These are a set of ninth-century Breton gospels, formerly in the possession of St Petroc's minster at Bodmin and now in the British Library.[45] At various points in the gospels, manumissions of slaves were recorded, ranging in date from the mid-tenth to the early twelfth century. Throughout the manumissions, the most prolific manumitter of slaves over the altar of St Petroc was the English crown.[46]

Similarly, the tenth century also saw the establishment of more structured English ecclesiastical organization in Cornwall, although the Cornish church remained distinctive beyond 1066. It is unclear how many churches exercised episcopal authority in Cornwall before the tenth century, although more than one seems likely. The church at Bodmin, the most important ecclesiastical landholder in Cornwall after the bishop of Exeter, seems to have been connected to episcopal authority, if it can be inferred that the *Dinuurin* of Bishop Kenstec's profession is to be identified with Bodmin. The church at St Germans, which became the seat of the Anglo-Saxon bishop in Cornwall after the 930s, may also have been connected with earlier episcopal jurisdiction; an anathema

---

43 Oliver Padel, 'Christianity in Medieval Cornwall: Celtic Aspects', in Nicholas Orme, *A History of the County of Cornwall II: Religious History to 1560*, Victoria County History (Woodbridge, 2010), pp. 110–25, at 122–23; Olson, *Early Monasteries*, pp. 75–78.

44 *Annales Cambriae, A.D. 682–954: Texts A–C in Parallel*, ed. and trans. David Dumville (Cambridge, 2002), *s.a.* 877: 'Dumngarth rex Cerniu mersus est'. His death may have been accidental, but drowning was used in Ireland as a form of execution which did not shed blood, so it is possible that Dumngarth was executed or murdered.

45 London, British Library, Add. 9381.

46 The Bodmin manumissions are printed in Max Förster, 'Die Freilassungsurkunden des Bodmin-Evangeliars', in *A Grammatical Miscellany offered to Otto Jespersen on his 70th Birthday*, eds Nils Bøgholm, A. Brusendorff, and Carl Bodelsen (Copenhagen, 1930), pp. 77–100; they are discussed in O. J. Padel, *Slavery in Saxon Cornwall: The Bodmin Manumissions* (Cambridge, 2009); see also Charles Insley, 'Kings and Lords in Tenth-Century Cornwall', *History* 98 (2013), 2–22, at pp. 16–17.

ascribed to the bishop of St Germans in the Lanalet Pontifical, a late tenth- or early eleventh-century combined benedictional and pontifical associated with the church at St Germans, describes the bishop as 'the bishop of Lanalet minster'.[47] This suggests at the very least a pre-Anglo-Saxon church exercising some sort of episcopal jurisdiction on the same site or near the tenth-century church of St Germans.[48]

Nonetheless, the tenth century saw the churches in Cornwall being brought under the authority of a bishop of St Germans, appointed by the kings of the English, a process that may not have been complete until Æthelred II granted full episcopal privileges to Bishop Ealdred of St Germans in 994, along with the 'rule of St Petroc' (*regimen Sancti Petroci*).[49] However, what remains striking about the Cornish church in Domesday Book is the extent to which native foundations remained privileged institutions, especially when compared to newer foundations of the bishop of St Germans (or, after 1050, Exeter), and the Devon abbey of Tavistock. In 1086, the estates of the Cornish minsters were geld-free, but not the estates of either the bishop of Exeter or the abbot of Tavistock.[50]

The Cornish church may have been subject to other pressures in the tenth century, including secularization; it seems likely that although native foundations remained legally privileged institutions they may have suffered what might have been a significant diminution of their property and jurisdiction. This is in part a process suggested by place-name evidence and partly by the charter evidence. The best examples are those place-names which contain the element *meneage*—for instance, St Martin-in-Meneage in south-western Cornwall—which is derived from the Cornish word *manach* (monk) and the adjective *menaghek* (monkish).[51] The *meneage* may simply indicate an area under monastic authority, perhaps a sanctuary area, but it may also indicate more direct monastic lordship in the form of ownership.[52] If the canons of St Keverne are taken as an example, it is clear that the *meneage* associated with their patronal saint, St Achebran, was larger in 1086 than their recorded property.[53]

---

47 Rouen, Bibliothèque municipale, 368; *Pontificale Lanalatense* (*Bibliothèque de la Ville de Rouen A. 27 cat. 368*), ed. G. H. Doble (London, 1937); Padel, 'Christianity in Medieval Cornwall', pp. 122–23; Olson, *Early Monasteries*, pp. 74–78.

48 Thomas, *Early Christian Archaeology*, pp. 49–51.

49 S 880 (KCD 686).

50 Olson, *Early Monasteries*, pp. 90–93.

51 Padel, *Cornish Place-Name Elements*, pp. 156 and 163.

52 *Pre-Conquest Charter-Bounds of Devon and Cornwall*, ed. and trans. Della Hooke (Woodbridge, 1994), p. 40; Olson *Early Monasteries*, p. 108.

53 Great Domesday Book, fol. 121a (*Domesday Book*, 10, *Cornwall*, eds Caroline Thorn and Frank Thorn (Chichester, 1979), 4, 23).

The canons of St Keverne are an apposite example, since some of the charter evidence also seems to indicate the loss of their property into secular hands. A diploma of King Edgar dated 967 records what appears to be property formerly associated with St Keverne being granted to a thegn with the hybrid Old English-Cornish name Wulfnoth Rumoncant,[54] while further St Keverne property seems to have been the subject in 977 of a diploma of King Edward (the Martyr) in favour of Ealdorman Æthelweard.[55] How we should view this process of secularization (and whether it really is secularization) is unclear.[56] Some of the land seems to have ended up in the hands of other churches, including in Normandy after 1066 (Robert of Mortain granted 'Lannachebran' to Mont-Saint-Michel in around 1070).[57] Equally unclear is whether we should see this transfer of property away from native foundations as a consequence of the intensification of Anglo-Saxon rule over the Cornish.[58] At least two of the beneficiaries of the surviving charters were men with both Cornish and Old English names, and it is possible that we are looking at the same fragmentation of large dispersed estates and the consolidation of smaller estate structures that we can see across southern England in the tenth and eleventh centuries—manorialization, perhaps.[59]

Cornwall in 1066 therefore presents a complex picture to the historian: a landscape apparently firmly under English political and ecclesiastical control, but also one which looks rather different from the neighbouring counties of south-western England. The Bodmin manumissions, as well as the charters, hint at a native landholding elite which is still identifiable in the eleventh century, while Domesday Book presents us with privileged local churches.[60] Although it is tempting to regard the hundreds of the south west as a West Saxon innovation of the ninth or tenth century, it is likely that the administrative geography of Cornwall that can be seen in Domesday Book was a palimpsest, rather than something constructed *ab initio* by English kings in the tenth century.[61] The hundred of Trigg, for instance, in north Cornwall may very well be the descendent of a much earlier administrative district. The *Vita prima* of St Samson of Dol describes an episode when the saint visited Cornwall on

54 S 755 (BCS 1197).

55 S 832 (ed. J. B. Davidson, 'On Some Anglo-Saxon Charters at Exeter', *Journal of the British Archaeological Association* 39 (1883), 259–303). For a text of the boundary, see Appendix 2.

56 Turner, *Making a Christian Landscape*, pp. 125–27.

57 Turner, *Making a Christian Landscape*, pp. 117 and 126.

58 Insley, 'Kings and Lords', pp. 14–15.

59 It is worth noting that it is this process that may lie behind the significant increase in Anglo-Saxon charters that survive from the tenth and eleventh centuries in comparison with earlier centuries.

60 Insley, 'Kings and Lords'; Olson, *Early Monasteries*, pp. 92–93.

61 Turner, *Making a Christian Landscape*, pp. 113–18.

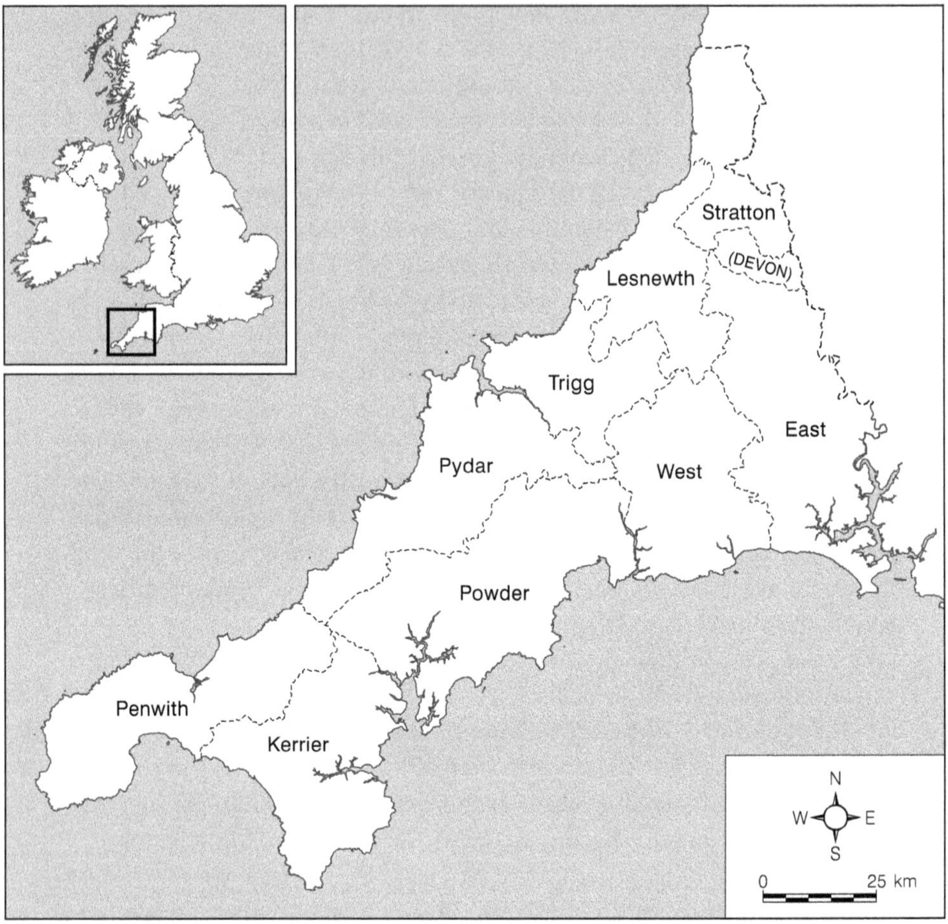

MAP 9.1 Cornish hundreds
DRAWN UP BY AND REPRODUCED WITH PERMISSION OF NICK SCARLE

his way from *Demetia* (Dyfed) to Brittany. During this visit Samson spent some time correcting the religious behaviour of a local *comes* called Vedianus and his followers in the *pagus Tricurius*, which is almost certainly an early form of Trigg.[62] As Oliver Padel and Duncan Probert have suggested, this name may be a form of the Brittonic *Tricorios* ('district/tribe of three armies'), which hints at some of the layers of sub-regnal lordship in early medieval Dumnonia.[63] It

62 *La vie ancienne de Saint Samson*, I, 48, ed. and trans. Flobert, p. 216; Turner, *Making a Christian Landscape*, p. 114; Olson, *Early Monasteries*, p. 16.

63 Charles Thomas, *And Shall These Mute Stones Speak? Post-Roman Inscriptions in Western Britain* (Cardiff, 1994), p. 216; Padel, *Cornish Place-Name Elements*, p. 64; Probert, 'New Light on Aldhelm's Letter', pp. 122–23.

would, of course, be over-simplistic to suggest that the administrative geography of the south west remained unchanged between the sixth and twelfth centuries, but it does at least suggest a complex and long history behind the administrative landscape that comes into historical focus at the end of the eleventh century.

The Charters

This has been a rather long prologue to a discussion of the charters, but it is important to emphasize just how unusual Cornwall was in comparison to the rest of south-western England, even in the tenth and eleventh centuries. The handful of pre-Conquest Cornish charters that survive, therefore, provide us with an invaluable window into this distinctive society. Given that for most Cornish settlements, Domesday Book or twelfth- and thirteenth-century manorial and exchequer records are their earliest recorded appearances, the topographical references in the charters, and in particular their boundary clauses, give us some of our earliest glimpses of the Cornish language.[64]

The total number of charters surviving from pre-Conquest Cornwall is not high. If we exclude references to lost documents, and just include specimens where we have all or most of the text, then there are 16 charters (not including the aforementioned manumissions contained in the Bodmin Gospels).[65] Of these, ten have some sort of boundary clause. The remaining six are all interesting documents. Three are connected with the relationship between the bishoprics of Crediton (Devon) and St Germans (Cornwall); two of these narrate the history of the bishoprics and the allocation of estates formerly belonging to the bishopric of Sherborne, while the third, a rather sumptuous gilded diploma issued by Æthelred II in 994, confirms the episcopal rights and jurisdictions of the bishop of St Germans.[66] In addition, we have a spurious grant in the name of Edward the Confessor of land at St Michael's Mount to Mont-Saint-Michel,[67] and a record of an authentic exchange of land between King Eadred and a thegn called Wulfric.[68] The last specimen is a private

64 B. Lynette Olson and O. J. Padel, 'A Tenth-Century List of Cornish Parochial Saints', *Cambridge Medieval Celtic Studies* 12 (1986), 33–71.

65 These are listed in Appendix 1.

66 S 1296, S 1451a, and S 880. S 880 is the gilded diploma; its modern shelfmark is Exeter, Dean & Chapter, 2070. See Padel, 'Christianity in Medieval Cornwall', pp. 122–23.

67 S 1061 (KCD 914).

68 S 552 (*Abing* 44).

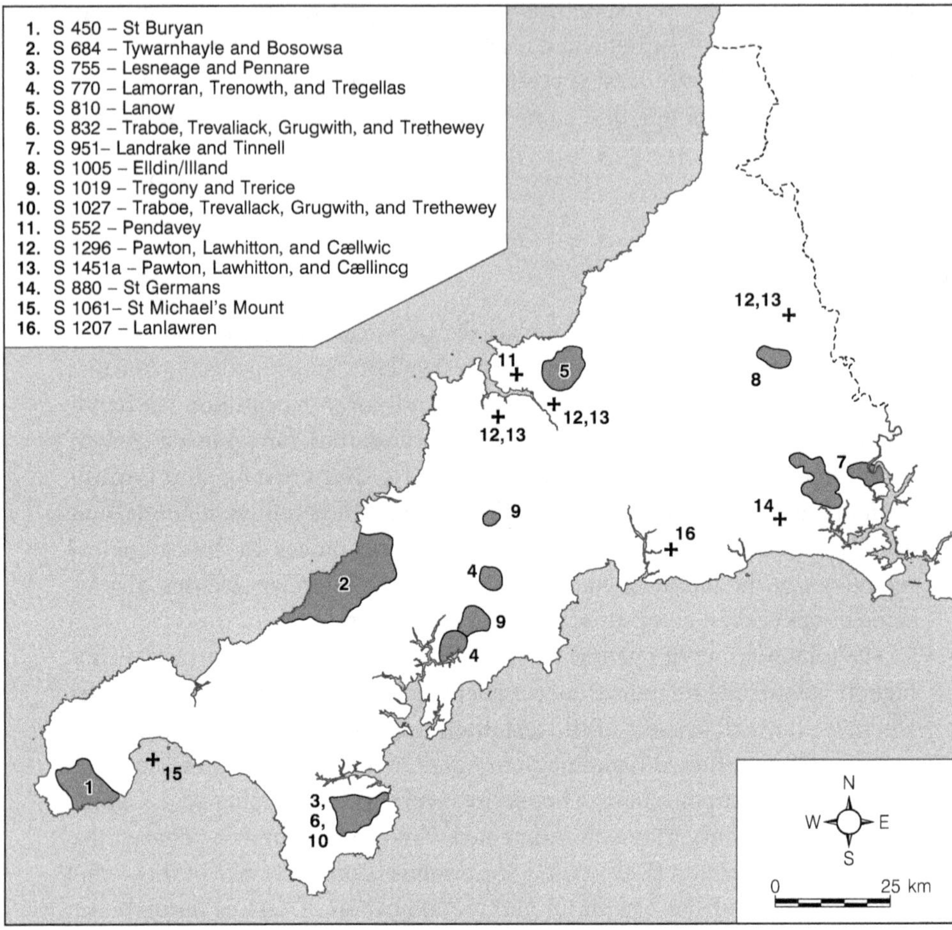

MAP 9.2 The estates of Cornish charters.
DRAWN UP BY AND REPRODUCED WITH PERMISSION OF NICK SCARLE

charter in the name of a Cornish nobleman called Maenchi for the community of St *Heldenus*.[69]

The ten charters with boundaries are a mixture of contemporary single sheets, later single-sheet copies and later medieval cartulary copies, of varying degrees of authenticity. All date from the reign of Æthelstan (r. 924–39) or later, and seven of the ten are preserved in contexts connected with Exeter

69 S 1207 (ed. O. J. Padel, 'The Charter of Lanlawren (Cornwall)', in *Latin Learning and English Lore: Studies in Anglo-Saxon Literature for Michael Lapidge*, eds Katherine O'Brien O'Keeffe and Andy Orchard (Toronto, 2005), pp. 74–85). See Padel, 'Two New Pre-Conquest Charters', pp. 22–23. Padel suggests St *Heldenus* was probably St Hyldren.

Cathedral (although one is really a stray from the archive of Bodmin Priory);[70] of the remaining three, two are preserved amongst the archives of Christ Church, Canterbury,[71] while one is all that remains of the archive of the minster of St Kew.[72] This archival preponderance towards Exeter material needs to be kept in mind when thinking about what the charters might reveal about the languages of diplomatic in Cornwall (especially given that Exeter lies in Devon, not Cornwall). The chronological bias also needs some comment. A charter purporting to be a diploma of Æthelstan is somewhat of an outlier,[73] as it is Edgar's reign (r. 957/9–975) which seems to have witnessed concerted issuing of diplomas for lands in Cornwall. The processes that lie behind this chronological bias are probably unrecoverable; intensified English royal interest in and control over Cornwall after the 930s might provide one context, but we should acknowledge the possibility that other processes around estate reconfiguration and landscape change might also have been at play.

The total absence of any surviving texts from before the 930s also requires comment, since in this case absence of evidence is unlikely to mean evidence of absence. Here the aforementioned private charter of Maenchi is particularly important,[74] since it attests to a non-English diplomatic tradition in Cornwall, namely the so-called 'Latin Celtic Charter' tradition first identified by Wendy Davies, of which this private document is the sole complete witness.[75] Davies argued that there was a range of diplomatic features specific to earlier medieval charters from Wales, Cornwall, and Brittany that might allow historians to talk of a distinct 'Celtic' Latin charter tradition. These features were (i) the use of the past tense for the verb of donation, rather than the present tense (as was generally the norm in Anglo-Saxon diplomas); (ii) the use of the third, rather than the first, person in the disposition (iii) the use of the phrase *in diocesim sempiternam* (in perpetual possession) and (iv) the grant being expressed as a gift to a particular saint, rather than a particular individual such as an abbot or a bishop.[76]

---

70 S 450, S 684, S 755, S 770, S 832, S 951, and S 1027. The stray from Bodmin Priory is S 684.

71 S 1005 (KCD 770) and S 1019 (KCD 787).

72 S 810 (ed. Picken, 'The "Landochou" Charter').

73 S 450 (BCS 785).

74 S 1207 (ed. Padel, 'The Charter of Lanlawren').

75 For the 'Latin Charter tradition' see Wendy Davies, 'The Latin Charter-Tradition in Western Britain, Brittany and Ireland in the Early Mediaeval Period', in *Ireland in Early Medieval Europe: Studies in Memory of Kathleen Hughes*, eds David Dumville and Rosamond McKitterick (Cambridge, 1982), pp. 258–80; Charles Insley, 'Athelstan, Charters, and the English in Cornwall', in *Charters and Charter Scholarship in Britain and Ireland*, eds Marie Therese Flanagan and Judith Green (Basingstoke, 2005), pp. 15–31, at 20.

76 Davies, 'Latin Charter-Tradition', pp. 266–67; Padel, 'The Charter of Lanlawren', p. 75.

Further references to now-lost charters elsewhere can be found in some of the later medieval Sherborne material that imply the recording of gifts of land in Cornwall, and we should not dismiss the possibility that if King Gerent did indeed grant *Macor* to the bishop of Sherborne, that grant was accompanied by some sort of document.[77] It is also worth remembering that although there are no surviving Cornish charters which pre-date the tenth century, Cornwall was in close contact with South Wales and Brittany, both places which certainly did have early medieval charter traditions.[78] If there were earlier charters, though, they have almost entirely been lost. Maenchi's charter only survives because it was copied into the Athelney cartulary at some point in the later Middle Ages.[79]

All 16 of these charters are predominantly or entirely in Latin. Where we find significant linguistic diversity is in the bounds, which can be divided into two broad categories: much the biggest group (eight) has bounds in Old English; two of the charters have bounds predominantly in Latin.[80] Those with Old English bounds, however, do not form a homogeneous group; most of them also make extensive use of Cornish topographical terms and habitative names.[81] Although some of the topographical terms here—*rið* (stream), *sæ* (sea)—are Old English, the majority are Cornish. We can contrast this with a diploma purportedly of King Cnut for land in the north east of Cornwall, in which the bulk of the topographical terms are Old English: only two boundary markers—*carrecron* and *nantnewion*—are in Cornish.[82] The same pattern can be seen in a diploma of Edward the Confessor, where the majority of the topographical terms are in Old English.[83] Both the diploma of Cnut and the diploma of Edward concern property in the very east of Cornwall, in Stratton and East Wivelshire; the remaining charters concern land much further west, in Trigg, Pydar, Kerrier, and Penwith hundreds. In this, the charters bear out the evidence of Domesday, which indicates a heavy concentration of English place-names (and one assumes, tentatively, settlement) in east Cornwall. The evidence suggests, therefore, that this pattern was in place by the end of the tenth century or early eleventh century at the latest.[84]

77 O'Donovan, *Sherb*, pp. xx–xxxi and xxxvii–li.
78 Davies, 'Latin Charter-Tradition'.
79 Bath, Downside Abbey, Philips 4810, p. 119.
80 S 450 (BCS 785) and S 810 (ed. Picken, 'The "Landochou" Charter').
81 See, for example, S 755 (BCS 1197) in Appendix 2.
82 S 951 (ed. Davidson, 'On Some Anglo-Saxon Charters'). See Appendix 2.
83 S 1005 (KCD 770).
84 Padel, 'Place-Names and the Saxon Conquest', pp. 216–19.

The presence of both Old English and Cornish topographical terminology in the boundaries is interesting from a code-switching perspective. In most of the charters where this occurs, this usage, especially in terms of syntax and phonology, seems to be symptomatic of genuine bilingualism rather than borrowings into one language or the other. None of the Cornish words exhibit any of the sound changes that occur to Brittonic words borrowed into Old English. Across western Wessex—Somerset, Dorset, and Devon—there are examples of Brittonic place-names or topographical features that have been borrowed into Old English and have undergone subsequent mutation.[85] We might cite, for example, the sound mutations that turned early Brittonic *crug* (hill, mound, tumulus) into 'crick' or 'creech' when taken into Old English.[86] That these sorts of sound shifts are seemingly absent from the Britonnic-derived boundary terms in our tenth-century Cornish charters, for instance the *crucou mereðen* in the bounds of the Lesneage charter, might suggest that those scribes who drew up the bounds and copied them into the charters were comfortable operating in two distinct linguistic spaces, rather than individuals who were predominantly Old English speakers borrowing Brittonic topographical terms.[87]

The bounds are also a rare witness to forms of Cornish that pre-date the later twelfth and early thirteenth century, when Cornish underwent a series of sounds shifts that produced the phonology of Middle Cornish. Indeed, the beginnings of this process can be seen in the surviving boundaries. The bounds of a mid-tenth-century single-sheet royal diploma for land in Tywarnhayle generally reproduce the orthography and thus phonology of earlier forms of Cornish, but one of the geographic markers in the bounds is the Old Cornish word for stream—*frot*—except that either the draftsman of the boundary or the scribe of the charter rendered it *fros*, with a final 's'.[88] This is one of the key sound shifts between Old and Middle Cornish; see, for instance, the shift from *bod-* (dwelling, farmstead) to *bos-* or *ryt* (ford) to *ris*/*res*. And while this is a change generally observable by *c.*1200, its presence in what is almost certainly a genuine, if rather idiosyncratic, charter suggests that this process was under way much earlier.[89] If this is what lies behind the spelling in this diploma, rather than just simple error, it again underlines the point that these bounds were being drafted by individuals who were generally bilingual and were—in

85 Probert, 'Mapping Early Medieval Language Change', pp. 234–40.

86 Probert, 'Mapping Early Medieval Language Change', pp. 236–37.

87 S 755 (BCS 1197); for the text, see Appendix 2.

88 Exeter, Dean & Chapter, 2522; S 684 (BCS 1056).

89 Padel, *Cornish Place-Name Elements*, pp. 100–1; O. J. Padel, 'The Boundary of Tywarnhayle (Perranzabuloe) in A.D. 960', *Journal of the Royal Institution of Cornwall* (2014), 69–92, at p. 89.

the orthography of their own writing—experiencing the instability and fluidity of their own language.

The content of these boundaries also raises a wider question about the production of these charters. I have argued elsewhere that the core group of surviving south-western charters, including a number of the ones referred to in this discussion, were produced locally in the south west, probably in the episcopal scriptorium at Crediton.[90] In almost all respects these diplomas conform to the somewhat fluid norms of tenth-century Anglo-Saxon diplomatic, what Simon Keynes calls the 'diplomatic mainstream'.[91] They might be rather conservative and depend to a great extent on the recycling of earlier formulation, but beyond that these Cornish specimens are unexceptional. Their palaeography, too, is unexceptional, in that the very small number of surviving contemporary single sheets were written either in English Square Minuscule or in Caroline Minuscule (or a combination of both). This might suggest that the bounds were perhaps drawn up separately before being incorporated into the final diploma; in the case of the above-mentioned diploma for land at Tywarnhayle, this is very clearly the case, since the bounds are along the foot of the single sheet, in a much smaller script in comparison to the main text of the diploma.[92] This should not surprise; there is plenty of evidence for multi-stage diploma production in the corpus of Anglo-Saxon charters;[93] what is more interesting is that there is relatively little garbling of the Cornish words and phrases in these boundaries. Is this because the charter scribes were simply very accurate copyists, or perhaps even in the scriptoria at Crediton or Exeter there were those who were familiar with Cornish? A number of our charters are actually eleventh-century single-sheet copies that can be identified as products of Bishop Leofric of Exeter's scriptorium of the period 1050 to 1072.[94] Again, the level of confusion seems relatively limited, especially in comparison with the way that later medieval scribes sometimes mangled what

90 Charles Insley, 'Charters and Episcopal Scriptoria in the Anglo-Saxon South-West', *EME* 7 (1998), 173–98; Pierre Chaplais, 'The Authenticity of the Royal Anglo-Saxon Diplomas of Exeter', *Bulletin of the Institute of Historical Research* 39 (1966), 1–34; reprinted in Pierre Chaplais, *Essays in Medieval Diplomacy and Administration* (London, 1981), xv.

91 Simon Keynes, 'Church Councils, Royal Assemblies, and Royal Diplomas', in *Kingship, Legislation and Power in Anglo-Saxon England*, eds Gale R. Owen-Crocker and Brian W. Schneider (Woodbridge, 2013), pp. 17–182, at 92.

92 S 684 (BCS 1056).

93 Keynes, 'Church Councils', pp. 68–92.

94 Namely S 755, S 770, and S 832. See Insley, 'Charters and Episcopal Scriptoria', pp. 186–88; Elaine Drage, 'Bishop Leofric and the Exeter Cathedral Chapter 1050–72: A Reassessment of the Manuscript Evidence' (unpublished D.Phil. thesis, University of Oxford, 1978), pp. 157–59.

was in front of them; were there Cornish speakers, or at least, those familiar with Old Cornish at Exeter in the late eleventh century?[95]

Here we are in the realms of speculation. Even if we can suggest a high degree of bilingualism (or trilingualism if we include Latin) among the monastic clergy of the south west, this does not explain why the basic language of most of these bounds was Old English, even for boundaries in those areas of Cornwall in the far west which were clearly Cornish speaking beyond the eleventh century. One might argue that the norm for Anglo-Saxon royal diplomas in the tenth century—at least those that were concerned with grants of lands—was to have an Old English boundary clause and this may indeed be the case. It is, therefore, worth pondering the two tenth-century Cornish charters that have boundaries where the base language is Latin, not Old English.

These two charters—purporting to be diplomas respectively of Æthelstan and Edgar—have boundary clauses where the underlying language is Latin, with topographical terms in either Latin or Cornish.[96] Unfortunately, both charters only survive in late medieval copies and neither is of unimpeachable authenticity. The diploma of Æthelstan in particular is regarded with scepticism by most commentators, although some argue that it has an authentic basis of some sort.[97] We need, though, to disentangle the authenticity of the whole document from that of the boundary, and allowing for a measure of mistranscription by their thirteenth- and fourteenth-century copyists, both boundaries can be seen to belong to the period they purport to be—the tenth century.[98] What is striking about both charters is how far outside of Keynes' mainstream they lie. If we accept that both documents contain authentic material beyond the boundaries, then their diplomatic is deeply idiosyncratic. This is especially noticeable with the Æthelstanian diploma, which has plausibly been argued to contain material which can be dated to 931, even if the surviving document is dated 943.[99] Generally speaking, Æthelstan's diplomas are characterized by a high degree of standardization in terms of their diplomatic, such that one individual—conventionally known as 'Æthelstan A'—is

95 For the problems copyists of the later medieval period had with Old English topographical and personal names see, for instance, Kathryn A. Lowe, 'Linguistic Geography, Demography and Monastic Community: Scribal Language at Bury St Edmunds', in *Interfaces between Language and Culture in Medieval England. A Festschrift for Matti Kilpiö*, eds Alaric Hall, Olga Timofeeva, Ágnes Kiricsi, and Bethany Fox (Leiden, 2011), pp. 147–78.

96 S 450 (BCS 785) and S 810 (ed. Picken, 'The "Landochou" Charter'). See Appendix 2.

97 Padel, 'Two New Pre-Conquest Charters', pp. 23 and 26; Olson, *Early Monasteries*, pp. 78–84.

98 *Pre-Conquest Charter-Bounds*, ed. and trans. Hooke, pp. 22–27 and 33–37.

99 Olson, *Early Monasteries*, pp. 78–84.

regarded by most commentators as being responsible for most, if not all, royal diplomas produced between 928 and 935.[100] The conclusion, therefore, is that if some sort of authentic charter lies behind the diploma of Æthelstan, it was not produced by 'Æthelstan A' and was, presumably, produced locally. The same seems to be the case with the diploma of Edgar, which, allowing for the transmission errors of its late medieval copyists, seems to have diplomatic links with the 'Dunstan B' group of tenth-century royal diplomas, but it is also quite distinctive.[101]

The most striking feature of both charters is their boundaries, which combine the detailed sequential perambulations typical of late ninth, tenth-, and eleventh-century charters, with the Latin that was used for the rarer and less detailed boundaries of earlier charters. Where boundary clauses do occur before the mid-ninth century—which is not very often—they tend to be predominantly in Latin but also very simple, generally the cardinal points of the compass ('... to the north ... to the west ...', etc.), although there are a few early examples of sequential bounds in Latin (for example, S 84, S 262, S 264, and S 267–68).[102] There does, as Susan Kelly argues, seem to have been a West Saxon tradition of sequential Latin bounds, but this had been superseded by bounds in Old English by the mid-ninth century.[103] Detailed perambulations combined with Latin are therefore extremely unusual in a tenth-century Anglo-Saxon context. Indeed, their presence in the above-mentioned diplomas of Æthelstan and Edgar could be argued to support their essential authenticity,[104] since one might expect an individual forging a tenth-century royal diploma to have incorporated an Old English boundary, as that was generally the practice. The combination of Latin and sequential bounds does, as we have seen, have an Anglo-Saxon precedent, but the surviving examples are much older—from the early eighth to the very early ninth century, respectively. It is not implausible that the use of Latin in the diplomas of Æthelstan and Edgar is a relic of this older Anglo-Saxon practice, but it is also possible to look elsewhere for parallels closer in time. We can point to what may have been a contemporary diplomatic tradition across the St George's Channel from Devon and Cornwall

100 Simon Keynes, *The Diplomas of King Æthelred the Unready, 978–1016: A Study in their Use as Historical Evidence* (Cambridge, 1980), pp. 39–44; D. A. Woodman, '"Æthelstan A" and the Rhetoric of Rule', *ASE* 42 (2013), 217–48, at pp. 219–20; Scott Thompson Smith, *Land and Book. Literature and Land Tenure in Anglo-Saxon England* (Toronto, 2012), pp. 37–46.

101 Simon Keynes, 'The "Dunstan B" Charters', *ASE* 23 (1994), 165–93.

102 Appendix 2; *Bath* 27, pp. 193–98, at 196.

103 Kelly, *Bath*, p. 196.

104 S 450 (BCS 785) and S 810 (ed. Picken, 'The "Landochou" Charter').

which did combine detailed perambulations with Latin text, namely that of the Llandaf charters from south-east Wales.

St Samson's life and career, as attested in the *Vita prima*, highlight what may have been significant early medieval links between South Wales and Cornwall.[105] It is clear that the later copyists at Llandaf sought to associate St Samson with their saint, Dyfrig, by incorporating Samson's *vita* into *Liber Landavensis*.[106] At the very least, continuing contacts between the Brittonic-speaking communities in Cornwall and South Wales might also provide the context for a sharing of diplomatic practice, and the example of Maenchi's charter, discussed above,[107] suggests that we can see Cornish diplomatic practice as part of a wider set of diplomatic traditions in western Britain and Brittany. The Llandaf charters themselves are contained in a twelfth-century cartulary chronicle, *Liber Landavensis*, associated with Bishop Urban of Llandaf, in south Wales. Although the charters contained in *Liber Landavensis* purport to date back to the seventh and in some cases sixth century, there is significant debate over their authenticity and the extent to which they were rewritten prior to and during their inclusion in *Liber Landavensis*.[108] This is not the time or place to delve into these debates, but even if we accept that the texts were significantly rewritten between the ninth and twelfth centuries, the bounds contained in many of them seem to have Old Welsh rather than Middle Welsh orthography and, as is the case with these two Cornish charters, the base language of some of the boundaries is Latin.[109] In other words, we should see the boundaries as products of the period between the ninth and eleventh centuries and, therefore, broadly contemporary with those in the aforementioned diplomas of Æthelstan and Edgar.[110]

105 Wooding, 'The Representation of Early British Monasticism', pp. 149–53; Probert, 'New Light on Aldhelm's Letter', p. 122.

106 Aberystwyth, National Library of Wales, 17110E; Karen Jankulak, 'Present and Yet Absent: The Cult of St Samson of Dol in Wales', in *St Samson of Dol*, ed. Olson, pp. 163–80, at 177–78; Ben Guy, 'The *Life* of St Dyfrig and the Lost Charters of Moccas (Mochros), Herefordshire', *Cambrian Medieval Celtic Studies* 75 (2018), 1–37, at p. 14.

107 S 1207 (ed. Padel, 'The Charter of Lanlawren').

108 Wendy Davies, *The Llandaff Charters* (Aberystwyth, 1979); Wendy Davies, *An Early Welsh Microcosm: Studies in the Llandaff Charters* (London, 1978); John Reuben Davies, 'Liber Landavensis: Its Date and the Identity of its Editor', *Cambrian Medieval Celtic Studies* 35 (1998), 1–11; John Reuben Davies, *The Book of Llandaf and the Norman Church in Wales* (Woodbridge, 2003), pp. 1–6 and 70–75.

109 Jon Coe, 'Dating the Boundary Clauses in the Book of Llandaf', *Cambrian Medieval Celtic Studies* 48 (2004), 1–43.

110 S 450 (BCS 785) and S 810 (ed. Picken, 'The "Landochou" Charter'). See Appendix 2 for an example of a Llandaf boundary; for the dating of the Llandaf boundaries, see Coe, 'Dating the Boundary Clauses'.

What is less clear, and is largely speculation on my part, is that we might be able to see detailed Latin perambulations with Brittonic topographical terms as part of a Celtic Latin charter tradition. As Oliver Padel has pointed out in his discussion of Maenchi's charter, in its key diplomatic components, it fits with the Latin 'Celtic' charter tradition identified by Davies, namely in its use of third-person, past-tense verbs, with the grant expressed as a gift 'to God, the saint and the individual/community'.[111] As an aside, we can also see similar formulation, combined with long Latin and Welsh boundaries, in the twelfth- and thirteenth-century charters associated with Strata Florida abbey in south-west Wales.[112] It is tempting, therefore, to see the Latin bounds of the diplomas of Æthelstan and Edgar as relics of an earlier Cornish diplomatic tradition, almost totally overwritten by the norms of tenth- and eleventh-century Anglo-Saxon royal diplomatic.

This does not get us any closer to answering the question about language choice—Latin or Old English—for Cornish charter bounds; indeed, if anything, if confuses it further, since the previous discussion suggests that there was an alternative model of boundary writing available to Cornish charter draftsmen. Why, then, in most cases, did they choose to use Old English, rather than Latin, or even Cornish? Again, this is probably not a question with an easy answer. Language choice in what were bi- or multilingual societies was never a simple matter and the choice of whether to use Latin or a vernacular language for writing could be a very political decision. As Elizabeth Tyler has most recently shown with the *Encomium Emmae Reginae*, the choice of Latin as the language of the text, which seems on the face of it to be a rather illogical choice for a text with very political aims, may well reflect a desire to avoid alienating an audience at the courts of Harthacnut and Edward the Confessor comprised of speakers of two or three vernacular languages (Old Norse, Old English, and Old Dutch).[113] In the context of diplomas, we also need to think of the various agencies involved in their production, not simply that of the scribe or draftsman. The beneficiary may well have played some sort of role in deciding the form that the document took, especially in areas which were towards

111 Padel, 'Two New Pre-Conquest Charters', pp. 20–24; Davies, 'Latin Charter-Tradition'; above, p. 357.

112 Charles Insley, 'Imitation and Independence in Native Welsh Administrative Culture, c.1180–1280', in *The Growth of Royal Government under Henry III*, eds David Crouch and Louise J. Wilkinson (Woodbridge, 2015), pp. 104–21, at 117–20.

113 Elizabeth M. Tyler, *England in Europe: English Royal Women and Literary Patronage, c.1000–c.1150* (Toronto, 2017), pp. 101–34, at 111–12; see also Elizabeth M. Tyler, 'Crossing Conquests: Polyglot Royal Women and Literary Culture in Eleventh-Century England', in *Conceptualizing Multilingualism*, ed. Tyler, pp. 171–96.

the peripheries of English royal power, such as the south west. The two Cornish diplomas whose bounds are anomalous in that they use Latin not Old English (namely the St Buryan and St Dawe and Kew charters) are also anomalous in other diplomatic ways and it is possible to see them having been produced in atypical circumstances, in which either the beneficiary or the scribe had distinct views on the form that the charter took, especially that part potentially most relevant to a lay audience (the boundary). The remaining Cornish diplomas, although typical in all sorts of ways of the wider body of tenth-century Anglo-Saxon royal diplomas, also raise questions. The relative lack of errors in the drafting and copying of the bounds suggest that some of the individuals involved in their production were probably bilingual (and possibly trilingual if Latin is added to the mix). The choice, then, of Old English as the language of the boundary may have been governed by a range of factors. Two of the beneficiaries (Wulfnoth Rumoncant and Ælfheah Gerent) had, as we have seen, both Old Cornish and Old English names, so also presumably occupied a cultural space where both languages were in play, but one (Old English) may have conferred particular political advantage. If these documents were drawn up, as I have argued elsewhere, in the episcopal scriptorium at Crediton, an institution with a long history as an Anglo-Saxon church, that too may have governed the drafting habits of its scribes, even if some of them were bilingual.[114] If the bounds were drafted elsewhere and then sent to Crediton to be included in the diploma, that merely adds a further layer of complexity to the interplay between text, individuals, and language.

Conclusion

This discussion has probably—hopefully, even—raised more questions than it has answered. It has necessarily been brief and confined to a particular body of source material—the surviving diplomas from Cornwall. Further light would almost certainly be shed by consideration of further sources, such as the Bodmin manumissions. Turning back to the diplomas, although the vast majority of surviving Cornish diplomas from the tenth and eleventh centuries look like 'typical' Anglo-Saxon royal diplomas (as far as such a thing existed), a deeper examination reveals them to be a valuable window onto society in south-western Britain, where language choice was far from a clear issue and where bi- or even trilingualism, at least among the clergy, was probably more common than we might think. It may also have been a society which had been

114 Above, p. 360; Insley, 'Charters and Episcopal Scriptoria'.

using charters or similar instruments to convey property for a very long time, certainly long before the oldest surviving documents, and where those older traditions have all but vanished from the diplomatic record.

Appendix 1: Cornish Charters with and without Bounds

With Bounds

S 450 King Æthelstan grants land in seven places in St Buryan to the church of St Buryan, A.D. 943 for 925×939
Earliest witness: Exeter, Devon Record Office, Chanter 4, f. 25v (s. xiv copy)
Editions: BCS 785; *Pre-Conquest Charter-Bounds*, ed. Hooke, pp. 22–27 (bounds only)

S 684 King Edgar grants land at Tywarnhayle and Besowsa to his thegn Eanulf, A.D. 960
Earliest witness: Exeter, Dean & Chapter, 2522 (s. x^{mid} single sheet)
Editions: BCS 1056; *OSFacs*, 2:Exeter 5 (with facsimile); *Pre-Conquest Charter-Bounds*, ed. Hooke, pp. 5 and 28–33 (with translation of bounds)

S 755 King Edgar grants land at Lesneage and Pennare in St Keverne to his faithful vassal, Wulfnoth Rumoncant, A.D. 967
Earliest witness: Exeter, Dean & Chapter, 2521 (s. xi^{ex} single sheet copy)
Editions: BCS 1197; *OSFacs*, 2:Exeter 6 (with facsimile); *Pre-Conquest Charter-Bounds*, ed. Hooke, pp. 37–40 (bounds only, with translation)

S 770 King Edgar grants land at Lamorran, Trenowth, and Tregellas to Ælfheah Gerent and his wife Moruurei, A.D. 969
Earliest witness: Exeter, Dean & Chapter, 2521, verso (s. xi^{ex} single-sheet copy)
Editions: BCS 1231; *OSFacs*, 2:Exeter 6 dorse (with facsimile); *Pre-Conquest Charter-Bounds*, ed. Hooke, pp. 41–45 (bounds only, with translation)

S 810 King Edgar grants land at Lanow in St Kew to the minster of St Dawe and St Kew, A.D. 961×963
Earliest witness: London, The National Archives, C47/52/1/1, m. 3 (s. xiv copy)
Editions: Picken, 'The "Landochou" Charter'; *Pre-Conquest Charter-Bounds*, ed. Hooke, pp. 33–37 (bounds only, with translation)

S 832 King Edward grants land at Traboe, Trevallack and Grugwith in St Keverne, and Trethewey in St Martin-in-Meneage to Ealdorman Æthelweard, A.D. 977
Earliest witness: Exeter, Dean & Chapter, 2527, verso (s. xi^{ex} single-sheet copy)
Editions: Davidson, 'On Some Anglo-Saxon Charters', pp. 284–85; *OSFacs*, 2:Exeter 14 dorse (with facsimile); *Pre-Conquest Charter-Bounds*, ed. Hooke, pp. 45–52 (bounds only, with translation)

S 951 King Cnut confirms a grant made by King Edmund to Bishop Burhwold of St Germans of land at Landrake and Tinnell in exchange for land at Throwleigh (Devon), A.D. 1018
Earliest witness: Exeter, Dean & Chapter, 2524 (s. xi^{ex} single-sheet copy/interpolated copy)
Editions: Davidson, 'On Some Anglo-Saxon Charters', pp. 287–89; *OSFacs*, 2:Exeter 9 (with facsimile); *English Historical Documents I*, ed. Whitelock, no. 131 (translation only); *Pre-Conquest Charter-Bounds*, ed. Hooke, pp. 55–62 (bounds only, with translation)

S 1005 King Edward grants land 'beneath Elddin' (Illand, in Northill) to Ordgar, A.D. 1044
Earliest witness: London, British Library, Cotton Augustus ii.59 (s. xi^{mid} single sheet)
Editions: KCD 770; *Pre-Conquest Charter-Bounds*, ed. Hooke, pp. 62–64 (bounds only, with translation)

S 1019 King Edward grants land at Tregony and Trerice in St Dennis to Eadulf, A.D. 1049
Earliest witness: Canterbury, Dean & Chapter, ChAnt C. 1281 (s. xi^{mid} single sheet)
Editions: KCD 787; *Pre-Conquest Charter-Bounds*, ed. Hooke, pp. 64–68 (bounds only, with translation)

S 1027 King Edward grants land at Traboe, Trevallack and Grugwith in St Keverne, and Trethewey in St Martin-in-Meneage to Bishop Ealdred, A.D. 1059
Earliest witness: Exeter, Dean & Chapter, 2527 (s. xi^{ex} single sheet)
Editions: Davidson, 'On Some Anglo-Saxon Charters', pp. 296–98; *OSFacs*, 2:Exeter 14 (with facsimile); *Pre-Conquest Charter-Bounds*, ed. Hooke, pp. 68–69 (bounds only, with translation)

Without Bounds

S 552 King Eadred to Wulfric, his faithful man; grant of 18 hides (*mansae*) at Welford, Berkshire, in exchange for land at Pendavey in Egloshayle, Cornwall, A.D. 949
Earliest witness: London, British Library, Cotton Augustus ii.44 (s. x^{mid} single sheet)
Editions: BCS 577; *Abing* 44

S 1296 Archbishop (Dunstan) to King Æthelred; letter in Old English concerning estates belonging to the diocese of Cornwall including Pawton in St Breock, *Cælwic*, and Lawhitton, Cornwall, A.D. 981×988
Earliest witness: Oxford, Bodleian Library, Eng. Hist. a. 2, no. xiv (s. x/xi single sheet)

Editions: *Councils and Synods*, eds Whitelock et al., no. 35 (ii); *English Historical Documents I*, ed. Whitelock, no. 229 (translation only)

S1451a Account in Latin of the consecration in 905 of seven bishops (for Winchester, Ramsbury, Sherborne, Wells, Crediton, Selsey, and Dorchester), and statement of the assignment to Crediton, on that occasion, of land at Pawton in St Breock, *Cællincg*, and Lawhitton, Cornwall
Earliest witness: London, British Library, Add. 7138 (s. x^{ex} single sheet)
Editions: *Councils and Synods*, eds Whitelock et al., no. 35 (i); Patrick W. Conner, *Anglo-Saxon Exeter: A Tenth-Century Cultural History* (Woodbridge, 1993), pp. 221–25; Alexander R. Rumble, 'Edward the Elder and the Churches of Winchester and Wessex', in *Edward the Elder, 899–924*, eds N. J. Higham and D. H. Hill (London, 2001), pp. 230–47, at 238–39 (translation only)

S 880 King Æthelred II to Ealdred, bishop of Cornwall; grant of privileges, A.D. 994
Earliest witness: Exeter, Dean & Chapter, 2070 (s. x^{ex} single sheet)
Editions: KCD 686; *OSFacs*, 2:Exeter 8 (with facsimile)

S 1061 King Edward to St Michael's Abbey (Mont-Saint-Michel); grant of land at St Michael's Mount, Cornwall; and at *Vennesire* (? Winnianton Hundred, Cornwall) and the harbour called Ruminella (? Old Romney, Kent), A.D. 1027×1035
Earliest witness: Avranches, Bibliothèque municipale, 210, fol. 32v (s. xii copy)
Editions: KCD 914; R. Allen Brown, *The Norman Conquest* (London, 1984), p. 139 (translation only)

S 1207 Maenchi, son of Pretnigor, *comes*, to St Heldenus; grant of land at Lanlawren (in Lanteglos), Cornwall, A.D. 924×939
Earliest witness: Bath, Downside Abbey, Phillips 4810, p. 119 (s. xvii transcript)
Edition: Padel, 'The Charter of Lanlawren', p. 75 (with translation)

Appendix 2: Cornish Boundary Clauses

Old English Bounds with Cornish Toponyms[115]

S 755

+ Ðis is þara . iii . hida landgemæru æt Lesmanaoc. Ærest up of Porðalap andlang riðe agean stream to hryt eselt þonne suð andlang riðe to Crousprah þonne forð suð to Cestell Merit fram Cestell Merit to crucou mereðen . þonne east ageriht to lein broinn þonne to hryt catpallon . þonne adún andlang cendefrion oð þa lytlan riðe . þonne up andlang riðe to fonton gén fram fonton gén andlang dices to þam herepaðe þanon aðan lytlan dic to þan miclan dice þonne for on þa dic to fos no cedu þonne adun

115 All editions and translations in this section are my own.

andlang riðe eft to Perdalau. Þonne is þis þæs anes æceres landgemæru æt Pennarð ærest fram sæ andlang dic to þa riðe. þonne andlang riðe eft on sæ.

['This is the boundaries of the three hides at Lesneage (Cornish *lys* = 'court' + Cornish *menaghek* = 'monastic'). First up from Porthallow (Cornish *porth* = 'cove' + *alaw* = 'lillies') along the stream against the stream to Eselt's ford (Cornish *hryt* = 'ford') then south along the stream to the Hag's Cross (Cornish *crous* + *gruah*) then straight south to Kestlemerris (Cornish *castell* = 'fort' + ?pers. name). From Kestlemerris to *mereðen* barrows (Cornish *cruc* = 'barrow' + ?*merthen* = 'sea fort') then east straight to rush pool (Cornish *lyn* = 'pool' + *bronnen* 'rushes') to Catwallon's ford (Cornish *hryt* = ford + pers. name) then down along the *cendefrion* (? Cornish *kendowrow* = 'joint waters') as far as the little stream then up along the little stream to the cold spring (Cornish *fenten* = spring + *yeyn*, 'cold'). From the cold spring along the dyke to the highway thence down the little dyke to the great dyke then forth on the dyke to *fos no cedu* (Cornish *fos* = 'dyke' + ?obscure) then down along the little stream to Porthallow. Then this is the one acres boundary at Pennare. First from the see along the dyke to the little stream, then along the little stream back to the sea.']

S 951

Þis sindon þa land gemæro þæs hiþisces to Tinieltune. Ærest of Carrecron on ða riðe þest to þæs þylles heafod þanon þest to ðam þege þonne norð on þone þeg to þam stybbe þonne þest to þam þylle adun on þa riðe to þam fleote up to cinges mylne up on þone broc to nantneþiou þonne suð riht to behrates þylle on þa riðe to þa gemyðo þonne up on þone broc to þelbricce norð on þone þeg to þære dic þonne þest on þa þale to þam þylle on þære riðe to þam gemyðo þonne þest on ða ealdan landscaru þonne norð to þære riðe þonne east on þæs slæd to þam broce þonne east to þam þege on þone hric to þam þylle adun to þam broce oð Tamer adun to Carrecron.

['These are the land bounds of the one hide at Tinnell. First from Cargreen (Cornish *karrek* = 'rock' + Cornish *ruen* = 'seal') to the stream west to the head of the spring thence west to the way then north to the way to the stump then west to the spring down by the stream to the creek up to the king's mill up by the brook to *nantnewion* (Cornish nans = 'valley' + ?obscure) then due south to *behrates* (?OE) spring to the stream to the confluence then up by the brook to the plank bridge then north by the way to the dyke then west by the ridge to the spring by the stream to the confluence then west to the old land boundary then north to the stream then east by the slade to the brook then east to the way by the ridge to the spring down the brook as far as the Tamar down to Cargreen.']

Latin Bounds with Cornish Toponyms[116]

S 450

Istis terminis ambitur predicta tellus, id est, a fonte usque ad fossam et a fossa quæ tendit circa kestel cromlegh usque ad Yolbrunnemian et inde usque ad Fimbol et inde usque ad Ponsprontiryon et inde usque ad Mahen halen et inde ad pelnagerens et inde usque ad Mankependoin ascendens contra montem usque ad Polmadice et inde circa fossam ad Kacregan et inde per rectitudinem viæ usque ad rivulum ascendens contra rivulum usque ad fontem

['These boundaries surround the aforesaid estate, that is from the spring as far as the dyke and from the dyke which extends around *cestel cromlegh* (Cornish *castell* = 'castle, fort' + *cromlech* = 'dolmen') as far as rush pool (Cornish *pol* = 'pool' + *bronnen*, 'rushes') and thence as far as the end of the pool (Cornish *fyn* = 'end' + *pol* = 'pool') and thence as far as the priests' bridge (Cornish *pons* = 'bridge' + *pronter*/*prontyryon* = 'priest/priests') and thence as far as the stone marsh (Cornish *men* = 'stone' + *hal* = 'stone') and thence to *pelnagerens* (?obscure, but possibly containing Cornish *pol* = 'pool') and thence to stone hedge spring (Cornish *men* = 'stone' + *pen* = 'head' + *kee* = 'hedge/bank' + *pendour* = 'water's end') ascending across the hill as far as ?fox pool (Cornish *pol* + ?*madoc* = 'fox') and thence around the dyke to *kacregan* (?Crean in St Buryan) and thence by the right of the road as far as the stream, climbing against the stream as far as the spring ...']

S 810

Hec sunt territoria istius agelluli. Primitus a pont Magano in longitudine riuolis usque ad puern golornan deinde ad pentalou usque per siluam de penfynfos. deinde ad fynnian Iacu. deinde usque penmayn cenpuerehit nahal de poll duu. iterum de pont Magano.

['Here are the lands of this little estate. First from Magano's bridge (Cornish *pons* = bridge +?pers. name) along the river as far as *galornan* (?obscure) alder-swamp (Cornish *guern* = 'alder swamp') thence to the end of the thicket (Cornish *pen* = 'end' + *tal* = 'brow' + *lon* = 'thicket') through the wood as far as the boundary dyke (Cornish *pen* = 'head' + *fyn* = 'end' + *fos* = 'dyke'), thence to Iago's boundaries (pers. name + Cornish *fyn*/*fynnion* = 'boundary/boundaries'). Thence as far as the end of the stone (Cornish *pen* = 'head' + *men* = 'stone') *cenpuerehit nahal* (?obscure). From the black pool (Cornish *pol* = 'pool' + *du* = 'black') again from Magano's bridge.']

116 All translations in this section are taken from *Pre-Conquest Charter-Bounds*, ed. and trans. Hooke. See my Appendix 1 for full details of Hooke's printed editions and translations.

Earlier Anglo-Saxon Charters with Latin Sequential Bounds

S 84: Diploma of King Æthelbald of the Mercians, from AD 718×727, Worcester
Hec sunt confinia huius ante nominati agelluli. Hoc est primum of bladene on bægan-wellan . inde in montem susibr[...] urbs antiqua et postea bi þære ealdan cestelbyrig on nunnena beorgas ac deinde on fearhom et sic of fearhom neoðeweardum iterum on bleadene.[117]

['These are the bounds of the aforesaid estate. First from the Bladen (R. Evenlode) to Bæga's spring, thence to the Susibr[...] hill, an ancient city, and after that by the old earthwork fort to the Nuns' barrows and then to the bull's enclosure and so from the bull's enclosure croft downwards once more to the Bladen.']

S 264: Diploma of King Cynewulf of the West Saxons, from AD 778, possibly Bedwyn, Wiltshire
... ab oriente uallem uocatem cymenes denu et sic in longum ...... nes geat et sic in africum uergens in longum illius septi tendit ad peadan stigele deinde per idem septum in filiðleage australem partem inde in longum prædicti septi in quoddam uallum in harandene sicque per hoc uallum pertingit ad illum agellum qui dicitur tatan edisc et sic per occidentalem plagam eiusdem agelli iacet in illos tumulos .... torum deinde in bedewindan et sic in longum illius spinet in horselget ...[118]

['... from the east the valley called Cymen's Dene and so turning south along the hedge it reaches Peada's stile, then by the same hedge to the south part of Hay lea thence along the aforesaid hedge to a certain dyke in Hare's dene and so by this dyke it reaches the field which is called Tata's paddock and so by the west side of the same field as it lies towards the barrows ...... then to Bedwyn Brook and so along the spinney to the gate of the horse hollow ...']

A Welsh Comparison? The Llandaf Charters

Grant by King Gwrgan to St Dyfrig and Bishop Inabwy of Two and Half unciae of Land at Lannbudgualan (?Ballingham, Herefordshire). Seventh Century.
Finis illius est, a vado selinam super transversum, usque in flumine magno iuxta rivulum Circhan, in circuitu fluminis Guy totus angulus datus est Deo et Dubricio et Lunapeio episcopo.[119]

117 BCS 139. The translation is my own.
118 BCS 225. The translation is my own.
119 *The Text of the Book of Llan Dâv*, ed. J. Gwenogvryn Evans with John Rhys (Oxford, 1893), p. 163. The translation is my own.

['... Its boundary is, from the willow ford upwards as far as the great river, near the brook Circhan, within the circuit of the River Wye. The whole angle is given to God, St Dyfrig and Bishop Inabwy.']

Bibliography

Primary Sources

Aldhelmi Opera, ed. Rudolf Ehwald, MGH Auct. ant. 15 (Berlin, 1919).

The Anglo-Saxon Chronicle: A Revised Translation, eds and trans. Dorothy Whitelock, David Douglas, and Susie Tucker (London, 1961).

Annales Cambriae, A.D. 682–954: Texts A–C in Parallel, ed. and trans. David Dumville (Cambridge, 2002).

Canterbury Professions, ed. Michael Richter (Torquay, 1973).

Cartularium Saxonicum: A Collection of Charters Relating to Anglo-Saxon History, ed. Walter de Gray Birch, 3 vols (London, 1885–99).

Charters of Abingdon Abbey, ed. S. E. Kelly, Anglo-Saxon Charters VII–VIII (Oxford, 2000).

Charters of Bath and Wells, ed. S. E. Kelly, Anglo-Saxon Charters 13 (Oxford, 2007).

Charters of Sherborne, ed. M. A. O'Donovan, Anglo-Saxon Charters III (Oxford, 1998).

Codex Diplomaticus Ævi Saxonici, ed. J. M. Kemble, 6 vols (London, 1839–48), paperback reprint, 6 vols (Cambridge, 2011).

Councils and Synods with Other Documents relating to the English Church, I: A.D. 871–1204, eds D. Whitelock, M. Brett, and C. N. L. Brooke (Oxford, 1981).

Domesday Book, 10, *Cornwall*, eds Caroline Thorn and Frank Thorn (Chichester, 1979).

English Historical Documents. I: c.500–1042, ed. Dorothy Whitelock, 2nd ed. (London, 1979).

Facsimiles of Anglo-Saxon Manuscripts, ed. W. B. Sanders, 3 vols (Southampton, 1878–84).

Die Gesetze der Angelsachsen, ed. Felix Liebermann, 3 vols (Halle, 1903–16).

Gildas, *De excidio et conquestu Britanniae*, ed. and trans. Michael Winterbottom, *Gildas: The Ruin of Britain and Other Works* (Chichester, 1978).

The Laws of the Earliest English Kings, ed. Frederick Attenborough (Cambridge, 1922).

Picken, W. M. M., ed., 'The "Landochou" Charter', in W. G. Hoskins, *The Westward Expansion of Wessex* (Leicester, 1960), pp. 36–44.

Pontificale Lanalatense (*Bibliothèque de la Ville de Rouen A. 27 cat. 368*), ed. G. H. Doble (London, 1937).

Pre-Conquest Charter Bounds of Devon and Cornwall, ed. and trans. Della Hooke (Woodbridge, 1994).

The Text of the Book of Llan Dâv, ed. J. Gwenogvryn Evans with John Rhys (Oxford, 1893).

La vie ancienne de Saint Samson de Dol. Texte édité, traduit et commenté, ed. Pierre Flobert (Paris, 1997).

Willibald, *Vita Bonifatii*, ed. Wilhelm Levison, MGH SS rer. Germ. (Hanover, 1905).

Secondary Sources

Alexander, Louis M., 'The Legal Status of Native Britons in Late Seventh-Century Wessex as Reflected by the Law Code of Ine', *Haskins Society Journal* 7 (1995), 31–38.

Bhreathnach, Edel, *Ireland in the Medieval World AD 400–1000* (Dublin, 2013).

Brooks, Nicholas, 'Latin and Old English in Ninth-Century Canterbury', in *Spoken and Written Language: Relations between Latin and the Vernacular Languages in the Earlier Middle Ages*, eds Mary Garrison, Arpad P. Orbán, and Marco Mostert (Turnhout, 2013), pp. 113–31.

Brown, R. Allen, *The Norman Conquest* (London, 1984).

Campbell, Ewan, *Continental and Mediterranean Imports into Atlantic Britain and Ireland, AD 400–800* (York, 2007).

Chaplais, Pierre, 'The Authenticity of the Royal Anglo-Saxon Diplomas of Exeter', *Bulletin of the Institute of Historical Research* 39 (1966), 1–34; reprinted in Pierre Chaplais, *Essays in Medieval Diplomacy and Administration* (London, 1981), XV.

Coe, Jon, 'Dating the Boundary Clauses in the Book of Llandaf', *Cambrian Medieval Celtic Studies* 48 (2004), 1–43.

Conner, Patrick W., *Anglo-Saxon Exeter: A Tenth-Century Cultural History* (Woodbridge, 1993).

Crick, Julia, 'The English and the Irish from Cnut to John: Speculation on a Linguistic Interface', in *Conceptualizing Multilingualism in Medieval England,* c.*800–*c.*1250*, ed. Elizabeth M. Tyler (Turnhout, 2011), pp. 217–38.

Davidson, J. B., 'On Some Anglo-Saxon Charters at Exeter', *Journal of the British Archaeological Association* 39 (1883), 259–303.

Davies, John Reuben, *The Book of Llandaf and the Norman Church in Wales* (Woodbridge, 2003).

Davies, John Reuben, 'Liber Landavensis: Its Date and the Identity of its Editor', *Cambrian Medieval Celtic Studies* 35 (1998), 1–11.

Davies, Wendy, *An Early Welsh Microcosm: Studies in the Llandaff Charters* (London, 1978).

Davies, Wendy, 'The Latin Charter-Tradition in Western Britain, Brittany and Ireland in the Early Mediaeval Period', in *Ireland in Early Medieval Europe: Studies in Memory of Kathleen Hughes*, eds David Dumville and Rosamond McKitterick (Cambridge, 1982), pp. 258–80.

Davies, Wendy, *The Llandaff Charters* (Aberystwyth, 1979).

Downham, Clare, *Medieval Ireland* (Cambridge, 2018).

Drage, Elaine, 'Bishop Leofric and the Exeter Cathedral Chapter 1050–72: A Reassessment of the Manuscript Evidence' (unpublished D.Phil. thesis, University of Oxford, 1978).

Dumville, David N., *English Caroline Script: Studies in Benedictinism 950–c.1030* (Woodbridge, 1993).

Dumville, David N., 'English Square Minuscule Script: The Background and Earliest Phases', *ASE* 16 (1987), 147–79.

Edwards, Heather, *The Charters of the Early West-Saxon Kingdom* (Oxford, 1988).

Finberg, H. P. R., 'Sherborne, Glastonbury, and the Expansion of Wessex', in *Lucerna: Studies of Some Problems in the Early History of England*, ed. H. P. R. Finberg (London, 1964), pp. 95–115.

Förster, Max, 'Die Freilassungsurkunden des Bodmin-Evangeliars', in *A Grammatical Miscellany offered to Otto Jespersen on his 70th Birthday*, eds Nils Bøgholm, A. Brusendorff, and Carl Bodelsen (Copenhagen, 1930), pp. 77–100.

Fulton, Helen, 'Negotiating Welshness: Multilingualism in Wales Before and After 1066', in *Conceptualizing Multilingualism in Medieval England, c.800–c.1250*, ed. Elizabeth M. Tyler (Turnhout, 2011), pp. 145–70.

Gallagher, Robert, 'The Vernacular in Anglo-Saxon Charters: Expansion and Innovation in Ninth-Century England', *Historical Research* 91 (2018), 205–35.

Grimmer, Martin, 'Britons in Early Wessex: The Evidence of the Law Code of Ine', in *Britons in Anglo-Saxon England*, ed. N. J. Higham (Woodbridge, 2007), pp. 102–14.

Guy, Ben, 'The *Life* of St Dyfrig and the Lost Charters of Moccas (Mochros), Herefordshire', *Cambrian Medieval Celtic Studies* 75 (2018), 1–37.

Hoskins, William, *The Westward Expansion of Wessex* (Leicester, 1960).

Insley, Charles, 'Athelstan, Charters, and the English in Cornwall', in *Charters and Charter Scholarship in Britain and Ireland*, eds Marie Therese Flanagan and Judith Green (Basingstoke, 2005), pp. 15–31.

Insley, Charles, 'Charters and Episcopal Scriptoria in the Anglo-Saxon South-West', *EME* 7 (1998), 173–98.

Insley, Charles, 'Imitation and Independence in Native Welsh Administrative Culture, c.1180–1280', in *The Growth of Royal Government under Henry III*, eds David Crouch and Louise J. Wilkinson (Woodbridge, 2015), pp. 104–21.

Insley, Charles, 'Kings and Lords in Tenth-Century Cornwall', *History* 98 (2013), 2–22.

Jankulak, Karen, *The Medieval Cult and Relics of St Petroc* (Woodbridge, 2001).

Jankulak, Karen, 'Present and Yet Absent: The Cult of St Samson of Dol in Wales', in *St Samson of Dol and the Earliest History of Brittany, Cornwall and Wales*, ed. Lynette Olson (Woodbridge, 2017), pp. 163–80.

Kelly, Susan, 'Anglo-Saxon Lay Society and the Written Word', in *The Uses of Literacy in Early Mediaeval Europe*, ed. Rosamond McKitterick (Cambridge, 1990), pp. 36–62.

Keynes, Simon, 'Church Councils, Royal Assemblies, and Anglo-Saxon Royal Diplomas', in *Kingship, Legislation and Power in Anglo-Saxon England*, eds Gale R. Owen-Crocker and Brian W. Schneider (Woodbridge, 2013), pp. 1–182.

Keynes, Simon, *The Diplomas of King Æthelred the Unready, 978–1016: A Study in Their Use as Historical Evidence* (Cambridge, 1980).

Keynes, Simon, 'The "Dunstan B" Charters', *ASE* 23 (1994), 165–93.

Lewis, C. P., 'Welsh Territories and Welsh Identities in Late Anglo-Saxon England', in *Britons in Anglo-Saxon England*, ed. N. J. Higham (Woodbridge, 2007), pp. 130–43.

Lowe, Kathryn A., 'Linguistic Geography, Demography and Monastic Community: Scribal Language at Bury St Edmunds', in *Interfaces between Language and Culture in Medieval England. A Festschrift for Matti Kilpiö*, eds Alaric Hall, Olga Timofeeva, Ágnes Kiricsi, and Bethany Fox (Leiden, 2011), pp. 147–78.

Morgan, Richard, 'Place-Names in the Northern Marches of Wales', in *A Commodity of Good Names: Essays in Honour of Margaret Gelling*, eds Oliver Padel and David Parsons (Donnington, 2008), pp. 204–16.

Olson, B. Lynette and Padel, O. J., 'A Tenth-Century List of Cornish Parochial Saints', *Cambridge Medieval Celtic Studies* 12 (1986), 33–71.

Olson, Lynette, *Early Monasteries in Cornwall* (Woodbridge, 1993).

Olson, Lynette, 'Introduction', in *St Samson of Dol and the Earliest History of Brittany, Cornwall and Wales*, ed. Lynette Olson (Woodbridge, 2017), pp. 1–18.

Orme, Nicholas, *The Saints of Cornwall* (Oxford, 2002).

Padel, O. J., 'The Boundary of Tywarnhayle (Perranzabuloe) in A.D. 960', *Journal of the Royal Institution of Cornwall* (2014), 69–92.

Padel, O. J., 'The Charter of Lanlawren (Cornwall)', in *Latin Learning and English Lore: Studies in Anglo-Saxon Literature for Michael Lapidge*, eds Katherine O'Brien O'Keeffe and Andy Orchard (2005), pp. 74–85.

Padel, O. J., 'Cornwall as a Border Area', *Nomina* 6 (1982), 18–22.

Padel, O. J., 'Place-Names and the Saxon Conquest of Britain and Cornwall', in *Britons in Anglo-Saxon England*, ed. N. J. Higham (Woodbridge, 2007), pp. 215–30.

Padel, O. J., *Slavery in Saxon Cornwall: The Bodmin Manumissions* (Cambridge, 2009).

Padel, O. J., 'The Text of the Lanlawren Charter', *Cornish Studies* 7 (1979), 43–44.

Padel, Oliver 'Christianity in Medieval Cornwall: Celtic Aspects', in Nicholas Orme, *A History of the County of Cornwall II: Religious History to 1560*, Victoria County History (Woodbridge, 2010), pp. 110–25.

Padel, Oliver, *Cornish Place-Name Elements* (Nottingham, 1985).

Padel, Oliver, 'Two New Pre-Conquest Charters for Cornwall', *Journal of Cornish Studies* 6 (1978), 20–27.

Pearce, Susan, *The Early Church in Western Britain and Ireland* (Oxford, 1982).
Pearce, Susan, *The Kingdom of Dumnonia. Studies in History and Tradition in South-Western Britain* (Padstow, 1978).
Petts, David, 'Cemeteries and Boundaries in Western Britain', in *Burial in Early Medieval England and Wales*, eds Andrew Reynolds and Sam Lucy (Leeds, 2002), pp. 24–46.
Picken, W. M. M., 'Callington and Kelliwic', *Devon and Cornwall Notes and Queries* 27 (1956–58), 225–6.
Probert, Duncan, 'Church and Landscape: A Study in Social Transition in South-Western Britain, A.D. c.400 to c.1200' (unpublished PhD thesis, University of Birmingham, 2002).
Probert, Duncan, 'Mapping Early Medieval Language Change in South-West England', in *Britons in Anglo-Saxon England*, ed. N. J. Higham (Woodbridge, 2007), pp. 231–44.
Probert, Duncan, 'New Light on Aldhelm's Letter to King Gerent of Dumnonia', in *Aldhelm and Sherborne. Essays to Celebrate the Founding of the Bishopric*, eds Katherine Barker with Nicholas Brooks (Oxford, 2010), pp. 110–28.
Rumble, Alexander R., 'Edward the Elder and the Churches of Winchester and Wessex', in *Edward the Elder, 899–924*, eds N. J. Higham and D. H. Hill (London, 2001), pp. 230–47.
Schrijver, P., 'Old British', in *Brythonic Celtic—Britannisches Keltisch. From Medieval British to Modern Breton*, ed. Elmar Ternas (Bremen, 2011), pp. 1–84.
Seaman, Andrew, 'Dinas Powys in Context: Settlement and Society in Post-Roman Wales', *Studia Celtica* 67 (2013), 1–23.
Smith, Scott Thompson, *Land and Book. Literature and Land Tenure in Anglo-Saxon England* (Toronto, 2012).
Stephenson, Rebecca, 'Byrthferth's *Enchiridion* and the Effectiveness of Hermeneutic Latin', in *Conceptualizing Multilingualism in Medieval England,* c.*800*–c.*1250*, ed. Elizabeth M. Tyler (Turnhout, 2011), pp. 121–44.
Stout, Matthew, *Early Medieval Ireland 431–1169* (Dublin, 2017).
Thomas, Charles, *The Early Christian Archaeology of North Britain* (Oxford, 1971).
Thomas, Charles, *And Shall These Mute Stones Speak? Post-Roman Inscriptions in Western Britain* (Cardiff, 1994).
Tinti, Francesca, 'Writing Latin and Old English in Tenth-Century England: Patterns, Formulae and Language Choice in the Leases of Oswald of Worcester', in *Writing, Kingship and Power in Anglo-Saxon England*, eds Rory Naismith and David A. Woodman (Cambridge, 2018), pp. 303–27.
Todd, Malcolm, *The South-West to AD 1000* (London, 1987).
Townend, Matthew, *Language and History in Viking Age England: Linguistic Relations between Speakers of Old Norse and Old English* (Turnhout, 2002).
Turner, Sam, *Making a Christian Landscape. The Countryside in Early Medieval Cornwall, Devon and Wessex* (Exeter, 2006).

Tyler, Elizabeth M., 'Crossing Conquests: Polyglot Royal Women and Literary Culture in Eleventh Century England', in *Conceptualizing Multilingualism in Medieval England, c.800–c.1250*, ed. Elizabeth M. Tyler (Turnhout, 2011), pp. 171–96.

Tyler, Elizabeth M., *England in Europe: English Royal Women and Literary Patronage, c.1000–c.1150* (Toronto, 2017).

Wooding, Jonathon, 'The Representation of Early British Monasticism and *Peregrinatio* in *Vita Prima S. Samsoni*', in *St Samson of Dol and the Earliest History of Brittany, Cornwall and Wales*, ed. Lynette Olson (Woodbridge, 2017), pp. 137–62.

Woodman, D. A., '"Æthelstan A" and the Rhetoric of Rule', *ASE* 42 (2013), 217–48.

Woolf, Alex, 'Apartheid Economics in Anglo-Saxon England', in *Britons in Anglo-Saxon England*, ed. N. J. Higham (Woodbridge, 2007), pp. 115–29.

Wormald, Patrick, *The Making of English Law: King Alfred to the Twelfth Century. I: Legislation and its Limits* (Oxford, 1999)

CHAPTER 10

Vernacular Writing in Early Medieval Manorial Administration: Two Tenth-Century Documents from Werden and Essen

Stefan Esders

The vast early medieval seigneuries managed by episcopal churches and monasteries in the eastern parts of the Frankish Empire possessed thousands of lay dependents who continuously worked for their lords, but for the most part could not read or write, nor had any command of Latin. For this reason, one would expect manorial organization to be an area in which clerics and their administrators came most closely into contact with the lay population and thus had to make extensive use of the vernacular. While this probably holds true for oral communication, our extant documentation relating to manorial administration from continental Europe—polyptychs, registers, charters[1]—is almost exclusively written in Latin. This predominance of Latin should not simply be explained by assuming that Latin writing was more likely to be preserved or that it was only clerics who were writing, as such an explanation has been challenged by recent studies on the role of lay scribes in early medieval charter production.[2] Rather, we should assume that Latin was in many respects a technical language informed by ancient traditions of tax record-keeping and of registering public domains and their income.[3] For this reason, it is understandable that ecclesiastical institutions continued this established practice,

1 See Dieter Hägermann, 'Quellenkritische Bemerkungen zu den karolingerzeitlichen Urbaren und Güterverzeichnissen', in *Strukturen der Grundherrschaft im frühen Mittelalter*, ed. Werner Rösener (Göttingen, 1989), pp. 47–73; Ludolf Kuchenbuch, 'Ordnungsverhalten im grundherrlichen Schriftgut vom 9. zum 12. Jahrhundert', in *Dialektik und Rhetorik im früheren und hohen Mittelalter. Rezeption, Überlieferung und gesellschaftliche Wirkung antiker Gelehrsamkeit vornehmlich im 9. und 12. Jahrhundert*, ed. Johannes Fried (Munich, 1997), pp. 175–268.

2 *Die Privaturkunden der Karolingerzeit*, eds Peter Erhart, Karl Heidecker, and Bernhard Zeller (Dietikon-Zürich, 2009); *Documentary Culture and the Laity in the Early Middle Ages*, eds Warren C. Brown, Marios Costambeys, Matthew Innes, and Adam J. Kosto (Cambridge, 2013).

3 See, e.g., John Percival, 'The Precursors of Domesday: Roman and Carolingian Land Registers', in *Domesday Book: A Reassessment*, ed. Peter H. Sawyer (London, 1985), pp. 5–27; Ralph H. C. Davis, 'Domesday Book: Continental Parallels', in *Domesday Studies: Papers Read at the Novocentenary Conference of the Royal Historical Society and the Institute of British Geographers, Winchester, 1986*, ed. James C. Holt (Woodbridge, 1987), pp. 15–39; Stefan Esders,

 | DOI:10.1163/9789004432338_011

with the consequence that any person dealing with such matters needed a very good command of Latin.

Vernacular writing in early medieval manorial administration thus was the exception to the rule. Furthermore, one may venture to say that this exception had fairly rigid geographical limits, for it is only from early medieval Saxony that vernacular texts relating to manorial administration have survived. Dating to the eleventh century, the famous manorial register of the Westphalian nunnery of Freckenhorst is the first example of this documentation type written more or less completely in the vernacular.[4] Prior to this, only two short manorial vernacular texts have come down to us from the religious communities of Werden and Essen. It is these two earliest documents that the following study deals with.[5] Both communities were situated in Westphalia's Ruhr area,[6] only about five miles from each other, in the territory conquered and Christianized under Charlemagne.[7] Both also possess a broad variety of vernacular documents from the ninth and tenth centuries.[8]

'Die römischen Wurzeln der karolingischen *inquisitio* in Fiskalsachen', in *L'enquête au moyen âge*, ed. Claude Gauvard (Rome, 2008), pp. 13–28.

4 *Kleinere altsächsische Sprachdenkmäler mit Anmerkungen und Glossar*, ed. Elis Wadstein (Norden and Leipzig, 1899), no. 9, pp. 24–45 and p. 137. On this text see Ernst Hellgardt, 'Bemerkungen zum Text des Freckenhorster Heberegisters (Handschrift M)', *Amsterdamer Beiträge zur älteren Germanistik* 52 (1999), 63–96; Joachim Hartig, 'Die Gliederung des Freckenhorster Heberegisters', in *Festschrift für Gerhard Cordes zum 65. Geburtstag, Vol. 2: Sprachwissenschaft*, eds Friedhelm Debus and Joachim Hartig (Neumünster, 1976), pp. 96–111; most recently Ernst Hellgardt, 'Freckenhorster Heberegister und Heberolle', in *Althochdeutsche und altsächsische Literatur*, ed. Rolf Bergmann (Berlin, 2013), pp. 88–91.

5 I dealt with the second text of this study at greater length in an article published recently; see Stefan Esders, '*Te usero herano misso*. Überlieferungs- und Gebrauchskontext des Essener altsächsischen Heberegisters aus dem 10. Jahrhundert', *Frühmittelalterliche Studien* 51 (2017), 57–86.

6 On relations between the two communities, see Thomas Schilp, 'Männerkloster und Frauenstift. Werden und Essen', in *Das Jahrtausend der Mönche. Kloster Welt Werden 799–1803*, ed. Jan Gerchow (Essen and Cologne, 1999), pp. 74–79.

7 On the vernacular documents from both places, see most recently Katrinette Bodarwé, 'Werden und Essen', in *Deutsche Schreiborte des Mittelalters. Skriptorien—Werke—Mäzene*, ed. Martin Schubert (Berlin, 2013), pp. 549–78. As has been shown by Hans-Werner Goetz, the manorial organization of the religious centres established following the Carolingian incorporation of Saxony has profoundly impacted this area's settlement structures up to the present day: see Hans-Werner Goetz, 'Das Ruhrgebiet im frühen Mittelalter', *Jahrbuch des Vereins für Orts- und Heimatkunde in der Grafschaft Mark mit Sitz in Witten an der Ruhr* 86 (1988), 7–36; Hans-Werner Goetz, 'Das Ruhrgebiet im frühen Mittelalter. Zur Erschließung einer Randlandschaft', *Blätter für deutsche Landesgeschichte* 126 (1990), 123–60.

8 See the surveys of the evidence by Heinrich Tiefenbach, 'Werden und die Anfänge der altniederdeutschen Sprachgeschichte', in *Das Jahrtausend der Mönche*, ed. Gerchow, pp. 212–17; Heinrich Tiefenbach, 'Frühmittelalterliche Volkssprache im Frauenstift Essen', in *Essen und*

That the only surviving vernacular texts of this type come from Saxony has always puzzled historians and philologists. More than half a century ago, Wolfgang Metz, an expert in the field of early medieval manorial documentation, pointed out that, from areas in which Old High German was spoken, we do not have any vernacular manorial documentation apart from some boundary descriptions, while Old Saxon manorial texts come from Saxon monasteries whose writing practice was influenced by Anglo-Saxon missionaries, who were probably more experienced in writing the vernacular. By contrast, the Saxon abbey of Corvey, founded as a filial monastery of the West Frankish abbey of Corbie, did not adopt this practice, instead producing Latin manorial records which resemble those of western monasteries such as Saint-Germain-des-Prés.[9] However, this sounds rather too simple, for the vast majority of manorial documents from Werden were also written in Latin. And if we look closer at these manorial documents, it becomes more obvious they are in fact a jumble of Latin administrative language and vernacular personal names, place-names, glosses, and more, which gives the texts (and the manuscripts transmitting them) a distinctly hybrid appearance. For this reason, one must find more nuanced explanations for such phenomena than that put forward by Metz. As will become clear, each document needs to be contextualized individually with regard to its manuscript tradition and its supposed administrative setting. Only on this basis is it possible to reconstruct the communicative contexts from which these texts originated or to learn for whom they were once produced.

A Tenth-Century Vernacular List of Possessions of the Monastery of Werden

The male monastery at Werden was founded close to the Ruhr river around 800 by the Frisian missionary Liudger, who shortly thereafter became bishop of

---

die sächsischen Frauenstifte im Frühmittelalter, eds Jan Gerchow and Thomas Schilp (Essen, 2003), pp. 113–28; Bodarwé, 'Werden und Essen'.

9 Wolfgang Metz, 'Zur Geschichte und Kritik der frühmittelalterlichen Güterverzeichnisse Deutschlands', *Archiv für Diplomatik* 4 (1958), 183–206, at pp. 193–6. See already Wolfgang Metz, 'Karolingische Güterinventare als Quellen zur Geschichte der althochdeutschen Hermeneumata', *Deutsche Vierteljahrsschrift für Literaturwissenschaft und Geistesgeschichte* 29 (1955), 151–66, at pp. 159, 163, and 166. In the same vein, Werner Rösener, 'Zur Struktur und Entwicklung der Grundherrschaft in Sachsen in karolingischer und ottonischer Zeit', in *La grande domaine aux époques mérovingienne et carolingienne. Die Grundherrschaft im frühen Mittelalter*, ed. Adriaan Verhulst (Ghent, 1985), pp. 173–207, at 186–87.

the newly founded see of Münster.[10] For this reason, Werden remained under the control of the Liudgerid family for much of the ninth century, until in 877 the monks managed to gain some degree of independence from their founder family by obtaining a royal privilege of protection.[11] Probably on account of the unstable situation following this transfer and the infringement of monastic property by Viking invasions, the earliest part of the famous 'Werdener Urbar' was drafted shortly before 900, the so-called 'Urbar A', which documents the enormous spread of the monastery's property holdings in the Ruhr area, along the lower Rhine, as well as into Frisia and what is today the Netherlands.[12] In addition to documenting the possessions Werden acquired by donation, it registers the rights to extract certain revenues from many places at length. Interestingly, the text also includes reports given by local officials administering Werden's property and rights.

'Urbar A' as we have it today consists of four parts arranged in six quires of forty folios, but obviously assembled at a later date in a non-chronological but nonetheless systematic order.[13] The part known as 'A 3', covering quire V and fols 27–34, was the oldest part, written between 877 and 890. It contains a register of revenues from possessions in Westphalia and western Frisia, and at the very end of it, we find the vernacular insertion on fol. 34v. This is actually a somewhat later entry which was squeezed into a gap left on the last folio of the fifth quire. The insertion exceeds the margin on the right and was obviously made on some space which had been created by an earlier erasure. It is preceded by a notice on an administrative centre (*ministerium*) held in the 'Lochtropgau' (*in pago Lohthorpe*), while the passage following deals with the 'Brukterergau' (*in pago Borathron*).[14] We thus find the newly inserted passage

10 The most important reference work on Werden is Wilhelm Stüwer, *Die Reichsabtei Werden an der Ruhr* (Berlin, 1980), published as part of the *Germania Sacra* series. On Liudger, see *Heiliger Liudger: Zeuge des Glaubens, 742–809. Gedenkschrift zum 1200. Todestag*, ed. Rudolf Ludger Schütz (Essen, 2009), especially the chapter by Michael Buhlmann, 'Liudger und seine Klostergründung Werden', pp. 162–67, for Liudger and Werden. See also Ingrid Rembold, 'Rewriting the Founder: Werden on the Ruhr and the Uses of Hagiography', *Journal of Medieval History* 41 (2015), 363–87.

11 See Michael Buhlmann, 'Die älteste Immunitätsurkunde für das Kloster Werden an der Ruhr', *Das Münster am Hellweg* 52 (1999), 55–74.

12 *Die Urbare der Abtei Werden a. d. Ruhr, A: Die Urbare vom 9.–13. Jahrhundert*, ed. Rudolf Kötzschke (Bonn, 1906), pp. 4–87.

13 See *Die Urbare der Abtei Werden a. d. Ruhr*, ed. Kötzschke, pt. 2, pp. cix–cxxii; and most recently Christof Spannhoff, 'Zur Datierung des ältesten Werdener Urbars (A)', *Nordmünsterland. Forschungen und Funde* 2 (2015), 192–99.

14 See Paul Derks, '*In pago Borahtron*. Zu einigen Ortsnamen der Hellweg- und Emscherzone', *Beiträge zur Geschichte von Stadt und Stift Essen* 99 (1984), 1–78; Thomas Bauer, *Die mittelalterlichen Gaue* (Cologne, 2000), pp. 17–18.

embedded in entries dealing with areas north and south of the Ruhr, close to the monastery. But there is no obvious reason behind its insertion at this particular place, for the vernacular passage actually deals with holdings situated almost two hundred miles further northwest in what is today the Netherlands:

[1] *An Naruthi thiu kirica endi kiric land.*
[2] *fan Almeri te Tafalbergon.*
[3] *An Uuerinon thiu kirica endi al that gilendi.*
[4] *Te Amuthon thiu kirica endi kiricland.*
[5] *an theru Fehtu en uuérr sancti Liudgeri alterum sancti Martini.*
[6] *Utermeri sancti Liudgeri totum.*
[7] *Spilmeri s* (?). *Pulmeri half.*
[8] *Suecsnon ubi natus est sanctus Liudgerus totum.*
[9] *An Upgoa siuun hof stadi. siuun uuerr stadi.*
[10] *Te Aiturnon sancti Liudgeri.*
[11] *Te Kinleson en alt giuuarki.*[15]

Taking a closer look at the document, it becomes clear that this is not a register of corvées owed to the abbey, nor does it give details of revenues. Rather, it is primarily a list of distant possessions belonging to the abbey. The 11 places mentioned are situated between Utrecht and the Zuiderzee along the river Vecht. In three places, reference is made to a church and to land belonging to that church. Two weirs are mentioned on the river Vecht, one of which belonged to Werden, the other to the church of St Martin in Utrecht. Two places called *Utermeri* and *Spilmeri* belonged to St Liudger, Werden's saintly patron, integrally, while he possessed a half-share of another, *Pulmeri*. Reference is made to a place north of Utrecht where St Liudger was born. This may be a hint as to why these pieces of land came to Werden, that is, they were most likely part of the family patrimony of the Liudgerids.

Focusing on the wording, it should be noted that the document betrays some influence of Latin vocabulary, or rather a 'nominal mishmash', most obviously when it refers to 'St Liudger' (*sanctus Liudgerus*), which probably became

15 *Die Urbare der Abtei Werden a. d. Ruhr*, ed. Kötzschke, pt. 2, pp. 73–74. Translation: '[1] In Naarden, the church and church land. [2] In Almer (= southern part of the Zuiderzee), the Tafelberg (n. Naarden). [3] In Wierum, the church and all that site. [4] In Muiden, the church and church land. [5] In the river Vecht, a weir of St Liudger and another of St Martin [of Utrecht]. [6] Uitermeer (n. Weesp) [belongs to] St Liudger as a whole. [7] Spilmer and Purmer, one half [of each]. [8] Zuilen (n. Utrecht), where St Liudger was born, as a whole. [9] In Opgooi, seven farmsteads. Seven fortresses. [10] Eiteren (n. IJsselstein), of St Liudger. [11] At Kinlosen, in the old boundary.'

a standardized phrase.[16] For one place-name, the scribe added a whole sentence in Latin: *ubi natus est sanctus Liudgerus*. Two lines above there is another Latin reference to the saint for a place called *Utermeri* (= Uitermeer n. Weesp), which belonged in its entirety to Werden's patron: *sancti Liudgeri totum*. The vernacular passage that follows quite obviously echoes this Latin formulation: *Spilmeri s(ive) / Pulmeri half*. The scribe began in Latin, but continued in the vernacular, juxtaposing Latin *totum* and vernacular *half*. There seems to have been some fluidity in writing, or even some kind of 'code-switching'.

How can we explain the use of the vernacular in this text? Heinrich Tiefenbach, who studied the toponymic evidence from Werden at some length, suggested that the text may have been added from a charter which the scribe simply copied when inserting the vernacular passage. He also pointed to parallels in the well-known vernacular boundary descriptions from Würzburg and Hammelburg, which likewise slip easily from Latin into Old High German when narrating place-names.[17] While these are useful considerations, one should not imagine a fully vernacular charter here, of course. It is clear that the vernacular passages were copied into the Urbar just as they were found in an earlier document, thus echoing the technique of its first draft. This was not a register of corvées or rents, but rather a simple list of possessions, so it was probably not the result of an official legal inquest.[18] The texts probably

16 On 'nominal mishmash', see Kuchenbuch, 'Ordnungsverhalten im grundherrlichen Schriftgut', p. 232; Katrinette Bodarwé, *Sanctimoniales litteratae. Schriftlichkeit und Bildung in den ottonischen Frauenkommunitäten Gandersheim, Essen und Quedlinburg* (Münster, 2004), pp. 197–98. For similar treatment of saints' names in Anglo-Saxon charters, see Francesca Tinti, 'Writing Latin and Old English in Tenth-Century England: Patterns, Formulae and Language Choice in the Leases of Oswald of Worcester', in *Writing Kingship and Power in Anglo-Saxon England*, eds Rory Naismith and David Woodman (Cambridge, 2018), pp. 303–27, at 325–26.

17 Tiefenbach, 'Werdener Urbar', pp. 509–10, who also suspected some long-term influence of Old English models here. On the use of the vernacular in boundary descriptions, see in general Reinhard Bauer, *Die ältesten Grenzbeschreibungen in Bayern und ihre Aussagen für Namenkunde und Geschichte* (Munich, 1988); Reinhard Bauer, 'Frühmittelalterliche Grenzbeschreibungen als Quelle für die Namensforschung', in *Frühmittelalterliche Grenzbeschreibungen und Namenforschung*, ed. Friedhelm Debus (Heidelberg, 1992), pp. 35–60; Edward Roberts, 'Boundary Clauses and the Use of the Vernacular in Eastern Frankish Charters, *c*.750–*c*.900', *Historical Research* 91 (2018), 580–604. Evidence comparable to that from Werden can indeed also be found in Anglo-Saxon England: see Rory Naismith, 'The Ely Memoranda and the Economy of the Late Anglo-Saxon Fenland', *ASE* 45 (2016), 333–77.

18 We occasionally find vernacular particles embedded in testimonies following inquests, as for example in the case of the manor of Friemersheim, which is part of the Werden Urbar. On inquests of this type, see Ludolf Kuchenbuch, 'Verrechtlichung von Erinnerung im Medium der Schrift (9. Jahrhundert)', in *Mnemosyne. Formen und Funktionen der*

represent a kind of memo that may have been written following the consultation of a vernacular speaker, perhaps a local official with a poor knowledge of Latin—indeed, quite possibly one of those individuals whose reports the Urbar mentions several times.

The distinct toponomy of this region may have caused the scribe to write in a 'vernacular mode', but there seems to be more behind this. Arend Quak argued that the text was not actually written in Old Saxon, but rather in Old Dutch, as there are no linguistic traits exclusive to Old Saxon, while Dutch place-names were combined with words like *alt*, *endi*, *en*, and *half*, which were also very common in Old Dutch.[19] If Quak is correct, the language used in the text was closer to the Frankish language and thus different from Old Saxon, and this may have induced the scribe to write in the vernacular. One may add that this region, as is attested by the *Lex Francorum Chamavorum* compiled under Charlemagne, was one whose Frankish character was emphasized in terms of law, and was rather distant from those areas in which Frisian and Saxon law predominated.[20] So, the document refers to an area of Frankish law with Old Dutch place-names, not one of Saxon or Frisian law, as would be typical for the heartland of Werden's holdings.[21]

---

kulturellen Erinnerung, eds Aleida Assmann and Dietrich Harth (Frankfurt am Main, 1991), pp. 36–47.

19 Arend Quak, 'Altniederländisch im neuen etymologischen Wörterbuch des Niederländischen', in *Current Trends in West Germanic Etymological Lexicography: Proceedings of the Symposium Held in Amsterdam, 12–13 June 1989*, eds Rolf H. Bremmer, Jr. and Jan van den Berg (Leiden, 1993), pp. 37–46, at 42–43; Arend Quak, 'Ortsnamen als Quelle des Altniederländischen', *Namn och bygd* 82 (1994), 31–50.

20 Peter Hoppenbrauwers, '*Leges nationum* and Ethnic Personality of Law in Charlemagne's Empire', in *Law and Empire: Ideas, Practices, Actors, Rulers and Elites*, eds Jeroen Duindam, Jill Harries, Caroline Humfress, and Nimrod Hurvitz (Leiden, 2013), pp. 251–74; Thomas Faulkner, *Law and Authority in the Early Middle Ages: The Frankish* leges *in the Carolingian Period* (Cambridge, 2016), pp. 9–45; Stefan Esders, 'La loi des Chamaves', in *Les lois barbares*, eds Sylvie Joye, Marcelo Cândido da Silva, and Bruno Dumézil (forthcoming).

21 In a huge donation of scattered possessions given to Werden by a nobleman called Folker in 855, the charter (as included in Werden's Urbar A) makes explicit reference to Salic and Ripuarian law as well as to Frisian custom (*ewa*). In doing so, Folker entered the monastery, ordered his progenitors' *memoria* to be celebrated and wanted his donation to be done for the protection of his and his parents' souls: 'Ego quasdam proprietatis meae res, quę mihi iure heredetario in pago Hamalande, in comitatu Uuigmanni, nec non et in Batuue, in comitatu Ansfridi, cum edificiis omnibus, et cunctis adiacentibus siluarum, et aquarum et pascuarum commodis, cultam et incultam terram, cum mancipiis utriusque sexus, coram testibus et nobiliorum uirorum presentia, secundum legem Ripuariam, et Salicam, nec non secundum euua Fresonum, de iure et potestate mea in ius et proprietatem predicti monasterii (sc. Uuerdiensis) ... perpetuo possidendas tradidi, et secundum predictas leges uestituram feci. [...] Item commentariolum de hereditate Folkeri, quam

It was thus the distant location of the property in the area of Utrecht and the IJsselmeer which caused the text to be written in the vernacular and eventually copied as a vernacular document into the monastery's pre-existing Latin polyptych sometime in the early tenth century. If this interpretation is correct, the wide dispersal of a large monastery's possessions caused a gradual shift towards new uses of the vernacular in order to allow for more appropriate documentation.

A Tenth-Century Old Saxon Manorial Register of the Women's Convent at Essen ('Essener Heberegister')

The second example of administrative vernacular writing from Saxony emerges from a completely different context. The women's convent of Essen was founded around 850 by a Saxon noble called Altfrid, who soon after became bishop of Hildesheim.[22] As in the case of their male counterparts at Werden, the Essen nuns managed to rid themselves of the yoke of a bishopric-based founding dynasty and became closely linked with the Liudolfing family, that is, the later Ottonian dynasty.[23] It seems that the rules for canonesses formulated at Aachen in 816 provided the normative basis for the women's way of life in the monastery.[24]

The Essen vernacular document does not come from a polyptych (which, in the case of Essen, survives only as a chained book from the fourteenth century),[25] but interestingly was rather written into a manuscript that served

habet in Frisia […] Hęc igitur traditio facta est coram pluribus et idoneis testibus. In pago cui uocabulum est Flethetti. In uilla quę uocatur Hlara. Sub die septima idus nouembris. Et in pago uocato Batue in uilla quę uicatur Hlegilo sub die IIII idus nouembris anno ab incarnatione domini nostri Jesu Christi DCCCLV indictione III Regnante domno nostro Hluouuico imperatore iuniore augusto anno XV. […] Hęc sunt nomina testium qui hanc traditionem secundum legem Ripuariorum fieri uiderunt et audierunt. Signum Folkeri qui hanc traditionem coram testibus subterius nominates manu propria perfecit et roborauit. Nomina testium qui in orientali ripa Hreni fluminis constituti esse noscuntur': *Die Urbare der Abtei Werden a. d. Ruhr*, ed. Kötzschke, pt. 2, pp. 10 and 13–15.

22 See Hedwig Röckelein, 'Altfrid, Gründer des Stifts Essen und international agierender Kirchenmann?', in *Frauen bauen Europa. Internationale Verflechtungen des Frauenstifts Essen*, ed. Thomas Schilp (Essen, 2011), pp. 27–64.

23 Bodarwé, *Sanctimoniales litteratae*, pp. 41–43, 45–47.

24 On this, see Thomas Schilp, *Norm und Wirklichkeit religiöser Frauengemeinschaften im Frühmittelalter. Die Institutio sanctimonialium Aquisgranensis des Jahres 816 und die Problematik der Verfassung von Frauenkommunitäten* (Göttingen, 1998).

25 Franz Arens, 'Das Heberegister des Stiftes Essen, nach dem Kettenbuch im Essener Münsterarchiv, 1332', *Beiträge zur Geschichte von Stadt und Stift Essen* 34 (1912), 1–111.

religious purposes. This vernacular text thus leads us into an altogether different world of communication between Latin and the vernacular. It is sensible to begin again with the manuscript in which the text is found, Düsseldorf, Universitäts- und Landesbibliothek, Ms. B 80. It was written in the tenth century, very probably in Essen, and contains homilies of Gregory the Great on the gospels with several Old Saxon glosses.[26] The manuscript appears to have been written as a supplement to another tenth-century Essen manuscript, which, in addition to sermons of Augustine and Alcuin's commentary on the Gospel of John, included the first twenty of Gregory the Great's homilies.[27] The manuscript B 80 adds homilies 21 to 40, and thus appears originally to have been completed on fol. 152v.[28] At some point later, three texts were added to this: first, a brief Latin manorial register on fol. 152v;[29] second, in a different hand, an Old Saxon homily on All Saints on fol. 153r (the final sentence of which was added to the bottom of the preceding folio);[30] and, finally, on the very last folio (153v), the vernacular register, the so-called 'Essener Heberegister', which like the preceding homily was written completely in Old Saxon.[31]

26 On the manuscript see Eef Overgaauw, Joachim Ott, and Gerhard Karpp, *Die mittelalterlichen Handschriften der Signaturengruppe B in der Universitäts- und Landesbibliothek Düsseldorf, Teil 1: Ms. B 1 bis B 100* (Wiesbaden, 2005), pp. 268–73. Accessible online: http://digital.ub.uni-duesseldorf.de/man/content/pageview/5588451. On the vernacular texts contained in this manuscript, see http://www.handschriftencensus.de/7058. See Kurt Otto Seidel, '*Vui lesed* ... Geistiges Leben im Essener Damenstift im Spiegel einer Handschrift des 10. Jahrhunderts', *Essener Unikate* 26 (2005), 50–59. On the script, see Bodarwé, *Sanctimoniales litteratae*, pp. 114–15 and 142; and Hartmut Hoffmann, *Schreibschulen und Buchmalerei. Handschriften und Texte des 9.–11. Jahrhunderts*, MGH Schriften 65 (Hanover, 2012), p. 46. On the Essen scriptorium in general, see Hartmut Hoffmann, 'Das Skriptorium von Essen in ottonischer und frühsalischer Zeit', in *Kunst im Zeitalter der Kaiserin Theophanu*, eds Anton von Eeuw and Peter Schreiner (Cologne, 1993), pp. 113–53.

27 Düsseldorf, Universitäts- und Landesbibliothek, Ms. B 8: Digitized: http://digital.ub.uni duesseldorf.de/ms/content/pageview/4624757; on the supplementary nature of the two manuscripts B 8 and B 80 see also Bodarwé, *Sanctimoniales litteratae*, p. 384.

28 Düsseldorf, Universitäts- und Landesbibliothek, Ms. B 80; see Bodarwé, *Sanctimoniales litteratae*, pp. 385–86 and Hoffmann, *Schreibschulen und Buchmalerei*, p. 46.

29 Digitized: http://digital.ub.uni-duesseldorf.de/man/content/pageview/5588758.

30 Digitized: http://digital.ub.uni-duesseldorf.de/man/content/pageview/5588759.

31 Digitized: http://digital.ub.uni-duesseldorf.de/man/content/pageview/5588760. It was written on erased text.

In terms of palaeography,[32] language,[33] and content, the relationship between these three additions is far from clear. As will be suggested here, however, the combination of these particular texts and their inclusion as supplements to Gregory's homilies may provide clues as to why two administrative registers and two very different vernacular texts were copied into a manuscript of sermons.

The Latin register seems to have been added first on some space created by an erasure of some sort. The sermon was copied next, followed by the Old Saxon register. The three works may each be in a different hand, though it is possible that the two vernacular texts were written by the same person. The Old Saxon register was clearly also written over something that was scratched out.[34] The transition between the two languages is fluid in the Latin register: vernacular place-names are introduced here with 'An'.[35] Interestingly, this register refers at the beginning to a piece of property exclusively belonging to an otherwise unknown female provost called Eila in a place called *Krey* (today in the eastern part of Essen): *De predio eilę preposituręȩ . Creia .x. siclos.*[36] This appears to presuppose a division of the monastic property between the abbess and the nuns that took place sometime earlier in the tenth century.[37]

32 It has been thought that both Old Saxon texts could have been written by one hand. See Bernhard Bischoff, 'Paläographische Fragen deutscher Denkmäler der Karolingerzeit', *Frühmittelalterliche Studien* 5 (1971), 101–34, at p. 130. The dating of the script is disputed, but there does not seem a way to arrive at a more precise date than the tenth century. See Bodarwé, *Sanctimoniales litteratae*, pp. 117, 135–6, 142, 197, and 330. Hoffmann, *Schreibschulen und Buchmalerei*, p. 46 argued that the manuscript's main part was written in the second third of the tenth century, while the vernacular texts were added by two different hands only shortly afterwards.

33 Bodarwé, *Sanctimoniales litteratae*, pp. 197–98 rightly stresses that too strict a separation between a Latin and a vernacular register is not very helpful. On the language employed in both Old Saxon texts more specifically, see Lars-Erik Ahlsson, 'Die altsächsische Bedahomilie', *Niederdeutsche Mitteilungen* 29 (1973), 30–41; and Thomas Klein, *Studien zur Wechselbeziehung zwischen altsächsischem und althochdeutschem Schreibwesen und ihrer sprach- und kulturgeschichtlichen Bedeutung* (Göppingen, 1977), pp. 539–43.

34 Bodarwé, *Sanctimoniales litteratae*, p. 198.

35 Similar observations can be made in the use of Old English in Anglo-Saxon charters: see Tinti, 'Writing Latin and Old English', pp. 310–13.

36 Quoted here after *Kleinere altsächsische Sprachdenkmäler*, ed. Wadstein, no. 7, p. 21. Translation: 'On the estate of Eila, of the office of the provost. In Krey, ten *sicli* (= unit of weight)'.

37 A charter given by Otto I in 966 provides evidence that by this time the property had been divided up between the abbess on the one hand and the female provost and the *sanctimoniales* on the other, whose part should not be encroached upon by the abbess, thus providing a safe *terminus ante quem*: MGH D Otto I, no. 325, p. 440; see Ute Küppers-Braun, *Macht in Frauenhand. 1000 Jahre Herrschaft adliger Frauen in Essen* (Essen, 2002),

To understand what this meant in practical terms, we can consider a similar situation in the neighbouring monastery of Werden, about which we are much better informed. Here, the abbot's use of the monastery's property for political purposes prompted the community to have their property rights codified by the introduction of a strict separation between the property of the abbot and that belonging to the convent.[38] In practice, this meant that the various manors were distributed either to the abbot or to the monastic community. Around the same time, or possibly even earlier, the manors developed into proper economic centres at which the renders in kind were delivered for further production and conservation. These *officia* became the actual centres of manorial administration.[39] If a comparable development may be assumed for the community at Essen, these important changes must be considered among the reasons for the writing of the Latin register and, indeed, as we shall see, of the vernacular register. The existence of a separate set of monastic belongings reserved exclusively for the provost is assumed in both Essen registers and may also hint at who might have been responsible for the manuscript.[40] In the manuscript there is a gap of several lines immediately after the listing of the provost's property. The remainder of the register lists recently acquired property (*De novo predio*) in sixteen places located close to the convent, as well as in Westphalia and even in Holland.[41] The register records monetary rents received by the convent in cash for its properties, in most cases paid in sums of *denarii* or *sicli*. It seems that these places were not part of the *servitium* extracted by the manors.[42]

The second addition is very different in nature. It is a famous Old Saxon homily for All Saints' Day,[43] which is based on a popular Latin text often

pp. 27–30 and 48–49. The Latin register refers to this when listing the provost's possessions, but may have been composed even earlier. See Seidel, '*Vui lesed*', p. 54.

38 See Rudolf Kötzschke, *Studien zur Verwaltungsgeschichte der Großgrundherrschaft Werden an der Ruhr* (Leipzig, 1901), pp. 19–20, 75–6, and 114–6.

39 Kötzschke, *Studien zur Verwaltungsgeschichte*, pp. 76–77.

40 See Küppers-Braun, *Macht in Frauenhand*, pp. 27–28.

41 *Kleinere altsächsische Sprachdenkmäler*, ed. Wadstein, no. 7, pp. 21–22. See on this Helmut Weigel, *Studien zur Verfassung und Verwaltung des Grundbesitzes des Frauenstiftes Essen (852–1803)* (Essen, 1960), p. 64.

42 See Küppers-Braun, *Macht in Frauenhand*, p. 25.

43 See Ahlsson, 'Die altsächsische Bedahomilie'; Verio Santoro, 'La versione in sassone antico della prima lectio del sermone *In festiuitate omnium sanctorum*', *Romanobarbarica* 12 (1992–93), 223–49; Tette Hostra, '*Vui lesed*. Zur volkssprachlichen Allerheiligenhomilie', in *Speculum Saxonum. Studien zu den kleineren altsächsischen Sprachdenkmälern*, ed. Arend Quak (Amsterdam, 1999), pp. 105–15; Heinrich Tiefenbach, 'Altsächsische Allerheiligenpredigt', in *Althochdeutsche und altsächsische Literatur*, ed. Bergmann, pp. 16–18.

erroneously ascribed to Bede, though interestingly it is transmitted here without the Latin version.[44] The homily refers to the donation of the Pantheon in Rome in 609 by the emperor Phocas (602–10) to Pope Boniface IV (608–15).[45] It was converted into a Christian church dedicated to St Mary, and a new feast day for all saints was arranged for 1 November.[46] The Old Saxon version of the homily has caused some debate. As preserved here, is it complete or fragmentary?[47] Was this particular homily translated into Old Saxon because the transformation of the Pantheon could be interpreted as a conversion from paganism to Christianity, and thus as a parallel to the conversion of Saxony?[48] The assumption that the text is fragmentary is contradicted by the fact that the homily's

---

44 On this text, which was also translated into Old English, see James E. Cross, '*Legimus in ecclesiasticis historiis*: A Sermon for All Saints, and its Use in Old English Prose', *Traditio* 33 (1977), 101–35. See also Maximilian Diesenberger, *Predigt und Politik im frühmittelalterlichen Bayern. Arn von Salzburg, Karl der Große und die Salzburger Sermones-Sammlung* (Berlin, 2015), pp. 175–92, at 188.

45 *Kleinere altsächsische Sprachdenkmäler*, ed. Wadstein, no. 4, p. 18: 'Vui lesed tho sanctus bonifacius pauos an roma uuas. that he bedi thena kiesur aduocatum. that he imo an romŏ en hus gefi. that thia luidi uuilon pantheon heton. wan thar uuorthŏn alla afgoda inna begangana. So he it imo tho iegiuan hadda. so wieda he it an uses drohtines era. ende usero fruon sanctę mariun. endi allero christes martiro. te thiu also thar er inna begangan vuarth thiu menigi thero diuuilo. that thar nu inna begangan uuertha thiu gehugd allero godes heligono. He gibod tho that al that folk thes dages, also the kalend nouember anstendit te kerikŏn quami. endi also that gŏdlika thianust thar al gedŏn was. So wither gewarf manno gewilik fra endi blithi te hus. Endi thanana so warth gewonohed that man hŏdigo ahter allero thero waroldi beged thia gehugd allero godes heligono. te thiu so vuat so vui an allemo themo gera uergomelosom that wi it al hŏdigŏ gefullon. endi that vui thur thero heligono gethingi bekuman te themo ewigon liua, helpandemo usemo drohtine'. The text's erroneous rendering of the name of the Roman emperor *Phocas* as *fogat* can be explained either as an incorrect reading from a Latin model text (as suggested by Santoro, 'La versione', p. 238), or, as I was kindly told by Wolfgang Haubrichs, as a 'learned mistake', for the Old High German loanword for the Latin term *advocatus* was *fogat* ('Vogt').

46 On the Christian reinterpretation of the Pantheon, see Susan Rankin, '*Terribilis est locus iste*. The Pantheon in 609', in *Rhetoric Beyond Words: Delight and Persuasion in the Arts of the Middle Ages*, ed. Mary Carruthers (Cambridge, 2010), pp. 281–310. On the origins of the establishment of the feast of All Saints, see Gisbert Knopp, '*Sanctorum nomina seriatim*. Die Anfänge der Allerheiligenlitanei und ihre Verbindung mit den *Laudes regiae*', *Römische Quartalschrift für christliche Altertumskunde und Kirchengeschichte* 65 (1970), 185–231; Pierre Journel, 'Le culte collectif des saints à Rome du VIIIe au IXe siècle', in *Le jugement, le ciel et l'enfer dans l'histoire du christianisme* (Angers, 1989), pp. 19–30; Martin Wallraff, 'Pantheon und Allerheiligen. Einheit und Vielfalt des Göttlichen in der Spätantike', *Jahrbuch für Antike und Christentum* 47 (2004), 128–43.

47 For the argument that it survives in its entirety, see Ahlsson, 'Die altsächsische Bedahomilie'. Compare, however, Bischoff, 'Paläographische Fragen', p. 130.

48 Seidel, '*Vui lesed*', p. 56 and Santoro, 'La versione', pp. 245–47.

last sentence has been added in the manuscript on the preceding page, not on the reverse of the last page, which would have provided much more space.[49] Scholars have also argued that the homily provides a conclusive argument and should therefore be regarded as complete.[50] The fact that the Old Saxon homily only translates the first 14 lines of its 214-line Latin model thus has to be explained differently, for the vernacular text may not have possessed the same functionality as a Latin sermon.[51] Explaining the texts' features by reference to the conversion of the Saxons is also unconvincing, for this had occurred more than a century earlier. My impression is that this vernacular text cannot be understood in quite such a simple fashion, for the main message conveyed by the sermon is actually a historical justification for the feast of All Saints and of the obligation for all Christians to attend it on 1 November. This is made clear when the text explicitly says that this initially Roman custom is now observed by Christians across the world in celebration of the memory of the saints: 'And what we did wrongly in the past year out of negligence ('so vuat so vui an allemo themo gera uergomeloson'), we should fulfil on the present day so that through the saints' intercession we may achieve eternal life'.[52] The argument employs the language of debt: if one did not fulfil their obligations completely in the course of the preceding year, they should now finally fulfil them on All Saints' Day, as it is the saints who can intervene on their behalf to secure eternal life.[53] This idea is important to bear in mind, as the emphasis on fulfilling obligations on All Saints' Day could be read and interpreted in various ways.

Finally, let us move on to the Old Saxon register, which comes next on the reverse side of the leaf containing the All Saints homily. This register mentions nine places in the area around Essen whose importance for the convent

---

49 See above, n. 31.

50 Stephan Müller, 'Altsächsische Allerheiligenpredigt / Essener Heberolle', in *Für Königtum und Himmelreich. 1000 Jahre Bischof Meinwerk von Paderborn*, eds Martin Kroker and Christoph Stiegemann (Regensburg, 2009), pp. 308–10, at 308.

51 See below, n. 100.

52 *Kleinere altsächsische Sprachdenkmäler*, ed. Wadstein, no. 4, p. 18. The Latin version is even more explicit on this: 'Out of ignorance, negligence, or involvement in secular affairs'. See Cross, '*Legimus in ecclesiasticis historiis*', p. 106: 'Ex hac ergo consuetudine sanctae Romanae ecclesiae, crescente religione christiana, decretum est, ut in ecclesiis dei quae per orbem terrarium longe lateque construuntur, honor et memoria omnium sanctorum, in die qua praediximus haberetur, ut quicquid humana fragilitas per ignorantiam vel negligentiam seu per occupationem rei secularis, in solemnitate sanctorum minus plene peregisset, in hac observatione solveretur, quatenus eorum patrociniis protecti, ad superna populorum gaudia pervenire valeamus'.

53 See also Seidel, '*Vui lesed*', pp. 56–57. The last sentence (*helpandemo usemo drohtine*) appears to be reminiscent of oath or prayer formulas, which is another argument that the text ended here. See Santoro, 'La versione', p. 237.

goes back to the time of its foundation by Bishop Altfrid.[54] Most of these possessions came under Essen's control in the later ninth century, while the Old Saxon register clearly dates to the earlier tenth century, that is, before a great fire in 946, which led to a confirmation of property by Otto I in a charter of the following year.[55] The text of the Old Saxon register goes as follows:

> Van Vehus ahte ende ahtedeg mudde maltes ende ahte brod, tuena sostra erito, uiar mudde gerston, uiar uother thiores holtes. te thrim hogetidon, ahtetian mudde maltes ende thriuu uother holtes. ende uiarhteg bikera. ende usero herino misso tua crukon.
>
> Van Ekanscetha similiter.
>
> Van Rengerengthorpa similiter.
>
> Van Hukretha similiter ana that holt te then hogetidon. that ne geldet thero ambahto neuuethar.
>
> Van Brokhuson. te then hogetidon nigen mudde maltes ende tuenteg bikera. ende tua crukon.
>
> Van Horlon nigen ende uiftech mudde maltes ende tue uother thiores holtes. tue mudde gerston. Uiar brot. en suster erito. tuenteg bikera. endi tua crukon. nigen mudde maltes te thenhogetidon.
>
> Van Nianhus similiter.
>
> Van Borthbeki similiter.
>
> Van Drene te usero herano misso tian ember honegas. Te pincoston siuondon haluon ember honegas endi ahtodoch bikera. endi uiar crukon.[56]

---

54 Winfried Bettecken, *Stift und Stadt Essen. Coenobium Astnide und Sieldungsentwicklung bis 1244* (Münster, 1988), pp. 38–42; Thomas Schilp, 'Die Grundherrschaftsorganisation des hochadligen Damenstifts Essen. Von der wirtschaftlichen Erschließung zur politisch-administrativen Erfassung des Raumes', in *Vergessene Zeiten. Mittelalter im Ruhrgebiet. Katalog zur Ausstellung im Ruhrlandmuseum Essen*, ed. Ferdinand Seibt, 2 vols (Essen, 1990), 1:89–92. More detailed references to the nine manors are given in Esders, '*Te usero herano misso*', p. 68 n. 54.

55 Bettecken, *Stift und Stadt*, p. 37 takes the fact that the manor Ehrenzell is not mentioned in the register as evidence that the register must have been written before 966 when this manor is first attested in a charter. The diploma is MGH D Otto I, no. 85, p. 167. On this document, see Bettecken, *Stift und Stadt*, pp. 38–39 and 43–69.

56 *Kleinere altsächsische Sprachdenkmäler*, ed. Wadstein, no. 7, p. 21. Translation: 'From Viehhof, eighty-eight bushels of malt and eight loaves of bread, two *sextarii* of peas, four bushels of barley, four cartloads of dry wood. At high feasts, eighteen bushels of malt and three cartloads of wood, and forty cups. And at our lord's mass, two jugs. From Eickenscheidt, likewise. From Ringeldorf, likewise. From Huckarde, likewise, but without wood, at high feasts. This is not provided by any of these office districts. From Brockhausen, at high feasts nine bushels of malt and twenty cups, and two jugs. From Hordel, fifty-nine bushels of malt and two cartloads of dry wood. Two bushels of barley.

As has been noted, the text is not a fragment of a larger register, but forms a complete entity (as does the All Saints homily preceding it in the manuscript).[57] The nine places were centres (*officia*) for the collection of certain revenues in kind such as malt, barley, bread, peas, and wood, but also cups and jugs, which were evidently produced by the peasants. The peasants are not mentioned here, as the register focuses exclusively on the produce to be delivered by the nine manors to the monastery, or rather to its provost. Among the nine manors, the first-mentioned, 'Viehhof', which was not far from the monastery, functioned as some sort of administrative and economic centre. Among the products to be delivered by the manors, malt, barley, honey, and wood figure most prominently. That we do not find wheat in this list, nor rye nor oat, attests to the highly selective nature of this register. Some of the deliveries were clearly not 'renders in kind', but rather produced goods, that is, malt, bread, honey, and, more significantly, jugs and cups. It seems to have been assumed that these would be produced at the nine manors. Taken together, these goods quite obviously constitute the requirements of the monastic brewery,[58] as the bread was often used in brewing for fermentation, while peas were often added to barley during malting or shortly thereafter to improve the flavour.[59] Significantly, the register also provides the dates these items were to be delivered: 'at high feasts' (*te then hogetidon*), that is, Christmas, Easter, and Pentecost, and in one case concerning the delivery of honey, 'at pentecost' (*te pincoston*) and twice 'at our lord's mass' (*usero herino misso*).

Why was this list written in the vernacular? Why do we not have a Latin sermon on All Saints in this manuscript? And how can we explain this strange assemblage of texts in a manuscript otherwise containing Latin sermons? Historians and philologists have hitherto found it hard to make sense of these documents. Katrinette Bodarwé suggested that the manuscript testifies to an intensified administrative concern on the part of the female provost or

Four loaves of bread; and one *sextarius* of peas. Twenty cups and two jugs. Nine bushels of malt at high feasts. From Nienhausen, likewise. From Borbeck, likewise. From Dreen, at our lord's mass, ten buckets of honey. At Pentecost, six and a half buckets of honey and eighty cups, and four jugs.' Note the use of Latin terms such as *similiter*, which may have become standardized to the point that it no longer mattered whether they were in Latin or vernacular.

57 See Müller, 'Altsächsische Allerheiligenpredigt, Essener Heberolle', p. 310.

58 Weigel, *Studien zur Verfassung*, p. 55. On Essen's late medieval brewery, see Küppers-Braun, *Macht in Frauenhand*, pp. 147–48.

59 For an ancient recipe using these ingredients see Johann Wilhelm Wasser, *Gründliche Anleitung zum Bierbrauen, zur Beförderung richtiger Grundsätze der vorzüglichen Bereitung des Braun-, Weiß und Englisch-Bier betreffend in systematischer Ordnung und in Berechnungen tabellarisch dargestellt* (Berlin, 1793), p. 60.

chamberlain, since the register had a very limited scope and evidently was not intended to give a full list of possessions or income. She has argued that the register was copied into a manuscript for purposes of lections, teaching, and study, on the assumption that the person who oversaw the codex also served as a functionary.[60] For Bodarwé, it made sense to augment a manuscript of Latin homilies with an Old Saxon homily and Old Saxon glosses, if we assume that the religious women of the Essen community were in some way involved in a process of communication between the worlds of Latin and vernacular speakers.[61] While Latin glosses could improve one's understanding of a Latin text, vernacular glosses enabled a speaker reading the manuscript to provide further oral explanation to his audience, especially in the contexts of teaching or delivering a lection.[62] Bodarwé also made the important point that the well-known homilies of Gregory the Great were used in the liturgy of the hours as part of the monastic office.[63] However, in this view, the insertion of the two registers into the manuscript would need to be explained by the fact that the person who compiled the codex also performed administrative functions. Kurt Otto Seidel, by contrast, thought that the vernacular texts may have been addressed to novices who were less familiar with Latin, or to lay people who either helped the monastery administer its property or attended masses in the community.[64]

It is possible to push this discussion further by making use of Bodarwé's observation that the manuscript contains a note that Gregory's homily 33 would be used in lections on the feast of Mary Magdalene. As Bodarwé also noted, according to a marginal note in the corresponding manuscript of Gregory's first twenty homilies, the seventeenth homily was to be read in six lections on the birthday of St Matthew.[65] Indeed, as they explicitly state in their headings,

60 Bodarwé, *Sanctimoniales litteratae*, pp. 198–99.

61 Bodarwé, *Sanctimoniales litteratae*, p. 264. On the uses of glosses in situations of reading and preaching see Markus Schiegg, *Frühmittelalterliche Glossen. Ein Beitrag zur Funktionalität und Kontextualität mittelalterlicher Schriftlichkeit* (Heidelberg, 2015), pp. 178–86.

62 Bodarwé, *Sanctimoniales litteratae*, pp. 235–36.

63 On the uses of Gregory's sermons see Diesenberger, *Predigt und Politik*, pp. 161–66 and 189–90; Werner Schröder, 'Die *Verwandtschaft der althochdeutschen Glossen zu Gregors Homilien*', *Beiträge zur Geschichte der deutschen Sprache und Literatur* 65 (1941), 1–105; Rolf Bergmann, 'Überblick über die Gregor-Glossierung', in *Die althochdeutsche und altsächsische Glossographie. Ein Handbuch*, eds Rolf Bergmann and Stefanie Stricker, 2 vols (Berlin, 2009), 1:525–48, at pp. 542–44 lists twenty-seven manuscripts of Gregory's homilies on the gospels with glosses written between the eighth and tenth century.

64 Seidel, '*Vui lesed*', p. 58.

65 Bodarwé, *Sanctimoniales litteratae*, p. 301 n. 446. On Gregory's seventeenth homily on the gospels as a relevant text for preaching, see Diesenberger, *Predigt und Politik*, p. 162.

many of Gregory's homilies were first given in Rome not only on major feasts, but also on the birthdays of the martyrs in the basilicas dedicated to them.[66] In the Essen manuscript, we also find specific references to these Roman elements.[67] Moreover, the codex contains general remarks such as 'Item de martiribus lectio sancti euangelii secundum Lucam',[68] or the note that a sermon was to be delivered on the feast day of Mary Magdalene: 'In celebratione sanctę Marię Magdalenę prima lectio'.[69]

The calendar of the Essen community and its functionaries corresponded to the high feasts and those of various saints. This, however, holds equally true for the convent's peasant dependents, as the presence of particular saints is a special feature of ecclesiastical lordship.[70] A monastery's patron was important in the expansion and cohesion of ecclesiastical seigneuries, as the churches of dependent villages often shared their relics, thus constructing the notion of a large ecclesiastical community protected by an individual saint.[71] As several manorial registers attest, peasants' payments in kind were often rendered on the feast days of saints.[72] This practice was already underway in the ninth century, and in the tenth century it was further developed in many ecclesiastical seigneuries.[73]

66 See, e.g., homily 3 (Felicitas), 9 (Silvester), 11 and 12 (Agnes), 13 (Felix), 27 (Pancratius), 28 (Nereius and Achilleus), 32 (Processus and Martinianus), 35 (Mennas), 37 (Sebastian).

67 Düsseldorf, Universitäts- und Landesbibliothek, Ms. B 80, fol. 76v (Mennas) and fol. 98v (Sebastian).

68 Düsseldorf, Universitäts- und Landesbibliothek, Ms. B 80, fol. 63r.

69 Düsseldorf, Universitäts- und Landesbibliothek, Ms. B 80, fol. 66r.

70 On the features of ecclesiastical seigneuries, see the important remarks in Ludolf Kuchenbuch, 'Die Klostergrundherrschaft im Frühmittelalter', in *Herrschaft und Kirche. Beiträge zur Entstehung und Wirkungsweise episkopaler und monastischer Organisationsformen*, ed. Friedrich Prinz (Stuttgart, 1988), pp. 297–343, at 341.

71 Weigel, *Studien zur Verfassung*, p. 163.

72 See the important article by Hans-Werner Goetz, 'Kirchenfest und weltliches Alltagsleben im früheren Mittelalter', *Mediävistik* 2 (1989), 123–71, at pp. 148–52, which was missed by Dmitri Starostine, '... *in die festivitatis*: Gift-giving, Power and the Calendar in the Carolingian Kingdoms', EME 14 (2006), 465–86.

73 In the polyptych of the abbey of Mettlach, the oldest parts of which date from the tenth century, the connection of saint's feasts and the dates of rendering tributes, etc. appears to have been very much at an advanced stage: see Hartmut Müller, 'Die Mettlacher Güterrolle', *Zeitschrift für die Geschichte der Saargegend* 15 (1965), 110–46, at pp. 116–22. We also encounter this in the third part of the eleventh-century register of Freckenhorst, where the payments made by the abbey are coordinated with the feasts of saints: *Kleinere altsächsische Sprachdenkmäler*, ed. Wadstein, no. 9, pp. 24–45, at 41–43; see also Hartig, 'Die Gliederung', p. 109. On this phenomenon, see in more general terms Ludolf Kuchenbuch, 'Abschied von der "Grundherrschaft". Ein Prüfgang durch das ostfränkisch-deutsche

The Old Saxon register states that the renders in kind were to be given on the three high feasts (Christmas, Easter, Pentecost), on Pentecost alone (for the delivery of honey by the manor Drehnhausen), and twice on the feast of the monastery's lords (*te usero herino misso*). To which date does this feast of the monastery's patrons refer? The convent's patrons were Cosmas and Damian, two eastern saints whose western veneration began in Rome.[74] Their feast day, 27 September, is first attested in a charter issued by King Zwentibold of Lotharingia in June 898.[75] It appears to have been introduced between 872 and 898 by means of a relic translation from Rome to Essen.[76] A sacramentary written around 870 that came to Essen in the late ninth century contains three texts for masses celebrated for the birthday of Cosmas and Damian on 27 September.[77] A calendar inserted into the codex refers to this date,[78] and the manuscript also contains an invocation related to the two saints' feast.[79] Contrary to what one might have expected for the church's patron saints, these texts were not highlighted in the manuscript, and it has recently been argued that the texts must have been written before the manuscript was at Essen. By contrast, another entry in the manuscript, a 'Praefatio in natale sanctorum Cosme et Damiani', was highlighted by the scribe with a red rubric. This was probably written at Essen as a preface to the above-mentioned calendar, but it was added at a later date.[80] It thus cannot be assumed that the feast of the female monastery's patron saints was already being celebrated on 27 September

---

Reich, 950–1050', *Zeitschrift der Savigny-Stiftung für Rechtsgeschichte, Germanistische Abteilung* 121 (2004), 1–99, at pp. 83–89.

74 On the spread of the cult of Cosmas and Damian in the West, see Anneliese Wittmann, *Kosmas und Damian. Kultausbreitung und Volksdevotion* (Berlin, 1967), pp. 54–58.

75 MGH D Zwentibold, no. 22, p. 59. See also *Essener Urkundenbuch. Regesten der Urkunden des Frauenstifts Essen im Mittelalter, Vol. 1: Von der Gründung um 850 bis 1350*, ed. Thomas Schilp (Düsseldorf, 2010), no. 10, p. 7.

76 See Katrinette Bodarwé, 'Roman Martyrs and their Veneration in Ottonian Saxony: The Case of the *sanctimoniales* of Essen', *EME* 9 (2000), 345–65; Röckelein, 'Altfrid', p. 51; though for a slightly earlier date, see Thomas Schilp, 'Überlegungen zur Sakramentarhandschrift D 1 als *Liber vitae* der Essener Frauenkommunität', in *Libri vitae. Gebetsgedenken in der Gesellschaft des Frühen Mittelalters*, eds Dieter Geuenich and Uwe Ludwig (Cologne, 2015), pp. 203–22, at 218–220.

77 Düsseldorf, Universitäts- und Landesbibliothek, Ms. D 1. Digitized: http://digital.ub.uni-duesseldorf.de/urn/urn:nbn:de:hbz:061:1–112892. On this manuscript see also Volkhard Huth, 'Die Düsseldorfer Sakramentarhandschrift D 1 als Memorialzeugnis. Mit einer Wiedergabe der Namen und Namengruppen', *Frühmittelalterliche Studien* 20 (1986), 213–98, at p. 234 for the texts relating to Cosmas and Damian (at fol. 122r of the manuscript).

78 Düsseldorf, Universitäts- und Landesbibliothek, Ms. D 1, fol. 221r.

79 Düsseldorf, Universitäts- und Landesbibliothek, Ms. D 1, fol. 207v.

80 Schilp, 'Überlegungen zur Sakramentarhandschrift', pp. 219–20.

in the ninth century. Moreover, based on inscriptions and liturgical calendars, Hedwig Röckelein and Katrinette Bodarwé have convincingly argued that the commemoration of the two Essen patrons on a special feast day may not have begun until the early eleventh century.[81]

This points towards a different explanation, as the martyrdom of Cosmas and Damian was also mentioned in several *Libri ordinarii*, sacramentaries, liturgical prayers, and litany calendars. From these we learn that it was celebrated on All Saints' Day, since they belonged to the canonical saints who were commemorated in the high prayer of the Roman church.[82] Carl Hammer drew attention to the Roman liturgical prayer *Communicantes*, which enumerates Christ, the Virgin Mary, the apostles, and the Roman martyrs, transforming the celebration of the mass into a commemoration of 'all saints', which was adopted north of the Alps as early as the late eighth century.[83] The reception of Roman liturgy in the veneration of saints by the Essen female community is attested early on by gospel manuscripts, sacramentaries, and calendars.[84] Given that there were close relations between Essen and the noble Liudolfing family, it is also conceivable that the liturgy of All Saints, which had been promoted by the Carolingians, may have influenced liturgical practice at Essen.[85] The Old Saxon sermon makes this even more plausible, for when it refers to the

81 Bodarwé, 'Roman Martyrs', pp. 356–57 and 359; see also Hedwig Röckelein, 'Leben im Schutz der Heiligen. Reliquientranslationen nach Essen vom 9. bis 11. Jahrhundert', in *Herrschaft, Bildung und Gebet. Gründung und Anfänge des Frauenstifts Essen*, eds Günter Berghaus, Thomas Schilp, and Michael Schlagheck (Essen, 2000), pp. 87–100, at 93, who points out that an annual fair on the two saints' day only became established in the eleventh century by a privilege for a market by Henry III in 1041. See also Küppers-Braun, *Macht in Frauenhand*, pp. 17–20. On liturgy in medieval Essen see the survey by Jürgen Bärsch, 'Die Essener Münsterkirche als Ort des Gottesdienstes. Zur Feier der Liturgie im mittelalterlichen Stift Essen', in *Herrschaft, Bildung und Gebet*, eds Berghaus et al., pp. 71–85.

82 See Carl I. Hammer, '"For All the Saints". Bishop Vivolo of Passau and the Eighth-Century Origins of the Feast', *Revue Mabillon* n. s. 15 (= 76) (2004), 5–26, at pp. 15 and 26. See also Carl Kammer, *Die Litanei von Allen Heiligen* (Innsbruck, 1962), pp. 52–53, emphasizing that Cosmas and Damian were the last saints to be introduced into the Roman canon of the mass.

83 Hammer, '"For All the Saints"', pp. 14–15, referring to Vincent Lorne Kennedy, *The Saints of the Canon of the Mass*, 2nd ed. (Vatican City, 1963). Hammer also pointed out that the list of saints in the Old Gelasian sacramentary composed around 600 originally ended with Cosmas and Damian.

84 See Bärsch, 'Die Essener Münsterkirche', pp. 71–72.

85 For references, see Astrid Krüger, *Litanei-Handschriften der Karolingerzeit* (Hanover, 2007); Astrid Krüger, '*Sancte Nazari ora pro nobis*: Ludwig der Deutsche und der Lorscher Rotulus', in *Ludwig der Deutsche und seine Zeit*, ed. Wilfried Hartmann (Darmstadt, 2004), pp. 184–202.

intercession of 'all the saints', the author may well have had specific litanies on All Saints in mind.

In the previously mentioned charter of Otto I issued in 947, the *monasterium* of Essen is referred to as having been 'built in honour of the holy Saviour, the holy mother of God Mary, the venerable martyrs Cosmas and Damian, and all saints' ('Asnidensis monasterii a bonę memorię Altfrido presule in honore sancti Salvatoris sanctaeque Mariae genitricis et venerandorum Cosmae et Damiani martyrum nec non et omnium sanctorum constructi').[86] This wording adapted a formula that had been developed in eighth-century Rome in response to iconoclasm; the hierarchical listing of the Saviour, Mary, apostles, and saints also became established north of the Alps in the Carolingian period and elevated the *Salvator* to the status of many churches' primary patron.[87] For this reason, if we assume that the wording in the Old Saxon registers referring rather vaguely to 'the feast of our lords' (*te usero herino misso*) also included the other saints apart from Cosmas and Damian, the only possible date for combining the veneration of Cosmas and Damian along with the Saviour and Mary would be 1 November, All Saints' Day.[88] It is here that a close connection to the vernacular sermon on All Saints becomes apparent, for the main point of this text was to emphasize the Roman character of the feast and the obligation of Christians everywhere to attend church on this day and commemorate the pantheon of saints.

The liturgical calendar and All Saints' Day thus provide important contexts for understanding the functions of the vernacular texts found in the Essen manuscript and their relevance for manorial organization. It is not merely coincidence that the homilies of Gregory the Great and the Latin register were appended with Old Saxon texts in the manuscript. A scribe appears to have added them because the addition made sense. It is thus likely that the person responsible for the codex had to communicate with lay people quite regularly.

86 MGH D Otto I, no. 85, p. 167; for a more recent edition see *Essener Urkundenbuch*, ed. Schilp, no. 15, pp. 9–10 and 349–50. The charter confirms Essen's possessions and bestows immunity on the monastery. See also Seidel, '*Vui lesed*', p. 57.

87 See Arnold Angenendt, '*In honore Salvatoris*. Vom Sinn und Unsinn der Patrozinienkunde', *Revue d'histoire ecclésiastique* 97 (2002), 431–56 and 791–823, at pp. 799–807. See also Philippe Le Maitre, 'Image du Christ, image de l'empereur. L'exemple du culte du Saint-Saveur sous Louis le Pieux', *Revue d'histoire de l'église de France* 68 (1982), 201–12.

88 It should be mentioned here that in a somewhat later period at Essen influences from Byzantium have been detected, where the feast of saints Cosmas and Damian was celebrated (as in many Eastern churches) on 1 November. On Greek influence on the Essen All Saints litanies of the eleventh century and on the feast of Cosmas and Damian, see Richard Drögereit, 'Griechisch-Byzantinisches aus Essen', *Byzantinische Zeitschrift* 46 (1953), 110–15, at pp. 113–14.

But how should we envisage a situation of communication for which these vernacular texts may have been designed, and why were they copied into the manuscript without a Latin version of either text? Answers to these questions must necessarily be somewhat speculative, as we have to consider a scenario that would probably be quite different from the scene we might imagine for liturgical and administrative texts written in Latin.

Given that preaching in the vernacular was prescribed by a number of Carolingian texts, such as the bilingual (Old High German and Latin) model sermon known as *Exhortatio ad plebem christianam*, we should first take a closer look at the Old Saxon sermon text for All Saints' Day.[89] As mentioned, the feast of All Saints was adopted in the Frankish realm in the eighth century.[90] During the reign of Louis the Pious (814–40), attempts were made to make the celebration of All Saints' Day a general obligation within the Christian calendar.[91] We find traces of this in the synodal canons collected by Bishop Halitgar of Cambrai between 829 and 831 for his diocese: 'Every priest should have the [text of the] mass of All Saints along with the relevant sermons and, having fasted, should take care to celebrate it at the vigil venerably. He should notify all the people in his parish to abstain from work on this day.'[92] This provision makes clear that it may have been quite difficult indeed to put such a rule properly into effect. The same collection suggests that the priests themselves might have been part of the problem: 'We absolutely forbid those perverse and harmful meetings that priests have lately been in the habit of convening on the first day of the month for eating and drinking.'[93] The provision also points to the popularity of feasts such as All Saints within lay culture. A vernacular text

89 On this aspect see Diesenberger, *Predigt und Politik*, pp. 175–92. For this text, see *Die kleineren althochdeutschen Sprachdenkmäler*, ed. Elias von Steinmeyer (Berlin, 1916), no. 9, pp. 49–54. See Achim Masser, '*Exhortatio ad plebem christianam*', in *Althochdeutsche und altsächsische Literatur*, ed. Bergmann, pp. 83–85.

90 For the eighth century, see Hammer, '"For All the Saints"'.

91 See Cornelia Scherer, *Der Pontifikat Gregors IV. (827–844). Vorstellungen und Wahrnehmungen päpstlichen Handelns im 9. Jahrhundert* (Stuttgart, 2013), pp. 208–13.

92 Edited in Wilfried Hartmann, 'Neue Texte zur bischöflichen Reformgesetzgebung aus den Jahren 829/831. Vier Diözesansynoden Halitgars von Cambrai', *Deutsches Archiv für Erforschung des Mittelalters* 35 (1979), 368–94, at p. 389. Fourth synod, c. 2: 'Ut unusquisque sacerdos missam omnium sanctorum cum omeliis suis habeat eamque cum ieiunio in vigilia honorifice celebrare satagat, et in ipsa die feriare omnibus in sua parrochia denuntiet'.

93 Edited in Hartmann, 'Neue Texte', pp. 389–90. Fourth synod, c. 5: 'Interdicimus omnimodis perversa et noxia conventicula, quae in Kalendis bibendo et epulando nova adinventione agere sacerdotes soliti sunt'. On the position of local priests, see now *Men in the Middle: Local Priests in Early Medieval Europe*, eds Steffen Patzold and Carine van Rhijn (Berlin, 2016).

on All Saints' Day may have been a means of addressing this problem with regard to lay people. This could also explain why only the introductory portion of the Latin model was translated into Old Saxon, for this part served to justify the very existence of the feast with a historical explanation. Furthermore, since the Old Saxon text was translated from the introductory passage to a Latin sermon, it is not necessary to assume that the vernacular text must have functioned in the same way as a sermon. Rather, the short nature of this document attests to the great variety of admonition texts that range from 'sermon' to 'exhortation' and thus to a different situation of communication than is commonly assumed for most sermons.[94]

Little is known about the nature and conduct of such feasts, but there is some evidence that they also prompted the writing of vernacular texts. Wolfgang Haubrichs pointed to the fact that vernacular poetry such as the Old High German *Georgslied* and *Galluslied* (preserved only in a Latin version today), as well as the Old French 'Sequence of Eulalia' were commemorative texts, the refrains of which are reminiscent of liturgical and paraliturgical vernacular formulas. As they presuppose some knowledge of the martyr's story (which they do not mention), they focus on the saint's faith, suffering, and miracles, just like a song of heroes, justified by clerics and monks as part of lay culture during processions.[95]

Saints' feasts were thus recurring situations of communication between clerics and laymen, for which ecclesiastical texts were (re)composed in the vernacular to access lay culture.[96] Furthermore, a line of the Old High German phrasebook known as the 'Pariser Gespräche' refers to All Saints in the context of such a situation: 'Trenchet cher guole in gotes min[n]e. in al[l]er goten

94 See Thomas Martin Buck, *Admonitio und Praedicatio: Zur religiös-pastoralen Dimension von Kapitularien und kapitulariennahen Texten (507–814)* (Frankfurt am Main, 1997); Diesenberger, *Predigt und Politik*, pp. 193–213; and the contributions to *Sermo doctorum. Compilers, Preachers, and their Audiences in the Early Medieval West*, eds Maximilian Diesenberger, Yitzhak Hen, and Marianne Pollheimer (Turnhout, 2013).

95 Wolfgang Haubrichs, 'Heiligenfest und Heiligenlied im frühen Mittelalter. Zur Genese mündlicher und literarischer Formen in einer Kontaktzone laikaler und klerikaler Kultur', in *Feste und Feiern im Mittelalter*, eds Detlef Altenburg, Jörg Jarnut, and Hans-Hugo Steinhoff (Sigmaringen, 1991), pp. 133–43.

96 On liturgical processions in Essen, for which we only have documents from the high medieval period, see Jürgen Bärsch, '… *processiones et stationes fiunt quatuor modis in monasterio*. Beobachtungen zu Theologie und Liturgie prozessionaler Vollzüge im *Liber ordinarius* des Frauenstifts Essen', in *Liturgie in mittelalterlichen Frauenstiften. Forschungen zum Liber ordinarius*, ed. Klaus Gereon Breuckers (Essen, 2012), pp. 49–69.

helien. mine s[an]c[t]e maria frauv[e]. un[d] der ihuer [m]in[n]e hu'.[97] These pieces of evidence provide useful background for understanding why the sermon text on All Saints' Day was composed as an abbreviated text in the vernacular. Since the manuscript contains only the first chapter of the sermon in the vernacular and does not include one of the widely circulating Latin versions,[98] one must assume that the text addressed a situation in which there was no place for a long homily in the vernacular. Instead, it sought to justify the feast of All Saints and to encourage the attendance of church on this day to a group of lay people.

The Old Saxon glosses of Gregory's homilies in the manuscript show that the person in charge of the manuscript sought to explain the sermons' contents in the vernacular.[99] Despite the fact that many, if not most Essen manuscripts were written by women, it remains possible that some of the Essen *sanctimoniales* lacked sufficient command of Latin.[100] It could also be that the glosses served as a starting point for *ex tempore* preaching in the vernacular on those ecclesiastical feasts for which Gregory's homilies were used time and again, as is attested by other early medieval sermon collections.[101] In this respect, one cannot rule out the possibility that the manuscript's owner was less familiar with Old Saxon because it was not her mother tongue and she thus had a prompt prepared to facilitate her own vernacular preaching.

Does such a scenario also make sense for understanding the function of the Old Saxon register, however? The register's context seems to suggest a somewhat different situation of communication. It is striking that apart from the shorthand symbol for *similiter*, there are no other abbreviations in the register. Even the numbers are spelled out in full. Apparently, it was important to be able to pronounce the text without error during recitation. At the same time, the very strict visual organization of the register's entries, beginning with a

97 Edited in Wolfgang Haubrichs and Max Pfister, *"In Francia fui". Studien zu den romanisch-germanischen Interferenzen und zur Grundsprache der althochdeutschen "Pariser (Altdeutschen) Gespräche" nebst einer Edition des Textes* (Wiesbaden, 1989), p. 90, ll. 106–7. The Latin translation interestingly left out 'all saints': 'id est. bibite in d(e)i amore do(mne) s(an)c(t)e marie mee a(mo)re (et) in a(mo)re v(est)ra'. See also the contribution by Wolfgang Haubrichs to this volume.

98 See the references above at n. 45.

99 *Katalog der althochdeutschen und altsächsischen Glossenhandschriften*, eds Rolf Bergmann and Stefanie Stricker, 6 vols (Berlin, 2005), no. 104, 1:321–33: the Düsseldorf manuscript contains a total of 58 Old Saxon glosses (written with stylus and a leaden nib, but also in ink) added to the sermons of Gregory the Great, apparently in the tenth century at Essen. According to the authors, there are no Latin glosses.

100 Bodarwé, *Sanctimoniales litteratae*, pp. 110–65.

101 See Diesenberger, *Predigt und Politik*, pp. 161–63.

systematic entry of the Viehhof and followed by *similiter*, suggests that the manuscript's user could easily locate and enunciate particular entries, for instance, in the presence of an official.

How should we imagine the deliveries of these renders in kind on feast days, and which groups should we envisage making them? We probably do not need to imagine here the Essen *cerocensuales* ('Wachszinser'), a special category of ecclesiastical dependents directly subordinate to saints Cosmas and Damian, who, according to a special legal privilege ('Wachszinsrecht'), paid an annual poll tax in either cash or wax during the mass celebration at the altar, but no renders in kind.[102] The renders and produce described in the register would have been too big to offer directly in the church. Rather, one should envisage an administrative context outside of mass. But which group of persons might have been addressed by the register? One should remember that these renders were not directly offered by the peasants, but rather had to be delivered by nine of Essen's principal manors to the brewery, as they were to a large extent goods that had been produced or manufactured at these manors. This makes it likely that the register was not composed for a specific occasion of thanksgiving, but instead for the recurring instances on certain feast days (or shortly before) when those lay persons responsible for the nine manors delivered renders in kind, natural products, combustibles, and containers to the brewery, which would soon begin the process of brewing.[103] The register may thus have been written in the vernacular because the manuscript's owner expected that he or, more likely, she would soon have to communicate with the lay administrators of these nine manors.

It should be emphasized that the Old Saxon register was most likely not written in the vernacular because it was the direct result of an oral inquest, as we can otherwise observe in the cases of early medieval boundary descriptions

102 The oldest extant piece of evidence dates to between 1011 and 1039: *Rheinisches Urkundenbuch. Ältere Urkunden bis 1100, Vol. 2: Elten—Köln*, ed. Erich Wisplinghoff (Düsseldorf, 1994), no. 171, pp. 55–56; *Essener Urkundenbuch*, ed. Schilp, no. 27, pp. 18–19. See Helmut Weigel, 'Das Wachszinsrecht im Stift Essen', *Beiträge zur Geschichte von Stadt und Stift Essen* 67 (1952), 23–136, at pp. 64 and 116; Gudrun Wittig, 'Frauen und Freiheit im Mittelalter. Fallstudie am Beispiel der "Wachszinsigkeit" in Stift Essen und Kirchspiel Gladbeck', in *Vergessene Frauen an der Ruhr. Von Herrscherinnen und Hörigen, Hausfrauen und Hexen 800–1800*, ed. Bea Lundt (Cologne, 1992), pp. 77–97, at 81. See in general Stefan Esders, *Die Formierung der Zensualität. Zur kirchlichen Transformation des spätrömischen Patronatswesens im früheren Mittelalter* (Ostfildern, 2010), pp. 13, 65, and 82.

103 It was usual to start the process of brewing soon after malting. On the legal aspects of brewing, see Andreas Deutsch, 'Brauen', *Handwörterbuch der deutschen Rechtsgeschichte*, Vol. 1, eds Albrecht Cordes, Heiner Lück, and Dieter Werkmüller, 2nd ed. (Berlin, 2008), pp. 671–73.

where the scribe slips from Latin into the vernacular when noting down place-names,[104] or in the vernacular registers from Werden dealt with above, which blend Latin and vernacular terms.[105] The Essen register is fundamentally different, as it betrays a very systematic structure with entries arranged uniformly.[106] While the calculation of these deliveries was probably based on the results of an inquest carried out some time before, the register itself was clearly not the result of an inquest, but rather a product of record-keeping. For this reason, it seems likely that this text was actually 're-oralized' for the administration of the brewery, meaning that a text originally written in Latin was completely translated into the vernacular in preparation for a recurring situation of vernacular communication. It was necessary for the text to be comprehensible to lay people who did not know Latin, be they the manor administrators or the brewers. It is thus possible that the Old Saxon register was originally derived from a larger Latin register, a portion of which was translated into the vernacular. The brevity of the vernacular register can only be explained if we assume that it had a very special and confined administrative and communicative purpose, designed for a higher level of manorial organization, between the female provost and the lay administrators of the monastery manors and the staff of the brewery.[107] The register thus also entails some sort of performative quality, as it could allow one to memorize the size and quantities of deliverables and to pronounce them on certain feast days. Here, we should of course think of All Saints' Day, as suggested by the vernacular sermon text also found in the manuscript, but such knowledge was also useful for the other feast days referred to in the register. Considered from this perspective, the Old Saxon register was the carefully elaborated result of advanced manorial administration, so to speak,[108] for a periodic transactional situation related to the monastery's brewery.[109]

104 See above, n. 18.

105 Kuchenbuch, 'Ordnungsverhalten im grundherrlichen Schriftgut', p. 232.

106 See also Bodarwé, *Sanctimoniales litteratae*, p. 198.

107 It thus seems well conceivable that the provost also supervised the brewery: see Seidel, '*Vui lesed*', p. 54.

108 See Ludolf Kuchenbuch, 'Teilen, Aufzählen, Summieren. Zum Verfahren in ausgewählten Güter- und Einkünfteverzeichnissen des 9. Jahrhunderts', in *Schriftlichkeit im frühen Mittelalter*, ed. Ursula Schaefer (Tübingen, 1993), pp. 181–206, at 193–95 on the manorial registers' standardized modes in systematizing and storing the peasants' knowledge that originally had to be gained by oral inquest.

109 It seems remarkable that the deliveries by the nine manors as contained in the Old Saxon register are to a considerable extent also to be found in Essen's late medieval 'Kettenbuch' (chained book), suggesting that the amounts and size of several deliverable goods remained constant over centuries. See Helmut Weigel, 'Aufbau und Wandlungen der

Conclusion

As quoted at the outset of this chapter, Wolfgang Metz argued that early medieval manorial documentation remained confined to Old Saxon-speaking areas due to the influence of Anglo-Saxon missionaries. Although we have no parallels in Old High German-speaking areas, the different character of the two earliest cases dealt with here should be emphasized. The Werden example arose from the fact that a register of distant property was produced in a region with distinct linguistic features, which led the scribe to slip into the vernacular when recording place-names. By contrast, the Essen register was deliberately composed in the vernacular to assist the female provost when she would meet the individuals responsible for the nine manors that supplied the brewery, as delivery of the required produce was needed on feast days, most notably that of the monastery's patrons, All Saints' Day. If we add to this the eleventh-century Freckenhorst register, the first Saxon document of manorial organization written almost completely in the vernacular, it becomes clear that a region's particular cultural and linguistic features or the presence of agents involved in the process of Christianization should be considered only as possible preconditions for writing in the vernacular, even in manorial administration. Even in these regions, for a long time it made much more sense to write in Latin rather than in Saxon, making use of an established Latin technical vocabulary of administration. The earliest examples dealt with here are exceptions to the rule and thus cannot be explained simply by reference to general cultural traits in the process of the Christianization of Saxony. It tends to be individual circumstances that lead scribes to depart from Latin custom and to write in the vernacular instead. As my colleague Heike Mierau and I previously noted in a study of the early ninth-century Old High German *Klerikereid*, one should perhaps not focus on vernacular texts as a genre or even as a distinct category of texts at such an early date, but rather seek to find contexts and situations where those trained in Latin (that is, predominantly clerics) and those who spoke only a vernacular would encounter each other.[110] Emphasis should thus be laid on single texts, and we should identify methods to contextualize

---

Grundherrschaft des Frauenstifts Essen (852–1803)', in *Das erste Jahrtausend. Kunst und Kultur im werdenden Abendland an Rhein und Ruhr*, eds Kurt Böhner and Victor H. Elbern, 3 vols (Düsseldorf, 1962), 1:256–95, at pp. 266–68; see also Küppers-Braun, *Macht in Frauenhand*, pp. 24–25.

110 See Stefan Esders and Heike Johanna Mierau, *Der althochdeutsche Klerikereid. Bischöfliche Diözesangewalt, kirchliches Benefizialwesen und volkssprachliche Rechtspraxis im frühmittelalterlichen Baiern* (Hanover, 2000), pp. 230–41; and Stephan Müller, 'Klerikereid (auch Priestereid)', in *Althochdeutsche und altsächsische Literatur*, ed. Bergmann, pp. 230–31.

these texts individually in a maximalist approach—not only by taking manuscript tradition into account,[111] but also by imagining situations in which the line between Latin and vernacular could not be drawn too firmly and rather began to blur. These situations, after all, were the moments when ecclesiastical institutions most visibly became parts of a larger society, involved in different areas of life and types of communication.[112]

Bibliography

Primary Sources

Essener Urkundenbuch. Regesten der Urkunden des Frauenstifts Essen im Mittelalter, Vol. 1: Von der Gründung um 850 bis 1350, ed. Thomas Schilp (Düsseldorf, 2010).

Die kleineren althochdeutschen Sprachdenkmäler, ed. Elias von Steinmeyer (Berlin, 1916).

Kleinere altsächsische Sprachdenkmäler mit Anmerkungen und Glossar, ed. Elis Wadstein (Norden and Leipzig, 1899).

Rheinisches Urkundenbuch. Ältere Urkunden bis 1100, Vol. 2: Elten—Köln, ed. Erich Wisplinghoff (Düsseldorf, 1994).

Die Urbare der Abtei Werden a. d. Ruhr, A: Die Urbare vom 9.-13. Jahrhundert, ed. Rudolf Kötzschke (Bonn, 1906).

Die Urkunden Konrad I., Heinrich I. und Otto I., ed. Theodor Sickel, MGH Diplomata regum et imperatorum Germaniae 1 (Hanover, 1879–84).

Die Urkunden Zwentibolds und Ludwigs des Kindes, ed. Theodor Schieffer, MGH Diplomata regum Germaniae ex stirpe Karolinorum 4 (Berlin, 1960).

111 See Ernst Hellgardt, 'Althochdeutsche Texte in liturgischen und kanonistischen Handschriften (8.–12. Jh.)', in *Liturgie und Literatur. Historische Fallstudien*, eds Cornelia Herberichs, Norbert Kössinger, and Stephanie Seidl (Berlin, 2015), pp. 23–46; see also Roberts, 'Boundary Clauses', p. 592. For a general perspective (not particularly concerned with the vernacular), see also Hanns Peter Neuheuser, 'Rechtssicherung durch Sakralisierung. Die Eintragung von Rechtstexten in liturgische Handschriften', *Zeitschrift der Savigny-Stiftung für Rechtsgeschichte, Kanonistische Abteilung* 90 (2004), 355–405.

112 This article was written as part of the research project 'After Empire: Using and not using the past in the crisis of the Carolingian world, c.900–c.1050', funded by the Humanities in the European Research Area (HERA). I am extremely grateful to Edward Roberts and Francesca Tinti for inviting me to the 2016 IMC Leeds sessions on 'Languages and Literacy in the Early Medieval West', and to Maximilian Diesenberger, Hans-Werner Goetz, Wolfgang Haubrichs, and Ludolf Kuchenbuch for advice on various matters. I would also like to thank Edward Roberts both for correcting my English and for clarifying criticism on several points.

Secondary Sources

Ahlsson, Lars-Erik, 'Die altsächsische Bedahomilie', *Niederdeutsche Mitteilungen* 29 (1973), 30–41.

Angenendt, Arnold, '*In honore Salvatoris*. Vom Sinn und Unsinn der Patrozinienkunde', *Revue d'histoire ecclésiastique* 97 (2002), 431–56 and 791–823.

Arens, Franz, 'Das Heberegister des Stiftes Essen, nach dem Kettenbuch im Essener Münsterarchiv, 1332', *Beiträge zur Geschichte von Stadt und Stift Essen* 34 (1912), 1–111.

Bärsch, Jürgen, 'Die Essener Münsterkirche als Ort des Gottesdienstes. Zur Feier der Liturgie im mittelalterlichen Stift Essen', in *Herrschaft, Bildung und Gebet. Gründung und Anfänge des Frauenstifts Essen*, eds Günter Berghaus, Thomas Schilp, and Michael Schlagheck (Essen, 2000), pp. 71–85.

Bärsch, Jürgen, '... *processiones et stationes fiunt quatuor modis in monasterio*. Beobachtungen zu Theologie und Liturgie prozessionaler Vollzüge im *Liber ordinarius* des Frauenstifts Essen', in *Liturgie in mittelalterlichen Frauenstiften. Forschungen zum Liber ordinarius*, ed. Klaus Gereon Breuckers (Essen, 2012), pp. 49–69.

Bauer, Reinhard, *Die ältesten Grenzbeschreibungen in Bayern und ihre Aussagen für Namenkunde und Geschichte* (Munich, 1988).

Bauer, Reinhard, 'Frühmittelalterliche Grenzbeschreibungen als Quelle für die Namensforschung', in *Frühmittelalterliche Grenzbeschreibungen und Namenforschung*, ed. Friedhelm Debus (Heidelberg, 1992), pp. 35–60.

Bauer, Thomas, *Die mittelalterlichen Gaue* (Cologne, 2000).

Bergmann, Rolf, 'Überblick über die Gregor-Glossierung', in *Die althochdeutsche und altsächsische Glossographie. Ein Handbuch*, eds Rolf Bergmann and Stefanie Stricker, 2 vols (Berlin, 2009), 1:525–48.

Bergmann, Rolf and Stricker, Stefanie (eds), *Katalog der althochdeutschen und altsächsischen Glossenhandschriften*, 6 vols (Berlin, 2005).

Bettecken, Winfried, *Stift und Stadt Essen. Coenobium Astnide und Sieldungsentwicklung bis 1244* (Münster, 1988).

Bischoff, Bernhard, 'Paläographische Fragen deutscher Denkmäler der Karolingerzeit', *Frühmittelalterliche Studien* 5 (1971), 101–34.

Bodarwé, Katrinette, 'Roman Martyrs and their Veneration in Ottonian Saxony: The Case of the *sanctimoniales* of Essen', *EME* 9 (2000), 345–65.

Bodarwé, Katrinette, *Sanctimoniales litteratae. Schriftlichkeit und Bildung in den ottonischen Frauenkommunitäten Gandersheim, Essen und Quedlinburg* (Münster, 2004).

Bodarwé, Katrinette, 'Werden und Essen', in *Deutsche Schreiborte des Mittelalters. Skriptorien—Werke—Mäzene*, ed. Martin Schubert (Berlin, 2013), pp. 549–78.

Brown, Warren C., Costambeys, Marios, Innes, Matthew, Kosto, Adam J. (eds), *Documentary Culture and the Laity in the Early Middle Ages* (Cambridge, 2013).

Buck, Thomas Martin, *Admonitio und Praedicatio: Zur religiös-pastoralen Dimension von Kapitularien und kapitulariennahen Texten (507–814)* (Frankfurt am Main, 1997).

Buhlmann, Michael, 'Die älteste Immunitätsurkunde für das Kloster Werden an der Ruhr', *Das Münster am Hellweg* 52 (1999), 55–74.

Buhlmann, Michael, 'Liudger und seine Klostergründung Werden', in *Heiliger Liudger: Zeuge des Glaubens, 742–809. Gedenkschrift zum 1200. Todestag*, ed. Rudolf Ludger Schütz (Essen, 2009), pp. 162–67.

Cross, James E., '*Legimus in ecclesiasticis historiis*: A Sermon for All Saints, and its Use in Old English Prose', *Traditio* 33 (1977), 101–35.

Davis, Ralph H. C., 'Domesday Book: Continental Parallels', in *Domesday Studies: Papers Read at the Novocentenary Conference of the Royal Historical Society and the Institute of British Geographers, Winchester, 1986*, ed. James C. Holt (Woodbridge, 1987), pp. 15–39.

Derks, Paul, '*In pago Borahtron*. Zu einigen Ortsnamen der Hellweg- und Emscherzone', *Beiträge zur Geschichte von Stadt und Stift Essen* 99 (1984), 1–78.

Deutsch, Andreas, 'Brauen', *Handwörterbuch der deutschen Rechtsgeschichte*, Vol. 1, eds Albrecht Cordes, Heiner Lück, and Dieter Werkmüller, 2nd ed. (Berlin, 2008), pp. 671–73.

Diesenberger, Maximilian, *Predigt und Politik im frühmittelalterlichen Bayern. Arn von Salzburg, Karl der Große und die Salzburger Sermones-Sammlung* (Berlin, 2015).

Diesenberger, Maximilian, Hen, Yitzhak, and Pollheimer, Marianne (eds), *Sermo doctorum. Compilers, Preachers, and their Audiences in the Early Medieval West* (Turnhout, 2013).

Drögereit, Richard, 'Griechisch-Byzantinisches aus Essen', *Byzantinische Zeitschrift* 46 (1953), 110–15.

Erhart, Peter, Heidecker, Karl, and Zeller, Bernhard (eds), *Die Privaturkunden der Karolingerzeit* (Dietikon-Zürich, 2009).

Esders, Stefan, *Die Formierung der Zensualität. Zur kirchlichen Transformation des spätrömischen Patronatswesens im früheren Mittelalter* (Ostfildern, 2010).

Esders, Stefan, 'La loi des Chamaves', in *Les lois barbares*, eds Sylvie Joye, Marcelo Cândido da Silva, and Bruno Dumézil (forthcoming).

Esders, Stefan, 'Die römischen Wurzeln der karolingischen *inquisitio* in Fiskalsachen', in *L'enquête au moyen âge*, ed. Claude Gauvard (Rome, 2008), pp. 13–28.

Esders, Stefan, '*Te usero herano misso*. Überlieferungs- und Gebrauchskontext des Essener altsächsischen Heberegisters aus dem 10. Jahrhundert', *Frühmittelalterliche Studien* 51 (2017), 57–86.

Esders, Stefan, and Mierau, Heike Johanna, *Der althochdeutsche Klerikereid. Bischöfliche Diözesangewalt, kirchliches Benefizialwesen und volkssprachliche Rechtspraxis im frühmittelalterlichen Baiern* (Hanover, 2000).

Faulkner, Thomas, *Law and Authority in the Early Middle Ages: The Frankish* leges *in the Carolingian Period* (Cambridge, 2016).

Goetz, Hans-Werner, 'Kirchenfest und weltliches Alltagsleben im früheren Mittelalter', *Mediävistik* 2 (1989), 123–71.

Goetz, Hans-Werner, 'Das Ruhrgebiet im frühen Mittelalter', *Jahrbuch des Vereins für Orts- und Heimatkunde in der Grafschaft Mark mit Sitz in Witten an der Ruhr* 86 (1988), 7–36.

Goetz, Hans-Werner, 'Das Ruhrgebiet im frühen Mittelalter. Zur Erschließung einer Randlandschaft', *Blätter für deutsche Landesgeschichte* 126 (1990), 123–60.

Hägermann, Dieter, 'Quellenkritische Bemerkungen zu den karolingerzeitlichen Urbaren und Güterverzeichnissen', in *Strukturen der Grundherrschaft im frühen Mittelalter*, ed. Werner Rösener (Göttingen, 1989), pp. 47–73.

Hammer, Carl I., '"For All the Saints". Bishop Vivolo of Passau and the Eighth-Century Origins of the Feast', *Revue Mabillon* n. s. 15 (= 76) (2004), 5–26.

Hartig, Joachim, 'Die Gliederung des Freckenhorster Heberegisters', in *Festschrift für Gerhard Cordes zum 65. Geburtstag, Vol. 2: Sprachwissenschaft*, eds Friedhelm Debus and Joachim Hartig (Neumünster, 1976), pp. 96–111.

Hartmann, Wilfried, 'Neue Texte zur bischöflichen Reformgesetzgebung aus den Jahren 829/831. Vier Diözesansynoden Halitgars von Cambrai', *Deutsches Archiv für Erforschung des Mittelalters* 35 (1979), 368–94.

Haubrichs, Wolfgang, 'Heiligenfest und Heiligenlied im frühen Mittelalter. Zur Genese mündlicher und literarischer Formen in einer Kontaktzone laikaler und klerikaler Kultur', in *Feste und Feiern im Mittelalter*, eds Detlef Altenburg, Jörg Jarnut, and Hans-Hugo Steinhoff (Sigmaringen, 1991), pp. 133–43.

Haubrichs, Wolfgang, and Pfister, Max, *"In Francia fui". Studien zu den romanisch-germanischen Interferenzen und zur Grundsprache der althochdeutschen "Pariser (Altdeutschen) Gespräche" nebst einer Edition des Textes* (Wiesbaden, 1989).

Hellgardt, Ernst, 'Althochdeutsche Texte in liturgischen und kanonistischen Handschriften (8.–12. Jh.)', in *Liturgie und Literatur. Historische Fallstudien*, eds Cornelia Herberichs, Norbert Kössinger, and Stephanie Seidl (Berlin, 2015), pp. 23–46.

Hellgardt, Ernst, 'Bemerkungen zum Text des Freckenhorster Heberegisters (Handschrift M)', *Amsterdamer Beiträge zur älteren Germanistik* 52 (1999), 63–96.

Hellgardt, Ernst, 'Freckenhorster Heberegister und Heberolle', in *Althochdeutsche und altsächsische Literatur*, ed. Rolf Bergmann (Berlin, 2013), pp. 88–91.

Hoffmann, Hartmut, *Schreibschulen und Buchmalerei. Handschriften und Texte des 9.–11. Jahrhunderts*, MGH Schriften 65 (Hanover, 2012).

Hoffmann, Hartmut, 'Das Skriptorium von Essen in ottonischer und frühsalischer Zeit', in *Kunst im Zeitalter der Kaiserin Theophanu*, eds Anton von Euw and Peter Schreiner (Cologne, 1993), pp. 113–53.

Hoppenbrauwers, Peter, '*Leges nationum* and Ethnic Personality of Law in Charlemagne's Empire', in *Law and Empire: Ideas, Practices, Actors, Rulers and Elites*, eds Jeroen Duindam, Jill Harries, Caroline Humfress, and Nimrod Hurvitz (Leiden, 2013), pp. 251–74.

Hostra, Tette, '*Vui lesed.* Zur volkssprachlichen Allerheiligenhomilie', in *Speculum Saxonum. Studien zu den kleineren altsächsischen Sprachdenkmälern*, ed. Arend Quak (Amsterdam, 1999), pp. 105–15.

Huth, Volkhard, 'Die Düsseldorfer Sakramentarhandschrift D 1 als Memorialzeugnis. Mit einer Wiedergabe der Namen und Namengruppen', *Frühmittelalterliche Studien* 20 (1986), 213–98.

Journel, Pierre, 'Le culte collectif des saints à Rome du VIIIe au IXe siècle', in *Le jugement, le ciel et l'enfer dans l'histoire du christianisme* (Angers, 1989), pp. 19–30.

Kammer, Carl, *Die Litanei von Allen Heiligen* (Innsbruck, 1962).

Kennedy, Vincent Lorne, *The Saints of the Canon of the Mass*, 2nd ed. (Vatican City, 1963).

Klein, Thomas, *Studien zur Wechselbeziehung zwischen altsächsischem und althochdeutschem Schreibwesen und ihrer sprach- und kulturgeschichtlichen Bedeutung* (Göppingen, 1977).

Knopp, Gisbert, '*Sanctorum nomina seriatim.* Die Anfänge der Allerheiligenlitanei und ihre Verbindung mit den *Laudes regiae*', *Römische Quartalschrift für christliche Altertumskunde und Kirchengeschichte* 65 (1970), 185–231.

Kötzschke, Rudolf, *Studien zur Verwaltungsgeschichte der Großgrundherrschaft Werden an der Ruhr* (Leipzig, 1901).

Krüger, Astrid, *Litanei-Handschriften der Karolingerzeit* (Hanover, 2007).

Krüger, Astrid, '*Sancte Nazari ora pro nobis*: Ludwig der Deutsche und der Lorscher Rotulus', in *Ludwig der Deutsche und seine Zeit*, ed. Wilfried Hartmann (Darmstadt, 2004), pp. 184–202.

Kuchenbuch, Ludolf, 'Abschied von der "Grundherrschaft". Ein Prüfgang durch das ostfränkisch-deutsche Reich, 950–1050', *Zeitschrift der Savigny-Stiftung für Rechtsgeschichte, Germanistische Abteilung* 121 (2004), 1–99.

Kuchenbuch, Ludolf, 'Die Klostergrundherrschaft im Frühmittelalter', in *Herrschaft und Kirche. Beiträge zur Entstehung und Wirkungsweise episkopaler und monastischer Organisationsformen*, ed. Friedrich Prinz (Stuttgart, 1988), pp. 297–343.

Kuchenbuch, Ludolf, 'Ordnungsverhalten im grundherrlichen Schriftgut vom 9. zum 12. Jahrhundert', in *Dialektik und Rhetorik im früheren und hohen Mittelalter. Rezeption, Überlieferung und gesellschaftliche Wirkung antiker Gelehrsamkeit vornehmlich im 9. und 12. Jahrhundert*, ed. Johannes Fried (Munich, 1997), pp. 175–268.

Kuchenbuch, Ludolf, 'Teilen, Aufzählen, Summieren. Zum Verfahren in ausgewählten Güter- und Einkünfteverzeichnissen des 9. Jahrhunderts', in *Schriftlichkeit im frühen Mittelalter*, ed. Ursula Schaefer (Tübingen, 1993), pp. 181–206.

Kuchenbuch, Ludolf, 'Verrechtlichung von Erinnerung im Medium der Schrift (9. Jahrhundert)', in *Mnemosyne. Formen und Funktionen der kulturellen Erinnerung*, eds Aleida Assmann and Dietrich Harth (Frankfurt am Main, 1991), pp. 36–47.

Küppers-Braun, Ute, *Macht in Frauenhand. 1000 Jahre Herrschaft adliger Frauen in Essen* (Essen, 2002).

Le Maitre, Philippe, 'Image du Christ, image de l'empereur. L'exemple du culte du Saint-Saveur sous Louis le Pieux', *Revue d'histoire de l'église de France* 68 (1982), 201–12.

Masser, Achim, '*Exhortatio ad plebem christianam*', in *Althochdeutsche und altsächsische Literatur*, ed. Rolf Bergmann (Berlin, 2013), pp. 83–85.

Metz, Wolfgang, 'Karolingische Güterinventare als Quellen zur Geschichte der althochdeutschen Hermeneumata', *Deutsche Vierteljahrsschrift für Literaturwissenschaft und Geistesgeschichte* 29 (1955), 151–66.

Metz, Wolfgang, 'Zur Geschichte und Kritik der frühmittelalterlichen Güterverzeichnisse Deutschlands', *Archiv für Diplomatik* 4 (1958), 183–206.

Müller, Hartmut, 'Die Mettlacher Güterrolle', *Zeitschrift für die Geschichte der Saargegend* 15 (1965), 110–46.

Müller, Stephan, 'Altsächsische Allerheiligenpredigt / Essener Heberolle', in *Für Königtum und Himmelreich. 1000 Jahre Bischof Meinwerk von Paderborn*, eds Martin Kroker and Christoph Stiegemann (Regensburg, 2009), pp. 308–10.

Müller, Stephan, 'Klerikereid (auch Priestereid)', in *Althochdeutsche und altsächsische Literatur*, ed. Rolf Bergmann (Berlin, 2013), pp. 230–31.

Naismith, Rory, 'The Ely Memoranda and the Economy of the Late Anglo-Saxon Fenland', *ASE* 45 (2016), 333–77.

Neuheuser, Hanns Peter, 'Rechtssicherung durch Sakralisierung. Die Eintragung von Rechtstexten in liturgische Handschriften', *Zeitschrift der Savigny-Stiftung für Rechtsgeschichte, Kanonistische Abteilung* 90 (2004), 355–405.

Overgaauw, Eef, Ott, Joachim, and Karpp, Gerhard, *Die mittelalterlichen Handschriften der Signaturengruppe B in der Universitäts- und Landesbibliothek Düsseldorf, Teil 1: Ms. B 1 bis B 100* (Wiesbaden, 2005).

Patzold, Steffen and van Rhijn, Carine (eds), *Men in the Middle: Local Priests in Early Medieval Europe* (Berlin, 2016).

Percival, John, 'The Precursors of Domesday: Roman and Carolingian Land Registers', in *Domesday Book: A Reassessment*, ed. Peter H. Sawyer (London, 1985), pp. 5–27.

Quak, Arend, 'Altniederländisch im neuen etymologischen Wörterbuch des Niederländischen', in *Current Trends in West Germanic Etymological Lexicography: Proceedings of the Symposium Held in Amsterdam, 12–13 June 1989*, eds Rolf H. Bremmer, Jr. and Jan van den Berg (Leiden, 1993), pp. 37–46.

Quak, Arend, 'Ortsnamen als Quelle des Altniederländischen', *Namn och bygd* 82 (1994), 31–50.

Rankin, Susan, '*Terribilis est locus iste*. The Pantheon in 609', in *Rhetoric Beyond Words: Delight and Persuasion in the Arts of the Middle Ages*, ed. Mary Carruthers (Cambridge, 2010), pp. 281–310.

Rembold, Ingrid, 'Rewriting the Founder: Werden on the Ruhr and the Uses of Hagiography', *Journal of Medieval History* 41 (2015), 363–87.

Roberts, Edward, 'Boundary Clauses and the Use of the Vernacular in Eastern Frankish Charters, *c.*750–*c.*900', *Historical Research* 91 (2018), 580–604.

Röckelein, Hedwig, 'Altfrid, Gründer des Stifts Essen und international agierender Kirchenmann?', in *Frauen bauen Europa. Internationale Verflechtungen des Frauenstifts Essen*, ed. Thomas Schilp (Essen, 2011), pp. 27–64.

Röckelein, Hedwig, 'Leben im Schutz der Heiligen. Reliquientranslationen nach Essen vom 9. bis 11. Jahrhundert', in *Herrschaft, Bildung und Gebet. Gründung und Anfänge des Frauenstifts Essen*, eds Günter Berghaus, Thomas Schilp, and Michael Schlagheck (Essen, 2000), pp. 87–100.

Rösener, Werner, 'Zur Struktur und Entwicklung der Grundherrschaft in Sachsen in karolingischer und ottonischer Zeit', in *La grande domaine aux époques mérovingienne et carolingienne. Die Grundherrschaft im frühen Mittelalter*, ed. Adriaan Verhulst (Ghent, 1985), pp. 173–207.

Santoro, Verio, 'La versione in sassone antico della prima lectio del sermone *In festiuitate omnium sanctorum*', *Romanobarbarica* 12 (1992–93), 223–49.

Scherer, Cornelia, *Der Pontifikat Gregors IV. (827–844). Vorstellungen und Wahrnehmungen päpstlichen Handelns im 9. Jahrhundert* (Stuttgart, 2013).

Schiegg, Markus, *Frühmittelalterliche Glossen. Ein Beitrag zur Funktionalität und Kontextualität mittelalterlicher Schriftlichkeit* (Heidelberg, 2015).

Schilp, Thomas, 'Die Grundherrschaftsorganisation des hochadligen Damenstifts Essen. Von der wirtschaftlichen Erschließung zur politisch-administrativen Erfassung des Raumes', in *Vergessene Zeiten. Mittelalter im Ruhrgebiet. Katalog zur Ausstellung im Ruhrlandmuseum Essen*, ed. Ferdinand Seibt, 2 vols (Essen, 1990), 1:89–92.

Schilp, Thomas, 'Männerkloster und Frauenstift. Werden und Essen', in *Das Jahrtausend der Mönche. Kloster Welt Werden 799–1803*, ed. Jan Gerchow (Essen and Cologne, 1999), pp. 74–79.

Schilp, Thomas, *Norm und Wirklichkeit religiöser Frauengemeinschaften im Frühmittelalter. Die Institutio sanctimonialium Aquisgranensis des Jahres 816 und die Problematik der Verfassung von Frauenkommunitäten* (Göttingen, 1998).

Schilp, Thomas, 'Überlegungen zur Sakramentarhandschrift D 1 als *Liber vitae* der Essener Frauenkommunität', in *Libri vitae. Gebetsgedenken in der Gesellschaft des Frühen Mittelalters*, eds Dieter Geuenich and Uwe Ludwig (Cologne, 2015), pp. 203–22.

Schröder, Werner, 'Die Verwandtschaft der althochdeutschen Glossen zu Gregors Homilien', *Beiträge zur Geschichte der deutschen Sprache und Literatur* 65 (1941), 1–105.

Schütz, Rudolf Ludger (ed.), *Heiliger Liudger: Zeuge des Glaubens, 742–809. Gedenkschrift zum 1200. Todestag* (Essen, 2009).

Seidel, Kurt Otto, '*Vui lesed* ... Geistiges Leben im Essener Damenstift im Spiegel einer Handschrift des 10. Jahrhunderts', *Essener Unikate* 26 (2005), 50–59.

Spannhoff, Christof, 'Zur Datierung des ältesten Werdener Urbars (A)', *Nordmünsterland. Forschungen und Funde* 2 (2015), 192–99.

Starostine, Dmitri, '... *in die festivitatis*: Gift-giving, Power and the Calendar in the Carolingian Kingdoms', *EME* 14 (2006), 465–86.

Stüwer, Wilhelm, *Die Reichsabtei Werden an der Ruhr* (Berlin, 1980).

Tiefenbach, Heinrich, 'Altsächsische Allerheiligenpredigt', in *Althochdeutsche und altsächsische Literatur*, ed. Rolf Bergmann (Berlin, 2013), pp. 16–18.

Tiefenbach, Heinrich, 'Frühmittelalterliche Volkssprache im Frauenstift Essen', in *Essen und die sächsischen Frauenstifte im Frühmittelalter*, eds Jan Gerchow and Thomas Schilp (Essen, 2003), pp. 113–28.

Tiefenbach, Heinrich, 'Werden und die Anfänge der altniederdeutschen Sprachgeschichte', in *Das Jahrtausend der Mönche. Kloster Welt Werden 799–1803*, ed. Jan Gerchow (Essen and Cologne, 1999), pp. 212–17.

Tinti, Francesca, 'Writing Latin and Old English in Tenth-Century England: Patterns, Formulae and Language Choice in the Leases of Oswald of Worcester', in *Writing Kingship and Power in Anglo-Saxon England*, eds Rory Naismith and David Woodman (Cambridge, 2018), pp. 303–27.

Wallraff, Martin, 'Pantheon und Allerheiligen. Einheit und Vielfalt des Göttlichen in der Spätantike', *Jahrbuch für Antike und Christentum* 47 (2004), 128–43.

Wasser, Johann Wilhelm, *Gründliche Anleitung zum Bierbrauen, zur Beförderung richtiger Grundsätze der vorzüglichen Bereitung des Braun-, Weiß und Englisch-Bier betreffend in systematischer Ordnung und in Berechnungen tabellarisch dargestellt* (Berlin, 1793).

Weigel, Helmut, 'Aufbau und Wandlungen der Grundherrschaft des Frauenstifts Essen (852–1803)', in *Das erste Jahrtausend. Kunst und Kultur im werdenden Abendland an Rhein und Ruhr*, eds Kurt Böhner and Victor H. Elbern, 3 vols (Düsseldorf, 1962), 1:256–95.

Weigel, Helmut, *Studien zur Verfassung und Verwaltung des Grundbesitzes des Frauenstiftes Essen (852–1803)* (Essen, 1960).

Weigel, Helmut, 'Das Wachszinsrecht im Stift Essen', *Beiträge zur Geschichte von Stadt und Stift Essen* 67 (1952), 23–136.

Wittig, Gudrun, 'Frauen und Freiheit im Mittelalter. Fallstudie am Beispiel der "Wachszinsigkeit" in Stift Essen und Kirchspiel Gladbeck', in *Vergessene Frauen an der Ruhr. Von Herrscherinnen und Hörigen, Hausfrauen und Hexen 800–1800*, ed. Bea Lundt (Cologne, 1992), pp. 77–97.

Wittmann, Anneliese, *Kosmas und Damian. Kultausbreitung und Volksdevotion* (Berlin, 1967).

CHAPTER 11

Royal Authority, Regional Integrity: The Function and Use of Anglo-Saxon Writ Formulae

Albert Fenton

The corpus of Anglo-Saxon writs, edited by Florence Harmer in her groundbreaking edition of 1952, occupies a unique space within the rich diplomatic traditions of England before the Norman Conquest.[1] Composed invariably in the Old English vernacular, these short, nimble, epistolary-form texts addressed the power brokers of a local or regional court and communicated announcements or instructions from rulers or members of the ecclesiastical or non-royal elite. Their vernacular form meant that they could reach out and convey ideas and information to broader and more diverse audiences than the royal diplomas that they often complemented, which were formulated almost exclusively in Latin.[2] Indeed, a substantial proportion of the surviving corpus of writs functioned ostensibly as a support to the role performed by Latin royal diplomas—by proclaiming to the hierarchs of the shire that a transfer of land, and the cluster of legal and fiscal privileges associated with it, had legitimately taken place.[3] As a result of the complex processes of textual preservation, transmission, and loss in the intervening centuries, a large proportion of these writs announce such dispositive action in favour of the religious communities and institutions in whose archives they would come to be preserved.

1 Harmer's edition formed the culmination of a sequence of volumes of vernacular charters, produced under the aegis of H. M. Chadwick: see *ASWrits*; and Simon Keynes, 'Introduction', in *Select English Historical Documents of the Ninth and Tenth Centuries*, ed. Florence E. Harmer, 2nd ed. (Cambridge, 1914; rev. ed. 2011), pp. i–v. Subsequent studies of vernacular diplomatic are indebted to the trailblazing work of this group of scholars.

2 Although it is important to note that Latin royal diplomas often contained Old English segments (typically their boundary clauses and endorsements), as well as vernacular topographical terms, names and other features. A small proportion of writs survive only in Latin and these all represent later translations of Old English originals.

3 In doing so, such writs helped publicize royal grants in local society; to borrow a useful term from Peter Johanek, the texts helped make such grants 'landeskundig': Peter Johanek, 'Zur rechtlichen Funktion von Traditionsnotiz, Traditionsbuch und früher Siegelurkunde', in *Recht und Schrift im Mittelalter*, ed. Peter Classen (Sigmaringen, 1977), pp. 131–62, at 132.

 | DOI:10.1163/9789004432338_012

Yet the writ form was malleable and these documents also fulfilled a range of other functions in early English legal and political culture. These functions included, for example, providing testimony concerning disputes around land and tax, and giving authorization for a particular ecclesiast to draw up a *priuilegium* or diploma regarding a royal grant of land.[4] It is highly likely that these sub-groups of Anglo-Saxon writs represent the fossil record of what was once a much larger and more varied body of documents concerning immediate but ultimately transitory political and administrative concerns, which would have appeared curious but ultimately insignificant to archivists in the intervening centuries.[5]

The question of precisely *when* pre-Conquest writs emerged in diplomatic usage is difficult to answer. The earliest writs with a reasonable claim to authenticity date to the reign of King Æthelred II (*c*.978×1016), and writs continued to be issued in Old English by successive rulers thereafter, down to *c*.1070.[6] As demonstrated below, writs drew on several more ancient, well-established diplomatic formulations, which involved adapting and rendering Latin formulae into the vernacular to reach new audiences and articulate ideas in new settings.[7] It is certainly possible that rulers prior to Æthelred II sent out writs and other missives to regional courts and localities before the late

4 For writs that weigh-in on disputes, see S 1404, S 1383, and S 1242, the so-called 'Ruishton Letter', for which see also Andrew Rabin, 'Female Advocacy and Royal Protection in Tenth-Century England: The Legal Career of Queen Ælfthryth', *Speculum* 84 (2009), 261–88. For the three writs giving royal permission for a charter (referred to within these texts as a *priuilegium* or *boc*) to be created, see S 1105, S 1067, and S 1115; and for the wider significance of this latter function of writs, see Simon Keynes, 'Church Councils, Royal Assemblies, and Anglo-Saxon Royal Diplomas', in *Kingship, Legislation and Power in Anglo-Saxon England*, eds Gale R. Owen-Crocker and Brian W. Schneider (Manchester, 2013), pp. 17–182, at 45; Kelly, *Malm*, pp. 247–48.

5 O'Donovan, *Sherb*, p. 48; Susan Kelly, 'Anglo-Saxon Lay Society and the Written Word', in *The Uses of Literacy in Early Medieval Europe*, ed. Rosamond McKitterick (Cambridge, 1990), pp. 36–62, at 46–47.

6 The earliest (albeit problematic) extant royal writs are Æthelredian texts: S 945 (issued 978×1016) and S 946 (issued 984×1001). A writ of King Harold for Bishop Giso, S 1163, was one of the last surviving documents to be written before the Norman Conquest. King William I continued to issue writs in the Old English vernacular until a uniform shift to Latin *c*.1070.

7 For discussion of the origins of the Anglo-Saxon writ, see Maurizio Lupoi, *The Origins of the European Legal Order* (Cambridge, 2000), pp. 305 and 311. See also Richard Sharpe, 'The Use of Writs in the Eleventh Century', *ASE* 32 (2003), 247–91, who locates the reign of King Edgar (959–75) as the possible period of origin. More recently, George Molyneaux has illuminated the rapid evolution of documentary culture in that period, with specific discussion of writs and writ-charters; see his *The Formation of the English Kingdom in the Tenth Century* (Oxford, 2015), p. 168.

tenth century—but the function of these texts as orders and statements rather than announcements of grants meant that even interested parties did not seek to preserve them.

This chapter seeks to investigate the language of Anglo-Saxon writs, and the distinctive patterns of formulae within them, to probe how those aforementioned relationships—in particular the relationship between the 'central' royal court and later Anglo-Saxon England's complex network of local and regional courts—were constructed and maintained. It will attempt therefore to re-assess Florence Harmer's remark that the appearance of sequences of such formulae, especially alliterative formulae, within writs can be taken to represent ossified forms of 'undoubtedly ancient alliterative jingles [...] arranged for remembrance among the Germanic peoples in rhythmical and alliterative patterns'.[8] Might it be possible to discern the function of such formulae? Who would have heard them, and what impact might they have had on their intended audiences? How might we conceptualize their setting-in-life?[9] In seeking to answer these questions, my analysis will draw on recent work concerning the use of symbolic language within Carolingian royal diplomas—in particular the question of the relative performativity of different diplomatic typologies, and the use of repetitive elements within them.[10]

8 *ASWrits*, p. 87.

9 This term, referring to the concept of *Sitz im Leben*, describes the contexts in which a given text or charter was originally generated and deployed, and its contemporaneous functions. Geoffrey Koziol recently emphasized the importance of such questions, and the potential performative functions of diplomatic formulae in his 'Making Boso the Clown: Performance and Performativity in a Pseudo-Diploma of the Renegade King (8 December 879)', in *Rituals, Performatives, and Political Order in Northern Europe, c. 650–1350*, eds Wojtek Jezierski, Lars Hermanson, Hans Jacob Orning, and Thomas Småberg (Turnhout, 2015), pp. 43–61, at 47.

10 'Performativity' here is defined as the propensity for a text or charter to be read aloud or performed at a forum or other public setting in order to announce, publicize or affect political action. My definition draws on the insights of, amongst others, Brian Stock, *The Implications of Literacy: Written Language and Models of Interpretation in the Eleventh and Twelfth Centuries* (Princeton, NJ, 1983), pp. 14–16, 42, 49–50; Geoffrey Koziol, *The Politics of Memory and Identity in Carolingian Royal Diplomas: The West Frankish Kingdom (840–987)* (Turnhout, 2012), pp. 3–5, 40–2; Levi Roach, *Kingship and Consent in Anglo-Saxon England, 871–978: Assemblies and the State in the Early Middle Ages* (Cambridge, 2013), pp. 11–20. The term itself derives from the work of John L. Austin, *How to Do Things with Words* (Cambridge, MA, 1962). For iterative language in diplomatic contexts and its relationship with the communication of authority, see Ildar H. Garipzanov, *The Symbolic Language of Authority in the Carolingian World (c. 751–877)* (Leiden, 2008), pp. 27–28.

Anglo-Saxon Writs on Single Sheets: Physical Appearance and Form

Before looking more closely at questions of language and formulae and how they might relate to the overall function of these texts, it is necessary first to consider the form, appearance, and character of one very important group of writs: those preserved on single sheets of parchment in script contemporary with their contents, the so-called single-sheet originals. Like the wider body of Anglo-Saxon charters, each writ has undergone a unique and partially obscured process of textual transmission, shaped by the ruptures and continuities of their respective archival histories.[11] Approximately 77 insular and continental institutional archives have preserved Anglo-Saxon charter material, and 27 of these preserved pre-Conquest writs amongst their diverse muniments (meaning that roughly 35 per cent of archives containing pre-Conquest diplomatic material preserved writs amongst their extant documentation).[12] Of the extant corpus of writs, seven have survived as single-sheet originals, all issued at the behest of Edward the Confessor (see, as an example, Figure 11.1).[13]

11 For the archival distribution of writs, see *ASWrits*, pp. xv–xvii, with the later addition to the corpus of Florence E. Harmer, 'A Bromfield and a Coventry Writ of King Edward the Confessor', in *The Anglo-Saxons: Studies in Some Aspects of Their History and Culture Presented to Bruce Dickins*, ed. Peter Clemoes (London, 1959), pp. 89–103. See also P. H. Sawyer, *Anglo-Saxon Charters: An Annotated List and Bibliography* (London, 1968), pp. 44–67.

12 These calculations are presented with the necessary caveat that they do not include those archives whose material was subsumed into other archives within the medieval period. When these archives are included in the calculation, the total number of archives preserving pre-Conquest charter material swells to some 86 known archives. In turn, this larger number does not include the likely far higher total number of ecclesiastical, royal, and non-royal lay archives that actually existed in Anglo-Saxon England. For discussion, see Keynes, 'Church Councils', pp. 53 and 62–63; Alexander R. Rumble, 'Anglo-Saxon Royal Archives: Their Nature, Extent, Survival and Loss', in *Kingship, Legislation and Power*, eds Owen-Crocker and Schneider, pp. 185–99; and for the wider European context to lay archives, see Warren C. Brown, Marios Costambeys, Matthew Innes, and Adam Kosto, 'Introduction', in *Documentary Culture and the Laity in the Early Middle Ages*, eds Warren C. Brown, Marios Costambeys, Matthew Innes, and Adam J. Kosto (Cambridge, 2013), pp. 1–16.

13 These are London, British Library, Cotton Augustus ii.80 (S 1071, *ASWrits* 11) and London, British Library, Cotton Augustus ii.49 (S 1084, *ASWrits* 24), both preserved at Bury St Edmunds; London, British Library, Campbell Charter xxi.5, preserved at Canterbury Christ Church (S 1088, *CantCC* 179); Paris, Archives nationales, Cartons de rois, K 19, no. 6 (S 1105, *ASWrits* 55), preserved at Saint-Denis, Paris; two Westminster writs: London, Westminster Abbey W. A. M. xviii (S 1125, *ASWrits* 81) and London, Westminster Abbey W. A. M. xii (S 1140, *ASWrits* 96); and London, British Library, Add. Ch. 19802,

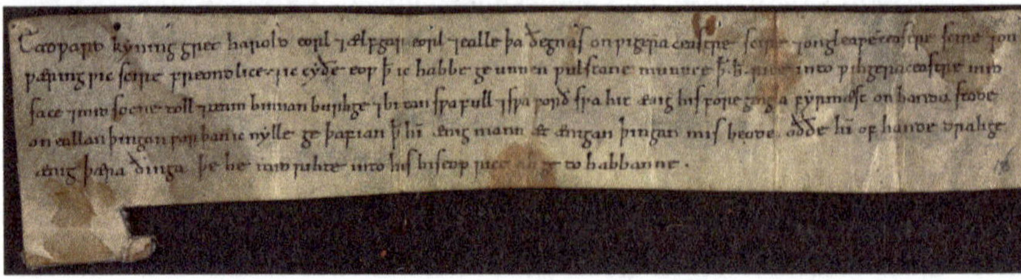

FIGURE 11.1 The face of London, British Library, Add. Ch. 19802 (S 1156, *Writs* 115). Writ of King Edward the Confessor concerning the monk Wulfstan, dated 1062

This group of seven documents, representing approximately six per cent of the surviving pre-Conquest writ corpus, was identified by Florence Harmer, and in 1957, was brought together by T. A. M. Bishop and Pierre Chaplais in their indispensable facsimile edition.[14] There, the single sheets issued by Edward the Confessor were presented alongside the larger corpus of seven extant contemporary single-sheet writs issued by William I, and 15 surviving contemporary single sheets issued by William II.

The first striking characteristic of the Edwardian single-sheet writs when observed as a group is their physical shape and proportions. They are small, highly compact documents that can be folded into a panel and easily stuffed into a pocket or small bag. When folded along their creases, they each have a measurement of between around 17 mm and 42 mm vertically, and 23 mm and 57 mm horizontally.[15] This relative uniformity is reflected by a concurrent uniformity of script size. Heights of minims typically stand at 2 mm, and ascenders vary slightly between 3 and 4.5 mm in height. The script used for all the texts is a tall, thin mid-eleventh-century Vernacular minuscule, developed in the early 990s and with strong similarities to the script found in late tenth-century charter-bounds from which they most likely evolved.[16] Possible

preserved at Worcester (S 1156, *ASWrits* 115) and reproduced as Figure 11.1. These texts can all be confidently dated to the period 1044×1066.

14 *ASWrits*, pp. 117–18; T. A. M. Bishop and Pierre Chaplais, *Facsimiles of English Royal Writs to A.D. 1100, Presented to Vivian Hunter Galbraith* (Oxford, 1957). For high-quality photographs of many of these documents, see the Digitised Manuscripts pages within the British Library website: https://blogs.bl.uk/files/list-of-anglo-saxon-charters.pdf.

15 Comparing the single-sheet writs to other typologies of pre-Conquest vernacular document, Susan D. Thompson notes that 'when other types of document are considered, no such uniformity is to be seen'; see her *Anglo-Saxon Vernacular Documents: A Palaeography* (Manchester, 2010), p. 7.

16 See Rebecca Rushforth, 'The Eleventh- and Early Twelfth-Century Manuscripts of Bury St Edmunds Abbey' (unpublished PhD thesis, University of Cambridge, 2002), p. 82; and

affinities and relationships between the respective hands of the single-sheet writs have previously been discussed, but none have proven conclusive, meaning that it is perfectly possible that each single-sheet writ was the product of a different scribe working under royal agency.[17] The king is consistently styled as *cyning* (albeit with orthographic variation), and there are two slight orthographic variations of Edward's name: *Eadpard* and *Eadpeard*. On five of the single sheets, small and delicate cross *signa* appear on the top line, directly in front of the king's name—this feature is also found, in the same location, on many contemporary single-sheet Latin royal diplomas as well as across other genres of vernacular charter.

A further distinctive feature of the single-sheet writs is the evidence of sealing, possible former sealing, and wrapping that appears on all but two of the documents. Of paramount significance are the three single sheets from Christ Church, Canterbury, Paris Saint-Denis, and Westminster.[18] All of these bear impressions of large (each between approximately 75 and 78 mm in diameter), imposing, double-faced wax royal seals, depicting Edward the Confessor crowned, enthroned, and carrying an orb and sceptre on the obverse, and sword and staff on the reverse.[19] Both sides of the wax impressions feature the circumscribed Latin legend + SIGILLVM EADVVARDI ANGLORVM BASILEI, invoking the Greek title for 'ruler' first employed by draftsmen of King Æthelstan (924–39) in some of his royal diplomas.[20] Seals—known in Latin as *sigillum*

in the context of earlier developments, Peter A. Stokes, *English Vernacular Minuscule from Æthelred to Cnut circa 990–circa 1035* (Cambridge, 2014), p. 202.

17 For example, the script of the non-erased portion of the Christ Church writ for Archbishop Stigand (S 1088, *CantCC* 179) has been tentatively compared to the two Bury St Edmunds single sheets (S 1071, *ASWrits* 11 and S 1084, *ASWrits* 24); see Bishop and Chaplais, *Facsimiles of English Royal Writs*, no. 3, and Simon Keynes, 'Regenbald the Chancellor (*sic*)', *Anglo-Norman Studies* 10 (1988), 185–222, at pp. 214–16. These scribal affinities are discussed in further detail in Chapter Two of my thesis, 'The Function of Writs in England before the Norman Conquest' (unpublished PhD thesis, University of Cambridge, forthcoming).

18 These are, respectively: S 1088 (*CantCC* 179), S 1105 (*ASWrits* 55), and S 1140 (*ASWrits* 96).

19 For images and discussion of the so-called 'second' (but only authentic) Edwardian seal impressions, see Simon Keynes, 'The Use of Seals in Anglo-Saxon England', in *Seals and Status: Power of Objects*, eds John Cherry, Jessica Berenbeim, and Lloyd De Beer (London, 2018), pp. 73–83, at 77–80; and for the sources of their symbolic iconography, see Brigitte Bedos-Rezak, 'The King Enthroned, a New Theme in Anglo-Saxon Royal Iconography: The Seal of Edward the Confessor and its Political Implications', in *Medieval Kings and Kingship*, ed. Joel Rosenthal (Binghamton, NY, 1986), pp. 53–88; reprinted in Brigitte Bedos-Rezak, *Form and Order in Medieval France: Studies in Social and Quantitative Sigillography* (Aldershot, 2003), IV.

20 For example, the royal diplomas S 429, S 430, and S 431. See Sarah Foot, *Æthelstan: The First King of England* (London, 2011), p. 213. The Graecism was also used by charter draftsmen of

and glossed in the vernacular as *insegel*—were clearly being produced, used, and circulated prior to this.[21] A small and coherent group of four non-royal seal matrices survives from the later Anglo-Saxon period, two cast in bronze and two in ivory, belonging to: Ælfric I, Godwine *minister* ('the thegn'), Wulfric and Ælfric II.[22] In addition, the seal of Godwine was later re-purposed, ostensibly for use by a certain Godgyth, styled *monacha Deo data* ('nun given to God').[23] It is clear from such evidence that the use of matrices to create wax seals was well-established, at least by the tenth and eleventh centuries, and that such items were in circulation amongst lay and ecclesiastical, as well as royal and non-royal, elites. Moreover, it has been noted that all these extant late Anglo-Saxon seal matrices, alongside the 'second' seal impression of Edward, share a common language.[24] They all feature a Latin inscription that begins with a cross *signum* and the word *sigillum*, followed by the Latinized name of the sigillant (e.g. ÆLFRICI or EÐILVVALDI).

With our small surviving sample, we can only speculate about why these inscriptions are so consistent—it may be the result of a conscious decision made by the seal-makers themselves, keen to standardize their creations and thus exercise a level of control over their production. Alternatively, it might reflect a more top-down attempt to construct (and then reproduce) a kind of commonly recognized symbolic language of authority, of the type described

other Cerdicing rulers including Edmund, Eadred, Eadwig, Edgar, and Æthelred II; for discussion see Ben Snook, *The Anglo-Saxon Chancery: The History, Language and Production of Anglo-Saxon Charters from Alfred to Edgar* (Woodbridge, 2015), p. 156; John R. Maddicott, *The Origins of the English Parliament, 924–1327* (Oxford, 2010), p. 44.

21 *Sigillum* ('little sign, figure, or seal, token') is a diminutive of *signum* ('sign, emblem'); see Jane Roberts, 'What did Anglo-Saxon Seals Seal When?', in *The Power of Words: Essays in Lexicography, Lexicology and Semantics in Honour of Christian J. Kay*, eds Graham D. Caie, Carole Hough, and Irené Wotherspoon (Amsterdam, 2006), pp. 131–57, alongside entries for *insegel* in the University of Toronto's *Dictionary of Old English Web Corpus*: http://tapor.library.utoronto.ca/doecorpus/.

22 In addition, the leaden *bulla* of Coenwulf, king of the Mercians (796–821), and a mid-ninth-century bronze seal matrix of Æthelwald, bishop of Dunwich, reveal that seals also fulfilled various functions in the earlier Anglo-Saxon period. A gold signet ring with the legend *Baldehildis*, recovered in Norfolk in 1998, may also have been used for sealing and possibly belonged to Queen Balthild of Neustria (d. *c.*680).

23 T. A. Heslop, 'English Seals from the Mid Ninth Century to 1100', *Journal of the British Archaeological Association* 133 (1980), 1–16. Note also the recent addition of a second seal-matrix in the name of Ælfric, a layman; see Jane Kershaw and Rory Naismith, 'A New Late Anglo-Saxon Seal Matrix', *ASE* 42 (2013), 291–98. For a panoramic overview with images, see Keynes, 'The Use of Seals'.

24 See P. D. A. Harvey, 'This Is a Seal', in *Seals and Their Context in the Middle Ages*, ed. Phillipp R. Schofield (Oxford, 2015), pp. 1–6, who argues that the word *sigillum* in the seal's legend refers not to the seal itself but to the cross *signum* at the start of the legend.

by Ildar Garipzanov in relation to Carolingian culture: 'Repetition was crucial in the symbolic language of the Carolingian world because it made the ruler's authority seem habitual or natural. Repetitive enactment of the royal liturgy, a constant use of specific titles and signs on objects connecting the rulers' courts with their aristocratic and free subjects, and the symbolic depiction of kings and emperors in different media made their authority an intrinsic part of the sociopolitical landscape'.[25] The idea of 'repetitive enactment' is all the more relevant when we consider just how many times these seal matrices must have been used over their lifetimes, given the ready availability of wax.

The Westminster writ for Abbot Edwin and the Worcester writ announcing the appointment of Wulfstan to that bishopric both display evidence of former wrapping and possible sealing,[26] the former with two long thin strips of wrapping membrane still intact, and the latter with a small fragmentary stub of wrapping-tie at the foot of the parchment. Meanwhile the two Bury St Edmunds single sheets have been trimmed in the post-medieval period, a process which sliced through the texts' ascenders and descenders and obliterated evidence of possible former wrapping and sealing.[27] It is perfectly plausible that the Bury St Edmunds single sheets could have been sealed in a similar way to the other documents of this group. This sealing of single-sheet writs can be contrasted to the general lack of evidence of former sealing and wrapping on other types of charter before the Norman Conquest.[28]

As such, due to the various aspects of their physical form, the single-sheet writs would have appeared—to literate, semi-literate, and non-literate observers alike—highly visually distinctive, and of a fundamentally different

25 Garipzanov, *The Symbolic Language of Authority*, p. 27.

26 Respectively S 1125 (*ASWrits* 81) and S 1156 (*ASWrits* 115).

27 S 1071 (*ASWrits* 11) and S 1084 (*ASWrits* 24).

28 For example, only three other vernacular single-sheet documents show signs of having once been wrapped (or possibly even sealed), with their very small 'steps' in the bottom left-hand corner of the documents. These are the so-called 'Fonthill Letter', S 1445; the will of the Ætheling Æthelstan, S 1503; and the will of Leofwine, S 1522. Similarly, the early eighth-century Wealdhere letter, a Latin single sheet preserved in its original form, has a gap left deliberately in the middle of its dorsal address so that, once wrapped, the address was still legible; see Pierre Chaplais, 'The Letter from Bishop Wealdhere of London to Archbishop Brihtwold of Canterbury: The Earliest Original "Letter Close" Extant in the West', in Pierre Chaplais, *Essays in Medieval Diplomacy and Administration* (London, 1981), ch. XIV, figs 5 and 6; and Jordan Zweck, *Epistolary Acts: Anglo-Saxon Letters and Early English Media* (Toronto, 2018), pp. 28–29. Anglo-Saxon royal diplomas, on the other hand, seem to have been consistently folded, with the sometime addition of a contemporary endorsement, but not wrapped closed or sealed *sur simple queue*; see Susan D. Thompson, *Anglo-Saxon Royal Diplomas: A Palaeography* (Woodbridge, 2006), pp. 19–26, and Robert Gallagher and Kate Wiles, this volume.

nature to other sorts of documentation such as royal diplomas, leases, records of dispute, and so on. Even when folded, where other kinds of documents might have borne contemporary endorsements summarizing the contents within, writs—from the evidence of the extant single sheets—typically bore no such mark, bound instead by their wrapping-ties and, if attached, their impressive wax seals.[29] When being transported across terrain, when being observed and read at local courts, and when sitting alongside other documents in private or institutional archives, writs would have been easy for contemporaries to recognize.

Textual References to Writs as Performatives

Our understanding of the setting-in-life of early English writs and their associated seals can be further enhanced by searching for references in other texts, which occasionally capture brief but highly telling descriptions of such documents and objects being deployed at local fora.

Two texts from Æthelredian England indicate that writs and seals had an important role to play as part of the proceedings and optics of shire court ceremonial from as early as the 990s. The first, dated *c.*990×992 and known as the Cuckhamsley chirograph, is a single-sheet *memoria causa* that alludes to the performative function of King Æthelred II's seal in a narrative describing a dispute between two individuals over land in Berkshire.[30] The two litigants are Wynflæd, a powerful woman—perhaps a widow—and Leofwine, a prominent man whose rank is not defined but who holds estates at Hagbourne and Bradfield in Berkshire, which Wynflæd is claiming as her own. As the dispute enters deadlock, Æthelred sends his seal to the meeting, by means of an individual whose identity and rank is stated emphatically: 'þa sende se cyning be Æluere abbude his insegel to þam gemote æt Cƿicelmeshlæƿe 7 grette ealle þa ƿitan þe þær gesomnode ƿæron þæt ƿæs Æþelsige biscop 7 Æscƿig biscop 7 Ælfric abbud 7 eal sio scir 7 bæd 7 het þæt hi scioldon Ƿynflæde 7 Leofƿine sƿa

29 The endorsements on the single-sheet writs date from the twelfth to fourteenth centuries and two of the single sheets (S 1084 and S 1105) lack endorsements entirely.

30 S 1454 (*CantCC* 133). A chirograph was any document drawn-up in duplicate, triplicate, or quadruplicate, with a word (typically *CYROGRAPHVM*) written across the parchment. If the claims of the document came into contention, the divided sections of the chirograph could be reunited, and the veracity of its claims publically asserted. For further context, see Kathryn A. Lowe, 'Lay Literacy in Anglo-Saxon England and the Development of the Chirograph', in *Anglo-Saxon Manuscripts and Their Heritage*, eds Philip Pulsiano and Elaine M. Treharne (Aldershot, 1998), pp. 161–204.

rihtlice geseman spa him æfre rihtlicost þuhte'.[31] The exact nature of the 'seal' here has been the subject of debate: Pierre Chaplais has posited that it could have been a loose token of credence, carried by Abbot Ælfhere to symbolically authenticate a pronouncement delivered orally.[32] Conversely, the word *insegel* could be functioning metonymically, as a sort of semantic abbreviation for the concept of *gewrit and insegel*, a collocation that appears in numerous other texts from our period.[33] Whilst the precise nature of this symbolic object is irrecoverable, it is clear that, through Abbot Ælfhere of Bath and the authority of the royal *insegel*, the king is able to articulate *in absentia* a direct command from wherever he might be to the venue of the Berkshire shire-meeting. There, it may have been set alongside other written testimonies which are also described being sent to the moot at Cuckhamsley Hill, no doubt to be seen, read aloud, and contested. We are told: 'Sigeric arcebiscop sende his sputelunga þærto 7 Ordbyrht biscop his'.[34]

A second text, a charter preserved in the *Textus Roffensis*, records a dispute between Godwine, bishop of Rochester, and a certain Leofwine (otherwise unattested) over the ownership of *bocland* at Snodland in Kent—and dates to a slightly later span of *c.*995×1005.[35] Bishop Godwine appears to have discovered, soon after his accession to Rochester in 994, certain *swutelunga* ('documents', 'testimonies') in the cathedral archive, and attempted to use them to lay claim to the estate. When news of the dispute reached the ear of Æthelred (he may,

31 'Then the king sent his seal, by means of Abbot Ælfhere, to that court at Cuckhamsley [i.e. *Scutchamer Knob*], and greeted all the councillors that were summoned there—namely Bishop Æthelsige and Bishop Æscwig and Abbot Ælfric and all the shire—and bade and commanded that they should reconcile Wynflæd and Leofwine as justly as they considered most just for ever.': trans. *CantCC* 133.

32 Pierre Chaplais, 'The Anglo-Saxon Chancery: From the Diploma to the Writ', *Journal of the Society of Archivists* 3 (1966), 160–76, at p. 172. For recent discussion, see Brooks and Kelly, *CantCC*, pp. 144–47, and for speculation about the nature of these Æthelredian seals and their hypothetical graphic elements, see Keynes, 'The Use of Seals', p. 77.

33 The earliest and perhaps best known example being the Alfredian passage in the Old English version of St Augustine's *Soliloquies*, in which the author invites the audience to visualize being sent their lord's *ærendgewrit and hys insegel* ('errand-writ/letter and seal') and thus being able to perceive their lord's will: *King Alfred's Version of St Augustine's Soliloquies*, ed. Thomas A. Carnicelli (Cambridge, MA, 1969), p. 62. See also Simon Keynes, *The Diplomas of King Æthelred 'the Unready', 978–1016: A Study in Their Use as Historical Evidence* (Cambridge, 1980), pp. 136–37, who notes that the syntactic position of *hys* in this passage implies that the letter and seal are conceived of as being separate—the two elements are associated rather than necessarily physically joined together.

34 'Archbishop Sigeric sent his testimony thither and Bishop Ordbriht his.': trans. *CantCC* 133.

35 S 1456 (*Roch* 37). The *Textus Roffensis* or 'Rochester Book' is Rochester, Cathedral Library A. 3. 5.

of course, have been petitioned by one or both of the litigants), the king dispatched his *gewrite and his insegl* to Archbishop Ælfric (the messenger or agent is not identified), and commanded that Ælfric, alongside the thegns of both East and West Kent, settle the dispute: 'Þa ða him seo talu cuð pæs þa sende he geprit 7 his insegl to þam arcebisceope Ælfrice 7 bead him þæt he 7 hys þegenas on East Cent 7 Ƿest Cent hy onriht gesemdon be ontale 7 be oftale'.[36] They are commanded to weigh the competing testimonies against each other, the process of adjudication expressed in the form of a neat, polyptotonic word-pair: *be ontale and be oftale*—claim weighed against counter-claim. As with the *insegel* of the Cuckhamsley chirograph, the writ and seal depicted in this account do not survive, and this is unsurprising if the main announcement of the writ amounted to little more than a court-summons.[37] Crucially, however, within the narrative of the Snodland account, the possession of the *gewrit and insegel* seems to provide a physical focal point for the action of the court itself. With the writ and seal in his possession, the litigants, their allies, and other suitors and interested parties gathered around Ælfric. With ownership of the document and symbolic object, he was effectively transformed into a conduit for the enacted performance of royal authority, instituting and publicizing the need for group solidarity and litigation.

We can complement these two formal, legalistic accounts with a passage from a third text—a description found within Ælfric of Eynsham's Old English homily *De populo Israhel*, composed around the turn of the millennium. In it, Ælfric discusses those in society who ignore Christian preachers, in order that they might plead ignorance and thus evade God's ultimate judgement. Then, Ælfric constructs a secular parallel, and in doing so alludes to an aspect of contemporary political culture: 'Nu cweðe we þærtogeanes, þæt gif se cyning asent gewrit to sumon his þegena, and he hit forsyhð swa swyðe þæt he hit nele gehyran, ne his aseon, þæt se cyning ne byð na swyðe bliðe him, þonne he geaxað hu he hine forseah'.[38] He compares rejection of Christian instruction

36 'When the claim was known to him, he sent a letter and his seal to Archbishop Ælfric, and gave orders that he and his thegns in East Kent and West Kent should settle the dispute between them justly, weighing both claim and counterclaim': *Roch* 37; trans. *ASChart*, no. 69, pp. 140–42.

37 Indeed, the twelfth-century endorsement on the Cuckhamsley chirograph itself reads *inutile*, a comment added to other, mostly vernacular, documents in the Christ Church archive which were perceived as ephemeral. It surely hints at the high level of destruction and loss of similar single sheets in the intervening centuries. Latin epistolary-form texts no doubt also suffered, since the aforementioned Wealdhere letter is also rendered *epistola inutilis* on its endorsement. See Brooks and Kelly, *CantCC*, p. 40.

38 'Now we say against this, that if the king sends his writ to any one of his thegns, and he despises it so greatly that he will not hear it, nor look at [any] of it, the king will not be

to the king sending his *gewrit* to a thegn only for it to be ignored—warning that the king (and by analogy, God) would not be gracious or *bliðe* if the thegn in question deigned not to hear or look at the document. Ælfric was known for his straightforward vernacular prose style and an aversion to convoluted or obscure metaphor—making it probable that this passage was constructed deliberately for its plausibility and intended to be relatable for his audience.[39] He neatly aligns royal and divine authority, and the *gewrit* itself is perceived as an extension of the king's will. Interestingly, the terms used to describe the thegn's interaction with the royal writ involve verbs of hearing and seeing rather than reading—hinting again at the propensity for such texts to be understood visually (by the semi- and illiterate) and performed to their intended audiences, rather than simply read privately.[40]

Another important depiction, some fifty years later, narrates the deployment of a *cynges gewrite and insegle* in a different, deeply politically charged, context. In 1051, King Edward had appointed the bishop of London, Robert of Jumièges, to the archbishopric of Canterbury, with Sparrowhawk (*Sparhafoc*), abbot of Abingdon, stepping up to fill the London vacancy created by Robert. These translations and appointments were two among several others designed to promote Edward's close allies and sideline local interests at this time. On his return journey from Rome, having gone to acquire his pallium, Robert was intercepted in England by Sparrowhawk; the account in the Peterborough Chronicle reads: 'Ða com Sparhafoc abbod be wege to him mid þæs cynges gewrite 7 insegle to þan þet he hine hadian sceolde to biscop into Lundene þa wið cweð se arcebiscop 7 cwæð þet se papa hit him forboden hæfde'.[41] Sparrowhawk has a writ and seal from the king in his possession declaring his valid appointment, and he uses it in an attempt to protect his position and

very gracious to him when he learns how he scorned him.': Ælfric, *De populo Israhel*, ed. John C. Pope, *Homilies of Ælfric: A Supplementary Collection*, 2 vols (London, 1968), 2:659; trans. Keynes, *The Diplomas of King Æthelred*, pp. 136–37.

39 For further context, see Frances R. Lipp, 'Ælfric's Old English Prose Style', *Studies in Philology* 66 (1969), 689–718, at p. 689; Catherine Cubitt, 'Ælfric's Lay Patrons', in *A Companion to Ælfric*, eds Hugh Magennis and Mary Swan (Leiden, 2009), pp. 165–92.

40 For more on the social function and importance of reading aloud in the early medieval period, see Daniel Donoghue, *How the Anglo-Saxons Read Their Poems* (Philadelphia, 2018).

41 'Then Abbot Sparrowhawk met him on the way with the king's writ and seal to the effect that he was to be consecrated bishop of London by the archbishop. But the archbishop refused and said the pope had forbidden it him': *The Anglo-Saxon Chronicle: A Collaborative Edition, Volume 7. MS E*, ed. Susan Irvine (Cambridge, 2004), p. 80, *s.a.* '1048' for 1051; translation from Dorothy Whitelock with David C. Douglas and Susie I. Tucker, *The Anglo-Saxon Chronicle: A Revised Translation* (London, 1961), p. 117.

gain or consolidate Robert's support for his translation to London. But the abbot and his writ are overruled, his appointment having been rejected by the pope, a prohibition which Robert himself may have purposefully obtained whilst in Rome.[42]

The function of the writ and seal described in the Peterborough Chronicle account can be usefully juxtaposed with the surviving writs that announce ecclesiastical appointments (sometimes alongside related privileges) at different levels of the church hierarchy.[43] Moreover, it indicates the usefulness of such documents to their respective 'beneficiaries', in the event that their ecclesiastical authority or jurisdiction came to be contested, for example amid accusations of simony. Having functioned originally as an ostensibly straightforward administrative royal pronouncement of a church appointment, the Peterborough Chronicle account highlights how writs of this function could be re-used and re-performed in other settings in order to defend the position, rights, and privileges of an individual (and, by extension, those of an entire community).[44] These accounts fit well with Brian Stock's conceptualization of 'textual communities', in which texts had the propensity to be written and then performed and re-performed orally by an 'individual who mastered it [the text], then utilized it for reforming a group's thought and action'.[45]

Aspects of Diplomatic Structure

Having discussed the physicality of these documents, as well as contemporary accounts of their setting-in-life, we can now turn to look at their internal

42 Frank Barlow, *Edward the Confessor* (London, 1970), pp. 104–6. Sparrowhawk remained bishop-elect of London for the summer and autumn of that year, before his eventual expulsion.

43 Five writs announcing episcopal appointments survive: S 1102 (*ASWrits* 50), S 1111 (*Wells* 33), S 1151 (*ASWrits* 109), S 1152 (*ASWrits* 110), and S 1156 (*ASWrits* 115), and two writs announcing abbatial appointments are extant: S 1083 (*ASWrits* 23) and S 1100 (*ASWrits* 47). The spread of this group across six different archives hints at their likely ubiquity in the later Anglo-Saxon period. For further discussion, see Molyneaux, *The Formation of the English Kingdom*, p. 217.

44 Writs were also used to extend such protections and privileges to other groups in society, beyond religious communities, as shown by the writ in favour of the London Cnihtengild (a pre-Conquest association of, ostensibly secular, landowners, administrators, and other power brokers): S 1103 (*ASWrits* 51). For wider context, see Robin Fleming, 'Rural Elites and Urban Communities in Late-Saxon England', *Past & Present* 141 (1993), 3–37; Rory Naismith, *Citadel of the Saxons: The Rise of Early London* (London, 2018), pp. 162–64.

45 Stock, *The Implications of Literacy*, pp. 42 and 90–91.

features, namely their diplomatic structure and formulae, with a view to discerning elements of residual performativity therein.[46]

Writs uniformly begin with an opening clause (or 'protocol') that took its form from a slightly modified, vernacularized version of the older Latin *ille illo salutem* ('*x* greets *y*') formula. This formula had its origins in Greek and Roman practice; it appears in some of Cicero's earliest missives, as well as letters of emperors, provincial governors and early popes.[47] In England, the basic Latin *salutatio* formulae were already becoming highly elaborate by the eighth century, thanks to the creativity of the likes of Aldhelm and Boniface, and it is used in Anglo-Saxon royal letters around this time.[48] In the ninth century, we observe an adapted vernacular version of the *salutem* formula in the well-known preface to the Alfredian translation of Gregory the Great's *Regula Pastoralis*: 'Ælfred kyning hateð gretan Wærferð biscep his wordum luflice and freondlice, and ðe cyðan hate ðæt …'.[49] In the later tenth century, Ælfric's Old English preface to his *Lives of Saints* similarly employs a *gret … eadmodlice* formula, indicating that a vernacularized form of the *ille illo salutem* construction was already well-established as our earliest writs emerge in the historical record.[50] Hence the tenth- and eleventh-century writ protocol was itself the product of a series of interactions between Latin and Old English that had continued throughout the eighth, ninth, and tenth centuries, traceable in literary and epistolary texts.

The writ protocols, then, identify the sender of the writ and their rank, and delineate the addressees, who are sometimes named individually, sometimes ranked and sometimes addressed generically as collectives. Predominantly the opening clause describes the principal power brokers of the shire court (the presiding ecclesiast, earl, and thegns), but the form had some adaptability: one writ, for example, addresses a hundred court, and four are directed to

46 Richard Sharpe stresses 'the need to understand systematically what the forms are really doing—when they are usually not explicit' in his 'The Use of Writs', p. 254.

47 Carol Dana Lanham, *Salutatio Formulas in Latin Letters to 1200: Syntax, Style, and Theory* (Munich, 1975), p. 17.

48 See, for example, the letter of King Alhred of Northumbria and his wife Queen Osgifu to Bishop Lul, in *English Historical Documents. I: c.500–1042*, ed. Dorothy Whitelock, 2nd ed. (London, 1979), no. 187, pp. 833–34, and the letter of King Cynewulf of Wessex to Lul, no. 190, pp. 835–36.

49 'King Alfred sends his greetings to bishop Wærferth with affectionate and friendly words and informs you that …': *King Alfred's West Saxon Version of Gregory's Pastoral Care*, ed. and trans. Henry Sweet (London, 1958), p. 3. For more on the origins of this tradition alongside other forms of dedicatory and epistolary prefaces, see Susan Irvine, *Uncertain Beginnings: The Prefatory Tradition in Old English* (Cambridge, 2017), p. 5.

50 'Ælfric gret eadmodlice Æðelweard ealdorman …' ('Ælfric humbly greets the nobleman Æthelweard …'): *Ælfric's Prefaces*, ed. Jonathan Wilcox (Durham, 1995), pp. 120–21.

the borough courts of London, Winchester, and Thetford.[51] It is worth stressing that these writ address clauses are, by their very nature, strictly formal in their tone and therefore narrow: when described in other kinds of vernacular document, shire meetings take on a much more varied appearance. For example, secular kin (the sons and brothers of earls and also bishops) loom large in these types of memoranda as witnesses to agreements at the shire court level, along with elite women and their allies, but they do not find themselves addressed explicitly in writ protocols.[52]

Through an analysis of the addressees and the ways in which they are described, it is possible to observe typological groups of protocol styles, which defy archival boundaries and therefore hint at centralizing practices and proclivities. These groups have been tabulated in Table 11.1, which shows the three main groups of writ protocol, the total number of pre-Conquest writs within each grouping, and the archival spread of these forms of protocol.[53]

TABLE 11.1 The nature and distribution of typologies of writ protocol (address clause)

Typology of writ protocol	**Number of pre-Conquest writs within this grouping**	**Number of archives represented**
Group A—Example structure: *Eadward kyng gret Heremann biscop 7 Harold eorl 7 ealle mine þegenas on Dorsætan freondlice* (S 1064, *ASWrits* 2).	74	19
Group B—Example structure: *Eadweard cyngc gret mine bisceopas 7 mine eorlas 7 ealle mine þegnas on þam sciren þær Sce Eadmund hafað land inne freondlice* (S 1071, *ASWrits* 11).	22	10
Group C—Example structure: *Ælfðryð gret Ælfric arcebiscop 7 Eþelwerd ealdarman eadmodlice* (S 1242, *ASWrits* 108).	6	6

51 For a hundred court, see S 1241, and for borough courts, see S 1096, S 1103, S 996, and S 1153.

52 For depictions of secular kin and their role in local dispute adjudication see, for example, S 1462, S 1473, and S 1406. For women (and especially widows, aristocrats, and royal women) as legal actors in local and central aulic contexts, see Rabin, 'Female Advocacy', p. 264.

53 See also the tabulation in Fenton, 'The Function of Writs', building on Harmer's summary of 'persons addressed' in *ASWrits*, pp. 45–54.

The largest group (termed here 'Group A') are those protocols that greet a fixed sequence of identified individuals: typically a named presiding bishop of the shire, a named ealdorman or, later, earl, followed by the thegns of the shire territories. To take an example: 'Eadward kyng gret Heremann biscop 7 Harold eorl 7 ealle mine þegenas on Dorsætan freondlice'.[54] This formulation is the most populous typology of writ protocol, and to my mind constitutes its 'standard' formulation, upon which other improvisations could be made, and within which other individuals could be slotted. The hierarchical formulation itself, describing ecclesiastical and secular power brokers beneath the king, is clearly a very old one; the prologue to the seventh-century laws of Ine, for example, describes how the king consulted his father, two bishops, and all his ealdormen and chief councillors before creating the code. Similarly Edward the Elder's first law-code takes the form of a directive to his reeves, greeting them and delineating their jurisdictional powers.[55] A rather more precise formulation of the perceived local hierarchy can be found in Æthelstan's London ordinance (or 'VI Æthelstan'): 'Endlyfte, þæt Æthelstan beot his bisceopum 7 his ealdormannum 7 his gerefum eallum ofer ealne mine anweald, þæt ge þone frið swa healdan swa ic hine gerædd habbe 7 mine witan'.[56] The structure of a local assembly is clearly being described here, with its constituents directly addressed by the king, subject to pledges and liable to compensation if they undermine the king's peace. The clause hints that a formulaic way of emphatically addressing regional authorities was developing in the later ninth and early tenth centuries—one that would later become formally embedded in the writ protocol. A similar protocol formulation is used in Cnut's letters of 1020 and 1027, the former surviving in the vernacular and targeted at ranked groups that mirror, albeit in a more elaborate phraseology, the ecclesiastical and secular suitors of the writ protocols.[57] Whilst these texts themselves are clearly not

54 'King Edward sends friendly greetings to Bishop Herman and Earl Harold and all my thegns in Dorset': S 1064 (*ASWrits* 2).

55 For Ine's code, see *Die Gesetze der Angelsachsen*, ed. Felix Liebermann, 3 vols (Halle, 1903–16), 1:20–27, and for Edward the Elder's first code, 1:138–40.

56 'Eleventhly: Æthelstan commands his bishops and his ealdormen and all his reeves over all my dominion, that you observe the peace just as I and my councillors have enacted it': *Die Gesetze*, ed. Liebermann, 1:182; translated in *English Historical Documents I*, ed. Whitelock, no. 37, p. 427.

57 'Cnut cyning gret his arcebiscopas 7 his leodbiscopas 7 Þurcyl eorl 7 ealle his eorlas 7 ealne his þeodscype, twelfhynde 7 twyhynde, gehadode 7 læwede, on Englalande freondlice' ('King Cnut greets in friendship his archbishops and his diocesan bishops and Earl Thorkel and all his earls, and all his people, whether men of a twelve hundred wergild or a two hundred, ecclesiastic and lay, in England'): *Die Gesetze*, ed. Liebermann, 1:273; translated in *English Historical Documents I*, ed. Whitelock, no. 48, p. 452.

writs, the generic overlap is striking and the nature of the greeting to the shire court is beginning to crystalize into a Group A-type standard formulation.

A number of important sub-typologies occur within Group A, in which other ranked groups and individuals are addressed. Sometimes a named shire-reeve is inserted, positioned between the earl and thegns: 'Eadward kingc gret Alfwolf biscop 7 Harold eorl 7 Alfred scyrgereuan 7 ealle mine þegenas on Dorsætan freondlice'.[58] At other times, a named but unranked individual (or individuals) is included, in the same position: for example, Godric, Ælfwine, Ælfric, Toli, Æthelric, and Osweard—deemed important enough to include in the clause above and distinct from the general address to the thegn collective.[59] The unranked Æthelric, who appears in the protocol of three Christ Church, Canterbury writs, for example, could have been the shire-reeve of the same name, or the wealthy Kentish landowner Æthelric bigga, who is described attending a shire court meeting in a mid-eleventh-century vernacular memorandum of an estate purchase.[60] Port-reeves (positioned between earl and thegns) and abbots (positioned immediately after the archbishop/bishop) are also addressed, albeit less frequently.[61]

The Group A-type protocol, with its various sub-typologies, can be distinguished from a second type, Group B, in which the address is given to ranked collectives rather than identified individuals, finishing with the specifics of the beneficiary, typically a religious community alongside a named churchman. For example, the protocol of one of the aforementioned Bury single sheets takes the form: 'Eadweard cyngc gret mine bisceopas 7 mine eorlas 7 ealle mine

58 'King Edward sends friendly greetings to Bishop Ælfwold and Earl Harold and Alfred the sheriff and all my thegns in Dorset': S 1063 (*ASWrits* 1). This is preserved at Abbotsbury, like the aforementioned 'standard' Group A-type protocol (S 1064, *ASWrits* 2).

59 See, for example, S 1066, S 1069, S 1070, S 1078, S 1080, S 1083, S 1084, S 1085, S 987, S 988, and S 1092 *inter alia*.

60 S 1473 (*CantCC* 171), which survives as the upper portion of a tripartite chirograph.

61 For port-reeves (administrators of towns), see S 1096, S 1103, S 1149, and S 1150 (the writs that contain these protocols are spread across the archives of Chertsey, London St Paul's, and Westminster), and for abbots see, for example, S 985, S 1111, and S 1137 (distributed across the archives of Canterbury Christ Church, Wells, and Westminster). As the Cuckhamsley chirograph demonstrated, abbots sometimes had an important role to play in the ritual of shire court proceedings, and they also appear as witnesses in other vernacular accounts of shire court adjudication. Stallers also appear in six protocols (positioned after the earl and above the general thegns), but these are all confined to the Westminster archive. As James Lloyd has suggested, it could well be that Westminster copyists and forgers, 'thinking stallers more prestigious, introduced them into the addresses themselves.' See his 'Reeves as Agents of Royal Government in the English Shires, from the Reign of Alfred to Domesday Book' (unpublished PhD thesis, University of Cambridge, 2014), p. 86.

þegnas on þam sciren þær Sce Eadmund hafað land inne freondlice'.[62] There is some discernible variation within the group: occasionally an archbishop or bishop is named alongside their community, and sometimes an abbot is identified.[63] How might we explain the formulaic difference, then, between the protocols of the Group A- and B-types? Thinking again in the context of performativity and audience, the Group B-type could represent a stylistic turn or innovation, in which the king's writ-draftsmen wished to address the shire suitors in general terms, and then isolate and emphasize the beneficiary regarding the specific terms of their grant or privilege.

In addition to Groups A and B, a further, highly heterogeneous group of protocols, Group C, can be identified for address clauses that do not fit the rigid established norms of the first two typologies.[64] The clauses in this 'tail' group are fascinating for their sheer diversity—they retain the *gret ... freondlice* formula, but are addressed to a wider array of sociopolitical communities: the shire, borough and hundred courts (see above), as well as individuals and smaller groups. In the case of the latter—exemplified by the non-royal writ of Bishop Æthelric, issued at some point between 1002 and 1014 and preserved at Sherborne—it seems possible that writs could be directed for the attention of individual shire court negotiators.[65] In this writ, the bishop complains of an alarming level of evasion of a local ship levy at eleven different locales, in a detailed list reminiscent of a vernacular boundary clause. It hinges around an active request for legal intervention from the ealdorman Æthelmær, who must have been the appropriate channel through which the levies could be renegotiated. The main announcement of Æthelric's writ has a strong personal voice, exemplified in the appeal: 'gif hyt þin pilla pære þu mihtest eaðe gedon þæt ic hyt eal spa hæfde'.[66] This is no doubt exactly the type of document referred to in passing as *swutelunga* by the Cuckhamsley chirograph, in other words a document (perhaps even a holograph) dispatched by an interested

62 'King Edward sends friendly greetings to my bishops and my earls and all my thegns in the shires in which St Edmund has land': S 1071 (*ASWrits* 11). Two other single-sheet originals (S 1088 and S 1125) have a protocol of the Group B-type, suggesting that it represents an authentic mid-eleventh-century formulation.

63 For archbishops and bishops addressed in Group B, see S 986, S 1086, S 1088, S 1089, S 1097, and S 1159 (represented across three archives); and for abbots addressed, see S 1065, S 1099, S 1125, and S 1099 (likewise spread across three different archives).

64 Examples from Group C include Archbishop Wulfstan's writ (S 1386), Queen Edith's writ (S 1241), the Ruishton Letter (S 1242), S 1154, and Gospatric's writ (S 1243).

65 The address reads 'Æþelric biscop gret Æþelmær freondlice': S 1383 (*Sherb* 13).

66 'If you were willing, you could easily bring it about that I had it in the same way': modified translation from *ASWrits* 63.

party of an ongoing dispute or negotiation, to be performed and used at court.[67] The Group C-type indicates the adaptability of the protocol, which could specify a more focused group of addressees and, in doing so, could function as a more effective instrument of legal leverage and control. As such, and as with Group B, a closer link can be observed between the protocol's form and the intended contemporaneous 'function' of the writ itself. The non-royal or 'private' writs that sit in this grouping provide another reminder, seen elsewhere in pre-Conquest diplomatic, of the ways in which royal diplomatic forms could provide paradigms for other elites drawing up documents to further their own interests in the eleventh century—and hints at the politics behind some of the connections and overlap we see between different diplomatic typologies. In doing so, they also illuminate the nature of diverse local fora as vibrant spaces of encounter, sociality, and petition.

Spatial Formulae—Nature, Form, and Aspects of Distribution

In light of our consideration of the content and structure of the writ address clauses, we can now turn to another key formulaic element of these documents, namely the main announcement clauses in which the specific notification is made. To introduce the clause, a verb of speaking is usually employed, typically a variant of *ic cyðe eow þæt* ('I make it known to you that'), invoking the personal voice of the king or issuer. And what follows is a very interesting sequence of formulaic word-pairs, often but not always alliterative, framing the extent of the given property or privileges in spatial terms. For example, in a writ of Cnut generated *c.*1035, the king declares:[68] '7 ic cyðe eop þæt ic hæbbe geunnan Æþelnoðe arcebisceope ealre þara landare þe

67 Æthelric's writ survives as an early eleventh-century copy entered onto the verso of the last leaf of the Sherborne Pontifical (Paris, Bibliothèque nationale de France, lat. 943, fol. 170v), and the copyist appears to have remained faithful to aspects of their single-sheet exemplar (the lost original single sheet from which it was most likely copied): the format is long and horizontal, and it begins with a small, unobtrusive *signum crucis* of the type found on the Edwardian single-sheet originals. For a divergent interpretation, see Chaplais, 'The Anglo-Saxon Chancery', p. 174, who posits that the writ was a *post eventum* written record of a purely oral declaration, and that no such document was in fact sent to Æthelmær.

68 S 988 (*CantCC* 157). This writ is one of a small group of writs copied into the MacDurnan Gospels (London, Lambeth Palace 1370); see also S 1386, S 986, and S 987. The writ now forms part of London, British Library, Cotton Tiberius B.iv, having been detached after moving into the library of Sir Robert Cotton.

Ælfmær hæfde 7 mid rihte into Cristes cyricean gebyrað binnan birig 7 butan on puda 7 on felda spa full 7 spa forð spa Ælfric arcebisceop hyre peold oþþe ænig his forgenegena'.[69] Lisi Oliver has argued that formulaic language such as this 'provides a masterly example of poetic form used in legal diction', noting the conjunction of opposites to describe alliteratively a totality, and finishing with the use of a hypermetric poetic line.[70] Indeed, to my mind this hypermetric line coincides with—and therefore works deliberately to emphasize—the identity of the previous owner of the land (perhaps a similar strategy to the syntactic emphasis put on the beneficiary of the writ's announcement in the Group B-type protocols).

Taking the corpus of writs as a whole, it is possible to isolate and categorize these spatial formulae into two distinct groupings. One group describes physical space, emphasizing its totality: *on wudan and on feldan* ('in woodland and in field'), *binnan burh ge butan* ('within borough and outside it'), *be strande ne be lande* ('by strand or by land'). Another set of formulae describes temporal space, sometimes looking backwards (*spa full and spa forð swa* ('as fully and completely as [somebody previously had owned it]')), and sometimes looking to the future (*on dæge and æfter* ('during my lifetime and after')) and so on.[71] This group is distinct from other sequences of word-pairs and formulae within writs that have more obviously legalistic meanings; for example, *sacu and socn* (sake and soke or 'cause and suit') and *toll and team* (toll/tax and profits from 'vouching to warranty'), as well as other constellations of judicial and financial rights: *infangenetheof* (right to receive forfeited possessions from thieves caught in the act; literally 'in-seized-thief'), *hamsocn* (attack on a house), *grithbryce* (breach of peace), *mundbryce* (breach of protection), *foresteall*

69 'And I make known to you that I have granted Archbishop Æthelnoth all the landed property that Ælfmær had and [which] rightly belongs to Christ Church, within borough and outside it, with woodland and open land, as fully and to such an extent as Archbishop Ælfric possessed it or any of his predecessors.': translation from *CantCC* 157.

70 Lisi Oliver, 'Legal Documentation and the Practice of English Law', in *The Cambridge History of Early Medieval English Literature*, ed. Clare A. Lees (Cambridge, 2013), pp. 499–529, at 519.

71 Of the 27 pre-Conquest archives that preserved writs, all except three contain writs that employ at least one of these spatial formulae in their main announcement clauses. This wide archival spread is strong evidence that such formulae were a central component of this diplomatic language from the later tenth century to *c.*1070. Moreover, of the group of single-sheet originals, all of them contain at least one of these spatial formulae (between one and four), suggesting that these formulae are authentically pre-Conquest in character, rather than the creation of later copyists.

(obstruction), *fihtwite* (fine for fighting), *fyrdwite* (fine for neglect of military service), and *flymenafyrmth* (fine for harbouring fugitives).[72]

In order to further probe the question of the function of these spatial formulae, I was interested in looking at their stability across the late tenth and eleventh centuries, and across the discrete kingships of the rulers whose vernacular writs have survived. In Table 11.2, we have the various issuers of writs, arranged chronologically, with the average number of spatial formulae per writ for each of these rulers (along with the total number of writs extant for each king), as well as the employment of spatial formulae in writs issued by individuals other than kings.[73]

The first, perhaps most striking feature of the royal group is that these formulae are maintained across five different kingships—they are not falling away from the documents, and survive the turbulent conquests of 1016 and 1066, being employed right down to *c*.1070. The passage of time appears to have had little influence on any changes that we observe in form, notwithstanding orthographic variation. Whilst writs themselves were adaptable in terms of their functions and uses, these formulae appear rigid and stable. Indeed, even between *c*.1066 and 1070, no new spatial formulae emerge. We also see the employment of the samc (or in the case of Gospatric's writ, modified) spatial formulae within the corpus of non-royal writs issued between *c*.995 and 1066 by various secular and ecclesiastical individuals, each with their own distinctive links to the royal court. Again, and as with the non-royal protocols of the Group C-type, it is tempting to see the employment of these formulae as

72 For these legalistic word-pairs, see *ASWrits*, pp. 73–85; David Roffe, 'From Thegnage to Barony: Sake and Soke, Title and Tenants-in-chief', *Anglo-Norman Studies* 12 (1990), 157–76; Stephen Baxter, 'Lordship and Justice in Late Anglo-Saxon England: The Judicial Functions of Soke and Commendation Revisited', in *Early Medieval Studies in Memory of Patrick Wormald*, eds Stephen Baxter, Catherine Karkov, Janet L. Nelson, and David Pelteret (Farnham, 2009), pp. 383–419, who emphasizes the economic dimension of these rights, which may have empowered the recipients to collect the profits of justice administered through royal courts, under the auspices or coercion of royal officials. The three main royal protections of *hamsocn, mundbryce*, and *forsteal* appear in royal legislation amongst other texts: for discussion, see Tom Lambert, *Law and Order in Anglo-Saxon England* (Oxford, 2017), pp. 308–10.

73 I have included here, for a cross-Conquest perspective, the vernacular writs of William I, which maintain many aspects of the language, style, and structure of pre-Conquest writs, but which uniformly shift to Latin after *c*.1070. For these, see *Regesta Regum Anglo-Normannorum: The Acta of William I (1066–1087)*, ed. David Bates (Oxford, 1998), pp. 44–50. The protocol structures of William I's vernacular writs also conform to the two styles of Groups A and B, described above; for the list, see *Acta of William I*, ed. Bates, p. 45.

TABLE 11.2 The distribution of spatial formulae in writs—*binnan burh ge butan, on wudan and on feldan, be strande ne be lande, swa full and swa forð swa, on dæge and after, inne tid and ut of tid*

a. Royal writs

Issuer of writ	Number of writs extant	Average number of spatial formulae per writ
King Æthelred II (*c.*978×1016)	2	1
King Cnut (*c.*1017×1035)	6	2
King Edward the Confessor (*c.*1042×1066)	83	2
King Harold (*c.*1066)	1	2
King William I (*c.*1066×1070)	32	2

b. Non royal-writs

Issuer of writ	Average number of spatial formulae per writ
Queen Ælfthryth (*c.*995×1002)	1
Bishop Æthelric (*c.*1001×1012)	0
Archbishop Wulfstan (*c.*1020)	0
Gospatric (*c.*1041×1055)	3 (*sui generis*)
Queen Edith (*c.*1061×1066)	1
Abbot Wulfwold (*c.*1061×1066)	5

evidence of private, lesser ranking individuals appropriating forms associated with royal writ announcements, in order to give their own testimonies and accounts further weight, formality, and authority in the local court settings in which they would be performed.

In Table 11.3, the spatial formulae have been tracked in documents outside the writ corpus, taking into account the wider body of pre-Conquest vernacular charters.[74]

74 My thanks to Professor Simon Keynes for sharing his 'Register of Vernacular Charters' (unpublished spreadsheet) with me, upon which this analysis is based.

TABLE 11.3 The appearance of spatial formulae in other typologies of vernacular charter

Formula	Found in
mid mete and mid manne	Agreements: S 1224, S 1476, S 1465, S 1468, S 1391, S 1471. Records of grants: S 1225, S 1659, S 1219. Wills: S 1486, S 1536, S 1538. Outcomes of litigation: S 1474. Leases: S 1422, S 1426.
on dæge and æfter dæge	Grant of land: S 1220. Record of land purchase: S 1473. Outcome of litigation: S 1460. Record of marriage agreement: S 1459. Wills: S 1527.
binnan burh ge butan	Agreement: S 1471. Grant of land: S 223, S 1234. Record of grant: S 1400. Lease: S 1280.
swa full and swa forð swa	Agreement: S 1470. Wills: S 1489, S 1519, S 1529. Leases: S 1399, S 1426. Record of grant: S 1222. Statement of estate history: S 1467.

Such spatial formulae are used far less consistently, but nonetheless can be found smattered across a range of texts including records of land grants, wills, and leases. Clearly these forms were not restricted in their use to the agencies responsible for drawing up royal (and private) writs, and would have been well-known to other parties and groups generating charters in their own interests. Where these formulae are employed, they typically frame or add emphasis to a discursive account of land acquisition or disposition.

Conclusions

This study has isolated aspects of the address and main announcement clauses of vernacular writs in an attempt to probe deeper into the nature of their forms and variations.[75] In doing so, I believe we can situate the protocols and spatial formulae of the main announcements within a wider context of aulic performativity, and posit that they functioned, to borrow Hagen Keller's phrase, as 'symbolic markers' for key moments of ceremonial at local courts.[76]

75 Of interest too, but outside the scope of this chapter, are the writ's prohibition clauses, statements of religious motive, sanctions, and valedictions. See *ASWrits*, pp. 66–73; Oliver, 'Legal Documentation', pp. 520–21.

76 Or 'als symbolische Kennzeichnung.' See Hagen Keller, 'Hülderweis durch Privilegien: symbolische Kommunikation innerhalb und jenseits des Textes', *Frühmittelalterliche Studien* 38 (2004), 309–21, at p. 314.

The clauses clearly disambiguate the personal voice of the king (his authority and identity also invoked through the concurrent use of seals), connect him to the local dignitaries, and make an announcement of a particular grant more emphatic by framing it with alliterative, symbolic language. This diplomatic discourse must have played a vital role in constructing seemingly natural, shared conceptions of royal authority, in a culture in which the stable and uncontested relationship between ruler and ruled was paramount, and in which there was an urgent need for royal and other announcements to be conveyed clearly and understood with minimal ambiguity.[77] In my view, it is their performative function, rather than an innate concern for preserving archaic forms, that helps explain the rise and persistence of these spatial formulae, as well as the rigid and enduring structures of the A- and B-type protocols. Furthermore, and fundamentally, in this tenth- and eleventh-century English context, the vernacular played a crucial and supporting sociopolitical role alongside the diplomatic usage of Latin, in that most fundamental business of articulating—and making tangible—grants of land, favour, and privilege.

Recent studies, mostly focusing on the language and content of Latin royal diplomas from later Anglo-Saxon England, have revealed that diplomatic texts were part of a nexus of legalistic and ritualized norms, and that we can use them to peer into the atmosphere and intrigue of tenth- and eleventh-century royal assemblies.[78] I hope that this study has shown that vernacular documentation can help us reconstruct political activity at a more parochial level—a world similarly permeated by the written word and by the use and performance of complex and sophisticated texts.

77 Alongside this, we must of course consider the practical likelihood that formulaic structures simply made it easier for Anglo-Saxon charter draftsmen to construct their texts. There is no positive evidence for the use of formularies in England before the Norman Conquest, and charter scribes seem to have recycled formulae and formulations from earlier documents; for discussion, see Keynes, *The Diplomas of King Æthelred*, pp. 115–20; Kelly, *Pet*, pp. 296–97; cf. Snook, *The Anglo-Saxon Chancery*, p. 41, n. 37.

78 See, for example, Levi Roach, 'Public Rites and Public Wrongs: Ritual Aspects of Diplomas in Tenth- and Eleventh-Century England', *EME* 19 (2011), 182–203; Simon Keynes, 'Welsh Kings at Anglo-Saxon Royal Assemblies', *Haskins Society Journal* 26 (2014), 69–122, at pp. 96–99, elucidating the performativity of the 'alliterative' Latin royal diplomas of the 940s and 950s and their likely court settings; and Charles Insley, 'Rhetoric and Ritual in Late Anglo-Saxon Charters', in *Medieval Legal Process: Physical, Spoken and Written Performance in the Middle Ages*, eds Marco Mostert and P. S. Barnwell (Turnhout, 2011), pp. 109–21.

Bibliography

Primary Sources

Anglo-Saxon Charters, ed. and trans. Agnes J. Robertson, 2nd ed. (Cambridge, 1956).

The Anglo-Saxon Chronicle: A Collaborative Edition. Vol. 7, MS. E, ed. Susan Irvine (Cambridge, 2004).

The Anglo-Saxon Chronicle: A Revised Translation, eds and trans. Dorothy Whitelock, David Douglas, and Susie Tucker (London, 1961).

Anglo-Saxon Writs, ed. and trans. Florence E. Harmer (Manchester, 1952; 2nd ed. Stamford, 1989).

Ælfric, *De populo Israhel*, ed. J. C. Pope, *Homilies of Ælfric: A Supplementary Collection*, vol. 2 (London, 1968).

Ælfric's Prefaces, ed. Jonathan Wilcox (Durham, 1995).

Charters of Christ Church Canterbury, eds N. P. Brooks and S. E. Kelly, Anglo-Saxon Charters 17–18 (Oxford, 2013).

Charters of Malmesbury Abbey, ed. S. E. Kelly, Anglo-Saxon Charters XI (Oxford, 2005).

Charters of Peterborough Abbey, ed. S. E. Kelly, Anglo-Saxon Charters 14 (Oxford, 2009).

Charters of Rochester, ed. A. Campbell, Anglo-Saxon Charters I (Oxford, 1973).

Charters of Sherborne, ed. M. A. O'Donovan, Anglo-Saxon Charters III (Oxford, 1998).

English Historical Documents. I: c.500–1042, ed. Dorothy Whitelock, 2nd ed. (London, 1979).

Die Gesetze der Angelsachsen, ed. Felix Liebermann, 3 vols (Halle, 1903–16).

King Alfred's Version of St Augustine's Soliloquies, ed. Thomas A. Carnicelli (Cambridge MA, 1969).

King Alfred's West Saxon Version of Gregory's Pastoral Care, ed. and trans. Henry Sweet (London, 1958).

Regesta Regum Anglo-Normannorum: The Acta of William I (1066–1087), ed. David Bates (Oxford, 1998).

Secondary Sources

Austin, John L., *How To Do Things With Words* (Cambridge, MA, 1962).

Barlow, Frank, *Edward the Confessor* (London, 1970).

Baxter, Stephen, 'Lordship and Justice in Late Anglo-Saxon England: The Judicial Functions of Soke and Commendation Revisited', in *Early Medieval Studies in Memory of Patrick Wormald*, eds Stephen Baxter, Catherine Karkov, Janet L. Nelson, and David Pelteret (Farnham, 2009), pp. 383–419.

Bedos-Rezak, Brigitte M., 'The King Enthroned, a New Theme in Anglo-Saxon Royal Iconography: The Seal of Edward the Confessor and its Political Implications', in *Medieval Kings and Kingship*, ed. Joel Rosenthal (Binghamton, NY, 1986), pp. 53–88;

reprinted in Brigitte Bedos-Rezak, *Form and Order in Medieval France: Studies in Social and Quantitative Sigillography* (Aldershot, 2003), IV.

Bishop, T. A. M. and Chaplais, Pierre, *Facsimiles of English Royal Writs to A.D. 1100, Presented to Vivian Hunter Galbraith* (Oxford, 1957).

Brown, Warren C., Costambeys, Marios, Innes, Matthew, and Kosto, Adam, 'Introduction', in *Documentary Culture and the Laity in the Early Middle Ages*, eds Warren C. Brown, Marios Costambeys, Matthew Innes, and Adam Kosto (Cambridge, 2013), pp. 1–16.

Chaplais, Pierre 'The Anglo-Saxon Chancery: From the Diploma to the Writ', *Journal of the Society of Archivists* 3 (1966), 160–76.

Chaplais, Pierre, 'The Letter from Bishop Wealdhere of London to Archbishop Brihtwold of Canterbury: The Earliest Original "Letter Close" Extant in the West', in his *Essays in Medieval Diplomacy and Administration* (London, 1981), ch. XIV.

Cubitt, Catherine, 'Ælfric's Lay Patrons', in *A Companion to Ælfric*, eds Hugh Magennis and Mary Swan (Leiden, 2009), pp. 165–92.

Donoghue, Daniel, *How the Anglo-Saxons Read Their Poems* (Philadelphia, 2018).

Fenton, Albert 'The Function of Writs in England before the Norman Conquest' (unpublished PhD thesis, University of Cambridge, forthcoming).

Fleming, Robin, 'Rural Elites and Urban Communities in Late-Saxon England', *Past & Present* 141 (1993), 3–37.

Foot, Sarah, *Æthelstan: The First King of England* (New Haven, CT, 2011).

Garipzanov, Ildar H., *The Symbolic Language of Authority in the Carolingian World (c. 751–877)* (Leiden, 2008).

Harmer, Florence E., 'A Bromfield and a Coventry Writ of King Edward the Confessor', in *The Anglo-Saxons: Studies in Some Aspects of Their History and Culture Presented to Bruce Dickins*, ed. Peter Clemoes (London, 1959), pp. 89–103.

Harvey, P. D. A., 'This Is a Seal', in *Seals and Their Context in the Middle Ages*, ed. Phillipp R. Schofield (Oxford, 2015), pp. 1–6.

Heslop, T. A., 'English Seals from the Mid Ninth Century to 1100', *Journal of the British Archaeological Association* 133 (1980), 1–16.

Insley, Charles, 'Rhetoric and Ritual in Late Anglo-Saxon Charters', in *Medieval Legal Process: Physical, Spoken and Written Performance in the Middle Ages*, eds Marco Mostert and P. S. Barnwell (Turnhout, 2011), pp. 109–21.

Irvine, Susan, *Uncertain Beginnings: The Prefatory Tradition in Old English* (Cambridge, 2017).

Johanek, P., 'Zur rechtlichen Funktion von Traditionsnotiz, Traditionsbuch und früher Siegelurkunde', in *Recht und Schrift im Mittelalter*, ed. Peter Classen (Sigmaringen, 1977), pp. 131–62.

Keller, Hagen, 'Hülderweis durch Privilegien: symbolische Kommunikation innerhalb und jenseits des Textes', *Frühmittelalterliche Studien* 38 (2004), 309–21.

Kelly, Susan, 'Anglo-Saxon Lay Society and the Written Word', in *The Uses of Literacy in Early Mediaeval Europe*, ed. Rosamond McKitterick (Cambridge, 1990), pp. 36–62.

Kershaw, Jane and Naismith, Rory, 'A New Late Anglo-Saxon Seal Matrix', *ASE* 42 (2013), 291–98.

Keynes, Simon, 'Church Councils, Royal Assemblies, and Anglo-Saxon Royal Diplomas', in *Kingship, Legislation and Power in Anglo-Saxon England*, eds Gale R. Owen-Crocker and Brian W. Schneider (Woodbridge, 2013), pp. 1–182.

Keynes, Simon, *The Diplomas of King Æthelred 'the Unready', 978–1016: A Study in Their Use as Historical Evidence* (Cambridge, 1980).

Keynes, Simon, 'Introduction', in *Select English Historical Documents of the Ninth and Tenth Centuries*, ed. and trans. Florence E. Harmer (Cambridge, 1914; rev. ed. 2011).

Keynes, Simon, 'Regenbald the Chancellor (*sic*)', *Anglo-Norman Studies* 10 (1988), 185–222.

Keynes, Simon, 'Register of Vernacular Charters' (unpublished spreadsheet).

Keynes, Simon, 'The Use of Seals in Anglo-Saxon England', in *Seals and Status: Power of Objects*, eds John Cherry, Jessica Berenbeim, and Lloyd De Beer (London, 2018), pp. 73–83.

Keynes, Simon, 'Welsh Kings at Anglo-Saxon Royal Assemblies', *Haskins Society Journal* 26 (2014), 69–122.

Koziol, Geoffrey, 'Making Boso the Clown: Performance and Performativity in a Pseudo-Diploma of the Renegade King (8 December 879)', in *Rituals, Performatives, and Political Order in Northern Europe, c. 650–1350*, eds Wojtek Jezierski, Lars Hermanson, Hans Jacob Orning, and Thomas Småberg (Turnhout, 2015), pp. 43–61.

Koziol, Geoffrey, *The Politics of Memory and Identity in Carolingian Royal Diplomas: The West Frankish Kingdom (840–987)* (Turnhout, 2012).

Lambert, Tom, *Law and Order in Anglo-Saxon England* (Oxford, 2017).

Lanham, Carol Dana, *Salutatio Formulas in Latin Letters to 1200: Syntax, Style, and Theory* (Munich, 1975).

Lipp, Frances R., 'Ælfric's Old English Prose Style', *Studies in Philology* 66 (1969), 689–718.

Lloyd, James, 'Reeves as Agents of Royal Government in the English Shires, from the Reign of Alfred to Domesday Book' (unpublished PhD thesis, University of Cambridge, 2014).

Lowe, Kathryn A., 'Lay Literacy in Anglo-Saxon England and the Development of the Chirograph', in *Anglo-Saxon Manuscripts and Their Heritage*, eds Phillip Pulsiano and Elaine M. Treharne (Aldershot, 1998), pp. 161–204.

Lupoi, Maurizio, *The Origins of the European Legal Order* (Cambridge, 2000).

Maddicott, John R., *The Origins of the English Parliament, 924–1327* (Oxford, 2010).

Molyneaux, George, *The Formation of the English Kingdom in the Tenth Century* (Oxford, 2015).

Naismith, Rory, *Citadel of the Saxons: The Rise of Early London* (London, 2018).

Oliver, Lisi, 'Legal Documentation and the Practice of English Law', in *The Cambridge History of Early Medieval English Literature*, ed. Clare A. Lees (Cambridge, 2013), pp. 499–529.

Rabin, Andrew, 'Female Advocacy and Royal Protection in Tenth-Century England: The Legal Career of Queen Ælfthryth', *Speculum* 84 (2009), 261–88.

Roach, Levi, *Kingship and Consent in Anglo-Saxon England, 871–978: Assemblies and the State in the Early Middle Ages* (Cambridge, 2013).

Roach, Levi, 'Public Rites and Public Wrongs: Ritual Aspects of Diplomas in Tenth- and Eleventh-Century England', *EME* 19 (2011), 182–203.

Roberts, Jane, 'What did Anglo-Saxon Seals Seal When?', in *The Power of Words: Essays in Lexicography, Lexicology and Semantics in Honour of Christian J. Kay*, eds Graham D. Caie, Carole Hough, and Irené Wotherspoon (Amsterdam, 2006), pp. 131–57.

Roffe, David, 'From Thegnage to Barony: Sake and Soke, Title and Tenants-in-chief', *Anglo-Norman Studies* 12 (1990), 157–76.

Rumble, Alexander, 'Anglo-Saxon Royal Archives: Their Nature, Extent, Survival and Loss', in *Kingship, Legislation and Power in Anglo-Saxon England*, eds Gale R. Owen-Crocker and Brian W. Schneider (Woodbridge, 2013), pp. 185–200.

Rushforth, Rebecca, 'The Eleventh- and Early Twelfth-Century Manuscripts of Bury St Edmunds Abbey' (unpublished PhD thesis, University of Cambridge, 2002).

Sawyer, P. H, *Anglo-Saxon Charters: An Annotated List and Bibliography* (London, 1968).

Sharpe, Richard, 'The Use of Writs in the Eleventh Century', *ASE* 32 (2003), 247–91.

Snook, Ben, *The Anglo-Saxon Chancery: The History, Language and Production of Anglo-Saxon Charters from Alfred to Edgar* (Woodbridge, 2015).

Stock, Brian, *The Implications of Literacy: Written Language and Models of Interpretation in the Eleventh and Twelfth Centuries* (Princeton, NJ, 1983).

Stokes, Peter A., *English Vernacular Minuscule from Æthelred to Cnut circa 990–circa 1035* (Cambridge, 2014).

Thompson, Susan D., *Anglo-Saxon Royal Diplomas: A Palaeography* (Woodbridge, 2006).

Thompson, Susan D., *Anglo-Saxon Vernacular Documents: A Palaeography* (Manchester, 2010).

Zweck, Jordan, *Epistolary Acts: Anglo-Saxon Letters and Early English Media* (Toronto, 2018).

Online Sources

British Library List of Anglo-Saxon Charters, https://blogs.bl.uk/files/list-of-anglo-saxon-charters.pdf.

Dictionary of Old English Web Corpus, http://tapor.library.utoronto.ca/doecorpus/.

CHAPTER 12

From Memorandum to Written Record: Function and Formality in Old English Non-Literary Texts

Kathryn A. Lowe

In this chapter, I consider a set of Old English non-literary texts of indeterminate date spanning the Conquest from the abbey of Bury St Edmunds within the context of other, more securely pre-Conquest, texts surviving from the archive. The texts discussed here, which range from booklists to funerary arrangements, are not well known, although all have been edited by Agnes Robertson.[1] Their marginalized status is reflected in the fact that three of them appear in appendices to Robertson's edition which contain, variously, post-Conquest documents, and undated documents. This partly accounts for their lack of discussion in scholarship, but another contributing factor is the way in which they have been classified, an issue which affects a number of documents from all archives. Together such vernacular texts constitute evidence for a wider use of the written word in Anglo-Saxon England than is still often acknowledged in scholarship.

Bury St Edmunds Abbey and its Archive

The early history of the abbey, located in West Suffolk, is difficult to establish, but it appears to have been transformed from some form of congregation dedicated to the cult of St Edmund into a monastic, Benedictine, foundation during Cnut's reign (1016–35); some years on, its first abbot, Ufi, was appointed. The Anglo-Saxon archive of this foundation is well known for its focus on the vernacular; this is surely the result of a peculiarity of the early history of the abbey whose wealth is due to the generosity of lay benefactors who donated lands to the foundation through bequest (customarily in Old English) rather than to royal grants of estates issued by diploma or grants of privilege (predominantly in Latin). The majority of charters from Anglo-Saxon England as a whole fall into this latter category; they constitute roughly two-thirds of the 1,500 or so of the total. By contrast, only seven charters (under 15 per cent) of

1 *ASChart.*

 | DOI:10.1163/9789004432338_013

Bury's pre-Conquest archive of 49 charters may be classified as diplomas or grants of privilege; three of these survive in both Latin and Old English versions.[2] The rest of the archive comprises a celebrated series of vernacular wills and bequests, first edited by Dorothy Whitelock in 1930 or by Robertson (1939; second edition 1956).[3] They are complemented by a sequence of writs from the reign of Edward the Confessor, edited by Florence Harmer.[4]

The Charter Corpus

The foundation for the modern study of Anglo-Saxon charters was laid in 1968, when Peter Sawyer published his handlist of the corpus together with a note of the manuscripts witnessing each charter, editing history, and a summary of scholarship.[5] Subsequently, this seminal reference aid has been put online and updated (comprehensively to 2010, sporadically thereafter), and there have been additions, both to that point and subsequently. These have been identified in a necessarily *ad hoc* way, generally as a consequence of preparing a particular archive for publication under the auspices of the British Academy Anglo-Saxon Charters series, or through the reporting of new discoveries. It is not straightforward to retrieve this information without trawling through the online index,[6] and I therefore supply the information here in Table 12.1 of the Appendix; it is unfortunate that subsequent additions to the database are not, it appears, identifiable as such, and therefore the procedure needs to be repeated in order to catch new entries.

Several of these new discoveries are entirely in the vernacular or incorporate text written in Old English, and are only just finding their way into the *Dictionary of Old English Corpus* with a new version including such texts scheduled for release before the publication of the next online fascicle (*La-Le*).[7]

2 S 980, S 1045, and S 1046. The tally of 49 charters excludes the records discussed further in this article which span or post-date the Conquest.

3 *ASWills*.

4 *ASWrits*.

5 S.

6 See http://www.esawyer.org.uk/browse/sawno.html.

7 *Dictionary of Old English: A to I*, eds Angus Cameron, Ashley Crandell Amos, Antonette diPaolo Healey et al. (Toronto, 2007–), https://tapor.library.utoronto.ca/doe/. Work on charter texts is reported in the 2019 progress report, available at https://doe.utoronto.ca/pages/index.html, where the editors report the inclusion of 'about a dozen' charters from St Albans (see note 105 below); they are yet to add the material included in Table 12.1 of the Appendix. The agreement of the British Academy to allow the *Dictionary of Old English* to use texts from the volumes in the Anglo-Saxon Charters series should in due course fill most gaps.

Other texts were already known but have since been reclassified for these purposes as charters (for example, the *Codex Aureus* inscription, *olim* Rec 6. 5, now S 1204a). Such reclassification disproportionately affects the *Dictionary of Old English* short-title series of Rec(ords). This is currently a group of 86 texts, some of which are multi-part. They total around 19,000 words. The majority of these are of post-Conquest date, incorporating material from David Pelteret's catalogue which appears in its entirety (although with some, presumably accidental, omissions) in various places across the *Dictionary of Old English Corpus*.[8] However, some of these texts cannot be dated; others are securely pre-Conquest. Of course, early volumes of the British Academy Anglo-Saxon Charters series, published before the *Dictionary of Old English Corpus*, the online Sawyer, and Pelteret did not include these texts. Thus, the first volume in the series, Rochester (1973),[9] omits Rec 16.1 (now S 1481d, a list of estates), Rec 16. 2 (S 1481f, a list of slaves) and Rec 16. 3[10] (a list of slaves). According to the Anglo-Saxon Charters Committee's guidelines, the following applies:

> The new edition of Anglo-Saxon charters is intended to be a complete corpus of all pre-Conquest title-deeds known to have survived. It will include all documents relating to grants of lands and liberties, whatever their grantor … whoever their beneficiary, whatever their diplomatic form … and whatever the language in which they are written … Documents which cannot be regarded as title-deeds, such as episcopal professions, will not be included. Such documents will be considered for separate treatment in one or more self-contained volume(s), within or outside the present scheme.
>
> All manumissions will be edited together, in a separate volume (one section for each church where the manumissions were recorded).[11]

The result of this is that some new, or newly reclassified, documents, despite being afforded a Sawyer number and thus canonical status, will nevertheless be excluded from the canonical series. However, despite this statement,

8 David A. E. Pelteret, *Catalogue of English Post-Conquest Vernacular Documents* (Woodbridge, 1990).

9 *Roch.*

10 David A. E. Pelteret, 'Two Old English Lists of Serfs', *Medieval Studies* 48 (1986), 470–513, at p. 493. Those omitted from the *Dictionary of Old English* are nos 32, 37, 40, 49, 52, 53, 55, 56, 58–60, 64–66, 69, 90, 111, 143, and 147.

11 *British Academy-Royal Historical Society Committee of Anglo-Saxon Charters Guidelines for Editors* (unpublished, 1990), p. 1. This document has been distributed to those individuals preparing editions for the British Academy Anglo-Saxon Charters series.

inclusion of a wider range of material is to an extent at the discretion of the editors. By way of example, the *Dictionary of Old English* Rec series include five items relating to Christ Church, Canterbury, four of which are pre-Conquest.[12] Two of these, Rec 6. 3 (a text inserted in a gospel-book outlining the boundary between Canterbury and Rochester), and Rec 6. 5 (now S 1204a), are included in the Christ Church volumes for the Anglo-Saxon Charters series,[13] but not Rec 6. 4, a notice of confraternity and list of names similarly inserted into another gospel-book datable by its contents to the reign of King Cnut,[14] nor Rec 6. 6, a manumission by King Æthelstan. The surprise here is not the omission of Rec 6. 4 or Rec 6. 6, given the guidelines for the editors, but rather the inclusion of Rec 6. 5, now S 1204a, the celebrated *Codex Aureus* inscription, which trumpets the return of the gospel-book in which the record is written to Christ Church following its ransom from the vikings. This does not appear to answer any more readily to the Committee's definition of a charter than does, for example, S 1451a, an account of consecration, omitted from the Christ Church volumes.

There thus appears some inconsistency relating even to those records that are securely dated to the pre-Conquest period. Those that post-date the Conquest, or are of uncertain date, are generally excluded. However, by their use of the vernacular and through their text type, these records show continuity of practice with those dating from the pre-Conquest period, both relating and responding to them. My contention is that such texts can only be understood within the context of other vernacular records from the archive to which they belong. I demonstrate this by attention to those texts currently classified within the Rec series from Bury St Edmunds, none of which has to date been included in the Sawyer catalogue.

Records from Bury St Edmunds

There follows a brief description of each of the items belonging to the Rec series from Bury St Edmunds:

- Rec 5. 2: an inventory relating to an unknown estate, including a list of people, animals, and foodstuffs (s. xi$^{4/4}$).[15]

---

12 The post-Conquest item, Rec 6. 10, a writ of William I, is misplaced in this series and should be reclassified (in *Dictionary of Old English* short-title terms) as Ch IWm.

13 *CantCC* 184 and 97.

14 N. R. Ker, *Catalogue of Manuscripts Containing Anglo-Saxon* (Oxford, 1957), p. 317.

15 *ASChart*, Appendix II.3, p. 248.

- Rec 5. 3: a fragmentary account of funerary arrangements (s. xii^{1}).[16]
- Rec 5. 4: a series of thirteen memoranda in six different hands regarding food-rents and charitable gifts. Contents include notice of food-farms due from estates, a list of holdings in various Norfolk hundreds, an inventory of movables (including books and ecclesiastical garments) in the church and treasure-house, charitable donations, gifts due to mark the anniversary of notables. Three are solely in Latin, one is glossed in Latin (s. xi^{med}–s. xii^{med}).[17]
- Rec 5. 5: two separate notes: a booklist, and a list of names associated with Bury St Edmunds, including that of Abbot Baldwin (1065×1097).[18]
- Rec 5. 6: an agreement with Ordric the cellarer relating to the collection of Peter's Pence. A rubric dates this to the reign of Edward the Confessor (1042×1066).[19]

Of these texts, two (Rec 5. 3, Rec 5. 5) seem to have been written on pieces of parchment subsequently deployed as flyleaves, while one (Rec 5. 2) is written into the back of a book.[20] The series comprising Rec 5. 4 is copied on a separate quire apparently designed to be added to an existing book. One (Rec 5. 6) survives in multiple cartulary copies. I discuss each of these separately below, except 5. 4, which has been the focus of my attention elsewhere.[21] I begin with those texts on flyleaves. The texts and translations presented here are from my and Sarah Foot's forthcoming edition of *Charters of Bury St Edmunds and St Benet at Holme* for the Anglo-Saxon Charters Series, included at our request because of the importance of vernacular texts from the foundation. I am responsible for the texts and translations themselves, the description of the manuscripts, and history of the archives; Prof. Foot for the history of the abbeys and their benefactors, together with historical commentaries to the editions.

Rec 5. 3

MS: Cambridge, Pembroke College 83, front flyleaf

16 *ASChart*, Appendix II.8, p. 252.

17 Oxford, Corpus Christi College 197, fols 106v–109r; *ASChart*, no. 104, pp. 192–200.

18 *ASChart*, Appendix II.7, p. 250.

19 *ASChart*, no. 119, p. 220. For a recent study of Peter's Pence, see Rory Naismith and Francesca Tinti, 'The Origins of Peter's Pence', *EHR* 134 (2019), 521–52, with discussion of the Bury text at pp. 542–43.

20 Manuscript details for each of these texts are supplied below.

21 Kathryn A. Lowe, 'Post-Conquest Bilingual Memoranda from Bury St Edmunds', *Review of English Studies* 59 (2008), 52–66.

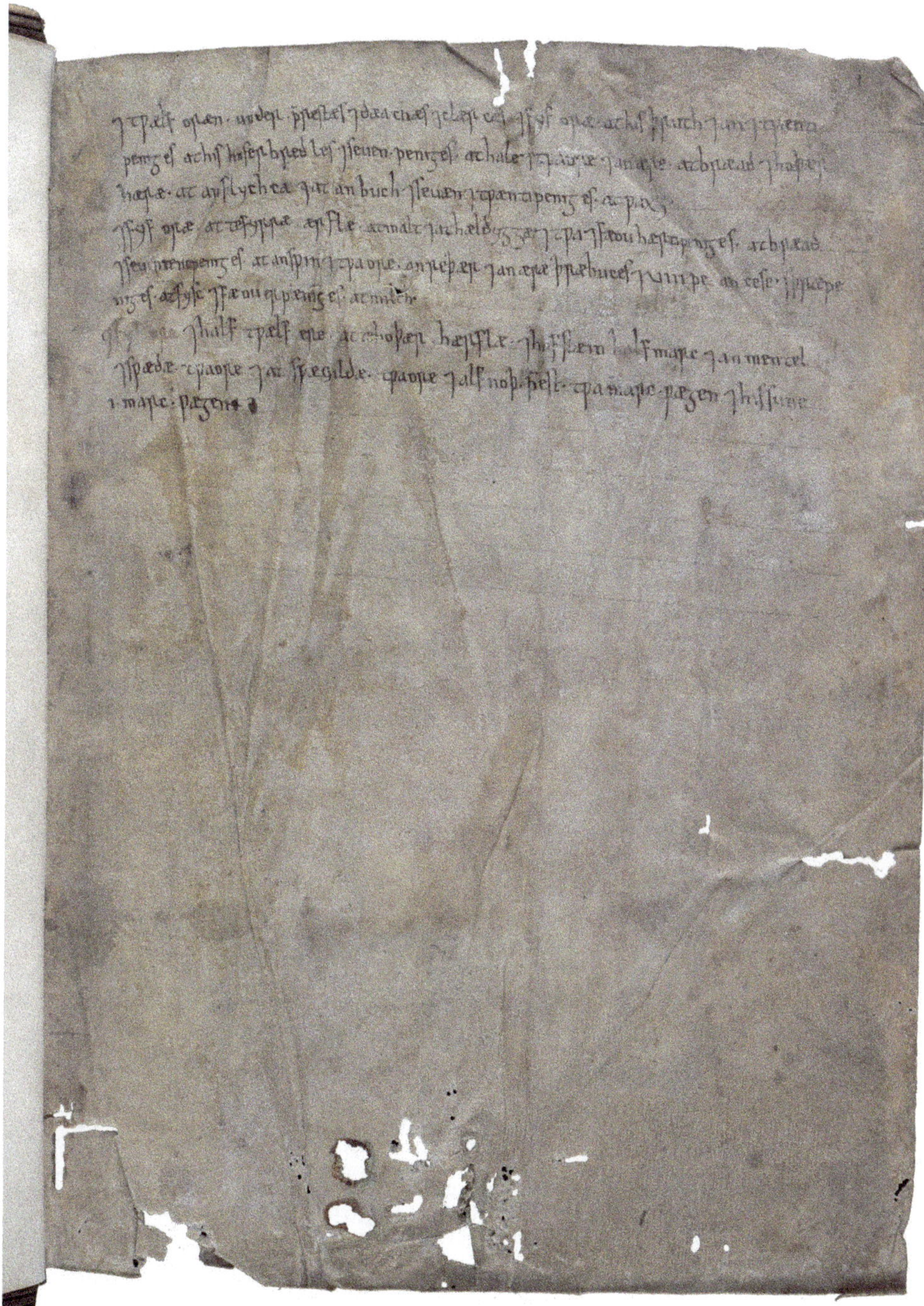

FIGURE 12.1 Cambridge, Pembroke College 83, front flyleaf
BY PERMISSION OF THE MASTER AND FELLOWS OF PEMBROKE COLLEGE, CAMBRIDGE

Text:

& tpælf oræn . under . prestæs & dæcnæs & clærcæs & fyf oræ . at his þruth & an & tpænti peniges at his hoferbredles & seuen . peniges . at hale & tpa ore [...]& an ære . at bræad & hoþær hæræ . at an flychca & at an buch & seuæn & tpænti peniges . at pax;.

& fyf oræ . at te fyrræ . ærflæ . at malt & at hældyggæ & tpa & fæouhærti peniges . at bræad & seuentene peniges . at an spin & tpa ore . an reþær & an æræ þræ buces & viii. pe . an cese & þræ peniges . at fysc & fæouer pæniges . at milch.

& half tpælf ere . at te hoþær . hærflæ . & Hafslæin half marc & an mentel & Spædæ . twa ore & at Spæg<n>ildæ . tpa ore & Alfnoþ . p*r*est . tpa marc . Ƿægen & his sune i. marc . Ƿægen

['... and twelve ores for the priests and deacons and clerics, and five ores for his coffin, and twenty-one pennies for his pall, and seven pennies for ale, and two ores [...], and one ore for bread, and another ore for a flitch of bacon, and for a (male) goat, and twenty-seven pennies for wax. And five ores for the first funeral feast for malt and for fuel, and forty-two pennies for bread, and seventeen pennies for a pig, and two ores [for] an ox, and one ore for three (male) goats, and eight pennies for a cheese, and three pennies for fish, and four pennies for milk. And eleven and a half ores for the second funeral feast, and to Hafstein half a mark and a cloak, and to Swathi two ores, and for Sweinhild two ores, and to Ælfnoth the priest two marks. To Wagen and his son one mark ...']

Rec 5. 3 is a most curious document recording a set of funerary arrangements. It is written on the recto of the front flyleaf added to a manuscript of Bede's commentary on Luke's gospel (*In Lucae euangelium expositio*), originally from Saint-Denis (now Cambridge, Pembroke College 83).[22] The manuscript itself dates to the first half of the ninth century, or to its middle. The hand of the record, described aptly by Rebecca Rushforth as 'very unpractised and difficult to date',[23] may perhaps best be compared with charter script as it develops after the Conquest. It is probably of the first half of the twelfth century,

22 The manuscript is listed with bibliography in Helmut Gneuss and Michael Lapidge, *Anglo-Saxon Manuscripts: A Bibliographical Handlist of Manuscripts and Manuscript Fragments Written or Owned in England up to 1100* (Toronto, 2014), no. 134.

23 Rebecca J. Rushforth, 'The Eleventh- and Early Twelfth-Century Manuscripts of Bury St Edmunds Abbey' (unpublished PhD thesis, University of Cambridge, 2002), p. 62.

perhaps somewhat closer to the middle of that century than to its beginning.[24] Attention to the verso of the leaf on which the memorandum appears confirms this *terminus ante quem*. It contains a statement 'Incipit epistola Accae epistoli ad Bedam de postulanda expositione in Lucam', written in the first half of the twelfth century, that generally prefaces the text itself of Acca's letter to Bede. The letter itself begins on the following folio. The surface of the folio containing the memorandum appears to have residue on it, perhaps of paste. If so, it may be taken as evidence that the statement postdates the memorandum, and was written on a piece of scrap parchment containing the record. The manuscript was catalogued by Henry of Kirkestede in the mid-fourteenth century;[25] its absence from earlier lists should not be taken as significant given the disorganization of the library before Kirkestede set to work; as a Saint-Denis book, it may well have arrived at Bury in 1065 with its new abbot, Baldwin, who had been a monk there.[26]

The record itself is markedly informal in terms of its execution, but nevertheless seems to be a copy of an existing text: what appears to be an error of copying <l> for <t> in 'Hafslæin' (cf. ON *Hafsteinn*) along with the erased phrase '& fyf oræ' at the start of the final section, apparently the result of accidentally restarting the previous section, suggests this.[27] The end of the text looks as though it has been blotted out by the scribe who perhaps thought that whatever remained of his exemplar was not worth the effort of recopying.

The language of the record similarly supports a dating of the twelfth century. We have the consistent writing of *a* for *æ* in *at* (no fewer than fifteen times) and in the personal name 'Alfnoth'.[28] There is monophthongization of *ea* and merger with *æ* throughout, for example, 'hale' (PDE *ale*), 'pax', 'malt', and 'half'.[29]

24 I am most grateful to Prof. Julia Crick for her opinion on the dating of the script and to Prof. Tessa Webber for hers on the dating of the incipit statement.

25 Henry of Kirkestede, *Catalogus de libris autenticis et apocrifis*, eds Richard H. Rouse and Mary A. Rouse (Oxford, 2004), K84. 23, p. 153.

26 Herman the Archdeacon and Goscelin of Saint-Bertin, *Miracles of St Edmund*, ed. and trans. Tom Licence (Oxford, 2014), pp. 60–61.

27 In this chapter standard headwords are printed in italics, while citations from original manuscripts are provided in quotation marks.

28 For the sound change and its chronology from the Old English perspective, see Richard M. Hogg, *A Grammar of Old English. Volume 1: Phonology* (Oxford, 1992), §5.216; and from the Middle English perspective, Richard Jordan, *Handbook of Middle English Grammar: Phonology*, ed. Eugene J. Crook (The Hague, 1974), §32.

29 Hogg, *A Grammar of Old English*, §5.212, §215; Jordan, *Handbook of Middle English Grammar*, §58. The <æ> of the stressed syllable of *dæcnæs* may derive from what the Oxford English Dictionary describes as a 'popular' form of the Latin loan (*Oxford English Dictionary Online*, Oxford University Press, www.oed.com, December 2018, *s.v.* 'deacon, n.1').

All of this suggests twelfth, rather than eleventh, century. However *ēa* retains its traditional spelling as a diphthong (to a degree, if <æa> can be described as traditional; see further below) in 'bræad'.[30] *eo* is consistently *e* (in 'seuen(tene)' on three occasions).[31] The fortunes of *ēo* are mixed, with monophthongization and unrounding in 'prestæs', 'þræ', but retention in 'fæouer', 'fæouhærti'. Hogg observes that such monophthongization is very infrequently represented in texts until the very end of the period, and it is generally characterized as a twelfth-century feature.[32] The spellings with <æ> are likely inverse, reflecting the collapse of the front vowels to /e/ exhibited in other Bury charters; this also accounts for the use of the graph <æ> for <e> in 'tpænti', 'tpælf'.[33] The Norse diphthong /øy/ in the singular form of Present-Day English *ora* 'a Danish unit of account' OE *ȳre* (cf. Olcel. *eyrir*) is monophthongized to /y:/. Here, with the merger of /y:/ to /e:/, considered a Kentish phenomenon, but recorded in several Bury charters, it is spelled 'ere',[34] together with a slew of inverse spellings in <æ> ('ære' etc.).[35]

Perhaps more striking is the use of <æ> for <e> in unstressed syllables ('oræn', 'prestæs', 'dæcnæs', 'clærcæs', 'hoþær', 'seuæn', 'oræ', 'fyrræ', etc.), and as the first element of diphthongs 'bræad', 'fæouer'. Other Bury records from this period do not exhibit such features. For example, the last in a series of texts constituting Rec 5. 4 was copied around the middle of the twelfth century by the sixth hand working on that set, in other words, no earlier than our funerary arrangements record. It reads as follows:

> Ðis is s*an*cte Eadmundes ferme on Byrtune .iiii. met maltes under masc & grut . halmet hpæte . an ryðer . & ii. spin .iiii. ges .xx. hennen . Of Ruham ealspa mycel . & of Redgraue ealspa Of Pakenha*m* & of Stantune ealspa mycel . Of Elmespelle & of Ƿulpet & of Grotene ealspa . Of Herningpelle & of Cunegestune ealspa mycel Of Palegraue & of Ðorpe ealspa mycel . Of Horningeseorðe & of Risby ealspa micel . Of Kokefelde & of Ceorlespurðe ealspa micel . Of Hpepstede & of Bradefelde ealspa

30 Hogg, *A Grammar of Old English*, §5.212; Jordan, *Handbook of Middle English Grammar*, §81.

31 Jordan, *Handbook of Middle English Grammar*, §73.

32 Hogg, *A Grammar of Old English*, §5.211; Jordan, *Handbook of Middle English Grammar*, §84.

33 Kathryn A. Lowe, 'Linguistic Geography, Demography, and Monastic Community: Scribal Language at Bury St Edmunds', in *Interfaces between Language and Culture in Medieval England. A Festschrift for Matti Kilpiö*, eds Alaric Hall, Olga Timofeeva, Ágnes Kiricsi, and Bethany Fox (Leiden, 2011), pp. 147–178, at 172 and discussion.

34 Hogg, *A Grammar of Old English*, §5.194; Lowe, 'Linguistic Geography', pp. 152–53 with examples, Appendix, pp. 171–75.

35 Sara M. Pons-Sanz, *The Lexical Effects of Anglo-Scandinavian Linguistic Contact on Old English* (Leiden, 2013), §2.2.1.3.

> mycel . Of Ƿyrlingpurðe & of Saham ealspa mycel . Of Rungetune . & of Culeforde & of Fornha*m* ealspa mycel . On Brokeforde & of Rikingehale ealspa mycel . Of Tifteshale .i. met maltes under masc & grut & .i. lepene hpæte . & feorðendæl an ryðer & an half spin & an gos & .v. hennen.
>
> ['This is St Edmund's food-rent from [Great] Barton: three measures of malt including mash and grout, a half-measure of wheat, one ox and two pigs, four geese, twenty hens. From Rougham just as much and from Redgrave the same. From Pakenham and from Stanton just as much. From Elmswell and from Woolpit and from Groton the same. From Herringswell and from Coney Weston just as much. From Palgrave and from Thorpe just as much. From Horringer and from Risby just as much. From Cockfield and from Chelsworth just as much. From Whepstead and from Bradfield just as much. From Worlingworth and from [Monk] Soham just as much. From Runcton and from Culford and from Fornham just as much. From Brockford and from Rickinghall just as much. From Tivetshall one measure of malt including mash and grout, and one basket of wheat, and a quarter of an ox, and half a pig, and one goose, and five hens.'][36]

While this text shares the late phonological features such as (in part) monophthongization of diphthongs noticeable in the funeral feast record ('ferme', 'half', 'malt', 'Rikingehale', 'Tifteshale'), it displays none of the confusion between *æ* and *e* in unstressed syllables manifest in Rec 5. 3. It seems that it was perfectly possible, then, to write unexceptional late Old English in the mid-twelfth century at Bury; none of the other records listed above, albeit shorter, manifest the kind of variation seen in Rec 5. 3.

Could the language itself of Rec 5. 3 result from the record's informality? It is certainly the case that the final text in Rec 5. 4 is far more carefully written than our funerary record. As a group, the texts constituting Rec 5. 4 were inserted on a separate quire, ruled similarly, to accompany a copy of the Rule of St Benedict. Rushforth has argued that the formality of the first hand suggests that it was always intended to be added to the book,[37] and this may have led to a greater degree of care taken in copying the subsequent records. Rec 5. 3, by contrast, is something of a mess, looking at best casual.

While this seems an attractive hypothesis on the face of it, it may not be the case. Such <æ> for <e> forms in unstressed syllables, while sporadic elsewhere,

36 The text and its translation are taken from our forthcoming edition.

37 Rushforth, 'Eleventh and Early-Twelfth Century Manuscripts', p. 16.

are a notable feature, for instance, of some of the charter copies produced by the main hand responsible for the earliest part (essentially to fol. 110v)[38] of the *Codex Wintoniensis* (London, British Library, Add. 15350) from the Old Minster, Winchester. This is similarly datable to the first half of the twelfth century (1129×1139), and is a most handsome production, written in a fine bookhand:[39]

> And heo þanne gæornlicæ of þam god geþæncæ and for uncre sawle geornlicæ beo and brucæ heo þæs landæs æt Batancumbæ hyræ dæg and æfter hire dæge ga hit an Ælfwærdes hand uncres suna gif hæ lifæs beo gyf hæ næ beo gyf hæ næ beo [*sic*] for mine broðorn[40]
>
> ['And she is to remember God zealously [with almsgiving] from the property, and be zealous for the welfare of our souls. And she is to possess the estate at Batcombe for her time and after her death it is to pass into the possession of our son Ælfweard if he is still alive. If he is not, my brothers are to succeed to it']

Although such spellings appear on occasion throughout the work of this scribe, there is, however, a marked cluster of them. This led R. A. Williams to argue that the *Codex Wintoniensis* scribe copied texts running from fols 91r–111v (beginning with his text of S 304 and ending with S 336) from an exemplar already including those texts.[41] Williams's work requires revision; it is impossible to identify the sequence with such precision, because the majority of charters in the manuscript contain only a small amount of English (in the form of bounds), and the end of the sequence as identified by Williams is in fact copied by another scribe. It is, though, certainly the case that the four wholly vernacular texts within the tranche (S 1485, S 1402, S 1484, and S 1476) are different in character from the rest of the scribe's copies of Old English texts elsewhere in the manuscript. While, then, the main text scribe of the *Codex Wintoniensis* produced a formal copy of his exemplar(s), we cannot tell what they in turn looked like. However, the range of charters included in the cluster suggests that the exemplar must also have been a product of the Old Minster scriptorium.

There is, however, a comparandum from the Bury archive itself, one that appears a century earlier. The same alternation appears in the single sheet

38 Alexander R. Rumble, *Property and Piety in Early Medieval Winchester* (Oxford, 2002), p. 6.

39 The hand is described by Rumble, *Property and Piety*, pp. 6–7.

40 S 1485 (*ASWills* 9, p. 22, l. 31–p. 24, l. 4 with translation p. 23, p. 25 as quoted here).

41 R. A. Williams, 'Die Vokale der Tonsilben im *Codex Wintoniensis*', *Anglia* 25 (1902), 393–517, at pp. 396–97.

of the wills of Ælfflæd and her sister, Æthelflæd (S 1486, S 1494), probably of the final quarter of the tenth century. This is a text whose language I have studied in some detail elsewhere.[42] The example below manifests all of the same features.

> ic an … twægra bæha on twera punda gewihte. & twa sopcuppan. & an sæolfran fæt; & þæ leof æadmodlice bidde for godes luuan. & for mines hlafordæs sawle lufan. & for minræ swystor sawlæ lufan þ*æt* þu amundie þa halgan stowæ et Stocæ þæ mine yldran on restaþ.[43]
>
> ['I grant … two armlets of two pounds in weight, and two drinking-cups and a silver vessel. And I humbly pray you, Sire, for God's sake and for the sake of my lord's soul and for the sake of my sister's soul, that you will protect the holy foundation at Stoke in which my ancestors lie buried']

It is worth noting in this regard that Bury is by no means the only (or even the major) beneficiary of either of these wills, and it seems most likely in fact that the surviving single sheet originated from the foundation of Stoke-by-Nayland, just over twenty miles to the south of Bury, close to the Essex border. The language, I have argued, is best explained as the output of a scribe working at a foundation less important than Bury and therefore less of a centre of scribal production.[44] However, the language of the wills is unusual because of its tenth-century date rather than the forms themselves, which are encountered with reasonable frequency in the twelfth century; we therefore cannot conclude that Rec 5. 3 was not written at Bury judging from morphology and phonology alone.

While the phonology of Rec 5. 3, then, does not preclude a Bury origin, what of its other features? The text includes unusual lexical items drawn from Norse. Norse vocabulary is studded through the Bury archive, owing both to its location in the eastern Danelaw, and the overwhelmingly eleventh-century skew of its surviving charters. The pre-Conquest names which appear throughout the benefactors' lists from the abbey are similarly testament to this shared heritage: Thurkil, Thurketel, Thurstan, Ulfktel, Ketel, and so on. Below appears a list of the Norse-derived terms in texts from the archive, compiled from Sara

42 Lowe, 'Linguistic Geography', pp. 153–55.

43 S 1486 (*ASWills* 15, p. 38, ll. 2, 6–10 with translation p. 39 as quoted here).

44 Lowe, 'Linguistic Geography', p. 155.

Pons-Sanz's monograph on Anglo-Scandinavian linguistic contact, with the exception of the almost ubiquitous *eorl* and the money term *mark*.[45]

> *elding*, 'fuel' (cf. OIc *elding*) Rec 5. 3; *erfle*, 'funeral feast' (cf. OIcel *erfiǫl*) Rec 5. 3; *brynige* 'coat of mail' (cf. OIcel *brynja*) S 1537, S 1531, S 1519; *fæt*, 'clothes' (cf. OIcel *fat*) S 1531; *feolaga*, 'partner' (cf. OIcel *félagi*) S 1531; *feolagscipe*, 'partnership' (cf. OIcel *félagskapr*) S 1519, S 1531; *fro*, 'from' (cf. OIcel *frá*) S 1083, S 1527; *fyrre*(*r*), 'first (of two things)' (cf. OIcel *fyrri*) Rec 5. 3; *goldwrecen*, 'inlaid with gold' (cf. OIcel *gullrekinn*) S 1537; *griðbryce*, 'breach of the peace' (cf. OIcel *griðabrek*) S 1078, S 1084; *hamsocn*, 'offence of attacking a man in his own home; privilege relating to the offence' (cf. OIcel *heimsókn*) S 1078, S 1084; *lagu*, 'law' (cf. OIcel *lǫg*) S 1083; *unlagu* 'illegality' (cf. OIcel *úlǫg*) S 1077; *lysing*, 'freeman' (cf. OIcel *leysingi*) S 1529; *maldæg*, 'covenant' (cf. OIcel *máldagi*) S 1531; *manslot*, 'share of land, holding' (cf. OIcel *mannshlutr*) Rec 5. 4; *mund*, 'bride-price' (cf. OIcel *mundr*) S 1531; *yre*, 'unit of account' (cf. OIcel *eyrir*) S 1531, Rec 5. 3, Rec 5. 4; *sceppe*, 'a dry measure' (cf. OIcel *skeppa*) Rec 5. 4; *scoru*, 'the number of twenty' (cf. OIc *skor*) Rec 5. 4; *toft*, 'homestead' (cf. OIcel *topt*) S 1525, S 1527, S 1531.

Rec 5. 3 includes four words (along with *mark*) that are demonstrably Norse-derived. *yre*, the money term, is found elsewhere in charters from Bury, including twice in the series of records comprising Rec. 5. 4. *fyrre*(*r*) (*Dictionary of Old English Online s.v. fyrre, fyrrer*) is also found in the first continuation of the Peterborough Chronicle in the entry for 1131 (written around that time) as a synonym for OE *forma*, the way in which it is used here.[46] *elding* 'fuel' and *erfle* 'funeral feast' are not found anywhere else in Old English. According to Oxford English Dictionary, *elding*'s (*s.v.* 'elding, n.1') next occurrence in the written record dates to the fifteenth century, although in a text believed to have been composed in the fourteenth century. *Erfle* (*s.v.* ''arval | 'arvel | 'arvill, n') is next recorded in the middle of the fifteenth century; neither *Oxford English Dictionary Online* entry currently includes this example.

It is not just the language that is unusual: the text, of course, makes provision for not one, but two, funeral feasts. Most recently Victoria Thompson has

45 Pons-Sanz, *Anglo-Scandinavian Linguistic Contact.*

46 *The Anglo-Saxon Chronicle: A Collaborative Edition. Vol. 7, MS. E*, ed. Susan Irvine (Cambridge, 2004), p. 132.

argued that this is a Scandinavian practice.[47] This milieu is also suggested by the names: all the people in the text, with the exception of the priest, Ælfnoth, have Norse-derived names: 'Hafslæin' (< ON *Hafsteinn*), 'Spædæ', perhaps the Norse byname *Svaði*, 'Spægildæ' <? **Sveinhildr* (an unattested feminine personal name), and 'Ƿægen' (< ODan *Wagn*).[48] The forms of *Hafsteinn* and *Sveinhildr* seem to have been corrupted in the course of transmission and, as noted above, the <l> instead of the <t> in 'Hafslæin', as well as the accidental repetition of the start of the first paragraph at the beginning of the second, suggests that this is a copy of an existing text. Although what survives describes funerary arrangements and therefore was relevant only until after burial, we have lost the start of the text. The garbling of the personal names indicates that they were unfamiliar to the copyist and/or that they were unclear in the original text, rather implying that they were copied at one remove or more in terms of time or location from the original. It is possible that the missing part outlined bequests of value (or which subsequently became of value) to Bury, which prompted its recopying. With no mention of any estates or the name of the testator in the text that survives, there is no way of testing this conjecture. Alternatively, and perhaps more likely, scrap parchment could have migrated to the foundation from outlying areas, perhaps (in this case) from a local church, where laymen were more commonly buried in the late Anglo-Saxon period.[49]

The next text I consider is similarly written on a flyleaf, and is one of two early booklists surviving from the archive.

Rec 5. 5
MS: Bodleian, Auct. D. 2. 14, fol. 173r

Text:

> Þas bocas haueð Salomon pre*o*st . þ*æt* is þe codspeltraht .
> & þe martyrliua .[50] [& þe ....][51] & þe æ<n>glisce saltere

47 Victoria Thompson, *Dying and Death in Later Anglo-Saxon England* (Woodbridge, 2004), p. 127.

48 I am grateful to Prof. John Insley for help with interpreting these forms.

49 Helen Gittos, 'Creating the Sacred: Anglo-Saxon Rites for Consecrating Cemeteries', in *Burial in Early Medieval England and Wales*, eds Sam Lucy and Andrew Reynolds (London, 2002), pp. 195–208. I owe this reference to Prof. Sarah Foot.

50 martyrluia MS.

51 This entry has been erased; traces of letters are visible; number of dots indicates likely number of letters affected.

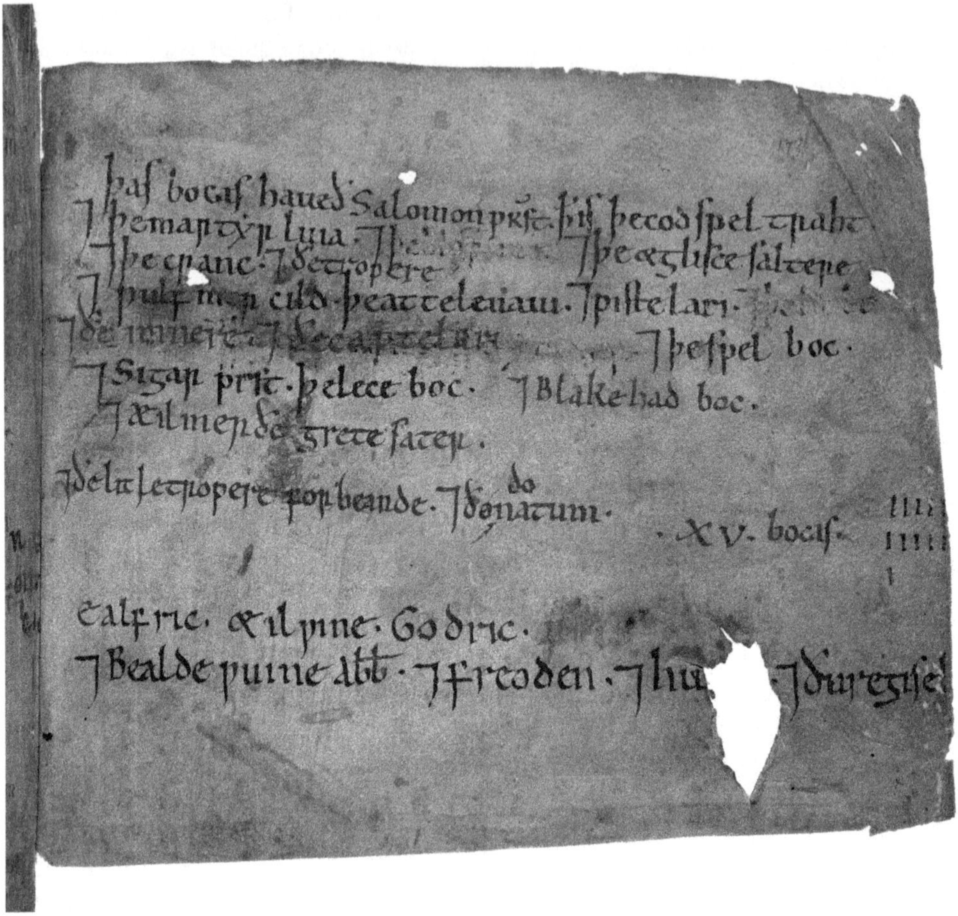

FIGURE 12.2 Oxford, Bodleian Library, Auct. D.2.14, fol. 173r

& þe cranc . & ðe tropere
& Ƿulfmer cild . þe atteleuaui. & pistelari . [& þe.....e][52]
[53]& ðe imnere . & ðe captelari[53] & þe spelboc .
& Sigar preost . þe leceboc . & Blake ha<n>dboc .
& Æilmer ðe grete sater .
& ðe litle tropere forbea[r]nde . & ðe \do/natum .

.xv. bocas .

52 This entry has been erased.

53 This passage is written over erased text.

Ealfric . Æilpine . Godric .[54]
Bealdepuine abb*ot* . & Freoden. & Hu[...][55] . & Ðuregisel

['Salomon the priest has these books: that is, the homiliary, and the lives of the martyrs [?], and the ..., and the English psalter, and the chronicle, and the troper.

And Wulfmær Cild the gradual, and an epistolary, and the ..., and the hymnal, and the collectar, and the homiliary.

And Sigar the priest the leechbook, and Blaca a manual, and Æthelmær the great psalter.

And the small burned troper and the Donatus.

Fifteen books.']

These two separate texts, a booklist, and a list of names, are written on the flyleaf to an Italian gospel-book dated by David Dumville to the sixth or seventh century.[56] The book seems to have arrived in England by the end of the eighth century, when annotations were made in it that link it to Mercia, probably Lichfield.[57] How, or whether, the book arrived at Bury is unknown; as Rushforth observes, there is no evidence that it was ever at the abbey, and the flyleaf may have been added following the book's acquisition by Sir Robert Cotton.[58] The flyleaf is considerably shorter than the volume to which it now belongs and looks to be a piece of scrap parchment. There is a large hole towards the bottom of the parchment which has led to the loss of perhaps three letters in the penultimate name. The reverse contains the Latin service *Ad introitum portae* in a hand of the second half of the eleventh century. It is unrelated to the text considered here.[59]

The texts are linked to Bury's monastic community as a result of the (separate) list of names towards the bottom of the leaf, which include Abbot Baldwin and Frodo, probably his brother. It is in a larger and slightly more formal hand than the booklist that precedes it on the parchment, and is similar in aspect to the hand of Rec 5. 2, discussed below. The mention of Baldwin and the general

54 A word of four or five letters has been erased following this name.

55 A torn hole in the parchment results in the lost of three or four letters at the end of the name followed by a punctus.

56 Gneuss and Lapidge, *Anglo-Saxon Manuscripts*, no. 529; David N. Dumville, *Liturgy and the Ecclesiastical History of Late Anglo-Saxon England* (Woodbridge, 1992), p. 102.

57 Dumville, *Liturgy and the Ecclesiastical History*, p. 102.

58 Rushforth, 'Eleventh- and Early Twelfth-Century Manuscripts', pp. 19–20.

59 Ker, *Catalogue of Manuscripts*, no. 290.

appearance of the hand has been used to date the texts to his abbacy (1065–97), but the language of both texts suggests a rather later, twelfth-century, date: the determiner is consistently levelled to 'þe' or 'ðe', 'bocas' has an analogical plural, not found elsewhere in the Old English corpus, and both texts include inverse spellings of <ea> for <æ> (in 'Ealfric' and, probably, 'forbea[r]nde') following the monophthongization of *ea* in the twelfth century (with sporadic forms recorded earlier). The list of names might, of course, have been recopied (for whatever reason) from an earlier list: the unusual spelling 'Bealdepuine', with <p> replacing one of the two <u>s which together represent the same sound, and what looks to be an oblique ending on 'Freoden' might support this theory.

The booklist itself is written in handwriting that Michael Lapidge describes as 'excessively crude'.[60] Two scribes appear to have been at work on the list, although their contributions are at times hard to distinguish. The messy appearance is compounded by the lack of ruling and by the series of erasures and overwriting. Both scribes use Caroline **a**, but a combination of long **r** and Caroline **r** (and once a majuscule), apparently at random. The first scribe seems to have written everything as far as 'leceboc' except '& ðe tropere'; the second adds the subsequent entries and supplies the total number of books. To the right of this is what seems to be a tally, a series of 11 vertical strokes disposed in two rows of five and a final single stroke. Although it is possible that further strokes could have been lost at the right-hand edge, the total could not have matched the sum of 15 books noted in the text if the first two rows were even in number.

The booklist seems to have been a working document updated over a period of time, perhaps as books were returned to the library; it is noteworthy that there are two erasures, and the first two items on the fourth line, '& ðe imnere. & ðe captelari', have been written over a longer set of entries, inexpertly erased. Despite the overall untidy effect, the total of 15 books given at the bottom is the total of the books as modified.

The booklist is entirely different in type from the other surviving specimen from the archive during this period, the third in the series of records comprising Rec 5. 4. Here ten books kept within the church are listed as part of an inventory of the abbey's possessions when Leofstan became abbot; they appear from their nature to be important volumes required for the celebration of mass and the saying of the Divine Office; also included is a *vita* of St Edmund. This

60 Michael Lapidge, 'Surviving Booklists from Anglo-Saxon England', in *Learning and Literature in Anglo-Saxon England*, eds Michael Lapidge and Helmut Gneuss (Cambridge, 1985), pp. 33–89, at 74.

record begins with an extraordinary preamble, which I have argued elsewhere may be a translation of a charter proem celebrating Leofstan's appointment as abbot in 1045.[61] After the list of books, the inventory continues with a list of vestments, fittings, and furniture for the church held in the treasury, and concludes with a list of (liturgical) books and related items in the possession of seven named individuals, four of whose names recur in another context in the first record in the series. This final part of the record runs directly on from what precedes it, and seems therefore to be part of this commemorative snapshot of a moment in the abbey's history.

Rec 5. 3 was written on a piece of parchment later deployed as a flyleaf to a book. Charters and records find their way into spare leaves or spare gaps in a variety of high-grade service books, bibles or other works, or, as in the case of Rec 5. 4, added on a separate quire. These seem deliberate attempts to preserve important transactions, produced at a time prior to the production of a general cartulary in the early thirteenth century. The next text I look at, Rec 5. 2, also appears to fall into this category, but such an interpretation presents a number of problems.

Rec 5. 2
MS: Cambridge, Pembroke College 88, fol. 167v

Text:

> [.x]l peorcpyrðra manna .xviii. oxana .
> [..]xxvi faldhriþera hundteontig spina & .ui.
> [hu]ndnigontig sceapa. sifon hund flicca .
> [ty]n hund ceasa .vii. systras huniges . oþar
> [ha]lf hund foþra cornes .ccc. æcera asapen.
>
> ['... forty able-bodied men, eighteen oxen, ... and ... stalled cattle, one hundred pigs and ninety-six sheep, seven hundred flitches of bacon, one thousand cheeses, seven sesters of honey, one hundred and fifty fothers of corn, three hundred acres sown.']

The inventory is written on the verso of the final (mutilated) leaf of a late tenth-century copy of Laidcenn's *Egloga de 'Moralibus in Job'*.[62] There is considerable debate about whether the host manuscript is English or Continental.

61 Lowe, 'Bilingual Memoranda', p. 60.

62 Gneuss and Lapidge, *Anglo-Saxon Manuscripts*, no. 135.

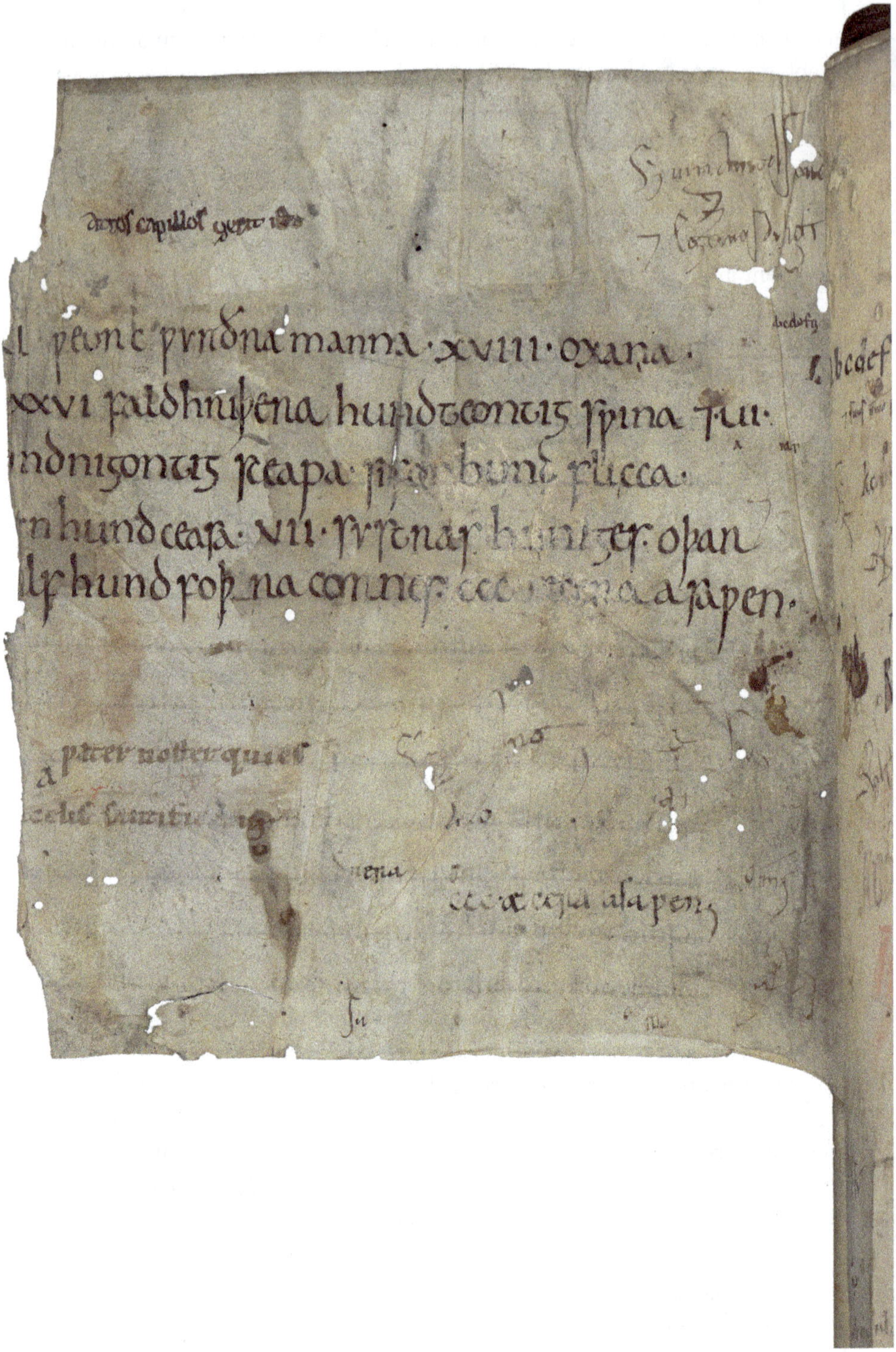

FIGURE 12.3 Cambridge, Pembroke College 88, fol. 167v

T. A. M. Bishop identified one of the hands working within it as one responsible for a stint in a manuscript (Oxford, Bodleian Library, Auct. D. inf. 2. 9) almost certainly produced at St Augustine's, Canterbury,[63] an attribution supported by the most thoroughgoing analysis of the script in the context of that scriptorium, that of Helen McKee.[64] She concludes that he was likely a Continental scribe working at the foundation,[65] and dismisses Gneuss's suggestion that the manuscript hailed from Saint-Denis, noting that the script has no connection with the script practised there at that time.[66] An *ex-libris* inscription places the manuscript at Bury around 1200.[67] The text of the *Egloga* is incomplete, but it seems as though a final ten- rather than the standard eight-leaf, quire, if James's collation is accurate, was used in order to fit what remained of the text.[68]

The text of the inventory occupies the first five ruled lines of what was a blank folio with a generous top margin. The bottom of the page has been cut away, and a narrow step of parchment has been roughly removed at the fore-edge extending from the top of the parchment to the bottom of the memorandum. The resultant loss is probably no more than a couple of letters from the beginning of each line. The text of the inventory is written in a large round minuscule which Rushforth dates to the late eleventh century;[69] it features a curious **y** with no tail, almost **v**-shaped, and an **n**-shaped **r** without descender, similar to the half-uncial type. **a** is occasionally Caroline.

The language of the record cannot certainly establish its provenance either. 'sceapa' is a West Saxon (hereafter WS) form, with *ǣ* > *ēa* through palatal diphthongization.[70] The expected form in non-WS would be *scepa*. 'sifon' is another

63 T. A. M. Bishop, *English Caroline Minuscule* (Oxford, 1971), p. xxv.

64 Helen McKee, 'St Augustine's Abbey, Canterbury: Book-Production in the Tenth and Eleventh Centuries' (unpublished PhD thesis, University of Cambridge, 1997). McKee rejects another scribal attribution by Bishop, p. 121.

65 McKee, 'St Augustine's Abbey', p. 122. It may be noted that the association is rejected by R. C. Barker-Benfield, *St Augustine's Abbey, Canterbury*, 3 vols (Oxford, 2008), 3:1824 as being without 'independent evidence of provenance'.

66 McKee, 'St Augustine's Abbey', p. 121, n. 265. Gneuss repeats the suggestion in the summary information to the entry in Gneuss and Lapidge, *Anglo-Saxon Manuscripts*, no. 135.

67 Henry of Kirkestede, *Catalogus*, eds Rouse and Rouse, p. xliv, n. 57.

68 Montague Rhodes James, *A Descriptive Catalogue of the Manuscripts in the Library of Pembroke College, Cambridge* (Cambridge, 1905), no. 88, p. 81. The text ends approximately halfway through Lathcen's final *Egloga XXXV* as edited by Adriaen (who only partly collates this manuscript), though the leaf has been cut away (*Egloga quam scripsit Lathcen filius Baith de moralibus Iob quas Gregorius fecit*, ed. M. Adriaen (Turnhout, 1969), p. 361, l. 106, ending 'omne malum').

69 Rushforth, 'Eleventh- and Early Twelfth-Century Manuscripts', p. 63.

70 Hogg, *A Grammar of Old English*, §5.19.

WS form. Here the normal development is *i* > *io* through *u*-umlaut.[71] Initial *sio* developed in Early WS to *sie*, and *y* in Late WS,[72] subsequently unrounded to *i* (evidenced in what Richard Jordan calls 'West Saxon subdialects' already in late Old English).[73] 'systras', however, seems to be an inverted spelling of *sestras*, with similar examples found in both Kent and Bury.[74] These is no sign of monophthongization of diphthongs, for example in 'weorc', nor evidence of the merger of /æ/ and /ɑ/ (so still 'æceras' rather than *aceras*); the only other late (i.e. eleventh-century) form is 'oþar', where the *a* of the unaccented syllable indicates that the back vowels had merged with /e/.[75] The form 'ceasa' is unexampled elsewhere and is perhaps to be explained as patterned on 'sceapa' earlier in the same line. *cesa* or *cysa* would be the expected form at Bury (or Canterbury), with i-mutation in WS of *ēa* giving *cīesa*. In sum, the language of this text looks broadly standardized, with only one clearly non-WS spelling which would be equally as likely found in Canterbury as Bury St Edmunds.

Similar lists can be found in a number of archives, including Bury itself, where the sixth in the series of memoranda comprising Rec 5. 4 itemizes a list of goods left at an estate in Egmere (Norfolk) after Cola (presumably a tenant) left it. The main text of this record is written by the first scribe producing the series, datable to the middle of the eleventh century, but it also has an interlinear word-for-word Latin gloss in a hand of the end of the eleventh or beginning of the twelfth century.

> Her onstent gepriten hpæt man funde æt Eggemere syððan Cole hit let . Ðæt is .vii. oxen .& .viii. cy . & .iiii. feldhryþera . & .ii. stottas . & .v. scora scæp . & .xv. scæp under ealde & iunge . & .viii. score æcere gesawen & .i. flicce & .i. swin & .xxiiii. cesen.[76]
>
> ['Here stands written what was found at Egmere after Cola left it: that is, seven oxen and eight cows, and four grazing bullocks, and two young horses, and 100 sheep, and 15 underage and young sheep, and 160 sown acres, and one flitch of bacon, and one pig, and 24 cheeses.']

---

71 Hogg, *A Grammar of Old English*, §5.24.

72 A. Campbell, *Old English Grammar* (Oxford, 1959), §299(c).

73 Jordan, *Handbook of Middle English Grammar*, §41.

74 Examples of inverse spellings in the single-sheet wills from the archive are provided in the Appendix to Lowe, 'Linguistic Geography', pp. 171–75.

75 Hogg, *A Grammar of Old English*, §5.215.

76 Oxford, Corpus Christi College 197, fol. 108r (also printed in *ASChart*, no. 104, p. 196, ll. 10–19).

Perhaps a closer comparator is S 1448 from Peterborough, again one in a series of memoranda:

> Þis is þ*æt* erfegeprit æt Geaceslea: þryttene pepmen peorcepyrþe, & .v. pimmen, & æhta geonge men, & .xvi. oxan, fal\d/reþere, & .iii. hund scepa & .v. scep, & .xxx. spina, & hundteongig fliccena, & eal þa smean ðe þerto gebyriað, & .xxx. forþer cornes, & hund ehtetig æcere gesapen, & an egþpirf, & .vi. bidenfate, & .ii. cuflas, & þry trogas & lead & trefet, & .ix. pinterstellas, & .i. fedels spin.[77]
>
> ['This is the inventory of the stock at Yaxley: thirteen able-bodied men and five women and eight young men and sixteen oxen, a stalled ox and 305 sheep and thirty swine and 100 flitches of bacon and all the delicacies that belong to them, and thirty fothers of corn and eighty acres sown and one *egthwirf* and six barrels and two tubs and three troughs and a cauldron and a trivet and nine year-old stallions and one fat pig.']

The estate in question (Yaxley, Huntingdonshire) seems to have passed to Thorney at an early stage, and therefore there appears no obvious reason for keeping the record; Susan Kelly conjectures that ongoing litigation concerning the estate may have prompted its retention. This is a possibility as well for the Egmere record in Rec 5. 4.[78]

Despite the loss of letters at the left of the page, Rec 5. 2 appears complete. It is significant that, while the bottom of the leaf is missing, there is plenty of space both above and below the existing text; it is therefore not in itself fragmentary, but seems instead to be an excerpt from a longer text. It does not include the name of the estate and as such has no obvious utility as a document. Nor was the text written on a spare piece of parchment later deployed as an endleaf; instead it was copied into an existing book, on the blank verso following the end of Laidcenn's text (as transmitted in this manuscript) on the recto; a further page completes this final ten-leaf quire of the original book. While the overall aspect of the script of the record is quite grand and therefore, as Rushforth notes, invites comparison with the script of other Bury productions such as Rec 5. 4 and Rec 5. 5, the scribe appears inexperienced, and the mixture of letter-forms is unusual.[79] I wonder if it is best explained as a copying exercise conducted on a temptingly blank page. The mutilated leaf has been

---

77 *Pet* 29e, p. 325, with translation p. 330 quoted here.

78 Kelly, *Pet*, p. 330.

79 I am grateful to Prof. Peter Stokes for very useful discussion on this hand.

subject to a series of rough pen-trials and jottings, including, towards what is now the bottom, an attempt to replicate the final three words. There are also a variety of post-Conquest pen-trials and short notes on this page and on the subsequent one, as well as activity elsewhere, including a name and captions dated to the eleventh century,[80] together with an untalented drawing seemingly captioned 'min hors' ('my horse').

The final text I look at, Rec 5. 6, is identified by its rubric as an agreement dating to the reign of Edward the Confessor. As such, it looks as though it should be included in the online Sawyer. Although its claims to authenticity are doubtful, were forgeries to be excluded from Sawyer, the result would be a slim volume indeed.

Rec 5. 6

MSS: Cambridge, University Library, Add. 6006, fol. 51r; Cambridge, University Library, Ee. 3. 60, fol. 161r; Cambridge, University Library, Gg. 4. 4, fol. 220r

Text (edited from Cambridge, University Library, Add. 6006 and Cambridge, University Library, Ee. 3. 60):

> Þis foreward was maked wid Ordric horder; þat is þat ælc man in s*anct*e Eadmu*n*des byri husfast on his owe land sal gifen to þe halegenes bidripe þe horder on peni at Peter mæsse on ginni*ng* herefest, & sea þe syt on ode*re*s la*n*d sea sceal giuen oan halpini, for þat he \a/alle scolden sceren þe halegenes corn. Fram þis sceal næfre no mæn be scyr buton s*anct*e Ædmu*n*des þewes. [81]& sea cnytes <h>agen[81] & seo preostes inne þeo singen [82]at þo wyuedes.[82]
>
> God seonde heore frieond þe worden s*anct*e Ædmund.

> ['This agreement was made with Ordric the cellarer; that is, that each man in Bury St Edmunds occupying a house on his own land shall give to the cellarer one penny for the saint's reaping-work on St Peter's Day at the beginning of harvest; and he who occupies the land of another shall give one half-penny, because they all ought to cut the saint's corn. No

80 These are indexed by Donald Scragg, *A Conspectus of Scribal Hands Writing English, 960–1100* (Cambridge, 2012), nos 188–193.

81 A space here is left in place of this phrase in both manuscripts. The gap is filled in Ee. 3. 60 by another hand. *agen* is corrected from *asen*.

82 Ee. 3. 60; *atco windes* Add. 6006.

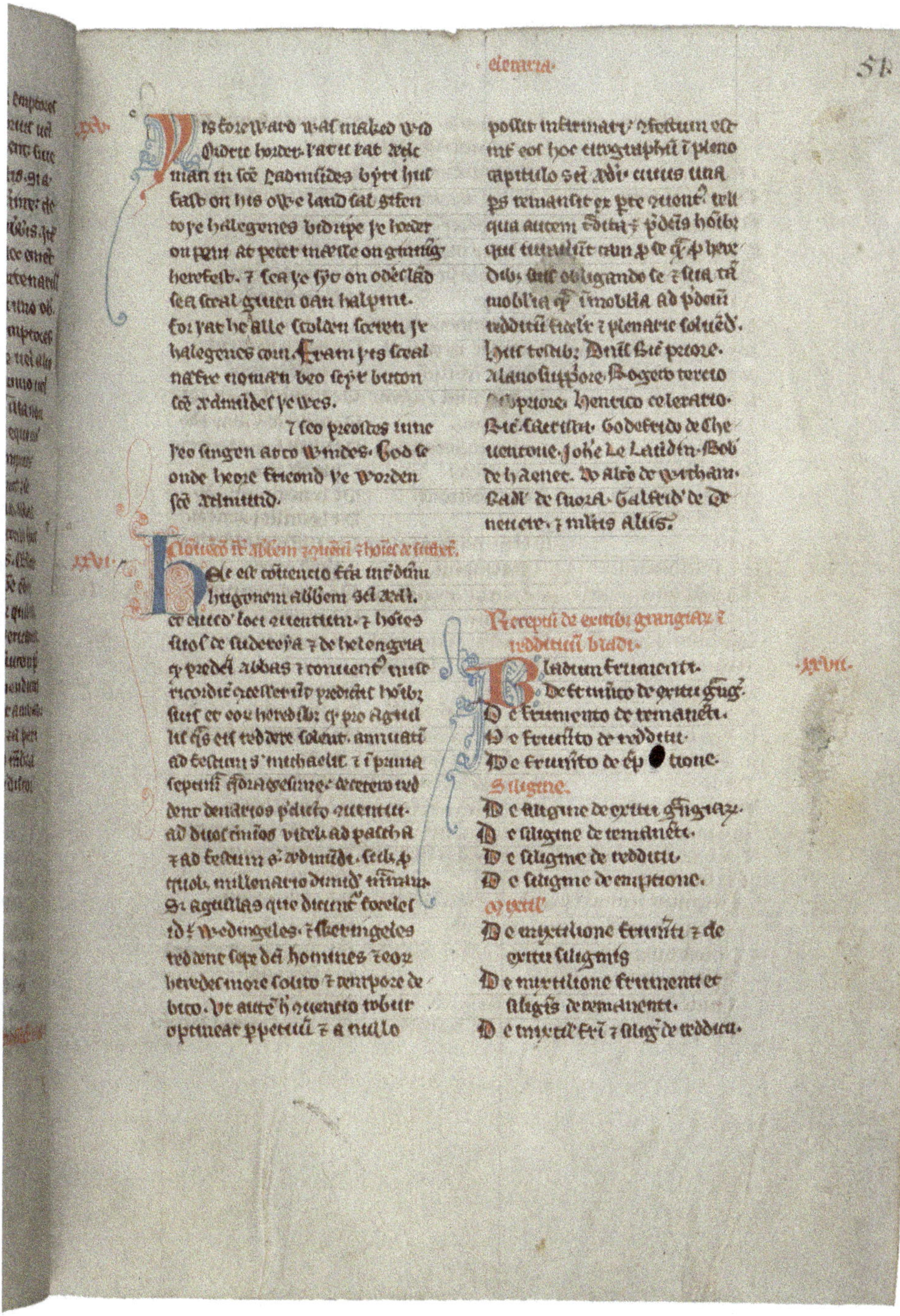

FIGURE 12.4 Cambridge, University Library, Add. 6006, fol. 51r
REPRODUCED BY KIND PERMISSION OF THE SYNDICS OF CAMBRIDGE UNIVERSITY LIBRARY

one shall ever be exempt from this except St Edmund's servants and the retainers' messuages and the priests within who sing at the altars.

May God be a friend of those who honour St Edmund.']

Copies of this text are found in three manuscripts, the earliest of which is Cambridge, University Library, Add. 6006, a thirteenth-century customary datable to after 1265.[83] The text appears in a section there relating to the cellarer's customers and rents, and is copied in a fairly formal book-hand with colour-tipped initials and penwork decoration to the opening initial. It is closely related textually to that of another surviving (fourteenth-century) copy in the abbey's Pinchbeck Register, Cambridge, University Library, Ee. 3. 60, although in a part that is not original to it. Cambridge, University Library, Add. 6006 has a gap between 'þewes' and '& seo preostes' and it seems that the exemplar could not be read at this point; the copy in Cambridge, University Library, Ee. 3. 60 has a similar gap but one that is filled subsequently, perhaps by the same scribe, apparently copying from the shared exemplar. A final copy, in the first part of the abbey's gargantuan Cellarer's Register (Cambridge, University Library, Gg. 4. 4), dates from the fifteenth century, and is copied from Cambridge, University Library, Ee. 3. 60.

The exemplar used by Cambridge, University Library, Add. 6006 and Cambridge, University Library, Ee. 3. 60 appears to have presented difficulties at other points: the opening instance of 'hordere' in the latter is inserted over an erasure and glossed 'Hordere, id est cellerario uel thesaurario' in a fourteenth-century hand. *Hordere*, while recorded in ME, is not especially common after the end of the thirteenth century (*MED Online*, *s.v.*).[84] This is considerably more successful than the same corrector's gloss of 'agen' (< OE plural *hagan*), mistaken for a form of the verb *āgān*, and glossed 'inire'. It is unsurprising that this baffled him (as it has baffled editors of the text), given the loss of the initial <h> on the noun, and the decidedly unhelpful morphology. The clue to its meaning is provided in the Latin account that precedes the copy of the charter 'Et antequam villa fuit libera solebant homines metere vt serui. Sola hospicia militum et capellanorum et seruiciencium metere vt serui',[85] in which 'sea cnytes [h]agen' is a reasonable approximation to 'hospicia militum'.

83 Rodney M. Thomson, *The Archives of the Abbey of Bury St Edmunds* (Woodbridge, 1980), p. 149.

84 *Middle English Dictionary*, ed. Robert E. Lewis, et al. (Ann Arbor, 1952–2001). Online edition (henceforth *MED Online*) in *Middle English Compendium*, ed. Frances McSparran, et al. (Ann Arbor, 2000–2018), http://quod.lib.umich.edu/m/middle-english-dictionary.

85 Printed in *ASChart*, p. 472.

Rec 5. 6 is unusual in a number of ways. It is not included in the Sacrist's Register (Cambridge, University Library, Ff. 2. 33), the major, late-thirteenth-century, cartulary that contains copies of almost all the pre-Conquest charters from the abbey. This is not in itself necessarily a suspicious feature: the text relates to the office of the cellarer, and may therefore not have been considered relevant. It does, though, make the language harder to gauge; the Sacrist's Register, itself descended from a lost exemplar of similar date,[86] modernizes its texts in a generally consistent way in terms of its morphology and phonology, and there is minimal updating, for example, of lexis. However, this text, if it is to be considered genuine at all, has been very substantially altered.

Several words appear in this charter that are otherwise either extremely rare or unrecorded in Old English: 'husfast', with only one comparable form, from the thirteenth century (*Oxford English Dictionary Online*, *s.v.* 'housefast, *adj.*'), 'bedrip' (with one other example in Old English in *Rectitudines* and examples in Middle English from the end of the twelfth century), *ginning* (not recorded elsewhere in OE; examples in the MED *Online* only from the fourteenth century). The sense deployed here of the verb 'giuen' (< OE *giefan*) in 'ælc man ... sal gifen ... to þe halegenes bidripe þe horder on peni' (*Oxford English Dictionary Online s.v.* 'give, *v.*', III a) as 'to make over to another in exchange for something else' is first recorded in the *Ormulum* (*c.*1180). Another difficulty with the charter's wording as it stands is the phrase 'oan halpini', which appears to imply a coin rather than cut coinage. This coin-type is generally believed first to have entered circulation during the reign of Edward I (1272–1307); it is certainly the case that examples of the noun in Middle English date to the beginning of that reign (MED *Online*, *s.v.* 'hal-penī n.'). However, sporadic recent finds have been made of halfpennies of Henry I (1100–35) and Henry III (1216–72). Other forms (*owe* < OE *agen*; updating of the preposition *mid* with *wid*) suggest that the exemplar for the surviving copies was produced, at the earliest, in the late twelfth or early thirteenth century.

The charter's opening words are couched in terms of an agreement. While *foreweard* is the term used in Old English for a contractual arrangement, it is accompanied in that period by the verb *wyrcan* rather than *macian* (e.g. S 1516 'þis is þe forward þe Wlfric and Eadwine ... wrouhten hem bituen'[87]). The Peterborough Chronicle has the older construction *s.a.* 1109 (probably copied

86 I reconstruct the pre-Conquest contents of this register in 'The Anglo-Saxon Contents of a Lost Register from Bury St Edmunds', *Anglia* 121 (2004), 515–34.

87 *ASWills* 33.

around 1121),[88] but uses *maken s.a.* 1140 (around 1154).[89] Rec 2. 1 (from Bath; after 1109 in a hand of the first half of the twelfth century)[90] has the formula with *makien*.[91] The end of the charter has some parallels (in broad terms) with the closing salutation of two writs from Bury St Edmunds: S 1085, Edward the Confessor's very frequently copied grant of a moneyer to Bury St Edmunds 'God seo eop alre freond' ('May God be the friend of you all'),[92] and Ch1Wm, a confirmation of S 1084 relating to the sokes of the eight-and-a-half hundreds 'God sy eower freond' ('May God be your friend').[93] The formula is not found elsewhere in documentary texts.

Some features which look early need careful assessment. One might perhaps expect that *sanctus* would be replaced by *seint* by the thirteenth century (its last recorded appearance in the MED *Online* is in the Trinity Homilies which were probably composed before 1200), though there is evidence that in a Bury context, the Latin loan was retained longer with conjunction with Edmund than with the names of other saints.[94] Similarly, forms such as 'Eadmund' or 'Ædmund' are found late in copies of Old English material from the foundation where other examples of the original *ēa* diphthong are spelled *e*.

Both the phonology of this text and its inflexional system is strange. The exemplar seems to have added either *-o* or *-a* variously to a number of <e>s in final position and sporadically elsewhere ('sea þe', 'sea cnytes hagen', 'seo preostes … þeo', 'frieond'). Comparable forms are found in the *Cartae antiquae* roll text of S 1045 and S 1084,[95] with examples including 'heo' for the masculine nominative singular personal pronoun and 'seo' for the nominative singular determiner accompanying grammatically masculine nouns. The roll dates to the end of the twelfth or beginning of the thirteenth century. The appearance of these forms in Rec 5. 6 suggest that the early-looking genitive form 'heore' and the otherwise unrecorded subjunctive singular 'seonde' may be

88 *Anglo-Saxon Chronicle E*, ed. Irvine, p. 115, p. xviii.

89 *Anglo-Saxon Chronicle E*, ed. Irvine, p. 138, p. xix.

90 Pelteret, *Catalogue*, no. 86 (p. 95).

91 *A Hand-Book to the Land-Charters, and Other Saxonic Documents*, ed. John Earle (Oxford, 1888), p. 270.

92 *ASWrits* 24.

93 *Regesta regum Anglo-Normannorum: The Acta of William I (1066–1087)*, ed. David Bates (Oxford, 1998), no. 38.

94 Lowe, 'The Anglo-Saxon Contents', pp. 531–32.

95 The National Archives: Public Record Office C 52/15, no. 1, no. 2. The charters have been edited from this manuscript in *The Cartæ Antiquæ Rolls 1–10*, ed. Lionel Landon, Publications of the Pipe Rolls Society 55, n.s. 17 (London, 1939), nos 443 and 444 (p. 87).

explained in the same way.[96] More surprising is the fact that 'sea'/'seo' appears twice to represent plural forms 'sea cnytes hagen' (< OE *þāra cnihta hagan*), 'seo preostes' (< OE *þā prēostas*). Elsewhere in the text the determiner is replaced by indeclinable 'þe', thus 'to þe halegenes bideripe', 'þe halegenes corn', with the generalized genitive *-es* inflexion additionally added onto the oblique *n*-stem ending.

While the language of Rec 5. 6, then, is exceptional, care needs to be taken in rushing to conclusions about the ultimate authenticity of the arrangement it describes. One other charter (S 1608) falls outside the run of pre-Conquest texts preserved in the Sacrist's Register.[97] This survives in another thirteenth-century customary (in this case, the prior's), but in an addition to it of the first half of the fourteenth century.

> Her kith and with song wrthe write þat forwarde þat Osulf and Leofroun wrouhte hem bitwen him be þat lond at Dicleburg and at Semer*e* swa ful and swa forth swa it hem on honde stod, on wode and on felde, Crist to loue & sancte Marie and alle C*ri*stes halgen her*e* soules to alesenesse. He it willetz þat þer singetz foure p*re*stes: to after Osulf, & to after Leofrounis day, and ilke woke to singen tuelue messes. And we willetz þat qwo so betz abbot at sancte Edmondes bery þat he betz þis minstr*e*s mu*n*d & her p*re*stes þat he ne mowen neyþer for hem ne for her*e* kin ferren ne forwerken.
>
> Þise sindon þise p*re*stes names: Godric & Alfric, and tweyne þat Leofstan abbot & Leofroun reden hem bytwen qwilke he mou*n* ben.
>
> He haue*n* gode stou*n*des þat up schulen holden; and qwo so nouth ne dotz as our*e* wille was, i*n* helle flod mote he drinklen witz þe tr*e*tour Iuda*s*. Fiat, fiat.
>
> ['Here is declared in this document the agreement that Oswulf and Leofrun made between them about the land at Dickleburgh (Nf) and at Semere (Nf) as fully and completely as it stood in their possession, consisting of woodland and open country, for the love of God and St Mary

96 The form *sende* is a strange one even if reinterpreted with the expected tonic vowel, though *MED Online* reports a singular present subjunctive 'sunde' in the London, British Library, Cotton Caligula A.ix version of Laȝamon's *Brut* (*s.v.* 'bēn v.'), perhaps composed before 1200.

97 The charter is printed in C. R. Hart, *The Early Charters of Eastern England* (Leicester, 1966), no. 133 (p. 86), but contains some errors. I therefore take the text below from our forthcoming edition.

> and all of Christ's saints, for the salvation of their souls. They wish it that four priests sing there, two after Oswulf's, and two after Leofrun's lifetime, and each week sing twelve masses. And we wish that whoever is abbot at St Edmund's *burh* that he is the guardian of these minsters and of their priests so that they cannot alienate them nor treat them improperly either for themselves or for their kin.
>
> These are the names of these priests: Godric and Ælfric; and two that Abbot Leofstan and Leofrun are to decide between them who they will be.
>
> May those who uphold [this] have good times, and whosoever does not do what our will was, may they drown in the river of hell with the traitor Judas. Let it be, let it be.']

This text, outlining an arrangement between a couple and the abbey concerning land in Norfolk, has also been substantially updated. The verb *drinklen*, 'drown', is recorded nowhere else in Old English, and is otherwise first recorded in manuscripts dating to the fourteenth century, although in copies of texts with an earlier (thirteenth-century) date of composition. The Anglo-Norman loan *traitour* appears in Old English only here and in the spectacular S 391, a vernacular version of a diploma of King Æthelstan from a lost manuscript, surviving only in a seventeenth-century transcript. The noun is otherwise earliest recorded in the second quarter of the thirteenth century. The verb-form 'mou*n*' derives from Old Norse *munu*, and is first recorded in the late-twelfth-century *Ormulum*. Conversely, ME *alesednesse* (< OE *alysednes*), common in Old English, is last recorded in 1225. Other forms are also best regarded as representing an earlier stage in the text's transmission, such as 'sindon', which is recorded in *A Linguistic Atlas of Early Middle English* only in Bury copies of Old English charters, and is not in *The Linguistic Atlas of Late Mediaeval English* (covering the period *c*.1350–1450) at all.[98] It is noteworthy that the scribe glosses this verb as 'sunt', suggesting that the form was unfamiliar to him. The opening 'Her kith and with song wrthe write' seems to be, as Cyril Hart noted, a garbling of the standard opening 'Her cyð on þissum gewrite'.[99]

98 Margaret Laing, *A Linguistic Atlas of Early Middle English, 1150–1325*, Version 3.2, http://www.lel.ed.ac.uk/ihd/laeme2/laeme2.html (Edinburgh, 2013–); M. Benskin et al., *An Electronic Version of A Linguistic Atlas of Late Mediaeval English*, http://www.lel.ed.ac.uk/ihd/elalme/elalme.html (Edinburgh, 2013–).

99 Hart, *The Early Charters of Eastern England*, p. 88.

Despite these features, there is no particular reason to doubt the authenticity of the grant itself: according to the finding-list to the charters contained in the late fourteenth-century Lakenheath Register, this charter survived as a single sheet with the pressmark F.23,[100] and Oswulf and Leofroun are remembered in copies of the benefactors' list surviving from the abbey for their gift of Bressingham.[101] Rec 5. 6 cannot therefore be rejected as a forgery on the basis of its language alone given the uncertainties surrounding when, and how, it was transmitted.

Conclusion

This set of records from Bury St Edmunds are varied in terms both of their form and their function, and are testament to the continued use of the vernacular at the abbey after the Conquest. The preservation of some appears the result of chance, while others are carefully planned. Two of the texts considered here (Rec 5. 3, Rec 5. 5), are certainly accidental survivals, owing their preservation solely to their redeployment as endleaves. Nevertheless, they manifest signs of continued utility after the moment of their original creation: one, Rec 5. 5, appears to be a working document, updated so as to remain of use for some time; the other (Rec 5. 3) is itself a copy of a text that had obviously been considered worth transmitting. Another text (Rec 5. 6), with charter-like qualities, has linguistic features that indicate production later than its avowed pre-Conquest date, though attention to the archival context of this text shows that such qualities may result from its unusual transmission history. A further set of records (Rec 5. 4) is copied into a quire designed to be bound with an important book explicitly to increase chances of preservation: these records seem, in part at least, to have an explicitly commemorative function. A text (Rec 5. 2) which appears similarly inserted into a book for the purpose of safe-keeping reveals itself through its contents to be an outlier, the one record from the archive copied without apparent purpose.

100 London, British Library, Harley 743, fol. 12v.

101 For example, Cambridge, University Library, Ee. 3. 60, fol. 324v.

The title of this essay, 'From memorandum to written record' is of course a play on that of M. T. Clanchy's monograph, *From Memory to Written Record: England 1066–1307*, first published in 1979, and now in its third edition.[102] Chapter 3 of this ground-breaking book is entitled 'Types of Record'[103] and attempts a 'general view over the whole area of writing activity'[104] during the period in question. It is both significant and instructive that Clanchy defines 'record' in a very broad sense. His headings under the section 'Statements issued by individuals' are as follows: Charters; Chirographs; Certificates (a term Clanchy uses to describe charter-like texts that 'do not exclusively concern gifts of property'); Letters; Writs. Under 'Memoranda kept by institutions' are the following: Financial accounts; Surveys and rentals; Legal records; Year books; Chronicles; Cartularies; Registers. Under 'Learned and literary works' are Learned works; Literary works; Liturgical books. There is little here that do not have equivalents in the pre-Conquest period; the difference is one of volume, not of kind.

The richness of the Anglo-Saxon written record as it pertains to Clanchy's first two categories is obscured by the terminology we continue to use. While the texts considered in this article are disparate, they share a host archive, and I hope to have shown that they are best assessed, discussed, and explained within that context. As the publication schedule for the Anglo-Saxon Charters Series progresses, texts such as these from other archives are likely to slip further from view as the old editions of collections containing them, apparently superseded by the new, are less frequently consulted. While this article has demonstrated throughout that the definition of 'charter' is a porous one, its association in an English context with land grants will always remain a barrier to inclusion under that heading. It would be better to ditch it altogether, and use instead 'record' as the umbrella term for the impressive range of vernacular non-literary texts produced during the pre-Conquest and transitional periods.

102 M. T. Clanchy, *From Memory to Written Record: England 1066–1307* (London, 1979, rev. editions 1993 and 2013).

103 Clanchy, *From Memory to Written Record*, pp. 83–115.

104 Clanchy, *From Memory to Written Record*, p. 83.

Appendix

TABLE 12.1 Additions to the Sawyer Catalogue[a]

Sawyer number	Date	Archive	British Academy Charter volume reference	Text type	Language
65a	*c.*693×709	Barking		Diploma	Latin
65b	*c.*693×706	Barking		Diploma	Latin
103a	716×745	London, St Paul's	*LondStP* 7	Diploma	Latin
103b	716×745	London, St Paul's	*LondStP* 8	Diploma	Latin
136a	793	St Albans	*StAlb* 2	Grant of land	English with bounds
270a	801	Glastonbury	*Glast* 16	Diploma	Latin, English bounds
286a[b]	838 for ?839	Canterbury, St Augustine's	*CantStA* 19	Diploma	Latin with bounds
294a[c] 294b[d]	844	Malmesbury	*Malm* 16	Grant of fiscal privileges	Latin with English
338a[e]	948 for 868	Abingdon	*Abing* 16	Diploma	Latin
342a	'835' for 871×899	Athelney		Diploma	Latin
343a	'872'	Athelney		Grant of privileges	Latin
367a	903	London, St Paul's	*LondStP* 10	Grant renewal	Latin

a To December 2018. It should be observed that additional vernacular summaries found of existing Latin texts since 1968 remain hidden under their original Sawyer number. Of particular note here is the extraordinary discovery by Simon Keynes of a seventeenth-century transcript of a lost cartulary from St Albans abbey which includes charters with vernacular sections or boundary clauses, or vernacular versions (including an exciting collection of wills) of texts otherwise known elsewhere only in Latin. For a list, see Simon Keynes, 'A Lost Cartulary of St Albans Abbey', *ASE* 22 (1993), 207–43.

b *Olim* S 1649.

c *Olim* S 314.

d *Olim* S 322.

e *Olim* S 539.

TABLE 12.1 Additions to the Sawyer Catalogue (*cont.*)

Sawyer number	Date	Archive	British Academy Charter volume reference	Text type	Language
418a	932	Barking		Diploma	Latin
517a	946	Barking		Diploma	Latin
522a	947	Barking		Diploma	Latin
552a	950	Barking		Diploma	Latin
662a	955×959	Evesham		Diploma	Latin, English bounds
676a	958	Coventry		Diploma	Latin, English bounds
705a	962	Athelney		Diploma	Latin, English bounds
712a	963	unclear		Diploma	Latin, English bounds
794a	974	Westminster		Diploma	Latin, English bounds
832a	964 for ?994	Athelney		Grant of tithes	Latin
931a	1013	Barking		Diploma	Latin
997a	1006 for 1016	Ghent, St Peter's		Undertaking to restore land	Latin
1037a	1065	York	*North* 11	Grant of see	Latin
1186a	799×801	Canterbury, Christ Church	*CantCC* 16	Confirmation of purchase of land	Latin
1204a	s. ix^2	Canterbury, Christ Church	*CantCC* 97	Book donation	English
1205a	?904	Malmesbury	*Malm* 23	Private grant	Latin
1205b	918	Ghent, St Peter's		Private grant	Latin
1218a	s. x^2	Ely		Record of grant	English
1243a	1042×1066	London, St Paul's	*LondStP* 31	Private grant	Latin
1251a	705	Malmesbury	*Malm* 11	Declaration	Latin
1428a	680	Winchester, Old Minster		Decree	Latin

TABLE 12.1 Additions to the Sawyer Catalogue (*cont.*)

Sawyer number	Date	Archive	British Academy Charter volume reference	Text type	Language
1428b	704×705	Canterbury, Christ Church	not included	Letter concerning dispute	Latin
1430a	798	Canterbury, Christ Church	*CantCC* 28	Council decree	Latin
1431a	803	Canterbury, Christ Church	*CantCC* 32	Council decree	Latin
1431b	803	Canterbury, Christ Church	*CantCC* 33	Council decree	Latin
1448a	983×985	Peterborough	*Pet* 30	List of sureties	English
1451a	s. x^{2}	Canterbury, Christ Church; Winchester, Old Minster; Exeter		Account of consecretation	Latin
1458a	*c.*1000	London, St Paul's	*LondStP* 25	List of estate contributions	English
1461a	*c.*1020	York, St Mary's	*North* 7	Survey of estates	English
1462a	1017×1027	Lichfield		Declaration regarding accusation	English
1481a	*c.*1055	Ramsey, Thorney		Settlement of dispute	English
1481b	s. xi^{2}	London, St Paul's	*LondStP* App 3A	Agreement	English
1481c	s. xi^{2}	London, St Paul's	*LondStP* App 3B	Agreement	English
1481d	?s. xi^{1}	Rochester	not included	List of estates liable for work	English
1481e	*c.*1000	Probably Ely		List of slaves; see Rec 9. 2	English
1481f	s. xi^{med}	Rochester	not included	List of slaves; see Rec 16.1	English

TABLE 12.1 Additions to the Sawyer Catalogue (*cont.*)

Sawyer number	Date	Archive	British Academy Charter volume reference	Text type	Language
1503a	?986	Ramsey		Will	Latin
1525a	s. x^2–s. xi	Bury St Edmunds		Will	English
1546a		St Albans	*StAlb* 2	Bounds	English
1546b		Exeter (ex Crediton)		Bounds	English
1552a		Malmesbury	*Malm* 47	Bounds	Latin
1561a		St Albans	*StAlb* 7A	Bounds	English
1569a		Bath	*Bath* 26	Bounds	English
1572a[f]		Abingdon	*Abing* 140A	Bounds	English
1590a		Worcester		Bounds	English
1591a		Evesham		Bounds	English

f Short version of bounds in S 967.

TABLE 12.2 The Rec Series in the *Dictionary of Old English*[a]

Rec	Manuscript	Scragg/ Pelteret[b]	Archive	Edited	Text type	Words	Date of manuscript
1	Oxford, Bodleian, Bodley 155, fol. 196v	Scragg 839	Barking	Hart, no. 106[c]	List of lands	50	s. xi^{ex}
2.1	Cambridge, Corpus Christi College 140, fol. 1v	Pelteret 86	Bath	Earle, p. 270[d]	Agreement of prior	175	s. xii^{1}
2.2	Cambridge, Corpus Christi College 111, pp. 55–6	Pelteret 78	Bath	Hunt, pp. 3–4[e]	Confraternity with other houses	475	s. xi^{2}
2.3	Cambridge, Corpus Christi College 111, p. 8 (s.xi^{2}); Cambridge, Corpus Christi College 140, fol. 1rv (s.xi^{2}–s.xi/ s.xii)	Scragg 45–51 Pelteret 73–77; 79–85	Bath	Earle, pp. 269–71	Twelve manumissions	525	s. xi^{2}–s. xi/ s. xii
2.4	Cambridge, Corpus Christi College 111, p. 7	Pelteret 70	Bath	Hunt, pp. lxxv–lxxvi	Relics	300	s. xi^{2}

a Almost all of the records in this table are contemporaneous with their copying into their host manuscript. There are a few clear exceptions: Rec 5.6, and Rec. 28.1–28.4, each of which claim, with varying degrees of credibility, to be pre-Conquest. Additionally, Rec 16.1–16.3 appear to be of the mid-eleventh century. Note also that in the following table, the number of words in each text, as provided by the *Dictionary of Old English Web Corpus*, has been rounded up or down to the nearest 25 (or to 5 up to 20).

b Scragg = Donald Scragg, *A Conspectus of Scribal Hands Writing English, 960–1100* (Cambridge, 2012); Pelteret = David A. E. Pelteret, *Catalogue of English Post-Conquest Vernacular Documents* (Woodbridge, 1990).

c Cyril Hart, *The Early Charters of Essex*, rev. ed. (Leicester, 1971).

d Earle = *A Hand-Book to the Land-Charters, and Other Saxonic Documents*, ed. John Earle (Oxford, 1888).

e Hunt = *Two Chartularies of the Priory of St. Peter at Bath*, ed. William Hunt (London, 1893).

TABLE 12.2 The Rec Series in the *Dictionary of Old English* (*cont.*)

Rec	Manuscript	Scragg/ Pelteret	Archive	Edited	Text type	Words	Date of manuscript
3	Bern, Stadtbibliothek, 671, fols 75v–76v		Bedwyn	Förster 1941, pp. 791–95[f]	Guild regulations; tithing instructions; manumissions	250	s. xi^{in}
4	BL,[g] Add. 9381, fols 1r, 7v, 8rv, 133v, 141v	Scragg 356–61 Pelteret 87–89	Bodmin	Förster 1930[h]	Manumissions	500	s. xi^{in}–s. xii^{in}
5.2	Cambridge, Pembroke College 88, fol. 167v	Scragg 188	Bury St Edmunds	See above, pp. 457–62	List of farm goods	25	s. xi^{ex}
5.3	Cambridge, Pembroke College 83, front flyleaf	Scragg 187	Bury St Edmunds	See above, pp. 444–53	Payments at a burial	125	s. xii^{1}
5.4	Oxford, Corpus Christi College 197, fols 106v–109r	Scragg 953–58	Bury St Edmunds	*ASChart* 104	Possessions, rents, and grants	925	s. xi^{med}–s. xii^{med}
5.5	Oxford, Bodleian, Auct. D.2.14, fol. 173r	Scragg 805–6	Bury St Edmunds	See above, pp. 453–57	Booklist	75	s. xi^{2}
5.6	Cambridge, University Library, Add. 6006, fol. 51r[i]		Bury St Edmunds	See above, pp. 462–69	Agreement with Ordric the Cellarer	100	s. xiii^{2}
6.3	London, Lambeth Palace 1370, fol. 114r	Scragg 780	Canterbury, Christ Church	*CantCC* 184	Boundaries	50	s. xi^{med}

f Förster 1941 = Max Förster, *Der Flussname Themse und seine Sippe. Studien zur Anglisierung keltischer Eigennamen und zur Lautchronologie des Altbritischen* (Munich, 1941).

g Note that in this table, BL = London, British Library.

h Förster 1930 = Max Förster, 'Die Freilassungsurkunden des Bodmin-Evangeliars', in *A Grammatical Miscellany Offered to Otto Jespersen on his Seventieth Birthday* (Copenhagen, 1930), pp. 77–99.

i And other copies.

TABLE 12.2 The Rec Series in the *Dictionary of Old English* (*cont.*)

Rec	Manuscript	Scragg/ Pelteret	Archive	Edited	Text type	Words	Date of manuscript
6.4	BL, Royal 1 D.ix fol. 43v	Scragg 670	Canterbury, Christ Church	Ker, p. 317[j]	Confraternity	50	s. xi[1]
6.5	Stockholm Royal Library, A.135, fol. 111r		Canterbury, Christ Church	See above, p. 472 (now S 1204a)	*Codex Aureus* inscription	175	s. ix[2]
6.6	BL, Royal 1. B.vii, fol. 15v		Canterbury, Christ Church	*SEHD* 19[k]	Manumission	75	s. x[2/4]
6.10	Canterbury, D&C, ChAnt C. 4[i]	Scragg 285 Pelteret 22	Canterbury, Christ Church	Bates, no. 66[l]	Writ of William I	200	s. xii[in]
7.1	BL, Cotton Domitian i, fol. 55v	Scragg 470	Canterbury, St Augustine's	*ASChart*, App. II, no. 6	Booklist	15	s. x[2]
7.2	Cambridge, Corpus Christi College 286, fol. 74v		Canterbury, St Augustine's	*CantStA* 24 (S 1198)	Grant of food-rent	175	s. x[1]
8.1	[BL, Cotton Otho B.ix]		Durham	*ASChart* 24	Gifts of King Æthelstan	75	MS destroyed
8.2	BL, Cotton Domitian A. vii, fol. 47v	Scragg 472	Durham	*North* 19, 20	Grants	100	s. xi[1/4]
8.3.1	BL, Cotton Domitian A. vii, fol. 47r	Scragg 471	Durham	BCS 1254	Manumissions	125	s. x[4/4]

j Ker = N. R. Ker, *Catalogue of Manuscripts Containing Anglo-Saxon* (Oxford, 1957).

k *SEHD* = *Select English Historical Documents of the Ninth and Tenth Centuries*, ed. and trans. Florence E. Harmer (Cambridge, 1914; rev. ed. 2011).

l Bates = *Regesta regum Anglo-Normannorum: The* acta *of William I (1066–1087)*, ed. David Bates (Oxford, 1998).

TABLE 12.2 The Rec Series in the *Dictionary of Old English* (*cont.*)

Rec	Manuscript	Scragg/ Pelteret	Archive	Edited	Text type	Words	Date of manuscript
8.3.2	[BL, Cotton Otho B.ix]		Durham	Craster, p. 190[m]	Manumissions	25	MS destroyed, manumissions s. x^{ex} or s. xi^{in}
8.3.3	[BL, Cotton Otho B.ix]		Durham	Craster, p. 190	Manumissions	75	MS destroyed, manumissions s. x^{ex} or s. xi^{in}
8.3.4	[BL, Cotton Otho B.ix]		Durham	Craster, p. 191	Manumissions	25	MS destroyed, manumissions s. x^{ex} or s. xi^{in}
8.4	Cambridge, Corpus Christi College 183, fol. 96v		Durham	*ASChart*, App. II no. 4	List of plate	50	s. xii^{med}
9.1	BL, Add. 61735, fol. 1rv	Scragg 370–73	Ely	*ASChart*, App. II, no. 9	Farm accounts	65	s. $xi^{1/4}$
9.2	BL, Cotton Tiberius B.v, vol I, fol. 76v	Scragg 271	Ely	Pelteret 1986, pp. 472–73 (now S 1481e)[n]	List of freeholders	300	s. x/xi
9.3	BL, Cotton Tiberius B.v, vol I, fol. 74v	Scragg 270	Ely	*ASChart* 71	Grant of land	75	s. x^2
9.4	BL, Cotton Tiberius B.v, vol I, fol. 74v	Scragg 269	Ely	Thorpe, pp. 610–13[o]	Guild regulations	450	s. x^2

m Craster = H. H. E. Craster, 'Some Anglo-Saxon Records of the See of Durham', *Archaeologia Aeliana*, fourth series, 1 (1925), 189–98.

n Pelteret 1986 = David A. E. Pelteret, 'Two Old English Lists of Serfs', *Mediaeval Studies* 48 (1986), 470–513.

o Thorpe = *Diplomatarium Anglicum ævi Saxonici, ed.* Benjamin Thorpe (London, 1865).

TABLE 12.2 The Rec Series in the *Dictionary of Old English* (*cont.*)

Rec	Manuscript	Scragg/ Pelteret	Archive	Edited	Text type	Words	Date of manuscript
10.1	Oxford, Bodleian, Auct. D.2.16, fols 1r–2v	Scragg 808 Pelteret 91	Exeter	*ASChart*, App. I, no. 1	List of books given by Bishop Leofric	725	s. xi^{2}
10.2	Exeter Cathedral 3501, fol. 7rv	Scragg 264 Pelteret 120–22, 124–34	Exeter	Earle, pp. 264–6 (incomplete)	Lists of guild members	500	s. xi^{ex} or s. xi/xii
10.3	BL, Cotton Tiberius B.v, vol. I, fol. 75r		Exeter	Conner, pp. 168–69[p]	Notice of guild assembly	225	s. x^{1}
10.4	Oxford, Bodleian, Bodley 311, fol. 1r	Scragg 843 Pelteret 92	Exeter	Ker, p. 360	Inscription of donation	5	s. x/xi
10.5.1	Cambridge, University Library, Ii.2.11, fol. 1r	Scragg 246 Pelteret 92	Exeter	Chambers et al., pp. 11–12[q]	Leofric inscriptions	20	s. xi^{2}
10.5.2	Cambridge, Corpus Christi College 41, fol. 244v	Scragg 32 Pelteret 92	Exeter	Chambers et al., pp. 11–12	Leofric inscriptions	25	s. xi^{2}
10.5.3	Cambridge, Trinity College B.II.2, fol. 121v	Scragg 202 Pelteret 92	Exeter	Chambers et al., pp. 11–12	Leofric inscriptions	25	s. xi^{2}
10.5.5	Oxford, Bodleian, Auct D.2.16, fol. 6v	Scragg 810 Pelteret 92	Exeter	Chambers et al., pp. 11–12	Leofric inscriptions	25	s. xi^{2}
10.5.6.1	Oxford, Bodleian, Auct F.1.15, fol. 77v	Scragg 106 Pelteret 92	Exeter	Chambers et al., pp. 11–12	Leofric inscriptions	25	s. xi^{2}

p Conner = Patrick W. Conner, *Anglo-Saxon Exeter: A Tenth-Century Cultural History* (Woodbridge, 1993).

q Chambers et al. = *The Exeter Book of Old English Poetry, Early English Manuscripts in Facsimile*, eds R. W. Chambers, M. Förster, and R. Flower (London, 1933).

TABLE 12.2 The Rec Series in the *Dictionary of Old English* (*cont.*)

Rec	Manuscript	Scragg/ Pelteret	Archive	Edited	Text type	Words	Date of manuscript
10.5.6.2	Oxford, Bodleian, Auct F.1.15, fol. 78r	Scragg 815 Pelteret 92	Exeter	Chambers et al., pp. 11–12	Leofric inscriptions	25	s. xi^2
10.5.7	Oxford, Bodleian, Auct. F.3.6, iii v	Scragg 335 Pelteret 92	Exeter	Chambers et al., pp. 11–12	Leofric inscriptions	25	s. xi^2
10.5.8	Oxford, Bodleian, Bodley 579, fol. 1r	Scragg 859 Pelteret 92	Exeter	Chambers et al., pp. 11–12	Leofric inscriptions	25	s. xi^2
10.5.9	Oxford, Bodleian, Bodley 708, fol. 113r	Scragg 872 Pelteret 92	Exeter	Chambers et al., pp. 11–12	Leofric inscriptions	25	s. xi^2
10.6.1	Exeter Cathedral 3501, fol. 7r	Pelteret 123	Exeter	Thorpe, p. 634	Manumissions	75	s. xii^1
10.6.2	Exeter Cathedral 3501, 4rv–6v + Cambridge, University Library, Ii.2.11, fol. 202v	Pelteret 93–100, 102–14	Exeter	Earle, pp. 257–64; Dickins, p. 366[r]	Manumissions	1825	s. xi/s. xii–s. xii^1
10.6.3.1	BL, Cotton Tiberius B.v vol. I, fol. 75v	Scragg 582	Exeter	Conner, p. 170	Manumissions	50	s. xi^1
10.6.3.2	BL, Cotton Tiberius B.v vol. I, fol. 75r		Exeter	Conner, p. 170	Manumissions	25	s. x^{med}
10.6.4	Oxford, Bodleian, Bodley 579, fols 1rv, 377v	Scragg 860–61; 864 Pelteret 135–40	Exeter	Earle, pp. 253–54	Manumissions	425	s. xi^{ex}- s. xi/xi

r Dickins = Bruce Dickins, 'The Beheaded Manumission in the Exeter Book', in *The Early Cultures of North-West Europe*, eds Cyril Fox and Bruce Dickins (Cambridge, 1950), pp. 363–67.

TABLE 12.2 The Rec Series in the *Dictionary of Old English* (*cont.*)

Rec	Manuscript	Scragg/ Pelteret	Archive	Edited	Text type	Words	Date of manuscript
10.7	Exeter Cathedral 3501, fol. $5r^{i}$	Scragg 253 Pelteret 101	Exeter	Earle, p. 260	Permission to ring bells	125	s. xi/s. xii
10.8	Oxford, Bodleian Auct D.2.16, fols 8r–14r	Scragg 811	Exeter	Conner, pp. 176–86	List of relics	1775	s. xi^{med}
10.10	Exeter Cathedral 3501, fol. 6v	Pelteret 115–19	Exeter	unprinted	Witnesses to sales of land	175	s. xii
11.1	Cambridge, Pembroke College 302, fol. 8r	Scragg 194	Hereford	Förster 1941, p. 769	Boundaries of see	50	s. xi^{1}
12	El Escorial, Real Bibliotheca, E. II.1, fol. 1r	Scragg 332	Horton	Ker, p. 152	Inscription recording gift of volume	5	s. xi^{2}
13	Lichfield, Cathedral 1, p. 4	Scragg 353	Lichfield	Earle, pp. 236–37	Record of lawsuit	25	s. xi^{1}
14	Cambridge, Corpus Christi College 383, fol. 107r		London, St Paul's	See above, p. 473 (now S 1458a)	List of *scipmen*	100	s. xii
15	BL, Cotton Otho C.i, vol. I, fols 68r–69v	Scragg 531–32	Malmesbury	BCS 106	Bull of pope Sergius	925	s. xi^{med}
16.1	Rochester, Cathedral Library A. 3. 5, fol. 162rv		Rochester	Pelteret 1986, p. 493 (now S 1481f)	List of serfs	95	s. $xii^{2/4}$
16.2	Rochester, Cathedral Library A. 3. 5, fol. 162rv		Rochester	Pelteret 1986, p. 493	Land transaction	30	s. $xii^{2/4}$
16.3	Rochester, Cathedral Library A. 3. 5, fol. 162rv		Rochester	Pelteret 1986, p. 493	Quittance	45	s. $xii^{2/4}$

TABLE 12.2 The Rec Series in the *Dictionary of Old English* (*cont.*)

Rec	Manuscript	Scragg/ Pelteret	Archive	Edited	Text type	Words	Date of manuscript
17	Sens, trésor de la cathédrale, 'authentique'			Ker, p. 455	Label inscriptions	15	s. ix^{1}?
19	Oxford, Bodleian, Bodley 579, fol. 8v	Scragg 865–70	Tavistock?	Earle, pp. 255–56	Manumissions	300	s. xi^{1}
20.1	BL, Add. 40000, fol. 4r	Scragg 366	Thorney	Ker, p. 163	Inscription recording gift	25	s. xi^{2}
20.2	BL, Add. 40000, fol. 10rv	Scragg 366.5	Thorney	unpublished	Names in *Liber vitae*	50	s. xi/s. xii
21.2	BL, Stowe 944, fols 28v, 29r	Scragg 737–40	New Minster Winchester	Birch 1892, pp. 64–72[s]	Names in *Liber vitae*	25	s. xi^{1}–s. xi^{2}
21.3.1	BL, Stowe 944, fol. 58r	Scragg 741	New Minster Winchester	Birch 1892, pp. 159–60	List of relics	25	s. xi^{med}
21.3.2	BL, Stowe 944, fol. 58rv	Scragg 742	New Minster Winchester	Birch 1892, pp. 161–62	List of relics	175	s. xi^{med}
21.3.3	BL, Stowe 944, fol. 58v	Scragg 743	New Minster Winchester	Birch 1892, pp. 162–63	List of relics	100	s. xi^{med}
22	BL, Harley 2965, fol. 40v		Nunnaminster	BCS 630 (S 1560)	Estate boundaries	100	s. ix/x
23.1	Cambridge, Corpus Christi College 367 Part II, fol. 48v	Scragg 166	Worcester?	*ASChart*, App. II, no. 5	List of books	25	s. xi^{med}
23.2	Oxford, Bodleian, Hatton 20, fol. 1r		Worcester	Ker, p. 385	Inscription on Pastoral Care	5	s. ix^{ex}
23.3	BL, Cotton Tiberius A.xiii, fol. 177r	Scragg 557 Pelteret 146	Worcester	*ASChart*, App I, no. 6	Payment to William I	100	s. xi^{2}
23.4	BL, Cotton Tiberius A.xiii, fol. 109r	Scragg 552	Worcester	Ker 1985, p. 58[t]	Dues	50	s. xi^{1}

s Birch 1892 = *Liber vitae of New Minster and Hyde Abbey*, ed. Walter de Gray Birch (London, 1892).

t Ker 1985 = N. R. Ker, 'Hemming's Cartulary: A Description of the Two Worcester Cartularies in Cotton Tiberius A.XIII', in N. R. Ker, *Books, Collectors and Libraries: Studies in the Medieval Heritage*, ed. Andrew G. Watson (London, 1985), pp. 31–60.

TABLE 12.2 The Rec Series in the *Dictionary of Old English* (*cont.*)

Rec	Manuscript	Scragg/ Pelteret	Archive	Edited	Text type	Words	Date of manuscript
23.5	BL, Cotton Nero E.i, pt ii, fol. 184v	Scragg 367	Worcester	BCS 1320	Calendar of lands	225	s. xi^{2}
23.6	BL, Cotton Tiberius A.xiii, fol. 181v	Scragg 556	Worcester	BCS 273 (= S 146 MS 3)	List of foods	50	s. xi^{2}
24.1	York, Minster Library, Add. 1, fols 156v–57r	Scragg 1045–48	York	See above, p. 473 (now S 1461a)	Survey of estates	450	s. xi^{in}
24.3	York, Minster Library, Add. 1, fol. 161r	Scragg 1050	York	*North*, App. 1	Inventory of church treasures	50	s. xi^{med}
24.4	York, Minster Library, Add. 1, fol. 161v	Scragg 1052	York	*North*, App. 2	List of *festermen*	125	s. xi^{ex}
26.1	BL, Add. 43703 (early-modern transcript of BL, Cotton Otho B.ix)[i]			*ASChart*, App. II, no. 1	Burghal hidage	250	s. xi^{1}
26.2	BL, Harley 3271, fol. 6v	Scragg 645		BCS 297	Tribal hidage	200	s. xi^{1}
26.3	BL, Add. 43703 (early-modern transcript of BL, Cotton Otho B.ix)[i]			*ASChart*, App. II, no. 1	Hidage for defence	200	s. xi^{1}
26.4	London, Soc. Ant. 60, fols 52r–54v	Pelteret 142	Northamptonshire	*ASChart*, App. I, no. 3	Northants geld roll	1300	s. xii^{1}
27.1	Dorchester, Dorset History Centre, D-FSI		Abbotsbury	Thorpe, pp. 605–8	Abbotsbury guild statutes	575	s. xi^{med}
28.1	BL, Cotton Roll, ii. 11		Crediton	Morsbach, p. 119[u]	Declaration of indulgences	300	s. xiii^{2}

u Morsbach = L. Morsbach, 'Umschriften ags. Urkunden in einer Pergamentrolle des Späten 13. Jahrhunderts: Texte und Erläuterungen', in *Britannica: Max Förster zum sechzigsten Geburtstage 1869 8. März 1929* (Leipzig, 1929), pp. 106–254.

TABLE 12.2 The Rec Series in the *Dictionary of Old English* (*cont.*)

Rec	Manuscript	Scragg/ Pelteret	Archive	Edited	Text type	Words	Date of manuscript
28.2	BL, Cotton Roll, ii. 11		Crediton	Morsbach, p. 117	Grants of indulgences	75	s. xiii^2
28.3	BL, Cotton Roll, ii. 11		Crediton	Morsbach, p. 117	Indulgence of Lifing	125	s. xiii^2
28.4	BL, Cotton Roll, ii. 11		Crediton	Morsbach, p. 119	Pledge of Eadnoth	200	s. xiii^2

Bibliography

Primary Sources

Anglo-Saxon Charters, ed. and trans. Agnes J. Robertson, 2nd ed. (Cambridge, 1956).

The Anglo-Saxon Chronicle: A Collaborative Edition. Vol. 7, MS. E, ed. Susan Irvine (Cambridge, 2004).

Anglo-Saxon Wills, ed. and trans. Dorothy Whitelock (Cambridge, 1930).

Anglo-Saxon Writs, ed. and trans. Florence E. Harmer (Manchester, 1952; 2nd ed. Stamford, 1989).

The Cartæ Antiquæ Rolls 1–10, ed. Lionel Landon (London, 1939).

Cartularium Saxonicum: A Collection of Charters Relating to Anglo-Saxon History, ed. Walter de Gray Birch, 3 vols (London, 1885–99).

Charters of Abingdon Abbey, ed. S. E. Kelly, Anglo-Saxon Charters VII–VIII (Oxford, 2000).

Charters of Bath and Wells, ed. S. E. Kelly, Anglo-Saxon Charters 13 (Oxford, 2007).

Charters of Christ Church Canterbury, eds N. P. Brooks and S. E. Kelly, Anglo-Saxon Charters 17–18 (Oxford, 2013).

Charters of Glastonbury Abbey, ed. S. E. Kelly, Anglo-Saxon Charters 15 (Oxford, 2012).

Charters of Malmesbury Abbey, ed. S. E. Kelly, Anglo-Saxon Charters XI (Oxford, 2005).

Charters of Northern Houses, ed. D. A. Woodman, Anglo-Saxon Charters 16 (Oxford, 2012).

Charters of Peterborough Abbey, ed. S. E. Kelly, Anglo-Saxon Charters 14 (Oxford, 2009).

Charters of Rochester, ed. A. Campbell, Anglo-Saxon Charters I (Oxford, 1973).

Charters of St Albans Abbey, ed. J. Crick, Anglo-Saxon Charters XII (Oxford, 2007).

Charters of St Augustine's Abbey, Canterbury, ed. S. E. Kelly, Anglo-Saxon Charters IV (Oxford, 1995).

Charters of St Paul's, London, ed. S. E. Kelly, Anglo-Saxon Charters X (Oxford, 2004).

Diplomatarium Anglicum ævi Saxonici, ed. Benjamin Thorpe (London, 1865).

Egloga quam scripsit Lathcen filius Baith de moralibus Iob quas Gregorius fecit, ed. M. Adriaen (Turnhout, 1969).

The Exeter Book of Old English Poetry, Early English Manuscripts in Facsimile, eds R. W. Chambers, M. Förster, and R. Flower (London, 1933).

A Hand-Book to the Land-Charters, and Other Saxonic Documents, ed. John Earle (Oxford, 1888).

Henry of Kirkestede, *Catalogus de libris autenticis et apocrifis*, eds Richard H. Rouse and Mary A. Rouse (Oxford, 2004).

Herman the Archdeacon and Goscelin of Saint-Bertin, *Miracles of St Edmund*, ed. and trans. Tom Licence (Oxford, 2014).

Liber vitae of New Minster and Hyde Abbey, ed. Walter de Gray Birch (London, 1892).

Regesta regum Anglo-Normannorum: The Acta of William I (1066–1087), ed. David Bates (Oxford, 1998).

Select English Historical Documents of the Ninth and Tenth Centuries, ed. and trans. Florence E. Harmer (Cambridge, 1914; rev. ed. 2011).

Two Chartularies of the Priory of St. Peter at Bath, ed. William Hunt (London, 1893).

Secondary Sources

Barker-Benfield, R. C., *St Augustine's Abbey, Canterbury*, 3 vols (Oxford, 2008).

Bishop, T. A. M., *English Caroline Minuscule* (Oxford, 1971).

British Academy-Royal Historical Society Committee of Anglo-Saxon Charters Guidelines for Editors (unpublished, 1990).

Campbell, A., *Old English Grammar* (Oxford, 1959).

Clanchy, M. T., *From Memory to Written Record: England 1066–1307* (London, 1979, rev. editions 1993 and 2013).

Conner, Patrick W., *Anglo-Saxon Exeter: A Tenth-Century Cultural History* (Woodbridge, 1993).

Craster, H. H. E., 'Some Anglo-Saxon Records of the See of Durham', *Archaeologia Aeliana*, fourth series, 1 (1925), 189–98.

Dickins, Bruce, 'The Beheaded Manumission in the Exeter Book', in *The Early Cultures of North-West Europe*, eds Cyril Fox and Bruce Dickins (Cambridge, 1950), pp. 363–67.

Dumville, David N., *Liturgy and the Ecclesiastical History of Late Anglo-Saxon England* (Woodbridge, 1992).

Förster, Max, *Der Flussname Themse und seine Sippe. Studien zur Anglisierung keltischer Eigennamen und zur Lautchronologie des Altbritischen* (Munich, 1941).

Förster, Max, 'Die Freilassungsurkunden des Bodmin-Evangeliars', in *A Grammatical Miscellany Offered to Otto Jespersen on his Seventieth Birthday* (Copenhagen, 1930), pp. 77–99.

Gittos, Helen, 'Creating the Sacred: Anglo-Saxon Rites for Consecrating Cemeteries', in *Burial in Early Medieval England and Wales*, eds Sam Lucy and Andrew Reynolds (London, 2002), pp. 195–208.

Gneuss, Helmut and Lapidge, Michael, *Anglo-Saxon Manuscripts: A Bibliographical Handlist of Manuscripts and Manuscript Fragments Written or Owned in England up to 1100* (Toronto, 2014).

Hart, C. R., *The Early Charters of Eastern England* (Leicester, 1966).

Hart, Cyril, *The Early Charters of Essex*, rev. ed. (Leicester, 1971).

Hogg, Richard M., *A Grammar of Old English. Volume 1: Phonology* (Oxford, 1992).

James, Montague Rhodes, *A Descriptive Catalogue of the Manuscripts in the Library of Pembroke College, Cambridge* (Cambridge, 1905).

Jordan, Richard, *Handbook of Middle English Grammar: Phonology*, ed. Eugene J. Crook (The Hague, 1974).

Ker, N. R., *Catalogue of Manuscripts Containing Anglo-Saxon* (Oxford, 1957).

Ker, N. R., 'Hemming's Cartulary: A Description of the Two Worcester Cartularies in Cotton Tiberius A.XIII', in N. R. Ker, *Books, Collectors and Libraries: Studies in the Medieval Heritage*, ed. Andrew G. Watson (London, 1985), pp. 31–60.

Keynes, Simon, 'A Lost Cartulary of St Albans Abbey', *ASE* 22 (1993), 207–43.

Lapidge, Michael, 'Surviving Booklists from Anglo-Saxon England', in *Learning and Literature in Anglo-Saxon England*, eds Michael Lapidge and Helmut Gneuss (Cambridge, 1985), pp. 33–89.

Lowe, Kathryn A., 'The Anglo-Saxon Contents of a Lost Register from Bury St Edmunds', *Anglia* 121 (2004), 515–34.

Lowe, Kathryn A., 'Post-Conquest Bilingual Memoranda from Bury St Edmunds', *Review of English Studies* 59 (2008), 52–66.

Lowe, Kathryn A., 'Linguistic Geography, Demography, and Monastic Community: Scribal Language at Bury St Edmunds', in *Interfaces between Language and Culture in Medieval England. A Festschrift for Matti Kilpiö*, eds Alaric Hall, Olga Timofeeva, Ágnes Kiricsi, and Bethany Fox (Leiden, 2011), pp. 147–178.

McKee, Helen, 'St Augustine's Abbey, Canterbury: Book-Production in the Tenth and Eleventh Centuries' (unpublished PhD thesis, University of Cambridge, 1997).

Morsbach, L., 'Umschriften ags. Urkunden in einer Pergamentrolle des Späten 13. Jahrhunderts: Texte und Erläuterungen', in *Britannica: Max Förster zum sechzigsten Geburtstage 1869 8. März 1929* (Leipzig, 1929), pp. 106–254.

Naismith, Rory and Tinti, Francesca, 'The Origins of Peter's Pence', *EHR* 134 (2019), 521–52.

Pelteret, David A. E., *Catalogue of English Post-Conquest Vernacular Documents* (Woodbridge, 1990).

Pelteret, David A. E., 'Two Old English Lists of Serfs', *Medieval Studies* 48 (1986), 470–513.

Pons-Sanz, Sara M., *The Lexical Effects of Anglo-Scandinavian Linguistic Contact on Old English* (Leiden, 2013).

Rumble, Alexander R., *Property and Piety in Early Medieval Winchester* (Oxford, 2002).

Rushforth, Rebecca J., 'The Eleventh- and Early Twelfth-Century Manuscripts of Bury St Edmunds Abbey' (unpublished PhD thesis, University of Cambridge, 2002).

Sawyer, P. H., *Anglo-Saxon Charters: An Annotated List and Bibliography* (London, 1968); revised as the Electronic Sawyer, www.esawyer.org.uk.

Scragg, Donald, *A Conspectus of Scribal Hands Writing English, 960–1100* (Cambridge, 2012).

Thompson, Victoria, *Dying and Death in Later Anglo-Saxon England* (Woodbridge, 2004).

Thomson, Rodney M., *The Archives of the Abbey of Bury St Edmunds* (Woodbridge, 1980).

Williams, R. A., 'Die Vokale der Tonsilben im *Codex Wintoniensis*', *Anglia* 25 (1902), 393–517.

Online Sources

Dictionary of Old English: A to I, eds Angus Cameron, Ashley Crandell Amos, Antonette diPaolo Healey et al. (Toronto, 2007-), https://tapor.library.utoronto.ca/doe/.

An Electronic Version of A Linguistic Atlas of Late Mediaeval English, eds M. Benskin et al. (Edinburgh, 2013-), http://www.lel.ed.ac.uk/ihd/elalme/elalme.html.

Laing, Margaret, *A Linguistic Atlas of Early Middle English, 1150–1325*, Version 3.2 (Edinburgh, 2013-), http://www.lel.ed.ac.uk/ihd/laeme2/laeme2.html.

Middle English Dictionary Online, in *Middle English Compendium*, eds Frances McSparran, et al. (Ann Arbor, 2000–18), http://quod.lib.umich.edu/m/middle-english-dictionary/.

Oxford English Dictionary Online, Oxford University Press, www.oed.com.

CHAPTER 13

Writing, Communication, and Currency: Dialogues between Coinage and Charters in Anglo-Saxon England

Rory Naismith

The inscriptions on Anglo-Saxon coins are deceptively straightforward in appearance. They are short and simple, extending to just a few words. Yet in order for these coins to be made with the right text on them, a number of more elaborate events had to take place. Someone needed to create the demand that led to the coin's manufacture: a customer.[1] A craftsman-official known as a moneyer needed to be commissioned to make the coin, and that moneyer (or his subordinates) needed to have the requisite skills in working silver or gold. The moneyer also had to have access to the tools of the trade, including dies of the appropriate type inscribed with his name and location, which would be used to stamp those details onto each coin he made. For those dies to be manufactured, a separate craftsman, potentially situated hundreds of miles away, had to have access to the precise details of what was needed, most importantly the name and location of the moneyer in question.

All in all, a series of challenging logistical operations were needed to produce the written component of the monetary system. Language and communication were consequently an inherent part of the minting process. Messages had to be sent, and meetings might have to be arranged, all within a very short timeframe. The present chapter is concerned with this background to the currency. It makes the case for there having been a whole world of oral and written interaction behind the polished final product; a world that has left precious little impression in surviving written records, and that can only be understood with recourse to the coins themselves. Yet the coinage could not have come into existence otherwise, and the volume and complexity of the currency implies a truly impressive level of activity behind the scenes. It is a fascinating

1 Michael Frank Hendy, 'From Public to Private: The Western Barbarian Coinages as a Mirror of the Disintegration of Late Roman State Structures', *Viator* 19 (1988), 29–78; and Rory Naismith, 'Gold Coinage and its Use in the Post-Roman World', *Speculum* 89 (2014), 273–306 on the transition to demand/customer-led production in early medieval Europe.

 | DOI:10.1163/9789004432338_014

case study in the application of administrative or, perhaps better, pragmatic literacy.[2]

In this respect the coinage is similar to the charter record. The two forms of evidence complement one another as dual windows onto how information was packaged for audiences who varied in their degree of education, but who appreciated the content writing conveyed, and needed to be able to access it in the interests of authenticity and validity.[3] In the words of Robert Bartlett, coins and charters together represented an 'incarnation [of] the most abstract aspect of social relations: rights and claims ... given tangible form'.[4] The presentation of text on an Anglo-Saxon coin—streamlined to just a few core details—therefore invites comparison with the treatment of core details in contemporary English charters (i.e. names of donor, recipient, and property, including boundary details). Both moneyers and charter draftsmen took pains to ensure clarity, including among users with limited literacy. Use of more widely comprehensible languages or registers, along with prescribed and well-known formulas, all helped the key elements of coins and charters stand out. A charter might carry a summary of its operative details on the dorse.[5] Coins and charters both also had a strong visual dimension: people understood information depending on where it was and how it looked. Charters normally opened with a pictorial invocation of greater or lesser complexity, and elements of the text could be identified visually too: the boundary clause was normally

---

2 Malcolm B. Parkes, 'The Literacy of the Laity', in *Literature and Western Civilization: The Medieval World*, eds David Daiches and Anthony Thorlby (London, 1973), pp. 555–76; *Pragmatische Schriftlichkeit im Mittelalter: Erscheinungsformen und Entwicklungsstufen*, eds Hagen Keller, Klaus Grubmüller, and Nikolaus Staubach (Munich, 1992), though both are primarily focused on a later period. For recent surveys of thought and scholarship on medieval literacy since the 1970s, see Charles F. Briggs, 'Literacy, Reading, and Writing in the Medieval West', *Journal of Medieval History* 26 (2012), 397–420; and Rosamond McKitterick's contribution to this volume. On literacy, and especially pragmatic literacy, from an Anglo-Saxon perspective, see R. M. Liuzza, 'Literacy', in *A Handbook of Anglo-Saxon Studies*, eds Jacqueline Stodnick and Renée R. Trilling (Oxford, 2012), pp. 99–114, at 106; and Susan Kelly, 'Anglo-Saxon Lay Society and the Written Word', in *The Uses of Literacy in Early Medieval Europe*, ed. Rosamond McKitterick (Cambridge, 1990), pp. 36–62.

3 Alice Rio, *Legal Practice and the Written Word in the Early Middle Ages: Frankish Formulae, c. 500–1000* (Cambridge, 2009), pp. 11–20.

4 Robert Bartlett, *The Making of Europe: Conquest, Colonization and Cultural Change 950–1350* (London, 1993), p. 287.

5 Simon Keynes, 'Church Councils, Royal Assemblies, and Anglo-Saxon Royal Diplomas', in *Kingship, Legislation and Power in Anglo-Saxon England*, eds Gale R. Owen-Crocker and Brian W. Schneider (Woodbridge, 2013), pp. 1–182, at 161–69. See also the contribution of Gallagher and Wiles to this volume.

written in smaller script from about 940,[6] while capitals or other forms of emphasis were sometimes used to highlight the key elements of the dispositive passage. Even without reading the whole text, it was possible to pick out the operative passages of a charter.[7] Coins had highly prescribed placements for all written elements too: king's name and title on obverse, moneyer's name and—sporadically from about 930, regularly from the early 970s—mint-name on the reverse, the latter two elements conjoined with a preposition or descriptive noun.[8] Crosses normally introduced both inscriptions, in the same way as pictorial invocations in charters. The highly standardized, signposted texts on coins may have been more readily comprehensible than the nuances of numismatic iconography. Greek letters, or symbolically charged religious content and royal portraiture, could only be fully appreciated by those with a significant degree of learned visual literacy.[9] In a sense, therefore, the more elaborate imagery of Anglo-Saxon coins fulfilled a similar function to the florid literary proems found in many charters, as an element that only educated audiences could fully grasp.

The analogy can be pursued into how coins and charters were put together. Both reflect mediation between local communities and institutions, and those charged with running a larger kingdom. The same challenges of distance and detail were faced by moneyers and draftsmen: they had to find ways to pass on the names of individuals and locations, along with other pertinent material such as boundary clauses; and they had to collaborate with people who varied in their grasp of Latin and who did not necessarily share the same dialect or speak the same vernacular. There is no doubt that oral processes of communication played a crucial part in accomplishing all of this, even if the ultimate aim was to produce documents or objects carrying text. Charters, as longer and more complex compositions, inevitably offer greater potential than coins for glimpsing responses to the obstacles posed. But charters have the severe limitation of surviving in comparatively restricted numbers (some 1500 in total), heavily concentrated at just a few archives such as the cathedrals or

6 Peter A. Stokes, *English Vernacular Minuscule from Æthelred to Cnut c. 990–c. 1035* (Woodbridge, 2014), p. 193.

7 Keynes, 'Church Councils', p. 138.

8 An exceptional case of a coin which breaks these rules is a penny of Edmund (939–46) found in the Forum hoard: Rory Naismith and Francesca Tinti, *The Forum Hoard of Anglo-Saxon Coins*, Bollettino di Numismatica 55–56 (Rome, 2016), no. 635. Made by a moneyer based in southern England (possibly at Shaftesbury), this coin places the moneyer's name where the king's would normally be, and the king's name and title where one would expect the moneyer's name and role.

9 On the rise of the related concept of 'graphicacy': Ildar Garipzanov, 'The Rise of Graphicacy in Late Antiquity and the Early Middle Ages', *Viator* 46 (2015), 1–21.

monasteries of Abingdon, Canterbury, Winchester, and Worcester. Coins, by contrast, survive in vast numbers: no exact total can be pinned down as new material is constantly coming to light and a significant portion is held in uncatalogued private collections, but an estimate of at least 100,000 surviving Anglo-Saxon coins with inscriptions is plausible. These include much stronger representation from northern and eastern regions poorly reflected in the charter record—and of course the survival of coins is governed by completely different factors than the preservation of charters. Even if each individual coin offers much less text than each individual charter, collectively they tell a much more balanced story.

The Content and Language of Coin Inscriptions

The written content which had to appear on coins in the early Middle Ages was short but important. Users looked at words and images to determine if what they held in their hand was indeed acceptable. Most Anglo-Saxons would probably only glance quickly at their coins to make sure they were broadly the same as others they knew well. Some might have looked more closely and—if they could—read the inscription, above all if they had any cause to doubt a coin's authenticity.

An example of what a late Anglo-Saxon coin-user would have seen is Figure 13.1. This specimen belongs to the reign of Æthelred II (978–1016). One face displays an elegant bust of the king, surrounded by the words +ÆÐELRÆD REX ANGLOR[*um*]; in this case the abbreviation *-orum* is indicated with a ligature of OR, as was common in contemporary manuscript contexts. A cross

FIGURE 13.1 Penny of Æthelred II (978–1016), *First Hand* type, London mint, moneyer Beornwulf
PRIVATE COLLECTION; AUTHOR'S PHOTOGRAPH

serves the practical purpose of establishing where the legend starts, and the symbolic purpose of sanctifying what comes after; we then learn that this coin was made under the authority of Æthelred, king of the English. Royal styles are virtually a constant on Anglo-Saxon coins: only in a few cases in the eighth century was this detail omitted altogether (so that one had, for example, just +ALDFRIDVS or EADBERHTVS for two Northumbrian monarchs), but very often it extended no further than REX.[10] In the time of Edgar and after, it settled on REX ANGLORVM, usually (as here) abbreviated to some extent. One does not see on coins the elaboration that often characterized royal styles in the main text of diplomas, though a better comparison is with the compressed style given in the witness list or the endorsement, where space and brevity were greater concerns. On the other side of the coin, a large central image of the Hand of God complements the small crosses that begin both obverse and reverse legends. The reverse inscription is separated from the central design by an outer circle, and consists of the words +BIORNVLF MO LVNDON. This indicates that the coin was made in London by a moneyer known as Biornulf.[11] There is also a short inscription embedded in the Hand of God design: A ω, alpha and omega, which again alludes to divine authority.

This last inscription fulfilled a symbolic role particular to this coin issue, but the king's name and title and the details of moneyer and mint-place all had clearly defined functions that persisted across reigns and kingdoms. The name of a ruler could serve a propagandistic role, since coins were one of only a few media (along with charters) that distributed a clear and literate assertion of power.[12] As such, even the act of issuing coins in one's own name could be a politically charged statement. Adherence to traditional norms of format and appearance might in fact help reinforce the significance of a new ruler's name on the coin, implying that he or she had taken up a legitimate position.[13] In a more direct sense, the ruler's name also acted as a guarantee. It explicitly identified the resultant penny as the king's penny. Forging a coin in the name of a king, or rejecting one for no good reason, was an insult to the ruler's

10 Rory Naismith, *Medieval European Coinage, with a Catalogue of the Coins in the Fitzwilliam Museum, Cambridge. 8: Britain and Ireland c. 400–1066* (Cambridge, 2017), pp. 372–74.

11 Although orthographic variations can be meaningful, it is conventional in numismatic literature to facilitate comparison across mints by representing moneyers' names according to a late West Saxon normalized form, which in this case would be Beornwulf. For the implications of variation in names, see below pp. 510-13.

12 Ildar H. Garipzanov, *The Symbolic Language of Authority in the Carolingian World (c. 751–877)* (Leiden, 2008).

13 Rory Naismith, *Money and Power in Anglo-Saxon England: The Southern English Kingdoms, 757–865* (Cambridge, 2012), pp. 50–51.

authority.[14] Details of the moneyer's name and location served as a kind of guarantee for those who had doubts about a coin's reliability, founded on a highly personalized conception of trust in money.[15] What mattered was being able to trace who had given the coin to whom, ultimately reaching back to the manufacturer.[16] Indeed, the mint-name was in a sense secondary, and became common only once the minting network grew in the tenth century and there was a realistic chance of several moneyers across the kingdom sharing common names.[17] The moneyers of tenth- and eleventh-century England have been extensively studied from a philological point of view, to determine how many moneyers in various places carried names of Old English, Old Norse, or other origin.[18] Similar research has been carried out on the Roman, Frankish, Gothic, and other name-forms found among moneyers of Merovingian Gaul.[19] Anglo-Saxon moneyers' status was relatively high, with many being drawn from minor landowners and urban elites.[20] A high proportion of them worked only occasionally, with minting being one role among many, perhaps carried out at multiple locations. Crucially, this meant that most moneyers would have been in a position to compel or employ others to do the more laborious work of minting; the moneyer himself served more as financier and overseer.[21]

---

14 Cf. IV Æthelred, c. 6, *Die Gesetze der Angelsachsen*, ed. Felix Liebermann, 3 vols (Halle, 1903–16), 1:234.

15 Elina Screen, 'Anglo-Saxon Law and Numismatics: A Reassessment in the Light of Patrick Wormald's *The Making of English Law*', *British Numismatic Journal* 77 (2007), 150–72; Rory Naismith, 'The Laws of London? IV Æthelred in Context', *The London Journal* 44 (2019), 1–16.

16 See below, pp. 516–17.

17 Naismith, *Medieval European Coinage 8*, pp. 132–33 and 191.

18 Two key studies (among many) are Veronica J. Smart, 'Scandinavians, Celts and Germans in Anglo-Saxon England: The Evidence of Moneyers' Names', in *Anglo-Saxon Monetary History: Essays in Memory of Michael Dolley*, ed. Mark Blackburn (Leicester, 1986), pp. 171–84; and Fran Colman, *The Grammar of Names in Anglo-Saxon England: The Linguistics and Culture of the Old English Onomasticon* (Oxford, 2014). Anglo-Saxon mint-names have not received the same degree of attention, though see Jayne Carroll and David N. Parsons, *Anglo-Saxon Mint Names. I: Axbridge-Hythe* (Nottingham, 2007).

19 Several papers on this theme may be found in *Die Merowingischen Monetarmünzen als Quelle zum Verständnis des 7. Jahrhunderts in Gallien*, eds Jörg Jarnut and Jürgen Strothmann (Paderborn, 2013).

20 Famously, the Domesday Book lawmen of Lincoln included a large number of moneyers, and some late Anglo-Saxon moneyers in London may have been members of powerful families: Francis Hill, *Medieval Lincoln* (Cambridge, 1948), p. 40; and Pamela Nightingale, 'Some London Moneyers, and Reflections on the Organization of English Mints in the Eleventh and Twelfth Centuries', *Numismatic Chronicle* 142 (1982), 34–50.

21 Naismith, *Medieval European Coinage 8*, pp. 240–43; R. Naismith, 'The Currency of Power in Late Anglo-Saxon England', *History Compass* 17 (2019).

In England, names on coins were normally rendered in the nominative of the original tongue (usually Old English).[22] The main exceptions, in which rulers' names were Latinized, can be found in some coin issues from Northumbria before and during viking rule, and in one exceptional coin-type of Edward the Confessor (1042–66) which will be discussed below. Other elements of coin-inscriptions were normally in Latin. Some concessions were made to wider use of the vernacular in late Anglo-Saxon England, as when the unusual *Agnus Dei* type of (probably) 1009 replaced the Latin abbreviation for *monetarius* in the reverse inscription with the Old English preposition ON ('in'); a practice which eventually became the norm.[23] Rendering other parts of the inscription in the vernacular was an exceptional measure. At viking York, in the years around 940, the moneyers famously adopted vernacular forms of title for both the king and moneyer (CYNING and MINETERE, respectively), probably as part of an initiative by the new regime to distance itself from Anglo-Saxon practice.[24] The same vernacular royal title was used occasionally on coins minted at Dublin at the end of the tenth century,[25] and it may be significant that this short-lived revival took place in the coinage of Sihtric Silkbeard (989–1036), son of one of the kings named on the earlier coinage of York (Olaf Cuarán (d. 980)). Only a few parallels to this use of the vernacular on coins can be found elsewhere in western Europe before the twelfth century. One can point to a rare group of coins from mid-eleventh-century Gittelde in Lower Saxony, with the inscriptions +HIR STEID TE BISCOP ('here stands the bishop') and +IELITHIS PENING ('penny of *Jelithe*/Gittelde'),[26] and a cluster of coins minted in Norway under Olaf Kyrre (1067–93) with runic reverse inscriptions in the vernacular that identify the moneyer's relationship to his coin or die: *askell a benek þen* ('Åskell owns this penny'), *kunar a mot þisa* ('Gunnar owns this die'), and the like.[27] Other languages featured in specialized contexts only. Greek occurred in religious formulations, most prominently alpha and omega,

22 It was more common to Latinize names in charters: see Seiler in this volume.

23 Simon Keynes and Rory Naismith, 'The *Agnus Dei* Pennies of King Æthelred the Unready', *ASE* 40 (2011), 175–223, at p. 190.

24 Naismith, *Medieval European Coinage 8*, p. 299.

25 R. H. M. Dolley, *Sylloge of Coins of the British Isles 8: The Hiberno-Norse Coins in the British Museum* (London, 1966), no. 28.

26 Hermann Dannenberg, *Die deutschen Münzen der sächsischen und fränkischen Kaiserzeit*, 4 vols (Berlin, 1876–1905), 2:633–34.

27 Kolbjørn Skaare, *Coins and Coinage in Viking-Age Norway: The Establishment of a National Coinage in Norway in the XI Century, with a Survey of the Preceding Currency History* (Oslo, 1976), p. 109.

in a few cases from the early ninth century onwards.[28] Exceptionally, Arabic was copied on the famous Offa dinar of the late eighth century, albeit with little likelihood that its meaning was understood.[29] For coin inscriptions besides names, Latin was the overwhelmingly dominant language across England and the rest of western Europe.

Although not a matter of language as such, the script used to convey these short texts was closely associated with their content, and helped to establish credibility. The preference across England and in other early medieval European kingdoms was for capitals. Use of them was inherited from the Roman Empire, and the specific form of capital script found on immediately post-Roman coins from Gaul, Italy, and Spain was heavily influenced by the prominently seriffed and ridged lettering on late Roman coinage.[30] When inscriptions became common on Anglo-Saxon coins in the mid-eighth century, capital script was the norm. In all areas of post-Roman western Europe, however, coin inscriptions included several non-classical letter-forms: A with a horizontal top stroke or a chevron-shaped bar, for example, or angular forms of C, G, or S. Uncial letter-forms of A, D, M, and other letters also occurred from time to time. As with display scripts in books, or inscriptions on stone or other materials, the canon of acceptable lettering was quite broad.[31] In a few cases particular letter-forms had specific connotations. In Mercia, uncial M became established under Offa (757–96) and his successors as the preferred shorthand for *Merciorum* in royal titulature.[32] Certain moneyers in Northumbria during the ninth century used a slightly greater admixture of half-uncial or minuscule letter-forms in coin inscriptions than their counterparts elsewhere.[33] The overall impression is that coin inscriptions did not stand significantly apart from other media in their epigraphy. Coins were part of a continuum of written culture that used a common range of scripts.

---

28 Naismith, *Medieval European Coinage 8*, p. 377; Naismith, *Money and Power*, pp. 70–71. The earliest English examples come from Wessex in the period 786–802.

29 Naismith, *Money and Power*, pp. 113–14. See also Rory Naismith, *Sylloge of Coins of the British Isles 67: British Museum: Anglo-Saxon Coins II. Southern English Coinage from Offa to Alfred c. 760–880* (London, 2016), no. 3. Other imitations of Arabic coins could be of Anglo-Saxon origin, but only the Offa dinar can be attributed securely.

30 Stanley Morison, *Politics and Script: Aspects of Authority and Freedom in the Development of Graeco-Latin Script from the Sixth Century B.C. to the Twentieth Century A.D.* (Oxford, 1972), pp. 90–91 and 155–57.

31 Elisabeth Okasha, 'The Non-Runic Scripts of Anglo-Saxon Inscriptions', *Transactions of the Cambridge Bibliographical Society* 4 (1968), 321–38.

32 Naismith, *Money and Power*, pp. 72–79.

33 Naismith, *Medieval European Coinage 8*, p. 378.

Die-Cutters, Moneyers, and the Projection of Royal Authority

Whereas texts on parchment were written out with quill and ink, and inscriptions on stone were marked out and carved into the surface, the letters on Anglo-Saxon coins were generally engraved using pre-made 'punches' that represented individual parts of letters (uprights, cross-strokes, curves, wedges, etc.). No such 'punches' have survived,[34] but their traces are readily identifiable if coin inscriptions are closely examined. An example is presented here as Figure 13.2, which shows a close-up of the lettering on a penny of Æthelred II. Special training was needed to make and use 'punches' effectively, especially as the inscription would have to be made in mirror-image on the die to appear correctly on the resultant coin.[35] In short, the technical process of creating

FIGURE 13.2
Penny of Æthelred II (978–1016), *Crux* type, Canterbury mint, moneyer Leofric, with detail of reverse showing punches used to make individual letters
PRIVATE COLLECTION; AUTHOR'S PHOTOGRAPH

34 Some possible examples—though implied by the relevant authors to be punches for jewellery—were found as part of the tools of a seventh-century smith at Tattershall Thorpe, Lincolnshire: David A. Hinton, *A Smith in Lindsey: The Anglo-Saxon Grave at Tattershall Thorpe, Lincolnshire* (London, 2000), nos 9–13.

35 Naismith, *Medieval European Coinage 8*, p. 379; David Sellwood, 'Medieval Minting Techniques', *British Numismatic Journal* 31 (1962), 57–65.

coin inscriptions was quite different from other forms of writing, meaning the individuals responsible for inscribing coin-dies were probably not the same as those who produced book-script or stone inscriptions—and yet their work had much in common with other inscriptions, pointing to participation in a common culture of writing, and to a measure of literacy on their part.[36]

The key figure in this process was the craftsman responsible for making the coin-dies. Already when moneyers' names first appear on coins regularly in the eighth century,[37] it is manifestly clear that they were not making their own dies, as several of them use dies of identical style. The roles of making coins and dies were usually distinct, but die-cutters are shadowy individuals. No information whatsoever is recorded about them, though certain characteristics can be inferred. Few if any would have been employed full-time making coin dies. Some may have worked as (or for) moneyers, or as makers of seal matrices and other fine metallic objects which required similar expertise,[38] potentially acquired in the service of a particular patron, such as a secular lord or ecclesiastical institution.[39] It is also likely that many die-cutters possessed a degree of pragmatic literacy. The evidence for this is circumstantial but collectively weighty. Dies were made in very large quantity, and most were rendered legibly yet with enough small variations in orthography and other details to suggest that each inscription was created afresh, rather than following a prescribed norm. This combination points to the makers themselves being responsible for their composition. In this respect coin-dies may have been distinct from most other kinds of inscription, which were not produced on the same routine basis and probably drew on a wider range of skilled individuals.[40]

36 On the circumstances behind stone inscriptions, see Elisabeth Okasha, 'The Commissioners, Makers and Owners of Anglo-Saxon Inscriptions', *Anglo-Saxon Studies in Archaeology and History* 7 (1994), 71–77; and Elisabeth Okasha, 'Literacy in Anglo-Saxon England: The Evidence from Inscriptions', *Anglo-Saxon Studies in Archaeology and History* 8 (1995), 69–74.

37 Derek Chick, *The Coinage of Offa and his Contemporaries*, eds Mark Blackburn and Rory Naismith (London, 2010), pp. 1–15.

38 T. A. Heslop, 'English Seals from the Mid Ninth Century to 1100', *Journal of the British Archaeological Association* 33 (1980), 1–16, at pp. 4–7.

39 For smiths who worked in the service of seventh-century lords, see Æthelberht, c. 7 and Ine, c. 63, *Gesetze*, ed. Liebermann, 1:3, 118–19. For metalworkers and other craftsmen in the orbit of large ecclesiastical institutions, see Sarah Foot, 'Reading Anglo-Saxon Charters: Memory, Record, or Story?', in *Narrative and History in the Early Medieval West*, eds Elizabeth M. Tyler and Ross Balzaretti (Turnhout, 2006), pp. 39–66.

40 Okasha, 'Literacy in Anglo-Saxon England', esp. p. 70: note the distinction drawn between patron, composer, and engraver.

The number and location of these die-cutters is often opaque. At times when standardized coin-types prevailed (as was generally the case after the early 970s) the contribution of each die-cutter can only be detected indirectly, through looking for small differences in the execution of dies that betray the hand of a particular craftsman (or group of craftsmen, though for the sake of clarity discussion will remain in the singular).[41] The technique is inevitably subjective, as it depends on the interpretation of modern scholars, but nonetheless it strongly suggests that arrangements for making and distributing dies were variable, sometimes changing very rapidly. Under these circumstances, the die-cutters could not have been a permanent, dedicated profession; rather, they would have been drawn, as circumstances dictated, from those available on the spot with appropriate expertise and status.

As might be expected, the relationship between die-cutters and moneyers varied over time. In the century between the reigns of Offa and Alfred the Great (871–99), the normal practice was to give the name of only the moneyer, and consequently it is extremely difficult to determine how die-cutters relate to mint-places. With mint-names being so rare, and with so few other reliable ways of determining even the general location of individual moneyers, all one can do is weigh up three possibilities for how a die-cutter's work was disseminated among multiple moneyers: he could have supplied all the moneyers in one mint-place, been one of several die-cutters catering to moneyers in one mint-place, or sent dies to moneyers in multiple separate locations. It is likely that all three applied at one time or another.[42] The main point to take away is that arrangements for selecting and transmitting inscriptions would often have been highly localized and flexible.

The tenth and eleventh centuries offer more fruitful material for analysis because the minting system became both more dispersed and easier to discern, most famously in Edgar's reform of the early 970s and after. Sometimes the dies used in these coinages were made at just one centre for the whole kingdom, sometimes at several. Under Æthelred II, there were different mechanisms in place for every one of his six or seven main types, although by about the middle of Cnut's reign the situation had stabilized, and seems to have been focused on workshops in London. It was there, according to Domesday Book, that moneyers from Hereford and Worcester had to travel in 1066 in order to obtain their dies.[43]

At times the design and distribution of dies seems in fact to have been handled in a very similar way to the production of royal diplomas, and it is

41 Naismith, *Medieval European Coinage 8*, pp. 245–47.

42 Naismith, *Medieval European Coinage 8*, pp. 120–22, 132–33, 138–39 and 149.

43 Naismith, *Medieval European Coinage 8*, p. 243.

worth looking in more detail at these periods when two of the clearest surviving projections of royal authority came into such close contact. In the early tenth century, both coins and charters were brought under tighter control at much the same time, in much the same way and by the same royal regime: that of Æthelstan.[44] Just as the scribe known to posterity as 'Æthelstan A' took in hand the writing of diplomas for the entire kingdom, coins in Æthelstan's name minted from York to Exeter and Dover were issued with the same design, and with the same innovative royal style as was used in diplomas, book dedication inscriptions, and poems celebrating the king:[45] REX TO[*tius*] BRIT[*anniae*] or similar.[46] A crowned bust introduced onto the coins minted in much of the kingdom a few years later was also the product of intervention at the highest levels, for its crown closely mirrors the three-pronged crown worn by Æthelstan in the famous donation miniature of him with St Cuthbert in Cambridge, Corpus Christi College 183.[47] One might draw a further parallel between the introduction of mint-names onto the coinage, and the emphasis on place of assembly given in the 'Æthelstan A' charters. Mint-names did, as noted above, serve a practical purpose, but also reflect an overarching authority concerned with specificity and geography.

Parallels between coins and charters can also be extended to arrangements in the decades between Æthelstan's death and the reign of Edgar. The common factor here is a degree of managed disunity. Among diplomas, a steady stream of 'mainstream' productions can be identified, probably made at royal assemblies by a core group of scribes connected with the king. But alongside them were clusters of documents produced by other agencies. These were still every inch 'royal' productions in that they called on the name of the king, but were written up under other regional or institutional auspices, and were not always the result of grants made by the king at a royal assembly. Two main groups can be identified in the mid-tenth century: the 'alliterative' and 'Dunstan B' charters. The former are thought to have been produced in association with Coenwald, bishop of Worcester (928×929–957/8), mostly for recipients and/or estates in the midlands, and the latter in association with the monastery of

44 For Æthelstan's diplomas, see Keynes, 'Church Councils', pp. 35–37 and 53–55; Sarah Foot, *Æthelstan: The First King of England* (New Haven, 2011), pp. 70–73 and 132–36; Ben Snook, *The Anglo-Saxon Chancery: The History, Language and Production of Anglo-Saxon Charters from Alfred to Edgar* (Woodbridge, 2015), pp. 86–124; and D. A. Woodman, '"Æthelstan A" and the Rhetoric of Rule', *ASE* 42 (2013), 217–48.

45 Naismith, *Medieval European Coinage 8*, pp. 202–4; and Christopher Blunt, 'The Coinage of Athelstan, King of England 924–939', *British Numismatic Journal* 42 (1974), 35–160.

46 Typically with no sign of abbreviation, and the exact presentation of the title varied: REX T B, REX TO BR, and REX TO BRIT can all be observed, suggesting that no specific abbreviation was stipulated.

47 Foot, *Æthelstan*, pp. 216–23.

Glastonbury. Delegation is probably a more accurate characterization of the background of these documents than breakdown. They represent the special favour and competence of certain parties in the kingdom who could be entrusted with the making of charters; in the case of the 'Dunstan B' charters, perhaps even the handling of the whole business of redistributing land while the king was incapacitated. Royal authority was as much a matter of mediation as direct assertion.[48]

The mid-tenth century coinage was strikingly similar in its general complexion. All areas continued to name the king and the appropriate moneyer, but five or six major regional areas can be distinguished in terms of typology and weight. The most idiosyncratic areas are the least well known from the charter record: East Anglia and the east midlands. The west midlands, meanwhile, moved in a separate but parallel orbit to England along and south of the Thames. The latter area for the most part operated as a single unit, and can perhaps be likened to the 'mainstream' of tenth-century diplomas.[49] In general, though, there is no hint that the coinage followed the same fault lines as the charters: they were the responsibilities of different agencies. It was a higher tolerance for delegation and regional autonomy under loose royal leadership that the coins and charters of this period shared.

The Composition of Charter Texts: Points of Contact

The middle decades of the tenth century are an important reminder that the coinage worked according to its own rhythm which ran alongside, and was not dependent on, that of the charters. Both kinds of source need to be understood on their own terms as products of a sequence of communications. Doing so enables points of contact involving language to stand out all the more clearly.

48 Keynes, 'Church Councils', pp. 92–102; with Simon Keynes, 'The "Dunstan B" Charters', *ASE* 23 (1994), 165–93. For a similar interpretation of royal power in tenth-century Italy see Barbara Rosenwein, *Negotiating Space: Power, Restraint, and Privileges of Immunity in Early Medieval Europe* (Manchester, 1999), pp. 137–55.

49 Rory Naismith, 'Prelude to Reform: Tenth-Century English Coinage in Perspective', in *Early Medieval Monetary History: Studies in Memory of Mark Blackburn*, eds Rory Naismith, Martin Allen, and Elina Screen (Farnham, 2014), pp. 39–83; George Molyneaux, *The Formation of the English Kingdom in the Tenth Century* (Oxford, 2015), pp. 116–41; Kenneth Jonsson, *The New Era: The Reformation of the Late Anglo-Saxon Coinage* (Stockholm, 1987), pp. 21–28; and Naismith, *Medieval European Coinage 8*, pp. 185–89.

Charters provide a more instructive beginning, for by their nature they are more liable to reveal information about the circumstances of their production. A royal diploma provided written title, bestowed in a ceremony by the king before witnesses, typically at a meeting which served a number of purposes. The beneficiary might come from far away, and the estate concerned might be situated just as far away in another direction. A scribe tasked with writing a diploma to substantiate such a grant consequently needed—even more so than his counterpart the die-cutter—to have everything ready on time. The scribe had to be comfortable with the general principles of formulation favoured at the time. On a more practical level, the scribe would also need the names and essential details of king, beneficiary and estate, the list of witnesses present at the crucial meeting, information about boundaries and any additional relevant points such as what price had been paid, if any. The overall result showcased royal authority as a way of securing the grant detailed by the diploma—in much the same way that the king's name and title guaranteed the authority of the coinage.

Despite these many moving parts, charter production was meant to be seamless. Most diplomas of the tenth and eleventh centuries which survive as probable originals are 'single-stage' documents: they were written in one go, with no evidence of hiccups in their production. In principle, they could have been written at any point in the proceedings relating to the grant, including after it was carried out. But there are enough 'multi-stage' documents to suggest that scribes often faced situations in which not all the relevant details (beneficiary, estate, boundary details, witness list, etc.) were available at the time of writing. Consequently they would leave gaps to fill in later, or add details on the foot or dorse of the charter.[50]

Scribes were most likely to have taken such measures if they were writing their documents in the course of royal meetings, with a time crunch looming in the form of ceremonies of presentation. Difficulties in assembling the dossier of information that lies behind a charter probably explain the occurrence of multi-stage documents. The key points could mostly have been communicated by word of mouth at the meeting in question (either by the parties involved or their delegates), but the witness list and boundary clause were a different matter. Short memoranda were composed to keep track of the former. Specimens of such notes survive appended to two charters from the late eighth and

50 Keynes, 'Church Councils', pp. 61–68 and 74–92. For similar observations in relation to Carolingian material, see Mark Mersiowsky, *Die Urkunde in der Karolingerzeit: Originale, Urkundenpraxis und politische Kommunikation*, 2 vols, MGH Schriften 60 (Wiesbaden, 2015), 2:722–29 and 897–900.

ninth centuries,[51] but traces of their use can be detected in identical witness lists of the tenth and eleventh centuries.[52] Boundary clauses depended on close familiarity with the land in question, which could only really be obtained by first-hand acquaintance. One sees how the matter could be handled in a text of the 890s from Worcester, which describes how—in order to settle a dispute raised by Wærferth, bishop of Worcester, at a meeting in Mercia—a *geneat* named Ecglaf was ordered by his landlord Æthelwald to show a priest from Worcester around the bounds of a group of estates in Gloucestershire while the priest read from 'the old charters' (*ðam aldan bocum*), presumably so as to verify how the church's privileges (issued by King Æthelbald (716–57) over a century earlier) mapped onto the ground and identify discrepancies with current claims.[53] Both the priest and the *geneat* (or more realistically the bishop and Æthelwald) would have benefited from the process, the point being to confirm for all sides the veracity of the church's claim. In this instance Æthelwald accepted the bishop's accusation that he had infringed on Worcester's land in several places, but won agreement that he and his son would continue to enjoy those lands for as long as they lived. Had Æthelwald chosen to contest the case, or had the bishop wanted to update his records so as to protect the church against the same threat in future, a perambulation of this kind might well have led to a short written memorandum of the relevant bounds which could then have been conveyed to a scribe writing a charter. Landlords like either the layman Æthelwald or Bishop Wærferth might well have kept an archive of boundary descriptions ready to deploy in case of any unforeseen need. This could be one reason for the occasional survival of isolated boundary clauses.[54]

Language was a major concern on several levels. It mattered, first, in the actual to and fro of oral exchange between groups and individuals, even though this can only be accessed indirectly and indistinctly. Writing, while potent in itself, became even more so when it served as an extension of authoritative speech, and written acts are often full of spoken drama. As might be expected,

51 S 163 (*CantCC* 40) and S 293 (*CantCC* 73). Cf. Mary Prescott Parsons, 'Some Scribal Memoranda for Anglo-Saxon Charters of the 8th and 9th Centuries', *Mitteilungen des österreichischen Instituts für Geschichtsforschung* 14 (1939), 13–32; and Keynes, 'Church Councils', pp. 67–72 and 77–78.

52 Keynes, 'Church Councils', pp. 91–92 and 113.

53 S 1441 (BCS 574).

54 S 1540–1602. Keynes, 'Church Councils', pp. 66–67; and Brooks and Kelly, *CantCC* 80, p. 719. A similar argument has recently been made by Ed Roberts regarding the occasional use of detailed and partially vernacular boundary descriptions in East Frankish charters of the Carolingian period: Edward Roberts, 'Boundary Clauses and the Use of the Vernacular in Eastern Frankish Charters, *c.*750–*c.*900', *Historical Research* 91 (2018), 580–604.

contentious documents, like the narratives of dispute settlements, tended to produce more overt speechifying. Important utterances that had burned their way into the memories of listeners or carried special jurisdictional weight might even be recorded as direct speech. One thinks of the case of a woman in Herefordshire in the time of Cnut whose response to a question about the inheritance of land forms the centrepiece of an Old English dispute record. Because the woman herself was not present at the key meeting, three named thegns were delegated to go and ask her wishes. Her response began with a clear statement about her intentions: 'here sits Leofflæd, my kinswoman, to whom, after my death, I grant my land and my gold, my clothing and my raiment and all that I possess'; her speech went on in more spontaneous fashion: 'act like thegns, and duly announce my message to the meeting before all the worthy men, and tell them to whom I have granted my land and all my property, and not a thing to my own son, and ask them to be witnesses of this'.[55] The unusual nature of the woman's wishes, plus her absence from the main meeting, probably contributed to the decision to record her words in this way, as part of a document that was put together and written in a gospel-book by Thurkil the White, husband of the heiress.

Language in a document itself was inextricably bound to language in performance, speech, and interaction, at least when the resultant text was meant to be accessible to as many members of the elite (lay and ecclesiastical) as possible, in order to set down and legitimize a particular understanding of past events.[56] To this end the vernacular might be used for some or all of a document, and highly familiar formulations in either English or Latin could be deployed.[57] But there were clearly also times when the 'shock and awe' factor of impressively intricate Latin was called for: in many royal diplomas of the tenth and eleventh centuries accessibility and inaccessibility could complement one another, reaching out to different audiences whose interests overlapped.[58] Even if an Anglo-Saxon layman or local priest was not capable of construing an especially knotty proem, they might recall with deep respect hearing the

55 'Her sit Leoflæde min mæge þe ic geann ægðer ge mines lands, ge mines goldes, ge ræglæs, ge reafes, ge ealles þe ic ah æfter minon dæge ... doð þegnlice, [ond] wel abeodað mine ærende to þam gemote beforan eallum þam godan mannum, [ond] cyðaþ heom hwæm ic mines lands geunnen hæbbe, [one] ealre minre æhte, [ond] minan agenan sunu næfre nan þing, [ond] biddað heom beon þisses to gewitnesse': S 1462, *ASChart*, no. 78.

56 Foot, 'Reading Anglo-Saxon Charters', pp. 49–56.

57 F. M. Stenton, *The Latin Charters of the Anglo-Saxon Period* (Oxford, 1955), p. 49.

58 For recent literary analysis of Anglo-Saxon charter proems see Snook, *The Anglo-Saxon Chancery*.

words read aloud at the meeting where the diploma was bestowed, and the gist of their meaning as explained by a more learned member of the company.

The instrumental and calculated—but also highly pragmatic—approach to writing on display in Anglo-Saxon charters gives a clue to what may have gone on behind the more taciturn façade of the coinage. Vast amounts of information needed to be exchanged, orally and in writing. This was a complicated, demanding, and (doubtless) expensive operation, driven by highly individual needs and wishes among the parties involved. One can readily imagine that tasks of this kind are one reason why the *geneat* of *Rectitudines singularum personarum* was obligated to 'carry messages far and near wheresoever he is directed'.[59]

The Composition of Coin Inscriptions

The challenge in turning to Anglo-Saxon coin inscriptions is that, compared with charters, they give so little away. How did they get there? What kind of communications lay behind them? Who decided what inscriptions should say, right down to details of orthography? The starting point must have been a similar background of speech, travel, and written communication. References to these processes in law-codes, Domesday Book, and other texts are few, and mostly take a top-down perspective that emphasizes the direction of moneyers through local intermediaries. These intermediaries—ealdormen, reeves, bishops, and others—are probably who Æthelstan, Edgar, and other late Anglo-Saxon kings targeted when they legislated on money and coinage.[60] There is also evidence that in the Carolingian kingdoms (e.g. Charles the Bald at Pîtres in 864) and in Norman England (Henry I at Winchester in 1124/5) the king might occasionally call together all the moneyers, or all magnates who had responsibility for overseeing moneyers, to issue general instructions.[61] Such meetings could have been the way new Anglo-Saxon coinages were inaugurated, especially in the tenth and eleventh centuries. Other mechanisms for distributing designs and inscriptions should also be considered. At times

59 'Ærendian fyr saw nyr, swa hwyder swa him mon to tæcð': *Gesetze*, ed. Liebermann, 1:445; *English Historical Documents. II: 1042–1189*, eds David C. Douglas and George W. Greenaway, 2nd ed. (London, 1981), no. 172.

60 Naismith, 'Laws of London'; and Screen, 'Anglo-Saxon Law'.

61 Philip Grierson, 'The *Gratia Dei Rex* Coinage of Charles the Bald', in *Charles the Bald: Court and Kingdom*, eds Margaret T. Gibson and Janet L. Nelson, 2nd ed. (Aldershot, 1990), pp. 52–64; and Martin Allen, *Mints and Money in Medieval England* (Cambridge, 2012), pp. 27–29.

of relative decentralization (but when the same essential design was observed across the kingdom), die-cutters in a number of locations could have worked from a model, perhaps seen at or brought back from an assembly by local elites; at times of tighter centralization, when just a few craftsmen fulfilled the needs of all the mints, a royal meeting could have been the occasion for conceiving, engraving and distributing the initial run of dies, with individual moneyers later reporting to the central workshop for new equipment on a case-by-case basis, as Domesday Book says was the practice in 1066.

The king's name and title would undoubtedly have been prescribed for the die-cutters during these initial stages of a new coinage, even if only in the sense that *some* form of the king's name and *some* title should appear. Under Offa, royal styles were diverse, suggesting that the exact form of title was not stipulated.[62] Before Edgar's reform introduced some part of ANGLORVM virtually as standard, names of peoples were uncommon in the obverse inscription. Some eighth- and ninth-century kings specified that they were ruler of the Mercians, West Saxons, or (East) Angles, and Æthelstan was hailed as king 'of all Britain', but the large majority of kings were simply REX. The orthography of the king's name can sometimes give a clue to what instructions were issued to the die-cutters. A century after Offa, the West Saxon king Æthelberht (860–65) was named AEÐELBEARHT on pennies minted in Kent: a form which shows raising and unrounding of the final diphthong, characteristic of Kentish Old English but not seen in Wessex (Figure 13.3). One suspects therefore that the king's name was given to the die-cutters of Kent orally via Kentish locals, with no specific written form prescribed.[63] Just as Kentish and West Saxon assemblies and diplomatic productions remained separate in the ninth century,[64] Kent and Wessex seem to have minted coins as largely dis-

62 Naismith, *Money and Power*, pp. 79–82.

63 Rory Naismith, *The Coinage of Southern England 796–865*, 2 vols (London, 2011), nos C160–217 and R42–43.

64 Brooks and Kelly, *CantCC*, pp. 120–23; Simon Keynes, 'The West Saxon Charters of King Æthelwulf and his Sons', *EHR* 109 (1994), 1109–49. A document which demonstrates the complexities that could arise from dealing across these divisions is the 838 agreement of Archbishop Ceolnoth with King Ecgberht and his son Æthelwulf (S 1438), which survives in three contemporary single-sheet versions that contain the work of three distinct scribes: one from Christ Church, Canterbury (who wrote two copies); one from Wessex (who endorsed one Canterbury copy and wrote the text of a third); and one from an unknown centre who may have been associated with a meeting *æt Astran* in 839 (who added endorsements to two of the three copies). See *CantCC* 69; Keynes, 'West Saxon Charters', pp. 1112–14; Keynes, 'Church Councils', pp. 26–27.

FIGURE 13.3
Penny of Æthelberht of Kent/Wessex (858–65), moneyer Se(le)frith
CLASSICAL NUMISMATIC GROUP AUCTION 101, 5 JANUARY 2016, LOT 908

crete entities.[65] In the tenth and eleventh centuries the situation was variable. Some regional preferences emerged in titulature—REX SAXORVM (or an abbreviation thereof) as the title for Æthelstan at Derby, for example.[66] Most of the time, there was enough minor variation in orthography (e.g. EADWARD as opposed to EDWEARD under Edward the Confessor) to suggest that die-cutters were crafting the obverse inscription on an individual basis while working around a prescribed set of core elements: the cross, the king's name, and *rex*, with (after the early 970s) the option of as much of *Anglorum* as there was space for. In short, die-cutters were provided with an envelope of expectations but often left to their own devices in composing the obverse inscription.

Yet the machinery was in place for more specific forms of name and title to be promulgated. On at least two occasions the king and his inner circle activated these mechanisms. Both came at times of innovation and centralization. The first was Edgar's reform coinage itself, instituted in the early 970s, and (at least initially) based on a single source of dies.[67] These were the first in Anglo-Saxon England to use an abbreviated form of *-orum*, at the conclusion of the word ANGLOR[*um*] on the obverse (Figure 13.4). This abbreviation was well known in manuscript contexts, and can be found extensively in books from the time of Edgar, not least the book-length foundation charter of

65 The rarity of West Saxon coins in the ninth century means that this part of the story is more difficult to follow. Under Ecgberht and Æthelwulf West Saxon mints used distinct types (one of which was copied at contemporary Canterbury), while a specimen from the time of Æthelred I (865–71) adapts the type current in contemporary Kent: Naismith, *Medieval European Coinage 8*, p. 155; Mark Blackburn, 'Alfred's Coinage Reforms in Context', in *Alfred the Great: Papers from the Eleventh-Centenary Conferences*, ed. Timothy Reuter (Aldershot, 2003), pp. 199–218, at 208–12.

66 Naismith, *Medieval European Coinage 8*, p. 203.

67 Naismith, *Medieval European Coinage 8*, nos 1764–70.

FIGURE 13.4
Penny of Edgar (959–75), Reform type, Derby mint, moneyer Oswulf/Ásulfr (with obverse inscription ANGLOR[*um*])
CLASSICAL NUMISMATIC GROUP AUCTION 85, 15 SEPTEMBER 2010, LOT 1445

the New Minster in Winchester, issued in 966.[68] Its appearance on the coinage at this point was surely not a coincidence. This new abbreviation points to the input of book-learned clergy with a strong vision for how Edgar's rule over England should be expressed.[69] The second came some eighty years later, in the 1050s, with the seventh main coinage of Edward the Confessor, now usually referred to as the Sovereign/Eagles type. It belongs to a period of greater experimentation in portrayals of the king, under German influence,[70] and is unique in showing him full-length and enthroned, holding a staff or spear and *globus cruciger*.[71] On some dies of this coinage, used at a range of mint-places but seemingly from a single source, the king's name was represented in highly unusual fashion, as +EADVVEARDVS (Figure 13.5). This form is exceptional for eschewing winn in favour of VV, and for Latinizing the ending of the king's name.[72] There are almost no parallels to this in the tenth- or eleventh-century coinage—although, as with the accompanying image, there is a parallel in the spelling of Edward's name on surviving impressions of his seal.[73] The likelihood is that the die-cutter was either himself a foreign craftsman, or that an Anglo-Saxon die-cutter was confronted with a model

68 London, British Library, Cotton Vespasian A.viii, fol. 35v.

69 Naismith, 'Prelude to Reform', pp. 80–83; and Molyneaux, *The Formation of the English Kingdom*, pp. 117–23.

70 Marion Archibald, 'The German Connection: German Influences on the Later Anglo-Saxon and Norman Coinages in their English Context', in *Fundamenta Historiae: Geschichte im Spiegel der Numismatic und ihrer Nachbarwissenschaften. Festschrift für Niklot Klüßendorf zum 60. Geburtstag am 10. Februar 2004*, ed. Reiner Cunz (Hanover, 2004), pp. 131–50.

71 Naismith, *Medieval European Coinage 8*, nos 2206–34.

72 See Seiler in this volume for the Latinization of Old English names, especially in the earlier Anglo-Saxon period.

73 Simon Keynes, 'The Use of Seals in Anglo-Saxon England', in *Seals and Status: Power of Objects*, eds John Cherry, Jessica Berenbeim, and Lloyd de Beer (London, 2018), pp. 73–83, at 79.

FIGURE 13.5
Penny of Edward the Confessor (1042–66), *Sovereign/Eagles* type, Winchester mint, moneyer Leofing (with obverse inscription EADVVEARDVS)
CLASSICAL NUMISMATIC GROUP AUCTION 105, 10 MAY 2017, LOT 1204

that specified an unusual form of inscription, inspired by the relatively new seal matrix.[74]

The potential thus existed for royal names and titles to be spelled out in a specified way, but evidently it was far from standard to do so. A negotiable relationship existed between die-cutters and the individuals who chose and disseminated coin designs, including the royal name and title. This was, however, only half the story. Turning to the other side of the coin, the details about the manufacturer offer more potential for illuminating monetary communication and language. These elements of numismatic inscriptions were based on connections between moneyers and die-cutters. There might be several hundred of the former at any one time, distributed at fortress-towns from Yorkshire to the south coast, and between one and a dozen workshops of the latter, situated in the kingdom's main towns. Domesday Book mentioned how the moneyers of the west midlands in 1066 were travelling to London for their dies. Long-distance journeys were virtually a necessity in keeping the monetary system running. Messengers would be needed in such cases, and could have served a number of purposes. Passing on the name and location of their master was one; paying fees might have been another; and a third might have been to carry dies in both directions—superseded or worn ones from the moneyer to the die-cutter, and fresh ones on the way back. Inter-mint die-links substantiate this last part of the operation. These refer to cases of the same obverse die—which of course referred only to the king and his title—being used at two (or occasionally three or more) different mint-places, potentially at widely separated locations (see Map 13.1). Dies have been identified as having been used at Oxford and York, Canterbury and Stamford, and Buckingham and Chester. London bulks especially large in inter-mint die-links, because of its growing

74 Naismith, *Medieval European Coinage 8*, p. 275.

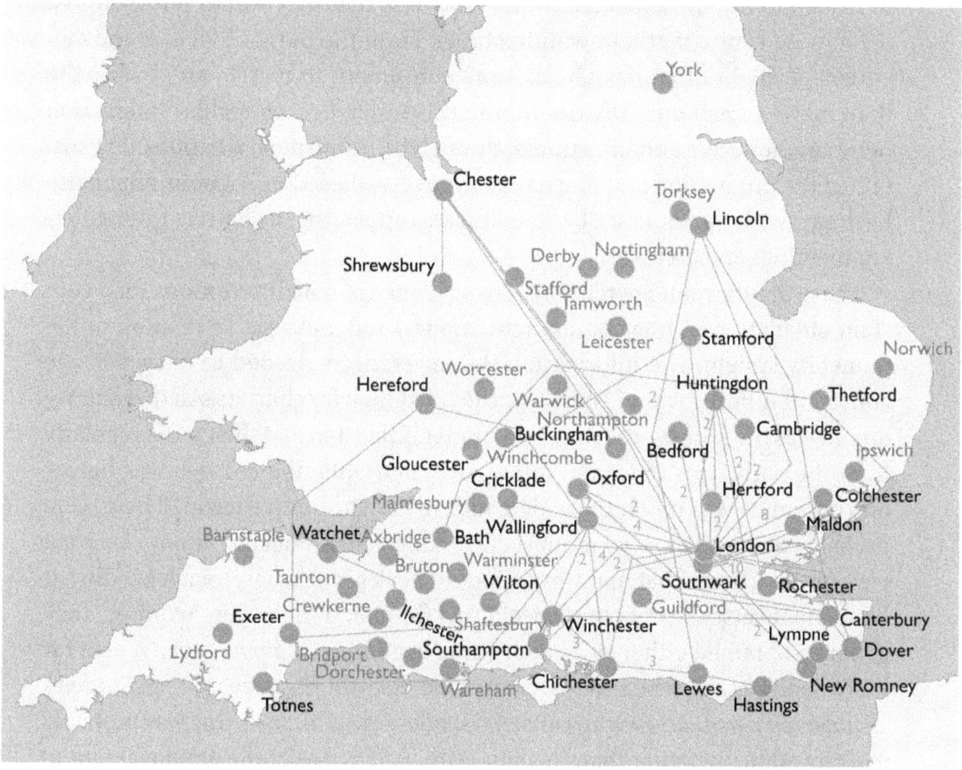

MAP 13.1 Map showing instances of obverse dies being used at different mint-places in the *Long Cross* type of Æthelred II. Each line represents an obverse die-link, with numbers indicating multiple dies used at the same pair of mint-places. Mint-places not featuring in inter-mint die-links are named with lighter text. Based on unpublished data gathered by Bill Lean and Stewart Lyon.
DRAWN BY THE AUTHOR

role in the distribution of dies in the late Anglo-Saxon period.[75] Several explanations might lie behind inter-mint die transfers. Some might have travelled with a relocating moneyer, especially when the moneyer at both mint-places had the same name (and was, therefore, probably the same individual). A few could also represent 'contamination': coins which were not actually made at one of the locations named on the reverse, for reasons that are now impossible to discern. But it is likely that most movements of obverse dies stem from very practical motivations. These objects could have a long life; longer than many moneyers might need them, and because dies were quite literally a license

75 Rory Naismith, 'London and its Mints *c.* 880–1066: A Preliminary Survey', *British Numismatic Journal* 83 (2013), 44–74.

to make money, the expectation probably was that they would returned to a die-cutting centre if still in working order. From the point of view of the die-cutters, it might often have been more convenient to recycle an obverse die than make a fresh one. Distribution in this way relied on regular interaction between moneyers and die-cutters, through the same peregrinations that sustained the production and movement of reverse dies. Comparisons might also be drawn with the same scribes or witnesses appearing in charters from different meetings and archives.

These die-movements reinforce the evidence of coin inscriptions for a constant circulation of men, equipment, money, and messages in relation to the monetary system. The information that messengers needed to convey in the context of minting was of course less detailed than for charters. All that was required was the moneyer's name and (under Æthelstan and then more regularly from the early 970s onwards) mint-place. But while the coinage was lighter on content, it was much more demanding in quantitative terms. There were probably at least 120 or so moneyers working across England at any one time (two or three times that many in periods of peak productivity), each needing at least one reverse die engraved specifically for him. If more were required, they could be obtained either as a batch at the beginning of a new type, or sent for individually as and when they were needed. As with the *geneat* of *Rectitudines singularum personarum* who carried the missives of his lord, this was probably a job for someone other than the moneyer, such as one of the employees mentioned in a tenth-century law-code.[76]

A *geneat* bringing a boundary clause to a royal assembly could well have crossed paths on the road with the employee of a moneyer on his way to a major town in order to obtain one or more coin-dies for his master. After parting company, the moneyer's agent would have travelled on, and eventually reached his destination at the workshop of a die-cutter. As all that was really required was a name and a location, the tentative presumption is that the agent would convey them to the die-cutter by word of mouth. The question that follows is how these names were then handled by the die-cutter. The scale of work that these craftsmen undertook surely required that they have sufficient literacy to be able to engrave names onto dies. Whether moneyers, or their operatives, had the same skill is less clear. The name that ended up on the die, therefore, probably derives from the die-cutter's interpretation of what the moneyer, or their proxy, had said.[77] There was room here for negotiation,

76 IV Æthelred, c. 9, *Gesetze*, ed. Liebermann 1:286. On the date and background of this text, see Naismith, 'Laws of London'.

77 Fran Colman, *Money Talks: Reconstructing Old English* (Berlin, 1991), pp. 159–62.

with potential for agency on both sides. By-names provide a good illustration. They appear on a small proportion of coins from about the 1020s and after.[78] A few are geared towards what might be termed contradistinction: to distinguish one individual from another of the same name, presumably operating at the same location. Epithets of this kind could have been mutually agreed on by the moneyers involved, and may or may not have been used for other purposes. At London in the 1030s and 1040s, for example, there appear to have been two men called Eadweald issuing coins. Two strategies were used to distinguish them: reference to one being the elder of the pair (EDWALD ĐE ALDA, 'Eadweald the Old'), and reference to the specific location within the city where one of them worked (EADWOLD ON ESTCEP LV, 'Eadweald on Eastcheap, London').[79] The majority of by-names on coins, however, seem to belong to a different background of self-representation. They reflect designations coined in the moneyers' own communities, and were used in other settings beyond minting.[80] By-names of this kind need not have been chosen because there was a second local figure with the same first name; all they denote is that some moneyers were keen to assert their own individuality. They often did so in prescribed ways, however. There is a refreshingly earthy quality to several of the appellations that moneyers received: ÆLFWIG SWENCEL ('Ælfwig the Troublemaker'), BRVNGAR PVCA ('Brungar Puck'), GODWINE COK ('Godwine Cock/Cook') and MATAĐAN BALLVC ('Matathan Bollock/ the Lad'). These ribald labels would not necessarily have been seen as disrespectful, or beyond the bounds of propriety—but they do suggest a new aesthetic among the up and coming members of local 'gentry' in which salty names were embraced as an assertion of group solidarity.[81] They surely represent a determined effort by the moneyers to have their own preferred designation recognized on the coinage. Another context for linguistic negotiation would be entered if names crossed from one linguistic milieu into another. Dialects of Old English might vary between moneyer and die-cutter, and one

78 Veronica Smart, 'Osulf Thein and Others: Double Moneyer's Names on the Late Anglo-Saxon Coinage', in *Studies in Late Anglo-Saxon Coinage in Memory of Bror Emil Hildebrand*, ed. Kenneth Jonsson (Stockholm, 1990), pp. 435–53.

79 The latter is the only known example of a street-name found in Anglo-Saxon coinage: Richard Ambrose and Rory Naismith, '"Eadwold on Eastcheap, London": A Street-Name on a Late Anglo-Saxon Penny', *British Numismatic Journal* 90 (2020), 202–9.

80 Cf. Gösta Tengvik, *Old English Bynames* (Uppsala, 1938).

81 James Chetwood, 'Re-evaluating English Personal Naming on the Eve of the Conquest', *EME* 26 (2018), 518–47, at 546. For a parallel in Milan around 1100, where by-names featuring the element Caca- ('shit') became popular, see Chris Wickham, *Sleepwalking into a New World: The Emergence of Italian City Communes in the Twelfth Century* (Princeton, NJ, 2015), pp. 51–52.

could be more familiar with names drawn from a different linguistic tradition. Old Norse names were common in eastern and northern England but occurred sporadically across the kingdom; a smaller number of names drawn from Continental Germanic, Irish, Welsh, and Latin or Romance might also be found. All could be subject to varying degrees of Anglicization.[82] In the tenth century, for example, some Latin names were left untouched, and still carry nominative case endings (e.g. STEFANVS), while others were adapted to an approximation of Old English (e.g. BENEÐIHT, for *Benedictus*).[83] They had, in other words, been Anglicized. Particular interest attaches to a pair of names which occur between about 920 and the 950s in the east midlands: PITIT and LITILMAN. The former appears under Edward the Elder, both are used under Æthelstan and Edmund, and the latter alone survived into the time of Eadwig. The two mean much the same thing—small (individual)—in Romance and Old English respectively, and it has been proposed that both names denote the same man.[84] If so, this would represent a surprising degree of linguistic expertise for a die-cutter to exercise independently, raising the possibility that 'Little' could have had significant input into his representation on coins. The varied treatment of other Latin/Romance and Continental Germanic names (often on coins of similar style, and thus probably struck from dies cut by the same hand) suggests that this case was not exceptional, at least in the context of the tenth-century east midlands, where most such names occur.[85]

Old Norse names in the century before the Norman Conquest present a rather different story. They often had readily identifiable English cognates, and a strong tradition of Anglicization developed around them from the mid-tenth century onwards: thus *-kell* (as in Thorkell the Tall) became *-cetel*, while *Ás-* (as in Áslakr) became *Os-*. The extent of this Anglicization—which took much the same form in contemporary charters and other records—means that it can sometimes be impossible to distinguish several linguistic possibilities: OSVLF might denote either Old English Oswulf or Old Norse Ásulfr, while OSBEARN could be Old Norse Ásbjorn or Continental Germanic Esbern/

82 Smart, 'Scandinavians, Celts and Germans', pp. 171–74.

83 Both these moneyers worked in the east midlands. On STEFANVS, BENEÐIHT and other moneyers with Latin and Continental Germanic names in England, see Veronica Smart, 'Economic Migrants? Continental Moneyers' Names on the Tenth-Century English Coinage', *Nomina* 32 (2009), 113–56.

84 Veronica Smart, 'Pitit and Litilman, an Onomastic Conundrum', *Nomina* 25 (2002), 133–38.

85 The distribution was more widespread under Edward the Elder, but became more concentrated in the course of the tenth century: Smart, 'Economic Migrants?', pp. 118–21.

Osbern.[86] But some names fitted less comfortably into customary forms, and when these were replicated by multiple die-cutters, it becomes possible to see that the die-cutter exercised a high degree of influence over the name-form that was actually placed on the coin. Two illustrative cases occur among the moneyers of Lincoln in the early eleventh century. This important northern mint generally produced its own dies but was also starting to turn to London on an increasingly frequent basis. In the final issue of Æthelred II (the so-called *Last Small Cross* type), one Lincoln moneyer was generally named IVSTAN or GVSTIN on reverse dies made in Lincoln itself.[87] This name is usually normalized in Old Norse as Iosteinn. On one occasion, however, a pair of dies was made in London and sent to him. The reverse names the moneyer IOSEDAN.[88] This very probably refers to the same individual, but the difference in orthography reflects how individual die-cutters interpreted names transmitted to them orally. One sees something similar with another Lincoln moneyer active about twenty years later, under Cnut. The normalized form of his name is Áslakr. Coin-dies of the first issue of Cnut (*Quatrefoil*), one of the most decentralized of the period, generally named him ASLAC. Those of the next type of the reign, in which a mix of local and central (probably London) dies were employed, used two name-forms: ASLAC and OSLAC. Finally, the third type, struck solely from central dies, only used OSLAC.[89] Other moneyers at Lincoln (and also York) are particularly good case-studies, because these mint-towns called on a mix of local and central die-cutters for longer than most, and had a diverse pool of moneyers' names.

Conclusion

Coins and charters are both the end-product of wide-reaching and sophisticated systems of communication, grounded in oral and written use of language. In this respect they are very much alike. But it is appropriate to end by

86 Individual names recorded on coins, including the examples here, are extensively paralleled in other English sources: Erik Björkman, *Nordische Personennamen in England in alt- und frühmittel-englischer Zeit* (Halle, 1910), pp. 10, 21–22, and 151–53. For in-depth exploration of three English sources and their varied treatment of Old Norse in the tenth century, see Matthew Townend, *Language and History in Viking Age England: Linguistic Relations between Speakers of Old Norse and Old English* (Turnhout, 2002), pp. 89–143.

87 H. R. Mossop, *The Lincoln Mint c. 890–1279* (Newcastle-upon-Tyne, 1970), pl. XXIV, nos 4–9.

88 C. S. S. Lyon, *Sylloge of Coins of the British Isles 68: The Lyon Collection of Anglo-Saxon Coins* (Oxford, 2016), no. 884 (with comment on p. 148).

89 Compare Mossop, *Lincoln Mint*, pl. XXXIII, no. 4, XLII, no. 19, and LIII, no. 28.

stressing how they differ: variations are just as important as similarities, and reinforce that these two sources confronted similar problems in relation to language and writing, but did so in different contexts and for different audiences. They need to be read as parallels which inform one another, rather than as part of a unified system.

Three major points of divergence stand out. First, there is the matter of *who* was involved. Charters were written for the benefit of the landowning elite as a whole, including laymen and women as well as ecclesiastics and church institutions, but the actual writing process probably remained the preserve of literate clergy. Coins were the preserve of an equally restricted yet quite distinct group of specialists: die-cutters and moneyers. Although these two groups are much less well understood than charter scribes, it is unlikely that there was any significant crossover between them. Die-cutters and moneyers appear to have been a body of laymen, exercising a highly targeted form of pragmatic literacy. Language for them was one of the tools of the trade. They dealt primarily with names, overwhelmingly drawn from the vernacular, as well as titles and occasionally other content in Latin. The two sat comfortably side by side, indicating a degree of comfort in handling both Latin and the vernacular, just as was also the case in contemporary charters. England's combination of consistent and frequently assertive royal dominance over the coinage with a very granular and personalized production system allowed an unusual degree of language interaction. Few other coinages of the early Middle Ages are comparable in this respect. The Carolingian Empire and its successors favoured names of rulers and mint-places together with appropriate Latin designations. Probably the closest parallel is the earlier Merovingian kingdom, though here the break between Latin and the vernacular is less easy to pin down.[90] England's coinage, in short, was a special case, and the interplay of Latin and the vernacular speaks volumes about the running of the currency. Royal names and Latin elements could at times be taken in hand and standardized by ruling authorities, while the tendency to Anglicize Old Norse and Romance names followed the same pattern as those found in other English settings. Monetary inscriptions thus did not operate in isolation; they formed part of a continuum of written culture, of which charters are one other well-represented branch. They reveal a whole new side of pragmatic literacy in the day-to-day life of the kingdom.

What these branches wrote down differed, however, and so in consequence did the networks and processes they called on. Die-cutters and moneyers needed names to be inscribed onto fresh minting tools. Charter scribes needed crucial names too, but also more extensive information such as boundary

90 See the papers in *Die Merowingischen Monetarmünzen*, eds Jarnut and Strothmann.

details, and the documents typically also required a more or less florid proem. Marshalling this information took significant effort on several sides. Moreover, charters were executed on a case-by-case basis: scribes did not necessarily know what direction their next task would come from, and although the parties involved had a vested interest in everything working as smoothly as possible, glitches were surely to be expected. The monumental air that surrounds Anglo-Saxon diplomas papers over what must often have been a messy and *ad hoc* process. Coin dies, by contrast, not only needed less information to be transmitted, but lent themselves to much more regular, predictable processes of communication. Moneyers needed dies when old ones were no longer functional, or when a new coinage was instituted. There are still uncertainties of course: how did moneyers know where to turn for their dies? Over the course of Æthelred II's reign, for instance, a moneyer in the same location might at times have been supplied from three or four different sources. The geographical breakdown of die-distribution only occasionally followed known political or administrative boundaries,[91] implying that it was a flexible and independent infrastructure; a much more robust one than charters depended on, and one in which the flow of language and information was pivotal.

This geographical dimension mattered in another way. *Where* dies and coins were produced differed substantially, with important ramifications for use of language. Charters, at least as represented by the corpus that survives, are largely a phenomenon of southern England and the west midlands. Their representation of the vernacular in terms of dialect, vocabulary, and input from other languages such as Old Norse, is heavily dependent on the distribution of material; their Latin too was guided by local diplomatic traditions, especially in the period before Æthelstan's reign. At a deeper level, the packaging of language in charters was also shaped by the setting in which they were created. These texts were written at, for, or as a result of meetings, royal and otherwise, in which physical presence and oral declaration were critically important. Latin and Old English were deployed partly to convey information in an accessible form, and partly to solemnize the act, often (especially in royal diplomas) with a degree of grandiose and highly deliberate obfuscation. These two needs allowed a charter to speak to twin audiences: one was immediate, consisting of the recipient, witnesses, and others on whom the act impinged; the other was a more restricted pool of future heirs, who might carry on using

91 Naismith, *Medieval European Coinage 8*, pp. 245–47. An interesting exception is the *Jewel Cross* coinage of the later 1030s, in which die-distribution seems to have followed affiliations to Harold and Harthacnut in their contest for the throne (Naismith, *Medieval European Coinage 8*, pp. 270–71).

the document for generations within a family or institution, and who would only produce it in another assembly if necessary. Audiences in both the present and the hereafter would be drawn from the secular and ecclesiastical elite. Coins were made more widely. Wherever moneyers worked, there would be a need to relay names back to a die-cutter. Coins were also made outside the orbit of elite assemblies that produced charters. On the one hand, their creation was much less public than charters, being dependent on an essentially closed circuit of specialists whose work would for the most part be held accountable only after the fact. On the other, the actual audience who might engage with coin inscriptions was massively larger and more diverse than was the case with charters. Public consumption can thus be contrasted with private production—precisely the opposite of charters.

The focus here has been on the producers of coin inscriptions, but the scrupulous attention to literacy on coins implies an expectation that users could read them too. Yet even basic literacy would have been exceptional among the mass of coin-users. The emphasis that coin inscriptions place on authority and accountability points the way to the most realistic audience of readers: reeves and other agents of justice who would have to hold moneyers to account. Even if a random Anglo-Saxon coin-user who recognized a problem with her or his pennies could read the names of the moneyer and the mint-place, they would nonetheless be expected to bring the issue to the attention of these same authorities. The reeve would then check the coins himself, and if necessary pursue the offending moneyer, or alert the local authorities in the relevant district if he lay elsewhere. How such a procedure might unfold is never explained in documentary texts from England, but one such case is known from contemporary Barcelona, where a charter records how in 990 an official referred to as the 'guardian of the mint/of the money' (*custos monetae*) identified some debased or forged coins in circulation and traced them back to the offending moneyer. Whether he did so by pursuing a sequence of transactions, or by reading an inscription, is not clear.[92] In England itself, there is no evidence for dedicated 'guardians' of this kind, but the Old English version of the Legend of the Seven Sleepers of Ephesus does suggest that reeves, bishops, and other upholders of justice might prosecute currency crimes. In this adaptation of a late antique

92 *Diplomatari de la Catedral de Barcelona: documents dels anys 844–1260. Volum I: documents dels anys 844–1000*, ed. Àngel Fabrega i Grau, Fonts Documentals 1 (Barcelona, 1995), no. 201. Translation and discussion can be found in Jonathan Jarrett, 'Currency Change in Pre-Millennial Catalonia: Coinage, Counts and Economics', *Numismatic Chronicle* 169 (2009), 217–43. No coins of this period can actually be identified from Barcelona, so it is not clear whether the moneyer's name would have been inscribed on the offending coins (though this was not the usual practice in Catalonia).

story, one of the sleepers arouses the suspicion of the townsmen for dealing in unusual currency. He is then brought before the *portgerefa* and bishop of the city, and questioned directly by the former in a public meeting.[93] Coin inscriptions as such are not referred to here, but it is easy to imagine them being one point to follow up in real-life cases of this kind. In terms of readership, therefore, coin inscriptions do not necessarily reveal anything about the literacy of the population as a whole, though they strengthen the case for pragmatic literacy among those responsible for upholding the law.

Bibliography

Primary Sources

Anglo-Saxon Charters, ed. and trans. A. J. Robertson (Cambridge, 1939).

The Anonymous Old English Legend of the Seven Sleepers, ed. Hugh Magennis (Durham, 1994).

Charters of Christ Church Canterbury, eds N. P. Brooks and S. E. Kelly, Anglo-Saxon Charters 17–18 (Oxford, 2013).

Diplomatari de la Catedral de Barcelona: documents dels anys 844–1260. Volum I: documents dels anys 844–1000, ed. Àngel Fabrega i Grau, Fonts Documentals 1 (Barcelona, 1995).

English Historical Documents. II: 1042–1189, eds David C. Douglas and George W. Greenaway, 2nd ed. (London, 1981).

Die Gesetze der Angelsachsen, ed. Felix Liebermann, 3 vols (Halle, 1903–16).

Secondary Sources

Allen, Martin, *Mints and Money in Medieval England* (Cambridge, 2012).

Ambrose, Richard and Naismith, Rory, '"Eadwold on Eastcheap, London": A Street-Name on a Late Anglo-Saxon Penny', *British Numismatic Journal* 90 (2020), 202-9.

Archibald, Marion, 'The German Connection: German Influences on the Later Anglo-Saxon and Norman Coinages in their English Context', in *Fundamenta Historiae: Geschichte im Spiegel der Numismatic und ihrer Nachbarwissenschaften. Festschrift für Niklot Klüßendorf zum 60. Geburtstag am 10. Februar 2004*, ed. Reiner Cunz (Hanover, 2004), pp. 131–50.

93 Catherine Cubitt, '"As the Lawbook Teaches": Reeves, Lawbooks and Urban Life in the Anonymous Old English Legend of the Seven Sleepers', *EHR* 124 (2009), 1021–49, at pp. 1028–31. For the text, see *The Anonymous Old English Legend of the Seven Sleepers*, ed. Hugh Magennis (Durham, 1994).

Bartlett, Robert, *The Making of Europe: Conquest, Colonization and Cultural Change 950–1350* (London, 1993).

Björkman, Erik, *Nordische Personennamen in England in alt- und frühmittel-englischer Zeit* (Halle, 1910).

Blackburn, Mark, 'Alfred's Coinage Reforms in Context', in *Alfred the Great: Papers from the Eleventh-Centenary Conferences*, ed. Timothy Reuter (Aldershot, 2003), pp. 199–218.

Blunt, Christopher, 'The Coinage of Athelstan, King of England 924–939', *British Numismatic Journal* 42 (1974), 35–160.

Briggs, Charles F., 'Literacy, Reading, and Writing in the Medieval West', *Journal of Medieval History* 26 (2012), 397–420.

Carroll, Jayne and Parsons, David N., *Anglo-Saxon Mint Names. I: Axbridge-Hythe* (Nottingham, 2007).

Chetwood, James, 'Re-evaluating English Personal Naming on the Eve of the Conquest', *EME* 26 (2018), 518–47.

Chick, Derek, *The Coinage of Offa and his Contemporaries*, eds Mark Blackburn and Rory Naismith (London, 2010).

Colman, Fran, *The Grammar of Names in Anglo-Saxon England: The Linguistics and Culture of the Old English Onomasticon* (Oxford, 2014).

Colman, Fran, *Money Talks: Reconstructing Old English* (Berlin, 1991).

Cubitt, Catherine, '"As the Lawbook Teaches": Reeves, Lawbooks and Urban Life in the Anonymous Old English Legend of the Seven Sleepers', *EHR* 124 (2009), 1021–49.

Dannenberg, Hermann, *Die deutschen Münzen der sächsischen und fränkischen Kaiserzeit*, 4 vols (Berlin, 1876–1905).

Dolley, R. H. M., *Sylloge of Coins of the British Isles 8: The Hiberno-Norse Coins in the British Museum* (London, 1966).

Foot, Sarah, *Æthelstan: The First King of England* (New Haven, CT, 2011).

Foot, Sarah, 'Reading Anglo-Saxon Charters: Memory, Record, or Story?', in *Narrative and History in the Early Medieval West*, eds Elizabeth M. Tyler and Ross Balzaretti (Turnhout, 2006), pp. 39–66.

Garipzanov, Ildar, 'The Rise of Graphicacy in Late Antiquity and the Early Middle Ages', *Viator* 46 (2015), 1–21.

Garipzanov, Ildar H., *The Symbolic Language of Authority in the Carolingian World (c. 751–877)* (Leiden, 2008).

Grierson, Philip, 'The *Gratia Dei Rex* Coinage of Charles the Bald', in *Charles the Bald: Court and Kingdom*, eds Margaret T. Gibson and Janet L. Nelson, 2nd ed. (Aldershot, 1990), pp. 52–64.

Hendy, Michael Frank, 'From Public to Private: The Western Barbarian Coinages as a Mirror of the Disintegration of Late Roman State Structures', *Viator* 19 (1988), 29–78.

Heslop, T. A., 'English Seals from the Mid Ninth Century to 1100', *Journal of the British Archaeological Association* 33 (1980), 1–16.

Hill, Francis, *Medieval Lincoln* (Cambridge, 1948).

Hinton, David A., *A Smith in Lindsey: The Anglo-Saxon Grave at Tattershall Thorpe, Lincolnshire* (London, 2000).

Jarnut, Jörg and Strothmann, Jürgen (eds), *Die Merowingischen Monetarmünzen als Quelle zum Verständnis des 7. Jahrhunderts in Gallien* (Paderborn, 2013).

Jarrett, Jonathan, 'Currency Change in Pre-Millennial Catalonia: Coinage, Counts and Economics', *Numismatic Chronicle* 169 (2009), 217–43.

Jonsson, Kenneth, *The New Era: The Reformation of the Late Anglo-Saxon Coinage* (Stockholm, 1987).

Keller, Hagen, Grubmüller, Klaus, and Staubach, Nikolaus (eds), *Pragmatische Schriftlichkeit im Mittelalter: Erscheinungsformen und Entwicklungsstufen* (Munich, 1992).

Kelly, Susan, 'Anglo-Saxon Lay Society and the Written Word', in *The Uses of Literacy in Early Medieval Europe*, ed. Rosamond McKitterick (Cambridge, 1990), pp. 36–62.

Keynes, Simon, 'Church Councils, Royal Assemblies, and Anglo-Saxon Royal Diplomas', in *Kingship, Legislation and Power in Anglo-Saxon England*, eds Gale R. Owen-Crocker and Brian W. Schneider (Woodbridge, 2013), pp. 1–182.

Keynes, Simon, 'The "Dunstan B" Charters', *ASE* 23 (1994), 165–93.

Keynes, Simon, 'The Use of Seals in Anglo-Saxon England', in *Seals and Status: Power of Objects*, eds John Cherry, Jessica Berenbeim, and Lloyd de Beer (London, 2018), pp. 73–83.

Keynes, Simon, 'The West Saxon Charters of King Æthelwulf and his Sons', *EHR* 109 (1994), 1109–49.

Keynes, Simon and Naismith, Rory, 'The *Agnus Dei* Pennies of King Æthelred the Unready', *ASE* 40 (2011), 175–223.

Liuzza, R. M., 'Literacy', in *A Handbook of Anglo-Saxon Studies*, eds Jacqueline Stodnick and Renée R. Trilling (Oxford, 2012), pp. 99–114.

Lyon, C. S. S., *Sylloge of Coins of the British Isles 68: The Lyon Collection of Anglo-Saxon Coins* (Oxford, 2016).

Mersiowsky, Mark, *Die Urkunde in der Karolingerzeit: Originale, Urkundenpraxis und politische Kommunikation*, 2 vols, MGH Schriften 60 (Wiesbaden, 2015).

Molyneaux, George, *The Formation of the English Kingdom in the Tenth Century* (Oxford, 2015).

Morison, Stanley, *Politics and Script: Aspects of Authority and Freedom in the Development of Graeco-Latin Script from the Sixth Century B.C. to the Twentieth Century A.D.* (Oxford, 1972).

Mossop, H. R., *The Lincoln Mint c. 890–1279* (Newcastle-upon-Tyne, 1970).

Naismith, Rory, *Sylloge of Coins of the British Isles 67: British Museum: Anglo-Saxon Coins II. Southern English Coinage from Offa to Alfred c. 760–880* (London, 2016).

Naismith, Rory, *The Coinage of Southern England 796–865*, 2 vols (London, 2011).

Naismith, Rory, 'The Currency of Power in Late Anglo-Saxon England', *History Compass* 17 (2019).

Naismith, Rory, 'Gold Coinage and its Use in the Post-Roman World', *Speculum* 89 (2014), 273–306.

Naismith, Rory, 'The Laws of London? IV Æthelred Reconsidered', *The London Journal* 44 (2019), 1–16.

Naismith, Rory, 'London and its Mints *c.* 880–1066: A Preliminary Survey', *British Numismatic Journal* 83 (2013), 44–74.

Naismith, Rory, *Medieval European Coinage, with a Catalogue of the Coins in the Fitzwilliam Museum, Cambridge. 8: Britain and Ireland c. 400–1066* (Cambridge, 2017).

Naismith, Rory, *Money and Power in Anglo-Saxon England: The Southern English Kingdoms, 757–865* (Cambridge, 2012).

Naismith, Rory, 'Prelude to Reform: Tenth-Century English Coinage in Perspective', in *Early Medieval Monetary History: Studies in Memory of Mark Blackburn*, eds Rory Naismith, Martin Allen, and Elina Screen (Farnham, 2014).

Naismith, Rory and Tinti, Francesca, *The Forum Hoard of Anglo-Saxon Coins*, Bollettino di Numismatica 55–56 (Rome, 2016).

Nightingale, Pamela, 'Some London Moneyers, and Reflections on the Organization of English Mints in the Eleventh and Twelfth Centuries', *Numismatic Chronicle* 142 (1982), 34–50.

Okasha, Elisabeth, 'The Commissioners, Makers and Owners of Anglo-Saxon Inscriptions', *Anglo-Saxon Studies in Archaeology and History* 7 (1994), 71–77.

Okasha, Elisabeth, 'Literacy in Anglo-Saxon England: The Evidence from Inscriptions', *Anglo-Saxon Studies in Archaeology and History* 8 (1995), 69–74.

Okasha, Elisabeth, 'The Non-Runic Scripts of Anglo-Saxon Inscriptions', *Transactions of the Cambridge Bibliographical Society* 4 (1968), 321–38.

Parkes, Malcolm B., 'The Literacy of the Laity', in *Literature and Western Civilization: The Medieval World*, eds David Daiches and Anthony Thorlby (London, 1973), pp. 555–76.

Parsons, Mary Prescott, 'Some Scribal Memoranda for Anglo-Saxon Charters of the 8th and 9th Centuries', *Mitteilungen des österreichischen Instituts für Geschichtsforschung* 14 (1939), 13–32.

Rio, Alice, *Legal Practice and the Written Word in the Early Middle Ages: Frankish Formulae, c.500–1000* (Cambridge, 2009).

Roberts, Edward, 'Boundary Clauses and the Use of the Vernacular in Eastern Frankish Charters, *c.*750–*c.*900', *Historical Research* 91 (2018), 580–604.

Rosenwein, Barbara, *Negotiating Space: Power, Restraint, and Privileges of Immunity in Early Medieval Europe* (Manchester, 1999).

Sawyer, P. H., *Anglo-Saxon Charters: An Annotated List and Bibliography* (London, 1968); revised as the Electronic Sawyer, www.esawyer.org.uk.

Screen, Elina, 'Anglo-Saxon Law and Numismatics: A Reassessment in the Light of Patrick Wormald's *The Making of English Law*', *British Numismatic Journal* 77 (2007), 150–72.

Sellwood, David, 'Medieval Minting Techniques', *British Numismatic Journal* 31 (1962), 57–65.

Skaare, Kolbjørn, *Coins and Coinage in Viking-Age Norway: The Establishment of a National Coinage in Norway in the XI Century, with a Survey of the Preceding Currency History* (Oslo, 1976).

Smart, Veronica, 'Economic Migrants? Continental Moneyers' Names on the Tenth-Century English Coinage', *Nomina* 32 (2009), 113–56.

Smart, Veronica, 'Osulf Thein and Others: Double Moneyer's Names on the Late Anglo-Saxon Coinage', in *Studies in Late Anglo-Saxon Coinage in Memory of Bror Emil Hildebrand*, ed. Kenneth Jonsson (Stockholm, 1990), pp. 435–53.

Smart, Veronica, 'Pitit and Litilman, an Onomastic Conundrum', *Nomina* 25 (2002), 133–38.

Smart, Veronica J., 'Scandinavians, Celts and Germans in Anglo-Saxon England: The Evidence of Moneyers' Names', in *Anglo-Saxon Monetary History: Essays in Memory of Michael Dolley*, ed. Mark Blackburn (Leicester, 1986), pp. 171–84.

Snook, Ben, *The Anglo-Saxon Chancery: The History, Language and Production of Anglo-Saxon Charters from Alfred to Edgar* (Woodbridge, 2015).

Stenton, F. M., *The Latin Charters of the Anglo-Saxon Period* (Oxford, 1955).

Stokes, Peter A., *English Vernacular Minuscule from Æthelred to Cnut c. 990–c. 1035* (Woodbridge, 2014).

Tengvik, Gösta, *Old English Bynames* (Uppsala, 1938).

Townend, Matthew, *Language and History in Viking Age England: Linguistic Relations between Speakers of Old Norse and Old English* (Turnhout, 2002).

Wickham, Chris, *Sleepwalking into a New World: The Emergence of Italian City Communes in the Twelfth Century* (Princeton, NJ, 2015).

Woodman, D. A., '"Æthelstan A" and the Rhetoric of Rule', *ASE* 42 (2013), 217–48.

CHAPTER 14

Epilogue

Janet L. Nelson

With this book, the editors and their other authors, severally and collectively, have made a very large contribution to linguistic and documentary scholarship. In these domains, several contributors, taking leaves from, among others, Geoffrey Koziol's 2012 book and from papers of Hagen Keller,[1] have endorsed the importance of performativity and the roles of laypersons in documentary culture. As Francesca Tinti points out in the introduction, meaning-packed gestures and ritual-soaked proceedings, and the reading of documents out loud, *viva voce*, 'often bridged the Latin of the charter and the early Romance pronunciation of the locality. However, in non-Romance-speaking regions, such as England and eastern Francia, the gulf between the written and the spoken word was much bigger'. Francesca Tinti has not only appreciated 'the impact of such a linguistic divide on the functioning of documentary culture': she has seen that it deserves 'far more attention than ... hitherto received'.

Anglo-Saxon England was a special case: its populations settled in lowland Britain and continued to use Germanic languages or dialects. The 'creation of a bilingual textual culture', that is, of Latin and the vernacular languages, was linked with the transfer of the Latin culture of early Christianity and its control of landed property.[2] Two of those with prime responsibility for the transfer, Augustine of Canterbury and Theodore of Tarsus, came from the Mediterranean world as middlemen: Augustine born in Rome, early sixth century, consecrated by Pope Gregory 597 and sent to England, d. 609,[3] and Theodore, born in Tarsus 602, consecrated in Rome, 668, d. 690. One or both of these men brought charters to England, a textual form that in time would prove to be an effective instrument of royal power, and a medium in which the shift from oral

1 Geoffrey Koziol, *The Politics of Memory and Identity in Carolingian Royal Diplomas: The West Frankish Kingdom (840–987)* (Turnhout, 2012); Hagen Keller, 'Hülderweis durch Privilegien: symbolische Kommunikation innerhalb und jenseits des Textes', *Frühmittelalterliche Studien* 38 (2004), 309–21.

2 Andy Orchard, 'Latin and the Vernacular Languages: The Creation of a Bilingual Textual Culture', in *After Rome*, ed. Thomas Charles-Edwards (Oxford, 2003), pp. 191–219.

3 Richard Shaw, 'When did Augustine of Canterbury Die?', *Journal of Ecclesiastical History* 67 (2016), 473–91.

 | DOI:10.1163/9789004432338_015

transaction to written record involved a change of linguistic code, traceable in one way or another in all the chapters of the present book.

As to East Francia, of fundamental importance is the rise to power of the Carolingian dynasty in the mid-eighth century, which involved the creation of an empire in the later eighth and early ninth. Although charter production certainly predated the Carolingians, their rule coincided with key archival innovations, including, most notably, the cartulary. In addition, the royal family and its ecclesiastical adjutants were the prime movers of intellectual change, and then became involved in the dissemination of a 'Carolingian Renaissance' to lay elites and peasant populations responsive to preachers in the vernacular. The Frankish Empire, some 1,112,000 square km in scale, could be imagined not as divided into Romance and Germanic parts, but rather as consisting of 'fluid contact zones characterized by a certain degree of bilingualism'.[4] Charlemagne might have 'sought to establish a universal Latin language, mastery of which was required of all members of the elite', but Francesca Tinti's observation that historians have tended to 'overlook the importance of vernacular languages and communication among the Carolingian upper classes' strikes the true note, as does the tenor of her general remarks in the book's introduction.

•••

Rosamond McKitterick's contribution on early medieval literacy, and in particular the role of charters in early medieval communication, provides both a starting-point and a mainstay for the rest of the book. It is a task to which she is ideally suited, given her profound and wide-ranging readings, over many wondrously productive years, on and in literacy and the communicative power of the Carolingians' world. She begins, indeed, by highlighting the multilingual character of that world, and its 'many different local realities'. Difference means variety, and in this case multifarious differences. These traits in turn mean large and variegated documents and archives, and attendant bibliographies and literatures dealing with different scholarly traditions and works in many languages. The author's own bibliographies are a godsend too, as their size suggests: she begins with the historiography and history of diplomatic and palaeography from the early modern period to the present. Charters, and the study of archives, are given pride of place, and at the heart of 'formative studies'. These working practices begin with monastic institutions and the networking among these. Marc Bloch's insight is one for all historians to share: '1681, the year of the publication of the *De Re Diplomatica*, was truly a great one in the

4 Tinti in this volume.

history of the human mind, for the criticism of the documents of archives was definitely established'.[5] The monastic archivists blossomed in time into 'world-wide networks of collaborative scholarship and friendship'.[6] Just as epigraphy and inscriptions on stones had been media that mattered in the early Middle Ages, so they came to matter in their own right. Other batons passed, in the twentieth and now the twenty-first centuries, to Spoleto, Kalamazoo, Leeds. Digital Humanities came to be regarded no longer as ancillary but as a discipline in its own right. Just as literacy came to be studied as an independent theme in social studies curricula, so it spread into such neighbouring fields as sociology, social anthropology, and social history.

Other approaches were adopted via manuscript studies and library studies, the connections between orality and literacy, and between pragmatic (legal, liturgical) and learned (literary, intellectual) literacy, as well as the boundaries between these. Boundaries can be traced between Latin and vernacular materials, between lay and clerical literacy, and between continuities and discontinuities with the Roman past. To follow up on such forms of distinction could mean to open the route to an oral-written continuum involving such verbal communications as commands and such gestural communications as rituals. Historians who have diagnosed an eleventh-century change to new 'formal aspects of written communication' have yet to convince colleagues.

McKitterick's chapter has much to say about charters and the multiple forms of literacy they present. A charter can be 'merely' a record, yet at the same time it can be a text 'with symbolic weight'. Such questions as that of the reliability of a written text, or the extent to which a written letter doubles as a way to remember or confirm the reader's belief in its 'truth', or the ways authority is conferred on texts by the application of memory, still await answers. The ways in which inscriptions preserved memory, public and potentially long-term as they were, brought new possibilities of individualizing. Letters, visual symbols, and coins bore new meanings about 'identity, religious faith, and social power', and those who issued coins chose those signs' precise placings and timings. The author of this chapter is alert to the connection of ritual practice in the liturgy with musical notation.

The practice of government in Charlemagne's empire would have been unthinkable without literacy, not just in Latin, crucial as that was, but in diverse vernaculars. Packed into the latter section of this chapter is a history of

---

5 Marc Bloch, *The Historian's Craft*, trans. Peter Putnam (Manchester, 2004; translation originally printed in 1954), p. 68.

6 McKitterick in this volume.

eighth- and ninth-century scripts and the varied forms of Caroline minuscule, treated within a wider context of administrative networks of communications across Mediterranean Europe, ‘not least where there was contact with Muslim or Jewish communities’. Ending this formidable chapter is an arresting discussion of glossaries, with a final query about their function and an account of their quantity and significance that skilfully avoids bursting the chapter’s buttons. Breathless readers at this point can both review the importance of a hitherto underrated genre in a variegated landscape of ‘networks of interdependence’ and make a perhaps first acquaintance with the up-to-the-minute notion of ‘entanglement’.

•••

Wolfgang Haubrichs’ mastery of linguistic acculturation as a phenomenon and of the evidence from the eastern and western parts of the late Roman Empire as a huge quarry of comparative material assures his work of a distinctive and very welcome place in the present volume. Processes of acculturation traceable from Theoderic’s Italo-Dalmatian kingdom to the kingdoms of the East Franks and of the Burgundians allow linguists to envisage in some detail a bilingualism that was ‘deep-seated’ and ‘long-lasting’ in various regions of the former Roman Empire. It takes a tracker of exceptional skill to follow the spoor through the hydronyms and toponyms, anthroponyms and ethnonyms, names and naming practices, and reconstruct the verbal landscapes of groups, peoples, and cultures. Bilingualism was no oddity: so much can be found, or rediscovered, that it is possible to be measured in extant evidence. Among the Franks in northern Gaul, and the Lombards in Italy, bilingualism and integration of Germanic-speakers into Romance-speakers can be tracked in names and ‘basic language contacts’. In what would become the ecclesiastical province of Trier could be found ‘a complex hotchpotch of bilingual zones of interference, Frankish linguistic islands’ in what would later be Old French-speaking districts. The lifespan of linguistic islands can be reconstructed by the aid of phonetic chronology. Striking in this evidence is the material culture of a region, and the toponyms reflect this. We find several hundred Frankish loan-words in Old French dialects, covering ‘nearly all areas of life’, from animals (Old French _froiz_, ‘frogs’ < _*froska_) to Old French _haschiere_ ‘agony’ < _harm-skara_, which appeared in the reign of Louis the Pious as ‘a humiliating punishment’. ‘In and around the Romance relic regions’, ‘there was a considerable degree of bilingualism’. Here, ‘the language border became increasingly fixed, but preserved a broad bilingual edge’. In some areas, such as south of the Upper Danube and in northern Italy, among the upper classes, multilingualism persisted until the end of the eighth century, when the Empire's disparate regions began to 'become more monolingual'. As with glossaries (Chapter 2), so with manuals for language acquisition: these aids to communication and handbooks for travellers existed in the ninth century, using both basic Old High German and Romance. Bilingualism and multilingualism were relatively frequent among ninth- and tenth-century elites. Haubrichs' chapter ends with some entertaining and edifying examples.

•••

In this volume, self-evidently, charters are a key theme *passim*. Annina Seiler seizes an ideal moment for investigating, and comparatively thinking with, two sets of documents both of seventh- and eighth-century date but of quite different size, from two quite distinct regions and kinds of repository, and weighing against each other Latin and vernacular elements to be found in the monastery of St Gall in Alemannia on the one hand, and a number of Southumbrian Anglo-Saxon archives on the other. In the story of the Old English and Old High German languages, this was a moment of 'incipient vernacular literacy'. Similar spelling variants similarly denoted a differentiation, both in witness-lists of charters in Southumbrian scriptoria and at St Gall, between more and less important charter witnesses. It was also a moment when there occurred 'a subtle shift from linguistic association to social distinction', differentiation implicitly involving plural axes of distinction. 'Subtle' would certainly describe this author's analysis. She goes on to detail the role of names in a whole variety of texts and contexts, including the 'mental grammar' of the scribes as well as the names' function in charters. She concludes that 'the creation of a written language in terms of its intensive development is … the process of putting it into writing—and involves the adoption and adaptation of a script'. The orthography of early Anglo-Saxon charters may not be everyone's cup of tea, but with the observation that 'the presence or absence of Latin inflections within the witness-list seems to be triggered by the social status of the referent', and the ensuing discussion of names in witness-lists, Annina Seiler succeeds in engaging the reader's attention throughout. The St Gall charters from this period are all written in Latin, but names are mostly Old High German and are subject to 'a certain individuality and variability'. Latinized forms frequently occurring among the names of people of higher status can be discussed in reference to the next chapter. But before leaving this one, it is worth noting the spelling variants in these charters' development of Old English and Old High German orthography, and the 'programmatic spellings' that indicate a writer's connection with a certain social group or region. In the Anglo-Saxon and St Gall charters, the Old English or Old High German nature of the names is foregrounded. Thus, spelling can be used 'to either highlight or downplay the distinctive elements of Old High German orthography'. A study of code-switching in tenth-century Anglo-Saxon leases suggests that names for which Old English spellings are used are clearly highlighted as vernacular. 'Spelling takes the place of the [sound-based] clues associated with code-switching in spoken language'.

•••

The charters of St Gall constitute a unique archive of over 800 original or contemporary single-sheet copies. Bernhard Zeller analyses these charters with respect to the monastery's extensive holdings across Germanic-speaking Alemannia and Romance-speaking Raetia. The formulae, script, and language of charters produced in Frankish-Alemannic contexts thus differed significantly to those from Raetia, an 'island of *romanitas*'; and close contacts between Chur and Raetia are documented in the *Liber professionis* of St Gall. In tenth-century St Gall, the monks told stories that revealed something of the languages spoken there and thereabouts. Bilingualism evidently thrived there among the monastic population, the teachers and students, and the patrons of the abbey. The charter-scribes increasingly monopolized the production of St Gall's charters. The language of these documents was '"scarcely regulated" early medieval Latin'—a language subjected to 'a profound influence and interference of spoken' or '"vulgar" Latin' and/or 'early Romance', including formulae 'individually adapted and adjusted by the scribes in the course of writing'. Prevalent was 'a general fuzziness concerning grammatical standards and orthography'. The Carolingian reforms began to hit monastic schools in Pippin's reign: they hit hard in Charlemagne's reign and new standards of Latinity were expected. Fuzziness ceased. At the same time, a 'pre-reform' Latinity persisted and this attested the opening of a gap between 'reformed Latin' and the vulgar *sermo rusticus*, also known to scholars as an emerging Romance language. In the St Gall charters there appeared an Old High German vernacular—unsurprisingly, given that the charter-scribes were mostly Alemans who spoke a High Germanic dialect. Vernacular terms proliferated in writing as well as speech. At its close, this chapter's author wisely pursues the question of why there is not more evidence for Old High German words in the St Gall charters. His answers are persuasive: one way or another, they reflect the real lives of the St Gall monks and their patrons.

• • •

In the next chapter, Edward Roberts and Francesca Tinti team up to take on the challenge of making comparisons. Since Anglo-Saxon England and East Francia shared a linguistic Germanic heritage, the documents in both territories unsurprisingly show developments in 'consciousness of language-use' and 'the alternating use of two languages in a single ... text' which linguists nowadays call code-switching. The co-authors, rather than regarding elements of Old English and Old High German in charters as simply aids to communication where Latin literacy was minimal, propose instead to view the use of the vernacular as a social tool. They also distinguish helpfully between royal and non-royal documents, compare the survival rates of English and East Frankish charters, and register the contrast between the impact of the invention of the cartulary *c.*800 in East Francia, which triggered a large increase in the survival chances of East Frankish 'private' charters, and the absence of Anglo-Saxon cartularies predating the eleventh century. In the remainder of this and the next section, the co-authors add further instructive comparisons and contrasts between East Francia and England in respect of the use of the vernacular in property-surveying and the tracing of boundaries. The final section on the evidence of 'language consciousness' in Anglo-Saxon and East Frankish charters is so substantial and so variously thought-provoking that it might well have rated a chapter in itself. The chapter's conclusion sets, quite briefly, the documentary sources beside such 'ambitious literary programmes' as the œuvre of King Alfred, and highlights the roles played by the emerging vernaculars. The co-authors end, though, with the exceptional contribution of the charters to early medieval history in general: 'charters take us deeper into society and offer a more expansive view thanks to their wide geographical distribution ... [and] by their very nature, they provide glimpses of language-use in day-to-day contexts ... charters are not just passive witnesses to transfers of property rights; they are active attempts to assert and formalize social relationships.'

• • •

In the next chapter (like the preceding one, co-authored), Anglo-Saxon endorsement practices come into their own as a topic unfairly consigned to obscurity that now receives the attention it deserves. A text written on the back ('dorse') of a single sheet of parchment has a purpose or function, and by the authors' count, 191 of such sheets survive from over 20 archives as possibly original pre-Conquest charters. Robert Gallagher and Kate Wiles meticulously catalogue these sheets, observing that the persons who made and kept them 'betray a concern to record and prove claims in writing', and that the maker's purpose was to 'summarize the contents of the charter in some capacity'. As to the languages of endorsements, 'the vast majority are in Old English, regardless of form and function.' The co-authors suggest that endorsements can be thought of as labels, and place-names are thus identified. The archive of Christ Church Canterbury kept an exceptional number of single sheets with endorsements, while other religious communities too used endorsements as a tool for organizing their documentary collections. For someone responsible for adding an endorsement to the sheet, the visibility of the addition once the sheet was folded was important.

The most notable development in the phrasing of endorsements can be identified in the 930s and 940s, with the appearance of a special endorsement formula, beginning 'this is the land' and ending with 'in perpetual inheritance'. The co-authors incline to agree with most earlier scholars that these endorsements were produced centrally and then disseminated, that the settings of these acts would have been royal assemblies at which multiple diplomas would often have been produced at the same time, and that the relevant formulae were 'adopted into wider documentary practice'. There were also endorsements in Latin. Much of the code-switching in them added a vernacular element to the Latin. These cases were unusual. 'It can be stated unambiguously that … endorsements were a vernacular phenomenon'. Finally the co-authors connect the endorsements of the late 930s with 'heightened interest in the performative value of [diplomas] as 'instruments of royal government''. 'The … importance of the single sheet over generations [is] emblematic of materiality as a crucial dimension to a documentary culture …'

•••

The landscape changes in Chapter 8 to early medieval northern and central Italy and the evidence of its private charters for traces of bilingualism. Marco Stoffella identifies Milan, Piacenza, Verona, Lucca, and Siena as holding the richest collections of early medieval charters in what had been the Lombard kingdom, and the eighth century as the period when there occurred a linguistic acculturation of the Lombards into late Latin/early Romance and also the emergence of early written Italo-Romance. In terms of methodology, charters provide the main evidence for these processes and the notaries responsible for the charters appear as key agents of language shifts. The term *ferquidem* in eighth-century Tuscan charters presents a significant case study.

In Italian scholarship, debate over bilingualism has been lively. There have been arguments over the way words of Germanic origin spread and what conditions allowed that spread; other arguments over the chronology of the ending of the use of the (Germanic) Lombard language and its replacement by late Latin/early Romance; and yet other arguments over whether bilingualism ever existed, and if it did, among which families or elites it persisted, and where. If there is a strong case for thinking a Germanic Lombard language was still being spoken in the mid-eighth century, then when and where did it become obsolete?

Rather than trying to resolve the question of Lombard bilingualism, Stoffella focuses his attention on Tuscany, whose dialect is distinctive and whose language boundaries are 'neatly defined'. Romance linguistic acculturation of the originally Germanic-speaking population became an irreversible process in the mid-eighth century when Romance elements increased, 'the two anthroponomical German and late-Latin traditions were interwoven', and 'the existence of a bilingual Lombardic-Romance society emerges …'. In the next section, 'archaisms and novelties', the use of early Italo-Romance words and expressions is attested by formulae, private charters and in 'dorsal notes of late eighth- and early ninth-century parchments.' Late in the ninth century, 'beneath the apparent oral spontaneity of direct speech, one must recognize the use of formularies'.

This chapter's author promised to come back to the term *ferquidem*: he is as good as his word. Present-day thinking is that *ferquidem* is of 'undoubtedly Lombard origin', and Marco Stoffella finds it occurring patchily in some parts of Tuscany and 'employed frequently in the second half of the eighth century'. Some scribes could have used the term, but very many ignored it. To put it mildly, the term and its variants were used 'rather arbitrarily'. Scribes had choices. Some gave the term 'an archaic nuance'. There was 'a progressive linguistic homogenization when formulae crystallized'. The form became 'part of the formulae'. To the question, 'can the use of *ferquidem* in Tuscan documents be read as evidence for the continuity of a spoken bilingualism in early medieval northern Italy?' Chapter 8's author ends with 'a cautiously positive answer'.

• • •

In Chapter 9, Charles Insley's insular vernaculars give entrées into Cornwall and Cornish charters by way of boundaries and borders, regions and realms, languages and language families, bilingualism and even trilingualism. In south-west Britain, the formation of place-names 'existed in a highly complex and fluid relationship'. The chapter's first and necessarily lengthy part supplies much contextual information on geography, settlement and lordship, ecclesiastical communities, and relations between the bishops of Sherborne and the Cornish. In 1066, Cornwall was 'apparently firmly under English political and ecclesiastical control' and its administrative landscape clear. The chapter's second and briefer part deals with the 16 surviving Cornish charters. Ten of these have boundary clauses and date from the reign of King Æthelstan. The remaining six are diverse: the last of them is of special interest as having been privately issued by a Cornish nobleman. This charter therefore constitutes evidence for 'a non-English diplomatic tradition in Cornwall', first identified in 1982 by Wendy Davies who termed it 'the Latin Celtic Charter-tradition'.[7]

The boundary clauses include both Old English and Cornish topographical terminology. Charles Insley, viewing this through a twenty-first-century lens, sees code-switching here, 'symptomatic of genuine bilingualism'. He goes on to suggest that scribes who drew up the bounds 'were comfortable operating in two distinct linguistic spaces'. He is particularly struck by the detail of the perambulations and the geographical extension of this charter-tradition into Wales. He concludes that his examination of the surviving diplomas from Cornwall 'reveals them to be a valuable window onto society in south-western Britain, where language choice was far from a clear issue and where bi- or even trilingualism, at least among the clergy, was probably more common than we might think'. This is a plausible proposition.

•••

In Chapter 10, Stefan Esders' account of vernacular writing in early medieval manorial administration bears similarities to Charles Insley's comparative approach to Anglo-Saxon and Cornish: he also, like some other contributors of the present volume, presents two contrasting case studies using different kinds of documents and putting each in its distinctive communicative context. Both documents were produced in monastic institutions in Germany in the tenth century. The vernacular list of possessions of the monastery of Werden is an addition to the earliest part of a much larger register of properties widely distributed in the area of the Ruhr and the lower Rhine. The vernacular list consists of 11 items of property, mostly churches but also at Opgooi seven farms

7 Wendy Davies, 'The Latin Charter-Tradition in Western Britain, Brittany and Ireland in the Early Mediaeval Period', in *Ireland in Early Medieval Europe: Studies in Memory of Kathleen Hughes*, eds David Dumville and Rosamond McKitterick (Cambridge, 1982), pp. 258–80.

(*hof stadi*) and seven fortresses (*uuerr stadi*), in the region between Utrecht and the Zuiderzee, far away from Werden itself. A very few little bits of Latin appear in the list, but rather than in Old Saxon, the rest is in the Old Dutch vernacular. What this is *not* is a register of labour-services or rents owed to the abbey. The text is rather a list of possessions, and its blending of Latin and vernacular, Esders suggests, could stem from its composition by a local official with poor Latin.

The second text in administrative vernacular is a manorial register of the women's convent at Essen of tenth-century date: designed for administrative purposes, it was also written into a manuscript that served religious purposes, as is clear from the presence of some of Gregory the Great's homilies on the Gospels. Sometime later, other texts were added. One was an Old Saxon homily for All Saints' Day which evidently functioned as 'a historical justification for the feast of All Saints and of the obligation to attend it on 1 November', while Cosmas and Damian were venerated on that day too. In Louis the Pious' reign efforts were made for their cult to become a general obligation for Christians with every priest being required 'to celebrate All Saints' Day venerably at the vigil', and at least one reforming bishop (Halitgar of Cambrai) 'absolutely forbidding priests who have lately been in the habit of convening on the first day of the month for eating and drinking'. Such feasts may also have encouraged the writing of such vernacular texts as the Old High German *Georgslied* and *Galluslied* and the Eulalia Sequence, the equivalent of heroic songs 'justified by clerics and monks as part of lay culture'.

The vernacular register, written in Old Saxon, listed nine places which were collection-centres for carefully chosen products in kind. On close examination, these products seem to have provided the wherewithal for the brewery and the brewing process supervised by the female provost of the Essen nuns. Stefan Esders suggests that the vernacular register 'had a very special and confined administrative and communicative purpose designed for a higher level of manorial organization between the female provost and the lay administrators of the monastery manors and staff of the brewery'. There was a performative quality to the register as well: its details could be memorized and declared aloud, especially on All Saints' Day. Yet these were situations in which the line between Latin and vernacular could become blurred, and they were 'the moments when ecclesiastical institutions most visibly became parts of a larger society'. These were situations in which a cadre of high-born women could become involved in otherwise unusual forms of everyday work and also play performative roles within their religious lives.

• • •

With Albert Fenton's Chapter 11 on 'the function and use of Anglo-Saxon writ formulae', the scene shifts back to Anglo-Saxon England. Invariably written in the Old English vernacular, these letters communicated information and commands in local and regional courts: at shire level, they reached out, so to speak, to wider audiences, and thus were functioned in a support-role for Latin royal charters. Writs often embodied and conveyed testimonies in land-disputes. In terms of form, they were small and compact, thus able to function in a 'go-between role' between court and region. Special traits were: that they were sealed, reflecting a commonly recognized symbolic language of authority, that their language was highly repetitive and couched in rhythmical and alliterative patterns, and that their single-sheet format was visually distinctive.

This chapter's author, having picked up on Geoffrey Koziol's concept, still as freshly imaginative and original as ever, of performativity, suggests that writs functioned in texts as performatives. Such uses of writs in several well-known case-studies of disputes (those of Wynflæd, or Bishop Godwine of Rochester come to mind) indicate their social function. 'Abbot Sparrowhawk met him [bishop-elect Robert of London] on the way back [to England from Rome] with the king's writ and seal to the effect that he was to be consecrated …'. In this case, Robert did his darndest to have himself consecrated bishop but was overruled by, in effect, the pope. Writs could be re-used and re-performed orally in other settings, apparently: good examples of the writ's *Sitz-im-Leben.*

Chapter 11's next section offers an analysis of a writ's diplomatic structure, noting that the writ was a product of a series of interactions between Latin and Old English, but also suggesting that 'the ways in which they [addressees] are described … hint at centralizing practices and proclivities'. The examples given bear out these hints. The next and final section on spatial formulae and aspects of distribution in the tenth and eleventh centuries gives convincing answers to searching questions on these topics: writs were at once adaptable and stable, standing the test of time. Albert Fenton concludes that spatial formulae can be situated within the context of courts' performativity—and he shrewdly borrows Hagen Keller's term 'symbolic markers' for key moments of ceremonial at local courts. In Fenton's words, 'this diplomatic discourse must have played a vital role in constructing seemingly natural, shared conceptions of royal authority, in a culture in which the stable and uncontested relationship between ruler and ruled were paramount, and in which there was an urgent need for royal and other announcements to be conveyed clearly and understood with minimal ambiguity'.

•••

A description of and commentary on the somewhat miscellaneous vernacular records of the archive of Bury St Edmunds and its pre-Conquest history is meticulously presented by Kathryn Lowe in Chapter 12. Thanks to her exceptional expertise, however, a first impression might understandably register a tone of impatience. Additions to the charter corpus have been identified in 'a necessarily *ad hoc* way', there is some inconsistency relating even to records that are securely dated. Still, this pre-Conquest vernacular material is historically invaluable, for it shows continuity of practice. Readers owe thanks for Kathryn Lowe's insistence that these texts 'can only be understood within the context of other vernacular records from the archive to which they belong'.

The records from Buȝry St Edmunds relate as much to such everyday matters of life and death as a ninth-century list for arrangements for funerary feasts, an eleventh-century listing of the abbey's people, animals, and foodstuffs, and a twelfth-century fragmentary account of funerary arrangements requiring, *inter alia*, 27 pennies for wax. Kathryn Lowe ventures to surmise that the vernacular language of that twelfth-century record may result from the record's informality. Some features of this record include items from Old Norse, and this surmise is strengthened when the rest of the Bury archive is also set in its pre-Conquest listing arrangements for funerary feasts and the listing eastern Danelaw location.

Booklists are special interest to manuscript scholars, and two such lists survive from Bury. Their owners were clerics connected to monastic communities: one of these lists was added to a book already with a long history, produced in Italy in the sixth or seventh centuries, having arrived in England by the end of the eighth century, with the list added in the twelfth century. An inventory fragment apparently from Wessex listed men, animals, and agricultural products, including 'one thousand cheeses'. A similar list included twenty-four cheeses. Another estate relates to harvest-time labour. The document ends, 'each man in Bury St Edmunds occupying a house on his own land shall give ... one penny ... on St Peter's day at the beginning of harvest ... No-one shall ever be exempt from this except for St Edmund's servants and the retainers' messuages and the priests within who sing at the altars'. Kathryn Lowe suggests a reasonable approximation for 'the retainers' messuages' would be *hospicia militum*, and offers some interesting comments on the circulation of coins (pennies and half-pennies) in the twelfth and thirteenth centuries. She concludes that these Bury records, varied in form and function, are 'testament to the continued use of the vernacular at the abbey', and that these documents are best identified as records—an umbrella term—rather than charters.

•••

The volume's thirteenth and last chapter provides a rousing finale with coins and charters making their entries in sympathetic counterpoint. In an arresting introductory section, Rory Naismith summons up a 'world of oral and written interaction' operating at once behind the scenes and at the same time in very public forms of pragmatic literacy. 'The two forms of evidence complement each other', rather as the moneyers and charter draftsmen fulfilled similar functions in their respective crafts. Whereas charters were few, coins existed in vast numbers, but 'though each individual coin offers less scope than each individual charter, collectively they tell a much more balanced story'.

The next section deals with the content and language of coin inscriptions. A coin-user in the reign of Æthelred II would have seen on one face 'an elegant bust of the king, surrounded by the words +ÆÐELRÆD REX ANGLOR[*um*]', the cross serving the practical purpose of indicating where the legend starts and the symbolic purpose of sanctifying the subsequent words, to the effect that the coin has been made under the authority of Æthelred king of the English. On the coin's reverse, a large central image of the Hand of God conveys divine authority, and the inscription of the moneyer +BIORNVLF MO[*netarius*] LVNDON. The king's name and title demonstrated his power, the details of the moneyer and mint-place had functions that persisted across reigns and kingdoms. 'Even the act of issuing coins in one's own name could be a politically charged statement ... The king's name worked as a guarantee, and identified the penny as the king's penny'. Coin inscriptions shared their epigraphy with that of other media: 'coins were part of a continuum of written culture that used a common range of scripts'.

The next section deals with die-cutters, moneyers, and 'the projection of royal authority'. In the period between the reigns of Offa and Alfred this projection reflected a notable enhancement of kingly power, but it was in the tenth and eleventh centuries that the minting system became more dispersed and 'easier to discern'. The similarities of coins and charters emerged clearly when both these manifestations of royalty and administrative power were brought under tighter control between the reigns of Æthelstan and Edgar. Rory Naismith sees here a common factor of 'a degree of managed disunity'. Documents were produced at royal assemblies by scribes commissioned by the king, but were often produced by other agencies such as episcopal churches. This implied not any kind of system-breakdown but delegation of responsibilities signifying devolution to elites: member of powerful families and senior churchmen. 'Royal authority was as much a matter of mediation as direct assertion'. Coins and charters evidently shared a 'higher tolerance for delegation and regional autonomy under royal leadership'.

More sense of what was involved in the system just described can be extracted by bringing together, as it were face-to-face, both coinage and charter production: both were products of sequence of communication. Here there emerge points of contact in which language was crucial. Contentious documents and narratives of dispute settlements in the nature of things produced speechifying, as for instance in the famous case of a Herefordshire woman who, in the reign of Cnut, had not been present at the key meeting and so delegated her business to three thegns. After stating her plans for bequests and grants of land, she spoke out boldly in the vernacular: 'Act like thegns! And duly announce my message to the meeting (*gemote*) before all the worthy men …'. Performance, speech and interaction were necessary parts of the event. Diplomas reached out to different audiences with overlapping interests.

The last section of this chapter concerns coin inscriptions. Many types of intermediary participated in business involving moneyers. King Charles the Bald, at an assembly held at Pîtres in 864, apparently summoned all the moneyers, or all magnates responsible for overseeing moneyers, to issue general instructions. It seems very likely that new Anglo-Saxon coinages were introduced in similar ways, and that moneyers were much involved. Often, though, the die-cutters were left to compose the obverse inscriptions on their coins. The machinery was there, and there are one or two snippets of evidence that the king and his agents activated it. Moneyers, of whom there were several hundred at any one time, must have had much truck with die-cutters. London's growing role in these transactions was an especially active one, and die-cutters were literate enough to engrave the names onto the dies: there was mutual intelligibility between moneyer and die-cutter. Mint-towns would need to call on both local and central die-cutters, and different naming traditions gave rise to quite a wide variety of different names, Old Norse, Continental Germanic as well as Old English. From the mid-tenth century onwards, Anglicization spread around these.

Coins and charters alike constituted 'wide-reaching and sophisticated systems of communications, grounded in oral and written use of language'. These systems and uses seemed very similar; but Rory Naismith concludes by giving weight to variations and differences, different contexts and different audiences—and to parallels which inform each other rather than unified systems. Charters were written for the landowning elite and not surprisingly called on different skills and processes; coins produced by the expertise of die-cutters and of moneyers differed greatly; and finally, the geography of dies and coins varied from place to place and with regional distribution, so that different languages were required and much was seen as unusual and surprising. To recapitulate the comments near the beginning of this chapter: most Anglo-Saxons would probably only glance at the quality of their coins to make sure they were broadly the same as others they knew well. Some might have looked more closely and—if they could—read the inscription, above all if they had any cause to doubt a coin's authority. The end-story of writing, communication and currency in Anglo-Saxon England is manifestly not one of uniformity: instead it is one of dialogue and of conversation.

Conclusion

Francesca Tinti has, not for the first time, shown her editorial flair and multilingual expertise, and come up with a project of great potential. Her knack for selecting research objectives and confronting the challenges inherent in a comparative approach, are evident throughout the present volume. With her co-editors and project team members—Robert Gallagher and Edward Roberts—she has brought together thirteen chapters, authored by fifteen contributors (two each in Chapters 6 and 7), many of them youthful, including an array of specialists in a number of disciplines and languages. What might hitherto have seemed obscure areas are now revealed as, instead, lively and distinctive culture-zones. New light is thrown on early medieval Europe. New generations of students are directed towards new approaches to languages and literacy. As such, it must be hoped that this volume will inspire further communication and fruitful collaboration drawing on historical, linguistic, and literary scholarship.

Bibliography

Secondary Sources

Bloch, Marc, *The Historian's Craft*, trans. Peter Putnam (Manchester, 2004; translation originally printed in 1954).

Davies, Wendy, 'The Latin Charter-Tradition in Western Britain, Brittany and Ireland in the Early Mediaeval Period', in *Ireland in Early Medieval Europe: Studies in Memory of Kathleen Hughes*, eds David Dumville and Rosamond McKitterick (Cambridge, 1982), pp. 258–80.

Keller, Hagen, 'Hülderweis durch Privilegien: symbolische Kommunikation innerhalb und jenseits des Textes', *Frühmittelalterliche Studien* 38 (2004), 309–21.

Koziol, Geoffrey, *The Politics of Memory and Identity in Carolingian Royal Diplomas: The West Frankish Kingdom (840–987)* (Turnhout, 2012).

Orchard, Andy, 'Latin and the Vernacular Languages: The Creation of a Bilingual Textual Culture', in *After Rome*, ed. Thomas Charles-Edwards (Oxford, 2003), pp. 191–219.

Shaw, Richard, 'When did Augustine of Canterbury Die?', *Journal of Ecclesiastical History* 67 (2016), 473–91.

Index

www.ingramcontent.com/pod-product-compliance
Lightning Source LLC
Chambersburg PA
CBHW071329230926
51849CB00002B/344

9789004428119